Critics and Criticism

Critics and Criticism
Ancient and Modern

By

R. S. CRANE

W. R. KEAST

RICHARD McKEON

NORMAN MACLEAN

ELDER OLSON

BERNARD WEINBERG

Edited with an Introduction by

R. S. CRANE

THE UNIVERSITY OF CHICAGO PRESS

CHICAGO & LONDON

THE UNIVERSITY OF CHICAGO PRESS, CHICAGO 60637
THE UNIVERSITY OF CHICAGO PRESS, LTD., LONDON

© 1952 by The University of Chicago. All rights reserved
Published 1952. Midway Reprint 1975
Printed in the United States of America

International Standard Book Number: 0-226-11795-2

CONTENTS

INTRODUCTION

THIS volume contains a selection from the writings on critical theory and method of a group of friends who came to know one another at the University of Chicago in the middle thirties and who have since carried on, in numerous conversations, the exchange of ideas on these and related questions which began among them at that time. Six of the twenty essays are new; the others are reprinted, with some corrections and additions, from the various journals and other publications in which they have appeared at intervals since 1936. The self-contained and limited character of all of them will be readily apparent. They are arranged in three sections, the first dealing primarily with representative critics of the present day, the second with figures and episodes in the history of criticism from the Greeks through the eighteenth century, the third with theoretical questions relating to the criticism of criticism and of poetic forms; and cross-references have been added to different and sometimes conflicting discussions of similar themes. The volume remains, however, essentially a book of miscellaneous studies, and such unity as it possesses must be looked for mainly in the general assumptions and aims with respect to the art of criticism, its existing state and future possibilities, which the six contributors, despite differences on incidental points, happen to have in common.

What these aims and assumptions are could perhaps be left to the detection of the reader, were it not that in the scattered comments evoked by some of the essays, as well as by others not reprinted here, positions have been ascribed to the so-called "Chicago school" for not all of which the present writers would care to take responsibility. It has been thought to follow from their concern with criticism that they are concerned with criticism alone and that they favor a radical reform of higher literary studies in which, as one writer has put it in a sympathetic allusion to the change he thinks has already been effected at the University of Chicago, the whole program would be "boldly reoriented from the historical to the critical." It has also been supposed that they are exclusive proponents of one special system of criticism among the many they have discussed; this being sometimes described as an extreme form of aesthetic atomism which, "denying the possibility of a general theory of literature, leaves us with unique and thus incommensurate and equal works"; and sometimes as a species of pseudo-Aristotelian formalism which defines all poetry, on a priori grounds, as imitation and its end as pleasure and, neglecting the

language of poems in order to concentrate on their "architecture," reduces
critical judgment to a consideration of how fully a given poem' exemplifies the
common structural principles of the genre to which it has been assigned. And
it has further been assumed that their attachment to this system is a matter
not of practical expediency but of doctrinal conviction, implying their commitment to a particular philosophic dogma the nature of which has been defined
variously as Aristotelianism or neo-Aristotelianism, as Croceanism, as a confusion of Croceanism and moral or logical positivism, as naturalism, scholasticism, nominalism, epistemological realism, absolutism, and relativism.

The contributors to this volume are grateful for the aids to reflection which
these comments have afforded them, but they would prefer a somewhat different version of their collective purposes and presuppositions.

I

In the first place, for all of them from the beginning, the problem of literary
criticism, upon which they have concentrated here, has been inseparable from
the much larger problem of how the humanities in general might be brought to
play a more influential role in the culture and action of the contemporary
world; and their conception both of the relations between criticism and other
humane studies and of the terms in which, at the present time, criticism may be
most fruitfully discussed springs directly from their views on this more inclusive issue. The humanities, they have assumed,[1] are distinguishable from the
natural and the social sciences by their special concern with those aspects of
man's achievements in sciences, in institutions, and in arts which are most
distinctively human in the sense that their causes are not completely reducible
either to natural processes common to men and animals or to superpersonal
conditions and forces affecting all the members of a given society. The humanities are therefore coextensive with the arts or methods that enable us to isolate
these aspects for our appreciation and use. And they are necessarily multidimensional, inasmuch as the humanistic properties of human achievements
vary independently according to the character of the symbolic medium in
which the achievements are embodied or through which they affect us; the
quality of the philosophic, scientific, moral, or religious ideas which they express or imply; the nature of the literary or artistic structures into which they
are built; and the peculiarities of the historical situations in the midst of
which they emerge. There are thus four distinct, but mutually supplementary,
groups of humanistic arts—linguistics (in the broad sense of the word), the
analysis of ideas, literary and artistic criticism, and history; and the humanities
in general tend to prosper in any generation—and to exert their power of

1. See Richard McKeon, *Journal of General Education*, III (1949), 290–303.

nourishing our minds, refining our sensibilities, and civilizing our actions—in the degree to which all four sets of arts are actively cultivated in the service of humanistic values and brought to bear, in a manner of co-operation that allows each of them to develop fully its own special potentialities, on the concrete matters of humanistic teaching and research.

It follows from these assumptions (or so it has seemed to the present writers) that the primary task of those who are disturbed by the current decline in the prestige and effectiveness of humane studies is at least twofold. They must aim, for one thing, at devising programs of higher education in which all the humane arts will be given an equal show—criticism no less than philology and bibliography, and history and the analysis of ideas no less than criticism—and in which everything possible will be done to break down the guild prejudices that nearly everywhere encourage specialists in one of the arts to think that there are no respectable methods of humanistic study other than their own or any real or important problems which these are incompetent to solve. They must stand out, thus, against the perennial jealousies of rhetoricians and philosophers, grammarians and rhetoricians, historians and critics; but they must be ready also to combat those latter-day reformers who see no hope for the humanities until the activities of humanists are "integrated" in terms of some rational plan, whether by putting together in separate departments, irrespective of the historical subject matters which give rise to their problems, all philologists, all critics, all students of ideas, and all historians or by elevating one of the humanistic disciplines—criticism or philosophy or religion or the history of culture or some doctrinaire version of one of these—into an architectonic status with respect to the others, and insisting that problems be posed, and studies directed, in ultimate reference to this unifying scheme. For the ideal of humanistic study is the fullest possible discovery, in every subject matter, of its varied humanistic aspects; and since, in any inquiry, only those aspects of an object are revealed which are pertinent to the questions asked and the techniques used, the humanities inevitably suffer whenever, on the one side, important subject matters, such as classical literature and philosophy or the plays of Shakespeare, become the monopoly of specialists in only one or a few of the humane arts or whenever, on the other side, the weight of academic authority is thrown in favor of a fixed hierarchy of the disciplines founded on a particular, and hence limiting, dogma respecting humanistic values.

The second major task of humanists at the present time is a necessary complement of the first. If the humanities are to exert a stronger influence in the future than in the recent past, something clearly is needed beyond the provision of more comprehensive programs for educating humanistic scholars and teachers and the invention of better ways for encouraging their co-operation in the solution of problems while safeguarding their liberty to inquire as they please. For the effectiveness of the contribution to humanistic ends which any of the arts can make at any time, even under the most favorable external conditions and given the best possible supply of talent, depends upon the existing intellectual state of the art itself, that is to say, upon the sufficiency of the principles and devices in vogue among its practitioners to a full discovery of the values that lie within its scope. And the history of the humanities, so far from being a chronicle of cumulative advance, has repeatedly illustrated—and in several fields illustrates all too well today—the tendency of the humane arts to lapse from time to time into contentment with simple and easy procedures and a narrow range of questions and distinctions, to substitute rhetoric or sectarian polemic for disinterested inquiry, to break with the past and make new starts by struggling afresh with problems long since solved, or (as in much contemporary linguistics, philosophy, and criticism) to seek renovation, unhumanistically, by assimilating themselves to the sciences of nature or society. It is little wonder, given the peculiar character of the humanities, that such should be the case; and this character, in turn, suggests the direction in which, whenever these corruptions appear in any of the arts, humanists must look for such remedies as the circumstances permit. It is characteristic of humane studies, in contrast especially with the experimental sciences, that they yield few results which can be tested objectively in application in such a way as to force their devotees to reconsider constantly the adequacy of the assumptions and techniques they have been in the habit of using. No matter how restricted or inappropriate the principles we employ in discussing poems, arguments, linguistic expressions, or historical events, statements of some sort, however irresponsible, can always be made and delivered to students or put into print without risk of consequences more serious than the scorn of our colleagues or the indifference of the public. We lack, in short, most of the compelling motives to re-examination of our basic premises and procedures which have played so conspicuous a part in keeping the sciences alive and promoting their growth. What, therefore, the humanities fail to provide naturally we must endeavor to supply by taking thought; and the most efficacious means would appear to be a combination of efforts directed (1) to subjecting the principles currently employed in the various humanistic arts to a systematic critique of their powers and limitations and (2) to investigating the possibilities of particular methods in the different arts which either have not been developed in the past or have been neglected in modern times because the questions to which they are suitable, though as pertinent as ever humanistically, have been allowed to disappear from view.

Such are the general notions about the humanities and what might be done to further them in our time that have chiefly guided the present essayists in their approach to literary criticism. They have taken it for granted that the advancement of the humanities entails giving much more respectful attention to criticism than has been accorded it, in most centers of higher learning, during the last half-century,[2] and they have therefore welcomed the multiplying signs that in many such centers criticism is now coming into its own. At the same time, they have been partisans of criticism in no exclusive sense that would question the equal importance of linguistics, philology, the philosophic analysis of ideas, and history; they have assumed, indeed, that the prosperity of these other studies is a condition of the prosperity of criticism itself. Their central problem in these essays, however, has not been the place of criticism among the other humanistic arts but its present internal state, as a branch of learning presumably capable of being made more nearly adequate than it has been so far, at least in recent times, to the humanistic uses it is fitted to serve; and with this problem they have attempted to deal, although in an obviously incomplete and tentative way, in terms of the two lines of inquiry indicated above.

II

Their first effort, accordingly, has been to explore the possibility of a general critique of literary criticism (defined as any reasoned and systematic discourse about the poetic arts and their products) such as might yield objective criteria for interpreting the diversities and oppositions among critics and for judging the comparative merits of rival critical schools. What are we to say, for example, when poetry is viewed by one group of critics as imitation and by other groups, opposed to the first but differing sharply among themselves, as expression, as communication, as language peculiarly marked by ambiguity or paradox, as symbolic action, as myth, or as imaginative "prehension" of the world? Or when one critic asserts and other critics deny that form in poetry is "meaning," or that the essential elements in all poems are logical structure and poetic texture, or that the primary determinant of value in poetry is diction, or that there are no real, but only conventional, distinctions of poetic kinds, or that plot and character in the novel or drama are mere "abstractions," or that *Macbeth* is a poem of the same order as *The Waste Land?*

The problem of accounting for such differences among critics—and the list could be extended indefinitely—has most often been solved in one or another of three ways. One is the way of the radical skeptics, who would have us believe that criticism, in so far as it involves commitment to a theory of poetry or literature, is a vain pursuit, since, if it were possible, critics, like scientists and

2. Cf. R. S. Crane, *English Journal*, XXIV (1935), 645–67.

scholars, would tend to agree, at least concerning the essential nature of the phenomena with which they profess to deal. A second solution, at the opposite extreme from this, is offered by those who not only hold that the true nature and attributes of poetry are discoverable but identify these, dogmatically, with the principles of a single critical theory, into the particular terms of which they then proceed to translate, for purposes of refutation or correction, the propositions of other systems—as Aristotle, for instance, translated the dialectic of Plato into the very different terms of his own metaphysics.[3] And there is, third, the still dogmatic but apparently more catholic approach of the synthesizers, i.e., of those who, when they are faced with a conflict of critical positions, insist on both the partial truth and the partial falsity of both of them and think to resolve the difficulty by formulating a new scheme of criticism founded on a combination of the best elements from each; as in the recent suggestion of R. P. Blackmur that the limitations of both the "new critics" and their opponents might be transcended through an alliance between Aristotle and Coleridge.[4]

That these three views, however, do not exhaust the possibilities of solution can be seen from an examination of the basic assumption about criticism upon which all of them rest. For the significant thing is that they all reduce criticism to a direct play of the critic's mind upon objects which, like the physical phenomena investigated in one of the established sciences, are taken to be constant in their natures for all observers; the notorious variability of critical theory, as reflected in the inconsistent or contradictory statements of different critics, being a simple function either of the peculiar difficulties incident to the study of objects of this kind (so that criticism, at best, can be only a record of subjective impressions) or of the natural proneness of most critics, because of the personal and historical circumstances that condition their writing, to be satisfied with incomplete or erroneous conceptions of their common subject.

There have been few, if any, critical controversies and few, if any, histories of criticism in which this assumption, though almost never explicitly stated, has not played a controlling part. Once it is put into words, however, its insufficiency appears. For it takes no account of the fact that criticism, as distinct from mere aesthetic perception or appreciation, is reasoned discourse, that is to say, an organization of terms, propositions, and arguments the peculiar character of which, in any instance, depends as much upon factors operative in the

3. Two recent examples of this very common way of dealing with variant critical principles are John Crowe Ransom's *The New Criticism* (Norfolk, Conn., 1941) and René Wellek and Austin Warren's *Theory of Literature* (New York, 1949), both of which, while treating other critics sympathetically, assume the possibility of only one true or adequate analysis of poetry.

4. *Hudson Review*, III (1951), 487–507; cf. Murray Krieger, *Sewanee Review*, LVIII (1950), 36–51. See also below, pp. 546–47.

construction of the discourse itself as upon the nature of the objects it envisages or the mind and circumstances of its author.[5] The reference of any critic's statements, general or particular, to the things he professes to be talking about is mediated, in the first place, by the special framework of concepts and distinctions which, out of all others that might be, or have been, thought relevant to the things in question, he has chosen for one reason or another to employ. There can be no intelligible discourse about literature or poetry or any of their branches or products (or, for that matter, about any other subject) that does not rest upon such a conceptual scheme; and, once chosen, whether deliberately or as a result of habit, it delimits what the critic can say about any of the questions with which he may be concerned—and this for the simple reason that we can discuss only those aspects of existent objects which are represented or implied in the terms we select or have available for the discussion; we cannot, for example, say anything about the specific forms of individual poems in a mode of criticism of which the distinctions used as principles in the argument pertain only to characteristics of the poet's mind or to the constitution of his medium or to the psychology of his audience. We are thus committed, in any instance of coherent critical discourse, to a particular subject matter, which can be said to be of our own making, not in the sense that it may not correspond to something real, but in the sense that, by our choice of one rather than another possible set of definitions and hypotheses, we have decided what it is to be. The subject matter of a given critical discussion is accordingly identical with its formulation in the necessarily finite system of general terms the critic uses in framing his problems and stating his conclusions; and it follows that, before we can judge fairly of either the meaning or the validity of any critical statement, we must first reconstruct the underlying and often only partly explicit conceptual scheme in which the statement appears—considering, for instance, whether it derives from principles that define and analyze poetry as a kind of knowledge or as a mode of speech or as an effect on the audience or as a variety of psychological, moral, or political activity or as a class of concrete objects, and so on.

This is one determinant of the differences among critical positions. A second determinant, no less important, derives from the fact that, given the same formulation of the basic subject matter of criticism, it is still a matter of choice for the critic whether his reasoning concerning it takes one or another of several radically divergent forms. It makes all the difference in the world for our interpretation and judgment of a critic's statements whether—to mention only the more significant diversities of procedure—he moves from assumed general principles to their applications by dialectical division and resolution or

5. See below, esp. pp. 148–49, 174–75, 463–545, 546–52.

from observed effects to their necessary and sufficient antecedents by hypothetical causal inference; whether he argues concerning the relation of parts to wholes in terms of the literally discriminable functions of the parts or in terms of their reflection of, or participation in, the characteristics he ascribes to the whole; whether he holds his terms constant and varies his treatment of things accordingly or holds things constant and allows the meanings of his terms to vary from context to context;[6] or whether he resolves his problems integrally "by referring poetry, for example, to some analogue of poetry" and "finding characteristics of poetry which are shared by the analogue," or differentially "by separating poetry from its analogues" and "finding characteristics which are peculiar to poetry."[7]

The combination of these two things—a particularly formulated subject matter and a particularly determined mode of reasoning about it—in the construction of any critical discourse, constitutes what we may call, in a broadened sense of the word, its "method." It is an aspect of critical writing of which few practicing critics have ever been consciously aware, and it has even less often been considered by historians of criticism in their analyses and comparisons of critics or critical schools. The necessary relativity of all critical utterances, whether statements of doctrine or observations on works, to the critic's choice of basic terms and operational devices—i.e., to the methodological principles which, as hidden premises, determine the sense and validity of his arguments— is a fact, nevertheless, that cannot safely be ignored; and it has three important implications for the general critique of criticism which the present writers have tried to develop.

1. The objects of the critique are the apparently inconsistent or contradictory positions advanced by different critics. It is clear, however, from what has been said, that there can be no genuine refutation of a critical position except within the particular framework of concepts and rules of inference in which it has been asserted; and it can easily be the case that a doctrine, like that, for example, which declares poetry to be a mode of imitation, while obviously meaningless or false in one such framework, can be both intelligible and true in another. It would seem, therefore, that most of the doctrinal polemics, with their catalogues of critical "fallacies" and "heresies," that have engaged critics in all times can be reduced to quarrels between opponents who are really talk-

6. Cf. below, pp. 160–61.

7. Cf. below, pp. 549–52. Comparison and classification of critical systems in terms of these two determinants of method will yield different schematisms according as one takes the first or the second major factor as the primary principle of differentiation or concentrates on particular aspects of the systems being compared because of their relevance to the special problems of theory or history that happen to be uppermost in the discussion. Some, but not all, of the possibilities of variation are illustrated in the third section of this Introduction and in the first two essays in Part III below.

ing about different things or talking about them in different ways. And, since there is nowhere any authority capable of deciding, among the many distinguishable aspects of poetry, which ones critics ought to fix upon as principles or how these ought to be discussed, it would appear that the only satisfactory approach to the existing diversities of criticism must be one that recognizes a plurality of distinct critical methods—each of them valid or partially valid within its proper sphere—and that insists, consequently, upon ascertaining, in methodological terms, what a given critic is doing, and why, before attempting either to state the meaning or judge the truth or falsity of his conclusions or to compare his doctrines with those of other critics.

2. It follows from this pluralistic and instrumentalist view of criticism that we must accord to critics the right of free choice as between different basic methods; this is as much a practical decision, and hence as immune to theoretical questioning, as is the decision (say) to study medicine rather than law. Granted, however, the initial choice by which a critic is committed to viewing aesthetic objects in a particular set of terms and to discussing them in a particular manner for the sake of arriving at a particular kind of knowledge or judgment, there are yet criteria by which the relative value or fruitfulness of different critical achievements may be appraised. For one thing, though commitment to method in this sense is inescapable, not even the soundest or most completely developed theory can compensate, in practical criticism, for the critic's want of sensibility and knowledge; these by themselves are not, as is often supposed, sufficient conditions of good criticism, but their absence is enough to make criticism bad, and we can always forgive a critic for poor theorizing whose erudition is extensive and whose taste is right. There is, again, a kind of tact in the use or application of principles (whatever their kind) which not all critics possess; we are disturbed, for example, when a critic, employing the analytical devices of the *Poetics*, finds the plot of *Samson Agonistes* defective for lacking a middle, or when another critic, for whom excellence in poetry consists in a certain quality of mind or language, argues inappropriately from this principle, which is more suited to deciding the relative merits of poets than of individual poems, that *Lycidas* and *Paradise Lost* would have been better works had they been written in the style of Donne.

But the criticism of criticism can go farther than this and, while still avoiding the mere confrontation of one dogmatism with another, raise questions about the comparative efficacy of methods themselves. Since any critical system must rest upon a finite number of terms and connections, every system necessarily has its characteristic limitations no less than its characteristic powers. There are kinds of questions which Aristotle, for example, can treat but Coleridge not, and other kinds of questions which Coleridge can deal with that find no place in Aristotle's poetic. Yet it is surely possible to say that, from the point of view of the relative adequacy or utility of their methods, Aristotle is a better critic than (say) Scaliger, and Coleridge a better critic than any of the neo-Coleridgeans of the present day;[8] and the reason lies in the considerably greater scope and flexibility of the analytical apparatus at the disposal of the earlier critics in each pair as compared with the latter. For, though we can never discuss literature or poetry systematically except within a particular conceptual framework, we do nevertheless have a common-sense apprehension, apart from any theoretical formulation, of the multiple likenesses and differences exhibited by literary works and of the variety of causes necessary to their production; and in the light of this precritical knowledge we can discriminate between critical systems, no matter how different their foundations, which permit a reasonably many-sided or comprehensive discussion of literary phenomena— i.e., which abound in pertinent and usable distinctions—and other systems, unfortunately more numerous, which content themselves with partial views while pretending to omit nothing essential.[9] The signs by which the latter can be detected are many, not a few of which appear in the criticism of our time: the tendency, for instance, to explain poetry in terms of only one or a small number of its causes, such as language, subject matter, or the psychology of the poet or his readers; the tendency to concentrate attention on the likenesses among poems to the neglect of all except their accidental differences, or at least to have one preferred mode of analysis for all poems; the tendency, as a consequence of the preceding, to reduce all operative distinctions to one or two pairs of contrary terms and to leave other terms (of which "experience" is a contemporary favorite) unanalyzed; the tendency to exclude as meaningless, rather than to translate and use, the distinctions of other systems; the tendency to set up restrictive canons of poetic excellence and, in the name of these, to "revaluate" negatively large parts of the established tradition; and so on.

3. To call attention, as is done in some of the following essays, to the methodological limitations of certain contemporary schools of criticism is not to deny the positive worth of many of the particular observations or insights into general principles which their representatives have contributed to the common store. What can perhaps be fairly said, however, is that these have been achieved to a considerable extent in spite of the critics' addiction to principles of inquiry and knowledge the limited range and restricted capacity for development of which are at the very least not matters for self-congratulation. And these deficiencies are not hard to understand when we consider how indifferent most of the influential critics of our day have been to the his-

8. Cf. Crane, (University of Kansas City) *University Review*, VIII (1942), 199–201.
9. Cf. below, pp. 60–63, 83 ff.

tory of criticism in all except the recent past[10] and how frequently, as a result, even the best of them have been forced to rethink old and difficult problems from the beginning without benefit of any of the short cuts which an acquaintance with preceding discussions might have afforded.

There is, indeed, some excuse for the belief that the history of criticism can be of little use to practicing critics, in the manner in which that history has commonly been written. It has been, for the most part, a history of doctrines and opinions only; and these, when separated from the methods that generated them and fixed the conditions of their meaning and validity, and when interpreted, in the usual fashion, as expressions of unique personalities or ages, can quite justifiably be thought of as dated museum pieces, having little or no relevance to contemporary needs. This is not the only way, however, in which the history of criticism can be studied. We can examine the critical writings of the past not merely doctrinally and circumstantially but methodologically as well—i.e., as successive efforts to cope with perennial problems of the literary arts and their products by means of principles of formulation and proof which, however they may differ from critic to critic or period to period, can yet be stated and compared in universal terms independently of the shifting particulars of the discourses in which they function. And a history of criticism of this sort (to which the essays in Part II of the present volume are intended as partial contributions[11]) can be made to serve a number of important purposes in the education of critics beyond the mere satisfaction of their historical curiosity.

Such a history is the pluralistic philosophy of criticism teaching by example; and perhaps the most general profit we can derive from it is the habit of viewing critical principles as neither doctrinal absolutes nor historically necessitated beliefs but instruments of inquiry and analysis, to which a critic therefore need not commit himself dogmatically, but only hypothetically, on the ground of their appropriateness to the particular kinds of problems he is interested in solving: this is the moral one is bound to draw from observing the interaction, in the past, between variations in the character of the principles critics have employed in their arguments and shifts in the nature of the questions they have asked. Such a history can also help to emancipate us from the always confining influence of a preoccupation with the up-to-date: partly by calling attention to

10. "Indifference" is, of course, much too mild a word for the exultant repudiation of all past criticism in the opening pages of I. A. Richards' *Principles of Literary Criticism*. The skepticism of F. R. Leavis is of a more moderate sort; see his *Education & the University* (London, 1943), pp. 85–86, 132–33.

11. Cf. also Bernard Weinberg, *Critical Prefaces of the French Renaissance* (Evanston, Ill., 1950), Introduction; and Elder Olson, "Criticism" (scheduled to appear in the *Encyclopaedia Britannica* [1952 copyright]). For a conception of the history of criticism in most respects the reverse of this, see E. M. W. Tillyard, *Cambridge Journal*, II (1949), 543–51.

the manner in which, in other periods as well as in our own, once new problems have brought new or at least different principles into use, the orthodoxy that inevitably comes to attach itself to these principles tends to restrict the range of questions which critics may properly ask; and partly also by placing the new criticism in the context of the various older systems which, on an analytical view, it appears to resemble in either purpose or method—it would be useful, for instance, to examine in some detail the relations of the current criticism of diction and imagery to the tradition of the ancient tropists[12] or to compare contemporary devices for expounding the mythical or symbolic "meaning" of poems with the apparatus developed for analogous uses by the experts in allegory of the Middle Ages. But, over and above all this, such a history, by its emphasis on methods as well as doctrines, can not only make us more clearly aware of what we are doing but help to suggest possible ways to a future reconstruction of criticism on broader theoretical bases than it has at present. Not all the potentialities of the many very different criticisms of the past were exhausted by their practitioners; we can at least learn from the example of the great critics what is the difference between partial and comprehensive critical views; and among the latter there are surely some that will bear revival and extension, as conceptual frameworks of a permanently valid sort within which a wide variety of still important critical questions, many of them obscured or neglected altogether by recent critics, can be brought to the fore again and discussed with rigor and finesse.[13]

III

The second major concern of the essays here collected is with the capacities for modern development and use of one such historical system—the poetic method of Aristotle. The writers would not wish to minimize their admiration for the *Poetics* and, indeed, for the other basic works of its author, for whose characteristic approach, as they interpret it, to problems of knowledge, action, and art they feel a strong temperamental affinity. They have not supposed, however, that this prevented their admiring and using for their own ends other great philosophers, from Plato to Dewey, who on all fundamental points of principle and procedure have taken a quite different line; and in criticism likewise they have viewed their "Aristotelianism" as a strictly pragmatic and

12. Cf. below, pp. 50–51.

13. Compare with the above a suggestive discussion of the nature and utility of the history of philosophy by Warner A. Wick, *Journal of General Education*, V (1951), 116–21. For a general approach to the question of variant "frameworks" with which, along with important differences, the present discussion of critical systems has something in common, see Rudolf Carnap, "Empiricism, Semantics, and Ontology," *Revue internationale de philosophie*, IV (1950), 20–40.

nonexclusive commitment—much like a modern physicist's preference for Einsteinian over Newtonian concepts—to hypotheses about poetry and poetics that seem to them capable of being developed into a comprehensive critical method, at once valid in itself and peculiarly adapted to the study of problems which they think are still significant but for the solution of which none of the prevailing modes of criticism affords the necessary analytic tools.

These are, stated generally, the problems that face us whenever we reflect on the undeniable fact that what a poet does *distinctively as a poet* is not to express himself or his age or to resolve psychological or moral difficulties or to communicate a vision of the world or to provide entertainment or to use words in such-and-such ways, and so on—though all these may be involved in what he does—but rather, by means of his art, to build materials of language and experience into wholes of various kinds to which, as we experience them, we tend to attribute final rather than merely instrumental value. The criticism of poetry (in the large sense that includes prose fiction and drama) is, on this view, primarily an inquiry into the specific characters and powers, and the necessary constituent elements, of possible kinds of poetic wholes, leading to an appreciation, in individual works, of how well their writers have accomplished the particular sorts of poetic tasks which the natures of the wholes they have attempted to construct imposed on them. For such criticism we obviously need analytic devices that will permit us to discriminate the various species of wholes that poets have made; to determine the number, character, and ordering of their functional parts; and to define the often quite different conditions of success or failure implied by the nature of each.

That it would be futile to look for devices of this kind in that variety of modern criticism which discusses poetry "integrally" in a broad context of social, political, psychological, or anthropological considerations perhaps goes without saying; but neither can they be found in the other major contemporary school—numbering most of the so-called "new critics"—which prefers to view poetry "differentially" as poetry and not another thing. Why this is so becomes clear when we consider the "new criticism" in the light of history. Its remote origins can be traced to the new critical methods developed in Alexandria and later in Rome after the decline of the philosophic criticism of the classical Greeks. It was then that the great shift took place from the view that poetry is a special class of made objects (analyzable by analogy with natural things and other artifacts) to the view that it is simply one of many modes of discourse, the differentia of which, as discourse, can be stated variously in terms of its language, its subject matter, its productive cause, its end or effect, or some relation of two or more of these factors. This is clearly the notion of poetry upon which most subsequent critical systems, for all their diversity in other respects, have been built; and there are few, if any, influential critics in our day who do not take it for granted as a principle obviously warranted by the nature of things,[14] though it should be evident that such a notion precludes any discussion of poems as concrete artistic wholes with distinctive forms which are analytically more than the sums of their parts.

A concern with differences among poetic kinds and techniques did indeed persist in the criticism of this tradition down to the eighteenth century, culminating in the exploitation by Renaissance and neoclassical critics of the doctrines and rules (though seldom the poetic method) of Aristotle. The "new criticism," however, is more directly a consequence of the profound reorientation of criticism, beginning in the eighteenth century, from an emphasis on poetic genres and their rules (considered usually in rhetorical terms) to an emphasis on common poetic qualities, no matter in what kinds of works they appear.[15] The manifestations of these, since they depend on particular and "local" configurations of thought or diction or of the two united, are immediately discernible in the parts of works and hence permit of definition and judgment, without recourse to specific structural principles, on the basis of general assumptions about the powers or operations of the poet's mind, the universal conditions of poetic pleasure, the objective characteristics of things, the nature of language and symbols, the genius of nations or of poetic traditions, or some selection or combination of these.[16] From Hume, Johnson, and Coleridge, through Arnold and Pater, to Eliot, Richards, Empson, Leavis, Ransom, Tate, and Brooks, most of our influential criticism, both speculative and applied, has been in this qualitative mode—a criticism, to use Coleridge's distinction, primarily of poetry or the poet rather than of poems. It has taken many forms in different men, some broader in scope and richer in conceptual content than others; and, though the tradition has been continuous since about 1750, it has naturally undergone various modifications in response to the changing circumstances of times. In our generation, for example, new bases of doctrine and new formulas for defining common poetic traits have been found in the sci-

14. The assumption emerges with startling explicitness in Ransom's *The New Criticism* (cf. esp. pp. 280–81), but it underlies most of the many contemporary efforts to differentiate poetry from "prose," "science," "rhetoric," etc.; cf., e.g., Wellek and Warren, *op. cit.*, pp. 11–18, 140–41, 152–54. See below, pp. 45 ff., 83 ff., and Olson, *Modern Philology*, XL (1943), 275–83.

15. Cf. below, pp. 459–60 and, for the distinction between "specific" and "qualitative" methods in criticism, pp. 63–65.

16. This is clearly evident in one of the classic places of this criticism, Coleridge's discussion of Wordsworth's poetry in the *Biographia literaria*. Consider also his distinction between "poem" and "poetry" in chapter xiv of the same work, and Ruskin, *The Stones of Venice*, chap. ii ("The Virtues of Architecture"), secs. iv–v. For what frequently happens to the concept of poetic "structure" in such a method, see below, pp. 95–96, and cf. Leavis, *Revaluation* (New York, 1947), pp. 60–61.

ences of neuropsychology, psychoanalysis, linguistics, and the anthropology of Frazer and others. Much contemporary criticism, also, has been dominated by a practical interest in explaining and promoting new directions in poetry itself, and this has led to a more or less exclusive concentration of some critics on problems of language (since the new poets were interested in reforming poetic diction) and of others on problems of symbolism and myth (since many of the poets were attempting didactic or quasi-didactic forms). And we must mention, as a recent development which might seem to promise an eventual return to specific criticism of some kind, the strong emphasis placed by academic representatives of the school on the "close reading" of texts. The promise, however, is as yet little more than that: most of the "new critics," under the still powerful influence of the assumption that poetry is best considered as a kind of discourse, continue to read all poems as if their authors had constructed them on identical principles, confusing, for instance, mimetic forms with didactic, and treating lyrics and novels, tragedies and essays, by means of the same distinctions;[17] and, more than that, for all the current insistence on "concreteness" and on the primacy of the "word," it is hard to think of any period in the long history of criticism in which the analytical concepts employed by most practical critics have been fewer in number or more abstract.

It is not surprising, then, that in the modern criticism inspired by this Hellenistic-Roman-Romantic tradition there should be no sufficient theoretical bases for the kind of discussion of poetic works which takes as its starting point the peculiar natures of the artistic wholes their writers were engaged in constructing and which attempts to explain and appreciate their parts, and the relations these bear to one another, as poetically necessary or desirable consequences of the writers' commitment to certain kinds of poetic structures and effects rather than others. The special power of the qualitative method, indeed, lies elsewhere, and the critics using it have succeeded best when they have taken poets or poetic schools and styles as their primary subjects and have treated individual works, or the parts thereof, mainly as signs or exemplars of the characteristics they ascribe to these. Yet it is difficult to see how we can form an adequate, or at least fair-minded, judgment of any work unless we have both the habit and the means of considering it—no matter what else we may think it important to say—from the point of view of its distinctive status as a "poetic" object. And this involves asking ourselves, first, what the specific constitution and power of the whole the writer has achieved or aimed at really is—taking care, however, lest we allow preconceptions as to what, e.g., "tragedy" must be to determine our analysis of a given work so called, or

17. Cf. below, pp. 85 ff., 108 ff., 138 ff.

identify the whole too easily with what is actually only an aspect or part,[18] or miss the crucial differences between it and broadly similar wholes. Having done this, we may then ask, in the second place, to what extent, and with what degree of artistic compulsion,[19] any of the particular things the writer has done at the various levels of his writing, down to the details of his imagery and language, can be seen to follow from the special requirements or opportunities which the kind of whole he is making presents to him—requirements and opportunities that are bound to differ more or less sharply according as the whole being constructed is a mimetic rather than a didactic form,[20] a dramatic form intended for the stage rather than one meant primarily for recitation, a tragic plot-form of the order of *Macbeth* rather than of *Othello*, or of *The Duchess of Malfi* rather than of *King Lear*, and so on.[21] To consider poetic works in these terms is obviously to raise a large number of questions about them, and about their relations with other works, which either never emerge or emerge only in partial or analogical formulation in other, and currently more flourishing, modes of criticism. If only, therefore, because of the neglect into

18. Cf. below, pp. 111 ff. Many other examples of such partial analysis can be found in recent Shakespearean criticism; cf., e.g., L. C. Knights, *How Many Children Had Lady Macbeth?* (Cambridge, 1933), pp. 34 ff. (where Shakespeare's tragedy is analyzed as "a statement of evil" in terms of a dialectical pattern imposed upon selected elements of dramatic "thought"); and John Arthos, "The Naïve Imagination and the Destruction of Macbeth," *ELH*, XIV (1947), 114–26 (where a different unifying pattern is attributed to the same play by erecting certain symptoms of Macbeth's personality into the principle of the action).

19. Cf. Joyce Cary, *New York Times Book Review*, April 30, 1950, p. 1: "Every professional artist has met the questioner who asks of some detail: 'Why did you do it so clumsily like that, when you could have done it so neatly like this?' And smiles, as on a poor dreamer without logic or understanding, when he gets the answer: 'It might have been better your way, but I couldn't do it because it wouldn't have belonged.' . . . They [i.e., critics like Horace and Boileau, who were also artists] learned in practice that there are rules of construction, mysterious relations in technique, which exist apparently in the nature of art itself, and which oblige the artist to respect them." These are not the same, however, as the abstract notions of literary kinds most modern critics insist upon when they discuss, e.g., the novel.

20. On the special meaning here assumed for this distinction see below, pp. 65–68, 588–92.

21. The scheme of inquiry outlined here is illustrated, in part, in the discussion, below, of *Tom Jones* (see esp. pp. 624–45). The scheme, of course, indicates only a logical order of questions; it is not intended to prescribe the actual steps of a critic's procedure in dealing with particular works, and it is in no wise incompatible with the contention of L. C. Knights (*op. cit.*, p. 7) that "our duty as critics is to examine first the words . . . , then the total effect which this combination of words produces in our mind." The point is merely that, wherever he starts, the critic's job is incomplete until he is able to join causally, in his conclusions, statements about parts and statements about the "poetic" wholes in which they are contained. The two are only analytically separable: thus an adequate study of the plot-form of *The Duchess of Malfi* would necessarily involve a detailed consideration of Webster's use of language in that play, and a study of the language in (say) the scene of the Duchess' death would necessitate asking to what extent the choice and collocation of words, the invention of imagery and metaphor, etc., were dictated, among other things, by Webster's sense of the particular mean between horrified indignation and pity which his plot-form required him to maintain in this part of his drama.

which they have fallen, it might be well that some critics at any rate should now deal with such questions: the influence of literary studies cannot but be greater in proportion to the variety of analytical resources at the disposal of literary scholars and teachers. But, in addition to this, the questions peculiar to specific criticism—being questions that turn primarily on the practical problems involved in making well different sorts of poetic works—possess an importance in themselves, not only for critics but likewise for literary historians and creative artists, which is surely not inferior to the importance that attaches to critical questions of a more general kind; and this alone is sufficient to justify an attempt to find theoretical bases for answering them that will be commensurate in some degree with their complex and ever changing nature.

It is the merit of Aristotle, uniquely among systematic critics, that he grasped the distinctive nature of poetic works as *synola*, or concrete artistic wholes, and made available, though only in outline sketch, hypotheses and analytical devices for defining literally and inductively, and with a maximum degree of differentiation, the multiple causes operative in the construction of poetic wholes of various kinds and the criteria of excellence appropriate to each. We have as a result a brief poetics of tragedy, which is still valid and usable provided we recognize that its most particular distinctions are relevant to only one of the many species of poems to which the name "tragedy" has been applied, and a partial poetics of Greek and especially Homeric epic. The important thing in Aristotle for the present essayists, however, is not so much the statements of doctrine and history contained in the *Poetics* itself as the method through which these statements are derived and validated in the arguments of the treatise when it is read in the light of the methodological principles stated explicitly in its author's other works or inferable from them. The Aristotle they have thus reconstructed[22] is not, it will easily be seen, the Aristotle of the Renaissance and neoclassical commentators or any of the more recent Aristotles of such interpreters as Butcher, Bywater, Murray, Lane Cooper, or Francis Fergusson. It may not, indeed, except in a general way, be Aristotle at all! They think it is; but, whether Aristotle's or not, the poetic method which they credit to him can be described in universal terms in such a manner as to remove it effectually from the circumstances of its historical origin and make it accessible, once its nature is clarified and its potentialities further developed, as a method for common use today.

Concerning the positive character of the method in general, enough perhaps is said in the essays collected in Parts II and III of this volume. It may be perti-

---

22. See below, esp. pp. 160–68, 176 ff., 463 ff., 552–66, 617, n. 7; McKeon, *The Basic Works of Aristotle* (New York, 1941), Introduction; and his article in the *Journal of the History of Ideas*, VIII (1947), 3–44.

nent, however, to mention some of the things which a commitment to it on the ground of its utility in formulating critical questions and suggesting observations on poetic works clearly does not imply. It does not, for one thing, imply any assumption that the concept of imitation, in its most general meaning, is more than an empirically verifiable hypothesis for distinguishing objects of art from natural things; or, taking the term in the more restricted sense in which it denotes one possible final cause in poetry, that all poems are imitations, though unquestionably many of them are.[23] It does not imply, again, that the critic must define the end of poetry or art as pleasure simply or consider its function, as one contemporary has supposed, to be only that of "ornamenting pleasurably, in a moment's leisure, the life of its beholder": it is one thing to say this and quite another to hold, not only with Aristotle but with most good critics, that when poems of any sort, didactic no less than mimetic, are well made, pleasure is bound to result, the peculiar quality of which, in any mimetic poem, is a sign of its form.[24] Such a commitment, once more, does not imply that the critic must think of distinctions among poetic species either as labels for conventionally determined classes of poems or as concepts signifying ideal values in the light of which individual productions may be compared and judged by considering the degree of their approximation to a previously determined norm: for the "Aristotelian" critic, definitions of kinds are causal formulas inductively derived from an inspection, in "poetic" terms, of poems, and his use of them in practical criticism is essentially as heuristic devices for discovering what are the relevant questions to be asked about the individual works he proposes to study. There is no implication, either, that poetic kinds can ever be completely enumerated or always differentiated accurately from one another— not only because new species are constantly emerging but because, when we go beyond such obvious extremes of form as tragedy and comedy, their bounds are often divided only by thin partitions. And, finally, there is nothing in the method that implies the impossibility, once the critic has grasped the principles of construction peculiar to different poems, of discussing their common elements and devices and arriving thus at comparative judgments or historical generalizations.

If the method, however, is to be of more than limited use today, it must be developed, through extension and refinement of its basic concepts, far beyond the relatively primitive state in which Aristotle left it. It is only of mimetic poetry, and only of two species of this, that the *Poetics* gives any account; and,

23. For a third sense of "imitation"—roughly equivalent to Henry James's "rendering" as opposed to "stating" and hence more closely related to the efficient cause of poetic form—see below, p. 623; and cf. *Poetics* 4. 1448[b]35, and 24. 1460[a]5–10.

24. Cf. below, pp. 588–89.

although many "Aristotelians" of the past have contented themselves with applying what is there said about Greek tragedy and epic directly to the criticism of modern works—even, in one instance, to *The Rime of the Ancient Mariner*—without considering that these may be founded on quite dissimilar principles, this is a use of Aristotle which clearly runs counter to the a posteriori and predominantly "differential" spirit of his approach. What is needed, accordingly, is much inductive theoretical research, based on wide knowledge and close analysis of modern and contemporary writings, into problems both of general poetics and of the specific poetics of literary forms as these are posed by the achievements of writers of all kinds since antiquity. In both fields unanswered questions of the first importance to practical critics, literary historians, and artists are to be met with on every hand. A few of them are touched upon in some of the essays in this volume,[25] but many others remain for future study: there is much more, for instance, to be found out about poetic imagery than can be revealed through the methods by which that subject is commonly investigated today; and we are reminded by the current vogue of didactic forms in lyric, novel, and drama that our resources for dealing with the problems raised by such works in other than a casual and undiscriminating way are still very meager.

No one, it is true, who uses this method for any length of time can help becoming aware of its limitations and hence of the need for supplementing it with other critical devices more sensitive to the various aspects of poetry which its characteristic selection of terms leaves out.[26] Poetry, as nearly all the critics of the last two centuries have correctly insisted, is much more than a productive art in Aristotle's meaning of the term; there can be no good or great poetry that does not presuppose natural genius, experience, mastery of language, moral seriousness, and (in some degree at least) philosophic wisdom; and it is surely a truncated criticism that takes no account of these dimensions of its subject. This is true enough; but, on the other hand, to abstract from certain factors in a given field of inquiry is not necessarily to imply their nonexistence or unimportance; we can never talk about everything at once, and, if we are to talk to good purpose about anything, we must hold various other things constant, at least for the time being. We must have many critical methods, therefore, besides the "Aristotelian"; but these in their turn, we must also recognize, are bound to have limitations which the "Aristotelian" method does not exhibit; and the limitations of that method, while indubitable, are perhaps after

25. Especially in the last four, but cf. also below, pp. 68–82, and Olson, "Verse" (scheduled to appear in the *Encyclopaedia Britannica* [1952 copyright]).

26. Cf. also below, pp. 645–47.

all not so narrow or cramping to the intelligence and sensibility of the critic as has sometimes been thought.

What is held constant in this criticism is the whole complex of accidental causes of variation in poetry that depend on the talents, characters, educations, and intentions of individual authors, the opinions and tastes of the audiences they address, the state of the language in their time, and all the other external factors which affect their choice of materials and conventions in particular works. The provisional exclusion of these is necessary if the analysis is to be concentrated upon the internal causes which account for the peculiar construction and effect of any poem qua artistic whole. Within the bounds thus set, however, the method is a comprehensive one in two respects. It is comprehensive, in the first place, because it embraces all the elements necessary, in some particular determination and ordering, to the existence of a poem of any kind as a made object productive of definite effects upon our minds, and because it considers these (as in *Poetics* 1–3) as independent variables in a fashion quite different from the reductive, and frequently monistic, treatment of poetic elements to be found in much criticism of the present time. It is not an analysis primarily either of poetic language or of poetic subject matter or of poetic technique but of the composite wholes which result from the union and interaction in poems of all three factors. And for all three it provides terms, appropriate to their status as internal causes of poetic effects, which can be further extended or specified in various ways to fit the peculiarities of different or newly developed species of poems without abandonment of their original analytic bases.[27]

The method is comprehensive, in the second place, by virtue of the devices it affords for discriminating a posteriori an indefinite number of different poetic forms or principles of construction and for dealing differentially with the common elements these involve, in terms not merely of their material content or technical configuration but of the functions they can be made to serve, directly or indirectly, in the constitution of different kinds of poetic wholes; with the result that, when the method is properly used, it permits a far wider range of relevant differentiations in the discussion not only of poems but of poetic devices and materials than any method in which such a functional treatment of elements has no place.

We are not confined, thus, to a consideration of diction in the light of its grammatically recoverable "meanings" only but can go on to speak of its uses as disclosure or action and, in so doing, uncover subtleties, even of "meaning," which would have escaped us otherwise.[28] We can similarly add new dimen-

27. Cf. below, p. 558.
28. Cf. below, pp 54–55, 68 ff.

sions to the technical criticism of the drama or novel by fixing our attention not simply on the material character of the devices used but on the often striking formal modifications which the same devices undergo when they are employed for different poetic ends. And so, too, with the subject-matter elements upon which, as they come to us through our inferences from the words of any poem, its peculiar "working or power" as an artistic whole most immediately depends. When viewed in abstraction from their forms and functions in particular poems, these elements are, in the aggregate, much the same in all species of poetry: there is no poetry that does not, in some fashion, deal with human fortunes, actions, feelings, characters, thoughts. In more limited forms of criticism these are often treated as constants under such general heads as "experience" or "life," or even, as by William Empson, collapsed into dictional "meaning."[29] The ultimate effect of such procedures is to dehumanize poetry by obscuring, or at least excluding from the sphere of discriminating critical observation, precisely those things which, not of course in themselves but as effectively constructed and rendered in the poet's language, are the most powerful causes of the interest which poetry excites. The method we are considering avoids any such generalized or reductive treatment of poetic "subjects." The form or "power" of a poem is determined primarily by the poet's representation of humanly significant or moving actions, characters, or thoughts, to the end of achieving a particular over-all effect, mimetic or didactic; but the form exists for our contemplation or edification only as it is realized in the succession of the poet's words in ways conditioned by his choice of manner or technique. For the "poetic" critic, therefore, the analysis of the "subject matter" of a poem must be both differential and functional; his first question concerning any selection the poet has made from the common ingredients of his or our experience is how, precisely, this has been made to serve final or intermediate ends within the particular kind of whole the poet is constructing. And, as different poetic wholes set different requirements in the constitution or handling of their parts, so the same material elements of action or thought may serve different—even radically different—functions in different poems and consequently take on, when viewed thus internally, quite different characteristics and values. To say this is to suggest, among other things, how little we have said about the plot of any novel or drama, at least in comparison with what might be said, when we have merely recounted the actions upon which it is based—actions that might easily be the matter of a plot with a very different "power" in another work—or when we have resolved the poet's construction into the substrate of legend or myth from which his story is

29. See the *Kenyon Review*, XII (1950), 600; and cf. below, pp. 52–54.

drawn.[30] And it is the same, too, with thought. There is a sense in which we can assert of the *Essay on Man*, for example, that its "structure" is a particular complex of themes which it shares with *King Lear* and *Paradise Lost;* but in speaking thus we surely obscure the obvious fact that no good reader has ever been affected in the same way by the similar noetic elements in the three poems. And this is not surprising when we consider that philosophic doctrines are only in a very remote and primitive sense the same when they come to us in such different combinations with other things and are put to such different artistic uses as is the case with the doctrines common to Shakespeare, Milton, and Pope.

It is a sign of the comprehensiveness of the "Aristotelian" method that it does not restrict us to such oversimplified considerations of poetic problems. And this is not all. The principles of the method, it is true, are the internal causes of poems, viewed as artistic products, in analytical separation from the activities that produced them; but it requires only a relatively easy shift in causal perspective to combine "poetic" propositions about particular poems with philological, biographical, or historical propositions about their materials and the conditions and circumstances of their making. We cannot infer the "poetic" nature or value of any artistic whole from its antecedents in the poet's life or in contemporary or earlier culture; but, having determined critically what the poem is in itself, we can then replace it in its setting of events and other writings and eventually develop a history of poetry in terms of the interaction of artistic and extra-artistic causes of change.[31] The relation is therefore peculiarly close between this mode of criticism and the other branches of humanistic scholarship which provide literally verifiable answers to questions about poetic texts. Bibliography, linguistics, textual criticism, philological exegesis, the study of sources, biography, the history of the theater, the analysis and history of ideas—these are all essential tools for the kind of critical research we are considering. And the relation is not one-sided only, for there are always many questions about poems which, though their investigation involves the use of non-"poetic" techniques, we are likely to overlook unless we approach the texts with "poetic" questions in mind.

The method, even on this generous view of it, is not, as has been said, a method of all work. Its peculiar virtue is that, more than any other critical method so far devised, it is suited to the literal investigation and explanation of poetic works in their uniqueness and particularity; in terms of their immediate

30. Cf. below, pp. 67–70, 618 ff.

31. The writer of this Introduction has dealt with some of the conditions of such a history in a short book, now nearly completed, on "The Critical and Historical Principles of Literary History."

and hence distinctively "poetic," rather than their remoter, causes and effects; with a complexity of analysis commensurate with the complexity of the poetic process and of poetic appreciation itself. For most readers of poetry (including the present essayists), however, poetry has other values besides those which this method is fitted to disclose—values, for example, which appear only when poems are considered in relation to the qualities of their authors' minds[32] or to the aspects of reality which they illuminate or to their moral, political, and social effects,[33] or which emerge fully only in a criticism (like Matthew Arnold's) that subordinates explicit principles to the direct response of a prepared mind to texts. To urge the claims of the "Aristotelian" method is not, therefore, to present it as a rival, but as a needed supplement, to the other methods now so long in vogue; and, in particular, it is not to deny that, as employed by writers like T. S. Eliot, F. R. Leavis, Allen Tate, R. P. Blackmur, or Kenneth Burke, these other methods have produced in our day much fine criticism, about which no sensible person can wish that its first principles were other than what they are.

One final thing, nevertheless, can perhaps be said. The criticism of the past generation has been prevailingly, as we have seen, qualitative and general rather than functional and specific, concentrating on selected parts or aspects of poems and treating these in terms of wholes which are not concrete artistic objects but compositions of qualities having their substrate in the poet or his tradition or age or in poetic language rather than in individual poetic works.[34] Much of it has been "differential" criticism in the sense that it has attempted to distinguish poetry sharply from other kinds of discourse; but within these bounds it has proceeded for the most part "integrally" by breaking down or neglecting distinctions of form and function as between different works. Its characteristic devices have therefore been comparison and analysis, controlled in their applications only by the critic's personal sense of what is made relevant by the very general basic analogy from which his principles derive. From this two consequences have followed which, in all except the best critics, have been inimical to both the prestige and the usefulness of the criticism thus produced: on the one hand, a great proliferation of different theories of poetry developed only slightly beyond the simple distinctions on which they are based, so that criticism itself seems constantly to be making new starts but never, as a discipline, getting anywhere in particular; and, on the other hand, an alarming kind of irresponsibility in the interpretation of individual works, of which many

32. Cf. Robert Roth, *Modern Philology*, XLVIII (1951), 193–204.

33. Cf. below, p. 566.

34. A classic instance is Eliot's "Andrew Marvell." Eliot, indeed, especially in his earlier essays on poets and dramatists, is the unrivaled contemporary master of this method.

examples could be cited in addition to those discussed in the first part of this volume. If there is a general remedy for these conditions, it is certainly not to be found in the proclamation of any new critical orthodoxy either of doctrine or of method. A plurality of critical approaches is not only inevitable but desirable in itself, both because the prosperity of the humanities depends on keeping all aspects of humanistic objects clearly in view and because, without the competition of radically different modes of criticism, the practice of the mode we may happen to prefer is bound to suffer. There is nothing, however, if our analysis of the relations between different critical methods is correct, that need prevent individual critics from understanding and using, with respect to questions for which each is appropriate, critical principles of several kinds. The critic of forms and functions can also be a critic of qualities, and the qualitative critic an "Aristotelian," without either of them losing his philosophic integrity, provided he views his commitment to both methods as hypothetical and pragmatic only. Nor is this all. It is generally true that we shall be safer and get farther in the long run in any field if, in our attempts to explore the similarities and unities of objects, we start with a prior understanding, in literal terms, of their specific differences of nature, than if, disregarding such differences, we proceed at once from our analogies to the particular applications they seem to permit. We might expect, therefore, that qualitative criticism would be all the better, as qualitative criticism, and almost certainly produce fewer glaring distortions of the "meaning" or structure of poems, if its practitioners were to form the habit of examining poetic works as concrete wholes before venturing to make statements about their parts in terms of a more abstract kind of theory. And the effects of such a habit, if it became widespread, might well be revolutionary for the collective development of criticism itself, by providing, in the multiple but compendent differentiations of the specific method, a broad base of ascertained literal knowledge about poetry in the light of which the many discrete and limited insights achieved by contemporary critics in the integral, or partly integral, modes might be coordinated with one another and developed more fully, to the great advantage of the critical art in all its modes and so ultimately of the humanities in general.

R. S. CRANE

I

I. A. RICHARDS ON THE ART OF
INTERPRETATION[1]

R. S. CRANE

No one in our time has written more voluminously than Mr. I. A. Richards on the difficulties that confront the interpreter of philosophical and literary texts, and no one has been more widely credited with the discovery of new principles and techniques by the aid of which, once they are fully elaborated, we may attain, in his own words, to "levels of intelligence in interpretation higher than those yet reached." The books which are cited in support of these high claims, from *The Meaning of Meaning* and *Principles of Literary Criticism* through *Mencius on the Mind* to *The Philosophy of Rhetoric*, *Interpretation in Teaching*, and *How To Read a Page*, constitute, indeed, an impressive series of disquisitions on what were once called the "Liberal Arts," which cannot be neglected by those curious about contemporary developments in intellectual criticism and exegesis. Their originality is undeniable; what is not so certain—and it is into this that I propose to inquire—is whether their contribution either of general concepts or of particular methods is substantial enough to justify the confidence of Richards' admirers that he has succeeded in putting the old art of interpreting texts on not only a new but a greatly improved basis.

I

Although he has written a great many pages in explanation of his doctrine, the doctrine itself is comparatively simple. Let us note two facts, to begin with, concerning the manner in which, according to him, correct thought about both the meaning of texts and the meaning of the meaning of texts must be derived. The two facts are closely related, and they are—as will become evident later—at once postulates of the right method of inquiry into both these questions and necessary consequences of the application of this method to the problems it allows or compels us to pose. In the first place, as Richards constantly reminds us, there is no thinking about anything that does not proceed inevitably by sorting and analogy. "Thinking," he remarks, "is radically metaphoric. Linkage by analogy is its constituent law or principle, its causal nexus. . . . To think of anything is to take it *as* of a sort." Nor is this true only of the "fluid" discourse which, because of its relaxation of definition, is nearly

1. Reprinted from *Ethics*, January, 1949; written in 1939.

related to poetry. Recognition of likes and discrimination of unlikes is the universal mode of generalization, and "Mathematics and the sciences, so often praised, and rightly, for the training in Logic they provide, are the leisurely, analyzed, explicitly recorded developments of the very same processes that, well or ill, operate in the main mode of metaphor." "To think of anything is to take it *as* of a sort." To think of the interpretation of discourse, as of discourse itself and of language in general, is, therefore, to think of it in terms of some fundamental analogy, some context or causal nexus with our past experience, by which the words we employ in the inquiry may be made to yield useful generalizations.

But—and this is the second postulate—since the end of our inquiry is knowledge, the only analogy which will serve our purpose is one that exhibits meaning and the meaning of meaning as instances of a sort of thing that in some sense can be pointed to rather than as instances merely of the theorist's attitudes or desires. We must endeavor, in other words, to rid our thinking about the subject from the fictions which have obscured it in the speculations of our predecessors, and to this end we must fashion our language in speaking of it as nearly as possible according to the pattern of natural science. And this means that we must dispense systematically with all terms which men have employed in the vain attempt to say *what* meaning or discourse is or *why* it is so and so, and confine ourselves to the terms we use to say *how* something behaves.

For science, which is simply our most elaborate way of *pointing* to things systematically, tells us and can tell us nothing about the nature of things in any *ultimate* sense. It can never answer any questions of the form: *What* is so and so? It can only tell us *how* so and so behaves. And it does not attempt to do more than this. Nor, indeed, can more than this be done. Those ancient, deeply troubling, formulations that begin with "What" and "Why" prove, when we examine them, to be not questions at all; but requests—for emotional satisfaction. They indicate our desire not for knowledge but for assurance, a point which appears clearly when we look into the "How" of questions and requests, of knowledge and desire.

The only meaningful way, then, in which we can talk about meaning is in terms of some analogy to the local motion of natural objects considered as a temporal sequence of events linked merely by efficient causes. It is a revealing fact that the terms and metaphors (in Richards' sense of the word) that recur most frequently in the key positions of his analysis are those designated by such expressions as "action," "motion," "behavior," "event." Thus thought "in the widest sense" is "any event in the mind"; "our knowledge is a reaction in us to something"; and the principles of Basic English—a language the theory of which recognizes no categories other than action and reaction—are "the oldest and most indubitable of all" (though, at the same time, the most modern and scientific) precisely because they represent "what we and our pre-human ancestors know most about," namely, how to perform those movements by which we maintain our vulnerable bodies in a world of "hard, moving, impenetrable and excarnificatory objects." The method of the inquiry is thus determined in a way strictly appropriate to the findings it seeks to obtain; and it will consequently occasion no surprise to the reader to learn from *The Philosophy of Rhetoric* that for Richards the true theory of interpretation—as distinguished from the superficial or erroneous theories of the past, which have been content with "bad analogies" based on unanswerable questions—not only has some affinities with physics but is "obviously a branch of biology."

It is at this point that the beautiful simplicity of Richards' scheme shines most clearly through the sophisticated diction and tortuous movement of the prose in which it is explained. Like the early Greek physicists who accounted for all things by means of one or two pairs of contrary terms, such as the dense and the rare or love and strife, he has found a way of reducing the whole problem of reading texts, even the most elaborately organized ones, to no more than two closely related distinctions, the one primarily psychological, the other (in the broadest sense of the term) linguistic. Meaning, he argues, is a kind of event which occurs whenever these two pairs of contraries mingle in the experience of any sensible creature, whether animal or human being, and there is no variety of meaning, at whatever level of intelligence or education, that cannot be adequately understood by considering it as an instance of this sort of behavior. Pavlov's dog hearing a bell from a distant part of the mansion and thereupon rushing incontinently to the dining-room; a man expecting a flame when he hears the scratch of a match; a scientist in the laboratory observing an instrument and writing down a formula in his notebook; a scholar expounding a passage in Plato—the only principles we need to interpret any of these examples of the universal "sign-situation" are, first, the fact that any response of an organism to a stimulus from its environment involves at once, though in varying proportions on different occasions, an appropriation of the stimulus and a reaction against it and, second, the circumstance that any awareness the organism may have of the relation between the felt impression and its antecedents or consequences in the environment or in the organism itself is a resultant of the interaction of the immediate experience with remembered experiences of like character in the past. Whether dog or scholar, we are all organisms living and functioning in the midst of things, capable of responding both to stimuli from without and to motions or feelings from within; and when we do respond, whether the result is to submit ourselves to things or to assert our purposes emotively with respect to them, the process is invariably one in which something taken as a sign is referred to something, real or fictitious, taken as a thing, by means of the co-operation in our minds of the present occasion with parallel or analogous events remembered from our past.

We need not ask *why* this is so; it is enough that we are so constituted that whenever a sign (as the sound of the dinner-bell or the occurrence of a puzzling word or construction in a text) is presented to our mind at a particular moment and in a particular set of circumstances, it acts upon us, through a kind of metaphoric attraction of like to like, by calling up the missing parts of the "context" of things or actions with which it has been linked in our previous experience. The meaning of any sign is thus the missing parts of its contexts; it is the "delegated efficacy" which any symbol acquires through its peculiar ability to serve as a substitute "exerting the powers of what is not there." We can have no sign-situation—no act of thinking or interpretation—of which this linking, by analogy, of past and present is not the essential feature; but it is obvious, given our nature as organisms in a world of things, that the process by which signs function as meanings may vary widely from time to time according as the major pull in the experience comes from the world of external objects to which the sign is being referred or from the needs and desires of the organism demanding emotional satisfaction. We may use signs or react to them, in other words, either in terms of their reference to objects or in terms of the effects in emotion and attitude which the reference produces; in the one case the mind is subjected to things, in the other it molds things to its own purposes and passions. No thought is possible in which the rivalry of the two functions is not to be discerned; however completely we teach our reactions to correspond with external states of affairs, the disturbing factor of the organism is always present.

The theory of discourse which Richards constructs by analogy with his account of the natural sign-situation is inevitably a theory in which the essential parts of any written composition—its meanings or our perceptions of its meanings—are treated as discrete events involving the co-operation or rivalry of "contexts." The term "context," as he points out, must be understood in a double sense:

(1) A word, like any other sign, gets whatever meaning it has through belonging to a recurrent group of events, which may be called its context. Thus a word's context, *in this sense*, is a certain recurrent pattern of *past* groups of events, and to say that its meaning depends upon its context would be to point to the process by which it has acquired its meaning. (2) In another, though a connected sense, a word's context is *the words which surround it in the utterance*, and the other *contemporaneous signs* which govern its interpretation. . . . For clarity we may distinguish the second sort of context by calling it the *setting*.

Whenever, in short, we use words to make a statement, or what looks like a statement, about anything, we are taking part in a process of analogical interaction between the "setting "in which our words are placed and the various "contexts"—there may be an indefinite number of them—which have surrounded the words in their past careers. A meaning is always an instance of a sort, its efficacy dependent upon a perceived likeness between present and former occasions—that is what is meant by the dictum that all thinking is radically metaphoric; and when the former occasions have been particularly numerous and conflicting, it is obvious that the pull of divergent possible interpretations upon the new "setting" must be severe. In his chapter on the meanings of the word "definite" in *Interpretation in Teaching*, Richards gives some striking examples, from the "protocols" of his students, of the force of these opposing attractions, but there is every reason to suppose that they operate more or less constantly in the literary prose of more expert writers. It is only rarely, indeed —and chiefly in the vocabulary of the rigorously limited laboratory sciences— that the "contexts" determining the meanings of terms approach a state of uniformity which allows us to say that the words and sentences in a passage "mean what they mean absolutely and unconditionally." The function of definition in the sciences is precisely to effect such a control over the interaction of contexts for the specific purpose in hand, but it is seldom, outside "the relatively *simple* fields of the sciences," that an equivalent control is possible, or even desirable.

Argument is a peculiar, specialized use of language to which it has not yet accommodated itself. To put it more strictly, the logical use of words, with single constant senses that are the same for each recurrence, maintained unchanged through a series of sentence manipulations, is an extremely artificial sort of behaviour to which our minds do not lend themselves until after a long and severe training. It is no more like our usual ways of talking than the goose-step is like our strolling gait. And the fluidity, the incessant delicate variation in the meaning of our words, which is a hindrance to explicit argument, is the virtue of language for our other purposes.

It is an error, consequently, to suppose that "if a passage means one thing it cannot at the same time mean another and an incompatible thing." The different contexts or types of context which supply the meaning for a single utterance are in constant rivalry one with another, with the result that we should "expect ambiguity to the widest extent and of the subtlest kinds nearly everywhere, and of course we find it."

The problem of the interaction of contexts is inseparable, for Richards, from the larger question, arising from the double character of all organic behavior, of the differences and connections among "the various aims of discourse, the purposes for which we speak or write." It is characteristic that here again, abandoning as unfruitful the traditional attempt to differentiate kinds of writing in terms of their specific traits of subject matter, method, and end, he reduces the problem to a distinction, by analogy with the facts of the universal sign-situation, among "the functions of language." The fundamental opposition thus derived—familiar to all his readers since the *Principles of Literary Criticism*—is that between "pure scientific impersonal or neutral statement," in which words are used to point to things, and "emotive utterance which expresses and evokes states of feeling." The theory of discourse, thus, must take account of all the complicated ways in which emotional attitude may be combined with reference and reference distorted by attitude; it must be prepared to distinguish the varieties of "statement, full and explicit, or condensed (by abstraction, ambiguity or implication, the hint, the aposiopesis); statement literal or direct, and indirect (by metaphor, simile, comparison, parallel, etc.); suasion, open (from cajolery) or concealed (either as mere statement or as mere ornament) and so on." And the principle which unifies the extremes is still the same principle of the interinanimation of contexts on which, as we have seen, all significances depend.

From Pavlov's dog responding meaningfully to the sound of the dinner-bell to the writer or reader of a prose masterpiece successfully contending with the divergent attractions of linguistic contexts and functions, the transition is thus perfectly clear: to understand the behavior of the one is to know by simple analogy all the truth that can be found out about the behavior of the other. The statement of that truth in words which must themselves necessarily exemplify it constitutes the scientific or theoretical aspect of the philosophy of interpretation. But interpretation, like any sort of animal response, exists only as event, so that to interpret a particular text is to function in a sign-situation in no way different in kind from those precipitated by the sound of the dinner-bell or the scratch of the match but, of course, immensely more complicated in the number of co-operating and conflicting stimuli, whether contexts or settings, that are brought to bear on the mind of the interpreter.

It is here, in Richards' argument, that we abandon, at least momentarily, the simplicities of theory for the paradoxes and duplicities of practice. It would seem, on the one hand, that, since interpretation is a natural process, nature herself, assisted by a kind of exercise similar to that which gives strength to the muscles, could well be trusted to make us all at least reasonably good interpreters of books. And this, indeed, is largely true. We are all born, Richards assures us, with a "natural skill in interpretation"—a skill that need not wait upon training in principles to be "inexplicably, unimaginably and all-but-triumphantly, successful already." Let us then avoid, in education, anything that will interfere with the working of the instinctive dialectic by which, as in all our thinking, we recognize likes and discriminate unlikes as a normal result of the process of contextual interaction. Yet nothing is more evident, we are also told (and the students' "protocols" quoted by Richards bear out the point), than that the natural skill in interpretation, when it is brought to bear on the words of a particular text, too often becomes confused and fails. An art of interpretation is therefore needed which will start with the "uncanny powers" we have already developed and help us develop them a little further.

For the outlines of such an art Richards reverts to the distinctions of the medieval trivium. "Less by design than from the nature, history and life of its subject," he says in the Introduction to *Interpretation in Teaching*, "this treatise has grown into three parts which correspond roughly to ancient provinces of thought. Rhetoric, Grammar and Logic—the first three liberal Arts, the three ways to intelligence and a command of the mind that met in the Trivium, meet here again." What is needed is precisely the training they are fitted to give, a training now almost entirely lacking in the curriculum; but such a training can be fruitful, can lead to better interpretations, only if Rhetoric, Grammar, and Logic are taught to students not as sciences but as arts, and as arts, moreover, which have in common, for all their differences in emphasis, the basic problems of the sign-situation.

For improvement of the natural skill in interpretation, however, even the minimum of theoretical analysis to which the arts are thus reduced is of little direct importance. The difficulty is not that our students are ignorant of principles; it is rather that they do not know "how to distinguish and meet the varying modes of language *in practice*." Our only sure reliance, therefore, must be the art of the teacher who, though he himself is an expert in the theory of meaning, takes care not to interfere with the natural growth of his pupils by imposing ideas upon them but contents himself with inventing occasions for self-discovery and with devising exercises which will bring his students to an awareness of their failures through comparison with the failures or only partial successes of others. The essential character of the method, as Richards expounds and illustrates it, is that of a free dialectic working on passages or sentences through exhibition of the contexts of their words or through construction of parallels between them and other passages or sentences. Controls are no doubt necessary, but they take the form not of explicit criteria for determining when a proper adjustment has been made between context and setting but rather of collections of the chief contexts of key words, such as "grammar" or "definite" or "is," or of translations into the vocabulary of Basic English.

The spirit of the procedure Richards recommends is well exemplified in his own "interpretation," in chapter xvii of *Interpretation in Teaching*, of a sentence from John Stuart Mill's *Inaugural Address at St. Andrews*. The problem is how we know what the pronoun "their" refers to in the last clause of the following: "Even as mere languages, no modern European language is so valuable a discipline to the intellect as those of Greece and Rome, on account of their regular and complicated structure."

How do we know what 'their' refers to? If we wrote 'their irregular and over-simple structure' the sentence would in several minor ways not mean the same, but most of Mill's main point would be preserved—only 'their' would have been switched over then to modern European languages, not to Greek and Latin. And equally it would be the context [i.e., our knowledge of the recurrent group of past events in which 'irregular' and 'simple' have referred to the structure of modern languages] which told us how to read it. . . . With the setting he is not likely to misread, for we know that Greek and Latin will be thought to be more regular and complicated than modern languages— whatever the facts in the matter, and the assumptions, as to the sorts of regularity and complication involved may be. Moreover, 'regular,' at least in such an occurrence as this, seems a word of praise [i.e., to have an emotive context] and so goes with 'valuable.' This joins with the setting to bar out the possibility that Mill (as others have sometimes thought) was thinking that the less regular a language the harder the task of learning it and therefore the better the discipline. There is an articulation between 'regular' and 'complicated,' which was lost by my rephrasing, 'their irregular and over-simple structure.' Mill's full point is 'though complicated yet regular.' And this articulation shows us that Mill is thinking of a certain sort of discipline which he expects from Greek and Latin.

It will have occurred to many readers that the problem of the reference of "their" in Mill's sentence—if problem it be—could have been solved much more expeditiously than it is solved here by the traditional devices of grammatical analysis. Richards seems to be aware of the objection, but he dismisses it as already outlawed by the original assumptions and analogies on which his system is erected:

This kind of analysis of the factors in interpretation can I believe usefully take the place of formal grammatical parsing. Parsing gave exercise in it incidentally, and had value as far as it did; but, in itself, it is an unnatural and distracting antic. This other sort of interpretative study follows closely the actual processes that take place in composition; parsing does not. No one asks, or should ask, himself in writing, 'What does this dependent phrase qualify?' We do all inquire, all the time we are writing, about the consiliences and the articulations of the meanings of the parts with one another; or, if we don't, we can very easily be made to.

It should be clear from what has gone before why he thinks this a completely cogent answer. For if the only questions that can give us the truth about things are questions concerning *how* something behaves, then obviously we are merely troubling our mind with fictions and seeking emotional assurance rather than knowledge if we permit ourselves, whether in writing something of our own or in reading the work of others, to put such queries as "*What* does this dependent phrase qualify?" The antic is indeed both unnatural and distracting— unnatural, since it is an arbitrary intrusion into the process of contextual interaction, and distracting, since it tends to mingle emotive with referential words. What we can know—and to know this is precisely the end of the art of interpretation—is *how* we have become aware, in so far as we have been successful in our reading, of *how* the words in a particular passage "behave."

Such, in its broad outlines, is the new art of interpreting prose and of teaching the interpretation of prose which Richards would have us substitute for the prescientific or magic-mongering systems of the past. His success in winning support for his proposals has been, as we all know, very considerable; and the secret is not hard to find. He has had the great advantage of knowing how to deal with perennial issues in a thoroughly modern style. In an age of faith in biology, he has contrived to frame the problems of literature, with rare consistency, in terms of primordial organic processes; in an age convinced beyond any in the past that the key to all philosophic mysteries, and to most of our practical difficulties as well, is to be found in the study of words, he has effected a remarkable renovation of the liberal arts by substituting for their traditional distinctions and devices a universal theory of signs. The natural appeal of his doctrine, moreover, has been greatly enhanced by the assured, not to say dogmatic, manner of its delivery. Nothing is more distinctive of his exposition, in all his many books, than the "damnatory clauses" in which, as Macaulay said of the Benthamites, his creed abounds "far beyond any theological symbol with which we are acquainted." "I neither am," he has said, "nor hope to be a scholar"; but this modesty has not prevented him from exposing, with his usual vigor of expression, the trivialities, the confusions, the absurdities, the false problems and unnecessary mysteries, the gross evasions of the most interesting issues, which have characterized, almost without exception, the efforts of scholars in the past to deal with the meaning of texts. It is no wonder that, armed with such credentials, he has succeded in convincing a wide public that only now at last, in this crucial matter of literary interpretation, have our eyes been opened to the reality of things, our first principles properly established, and the one true method of procedure clearly revealed.

It behooves us, therefore, if we are to form an independent judgment of a system so alluring in its modernity, so imposing in its dogmatic rigor, to look a little more closely both at the first principles upon which it is founded and at the practical consequences which appear to flow inevitably from them.

II

It is evident, first of all, that Richards' consideration of discourse is organized about three fundamental terms—the venerable triad which has served countless writers on logic, grammar, and rhetoric since Plato and Aristotle: the words in which texts are composed, the ideas or thoughts they symbolize, and the "real" things or events to which their words and statements refer. This triple distinction is the basis of the famous triangle of meaning first presented in *The Meaning of Meaning* and since then employed consistently in all his linguistic or rhetorical arguments. There is nothing in this fact by itself, of course, that is in any way unique: how else, indeed, could we say anything intelligible about any human discourse save by reference to the subject matter dealt with in its statements, the doctrines or beliefs set forth concerning this subject matter, and the words by which these doctrines are expressed? Everything turns, therefore, on the manner in which, in any given theory of discourse or interpretation, the three indispensable factors are related to each other as organizing principles of the discussion. There are only two major possibilities: on the one hand, we may recognize that, since the three terms are in themselves, apart from any use we make of them, completely equivocal words, the literal senses we give to them and the relations constructed among these senses may legitimately vary from context to context, so that our treatment of words or of thought or of subject matter may be quite distinct according as we are concerned, let us say, with the analysis of poems or of rhetorical compositions or of philosophical arguments. Or, on the other hand, we may prefer, once and for all, to fix the relation of words, thoughts, and things in a single pattern, determined by a fundamental analogy, which will henceforth persist throughout our consideration of individual problems as a device by which the particularities of our subject matter may be resolved into a set of simple universal laws. Now the choice between these two primary modes of procedure is obviously one that cannot be avoided by any writer who proposes to treat of the problem of interpretation; and, once made, it just as obviously entails consequences which, if the resulting analysis is self-consistent, must be expected to manifest themselves even in the least details of the system. And the essential point is that the choice itself is a choice that involves, for the theorist of discourse, simply a decision as to the way in which he intends to use his own words—whether, on the one hand, to mark off sharp distinctions of meaning, so that no one distinguishable aspect of an object is resolved into anything else, or, on the other hand, to make possible a reduction of such distinctions in the interest of a single unified truth. The choice is therefore independent of the nature of things, except as the nature of things may be held responsible for the necessity of such a choice; and it is logically prior to any true conclusions that may be reached about characteristics of writings which can be attributed to them only through use of the particular mode of definition and argument that has been selected.

Richards, it need hardly be said, has chosen the second rather than the first of these two ways of dealing with words, thoughts, and things as basic factors in the interpretation of discourse. He has chosen to fix the meanings and relations of his three central terms prior to his use of them in any particular inquiries; and he has chosen to fix them by means of a fundamental analogy or "metaphor" (in his sense of that word) which takes various forms in his writings, but is perhaps best represented by the parallel, in *The Meaning of Meaning*, of Pavlov and his dog.

The basis of that metaphor, it will be recalled, is a situation involving two distinct elements, one of which—the dog moving toward the dining-room—is biological strictly, and the other—Pavlov conditioning the dog so that it will perform this action whenever the dinner-bell rings—biological only in an indirect and unimportant sense, its essential character being that of an interference by human art with the processes of nature. From each of these elements Richards derives one of the two basic distinctions of his scheme. From the motions of the dog considered as an organism capable both of attending to things outside itself and of responding to stimuli from within, he takes the distinction which emerges on the level of human speech as the contrast of emotive and referential language or of fluid and rigid discourse. From the purposive actions of Pavlov so connecting food and the sound of the dinner-bell in the reflexes of the dog that, whenever the bell is heard, a motion is set up toward the usual place of food, he borrows the distinction, central to the art of interpretation as he conceives it, between linguistic "contexts" and "settings." The device whereby he brings the two elements of the analogy together in his system involves taking the sound of the dinner-bell as at once a sign of the previous situations, arranged by Pavlov, in which it had been connected with food, and as a stimulus to biological reactions on the part of the dog when it is again heard. When symbols are interpreted thus, the terms of the original triad of words, thoughts, and things fall into a characteristically simple pattern: the only problem we need consider is that of the function of individual words as the medium by which, in the uninterrupted flow of experience, human thought is shaped by reference either to things (considered always as "sorts") or to fictions that take the place of things. In this function words may obviously become important instruments for manipulating thoughts to one or another of the two purposes, given by the biological part of the analogy, for which symbols may be employed—to point to things or to express our own emotions; but the ways in which they work are determined by things in the sense of the contexts of past events, whether involving things or thoughts, in which they have been used. The processes of nature, of meaning, and of intention are thus separable only dialectually, as a consequence of our acquired ability to discriminate signs; no independent consideration of any of the three is possible, and hence no independent analysis, such as has been attempted by writers in the past, of words as applied to things or to ideas or to words or of ideas in relation to their objects or of objects in relation to other objects;[2] rather all the problems tend to merge into one, which can be examined with profit—that is, as a problem of things rather than merely of thought or words—only by considering how particular words "behave" with respect to one another and to the things and thoughts they bring before our minds.

It is this radical unification of the whole traditional analysis in terms of the "behavior" of individual words that impels Richards to dismiss, with such telling effect, not only the notion that any art or methodology is involved in his firsthand dealings with language, but likewise all the various systems of grammar, logic, and rhetoric in which previous writers—more concerned, in his view, with theories than with applications—have developed principles for an analysis of the structural aspects of discourse or for a particularized consideration of its various kinds. Preoccupied as he is with inducing a heightened awareness of individual sign-situations by comparisons of words, he has nothing to offer but a universal method for the reading of texts—a method without any devices for discriminating differences in subject matter or in method or in intention in the sense of the specific ends, peculiar to the given work, to which means have been rationally adapted by the author.

The causes of this curious dialectical asceticism will perhaps become clear if we revert to the analogy in the light of which Richards' system has been constructed.[3] The difficulty is not, of course, that the facts upon which one half of the metaphor is based involve nothing more exalted than the natural motions of a dog; readers of Plato, at all events, will not have forgotten the excellent use which Socrates makes of this same animal in the *Republic* when it is a question of determining what virtues are appropriate to the guardians of the state. And there is surely no reason why an analysis of argument, more nearly adequate than any Richards gives us for the explanation of structural characteristics in prose, could not be developed from postulates as strictly biological as his. The proof, if proof were needed, is afforded by John Dewey's *Logic: The Theory of Inquiry.* The condition of such a development, as Dewey shows, is simply the recognition that organic behavior is typically sequential; that, as appears plainly in such "unified and continuous" animal responses as hunting and stalking prey, it is not merely "a succession and compounding of independent discrete reflex-arc units" but a kind of elementary problem-solving with direction and cumulative force. If this is granted and if we assume a continuity of evolution from animal forms and activities to those of man, then,

2. Cf. below, pp. 176 ff.

3. I am not assuming, of course, any such deliberate and explicit use of the analogy, especially in his later writings, as my somewhat oversimplified argument might seem to imply.

given the potentiality, on the human level, of a cultural environment and of discursive thought, we need no other principles whereby to justify, in purely naturalistic terms, a fairly elaborate analysis of intellectual discourse as an art of fitting logical means to consequences in the solution of problems. Richards, however, although he can insist that the theory of interpretation is obviously a branch of biology, is not free to push the biological part of his metaphor as far as this; the dog is not simply a dog, it is Pavlov's dog; and, this being the case, its contribution to the explanation of language is necessarily limited to those aspects of its natural behavior which are adequately described—to borrow Dewey's phrase—as "simply a succession of isolated and independent units of excitation-reaction," or, in other words, as discrete events considered apart from any possible sequence of actions in which they function as means to an intelligible end. To the extent, therefore, that the problem of discourse and of the interpretation of discourse is determined by this part of Richards' analogy, the most we can expect in the way of principles is a simple pair of contraries applicable only to particular words.

The relation of means and consequences, however, is clearly implied in the part of the metaphor which concerns Pavlov; and the beginnings at least of an analysis of intellectual method, relevant to many kinds of prose literature, might easily have been derived by considering what is involved when a scientist selects one experiment rather than another as more directly conducive to a specific end. Needless to say, it is not this aspect of Pavlov that interests Richards, but rather two more limited aspects, one of which has to do with the results of his acts of conditioning as these appear in the subsequent operations of the dog whenever the dinner-bell rings, and the other of which relates to the processes and immediate intentions of the experiment itself. From the first comes the idea of the interaction of "contexts" and "settings" which is, for Richards, the essence of "meaning" interpreted as a natural event. But it is still necessary to account for the contexts themselves which determine materially the behavior of signs whenever these occur in a novel setting; and, since, when the problem is transferred to the level of human discourse, there can be no longer a Pavlov conditioning our reflexes, some substitute, less external in a literal sense to the individual organism but still in a way external, must evidently be discovered for the function he performs as experimenter in the original situation. That substitute is, in the first place, the long history of contextual interactions, in other men and in our past lives, which we call our cultural and linguistic inheritance. By this, as represented, for example, in the vast proliferation of meanings contained in the *OED* or in Richards' lists, we are all controlled, much as Pavlov's dog was controlled, in each of our uses or interpretations of any of the words we write or read, so that ambiguity—i.e., the intrusion into a particular setting of many contexts—is an ever present and never entirely soluble problem. But what has been conditioned may also, to a certain extent at least, be reconditioned; and if Pavlov persists in Richards' account of language and discourse as the more or less external control exercised over our words and thoughts by past associations of words with things, he also re-emerges, especially in practical treatises like *Interpretation in Teaching*, in the person of the teacher who sets his pupils exercises in verbal comparisons and translations to the end of heightening their awareness of how words behave in relation to other words and to things and ideas. He is the enlightened teacher, but he is also that most valuable instrument of the enlightened teacher, Basic English—a language that contributes to our understanding of both things and words by reducing the vocabulary of English to those words which are closest to things, inasmuch as their primary contexts are the organic motions of putting and taking, giving and getting, pointing and feeling; a language, moreover, that enables us to cope more efficiently with the problem of ambiguity by increasing still further that disproportion between the finiteness of words and the infiniteness of things from which ambiguity arises!

It would be unfair to say of the procedure Richards recommends for the practice and teaching of interpretation that it consists merely of a technique of lexicographical exercise without other ends than the exercise itself. The ends are there, and they are stated variously as understanding, as intelligence, as heightened awareness, as intellectual discernment, as insight, as self-discovery, as improvement of our command of all the interconnections of thought, nonverbal as well as verbal. Yet, however distinct these aims may appear in statements of them taken out of their context in Richards' system, it is evident, when we recall the basic principles of that system, that they are all ends as nearly identifiable with the means devised for their realization as was Pavlov's awareness of the behavior of his dog with the experiment he conducted for the sake of inducing that behavior. What Richards gives us, in short, in following out this aspect of his analogy, is simply a set of experimental devices for bringing about in the reader a sharpened consciousness of linguistic particulars as "sorts" of universal motions.

To go beyond this either by traveling the biological road taken by Dewey or by developing the implications of Pavlov as the artist in experiments would entail the elaboration of a general scheme of analysis applicable to particular texts in such a way that the particularity of their structure rather than the universality of their material constituents would become the center of attention. He is restrained, however, from adopting either of these courses by the peculiar character of the metaphor from which his whole method springs. It is a metaphor resting on what is clearly a constructed situation, partly natural and partly artificial, with the two elements so related that any full development of one of them is immediately checked or interfered with by some trait in the other. In the end, for Richards, it is nature which exerts the stronger dialectical pull, and it does so by virtue of the skeptical implications for our understanding of the terms of philosophy and the arts contained in his biological distinction between pointing and feeling, with its equivalent in the linguistic contrast of referential and emotive words. We have seen that this distinction underlies his doubt about the scientific meaningfulness of any other questions than those which ask *how* something behaves, and so deprives him from the start of all explanatory resources except such as are furnished by his very limited conception of the efficient cause. We have seen how it leads him to posit, as the ideal mode of interpretation, a procedure which, unlike the unnatural and distracting antic of parsing, follows closely the actual processes of composition as these should be if not as they are. And we may suggest that the strong suspicion of previous theories of criticism and interpretation which runs throughout his works, and which confirms him in his preference for a method so nearly universal that it seems to him no method at all, gains much of its force from precisely this bias in favor of one rather than the other of the two components, not quite perfectly fused, of the original analogy.

III

The method is indeed universal, but it *is* a method, and as such it is only fair to judge it, finally, in terms of its consequences apart from the somewhat arbitrarily constructed first principles by which it is validated theoretically. And, first of all, as we have noted so often, there is a whole range of problems—real problems, too, since they force themselves on us, independently of any theories of interpretation, whenever we attempt to understand a text as a whole or to compare two writings on the same subject—for the solution of which his scheme provides no apparatus whatever. Thus we are constantly tempted to ask, in reading prose works of any distinction, on what principles the words or sentences are ordered in this or that passage, or why the parts of the argument are arranged as they are, or how we may account for the author's insistence on certain aspects of his problem and his neglect of other aspects which, in the writings of his predecessors or successors, have usually been given a prominent place. In order to find answers to such questions, we obviously need devices which will enable us to discover a writer's basic terms, not merely as so many recurrent words, but rather as the fundamental scheme of concepts by means of which his problem is stated and the parts and order of his argument determined; we need principles by which, once the terms have been established, possible modes of working with them may be distinguished; and we need other principles, involving still more particularized discriminations of ends and means, in the light of which the peculiar structural characteristics of individual works may be understood and appreciated. It is evident that no such principles or devices are to be looked for anywhere in Richards' many publications. He speaks much of purposes in writing, but what he has in mind are the universal purposes, or linguistic "functions," common to the sophisticated author and the simplest biological organism, not those which differentiate writers as voluntary agents. He writes books which expound, as we have seen, a highly characteristic system of thought; but nowhere in these books does he provide means whereby the system may be understood in its distinctive outlines or whereby we may progress, in our reading of his books, beyond what is stated in separate paragraphs and sentences.

It is to these, indeed—the significant wholes to which his method tends to reduce all literature—that he systematically endeavors to confine our attention. For the Richardsian interpreter of discourse there can be only one problem; and, whether that problem is stated generally as the interaction of contexts and settings or is specified as ambiguity or metaphor or confusion of statement and definition, it is clearly one which can be adequately posed and solved in terms of isolated statements considered apart from the total artistic or logical structure of the works in which they appear. For the problem is really one of the universal behavior of words as determined by events which in any strict sense are extra-literary, and a solution is possible just as soon as we have enough of the immediate setting of the word before us to permit an estimate of what various contexts have been at work. Thus—to adapt an example from *Basic Rules of Reason*—it is not necessary to read the whole of the *Preface to the "Lyrical Ballads"* in order to deal with the question of what is meant by "poetry" in Wordsworth's assertion that "poetry is the look on the face of science"; instead we have only to recognize that the problem turns essentially on the meaning of "is," that "is" may have different meanings according as the sentences in which it occurs are definitions of words or statements about the things of which the word is the name, that if we compare the saying of Wordsworth with other sayings about "poetry" (Richards gives a good many of them), we see that it is more like a statement than a definition, and that as such, separated from a definition, it may have as many senses as Wordsworth or we ourselves at any time have attached to the word.

All this, granted the way in which the problem is stated, is no doubt true, and there is abundant justification in the circumstance for Richards' insistence on our need of a "better apparatus for controlling the senses of our words." A twofold difficulty, however, immediately confronts us. On the one hand, even if we allow that the question of Wordsworth's meaning in the sentence quoted can be intelligibly discussed in terms of that sentence alone plus the "contexts" of its words, there is nothing, so far as one can see, in the "better apparatus" Richards gives us—neither in his lists of the senses of "is" or of "poetry" nor in his directions for translation exercises into Basic English— that can do anything more than heighten our awareness of the problem. And, on the other hand, if we are seriously interested in discovering Wordsworth's intention rather than simply in playing a new and somewhat complicated linguistic game and if, consequently, we insist on considering the question not in the vacuum of a single sentence but in the total context, highly particularized as it is, of Wordsworth's argument and method in the *Preface*, then we are already provided, in various of the devices afforded by traditional dialectic, with much of the apparatus we need. For the problem of ambiguity is not, as many of Richards' disciples suppose, a new one; and, if the problem is what we have always thought it to be, the means of dealing with it available to us in (say) the first book of the *Topics* would still seem adequate to most of our uses. It is not easy, therefore, to escape the suspicion that what is at issue for Richards is not the question of ambiguity, in the usual meaning, at all; that his concern is less with solutions that make sense of difficult texts in their authors' terms than with the discovery or manufacture of problems by which linguistic wonder may be excited, and that that method is best, accordingly, which so restricts its means of solution that what emerges from any act of interpretation is not so much understanding of the author as increased insight into our own marvelous but somewhat confused minds.

There would be no objection to this, were it not that the reading of a book in any sense that involves doing justice to the distinctive intentions of its author is rendered impossible thereby. For the essence of Richards' method, so far as it assumes a positive character at all, is translation; and what inevitably happens when that technique is applied to a writer of any intellectual sophistication or systematic integrity will be plain to whoever meditates on the strange fate of John Stuart Mill in chapter xvii of *Interpretation in Teaching*. But translation in the mode exhibited in this chapter is innocent enough when compared to the fundamental distortion necessarily undergone by any writer who philosophizes in other categories than action and reaction when his statements are subjected to the Procrustean dialectic of Basic English—a language whose key terms have been selected in explicit opposition to most of the varied ways of dealing with the problem of words, ideas, and things to be found in the important prose writers of the past.

It is at this point that the question of method and the practical consequences thereof rejoins the question of principles. For if it be indeed true, as has been occasionally insinuated by followers of Richards, that his is a theory that ends all theories except itself and the better thought about language we may look for in

the future, then the objections we have brought against his program for the reform of interpretation are not only irrelevant but philosophically unsound—
expressions of our wishes that carry over into a new age the fictions and magic-
charged concepts of the past. Our examination of Richards' views will perhaps
have been justified if it has revealed the essential circularity of all such retorts.
For what is the force of an appeal to the nature of things against rival doctrines
of language or discourse when that nature itself has been determined by a
decision, prior to any inquiry, to identify reality only with what can be signified in a particular fixed relationship among three equivocal words? And what is
there to compel an abandonment of the distinctions of traditional grammar or
logic in an argument which derives all its negative cogency from a metaphor so
admirably adapted to the end of destroying such distinctions as that upon which
Richards' system is based?

WILLIAM EMPSON, CONTEMPORARY CRITICISM AND POETIC DICTION[1]

ELDER OLSON

THE last quarter of a century has seen the rise, in England and America, of a new critical movement. Its mere longevity would perhaps entitle it to some importance in the eyes of future literary historians; but that importance is guaranteed and augmented by the esteem which it has won and by the distinction and persistent fame of the persons who are regarded as its chief practitioners. The "new criticism," as this movement is called by both its friends and its foes, seems to be almost universally regarded as having at last brought literary study to a condition rivaling that of the sciences. It has, we are frequently told, established itself upon principles the scientific character of which is assured by the fact that they are drawn from such sciences as psychology, biology, anthropology, linguistics, economics, and so on, in their most modern development; it has led, according to its proponents, to an unparalleled accuracy and minuteness in the treatment of texts, and in the employment of terminology and critical techniques; it has, we are assured, an over-all, if not specific, unity of method, as well as a doctrine sufficiently established to permit a list of "heresies" and "fallacies"; finally, and best of all, it not only can discuss more and explain it better than the outworn criticisms which it supplants, but it is still, like the sciences, in a happy condition of growth.[2]

Mr. William Empson is among the principal exponents of this movement, and it might almost be said that where he is mentioned, it is mentioned, and where it is, he is. Nor is this extraordinary; in certain respects it can be said that he has produced it, and it, him. His prestige, briefly, is enormous; his theories, never too vigorously assailed, have gained wider acceptance with the years, and his particular interpretations of texts are regarded as pretty nearly exhaustive and definitive. The recent re-publication of one of his prin-

1. Reprinted from *Modern Philology*, May, 1950.

2. I do not, of course, imply that every one of these views is held by every critic, and with equal conviction and enthusiasm. But I have taken pains to construct a statement which should convey as fully as possible, and without too great inaccuracy, the general attitude which the "new critics" assume toward their criticism. See John Crowe Ransom, *The New Criticism*, Preface; William Elton, *A Glossary of the New Criticism* (Chicago, 1949), pp. 3–5; Robert W. Stallman, "The New Critics," in *Critiques and Essays in Criticism* (New York, 1949), p. 506.

cipal works, *Seven Types of Ambiguity*,[3] as a "classic of modern criticism," affords us an occasion to examine the critical method of Empson and, in that connection, of the "new criticism" as well.

I

For Empson, as for his master I. A. Richards, poetry is simply an aspect or condition of language; it is therefore definable in terms of its medium; it is language differentiated from other language by a certain attribute. Richards first proposed that this distinguishing feature was ambiguity, and occupied himself with exhibiting the complexities of response which ambiguity engenders; Empson has followed by enumerating seven kinds of ambiguity.

The term "ambiguity" here does not carry its usual meaning. Ambiguity as Empson conceives it is not the mere possession of double meaning; an obvious pun or a patent irony is not ambiguous, for instance, "because there is no room for puzzling";[4] although such expressions when less obvious are called ambiguous "even by a critic who never doubted their meaning," since they are "calculated to deceive at least a section of their readers."[5] Nor is ambiguity simply concision, nor the quality of language which produces mixed emotions; it is, rather, "any verbal nuance, however slight, which gives room for alternative reactions to the same piece of language."[6] The important point here is that of alternative reactions; Empson illustrates his meaning by remarking that a child might view the sentence "The brown cat sat on the red mat" as part of a fairy story or as an excerpt from *Reading without Tears*.[7]

The ambiguities are types of "logical disorder," arranged as stages of advancing disorder,[8] or, what is apparently the same thing, "in order of increasing distance from simple statement and logical exposition."[9] The seven types, then, are kinds in which (1) "a detail is effective in several ways at once"; (2) "two or more alternative meanings are fully resolved into one"; (3) "two apparently unconnected meanings are given simultaneously"; (4) "alternative meanings combine to make a complicated state of mind in the author"; (5) "a fortunate confusion" is present, "as when the author is discovering his idea in the act of writing or not holding it all in his mind at once"; (6) "what is said is contradictory or irrelevant and the reader is forced to invent interpretations"; and (7) "full contradiction" is present, "marking a division in the author's mind." These kinds are general and have subdivisions; the first, for example, divides into "comparisons with several points of likeness," "antith-

3. 2d ed., rev. and reset; New York: New Directions, 1947.

4. P. x.   7. P. 2.

5. *Ibid.*   8. P. 48.

6. P. 1.   9. P. 7.

eses with several points of difference," " 'comparative' adjectives," " 'subdued' metaphors," and ambiguities of rhythm, or, as Empson puts it, "extra meanings suggested by rhythm."[10]

One of his best-known passages is in illustration of "comparison with several points of likeness," and is a good example of his method in operation:

There is no pun, double syntax, or dubiety of feeling, in

> Bare ruined choirs where late
> the sweet birds sang,

but the comparison holds for many reasons: because ruined monastery choirs are places in which to sing, because they involve sitting in a row, because they are made of wood, are carved into knots and so forth, because they used to be surrounded by a sheltering building crystallized out of the likeness of a forest, and coloured with stained glass and painting like flowers and leaves, because they are now abandoned by all but the grey walls coloured like the skies of winter, because the cold and Narcissistic charm suggested by choir-boys suits well with Shakespeare's feeling for the object of the sonnets, and for various sociological and historical reasons (the protestant destruction of monasteries, fear of puritanism), which it would be hard now to trace out in their proportions; these reasons, and many more relating the simile to its place in the Sonnet, must all combine to give the line its beauty, and there is a sort of ambiguity in not knowing which of them to hold most clearly in mind. Clearly this is involved in all such richness and heightening of effect, and the machinations of ambiguity are among the very roots of poetry.[11]

The broad theory underlying Empson's method seems to be as follows: Poetry uses language, and language is meaningful and communicative; hence poetry is communicative. In analyzing communication, there are three possibilities: one may speak about what happened in the author's mind, about what is likely to happen in the reader's mind, or "about both parties at once," as involved in the communication itself.[12] The first two kinds of discussion, according to Empson, make the claim of knowing too much; "the rules as to what is conveyable are so much more mysterious even than the rules governing the effects of ambiguity" that the third possibility is best. Hence in the main he talks about the third, although he is by no means, he says, "puristic" about this.[13] Apparently the poet communicates ideas, like everyone else, and the reader is affected by these ideas according to their kind; the poet, however, would seem to be a poet, not in virtue of the emotional quality of his ideas, but in virtue of the devices of ambiguity which he consciously or unconsciously employs. Moreover, the effects *proper* to poetry are not the emotions evoked by the ideas; rather, since ambiguity is the essence of poetry, the process of

10. These quotations have been extracted from the analytical Table of Contents, pp. v–vi.

11. Pp. 2–3.

12. P. 243. 13. P. 235 n.

reading is a process of "inventing reasons" why certain elements should have been selected for a poem, as in the passage just quoted, and the peculiar pleasure derived from poetry is produced by the mental activity in response to these ambiguities.[14] It is, to use Empson's own word, a pleasure of "puzzling," apparently different from the pleasure afforded by riddles, charades, and anagrams in that these latter involve matters emotionally indifferent.

The method of interpretation which rests upon this theory is, as we might expect, one reducing all poetic considerations to considerations of poetic diction, and one reducing all discussion of diction, even, to problems of ambiguities. The method might be described as the permutation and combination of all the various "meanings" of the parts of a given discourse, whether these parts be simple or complex; out of the mass of "meanings" so found, Empson selects those which "give room for alternative reactions," i.e., which satisfy the fundamental condition of ambiguity. The instrument by which he detects the possible meanings of words is the *Oxford English Dictionary;* although it is seldom mentioned by name, its presence everywhere is neither invisible nor subtle. Its lengthy lists of meanings seem to have impressed no one so much as Empson. Apparently he reasons that, since poetry is language highly charged with meaning, the poetic word must invariably stagger under the full weight of its dictionary significances. Since the mass of significances achieved by permutation and combination is often very great, and since ambiguity is so extensive a principle of selection, the discovery of the main meaning or meanings of a passage often becomes for Empson an embarrassing matter. At such points he invokes the aid of rather general and often highly dubious historical, ethical, and psychological propositions about the poet and the audience. I suspect that such propositions are mainly conveniences for him; he does not, at any rate, worry too greatly when he finds they are false.[15]

The resulting interpretation is not always so prettily fanciful as the remarks on the Shakespearean sonnet may suggest; fanciful it is always, indeed, but the method of "permutation and combination," as I have called it, is a mechanical method, and it is capable of all the mindless brutality of a machine. Witness the treatment of a famous speech of Macbeth:

If it is an example of the first type [of ambiguity] to use a metaphor which is valid in several ways, it is an example of the second to use several different metaphors at once, as Shakespeare is doing in the following example. It is impossible to avoid Shakespeare

14. "Two statements are made as if they were connected, and the reader is forced to consider their relations for himself. The reason why these facts should have been selected for a poem is left for him to invent; he will invent a variety of reasons and order them in his own mind. This, I think, is the essential fact about the poetical use of language" (p. 25; see also p. 57).

15. See, e.g., p. 21 n.

in these matters; partly because his use of language is of unparalleled richness and partly because it has received so much attention already; so that the inquiring student has less to do, is more likely to find what he is looking for, and has evidence that he is not spinning fancies out of his own mind.

As a resounding example, then, there is Macbeth's

> If it were done, when 'tis done, then 'twere well
> It were done quickly;

(double syntax since you may stop at the end of the line)

> If th' Assassination
> Could trammel up the Consequence, and catch
> With his surcease, Success; that but . . .

words hissed in the passage where servants were passing, which must be swaddled with darkness, loaded as it were in themselves with fearful powers, and not made too naked even to his own mind. *Consequence* means causal result, and the things to follow, though not causally connected and, as in 'a person of consequence,' the divinity that doth hedge a king. *Trammel* was a technical term used about netting birds, hobbling horses in some particular way, hooking up pots, levering, and running trolleys on rails. *Surcease* means completion, stopping proceedings in the middle of a lawsuit, or the overruling of a judgment; the word reminds you of 'surfeit' and 'decease,' as does *assassination* of hissing and 'assess' and, as in 'supersession,' through *sedere*, of knocking down the mighty from their seat. . . .

He continues this at some length, concluding: "The meanings cannot all be remembered at once, however often you read it. . . ."[16]

Such a passage as this needs only attentive reading to make manifest its utter absurdity; but then that very absurdity in a fashion protects it, and gains a certain credence for it; it is so absurd that we in a measure believe it, merely because we are loath to believe that anything could be so absurd. To escape such spurious persuasion, we must, I think, forcibly remind ourselves of the facts. We are actually being asked to believe that the speech actually *means* all these various things; that Macbeth, trembling on the brink of murder, and restrained only by his fears of what may follow, is babbling of bird-nets, pothooks, levers, trolleys, assessments, lawsuits, and what not; and all this on the shadowy grounds that the *OED*, or whatever dictionary, lists alternative meanings for "trammel," "surcease," and "assassination," and that poetic language is ambiguous. This is a wrenching of a text if I ever saw one; what is worse, it is a wrenching to no rational purpose. The remark about "double syntax" is typical; there is no double syntax in

> If it were done, when 'tis done, then 'twere well
> It were done quickly . . . ;

for if you pause at the end of the line, as Empson suggests, you leave an unaccounted-for and absolutely unintelligible residue in the next line; and as a

16. Pp. 49–50.

Elder Olson

matter of fact you make nonsense, anyway, of the first. In short, the "double syntax" here owes its existence only to the supposition that poetry is necessarily ambiguous.

There are many other marvels of interpretation: at one point Empson not only confuses Macbeth with the witches, but the play itself with *King Lear;*[17] in *Hamlet*, the line "In the dead vast and middle of the night" is made to suggest a personification of Night as one of the terrible women of destiny, on the grounds of possible puns (*vast: waste: waist, middle* of night:*middle* of body);[18] and Crashaw's translation of the *Dies Irae*, on equally compelling grounds, refers to the defecation of God—hence the poet, "to find an image for the purest love . . . falls back on sexuality in its most infantile and least creditable form."[19] But one of the most common results of Empson's procedure is that poets appear to him unintelligible, or, to use his own word, "muddled." For example, Shakespeare's Sonnet XVI, with which I imagine few readers have found difficulty, is "muddled."[20]

These things of course result, as I have said, from the theory of ambiguity; and one would suppose that a principle so ruthlessly applied would be of absolute force, especially since it is the "essence" of poetry. As a matter of fact, Empson is not quite willing to credit it with as much authority as he demands from it. An ambiguity, while it can be "beautiful,"[21] is "not satisfying in itself, nor is it, considered on its own, a thing to be attempted; it must in each case arise from, and be justified by, the peculiar requirements of the situation."[22] "On the other hand, it is a thing which the more interesting and valuable situations are more likely to justify."[23] This is an admission, I take it, that ambiguity is not even in Empson's view the *principle* of poetry, since its propriety or impropriety is determined by something else—an unanalyzed thing vaguely called "the situation." Rather, it is a sign, and by no means an infallible sign even for Empson, that an interesting and valuable situation is involved. (The statement even of that much is, by the way, left undefended and unsupported by Empson, although his whole position depends upon it.) And he seems to discuss the sign—ambiguity—rather than the "interesting and valuable situation" of which it is a sign only because the sign is "less mysterious."[24] In short, he appears to be in the position of many of the ancient theorists who sought to discuss the elevated style; the style itself evaded their formulations, but since it predominantly involved certain tropes, the tropes might be ana-

17. P. 18, par. 3.

18. Pp. 96–97.

19. Pp. 222–24.

20. P. 57. The sonnet is analyzed on pp. 54–56.

21. P. 235.

22. *Ibid.*

23. *Ibid.*

24. P. 243.

lyzed, although, it was recognized, the mere production of tropes would not constitute elevation of style.

Indeed, Empson is really a tropist *manqué,* and the seven types are really tropes, as can be seen from the fact that the regular tropes fall under his divisions; the first type, for instance, includes metaphor and antithesis, and the subclasses are clearly subclasses of tropes. But there are certain important differences between the types of ambiguity and the ancient tropes; the types are not nearly so comprehensive; they do not offer nearly such clear distinctions between figures of language; they are not organized upon nearly so clear a principle; and, what is most crucial, they are not nearly so useful. The main difficulty with the tropes, as they were generally treated, was that, in Samuel Butler's phrase, "All a rhetorician's rules/Teach nothing but to name his tools"; that is, their treatment was not sufficiently functional; but they did offer a precise and exhaustive distinction, at their best, between kinds of grammatical devices. Hence, once a trope has been identified, one is in a position to inquire how it has been used, and thereby arrive ultimately at judgments of value. Empson's types, however, do not even permit the distinction of the device; I fear that only Empson can find instances of them, and even he is sometimes unsure.[25]

But, indeed, to deal rigorously with Empson's ideas, to attempt to state them clearly, to demand precision and adequacy of proof for them, is in a sense to be very unfair to him. It is unfair, perhaps, even to inquire into his exact meaning. As a matter of fact, I am not sure that he means anything exactly. He is constantly offering statements; but there is not one—even of his cardinal doctrines—which he is willing to stand by. It would appear that he is offering a method of verbal analysis based on ambiguity; but he is not quite sure what he means by "ambiguity."[26] It requires certain conditions; but these conditions are not always satisfied by his examples.[27] His first definition of ambiguity was that it "adds some nuance to the direct statement of prose." But, he continues, "this begs a philosophical question and stretches the term ambiguity so far that it becomes almost meaningless." Even his new definition "is not meant to be decisive but to avoid confusing the reader; naturally the question of what would be the best definition of ambiguity . . . crops up all through the book."[28] Elsewhere, he remarks in a footnote: "Effects worth calling ambiguous occur when the possible alternative meanings of word or grammar are used to give alternative meanings to the sentence"[29]—but this would disallow much of his

25. E.g., "The fundamental situation, whether it deserves to be called ambiguous or not . . ." (p. 2).

26. See Preface to the 2d ed., pp. vii–xv.

27. E.g., p. 214, par. 2.

28. P. 1 n.

29. P. 70 n.

own practice, for he constantly confounds potential with actual meaning, as in the examples we have just considered. The real truth of the matter is, I suspect, in the following sentence: "Apart from trailing my coat about minor controversies, I claimed at the outset that I would use the term ambiguity to mean anything I liked, and repeatedly told the reader that the distinctions between the Seven Types which he was asked to study would not be worth the attention of a profounder thinker." And he remarks, briefly afterward: "I have tried to clear the text of the gratuitous puzzles of definition and draw attention to the real ones."[30]

After such admissions it is almost improper to remark what is nevertheless plain to behold. Empson is not sure of the types of ambiguity; for instance, he is not sure that the first type *is* ambiguous.[31] He is not sure of the principles of classification. He is not sure that his method is useful to poets—on the contrary, poets ought to avoid ambiguity[32]—nor that it is of too much use even to readers, for, he says, they need not remember or apply it.[33] In short, it would seem that his only safeguard against complete and utter refutation is his slipperiness of statement and his ability to insist that any counterargument, any refutation, does not affect his ideas, but is merely a criticism of his expression.

These traits might seem to convict him of sophistry also; but they are rather a clue to the interpretation of his work. He is pointing to a problem; whatever we may think about his statement and treatment of it, the problem itself undoubtedly exists: what kind of minute and precise discussion of poetic language is requisite in order to make manifest the subtleties of genius and art? His principal difficulty is that contemporary criticism, for reasons that we shall examine later, affords no devices by which such a problem can be handled. In fact, it cannot even be accurately stated; for the only alternatives to his theory which Empson can conceive are the theories of "Pure Sound" and of "Atmosphere," as he calls them;[34] since neither of these is tenable, he pursues his own course. He seems utterly innocent of any knowledge of the history of criticism; as a consequence, he is a victim of the collapse of the theory of art in his own day. Possessing no clear or adequate poetic principles, he nevertheless has his intuitions, and he must use language to express these. If the language permits the concept to shine through, well and good; if not, one must alter the language. Recognizing that poetic language can be enormously effective, he supposes that this is due to denseness of meaning; and since denseness of meaning implies ambiguity, one must discuss ambiguity.

It is, indeed, on this topic of meaning, so crucial to his system as well as to

30. Preface to the 2d ed., pp. vii–viii.

31. P. 2.   33. P. 256.

32. Pp. 235–36.   34. P. 8.

that of Richards, that his confusions are least manifest and most serious. Perhaps most serious of all is that between meaning and implication or inference.

The discrimination of four conditions of meaning and inference may perhaps clarify this issue. First, meaning may be present without inference, or, if inference is present, it is based wholly upon linguistic or other semantic matters —for example, if language is involved, upon the meanings of words and upon syntactical laws. Meaning here is the simple resultant of the significant powers of words and of their combinations; the meaning of what Empson calls "direct" statement or expression is of this order. Inference, if present at all, is here minimal; from what a child knows, for instance, of the elemental parts (word-meanings) and of types of construction (attribution, predication, etc.) he may infer the meaning of the primer sentence. This would be simple part-whole inference, and wholly linguistic in character; if the child fails to infer the whole, he is reminded by analysis into parts and types of construction. Sentences which have a meaning of this order may be of infinite grammatical complexity; they will still be direct or simple in meaning, since the meaning is the resultant only of verbal signs.

But, secondly, meaning may be the resultant of more than verbal signs. It may, that is, result from inferences based on the character or purpose of the speaker, the manner of delivery (e.g., facial expression, gesture, etc.), our presupposed knowledge or opinions of the subject, the situation, and many other circumstances; and—while such inferences are frequently unrelated to the meaning, or do not affect it—frequently also they serve to modify, emphasize, or even contradict the meaning of the words uttered. For instance, irony, as we now conceive it, is possible because we can infer from something over and above the verbal expression that the expression means the opposite of what it says. Sentences affected by such inferences never mean quite what they say; however simple their form, their meaning is never a simple resultant of the verbal expressions.

Thirdly, meaning, if it is produced by inference, also produces inference which is not, however, part of the meaning. Not every inference which can be drawn from a fact is *meant* by the sentence which states the fact. An axiom of geometry does not, in its statement, *mean* every theorem which can be drawn from it. Similarly, a sentence is in itself a fact, but inferences drawn from that fact are no part of its meaning. For example, if a certain sentence is possible, it is inferable that language is possible; but the sentence itself—say, Empson's "The brown cat sat on the red mat"—does not, as he thinks, *mean* "Language is possible" or "This is a statement about a cat."

Fourthly, inference is possible quite apart from meaning. If I see a bloody ax and infer that something was killed with it, no question of meaning is involved, for all arbitrary signs are absent; a fact implies a fact, even in the absence of language and meaning.

Now while Empson talks of meaning and implication, he makes no effective distinction between these four cases. All are equally "meaning" for him. The cat sentence does not have merely its obvious meaning (case 1), but it *means* that it might have come out of a fairy story or a primer (case 2) and that it is a statement about a cat (case 3). The confusion would not be so serious, perhaps, if it did not carry with it his commitment to dictionaries. As one can readily see, dictionary meanings are absolutely determinative, if anywhere, only in the first case; and they grow less and less so, until they are not involved at all in the last case.

The confusion becomes particularly important when Empson is talking of the "meaning" of poetry. For, strictly speaking, a *mimetic* poem, an imitation— and he is mainly concerned with poems of this kind—has no meaning at all. It is a certain kind of product, like a picture, a symphony, or a statue; like an ax, a bed, a chair; it has no more meaning *as a poem* than these have.[35] It is a fact; from that fact we may make inferences, to which we respond emotionally and about which we make judgments; but it means nothing; it *is*. In short, to speak of the "meaning" of a poem is to confuse meaning with the implication of a fact.

Presumably, however, Empson means the diction of the poem when he speaks of poetry. In that case he confuses the diction with the poem; but his question may be very readily answered. In the broadest sense, what the diction means, precisely, is the poem itself.

The importance of these distinctions, which at first sight may seem pedantic and useless, is that they lead, so far as poetics is concerned, to a distinction—a very important one for the problems in which Empson is interested—between *lexis* and *praxis;* between speech as meaningful and speech as action. What the poetic character says in the mimetic poem is speech and has meaning; his *saying it* is action, an act of persuading, confessing, commanding, informing, torturing, or what not. His diction may be accounted for in grammatical and lexicographical terms; not so his action. And the profundity and complexity in poetry which so much interests Empson is due primarily to action and character, which cannot be handled in grammatical terms, rather than to diction, which can. That profundity is only in a small degree verbal, in the sense that verbal analysis will yield the whole of it; and even then it is very seldom a

---

35. I trust that these statements will not seem to make me a member of what Empson calls the "cult of Pure Sound" and that they will give no encouragement to slovenly and irresponsible reading. I do not imply here that the attempt to discover meaning should be foregone but that more than meaning is involved in poetry. The ensuing discussion will, I hope, clarify the somewhat terse statement here.

matter of verbal ambiguity. Shakespeare's profoundest touches are a case in point. "Pray you, undo this button" and "The table's full" are profound, not as meaningful verbal expressions but as actions permitting an extraordinary number of implications, in that they are revelatory of many aspects of character and situation. We shall not explain them by jumbling the dictionary meanings of "button" and "table," but by asking, among other things, why Lear requested the unfastening of a button and why Macbeth thought the table was full. This is true even in lyric poetry: the "Once more" of "Lycidas," for instance, has no profound verbal meaning; it is affecting because it implies the repeated suffering of bereavement.

The theories of Richards and Empson illustrate a tendency, very prevalent among critics who rate diction as important, to rate it as entirely too important. In the order of our coming to know the poem, it is true, the words are all-important; without them we could not know the poem. But when we grasp the structure we see that in the poetic order they are the least important element; they are governed by everything else in the poem. We are in fact far less moved by the words as mere words than we think; we think ourselves moved mainly by them because they are the only visible or audible part of the poem. As soon as we grasp the grammatical meaning of an expression in a mimetic poem, we begin drawing inferences which we scarcely recognize as inferences, because they are just such as we habitually make in life; inferences from the speech as to the character, his situation, his thought, his passion, suddenly set the speaker vividly before us and arouse our emotions in sympathy or antipathy; our humanity is engaged, and it is engaged by humanity. But where we can draw no such inferences, where no such impression of humanity is conveyed, we remain largely indifferent in the face of the finest diction. These inferences, moreover, largely determine our interpretation of the language itself; we recognize a pun or an ambiguity when we see a human reason why the character should deal in puns and ambiguities, and not when the dictionary lists a variety of meanings.

We do indeed say the character must be so-and-so *because* his words are such-and-such, as well as that the words must be such-and-such *because* the character is so; thus, at first sight, diction and the other parts of the poem seem mutually determinative; on closer inspection, however, we see that *because* has a different sense in each case, since it refers to a cause of a different order. The words are a cause of our conjecturing the character; the character is a cause of the words being said. We can see this even if we are speaking merely of words and meaning: the words are a cause of our knowing the meaning; but the meaning is the cause of the words in their selection and ordering.

If the words, then, are not what is primarily responsible for the effect, purely verbal interpretation, however essential, will not explain poetry, any more than stringing fine diction together will constitute it. Indeed, even Empson in a manner admits this; for he tells us that ambiguity must be justified by the "situation"; but he makes the fatal error of supposing that, because the situation is not something verbal, it is therefore outside the bounds of poetic consideration. As a consequence of this, he defines the poetic pleasure itself much too loosely; that pleasure is not, as he thinks, a logical pleasure produced by puzzling over the relation between statements; it is a pleasure produced by a play of emotions aroused in us by an exhibition of the actions and fortunes of men. Inference is indeed involved, and carries a pleasure of its own; but inference is only a necessary condition, and not a sufficient cause, of the poetic pleasure.

This looseness of treatment might seem to broaden the scope of Empson's inquiry; but it tends rather to restrict. He can conceive of metaphors, for instance, only as comparisons based upon real similarity; the more real likenesses present, the better the metaphor; the better the metaphor, the better the poem. His treatment of "Bare ruined choirs" is an instance. What he misses entirely is the governance of metaphor by thought, of thought by character, or character by action. For a metaphor is not simply a figure of diction in poetry; it is also someone's thinking, significantly, that something resembles something; it is the thought, that is, of a certain character in a certain situation, and it is significant of these things. The best similitudes are not always good metaphors in a given poem, and the best metaphors are not always good similitudes.[36]

In short, something is missing in all this; and what is missing is the nature of poetry.

II

Empson's theory, then, deals only with a single part of poetry, and that part the least important one poetically; indeed, only with a single attribute of that part, and one only vaguely and suppositiously attached to poetry, for ambiguity is neither peculiar to poetry nor universal to all, or to the best, poetry. Moreover, his treatment even of that attribute is so limited as not merely to send inquiry in the wrong direction, but also to preclude proper explanation and supplementation of whatever truths it may, as a system of discussion, contain. Nor are these faults peculiarly Empson's; they abound everywhere in the "new criticism," and, for that matter, in contemporary criticism generally. Scrutinizing the "new criticism" as a whole, I do indeed find that "unity of method" which Ransom, Elton, and others have claimed for

36. Mr. Empson has replied to these criticisms (*Kenyon Review*, XII [1950], 599–601). His chief point is that by "meaning" he means everything: plot, character, thought, and all. This makes his extreme dependence upon the dictionary all the more incomprehensible to me.

it;[37] I find it also in contemporary criticism generally; and on examining that method, I find it directly responsible for all the faults I have noted.

Contemporary criticism seems, for a variety of reasons, to have broken with the past, and to have begun afresh upon a discussion of principles. Such a venture required a new determination of the subject matter of criticism and re-opened the question of the nature of poetry, thereby giving rise to an indefinite number of definitions and hypotheses. The principal reason for the rejection of preceding theories was the belief that these were incommensurate, and in-capable of being made commensurate, with the growth of poetry in our time, having been, it was supposed, founded upon conceptions of poetry entirely too narrow and limited. The "new criticism" was to comprehend all that has been called "poetry," to discover its true nature and determine methods of its proper criticism and construction. A second important reason stemmed from the ad-vances made in certain sciences which might have some bearing on poetry; psychology, for instance, was thought to have advanced considerably and to possess new techniques and hypotheses that applied immediately both to the creative process of the artist and the emotional responses of the audience.

Commendable as these motives may be, the task of establishing and develop-ing the principles of art is a formidable one always, even for the philosopher, and in this instance it was complicated by certain difficulties. Chief among these was the absence of any clear, fruitful, and widely accepted metaphysics, episte-mology, philosophy of science; a discipline—call it what you will—capable of articulating and organizing the arts and sciences, establishing and criticizing their principles and methods, and, in short, settling the broader and more gen-eral questions which the pursuit of any department of inquiry must involve. How seriously this lack has affected contemporary criticism may be seen by anyone who takes the trouble to note the frequency of metaphysical questions, as well as the infrequency of happy solutions to these, in any critical discussion which seeks, nowadays, to rise above the mere particulars of art. Definitions are made by men who know neither what a definition is, nor how it is con-structed, nor what it is for, and methodology is discussed by men who would be hard put to it to say what method is. The excellent amateur of poetry has become a sadly amateurish philosopher. But the fault in this instance must be laid at the doors of the philosophers.

A second difficulty lay in the fact that the term "poetry," or its equivalents, had from antiquity been applied to a great number of things of widely different natures. The attachment of a name to something is, after all, only the reflection of an opinion of likeness; and custom had quite naturally extended the applica-

---

37. Ransom, *op. cit.*, Preface, p. x. While, strictly speaking, Ransom is speaking of R. P. Blackmur, he is clearly discussing him as a representative instance of a "new critic."

tion of the name of poetry, not merely to poetry itself, but to anything that involved the use of poetic devices such as verse, rhyme, ornamental diction, etc. Now it is impossible to have a single art, science, or discipline unless some homogeneity can be found in the subject matter; and criticism was thus faced with the impossible task of finding homogeneity among heterogeneous things: that is, of finding a common principle among things that had no common principles, and of finding a single definition that should state the common nature of things that had no common nature.

Criticism had to find points of likeness among an accidental accumulation of things of diverse natures, which had been called "poetry" because in accidental respects they resembled it; and likenesses it found; but these were *accidental* likenesses, as one might expect under the circumstances. Even where the characteristic selected was itself a necessary condition of poetry—as, for example, the use of language—there remained the difficulty of discerning in what special respects it was related to the nature or essence of poetry. Language functions very differently in the epigram, the didactic verse-treatise, and mimetic tragedy; if you call all of these "poetry" and inquire into the nature of poetic language, you will end up with some description which, because it must be common to all of these, will be very general and will shed little light upon the special functioning of language in, say, mimetic tragedy. Moreover, it was in the nature of the case that certain of these characteristics, being very general, should turn out to be common to things which were obviously not poetry, in any of the accepted senses, at all. For example, language is common to all the things called "poetry"; but nothing is more evident than that scientific prose, for instance, is very different from poetry, although it too is language; it must therefore be differentiated from poetry—but what is the proper differentia? You decide, at this point, that scientific prose is bare, poetic diction ornamented; or the latter is more highly charged with meaning than the former, or something of the sort; and if this does not sufficiently distinguish it, you proceed further, through differentiae of the differentia, until definition is finally achieved. Despite the fact that the definition was founded on a characteristic accidentally found in common among an accidental collocation of things, you will now, if you are a typical modern critic, consider that you have stated the nature or essence of poetry.

These "definitions" are not necessarily false, in the sense that they attribute to poetry characteristics which it does not have; but they are certainly not definitions; they certainly do not state the nature of poetry. The accidental characteristics of things, and hence the possible comparisons in terms of these, are limitless; thus an infinite number of definitions of the same thing can be generated in this fashion, all equally valid, since they are based upon and warranted by precisely the same procedure of definition. If so, they are equally "essential"; but—which of these "essences" is the *essence?* An examination of the construction of these definitions will disclose in every instance that the definition has a minimum reference to the object defined, or it touches only a certain attribute which is itself not shown to be essential to the object; all the rest is provided by the apparatus and mechanism of comparison. In short, these "definitions" are at most indications of the light in which the object "poetry" is to be viewed.

But may not these definitions even in that case have some value? Doubtless they may, as devices for permitting the discussion of a subject the nature of which is unknown, and where they function so, they are unexceptionable. It is frequently the case that, before we can state the nature of a thing, much preliminary discussion is needed: the properties, even the accidents, of the subject must be considered in order to be dismissed; and even when erroneous definition results, no great harm is done, for inquiry is still in progress; definition serves as matter for inquiry, and not as the basis of inquiry; it is itself examined and tested, it does not as yet fix and determine the whole approach to the subject. The definitions proposed by contemporary criticism do not, however, function thus heuristically; instead, they operate as a basis for proof, as principles of demonstration; and as such they are sources of misreasoning and error, and hinder rather than foster further discussion. It is one thing to suppose tentatively that poetry is language characterized by ambiguity, and then to inquire whether this characteristic is common to all poetry, whether it is peculiar to poetry, whether it accounts for all that poetry is and does; it is quite another thing to employ it to insist that any interpretation of poetry must turn upon ambiguities, and to twist the language of *Macbeth* into a meaningless and tasteless muddle, merely because, according to the definition, poetry must be ambiguous. It is the reverse, not merely of science, but also of sense, to erect a hasty guess into a principle of method, so that, far from being tested by the data, it tests the data by itself, silencing all adverse testimony, and forcing assent where it should itself yield to correction.

If the definitions of contemporary criticism are thus not strictly definitions, the hypotheses which are framed to support or supplement them are also not strictly hypotheses. In Empson's case, for instance, the definitive property of poetry, ambiguity, rests upon the hypothesis that there is a connection between ambiguity and interesting or valuable situations; that is, if poetry deals with interesting and valuable situations, and these tend to involve ambiguity, poetry must involve ambiguity. Such a hypothesis does not really give the *cause*, for it does not state why the *thing* is such-and-such; it is merely a *reason*, a ground of belief, stating why the theorist *thinks* the thing is so. It is not a poetic principle; it is the rationalization of an opinion. Even if the opinion and its ground were not false, however, both would still be inappropriate, for the terms in which they are couched are much too general: neither ambiguity nor a concern with interesting and valuable situations is peculiar to poetry. Moreover, even if they were appropriate, they would be falsely reductive; ambiguity, when it is present in poetry, is present through a variety of causes, and not simply through the fact that a certain kind of situation tends to involve it.

The hypotheses of contemporary criticism are not, as a matter of fact, hypotheses in any technical sense at all; they are rather a sort of postulate. We may distinguish, I think, three sorts of hypotheses: the heuristic, the demonstrative, and the nameless kind that serves both functions. The heuristic hypothesis is the first principle of a given science, used as a basis for inquiry into more general principles; thus dialectic, according to Plato, "uses hypotheses not as first principles, but as genuine hypotheses, that is to say, as stepping stones and impulses, whereby it may force its way up to something that is not hypothetical, and arrive at the first principle of everything."[38] The demonstrative hypothesis is a first principle in a given science, without which scientific knowledge in that particular sphere is impossible. Both of these imply completed inquiry within the given science; the third kind, which is hypothesis in the sense intended in modern science, implies no such completion; it is a tentative principle, a supposition either of "fact" or of the cause of a "fact." Obviously the hypotheses of contemporary criticism are not hypotheses in the first two senses; nor are they hypotheses in the third sense, although they have the same function as the tentative suppositions of modern science, viz., to explain facts or other hypotheses, or to render them consistent and compendent. For the true hypothesis, in this third sense, is characterized by reciprocal implication; as Descartes remarks, the facts must imply the hypothesis, and the hypothesis must imply the facts; and these are conditions which the modern critical "hypotheses" fail to satisfy. Empson's hypothesis, for instance, satisfies neither condition: it neither implies the data nor is implied by them. A canvass of interesting and valuable situations will not show that they "tend to involve ambiguity"; conversely, even if they did, this would prove nothing about individual instances, for a statistical attribute of a large class ("tend to involve ambiguity" is of this order) does not belong, affirmatively or negatively, necessarily or probably, to any subclasses of that class.

The characteristic hypotheses of contemporary criticism tend, finally, to have two salient traits which vitally affect the systems based upon them. First, they are inadequate; second, they are preclusive of supplementary hypotheses which might compensate for their inadequacies.

38. *Republic* vi. 511.

A very little discussion will, I hope, make this clear. All poetic theory is a form of causal explanation; and such explanation must comprise all the causes requisite to make a thing what it is. Unless the causal account is complete, the explanation is inadequate; if it is insisted upon as adequate, if it is claimed to account for the whole and not merely for the part, it is also preclusive. The theories of the early Greek physicists offer an example. Thales, for instance, thought to account for the phenomenal universe in terms merely of its material cause, the principle of water; but, as numerous philosophers have pointed out, this would at most account for the substrate; it does not explain the distinctive forms which water assumes as rain, cloud, ice, or snow, nor the motive forces which cause water to assume such forms, nor the functional organization of animate things; it offers only one principle of explaantion where several are required.

Modern criticism is very much in the condition of Thales.[39] It may be divided into two principal kinds: criticism based upon hypotheses concerning the medium of poetry, and hence given to the explanation of poetry as language, or language of a certain kind, and criticism based upon hypotheses concerning the subject matter of poetry, and hence given to the explanation of poetry as myth, as knowledge, as experience, or something of the kind. The first seeks to establish some distinction between poetic language and language in any other form or use. Thus Richards opposes poetry to scientific discourse, finding the latter ordered to clarity and the former to ambiguity, the latter informative and the former emotive;[40] Yvor Winters opposes poetry "to other kinds of writing," finding that poetry takes "special pains . . . with the expression of feeling";[41] John Crowe Ransom opposes poetry to unmetrical and unrhymed language, finding poetry a "compromise" between "meaning and metre";[42] but the end result is largely the same: in each case the nature of poetry is ultimately determined solely by the critic's hypotheses as to the nature or functions of language. All these statements contain a measure of truth; but they are inadequate as hypotheses. If tragedy, comedy, epic, and lyric be poetry, how shall they be described as distinctive species of language? Upon what special properties of language does each depend, so that, once these are determined, we shall have a given species of poetry? Is the difference between drama and narrative a difference of language? Are the differences between the large and complicated actions of epic and the small and simple of lyric, the differences between tragic

39. See above, p. 29, and below, pp. 84 ff.

40. *Principles of Literary Criticism* (New York, 1930), p. 267.

41. *The Anatomy of Nonsense* (Norfolk, Conn., 1943), p. 12.

42. *Op. cit.*, pp. 294–95. But see the whole final chapter, "Wanted: An Ontological Critic."

and comic action and character, the differences between the emotional effects of tragedy and those of comedy—are all these differences of language? Can we account for any differences of poetic language without taking into consideration such differences of poetic form as these? As a matter of fact, is there any attribute of poetic language which cannot also be found, and that abundantly, in other forms of discourse?

These positions are like arguing that ice is ice because it is water; they are attempts to derive the form from the matter. All such argument runs, obviously, in the wrong direction; it would infer the design of a house from the shape and weight of the bricks. No product is what it is simply because its matter is such-and-such; its matter is indeed a necessary, but not a sufficient, condition of its existence and nature. A saw, for instance, is not a saw because the steel determined it should be. The reverse is the case; I wish to cut the fibers of wood a certain way: I must therefore have a blade of a certain kind; it must therefore be made of a substance capable of assuming a certain shape, and hard enough to retain that shape; hence the steel. And, if I am to give a complete account, I must talk not merely about the steel but about the form given it, and how it was given it, and the function of cutting.

The hypotheses concerning subject matter take a variety of forms: poetic fiction is set against truth, or poetic truth against other truths; certain concepts or orderings of concepts are opposed to others, imaginables against credibles, and so on. The principal position is that poetry is myth, or at any rate closely related to myth; it is currently fashionable, numbering among its proponents Maud Bodkin, Robert Penn Warren, nearly all the psychological and political critics, and the critics who talk of "symbolic structure."[43] Superficially various as these hypotheses are, all are based, like those concerned with the medium, upon a simple dichotomy between what is poetic and what is not. With a little translation, the objections against the linguistic theories also apply to them.

Indeed, the subject-matter hypotheses and the linguistic hypotheses are fundamentally the same, being only separate developments from the same general hypothesis: viz., that all discourse is differentiable in terms of subject matter and style. This supposition, which may be traced at least as far back as the Ciceronian distinction between *res* and *verba*, has proved less profitable and more influential than any other single proposition in the history of criticism.[44] To apply it to poetry is to assume that poetry of whatever kind is a form of discourse, and to suppose that poetic organization is necessarily comparable to the organization of any other form of discourse. Such a supposition makes it

43. See below, pp. 108 ff., 138 ff.
44. Cf. *Modern Philology*, XL (1943), 278–79, 281–82.

impossible to differentiate any form of poetry except in terms of characteristics which it has in common with other discourse; it burkes all discussion of important peculiar characteristics of poetry for which there is no analogue in other discourse. That is, it provides no distinctions whereby any kind of poetry—whatever we may mean by the term—may be isolated and discussed as a separate kind.

III

I have remarked already that the term "poetry" is ambiguously used. On the one hand, it stands for such works as *Hamlet*, the "Ode to a Nightingale," and "Sailing to Byzantium," all of which are imitations; on the other hand, it stands for any works which, although nonimitative, involve devices or characteristics especially associated with mimetic poetry. In this latter sense, philosophical treatises like Parmenides' *On Nature*, Lucretius' *De rerum natura*, Sir John Davies' *Nosce teipsum;* medical treatises like Fracastoro's *Syphilidis;* histories like the chronicles of Geoffrey Gaimar and Wace or the *Dittamondo* of Fazio; ethical works, like Pope's *Essay on Man* and his *Moral Essays* have all been called poetry. The distinction is not one of value, but of kind; witness the fact that the *Divina commedia* belongs to the second class. The works of the first class are of a quite different order and are constructed on, and hence have to be judged by, quite different principles from those of works in the second.

This distinction, simple as it is, is likely to prove difficult if not repugnant to a twentieth-century mind. Distinctions of kind are nowadays likely to be called "scholastic"[45]—an epithet which means, I presume, that they are pedantic and useless; and, even if that charge be waived, we have become so used to considering poetry a matter of quality, or even of a degree of a quality, that the distinction is likely to seem a wrong one. Surely, one may say, the *De rerum natura* has more in common with *Hamlet* than with the *Critique of Pure Reason* or the *Essay Concerning Human Understanding;* obviously it ought, therefore, to be considered as poetry rather than as philosophy, especially since the philosophic content is quite incidental, in the view of most readers, to the beauty of the poetry; hence, if kinds are to be distinguished, they must be distinguished on different principles. The proper distinction, however, is not one of kind but of quality transcending all such schoolmasterly distinctions of kinds; one finds poetry in any kind of composition if the *poetic quality* is present.

This skeleton of argument underlies, I am sure, much of modern criticism; and it is by no means pointless or baseless. The objection that no one has yet

45. The latest instance occurs in an article by Murray Krieger, "Creative Criticism . . . ," *Sewanee Review,* LVIII (1950), 41.

defined the poetic quality is scarcely a fair one, and the objection that investigation of a quality common to all literature cannot produce sound or fruitful criticism is patently absurd; great critics, Longinus, Sainte-Beuve, and Arnold among them, have done just that. The weaknesses of contemporary criticism are not due to this position but to inept treatments of this position; to the position itself perhaps only two rejoinders can be made. First, the legitimacy of inquiring into a quality common to all art, if granted, does not imply the illegitimacy of inquiring into the distinctive characteristics of each art; and, second, inquiry of the first kind cannot provide such knowledge as the second kind would provide. Inquiry into a common quality as such cannot of itself provide knowledge of distinctive qualities. Qualitative criticism can at best tell the poet how to construct, the critic how to judge, poetry generally; it can scarcely give information for the construction and judgment of a poem of a given kind. In short, in so far as the problems of constructing and judging the various kinds of poetry are the same or similar, qualitative criticism may be useful; but, in so far as these problems differ, it is useless, and may sometimes be pernicious.

It has, for instance, a dangerous tendency to bring about the discredit of principles perfectly valid within a given sphere of art, simply because they are not universally valid. The result is to make most literary theories and judgments curiously unstable, and to make the surviving principles, supposedly universal to a whole art or group of arts, few and very far removed from any particular artistic problems. Art is not composed wholly of universal and absolute principles; if we look at the whole range of art without prejudice, with absolutely open eyes, it is not difficult to see that universality and validity are not necessarily connected. Certain principles underlie all art; others apply only to the temporal, or only to the spatial arts; others apply only to certain arts below these, and so on; but a principle is not less valid in a certain art merely because it happens to be specific to that art, and is invalid in any other. Yet, if we look at the history of criticism, we can readily see that many of its revolutions and counterrevolutions have turned precisely upon this confusion of validity with universality; false universalization—the elevation of something to absolute truth and force when it had only conditional truth and force— and a false demand for universality—the insistence that a principle could not hold for anything unless it held for everything—are the offspring of this confusion; and have time and again thrown criticism into chaos.

Criticism is likely, in the course of its development, to provide many propositions of conditional truth only, and to forget, because such propositions fitted the conditions exactly, that they were only conditionally true. In this fashion many a convention became a rule, many a rule a principle. Such tyranny usually brings revolt; but those who revolt tend to forget, in turn, that if what is conditionally true is not so absolutely, the false conditionally is also not false absolutely. The Three Unities, after long tyranny, have been utterly destroyed as false; but with them was destroyed the little measure of truth which they as doctrines contained. Not every play, it is true, need confine its action within one day and one place; but it is also true that the actions of certain plays would have been much more effective if they had been so confined. The theory of genres has been demolished; but what was true and useful in it perished along with what was false and dangerous. Criticism has been either wholly general or wholly particular ever since; and its present plight, indeed, is in great part due to its lack of such *specific* principles as might have eventually developed out of the theory of genres.

A second dangerous tendency of qualitative criticism is that, in emphasizing the common poetic quality, it is likely to blind us to the great variousness of poetry. We need, I think, to consider only the two major branches of poetry mentioned above to realize that their differences of kind must be respected if they are to be properly constructed, interpreted, or judged.

Greek epic and drama are mimetic poetry; despite their origin in ritual and myth, they require no reference to these in order to be intelligible and effective. Whatever the mythical origin of an Odysseus, an Achilles, or an Orestes, these are characters simply, and must be interpreted as such; neither they nor their actions and fortunes require allegorical interpretation; whatever symbolic significance they may have possessed as myth they have lost as materials of poetry. Plato, it is true, practiced the allegorical interpretation of poetry which Theagenes and Anaxagoras are said to have initiated in Greece; but he did so clearly as a consequence of his philosophic approach, rather than as a consequence of any characteristics of Homer and the dramatists; and doubtless the case was the same with his predecessors.

Such interpretations indicate, not the inherent necessity of interpreting epic and dramatic poetry as allegory, but the tendency to interpret them so when in their literal interpretation they conflict with doctrine. When the Christian doctrine arose, pagan poetry, literally interpreted, conflicted both with its theological and its moral teachings; and those who sought to defend such poetry were forced by the nature of the case, not only to interpret it allegorically, but also to insist that allegory was the essence of poetry. Moreover, if poetry was to be brought into accord with doctrine, it had itself to become doctrinal, and hence didactic. It is not surprising, in these circumstances, that poetry came to be thought of as didactic allegory.

Didactic allegory presents many superficial resemblances to mimetic poetry; but the differences between them, while perhaps few and obscure, are fundamental. Didactic poetry, whether allegorical or not, must always either propound a doctrine or determine a moral and emotional attitude toward a doctrine in such a way as to command action in accordance with it. The didactic structure must always, therefore, involve explicitly or implicitly some pistic or argumentative element: either the poem argues the doctrine directly, or the argument is left to the reader, as in the case of parables and fables. Argument of some form, however, is always involved; and, whatever form it takes, it inculcates either knowledge or action. In this respect it resembles either the theoretical or the practical syllogism. The principle of didactic poetry, therefore, is its doctrine or thesis, in the peculiar acceptance, theoretical or practical, required for it. Everything in the work mediately or immediately exists and has its peculiar character in order to enforce the doctrine; for instance, the argument itself exists only to prove the thesis and is absolutely determined by it. Such poetry is, of course, really a kind of dialectic or of rhetoric; and it is not surprising that ages which gave themselves over to such poetry should have identified poetry with rhetoric or dialectic in their critical treatises.[46]

Didactic allegory, as a branch of this kind of literature, comes about when the argument is given a particular metaphorical turn. Like fable and parable, it depends upon the possibility of extended metaphor, which in turn depends upon the possibility of discovering multiple analogies between a thing and its analogue, not only as wholes, but as wholes corresponding part for part. The salvation of the soul, for example, can be allegorically represented as a journey because likenesses can be found not merely between salvation and a journey, but also between the stages of salvation and the stages of a journey. The metaphor or symbol may, moreover, be an action, and as such be narratively or dramatically represented. It then bears, to a superficial view, a close resemblance to a plot—particularly to the episodic plot; and readers who are unaware of, or uninterested in, its metaphorical import are quite likely to disregard the import and become interested in the action for its own sake, treating it, consequently, as if it were a plot. *The Faerie Queene* and *Pilgrim's Progress* are very commonly read in this fashion, as romances rather than as allegories. Anyone who wishes to read them so, purely for the excitement and pleasure which they produce, of course may do so; but he is reading them only in part, and for the sake of certain qualities of that part which are incidental to the primary intention; and if he proceeds to judge these works as romances, to complain that the "plot" is not as effective or that the characters are not as convincing as might be, he is being unreasonable: he is insisting that, because a work happens in part to conform to his accidental interest, it should conform to his interest wholly. For the action of an allegory is quite different from a

46. See below, pp. 285 ff.

plot. Its characters and incidents are determined, like those of a thesis-novel, by the doctrine to be urged; the only difference is that they are metaphorical, whereas the thesis-characters and -incidents are literal and instantial. The characters very generally represent the subjects, and the incidents the predicates, of the doctrinal proposition; such is the case, for example, in the *Divina commedia*. They exist because the doctrine exists and because it must be presented in a certain way; they are what they are because the doctrine has certain characteristics. The allegorical incident happens, not because it is necessary or probable in the light of other events, but because a certain doctrinal subject must have a certain doctrinal predicate; its order in the action is determined not by the action as action, but by the action as doctrine; and whatever emotional quality and force it may have is determined rather by the emotional attitude which the doctrine must inculcate toward a certain object than by the context of action in which it occurs. Allegorical characters are what they are because we must view virtue or vice or whatever is involved in a certain light; not because we must adopt a certain attitude toward agents and patients if the action is to affect us in a certain way. Such poetry is a mode of statement; everything in it is representative of parts of discourse.

The construction of such mimetic poetry as epic, tragedy, and comedy is very different; these are ordered, not to a doctrine, but to a plot. And the construction of a plot is very different from that of an allegorical action. A plot is not a string of interesting incidents, but a system of incidents so constructed as to give us a specific pleasure by arousing and allaying our emotions.[47] It is not, like allegorical action, complete because it completely expresses a given doctrine but because, as action, it resolves those issues out of which it has begun. It does not, like allegorical action, seek to inculcate certain moral attitudes by arousing our emotions; on the contrary, it makes use of our moral attitudes to arouse our emotions. It does not engage our interest and emotions in particulars of the action in order to instruct us generally; on the contrary, it instructs us about particulars of the characters and actions in the poem in order to engage our emotions and interest in behalf of these very characters and actions. Whereas didactic poetry assumes that if we can be made to feel a certain way in the presence of certain objects we shall be able to make certain moral distinctions, mimetic poetry assumes that if we make certain moral distinctions we shall feel a certain way in the presence of certain objects. Didactic is antecedent to the formation of moral character; mimetic, subsequent. The former assumes that the reader is imperfect and requires to be perfected; the latter, that the reader is perfect and may enjoy a virtuous pleasure.

The characters in plot are present because an action, if it is to effect emotion,

47. Cf. below, pp. 621 ff.

must be morally determinate and hence must involve agents and patients of a determinate moral cast, or because they are convenient to the effective representation of that action. The incidents in plot occur because they are necessary or probable, or because they increase the emotional effectiveness of the work. We are not required in mimetic poetry, as we are in allegory, to ask what the characters or the incidents stand for; we are required to interpret the characters only as men and women, and the incidents only as fortunate or unfortunate, and seriously so or not. Mimetic poetry is not statement; doctrine appears, not as something urged, but as something assumed, and chiefly as what the poet assumes to be necessary or probable, or to be evocative of this or that emotion or moral attitude.

The language of didactic allegory is always many-meaninged or "polysemous," as Dante called it, because the things for which the words stand always stand for something further. The language of mimetic poetry, however, is ambiguous only when plot, character, thought, or the exigencies of representation demand that it be so. Hence these forms must differ even in the analysis of their language.

Custom has given these kinds of poetry the same general name; and perhaps courtesy requires that we should withdraw it from neither. But we need not therefore be misled by the name to suppose that these kinds are the same and to be given the same treatment. The critic who reads the *Divina commedia* as if it were mimetic poetry is likely to feel severely rebuked if he ever encounters the Epistle of Dante to Can Grande della Scala; for the poet makes clear that he is writing a scholastic treatise. The critic who, on the other hand, reads mimetic poetry as allegory commits the converse fault of Fulgentius, whose *Continentia Virgiliana* contains interpretations as far-fetched as any in our contemporary mythologists.

IV

There are no necessary differences between poetic diction, as diction, and the diction of any other kind of composition. There are no devices of language which can be pointed to as distinctively poetic; any other kind of composition may utilize metaphor, images, rhythm, meter, rhyme, or any of the "devices of poetic language," and poetry may utilize any of the devices associated with any other literary kind. We talk properly, therefore, about poetic diction as ''poetic''—whatever we may mean by poetry—not when we deal with a given order of diction but when we talk about language in its poetic employment. It is true that in given poetic works the language is markedly different from language in nonpoetic functions; but in any properly constructed work these differences are brought about, not by any fixed rule of poetic language, but by the functions which the language serves. Whether we refer to didactic, mimetic, or other forms of poetry, language can never be the sole issue, it can never even be the principal issue of poetic analysis. Language is always merely a medium, a material, never a form. Even in the extreme case of Arthur Machen's hero,[48] who wrote meaningless verses purely for their sound, diction is subsidiary; in this case rhythm and melody were formal. If, therefore, we must always talk about poetic diction in terms of some principle over and above language, it follows that discussions of poetic diction must differ, to some extent at least, in accordance with the different principles on which different kinds of poetry are composed.

It might seem at first sight that any such discussion must turn on tropes and figures;[49] but, in fact, it need not, and perhaps it should not. Important as tropes and figures may be, they are devices with many possible uses, and consequently the mere fact of their employment cannot tell us much about their actual function in given works. Moreover, most, if not all, of them are capable of being used for quite different, in fact opposite, ends, especially when they are used in combination. A metaphor indicates likeness; but a metaphor coupled with irony indicates difference. Furthermore, tropes and figures have been so repeatedly arranged in impressively exhaustive classifications that we are likely to be given two false impressions: first, that they are really complete and cannot be added to, because it is "against logic" that anything should be added to an exhaustive division; secondly, that their uses or functions have also been exhaustively treated. The first impression is false because it takes no account of development and growth; the second impression is false because poets are inventive and because new uses for old devices and old uses for new devices are among the things they invent.

Discussion ought therefore to proceed, not from devices to functions, but from functions to devices. In the remaining pages of this essay I shall try to illustrate how language functions in relation to some of the most general aspects of mimetic form. In order to do so, it will be necessary first to consider what might be called the general mechanism of such form; that is, how it is constructed and how it operates.

The vicissitudes of literary criticism have made it almost impossible to convey a notion of mimetic form by the simple enumeration of such names as tragedy, comedy, epic, and lyric; for these have all been applied to nonmimetic forms. Furthermore, if the names of literary kinds have broadened in meaning, they have also narrowed in other respects; for example, the name "poetry"

---

48. In *The Hill of Dreams.*

49. Cf., e.g., W. K. Wimsatt, Jr., "Verbal Style: Logical and Counterlogical," *PMLA*, LXV (1950), 5–20, and the earlier articles by the same writer cited *ibid.*, p. 13, n. 13; also Maynard Mack, " 'Wit and Poetry and Pope': Some Observations on His Imagery," in *Pope and His Contemporaries: Essays Presented to George Sherburn* (Oxford, 1949), pp. 20–40.

itself is today denied to the types of narrative and dramatic prose, although these were commonly regarded as poetry, and their authors as poets, until the early nineteenth century. On the whole, therefore, it is safer to say that mimetic form includes *some* tragedies, comedies, epics, lyrics, novels, short stories, and so on. Differ as they may from each other, all these have in common the fact that they present to us some spectacle of human happiness or misery, of actualized virtue or vice, or of pleasure and pain; that is, some human action or suffering. It is to the effective emotional presentation of this action or suffering that they are ordered as to a principle; that is, the action or suffering is the part which is chief, which gives form to the work, and to which all else is ordered. By that human spectacle, if I may call it thus, they evoke emotion in us. This is not to say, with Maud Bodkin and others, that they evoke emotion by the reference of their action to one or more generalized myths; on the contrary, they affect us by their particular representation of their respective objects; we react, not to man, but to Oedipus and Hamlet, and to these as presented by Sophocles and Shakespeare, and not to these as detached from the poems in which they are found. Our basic human nature, of course, underlies our reactions; but the capacity for moral or merely sympathetic emotion is a capacity only; what we actually feel is what is actually called forth by the poet through his representation of objects capable of so affecting us. We feel, both in art and in life, what we are capable of feeling; but we feel a given emotion only when there exist the proper conditions for that emotion; otherwise we should suffer all emotions simultaneously and continually.

The emotions are states of consciousness attended by pleasure and pain; their exciting causes are our opinions; for instance, we grow angry when we think we have been offended, fearful when we think we are in danger, and we do not feel these emotions unless we have these opinions. But emotions do not result merely from the operation of an exciting cause upon our basic human nature; the same exciting cause may produce different and in fact opposite emotions in different persons, or even in the same person at different times. Emotion is also a product of the frame of mind in which we are—of, that is, our disposition as determined by what we have experienced and felt—and of our moral character. Moreover, our opinion is twofold: we opine about persons and about the occasions on which they do or suffer something. There are, therefore, three factors in any emotion: our disposition, the person, and the occasion; for instance, we feel angry when we are disposed to be angry, with persons capable of arousing our anger, when the occasion for anger arises.

We feel a given emotion precisely when these three factors have been brought to concur; the history of the emotions invoked in us by a mimetic poem is precisely, therefore, the history of such concurrences effected by the poet through his imitation. Thus the analyst who would know what the audience is feeling from time to time in the course of a poem—in so far as their emotions are controlled by the poem—must follow the line of such concurrences, taking them, of course, in their proper sequence.

Most broadly, our emotions are determined by the object which is imitated; e.g., in tragedy, by the action. But, while the object is thus the foundation of what we feel, our emotions are very much modified by the particular manner in which the incidents and characters are disclosed to us; in fact, what we feel at a given moment is much more particularly determined by the manner of representation than by the object. Finally, the words employed by the poet modify still further the emotions produced in us by object and manner, and determine even more particularly what we feel. What we feel concerning the object of imitation, in short, is dependent upon the devices of disclosure which reveal that object to us.

Language is the device of disclosure in most mimetic poetry; in theatrical productions it is, of course, supplemented by the spectacle and sometimes by music (only, however, when the music interprets what is happening or may happen). But it would be a mistake to suppose that language can be adequately analyzed as an instrument of disclosure merely by talking about its *meaning*. I have already distinguished, in the first part of this essay, between speech as action (*praxis*) and speech as meaningful (*lexis*); to neglect that distinction is, I think, to blind one's self to a great deal of the poetic mechanism. Most of what is termed "meaning" by critics and poets is not meaning at all, but implications of character, passion, and fortune derived from the interpretation of speech as action. Unless the meaning of the words is grasped, we cannot, to be sure, grasp the nature of the speech as action; but when we grasp the nature of the speech as action, we make inferences—which, as I have argued, are not *meanings*—as to the character and his situation; we perceive an object which is the principal cause of our emotions in poetry.

How far language as diction affects us can be seen if we consider that, from one point of view, the causes of emotion in mimetic poetry fall into four classes: (1) the precedent context, not of words merely, but of the action as a whole up to a given point; (2) the particular speech-action, together with its implications; (3) the speech as diction; (4) ornament. The "Pray you, undo this button" speech of Lear affects us, according to this division, (1) because the whole poem has, up to this point, excited certain emotions with respect to Lear and his fortunes, and has left us in a certain frame of mind; (2) because the plea sets before us his utter helplessness, his anguished hope to save Cordelia, the bitter repentance implied in that hope, and so on; (3) because the diction simply and starkly expresses that plea; and (4) because the ornament—

in this case, the rhythm merely—affects us as well. Of these four classes of emotional causes, only the last two depend upon the particular choice and arrangement of words. A translation good enough to permit the operation of the first two would not be greatly inferior; indeed, the principal difficulty of translations, even in lyric poetry, is not so much that the translator fails in respect to the last two, as that, in his efforts to achieve a certain literary manner or a certain rhythm, or even to give the literal meaning, he fails to preserve the significance of the speech as action; he loses the passionate anger, or the fright; he loses the characteristic marks of nobility or meanness; he translates the meaning only, or the style, or the rhythm.

It is speech as action which plays more powerfully upon our emotions; it provides us with the signs from which we infer such things as plot, character, and thought, the most powerful elements in the work; but the signs which it offers us are natural, and not arbitrary, signs. The signs by which we infer from speech that a man is, say, frightened or resolute, or of this character or that, are not fixed by any convention of language; they differ no more from one tongue to another than weeping in Africa differs from weeping in Alaska, or a groan in Italy from a groan in Spain. And much of the "richness" of poetic language is due to this aspect of it. Much of what is currently discussed as "meaning" is this implication of the speech as act.

A great deal, then, of suspense, surprise, and emotion is effected by something other than diction as diction; nevertheless, diction can enhance these, and on occasion even generate them itself. It is this aspect of poetic language— of diction as diction—that I wish particularly to examine. Its problems are problems of word-choice and word-arrangement; they can never be solved without reference to conventional signs, although they can be discussed generally apart from a given language. The problem of diction is not one of how a frightened man, say, would talk, or of how, more generally, speech serves as an indication of character, passion, or situation; it is one of how, given all such determinations of the speech, words as words may prove most effective. As I have said, this is in one sense the least important part of poetics, for the words are determined by everything else in the poem; in another sense, it is the most important, because the words are all we have to go by, they alone disclose the poem to us. The effectiveness of what they disclose must be kept distinct from their effectiveness as instruments of disclosure; the "startling statement" in drama is startling because it discloses something startling, usually, not because it is startling as a matter of words and their arrangement; but what the words disclose can be effective only if the words are effective in their disclosure of it.

But, while disclosure is the general function of the words, what is disclosed must be disclosed properly and in the proper order. Language is a temporal medium; its parts are not coexistent, like those of a spatial medium, but successively existent; when one part is existing, one has ceased or will come to exist; its effects can never have the simultaneity of the effects of color and line in a painting. Moreover, the object imitated in mimetic poetry is always an activity, however minute; even a mood which is momentary is not something static and timeless; hence the object is temporal, too. Consequently, the activity must be remembered, if it is to be seen as a whole and have its whole effect; the language must be such as to permit this. This means that certain parts of the action must be rendered vivid, to have this full and proper emotional force, while others must be dimmed; language can produce such vividness or lack of it by the direction of our attention. Again, all arts that have temporal media, since they cannot exhibit everything at once, involve anticipation, as the spatial arts do not, since they present everything to perception simultaneously; and where anticipation is present, we have also suspense and the unexpected, since our anticipation can be played upon and can be surprisingly foiled. It is clear, therefore, that language can be artfully used to conceal or half-conceal. Finally, since language can be pleasing in itself, it has an ornamental function in poetry as well.

While language, then, has, strictly speaking, the general functions of disclosure and of ornamentation, it is useful to treat it under more special heads which follow from the foregoing argument. The mimetic poet, like any other, may be said to have seven subsidiary aims, with respect to language; I call them "subsidiary" because this essay has made it obvious that they could not be principal. These aims are disclosure, partial disclosure, concealment, direction of attention, evocation of suspense, production of the unexpected, and ornament. What must be disclosed, concealed, etc., belongs to the parts of poetics which deal with plot, character, and thought, and cannot be analyzed here; our present concern is simply the functioning of language as meaningful with respect to these aims.

Disclosure is at a maximum when language is as concise and clear as possible. There are two kinds of concision in language: one is obtained by the use of as few words as possible to express the meaning, while nevertheless expressing the full meaning; the other by expressing only part of the meaning, leaving the rest to inference. Thus the use of enthymeme for syllogism is concise in the latter way; and the famous Lacedaemonian dispatch "Dionysius in Corinth" is of this order. The implication involved here is different from the implications of character, etc., by speech as action in that what is implied is *meaning*, whereas the implications of speech as action are derived from meaning. For instance, the full meaning of the dispatch is "If you attack us, you will be served like a similar aggressor, Dionysius, who was also a great king and is now living, an exile and a private citizen, in Corinth." With the meaning clear, the speech may now be interpreted as an act of defiance implying the moral qualities of Spartans. Concision is possible also apart from language, when an act is a concise sign, i.e., one which has many implications; and poetic concision is greatest when both language and action are concise. For example, the "Who's there?" of *Hamlet* is not only concise as diction; the fact that the wrong man challenges shows tension, fright, doubt whether the sentinel on duty had suffered some unknown misfortune, an expectation of some foreign and possibly hostile presence, etc. The particular devices for obtaining concision of diction when the meaning is fully expressed vary according to the linguistic structures of the various languages; in general it may be said that such languages as have the same syntactical elements (e.g., the same parts of speech) tend to permit the same abridgments; thus asyndeton is possible in all tongues having conjunctions; and similarly such languages as form their words in the same way permit of the same devices of compounding several words into one. Concision of diction where only part of the meaning is expressed varies similarly with the language; it is also based, perhaps more importantly, on expectation and on logical implication.

Clear language is not language which raises no problems—for example, a scientific fact raising numberless problems may be clearly expressed; indeed, if language when clear never raised problems, questions could never be clear. It is, rather, language which raises no problems as to its meaning for those adequately acquainted with the tongue in which it is couched, however many and however profound the problems arising when its meaning is grasped. Anyone who thinks clear language is possible thinks that it consists in using clear words clearly; and in fact, generally speaking, that is all there is to it. But it is useful to analyze further, especially since the devices of ambiguity and indirection depend upon such analysis.

Whether we think of language as evocative, as evoking concepts, or as significative, as standing for something, the possibility of language depends upon a certain condition: the condition that the powers assumed for language by the speaker in his act of speech—whatever the extent and nature of such powers—should not also simultaneously be denied by the speaker, as evinced by the mode of utterance. I do not mean that he may not decide a given expression is inappropriate or incorrect, or change his mind, or reveal his true opinion by offering us an apparent statement and then withdrawing it; I mean that, since language consists of arbitrary signs, which have only such powers as we assign them, the speaker cannot at once assign and refuse to assign them. This is different from the principle of contradiction; the principle of contradiction is not the source of this condition but a consequence of it—indeed, operates only when certain powers of language are assumed. This fundamental condition is the linguistic warrant, without which language is impossible as language, although it may produce effects in us merely as sound. When it is really violated, lack of clarity does not result because there is no language to be clear; but apparent violations of it result in lack of clarity. Such apparent violations occur when any unit of speech seems to negate itself, either openly, as in oxymoron and paradox, or covertly, as when the things stated do not constitute oxymoron, paradox, etc., but imply them. An example is Donne's analogy of a woman's virtue to a snake's venom. All of these apparent violations relate to the conditions of clarity, and not those of language.

The conditions of clarity itself can be seen if we consider that it is dependent upon three things: the words, the syntactical arrangements, and the relations of sentences. Clarity is produced by the words in so far as they are prime, immediate, commensurate, consonant, and familiar. Words are prime if their use does not suggest that they are not being used in their first literal meaning; for example, "dog" or "animal" are both prime as applied to the beast on the hearthrug. Any word is capable of ambiguity; but, conversely, any ambiguous word is capable of being made prime. Words are immediate if they do not in themselves require any special calculation before they yield their meaning; thus the "not-not-not man" of logic-books is not immediate because it requires a calculus of negations, and Eliot's "polyphiloprogenitive" requires etymological calculation. In general, no word is immediate unless it is intelligible as a synthesis. This is merely a distinction between simple and familiar compounds, on the one hand, and unfamiliar compounds, such as coined words, on the other; and it is different from the question of being prime—once we have calculated what "not-not-not man" means, nothing leads us to suppose that it is not prime. Words are commensurate when they are neither too general nor too particular for the thing they stand for; thus "animal" or "Socrates" is incommensurate with "man." Words are consonant if they belong to the same order or level of discourse, in that they contain, as words, no implication of incompatible or inconceivable predication or attribution. For example, a pejorative word used to denote something admirable is used inconsonantly, and is unclear, since we have to wonder about its use. Words are familiar when they not only are commonly employed but are used in their customary grammatical functions, i.e., qua parts of speech; for instance, if a given word is commonly used as a noun and rarely as a verb, it is not wholly familiar when it is used as a verb.

Clarity is produced by syntactical arrangement when amphibology is absent, when grammatical construction is familiar, when the order is the common order, when the material sequence is observed, when predication and attribution are immediate, when the sentence is unified and complete, when the sentence form is primary, when the rhythm is appropriate to the emphasis, and when the sentence is of the proper magnitude. Not all of these need explanation. By observing the material sequence I mean such things as observing the natural order of events; for instance, Shelley's "I die, I faint, I fail" does not observe the material sequence. By immediate predication or attribution I mean that the predicate or the modifier lies adjacent to the subject to which it attaches. Thus parenthetical expressions of any length between subject and predicate produce lack of clarity. By unified sentence I mean one which connects matter which ought to be connected. For example, "She mourned his death and subsequently became very proficent in athletics" is not a unified sentence. By primary sentence form I mean the posing of a question in the interrogative, a statement in the declarative form, and so on. By proper magnitude I mean that the sentence should not be so long that the beginning is forgotten before the end is reached.

Clarity is produced in the relations of sentences when the proper signs of subordination, co-ordination, and transition are employed; when the material sequence is observed; and when the whole correlation (the paragraph) is unified, complete, and of the proper magnitude. Sentences are related to each other in four ways: additively, qualificatively, antithetically, and inferentially; they either add fresh information, qualify what has been said, oppose each other in some way, or are related as parts of an argument. Question and answer and command and compliance are not separate relations, but types of additive relation. The interrogative sentence always presents a subject and demands an attribute, or presents an attribute and demands a subject, or presents both and demands to know their connection; the answer adds the missing point, just as a blank is filled in a questionnaire. The compliance similarly adds information. Clarity results from the relations of sentences when grammatical signs make explicit, in any doubtful cases, which of the four relations is involved; this is particularly necessary when the words or the syntactical arrangements have not been clear.

In general, language is clear in proportion as it requires fewer mental operations to derive its meaning, however many mental operations may result from the meaning once it is known. Hence clear language never involves any misdirection of the mind of hearer or reader, except as this is caused by the tongue in which it is couched; hence language is clear in proportion as it follows normal expectation in all things, for we are not misdirected if what follows is what we expected, whereas any unexpectedness necessitates readjustment; hence familiar words in familiar arrangement are always clearest, since familiarity determines expectation. Language which follows expectation can always be more concise than other language, without sacrificing clarity; for we need only occasional indications that we are on the right track.

It is far from true that ambiguity is the essence of poetry; on the contrary, poetic language should always be as clear as possible, not in the absolute sense, but in the qualified one of maximum clarity consistent with the requirements of the individual poem as a whole. That is, there should be no *unnecessary* misdirection of the reader; and in this respect the greatest poetry is not "puzzling" or unclear, but amazingly clear. Indeed, it would seem that in proportion as the *implications* of the language increase in number and in importance, the language itself is clearer; compare the later poetry of Yeats.

Clarity is not, however, always consistent with the maximum effectiveness of the poem. If everything were disclosed as quickly and clearly as possible, interest, suspense, and surprise and, indeed, the poet's whole control of our emotions would be minimized, and the emotional force of poetry would be greatly lessened. In proportion as characters and situations are made vivid to us, they exert more powerfully their peculiar emotional force, and they can be disclosed too rapidly to be vivid. We are, for instance, more vividly aware of the vice of a man when we realize that we were mistaken in the supposition that he is virtuous, and we are more vividly aware of virtue which we have misjudged; our reaction in each case is proportional to our vivid awareness. Interest and suspense must diminish, once we know all; and surprise is impossible when only the expected happens. Hence, obviously, the poet must, if merely upon these grounds, conceal some aspects of his subject and misdirect us in our interpretation of it; and, although language is not the only instrument of concealment and misdirection, it is nevertheless an important one.

All the points involved in disclosure, as analyzed above, generate devices of partial disclosure and concealment. An example or two must suffice here. Partial disclosure is produced by vagueness, among other things; and vagueness is produced most generally by the incommensurateness of terms, by ambiguity either of terms, syntax, or sentence-relation, and by altering circumstances within the poem. All but the last are clear; I mean by it such phenomena as are produced when a verbal expression changes meaning as the poem advances, not because of verbal ambiguity as such, but because of changing circumstances, just as "King of England" may now mean one man, now another. This is different from ambiguous prophecies such as those in *Macbeth*. The powerful effect of vagueness in inducing suspense and otherwise augmenting attention and emotion is admirably exemplified, as Coleridge has observed, by Shakespeare's treatment of the ghost in *Hamlet*; it is first disclosed to the audience as a "thing" which "appears," has appeared before, and may momently be expected to appear again, then as something that may be fantasy, as something that might not be believed, then as a "dreaded sight" twice seen, and as an "apparition"; after such verbal preparation the ghost appears, and that unexpectedly. This is indeed, as Coleridge says, "admirable indefiniteness," and it is particularly effective, since the prior discussion has induced a certain frame of mind in the audience. Complete disclosure here, by the use of the word "ghost," would have ruined the effect. The vagueness of the incommensurate word is not necessarily a matter of generality; for instance, T. S. Eliot achieves many effects by the use of words more specific than his meaning, e.g., the proper names which turn out, after all, not to have an individual reference. In general, it may be said that the poet must disclose as much of his subject, and only so much, as is requisite to produce the opinion and frame of mind on which the desired emotion depends; and obviously language can help or hinder in this.

Since emotions are produced, not from mere opinions, but from opinions actively entertained, and since this active entertainment results from the focusing of our attention, clearly the direction of attention is of great importance. It is achieved in many ways: by the mere mention of something where other things are left unmentioned; by repetition; by the repeated omission or avoidance of the obvious word where the whole context insists upon it; by implication, especially when the premise given is dull, but the conclusion implied is shocking or startling, or vice versa when the conclusion is given; by treatment on a larger scale than that afforded other things, provided that the scale is not so large as to weary the attention; by use of suspense and surprise; by understatement, overstatement, or irony; by changes of style, as from the circumlocutory to the terse; and by images and metaphors.

Only a few of these require explanation. Omission of the obvious word can be achieved by breaking off the grammatical member short of the word, or by substituting an incommensurate or an inconsonant word; or, what is rather a matter of invention than of diction, by substituting attributes for subjects, antecedents for consequents, and so on. The chapter called "The Grindstone" in *A Tale of Two Cities*, for example, directs atttention to the bloodiness of Paris not merely by repeatedly using the word "blood," but by naming attributes of blood such as redness and imparting them to the whole scene. Attention is produced by the unexpected in various ways, and especially when the whole meaning is reversed so that, for example, a compliment becomes an insult. Thus the speech of the elder Yeats at the Abbey Theatre: "This Ireland, this land of saints—plaster saints"; and thus John Barrymore's declining of an invitation: "I have a previous engagement which I shall make as quickly as possible."

Suspense and the unexpected are based upon disclosure and concealment;

nevertheless, not everything concealed or disclosed produces these. The matter disclosed or concealed is, of course, the primary determinant, and it must be matter which engages interest and anticipation; but, this granted, suspense and surprise may nevertheless be enhanced by the diction. Broadly speaking, we are in suspense until we have found the meaning of any discourse that engages our attention, merely because of the nature of language as temporal; but suspense can be artificially produced by delaying what we wish to know; hence, by stopping the sentence short of the informing word, or by using vagueness at the point that should inform, e.g., paraphrasis, especially where the paraphrasis resolves the familiar into the unfamiliar, so that we are delayed by having to conjecture (cf. Stefan Zweig's "wooden wedge affixed to a hollow tube" for "rifle"); by interruption of predication through apposition, parenthesis, and so on; by oxymoron, paradox, and the other devices that rest on apparent contradiction (for we must pause to consider how "rash timidity" or "drunken sobriety" is possible); by extension of the grammatical parts, e.g., making an attributive adjective into a predicate or a relative clause, etc.; by giving the facts in such order that knowledge is incomplete until the last (e.g., by saying "There, in the drawer, lay a shiny cylinder . . . fitted with a needle, the tip of which was still stained dark brown" instead of "There . . . lay the hypodermic syringe which had been the instrument of murder"). In general, suspense will be produced by every device of diction which delays the discovery of meaning.

An image is a verbal expression capable of conveying a conception of the form either of some sensory presentation or of some bodily feeling. Images therefore derive from three sources: the "common sensibles," which are perceptible to all senses or more than one, such as magnitude, motion, rest, figure, and number; the external sensibles, e.g., an object of vision; and bodily feelings, such as pain, heat, cold, pressure, fatigue, tension, etc. As our perceptions are limited—we do not, for instance, see all that is presented to the eye—so images are limited; an image must not therefore be a complete depiction, but the formula of an *aperçu.* An image, moreover, must consist of parts (a subject and its attribute, as the minimum); yet the statement must be concise enough so that all details fuse and operate as one perception. Such a synthesis is impossible if the elements are too many or too indeterminately related to each other. For instance, a contemporary novelist takes several sentences to say that a man's face was composed of V's, which effects nothing despite the elaborate statement of how it was so composed, because the V's have to be imagined in various positions and because the memory cannot retain them all; a second description of the man as "a blond satan" conveys a better picture, but it is still not really an image. For an image must be distinguished from a mere description of an object; otherwise every descriptive catalogue would be full of images;

and it is also different from a word effecting a picture, or every concrete noun would be an image. What distinguishes the image from ordinary description is that it effects a mental representation such as a particular perception might, with a speed as nearly approaching simultaneity as words permit. Thus it must consist of elements readily conceivable and simultaneously conceivable as what a single perception would present; any change of point of view or other condition of perception is fatal: Coleridge was right in rejecting "the furrow followed free," because this necessitated a change of place. The novelist mentioned above speaks of a speeding car appearing to one of its passengers as "a tan streak beneath us"; this similarly refuses to synthesize into an image. From what has just been said about the content of an image, it follows that the diction of an image should be clear, concise, and "heightened." By "heightened" language I mean slightly exaggerated; the words should suggest a color clearer or brighter than would apply to the real perception, since mental images are necessarily fainter than real perceptions; this increases vividness.

"Vivid images" are commonly confused with images of vivid things; but a vivid image is so because of its depiction and not its object. Thus the imagery of Yeats's early poems is vivid, although it depicts dim things like "moth-like stars" and "glimmering moths." Obviously, images should always be vivid; whether the things they present should be made vivid is another question. Poets frequently try to gain a kind of spurious vividness of imagery by the insertion of words like "bright" and "vivid," but this is, on the whole, bad; anyone can make vivid imagery of that sort. The effect of imagery ought to be more like that of dramatic presentation than of narration; we must feel as though we are seeing or hearing, not as though someone were describing something to us. The "brightness" should be brought out by an accurate word, or implied, or suggested by metaphor. Images are made more vivid by contrast or by the inclusion of an uncommon or unexpected element, just as objects themselves are—for instance, Wallace Stevens' "rouged fruits in snow." Vividness results also from the selection of an unusual object—cf. Eliot's "jeweled unicorns draw by the gilded hearse"—or from an unusual perception of it; this is, however, a matter of content. Much more might be said; perhaps it will suffice here to say one thing further: that, while good images do not necessarily make a good poem, bad ones can damage a poem greatly.

Aristotle has distinguished four kinds of metaphor; we may supplement his remarks by observing that such metaphors as he calls "proportional" divide into the simple and the complex, according as the likeness on which the metaphor is based is in terms of a single attribute or several. For instance, "pearl-pale hand" is simple, whereas "angelic hair" is complex; the former sets only a certain pallor before us, whereas the latter suggests sheen, delicacy, length, color, etc. Complex metaphors give us either a mere conjunction of attributes or a correspondence of whole with whole and part with part. The latter is exemplified in the famous analogy, in Ecclesiastes, of the body to a citadel; in the comparison of the body to a castle in *The Faerie Queene;* and of the state to a body in *Coriolanus.*

There are three elements in every metaphor: perhaps we may call them the "referent," or thing analogized; the "analogue," or thing to which the referent is analogized; and the "continuum," or ground of likeness, whether in fact or thought, which permits the analogy. A metaphor is clearly stated as metaphor when these are explicit and when the grammatical indications of similitude are present or easily understood. But a metaphor to be clear as metaphor must be something more than the clear statement that something resembles something in a certain respect; it must be intelligible as a likeness. A metaphor can never be false; it must be true, either in that the analogy is real, or in that someone in a certain condition might think it real. Hence a metaphor can be "difficult" in three principal ways: through omission of one of its elements, through unclear statement grammatically, through apparent falsity. Difficult metaphor always produces suspense and is useful for forcing inference; that is, the difficulty produces curiosity which impels the reader to infer; the inference involves delay, and thus suspense. When one element of the metaphor is suppressed, a riddle always results: for example, "Why is a snake's venom like a woman's virtue?" Curiosity, and therefore suspense, are heightened when the things involved are seemingly disparate, and heightened even more when seeming paradox is involved, as in Donne's metaphor just mentioned; for the comparison of a snake's venom to a woman's virtue implies that good is like bad.

When the continuum is a sensible quality, the metaphor is bound to be easy; where it is not, it always involves some difficulty. Anyone knows that the sun is like a lamp in respect of light; but why a flea is like marriage, or why lovers resemble compasses, is another matter. The metaphysical metaphor takes referents and analogues with no apparent continua; or states the continua last.

When both referent and continuum are suppressed, or only vaguely intimated, the metaphor becomes a symbol; what we speak of as "symbolism" is, so far as diction is concerned, merely the employment of symbolic metaphor.[50] When even the symbol is ambiguous, either because it involves the unfamiliar use of the familiar, or because it has been vaguely or partially stated and must be clarified by the context, suspense due to metaphor is at a maximum. Eliot's "little old man" is an example; for when we have translated *gerontion* into that, the familiarity of the expression keeps us from realizing that it is a symbol.

50. But see below, pp. 586–87.

Many other kinds of metaphor may be distinguished; among them what might be called the "correlative metaphor." Hart Crane's "adagios of islands" is of this kind. This type makes an attribution to the correlative of one of the terms of the metaphor, rather than to the term. For example: *motion of ship: motion of adagio music;* the motion is now transferred to the correlative, i.e., to that with reference to which the ship moves; hence *adagios of islands.*

Among kinds of unexpected metaphor, there is the kind which unites terms commonly united, so that the likeness appears trite; a new continuum is involved, however, in the light of which the metaphor is suddenly vivid and startling.

Again, there is what I shall call the "subsumptive metaphor" or the "subsumptive symbol." This is a general metaphor comprising many metaphors as its parts, and uniting all; the Platonic process of "combination" must be used in order to produce such metaphor. It is particularly powerful because of the dialectic which it entails. The magical mythology of Yeats's *Vision* involves it, and Eliot's Wheel is of the same order.

Somewhat akin to metaphor is the use of words which, while not constituting metaphor, have metaphorical suggestion, either determinately suggesting some analogue, or leaving the analogue vague. For instance, "The train glided out of a hole in the mountain and slid into a dark wood" suggests a serpent determinately, although without real metaphor, for these are perfectly literal attributes. Use of more general attributes in this instance would render the analogue indeterminate, but have the effect of metaphor still. This is very useful for producing "atmosphere."

Many other developments of diction are, like these last kinds, fairly new; the study of diction, even as tropes and figures, may scarcely, therefore, be regarded as completed; and still less the investigation of its complex uses in relation to the various kinds of poetic ends.

THE CRITICAL MONISM OF CLEANTH BROOKS[1]

R. S. CRANE

CERTAIN skeptical doubts which I have long felt concerning "the new criticism" have been considerably sharpened by Mr. Cleanth Brooks's latest volume, *The Well Wrought Urn*,[2] as well as by his recent essay on "Irony and 'Ironic' Poetry."[3] I am not happy about this, since on a number of points I am in sympathy with the purposes which differentiate Mr. Brooks and the writers commonly associated with him from most of the other critical schools of the day. I applaud them for having rejected the temptation to assimilate poetry, by large analogies, to metaphysics or rhetoric or history or the spirit of the age, and for having insisted on considering it, in Eliot's phrase, as poetry and not another thing. I welcome their efforts to shift the emphasis in practical criticism from generalities about authors to particularized studies of texts; and I have only praise for their desire to rescue poetics from the dictatorship of factual science and relativism and to reorient it toward normative judgments. These seem to me valuable contributions, and, were it not for other and, as I think, more essential aspects of the philosophy common to the group, I should be inclined to let my gratitude for them outweigh my misgivings.

It is not so much the particular theses advanced by Brooks in "Irony and 'Ironic' Poetry" that disturb me as the tacit assumptions about critical theory and method which have made the questions debated in this essay seem of such crucial importance to him. On the immediate issues of his polemic against those who object to his enlargement of the term "irony" I think he is right. There is no reason why a critic who has chosen to make a common word like "irony" or "paradox" the central term of his system should not enjoy the privilege "of wrenching the word from its usual context—of at once specializing and broadening it"; all critics from the beginning have done this, and their readers can legitimately complain only when the wrenching is unsystematic or when the motive to it, as is sometimes the case in contemporary criticism, is merely ignorance of the existence in earlier literature of an equally good and, to the educated public, better-known word for the same idea. If Brooks is guilty of these faults, his detractors have not pointed it out. And he cannot be fairly

1. Reprinted, with minor alterations, from *Modern Philology*, May, 1948.
2. New York: Reynal & Hitchcock, [1947].
3. *College English*, IX (1948), 231–37.

accused, either, of having so narrowed the meaning of "irony" as to deny the benefit of the concept to any poem, however apparently "simple," which he can convince himself is poetry. At all events, if there was ever substance to this charge, it is probable that few readers of his chapter on "Tears, Idle Tears" in *The Well Wrought Urn*, in which Tennyson's handling of ironic contrast and paradox is exhibited in detail, will care to press it in the future.

I do not question, either, that "irony," in Brooks's sense of the term, is a constant trait of all good poems, and I should have no quarrel with him had he been content to say so and to offer his analyses of texts as illustrations of one point, among others, in poetic theory. What troubles me is that, for Brooks, there are no other points. Irony, or paradox, is poetry, *tout simplement*, its form no less than its matter; or rather, in the critical system which he has constructed, there is no principle save that denoted by the words "irony" or "paradox" from which significant propositions concerning poems can be derived. It is the One in which the Many in his theory—and there are but few of these—are included as parts, the single source of all his predicates, the unique cause from which he generates all effects.

In this, it is true, he is not alone among the "new critics." The terms may differ, but the same tendency toward a monistic reduction of critical concepts is manifest in Allen Tate's doctrine of "tension," in John Crowe Ransom's principle of "texture," in Robert Penn Warren's obsession with symbols, above all in I. A. Richards' Pavlovian mythology concerning the "behavior" of words. The doubts which Brooks inspires thus become doubts about the general state of critical learning. I shall treat him, therefore, rather as a sign than as an individual, and I take him in place of any of the others, partly because he has expounded his position in full most recently, and partly because the position itself, as I shall indicate, is set forth in language which at once affords an easy clue to what has happened to critical theory in our age and at the same time is prophetic, however unconsciously, of new directions it may yet take.

I

It will be well to begin at the climactic point where Brooks's analysis of poetry leaves off. "One of the critical discoveries of our time—perhaps it is not a discovery but merely a recovery—" he says in his essay, "is that the parts of a poem have an organic relation to each other." It is "this general concept of organic structure which has been revolutionary in our recent criticism; our best 'practical criticism' has been based upon it; and upon it rests, in my opinion, the best hope that we have for reviving the study of poetry and of the humanities generally."[4]

4. *Ibid.*, pp. 231–32, 237.

What the concept of organic structure means for him is made clear in *The Well Wrought Urn*, the subtitle of which is *Studies in the Structure of Poetry*. We must draw "a sharp distinction," he writes, "between the attractiveness or beauty of any particular item taken as such and the 'beauty' of the poem considered as a whole. . . . Unless one asserts the primacy of the pattern, a poem becomes merely a bouquet of intrinsically beautiful items." We must describe poetry, therefore, "in terms of structure"; but the nature of the "structure" which distinguishes poetry requires careful definition. "The structure meant is certainly not 'form' in the conventional sense in which we think of form as a kind of envelope which 'contains' the 'content.'" Nor is it a logical structure or a "rational meaning" which can be apprehended adequately by paraphrasing it in prose. Poetry, it must always be remembered, is the opposite of science.

The structure meant is a structure of meanings, evaluations, and interpretations; and the principle of unity which informs it seems to be one of balancing and harmonizing connotations, attitudes, and meanings. But even here one needs to make important qualifications: the principle is not one which involves the arrangement of the various elements into homogeneous groupings, pairing like with like. It unites the like with the unlike. It does not unite them, however, by the simple process of allowing one connotation to cancel out another nor does it reduce the contradictory attitudes to harmony by a process of subtraction. . . . It is a positive unity, not a negative.

It is the presence in poetry of a structure such as this, he remarks, that accounts for his choice of key terms, and explains the recurrence in his pages of such words as "ambiguity," "paradox," "complex of attitudes," and, most frequently of all, "irony." These words may perhaps give way to other better ones in the future, but any substitutes for them will "have to be terms which do justice to the special kind of structure which seems to emerge as the common structure of poems so diverse on other counts as are *The Rape of the Lock* and 'Tears, Idle Tears.'"[5]

"The structure meant is a structure of meanings, evaluations, and interpretations; and the principle of unity which informs it seems to be one of balancing and harmonizing connotations, attitudes, and meanings." Whatever may be said of the first part of this formula, the second part will surely recall to every reader the famous passage in chapter xiv of the *Biographia literaria* in which Coleridge describes the operation of "that synthetic and magical power," constitutive of poetic genius, "to which we have exclusively appropriated the name of imagination":

This power, first put in action by the will and understanding, and retained under their irremissive, though gentle and unnoticed, controul . . . reveals itself in the balance or reconciliation of opposite or discordant qualities: of sameness, with difference; of the general, with the concrete; the idea, with the image; the individual, with the repre-

5. *The Well Wrought Urn*, pp. 178–79.

sentative; the sense of novelty and freshness, with old and familiar objects; a more than usual state of emotion, with more than usual order; judgement ever awake and steady self-possession, with enthusiasm and feeling profound or vehement; and while it blends and harmonizes the natural and the artificial, still subordinates art to nature; the manner to the matter; and our admiration of the poet to our sympathy with the poetry.[6]

Brooks prefers to talk about the structure of poetry rather than about the imagination, but the parallelism of his doctrine with that of Coleridge is none the less evident, and, what is more to the point, it has been acknowledged by Brooks himself, recently in *The Well Wrought Urn*[7] and earlier in *Modern Poetry and the Tradition*. There he was interested in defining metaphysical poetry in such a way as to reveal its community with all poetry, or at least all good poetry; and among the pronouncements of other critics which he finds most to his purpose he singles out particularly the passage I have quoted from Coleridge and, as a "development" from it, I. A. Richards' definition of the "poetry of synthesis," that is to say, the poetry in which impulses are brought ironically—the term is Richards'—into conflict with their opposites and the apparent discords finally resolved.[8] Brooks can hardly object, therefore, if I state my dissatisfaction with his critical method, first of all at least, in terms of its departures from the method of Coleridge.

II

The theory of poetry set forth in the *Biographia literaria* forms a coherent whole, but it is too good a theory, for all its limitations, to permit of reduction to a single principle or cause. For this reason various modern commentators, including I. A. Richards and Allen Tate, have naturally discovered that Coleridge, great as he was, had only a confused glimpse of the simple truth about his subject. The confusion, however, appears less glaring on a close reading of the text of the *Biographia* than in the pages of these recent interpreters; and much of the trouble disappears when it is observed that Coleridge had not one source for the distinctions he employs but several sources, which are nevertheless correlated in a scheme that allows him to discriminate aspects of poems as determined now by their medium or manner, now by their substance, now by their origin in the mental powers of the poet, now by their immediate or remote ends. The unity of his system derives, indeed, from the primacy of one of these causes relatively to the others: "I labored at a solid foundation," he says, "on which permanently to ground my opinions, in the component faculties of the human mind itself, and their comparative dignity and im-

6. *Biographia literaria*, ed. J. Shawcross (Oxford, 1907), II, 12.

7. Pp. 17, 230.

8. *Modern Poetry and the Tradition* (Chapel Hill, 1939), pp. 40–43.

portance."[9] But the faculties of the mind, though ideally they form a hierarchy, can yet be distinguished as to their particular objects and operations, with the result that, whereas poetry can be analogized, on the philosophical level, to the other arts and to science and philosophy itself, a special consideration of it in criticism is still possible in terms of the variable factors which enter into its production.

Thus it is that Coleridge, as one can see from chapters i and xvi of the *Biographia*, as well as from many other passages, can make intelligible use of the old distinction, so abhorrent to modern critics, between the diction or language of poems and their "matter and substance." He knew from his own experience in writing verse, as well as from literary history, that the fitting of the right manner to the right objects, or vice versa, is a problem which poets actually face, and that in criticism, therefore, terms and distinctions are needed, on both sides of the disjunction, in order to formulate the degree of success achieved in its solution. The distinction is saved from becoming a merely sterile dichotomy by virtue of a further distinction, to which Coleridge himself attached great importance, but which has not been too well understood by some of the "new critics"[10]—the distinction, which he insists is not a division, between "poetry" and "poem." I have quoted his definition of "poetry": it is a much wider term than "poem," since, on the one hand, what is essential to poetry may be found in writings, like those of Plato, Jeremy Taylor, and Thomas Burnet, which lack not only meter but also "the contra-distinguishing objects of a poem," and since, on the other hand, no poem of any length either can be or ought to be "all poetry." The reason is that "poetry" comes into being, no matter what the medium, whenever the images, thoughts, and emotions of the mind are brought into unity by the synthetic power of the secondary imagination. The definition of poetry, therefore, is the same as the definition of what "the poetic genius" does with whatever materials it operates upon: whenever "opposite or discordant qualities" of any sort are balanced or reconciled, poetry results, though we may call it, judging by other criteria, poetry (in the narrower sense) or philosophy or pictorial art. Poetry is thus architectonic thought, but a "poem," or "poetry" in its limited meaning, is a composition in words of a special kind; it contains the same elements—afforded by the mind interacting with the things of its experience—as a prose composition, but differs by virtue of "a different combination of them, in consequence of a different object being proposed." It is at this point, with the introduction of ends, that Coleridge's criticism becomes specifically poetic, and the result

9. *Biographia literaria*, I, 14.

10. Cf., e.g., I. A. Richards, *Coleridge on Imagination* (New York, 1935), pp. 112–19; and Allen Tate, *Reason in Madness: Critical Essays* (New York, 1941), pp. 45–51.

is a definition of poem in separation, first, from works of science and history and then from such works in prose as novels and romances: "A poem is that species of composition, which is opposed to works of science, by proposing for its *immediate* object pleasure, not truth; and from all other species (having *this* object in common with it) it is discriminated by proposing to itself such delight from the *whole*, as is compatible with a distinct gratification from each component *part*."[11] Or again: "It [namely, poetry in the narrower sense] is an art . . . of representing, in words, external nature and human thoughts and affections, both relatively to human affections, by the production of as much immediate pleasure in parts, as is compatible with the largest sum of pleasure in the whole."[12]

The comprehensiveness of Coleridge's scheme is apparent. "Imagination" is the key term in the sense that it designates the common source in the mind from which poetry as the balancing and reconciliation of opposites necessarily derives, along with philosophy and other things; and as are the differences in the operation of the imagination, so are the major distinctions—evident, for example, in the contrast between Shakespeare and Milton—which separate kinds of poetic genius. But poetry is also the art of making poems, and the consideration of these must take account, not merely of the imagination as the source of all excellence in thought, but of particular differences in ends pursued, objects represented, and kinds and qualities of language and verse selected for the purpose. Multiple and converging lines of differentiation are hence made possible, with the aid of which the critic—as Coleridge himself showed—can explore a wide variety of problems and arrive at solutions in which the obvious complexity of poetic composition is not obscured by the reduction of all effects to a single cause.

The scheme has a characteristically Platonic structure, but of the better sort, inasmuch as it formulates its idea of excellence in terms applicable to all synthetic activities of the mind and at the same time preserves the identity of poetry, as poetry and not another thing, by discriminating differences in ends, subject matters, and linguistic forms. It is a scheme with two levels, signified respectively by the words "poetry" and "poem," and the principle which relates the two is the principle, common to most of the Platonisms, of reflection or imitation. A poem in itself is a composite of diction with such-and-such qualities and of thought or matter determined by this or that faculty of the mind acting on the objects of human experience, the composite so organized as to produce as much immediate pleasure by its parts as is compatible with a maximum of pleasure from the whole. But a poem is likewise the work of a

11. *Biographia literaria*, II, 8–10.
12. *Coleridge's Shakespearean Criticism*, ed. T. M. Raysor (London, 1930), II, 66–67.

poet, and as such it reflects, in so far as it is successful, the secondary imagination "co-existing with the conscious will," just as this reflects the primary imagination operative in all human perception, and just as this in turn reflects "in the finite mind . . . the eternal act of creation in the infinite I AM."[13]

It is illuminating to see what has happened to this multidimensional and hence relatively sophisticated theory, to which he is admittedly indebted, in the criticism of Brooks. He has retained two of Coleridge's points: the proposition that the "imagination" reveals itself in the balance or reconciliation of opposite and discordant qualities; and the proposition that the contrary of poetry is science. But the new scheme in which these doctrines are embraced is a much simpler scheme than Coleridge's, and one capable of generating far fewer distinctions and criteria for the analysis and judgment of poems. The most obvious contrast is that, whereas Coleridge was concerned alike with indicating differences, both as between poems and other forms of composition and as between different sorts of poems (witness the beginning of chap. xiv), and with establishing the unifying basis of all these distinctions in the powers and creative operations of the mind, Brooks is concerned solely with constituting poetry—that is, poems considered collectively—as homogeneous by attributing to poetry a "special kind of structure," to be found in all poems—in the *Odyssey* no less than in *The Waste Land*, as he says[14]—but distinctive of poems as opposed to works of science. His problem is one of literal differentiation, and he has no need, consequently, for the elaborate "Platonic" dialectic underlying the *Biographia*. But the result of his decision to look for differences only as between poetry and other things and not within poetry itself is a notable impoverishment of poetic theory.

The nature of this impoverishment will perhaps become clear if we observe the manner in which his two major propositions have been separated from the argumentative context in which their originals were placed in chapter xiv of the *Biographia*. In that context the antithesis of poetry and science formed a part, as we have seen, of Coleridge's definition of "a poem," and the concept of the balancing and reconciliation of opposites formed a part of his definition of "poetry" in terms of the "poet." And the two definitions were philosophically distinct, the term "poetry" being a much more inclusive term than "poem." Brooks has abolished this difference, and has done so by fusing the two concepts, with a consequent loss of analytical values on both sides. His discourse is uniformly of "poems" in Coleridge's sense, that is to say, compositions in words of a special kind, and these he opposes, as Coleridge did, to works of science and other similar modes of writing. He also follows Coleridge in assign-

13. *Biographia literaria*, I, 202.
14. *The Well Wrought Urn*, p. 191.

ing to poems a peculiar kind of structure, or relationship of parts to whole. But—and this is the crucial shift—he derives his formula for this structure from what had been Coleridge's formula for "poetry" considered as the creative activity of the poet, and in doing so he decisively narrows the scope of the formula by dissociating it from the universal operations of the mind—the same, for Coleridge, wherever the highest excellence is achieved, whether in poetry, philosophy, eloquence, or science—and attaching it as a distinctive predicate to one species of linguistic objects. "Poems" thus become either all "poetry" or not-poems, and it would be an error to look for "poetry" elsewhere than in "poems."

One consequence of this is the disappearance from his treatment of poems in contrast with scientific works of Coleridge's differentiation of ends—truth for works of science, pleasure (entailing the special relationship, already noted, of parts and whole in the composition) for poems. So far as I have noticed, Brooks never treats poems in relation to the kinds or degrees of delight they afford; if the word "pleasure" occurs, it is surely only as a nonfunctional appendage to his system. It is otherwise with "truth"; being intent upon distinguishing poetry from science in terms of their different linguistic "structures," he is obliged to assume some common reference, and this turns out to be the term "truth" employed in a highly analogical sense, as one thing for the "rational" and "abstract" statements of science, and another thing for the "paradoxes" of poetry. Strictly speaking, however, poetry has no final cause, in his system, that is anyway analytically distinct from what poems read as ironic contexts "say"—even his remark that the "task" of the poet is to "unify experience"[15] signifies only that the parts of a poem necessarily have an organic —that is, an "ironic"—relation to each other.

Another consequence is the disappearance of the distinction between the "manner" and the "matter," or the "form" and the "substance," of poems. The warrant of this in the *Biographia* derives from the position that "poems," as distinct from "poetry," are compositions in words possessing the same "elements" as other kinds of composition and differing only, as we have seen, in "a different combination of them, in consequence of a different object being proposed." Poems may thus be characterized and differentiated specifically in terms of the varying mental faculties operative in them and the varying kinds of phenomena, human or natural, they represent, and questions may be raised concerning the appropriateness to these of the diction and meter: the reader of Coleridge's practical criticism will recall many passages in which precisely this is done. For Brooks, on the other hand, any such procedure is necessarily suspect; it is a sign that the critic who employs it is ignorant of the principle

15. *Ibid.*, p. 194.

which essentially separates poetry from science. The distinction between language and thought is still reflected, to be sure, in his vocabulary, so that he can designate the "elements" of a poem sometimes as "attitudes," "evaluations," or "interpretations" and sometimes as "connotations" or "meanings." But the different words are merely names for different aspects of one thing—the "structure" which distinguishes poems. To treat them otherwise would be to revert to what he calls "the old form-content dualism" or to fall victim to "the heresy of paraphrase," with its implication of a "logical structure" detachable from the poem. Most of our difficulties in criticism, he remarks,

are rooted in the heresy of paraphrase. If we allow ourselves to be misled by it, we distort the relation of the poem to its "truth," we raise the problem of belief in a vicious and crippling form, we split the poem between its "form" and its "content"—we bring the statement to be conveyed into an unreal competition with science or philosophy or theology.

The most subtle examples of this error "are those which, beginning with the 'paraphrasable' elements of the poem, refer the other elements of the poem finally to some role subordinate to the paraphrasable elements."[16] But the parts of a poem are related "organically," and hence there can be nothing to which any of them can be said to be subordinate except the poetical "structure" itself which balances and harmonizes them.

The definition of this "structure," as we have observed, derives from Coleridge's definition, not of "poem," but of "poetry." But it, too, undergoes a profound change in its transfer from one system to the other. In Coleridge the concept of "poetry" is not a differentia of poems (since it may appear in works of philosophy and science) but a criterion of their value, the ideal of perfection to which they, or passages in them, are to be referred. They approach perfection whenever the poetic genius, or the imagination, put in action by the will and understanding and retained under their control, succeeds in reconciling or reducing to unity any of the various "opposite or discordant qualities" involved in the substance or the diction of a poem, and they depart from perfection in proportion as such unification is not achieved. It is in these terms, for example, that Coleridge distinguishes between the beauties and the defects of Wordsworth in chapter xxii of the *Biographia*. When Wordsworth is at his best, the unity is complete—there is a perfect appropriateness of the language to the meaning, there is a union of deep and subtle thought with sensibility, there is, above all, imagination. On the other hand, the unification does not always take place, and signs of the failure may be seen, throughout Wordsworth's poetry, in the occasional inconstancy of the style, in the un-

16. *Ibid.*, pp. 184, 183.

necessary matter-of-factness of certain passages, or in thoughts and images too great for the subject.

In making what remains of Coleridge's definition of "poetry" the differentia of "poems" as contrasted with works of science, Brooks has cut himself off from any such critical use of the concept as this. It is not strange, therefore, that he feels no need, as Coleridge did, for an analysis of the "component faculties of the mind and their comparative dignity and importance," or that, in speaking of poetic "structure," he introduces no distinctions that depend on a conception of the poetic process such as Coleridge expressed when he spoke of the "imagination" as being set in motion and kept under the control of the "will and understanding." Any such reference of poems or poetic values to the mental powers of the poet and their operations would be fatal to Brooks's central position, since it would derive the peculiar "structure" of poems from a cause in no way distinct from that which generates works of science, philosophy, theology, and rhetoric.

Some enabling cause of poetic "structure" must, however, be found; and what more natural—since this is the one remaining possibility—than to locate it in the poet's language as an instrument determined to poetry rather than to science or propaganda? That this is indeed Brooks's position is indicated by several passages in *The Well Wrought Urn*. Thus, after commenting on the quality of the "irony" in one stanza of Gray's *Elegy*, he remarks that "I am not here interested in enumerating the possible variations; I am interested rather in our seeing that *the paradoxes spring from the very nature of the poet's language:* it is a language in which the connotations play as great a part as the denotations." And again:[17]

> I have said that even the apparently simple and straightforward poet *is forced into paradoxes by the nature of his instrument.* Seeing this, we should not be surprised to find poets who consciously employ it to gain a compression and precision otherwise unobtainable. . . . The method is an extension of the normal language of poetry, not a perversion of it.[18]

The causal efficacy thus runs, not from the poet to the poem, but from "the language of poetry" to the ironical or paradoxical "structure of poetry," which the poet's choice of this kind of language, instead of that of science, makes inevitable. But "the language of poetry is the language of paradox";[19] in other words, the two terms signify the same thing, or at most different degrees of the same thing; and thus all the multiple principles which Coleridge found it necessary to invoke—in proper subordination—for the adequate criticism of poetry are collapsed into one—the single principle, essentially linguistic in its

17. *Ibid.*, p. 8; italics mine.

18. *Ibid.*, p. 10; italics mine.   19. *Ibid.*, p. 3.

formulation, which is designated as "irony" or "paradox." Brooks, in short, is a complete monist, and, given his choice of language rather than subject matter or the poet or the ends of poetry as the unique basis of all his explanations, a materialistic monist at that.

III

The last point can be put in another way by saying that whereas for Coleridge at least three sciences are necessary for criticism—grammar, logic, and psychology—Brooks finds it possible to get along with only one, namely, grammar; and with only one part of that, namely, its doctrine of qualification. His whole effort can be described not unfairly as an attempt to erect a theory of poetry by extending and analogizing from the simple proposition of grammar that the meaning of one word or group of words is modified by its juxtaposition in discourse with another word or group of words. The paradoxes and ironic oppositions and resolutions of discrepant "attitudes" which, in his system, distinguish poetry sharply from science and other nonpoetical modes of writing are merely the more striking forms which such qualification takes when it is considered, merely qua qualification of meaning by context, apart from, and in contrast with, what he takes to be the self-contained and "abstract" meaning, not dependent on any special context, of predications of fact or universal truth, such as "Two plus two equals four" or "The square on the hypotenuse of a right triangle is equal to the sum of the squares on the other two sides."[20] To talk about the "prose-sense" of poems is to reduce them, or some part of them, to the status of assertions of this kind; and it is for the sake of eradicating this error—the source of "the heresy of paraphrase"—that he insists on finding the essence of poetry in its exclusive reliance on properties of speech which in earlier analyses of language were treated between the consideration of individual words and the consideration of linguistic wholes determined differently by the different ends of logic, dialectic, poetic, and rhetoric; as, for example, in Aristotle's discussions of ambiguity and equivocation; the modes of opposition or contrariety; the different senses of sameness and difference; the kinds of metaphor, including that which involves antithesis; amplification and depreciation in thought and words; the ways of making discourse lively and dramatic; the technique of the unexpected; and so on. Brooks has retained very little of the complexity and precision of this old "grammatical" teaching, and he presents what remains of it as peculiarly relevant to poetry rather than as applicable generally to discourse, and, indeed, as constitutive by itself of the whole of poetic theory. For all his simplification and distortion of the ancient analyses, however, it is clear that the apparatus of terms and distinctions he brings to the study of poetry is a composite of elements that can be

20. *College English*, IX, 233.

traced historically to the pre-propositional sections of logic and dialectic, the theory of diction, merely qua diction, of poetic, and the stylistic part of rhetoric.

His key concepts, "paradox" and "irony," reflect unmistakably their grammatical origin. They are terms that designate the mutual "qualification"—and especially one mode of it—that inevitably occurs when the meanings of individual words or sentences or passages are not fixed by prior definition but are determined immediately, in the discourse itself, by the "contexts" in which they stand. "Irony," he says, "is the most general term that we have for the kind of qualification which the various elements in a context receive from the context. This kind of qualification . . . is of tremendous importance in any poem. Moreover, irony is our most general term for indicating that recognition of incongruities—which, again, pervades all poetry to a degree far beyond what our conventional criticism has been heretofore willing to allow."[21] And "paradox" would seem to differ from "irony" only as it signifies "irony" especially in its narrower sense—not the general phenomenon of contextual qualification (the importance of which, Brooks tells us, we, or at least the "new critics," have at last come to see)[22] but the special kind of qualification, so long neglected, which involves the resolution of opposites: in short, the antithetical metaphor of Aristotle, Johnson's "heterogeneous ideas yoked by violence together," and Coleridge's "imagination."

So much for the manner in which Brooks constitutes the distinctive "language of poetry." His main interest, however, is in its distinctive "structure," and this would seem, on first thought, to be something requiring formulation in different, and even nongrammatical, terms. He tells us indeed, in his recent essay, that the statements made in a poem—including those which look like philosophical generalizations—"are to be read as if they were speeches in a drama,"[23] and in *The Well Wrought Urn* he remarks that "the structure of a poem resembles that of a play."[24] This sounds promising—and the analogy does, in fact, as we shall see, imply one idea which, if Brooks had worked it out, might have led to a more adequate theory than the one he gives us; but the promise is dimmed when we recollect that a "drama" is after all, when considered apart from the specific emotional quality of its plot, merely a grammatical entity, that is, a sequence of speeches with conflicting contexts.

Again, he has much to say about "unity," as when he remarks that the poet "must perforce dramatize the oneness of the experience, even though paying tribute to its diversity," and that the poet gives us "an insight which preserves the unity of experience," his final task being, indeed, "to unify experience."

21. *The Well Wrought Urn*, pp. 191–92.
22. *College English*, IX, 232.
23. *Ibid.*, p. 233.
24. P. 186.

"He must return to us the unity of the experience itself as man knows it in his own experience."[25] But this, too, is disappointing, for it merely attributes to the poet the same necessity for "balancing and harmonizing connotations, attitudes, and meanings" which elsewhere in Brooks—and more typically—is said to follow from the nature of the linguistic instrument the poet uses, as contrasted with the fixed statement-making language of science. It is not, therefore, any special principle of unity derived from the nature of the "experience" or object represented in a given kind of poem that determines poetical structure; rather it is the presence in poems of poetical structure—i.e., ironical opposition and resolution—that determines, and is the sign of, the unification of experience. And, as Brooks makes abundantly clear, the "structure of poetry" is a structure common to all poems.

Only one alternative remains: to get the "structure" of poems out of their linguistic elements or parts. And this is what Brooks tells us explicitly that he is doing. "The structure obviously is everywhere conditioned by the nature of the material which goes into the poem. The nature of the material sets the problem to be solved, and the solution is the ordering of the material."[26] And again, and most plainly: "What is true of the poet's language in detail is true of the larger wholes of poetry."[27] But what is true of the poet's language in detail, in Brooks's account of it, is that it is a language—"of paradox," as he says—which inevitably organizes itself, when two words are put together, into "organic" relations according to some pattern of ambiguity, metaphor, or ironic contrast. And nothing less, or more, than this can be said about the total organization of parts—that is to say, of lines and passages—in the poem as a whole. Brooks devotes a short paragraph in *The Well Wrought Urn* to a familiar line of Gray's *Elegy:*

> Grandeur is not to smile at the "short and simple annals of the poor." Properly speaking, of course, the poor do not have "annals." Kingdoms have annals, and so do kings, but the peasantry does not. The choice of the term is ironical, and yet the "short and simple" records of the poor are their "annals"—the important records for them.[28]

Here is poetry, the whole of poetry, so far as its essence as "paradoxical" language is concerned, for here is ironic contrast and its resolution; and the only difference between this one line and the whole *Elegy* is merely a matter of the degree of complexity exhibited by the ironic interrelationships. We may speak, indeed, of partial "contexts" and of total "contexts," the latter being built up, as Brooks suggests in one place,[29] out of the former; but the two are

---

25. *The Well Wrought Urn*, pp. 194–95.

26. *Ibid.*, p. 178.   28. *Ibid.*, p. 102.

27. *Ibid.*, p. 192.   29. *Ibid.*, p. 226.

completely homogeneous in their elements and structure, and the relation between them is best described as that of microcosm to macrocosm.

The limiting consequences of this radical reduction of poetics to grammar become apparent as soon as we consider what problems of criticism Brooks's
system will not permit us to solve. Thus we cannot, by any legitimate extension
of his principles, develop an apparatus for discriminating essentially and not
solely in terms of accidents of subject matter or historical style—between
poems so obviously different in the special kinds of pleasure they give us as
are the *Odyssey* and *The Waste Land*, "Who Is Sylvia?" and "The Canoniza-
tion," "Westminster Bridge" and Gray's *Elegy*, *The Rape of the Lock* and
"Tears, Idle Tears." What is revealed, if we stay with Brooks, is merely the
ironical "structure" which all these, and other, poems have in common as contrasted with nonpoetical works or bad poems. But this is to shut our eyes to a
whole range of questions, turning on specific differences in poetic ends and the
means suitable for their realization, which are real problems for poets writing
poems and hence, one would suppose, important problems for critics. For,
literally speaking at any rate, a poet does not write poetry but individual
poems. And these are inevitably, as finished wholes, instances of one or another
poetic kind, differentiated not by any necessities of the linguistic instrument of
poetry but primarily by the nature of the poet's conception, as finally embodied
in his poem, of a particular form to be achieved through the representation, in
speech used dramatically or otherwise, of some distinctive state of feeling, or
moral choice, or action, complete in itself and productive of a certain emotion
or complex of emotions in the reader. It is thus only relatively to the form of
the poem, as the representation of a particularized human activity of a given
emotional quality, that the poet can know whether his poem is too long or too
short, whether the things to be said or left unsaid are properly chosen, whether
the parts are rightly ordered and connected, or whether the words, metaphors,
and "paradoxes" are appropriate or not to the thought, emotion, character,
situation, or general effect. In other words, the principles of the poet's artistic
reasoning (however instinctive this may be) are always, and necessarily, ends
or effects of some determinate sort to be accomplished in his poem, whether
ultimately in the poem as a whole or mediately in some part of it; and the principles will differ, and along with them his decisions as to what must or can be
done in constituting his action and its mode of representation, rendering his
characters and their thoughts, and fashioning his diction, according as he is
writing a simple lyric of feeling or a moral lyric of character, a tragedy or a
mock-epic. A sign of the adequacy to its subject of any theory of poetry which
aims, as Brooks's theory does, to treat poetry as poetry and not another thing,
is surely the extent to which it is able to cope, in specific terms, with problems

of this nature. The construction of an adequate theory is not an impossible task, but it requires a basic analysis that will take account, as Brooks never does, of more than one among the several variable "parts" which are combined in different ways in each of the many distinguishable species of poetic works.

It would be false to say that Brooks's preoccupation with language to the exclusion of the other more controlling causes of poetry deprives his criticism of any basis for judgments of value. He insists repeatedly, in fact, that they must be made. "The Humanities are in their present plight," he says, "largely because their teachers have more and more ceased to raise normative questions, have refrained from evaluation";[30] and he remarks that his studies of particular poems in *The Well Wrought Urn* are based on the assumption that "there are general criteria against which the poems may be measured."[31] The criteria as finally stated, however, turn out either to be excessively general or to have little direct applicability to individual poems. He refers to T. S. Eliot's test, which he puts in the form of the question, "Does the statement seem to be that which the mind of the reader can accept as coherent, mature, and founded on the facts of experience?"[32] We must indeed ask this question about poems, but the test is equally relevant to other kinds of works, as when one says of an argument that the conclusion seems true enough, but the conception of the subject is simple-minded. Elsewhere the standard is formulated in terms of deficiency and excess. On the one hand, poems lacking in irony are vulnerable to it, and hence "sentimental" and hence bad; on the other hand, as he suggests may be true of "Who Is Sylvia?" the "complexity" may be greater "than is necessary or normal."[33] Between these extremes, a hierarchy of poems, he thinks, may be established by the test of "complexity of attitude," with poems of simple affection at the bottom and probably tragedy at the top.[34] In so far as this reiterates the old doctrine that the excellence of art consists in a mean, there is no difficulty. But relatively to what is the too much or the too little to be determined in any particular case? Relatively to the maximizing, without diminishing returns, of the peculiar emotional effect proper to the object represented in a given poem? Or relatively to some standard of complexity fixed apart from the poet's problems in writing an individual poem of a certain form, and hence, in some sense, absolute? Brooks does not clearly say; but his notion of a hierarchy of poems based on the quantity and "sharpness" of the ironical oppositions they subsume suggests that he means by "normative" judgments the measurement of poems by a predetermined norm assumed to have general validity for all poems no matter what their kind or intended effect. He cannot,

30. *Ibid.*, p. 212.
31. *Ibid.*, pp. 198–99.
32. *College English*, IX, 234.
33. *Ibid.*, p. 235.
34. *The Well Wrought Urn*, pp. 229–30.

in fact, hold anything else but this, lacking any premises that would warrant judgments of individual poems founded on a mean relative to their peculiar ends and forms. And he lacks such premises because he has no concept of poems as concrete wholes the unity of which requires that the parts should be of a certain quality and magnitude and present in a certain order if the desired poetic effect is to be fully achieved.

But this is equivalent to saying that he has no distinctions for dealing with individual poems otherwise than as instances, to be grammatically construed, of a universal poetic "structure." His many *explications de textes* are accordingly better described, in his own term, as "readings" than as critical studies proper. Their method is the repeated application of his central paradigm of poetry to particular poems for the sake of uncovering, in the significances which can be attributed to their statements when taken in context, hitherto unnoticed occurrences of ironical "complexity," first on the level of single words and lines, and then on the level of the interrelationships between larger passages, until the end of the poem is reached.

A typical example of the method is the chapter on Gray's *Elegy* in *The Well Wrought Urn*, from which I have already quoted a passage illustrative of the manner in which the technique works in detail. The essay considers successively, first the effect of the many "echoes" of Milton and others in making the *Elegy* an ironical rather than a "simple" poem; then the ironic contrast implied in the opening description of the churchyard; then the ironic function of the personifications, together with their "supporting ironical devices" in phrases like "homely joys," "the short and simple annals of the poor," "animated bust," the stanza beginning "Full many a gem," and the lines on Hampden, Milton, and Cromwell; then the passage on the tombstones in the churchyard, which, according to Brooks, brings together opposites so far held apart; and, finally, the poet's lines about himself and his imagined epitaph, which are said to center in the speaker's "choice" between the two alternatives of burial contrasted earlier in the poem.

Brooks is concerned, in this chapter, to put us on guard against what he fears is the common temptation "to think of the prose-sense as the poetic content, a content which in this poem is transmitted, essentially unqualified, to the reader by means of the poetic form, which, in this case, merely supplies a discreet decoration to the content." This should certainly be discouraged; but Brooks appears to have fallen victim to an equally unfortunate temptation, which his critical principles, in fact, make irresistible, namely, to disregard the "poetic content" altogether. For surely there is a kind of "content," distinctive of poems like Gray's, which cannot be reduced, by paraphrase, to any proposition or idea, and which is not so much "transmitted" as represented: it is that which primarily constitutes the *Elegy* a complete and ordered serious lyric, productive of a special emotional pleasure, rather than simply a statement of thought. It is to be discovered by inquiring about the moral character of the speaker (as distinct from his "attitudes") and the particular problem which confronts him; about the relation between what Gray has chosen to present, namely, the calm and aphoristic but solemn deliberation in the churchyard, and the emotions which the speaker's situation and outlook had previously generated; about the sequence of his thoughts and feelings as thus made probable or necessary; and so on.[35] Brooks raises none of these poetic questions. The *Elegy* as he exhibits it is indeed ironical discourse, in which the "prose-sense" (that is, what is contained in bad paraphrases of the poem) is "qualified" at each step. But it is still merely discourse, with an arrangement dictated solely by the contrast the speaker is supposed to be making between two possibilities of burial and his (at least in Brooks's account) unmotivated choice between them. It has an outline, to be sure, but an outline of the kind that any sermon might have, or any serious familiar essay. The "reading" gives us, in short, not a poem but simply a piece of moderately subtle dialectic: an

35. More explicitly, I take the poetic form of the *Elegy* to be that of an imitative lyric of moral choice (see below, p. 564), representing a situation in which a virtuous, sensitive, and ambitious young man of humble birth confronts the prospect of his death while still to "Fortune and to Fame unknown," and eventually, after much disturbance of mind, reconciles himself to his probable "fate" by reflecting that none of the rewards of successful ambition can "sooth the dull cold ear of Death," which comes as inevitably to the great as to the obscure; that a life passed "far from the madding crowd's ignoble strife," though circumscribing the exercise of virtue and talent, may yet be a means of preserving innocence; and that he can at any rate look forward to—what all men desire as a minimum—living on in the memory of at least one friend, while his merits and frailties alike repose "in trembling hope" on the bosom of his Father and his God. What is embodied in the words of the poem is the final stage of this "action"—the resolution of the speaker's internal conflict (hinted at in ll. 101-8); with respect to this, his evening meditation in the churchyard on the "unhonour'd Dead" serves the double function of a dramatizing and externalizing device and, more importantly, of an analogy in his reconciling argument. He stands apart from both the great of the world and the humble rustics whose tombs are before him; but he resembles more closely, in his fortune, the latter than the former. Hence it is natural for him to infer that the advantages and consolations he finds in their lot can likewise be advantages and consolations for himself.

This is not, of course, the poem, or even a "paraphrase" of it; nor is it an attempt to state what Gray must have had explicitly in mind when he gave his *imprimatur* to the *Elegy* in its final form. It is rather an effort to formulate, hypothetically, the over-all principle of construction which appears to me to account most adequately for the detailed character and interrelations of the parts which the finished poem combines and for the effect which it is calculated to produce on a normally sensitive reader. Discussion of its value as a hypothesis in practical criticism would therefore turn on the extent to which, relative to alternative hypotheses, it, on the one hand, makes both grammatical and poetic sense out of the total succession of words and sentences in the *Elegy* and, on the other hand, receives further confirmation from repeated and independent considerations of these. The hypothesis itself is a correlation of three elements: the moral character of the speaker, the situation which compels his effort at resolution, and the steps of the meditation through which his choice is expressed; of these, only the last appears, abstracted from the others, in Brooks's "reading." Cf. below, pp. 632 ff.

inferior specimen of the genre represented—to choose an example consonant with the title of Brooks's volume—by Sir Thomas Browne's *Urn Burial*. What excitement and dramatic life the poem has, no less than its peculiar ethical quality, accordingly disappear, and we have instead an inconsequential and unmoving "theme" (largely read into the poem) on modes of burial. Why is it, if it is, a great poem? Or is it that "irony," in Brooks's view, is really a final good and not merely, as he indicates at times, a means or device?

The neglect of poetic content or form—the words here mean the same—is responsible, furthermore, for difficulties in the "reading" itself. This is inevitably so since, without a clear principle of control, in an adequate hypothesis about the poetic whole, the purely grammatical scrutiny of a poem for instances of "ambiguity," "paradox," "complex of attitudes," or "irony" is bound to lead to *contresens*. Not all of Brooks's remarks about the *Elegy* fall into this class, and the chapter contains, indeed, a number of shrewd and sensitive observations which any student will be glad to have. But I am disturbed, among other things, by his misconstruction of the thought in lines 45–76—a misconstruction which a prior inquiry into the unifying action of the poem would have prevented—and especially by his much too respectful view of William Empson's commentary on stanza 14—a masterpiece of critical irresponsibility surely unmatched in modern times, except elsewhere in Empson.

IV

I have hitherto gone along with Brooks in his contention that the qualities he calls "paradox" or "irony" are somehow peculiar to poetry, and have been content to urge the inadequacy of his theory in terms of what his exclusive concern with "the language of poetry" forces him to leave out. I now want to examine the proofs on which this major proposition of his theory—as a theory of poetry—ultimately rests.

The first step in the argument is simple enough. It consists in a division of all discourse into two kinds: that in which the statements are "abstract," in the sense that their meaning is "unqualified by any context," and that in which the statements are not "abstract" but bear "the pressure of the context" and have their meanings "modified by the context"; an extreme form of the latter is discourse which achieves "the stability of a context in which the internal pressures balance and mutually support each other."[36] The term "irony" applies, as we have seen, to the second type of discourse: in its "obvious" meaning to the general phenomenon of contextual qualification, in a "further sense" to the degree of qualification which is manifest when opposing or discordant meanings are fused.

36. *College English*, IX, 234.

The initial problem is to demonstrate that this division corresponds to the distinction between "science" and "poetry." That scientific discourse is made up of "denotations," that is, terms with fixed meanings, and hence of "abstract" statements, is assumed rather than proved; that poetry, on the other hand, is discourse which never contains "abstract" statements is argued instantially by presenting "readings" of various poems so chosen as to embrace representatives of the whole English tradition from Shakespeare to Yeats and of the extremes, within this tradition, of admittedly witty poems and of poems apparently "simple" and "spontaneous." All these are analyzed exclusively with a view to the manner in which single words, phrases, lines, and passages have their meanings determined "ironically" (in both senses of the term) by contexts; whence the conclusion follows that "the special kind of structure" thus revealed—a structure from which "abstract statements" are necessarily excluded by the very technique of reading—is "the common structure" of poems of all kinds, since it occurs not only in those where we would expect it from obvious signs but also in those where its presence has often been denied. And it follows, as a corollary of this, that to read poems as expressions of "rational" meanings rather than as patterns of "ironical" qualification is to do violence to their true nature and to bring them "into an unreal competition with science or philosophy or theology" or, as other passages indicate, moral rhetoric and propaganda.

If we ask, then, what the "readings" prove, the answer must be that they prove what they were designed to prove, namely, the possession by poems of a kind of structure which, on Brooks's assumptions, poems must have inasmuch as there are only two kinds of structure possible and the other is preempted by science, of which poetry is, also by assumption, the necessary opposite. He has got himself into this difficult logical position, I would suggest, precisely because, although his analysis is set up in terms derived from Coleridge, he has insisted, unlike Coleridge, on identifying "the structure of poetry" literally with poems in the usual sense of that word, while retaining, but reducing to linguistic differences, the opposition, in Coleridge, of "poems" and "science." As a result, he is committed to saying, or at least implying, not merely that "irony" or "paradox" is universally present in poems—which, granted his definitions of the two words, is doubtless true—but that the "structure" these terms signify is the differentia of poems, the sufficient cause which distinguishes them essentially from all other kinds of works in which language is employed. If he does not mean this, then it is hard to understand why he gives instances of "irony" only from poems or why he supposes that recognition of "the concept of poetry as an organism" with its corollaries of "the ultimate importance of context and the fact of contextual qualification," is "the best hope

that we have for reviving the study of poetry and of the humanities generally."
But if he does mean that "irony" is a quality peculiar to poems, then—especially in view of the claims he makes for the novelty of the theory—we might
reasonably expect him to offer some evidence that this is indeed the case. The
evidence would consist in a series of "readings" of complete works other than
poems leading to the conclusion that, when they are analyzed in the same way
his poems are analyzed, the same phenomena of contextual qualification and
"irony" do not appear. No such evidence, however, is forthcoming, with the
result that what would seem to be the crucial proposition of his theory is advanced as a mere assertion, without argumentative support.

How, if he had raised the question, he could have resolved it in favor of his
hypothesis, I confess I do not see. It is surely not a self-evident truth that it is
only, or peculiarly, in poems that the "relevance," "propriety," "rhetorical
force," and "meaning" of statements "cannot be divorced from the context in
which they are imbedded," or only, or peculiarly, in poems that systematic
ambiguities occur, or that "incongruities" are recognized, or extremes of opposition reconciled, or the claims of discordant and apparently irrelevant "attitudes" adjusted to one another. Merely to state the point should be sufficient,
it would seem, to convince anyone that these are "structures" common not
only to all poems but to all species of connected discourse—and necessarily,
since all words as they present themselves to a writer are ambiguous (there
being many more things or ideas than verbal symbols for them) and therefore
have to have their significances fixed by the particular contexts, of whatever
sort, in which they are used. There are many devices for doing this, but there
are none, as far as I can recall, that have not been used indifferently in poems,
essays, histories, orations, philosophic treatises, or scientific expositions. Nor
is any meaningful distinction to be made in this connection, as Brooks supposes,[37] between "context" and "universe of discourse": the one is the grammarian's term, the other the logician's; but if we wish to talk about discourse
apart from the various specific ends it serves (as Brooks talks about poetry),
we must inevitably speak of contexts and of statements in relation to them, that
being all that discourse, qua discourse, consists of.

Why, then, all the to-do about "irony" in poetry? Why not look for
"irony" everywhere? For, if we look, it will assuredly be found. It even pervades this essay I am writing, from the "echo" in the opening phrase on through:
there is no essential difference, in terms of anything Brooks's analysis can
show, between, for example, my "qualification" of Brooks by Coleridge and
Gray's "qualification" of the graves in the churchyard by the tombs in the
church. The full and proper meaning of "Beauty is truth, truth beauty," is no

37. *Ibid.*, p. 233 n.

doubt dependent, as Brooks makes clear in some detail, upon the total context of the character and "attitude" of the speaker in Keats's ode; but it would take almost as many words to exhibit adequately the "pressure" of the context upon Gibbon's statement in his fifteenth chapter that he intended to write "a candid but rational inquiry into the progress and establishment of Christianity." And it would require many more words—Coleridge needed thirteen chapters—to trace the contribution of the context to the very rich meanings which the words "poem" and "poetry" have when they are opposed in the *Biographia literaria*.

But we may go farther than this. Brooks finds his extreme of "irony" in I. A. Richards' "poetry of synthesis"—"a poetry which does not leave out what is apparently hostile to its dominant tone, and which, because it is able to fuse the irrelevant and discordant, has come to terms with itself and is invulnerable to irony"—invulnerability to irony being "the stability of a context in which the internal pressures balance and mutually support each other."[38] This is excellent, but it is a perfect formula for what is achieved, more completely than in any poem I have ever read, by the dialectic of the *Phaedrus* or *Republic* or by Hume's *Dialogues concerning Natural Religion*. No more than for any poem can the "insights" communicated by these marvelous discourses be summed up in a "paraphrase," however elaborate: they are supreme instances of "irony" in every sense which Brooks attaches to the word; and, although it is true that his method of "reading" would exhibit only a few of their more material and hence less essential traits, it would certainly leave out no more than the same method does when applied to poems.

There is, finally, science—or rather, since the comparison must be made in terms of uses of language, scientific works. Brooks would have it that the words of science, unlike those of poetry, do not change under the pressure of the context. "They are pure (or aspire to be pure) denotations; they are defined in advance. They are not to be warped into new meanings. But where is the dictionary which contains the terms of a poem? It is a truism that the poet is continually forced to remake language."[39] In these statements we have the keystone of his whole position: remove it, and his account of the structure "characteristic" of poetry crumbles. And at first sight this would seem hard to do. For it is undoubtedly the case that scientists, in the physical sciences at any rate, aspire to definitions of terms which will remain constant in all the treatises or papers in which the terms are used, and it is just as clearly the case that poets, in writing new poems, do nothing of the sort. But this difference follows as a consequence from the quite different ends which poets and scientists

38. *Ibid.*, p. 234.
39. *The Well Wrought Urn*, p. 192.

pursue and is not in any sense an antecedent cause of the differences between poetry and science. And in particular it is not a sign that the principle of "contextual qualification," which evidently operates in poetry, does not also function in scientific discourse, when this is considered, as Brooks considers poetry, purely in terms of interrelationships of significations. The terms of science, says Brooks, "are defined in advance." In advance of what? Surely not of the particular framework of meanings in which they are used: the definitions of Euclid are not separate from, but an integral part of, the "context" in which all his subsequent theorems are set up, and by the "pressure" of which the terms employed in the theorems are qualified in this way rather than in that. And what, for that matter, is a definition but a qualification of a common word, ambiguous otherwise, by a context? Moreover, as the context, in the sense of the total system of meanings, shifts, so do the meaning, propriety, relevance, and so on of any term or statement. Thus the vocabulary with which Aristotle discourses scientifically about poetry in the *Poetics* is in large part identical with the vocabulary of Plato in Books ii, iii, and x of the *Republic;* the meanings of the corresponding terms and statements in Aristotle, however, are entirely different, and the difference is produced (it is recorded in part, but only in part, in explicit definitions) by a radical change in "context," which can be described in the same grammatical fashion as Brooks describes differences or changes of "context" in poetry. And the shifts go on within the *Poetics* itself, as anyone can see, for example, who will trace what happens to the word *ethos* in chapter 6. Nor is modern science an exception. Where is the dictionary which contains the terms of Newton? He, too, like any innovating poet, inherited a vocabulary; but the *Principia* is an original system of verbal and ideational "contexts"—it is more than that, of course, but so, in a different way, is any good poem—under the pressure of which all the old words and "attitudes" take on new senses, with the consequence that the traditional language is completely "remade." In contemporary physics, also, as I am informed, contextual qualification occurs whenever a statement is moved from the macroscopic level of classical to the microscopic level of relativity mechanics. It is true that the rules for such shifts, in modern science, can be explicitly stated and are well known; but even this has its analogue in poetry in the persistence of conventions and formularized techniques for getting "paradoxical" effects.

The syntheses of science, too, can be described, omitting questions of their truth, in much the same terms as Brooks uses to distinguish the "poetry of synthesis." One example will suffice—the formula in which Einstein brought together in a single unified equation the hitherto "discordant" qualities of mass and energy:

$$E = mc^2.$$

I offer this, judging it solely by Brooks's criterion for poetic "structure," as the greatest "ironical" poem written so far in the twentieth century.

The moral of all this is surely not that there is any fundamental similarity between poetry and science, or poetry and dialectic, which can be made to lead to fruitful and precise practical criticism, but simply that Brooks's attempt to differentiate "the structure of poetry" by deriving it from basic distinctions in language is self-defeating. He has assumed, in his initial divisions, with no warrant from the facts, what he has to prove, and he has thus begged the entire question.

V

His fundamental error, I suggest, is that he has begun to theorize about poetry at the wrong end—starting not with concrete poetic wholes of various kinds, the parts of which, with their possible interrelationships, can be inferred as consequences from inductively established principles, but rather with one only of the several internal causes of poems, and the cause which they have most completely in common with all other literary productions, namely, their linguistic matter: here he begins, and here also he ends. The choice is regrettable, since it prevents him from dealing adequately with poetic works in terms of the sufficient or distinguishing causes of their production and nature; but it would be unfair to blame him unduly for making it, inasmuch as it has been a characteristic methodological choice, as I have said before, in the school of "new critics" to which he belongs. Nor are the reasons hard to assign. Chief among them is what I can only call the morbid obsession of these writers with the problem of justifying and preserving poetry in an age of science. This has resulted in an extraordinary florescence of modern apologies for poesy, the majority of which, in spite of much diversity in the rhetorical topics, have turned on the antithesis expressed in the title of one of the most famous of them, science and poetry. The question of the differences between poetry and science is as old as the Greeks, but whereas, with earlier critics, it was only one among many problems—and, for most, a problem preliminary to criticism proper—it has become, for our contemporaries, *the* crucial issue upon the successful resolution of which the fate of poetry, and even of the humanities in general, is thought to depend. How, with science everywhere dominant and the method of science universally accepted as the one road to truth, can poetry still be made to seem a valuable and respectable form of mental activity, rather than merely a survival of prescientific modes of thought destined to disappear in the future? Obviously—so goes the common answer—only by returning to first principles and seeking to define afresh the nature and peculiar sphere of poetry in terms which will at once mark it off sharply from the factual and "rational" sphere of science and exhibit it as a natural, and hence permanent, effect of causes distinct from, but no less basic in, man's life than those which operate in the scientific sphere.

It is not strange, therefore, that critics thus preoccupied with the single problem of establishing a division of labor between science and poetry should largely give up, as irrelevant to their purpose, the discrimination of particular poetic kinds and effects. What has to be saved, or reconciled with science, is poetry itself *en bloc;* and, that being the case, the inquiry resolves itself into a search for some one fundamental difference between the two which can be shown to depend, not upon the arbitrary determinations of poets or critics, but upon divergent tendencies in the underlying natural conditions from which both science and poetry spring. Such a common basis was frequently found in earlier times in the faculties of the soul (as in Bacon and Macaulay); in the twentieth century, however, this will no longer do; the golden key which is counted on to unlock all doors is now not the mind but language. It is here, accordingly, and not either in the final character of poetic works as opposed to scientific, or in the differentiation of ends or subject matters or techniques, that most of the "new critics" have sought their first principles, in the simple faith, that, because language is the instrument of both scientists and poets, the high claims of poetry can be asserted most effectively by deriving all its essential characteristics from a consideration of those potentialities of language which are left over, once the specialized use of words in science has been defined. So everything turns, for I. A. Richards, on the opposition of "referential" and "emotive" speech; for John Crowe Ransom, on the antithesis of logical "structure" and poetic "texture"; and for Brooks, as we have seen, on the contrast between the "abstract" language of science and the "paradoxical" language of poetry. The words of poetry have thus become all-important, to the neglect or obscuration of all the factors in poetic production which determine, for the poet, what the words ought to be; and poetry, ironically enough, is defended against materialistic science by arguments which attempt, materialistically, to deduce poetic form from an examination of the medium alone.

I am convinced that this has led only to a blind alley and that a "newer" criticism is needed which will not worry so much about saving poetry—this, after all, has been with us a very long time and, besides, contains within itself powerful springs of natural human interest, surely not yet exhausted—but will devote itself to a scholarly and philosophically comprehensive study of poetry calculated to refine our instinctive response to poems by giving us an adequately sensitive critical apparatus for discriminating among them. I have tried to show how Brooks, having made a false start, is prevented, by the pressure of the limited context he has selected, from developing such an apparatus. Not everything he says or implies in his writings, however, is strictly functional in terms of his characteristic method; and among the pale ineffectual ghosts from earlier and better systems which hover, in the shapes of undefined and inoperative words, on the confines of his argument and make possible critical insights frequently much better than his theory, there are several which, if brought back to life, might do serviceable work. Among these peripheral terms we find "beauty," "unity," "propriety," "drama," "character," and, especially, "imitation." "The poem," he writes, "if it be a true poem is a simulacrum of reality—in this sense, at least, it is an 'imitation'—by *being* an experience rather than any mere statement about experience or any mere abstraction from experience."[40] If he had started here rather than with "the language of paradox," he might have got somewhere (and incidentally been able to give a better account of "irony" itself), for here is clearly a first principle by which poetry may be distinguished essentially, and not merely accidentally, from science, philosophy, history, and rhetoric, and precise consequences drawn concerning the construction and peculiar beauty of poems of different kinds. But the statement is isolated in his system: it does not follow from his theory of language, nor is it made a starting point for any significant deductions. So, too, with the other terms: they remain "irrelevant and discordant" elements, meaningful enough in other critical analyses, but never, in Brooks, subsumed under any general poetic principles. Yet the presence of such words in his exposition may be taken as a sign of his own half-conscious awareness that grammar is not enough; and at all events we may regard them as encouraging portents, suggestive of a direction which criticism might take if only it freed itself from the despotism of linguistics and the unique cause and aimed at a multidimensional theory of poetry that would be, like Brooks's, literal rather than Platonic in method, but much more adequate than his to the discrimination of peculiarly poetic values and to the development of normative judgments relative to *all* the complex problems—of object, manner, and effect as well as of medium—that enter into the various poetic arts.

To reconstruct criticism in this way would obviously be to reverse the whole tendency of critical reasoning as practiced by the "new critics." It would be to substitute the matter-of-fact and concrete for the abstract; the a posteriori for the a priori; the argument from immediately sensible and particular poetic effects to their proximate poetic causes for the argument from remote and nonpoetic causes to only general and common poetic effects. It would be, in a word, to study poems as complete wholes possessed of distinctive powers rather than merely the materials and devices of poetry in a context of extrapoetic considerations. And that would be new indeed.

40. *Ibid.*, p. 194.

THE "NEW CRITICISM" AND *KING LEAR*[1]

W. R. KEAST

SINCE the publication in 1935 of Caroline Spurgeon's elaborate investigation of the imagery of Shakespeare's plays, an increasingly large proportion of critical studies of the plays, whatever the differences of theory that have distinguished them, have taken the recurrent images of the plays as their primary data, often with the more or less explicit assumption that a careful study of these apparently less obvious and calculated elements is likely to bring us nearer to Shakespeare or his meaning than is the study of such more obvious elements as plot, character, and thought. It is probably safe to say that, at the present time, studies of Shakespearean imagery constitute, along with investigations of the relation of the plays to Renaissance or medieval thought (and the two sorts of study are frequently combined), the dominant modes of critical scholarship dealing with Shakespeare. Professor Heilman's book on *King Lear*[2] is, I believe, the most extensive single analysis of a Shakespearean play using its poetic imagery as the basic materials of investigation. Although it seems to me to be in almost all respects a bad book, it raises, in crucial form and with respect to a very great text, so many questions of importance both to the criticism of Shakespeare and to the study of literature generally as to justify fairly extended consideration.[3]

Heilman finds that the "meaning" of *King Lear*, and hence its structure and unity as a work of art, are most fully indicated in the patterns of recurrent images. When so read, it is "finally a play about the ways of looking at and assessing the world of human experience" (p. 28; cf. also pp. 133–34): its theme is intellectual conquest and salvation through imaginative vision.[4] It

1. Reprinted from *Modern Philology*, August, 1949.

2. Robert Bechtold Heilman, *This Great Stage: Image and Structure in "King Lear"* (Louisiana State University Press, 1948).

3. Since completing this article, I have seen Oscar James Campbell's discussion of "Shakespeare and the 'New Critics,' " (*Joseph Quincy Adams Memorial Studies* [Washington, D.C., 1948], pp. 81–96); the general views expressed in this essay are in most respects similar to his. For other criticism of symbolic interpretations of Shakespeare see E. E. Stoll, "An *Othello* All-Too Modern," *ELH*, XIII (1946), 46–58, and "Symbolism in Shakespeare," *MLR*, XLIII (1947), 9–23.

4. See, e.g., Heilman, *op. cit.*, pp. 70, 83, 84–85, 86, 87, 91, 98, 100, 112, 115–16, 129–30, 144, 164, 179, 197, 217, 221–22, 228–29, 263, 278, 283.

exhibits "the efforts of a sensitive but, in its haste and passion and initial inflexibility, not very well-equipped, mind to come to terms with, to master, a cosmos whose complexity and recalcitrancy we have always tangible and solidly visible before us" (p. 214). In his plans for dividing his kingdom and in his treatment of his daughters, Lear imposes upon the world a false, rationalistic standard of values when he should have relied upon imaginative insight, which alone is capable of making essential determinations of quality; this imposition, which is Lear's tragic flaw, brings to power the daughters, who embody in a pure form this shrewd, but ultimately false, rationalism; and, when he tries to accommodate their actions toward him to his innate, but hitherto unrecognized, standard of values, Lear goes mad. But in his madness, which is structurally the climax of the play, is regeneration: Lear, "by expiatory suffering, undergoes a spiritual recovery, an imaginative wakening; Shakespeare pictures him as coming again to an apprehension of values of which he had lost sight" (pp. 228–29). Since the play is a tragedy and not a melodrama, the inner and private conflict in *King Lear* coincides with a public or outer struggle—the conflict in Lear and Gloucester between reason and imagination as appropriate sources of values and faculties of understanding is paralleled and intensified by the external conflict between a set of shrewd, worldly people (Goneril, Regan, Edmund, Cornwall) and a set of apparently helpless incompetents (Edgar, the Fool, Lear), in which the first group, despite initial successes, stops at superficial understanding, and the latter, despite apparent failure, achieves profound insight into the nature of the world and man. The "central paradox" of the play, illuminating the spiritual progress of Lear and the external conflict alike, is that "the poor naked wretches of the play, the victims of the world, will survive in spirit. The gorgeous are doomed. In proud array, Lear failed; uncovered, half-naked, he is saved" (p. 86).

After a chapter of "Critical Preliminaries" in which he sets forth some of the elements of his theory and gives a general account of the play, Heilman devotes a chapter of his book to each of the chief patterns of poetic imagery in which he finds the meaning and structure of *King Lear* conveyed. The *sight pattern* (chap. ii), in which such "dramatic facts" as the blindness of Gloucester are combined with metaphors and explicit references involving sight and blindness, points the importance and difficulty of seeing and judging correctly; it is allied most closely to the *madness pattern* (chaps. viii and ix), in which Lear's madness co-operates with many images of madness and folly to suggest that man's fate in the world, and the possibilities of his salvation, depend on his mode of understanding. These two patterns, to which is joined a scheme of images based on the root concept of *values* (chap. vii), are concerned generally with "the process and method of *understanding* and coming to terms with" a complex world (p. 179; Heilman's italics)—the sight imagery with man's ability to recognize and identify phenomena, the madness imagery with his ability to interpret them. Taken together, these three patterns illuminate the problems faced by man as a perceptive moral agent; the remaining patterns set forth "in complex detail" the reality he seeks to understand. The *clothes imagery* (chap. iii) underlines the problem of distinguishing between appearance and reality; the many *animal* images (chap. iv) join to form a pattern that suggests the ease with which man may be degraded from his proper humanity; the references to *nature* and to deviations from the natural (chap. v) bring into play rival conceptions of nature as a norm and emphasize the dependence of judgment and action on man's conception of the natural; another scheme, centering on the concept of *age* (chap. vi), points to the relativity of such a human condition to the values by which it is judged; and the *justice pattern* (chap. vi), extending the implications of the nature imagery, emphasizes the difficulties of just action in a complex world. All these patterns and the dramatic facts to which they are related set forth "the problem of The World": "the great in the world seem to use their greatness badly or to achieve it at the cost of all spiritual values; these values are preserved best by those whom the world rejects" (p. 252). But *King Lear* does not rest in the assertion of an enigma; we are not left to wonder what security the victims of the world may hope to achieve. A final, and culminating, pattern implies, if it does not directly assert, the resolution. The *religion pattern*, composed of the many references in the play to the gods, "ties together the other observations upon man and gets hold of the nature of man in the most inclusive terms" (p. 255; cf. also pp. 277–78), resolving the paradoxes implied in the other patterns by suggesting that

in the face of injustice man may believe in justice because the eternal gods will execute it. Man may speak in terms of a Nature which is Law because it is ordained by the gods whom he can invoke. The blind man sees because he can have insight into the divine reality. The sanity of the mad is that they can understand eternal truth [p. 255].

This summary, while it is, I believe, just to the main lines of Heilman's interpretation, gives no indication of the detail in which the various patterns of imagery are worked out, of the manifold interconnections and paradoxical linkages that he discovers between the various parts of the play, or of the numerous subsidiary and cooperating significances which he integrates into the larger thematic movements. But it will suffice, perhaps, as background for discussion of some of Heilman's assumptions, methods, and discoveries.

I

We may begin by noticing some features of his theory of drama set forth in the "Critical Preliminaries."[5] It is, he tells us, "a theory of meaning" (p. 12): a play or a tragedy or, at any rate, *King Lear* (Heilman is not very much interested in distinctions of this kind; I suspect, although he nowhere says so, that his remarks apply to any literary work whatsoever) is a "structure of meanings." It makes, however indirectly or ironically, an ultimate assertion; it conveys a "total meaning," usually in the form of a paradox, of which a considerable number of subordinate meanings are the parts (parts related to the total meaning not as items to an arithmetical sum but "organically," the parts often "scarcely distinguishable parts of a whole" [p. 175]). What is fundamental in Heilman's analysis is therefore the subject or "problem" to which the total meaning of the play and its parts is related; to this subject everything in the play metaphorically refers:

A series of dramatic statements about one subject does constitute a bloc of meaning which is a structural part of the play. This bloc may be understood as one of the author's metaphors. It is a metaphor just as a body of recurrent images, with its burden of implications, is a metaphor. The dramatist's basic metaphor is his plot. All of his metaphors are valid parts of his total meaning, the search for which must include a study of the relationship among the parts. All the constituent metaphors must be related to the large metaphor which is the play itself [pp. 11–12; cf. also p. 153].

Though equally valid, the various metaphors which constitute the play's meanings are not equally revelatory: they form a hierarchy, in which the plot—the overt "dramatic facts"—is basic in the sense of being at the lowest level and expressing the meaning least fully. Although the play may be summarized in a fashion by taking it "simply at the level of plot," such a procedure gives us only "partial outlines" of its tragic form; "in its fullness," we are told, "the structure can be set forth *only* by means of the pattern of imagery" (p. 32, italics mine; cf. also pp. 33, 38). That the poetic imagery should express the play's "inner" or "symbolic" meanings more adequately than do the characters and their actions, that the patterns should be parts in a more essential way than the latter, is, of course, inevitable in such a scheme as Heilman's: if a play is a large metaphor for the author's attitude toward a problem, we must expect to find that words, with their manifold potentialities for combination and suggestion, provide a more appropriate vehicle for the expression of inner symbolic meanings than do the more severely limited happenings and their agents; and

5. My discussion of Heilman's literary theory is limited to a few of its more serious disadvantages for dramatic interpretation. For a more comprehensive criticism of a critical theory with which his has much in common see above, pp. 83 ff.

since the theory posits that metaphor is the "basic constituent of form" and takes the language of drama as the primary object of critical investigation (p. 4), it is not surprising that words should turn out to be the most significant feature of the play.

But if the play as a whole and its constituent parts are metaphors, if they signify their meanings not literally but symbolically, then it follows that when Heilman assigns a meaning to something in *King Lear*, his statement must take the form of "A is *like* B" rather than of "A *is* B," where A is some element of the play and B its alleged meaning. We must keep this fact always in mind in reading what he has to tell us about *King Lear*; for the exigencies of composition sometimes permit him a license in the use of the copula through which a literal reading of the play might be mistakenly inferred. Thus, when he says (p. 35) that Lear's abdication is "a kind of refusal of responsibility, a withdrawal from a necessary involvement in the world of action," we must not take him literally; what he means, if the play is a metaphor, is that Lear's action is *like* a refusal and a withdrawal. These terms—like "the immaculateness of nonparticipation" and the "attempted elusion of the fettering of circumstance"—have only a remote relation to Lear's plan to "unburthen'd crawl toward death" and to prevent future strife by immediate publication of his daughters' dowries. No character in the play criticizes Lear's aims in the abdication, but only his means of effecting them—the transfer of the kingdom to Goneril and Regan and the banishment of Kent and Cordelia.

This example illustrates a consequence of Heilman's theory more important than the symbolism it entails: the primary source and guaranty of the symbolic values he attaches to elements of the play are not in his inductions from the evidence of the text but in the necessities of his own theories of tragedy and morality; as in the passage just quoted, the symbolism contradicts, or is irrelevant to, the plain meaning of the text. The critic's theory functions in his analysis not so much in suggesting possible modes of artistic combination or effect that *may* be found as in stipulating what *must* be found; and his reading is therefore arbitrary in the sense that fundamental control over it is exercised not by the work but by a preclusive doctrine which dictates the nature of the basic symbolic relations in the play. The essentially arbitrary procedure to which his theory of tragedy leads can be seen in a few examples of symbolic interpretation as Heilman practices it, first in the explication of details of diction and then in the elucidation of the large metaphorical meanings of the play as a whole.

Heilman's chapter on the sight pattern supplies several characteristic examples of the strange results which follow his effort to work into the pattern all the references to sight and blindness in the play. To the ordinarily acute reader, I venture to say, the following exchange between Edmund and Gloucester would seem innocent enough of ulterior significance:

GLOU.: What paper were you reading?
EDM.: Nothing, my lord.
GLOU.: No? What needed, then, that terrible dispatch of it into your pocket? the quality of nothing hath not such need to hide itself. Let's see: come, if it be nothing, I shall not need spectacles.
EDM.: I beseech you, sir, pardon me. . . .
GLOU.: Give me the letter, sir.
EDM.: I shall offend, either to detain or give it. The contents, as in part I understand them, are to blame.
GLOU.: Let's see, let's see.[6]

Heilman finds a fine irony in the diction: "just when Gloucester most fails to see where he is going, he feels, like Oedipus, most shrewd and observant." The sight pattern, he says, "points the issue for us": "while he is being made to see things as Edmund wishes Gloucester feels that he is detecting the truth" —three times he says "Let's see," but he does not see (p. 45). But it is obvious that when Gloucester asks to see the letter, he does not feel shrewd or observant or as if he were detecting the truth—he feels the impatience of the curious and interested man when teased; his remarks would be appropriate to anyone, however illuminated he might be spiritually, in such a situation. And, since Edmund's plan unfolds only as the scene progresses and since we do not yet know that Gloucester will be taken in by it, we are scarcely in a position to appreciate the irony, even if it were present.

Having got this far from Shakespeare, Heilman forges ahead into the darkness:

It is altogether logical, then, that Edmund's next move against Edgar takes place *at night* (II. i): the physical darkness betokens Gloucester's failure to see into what is going on. The actors in the nocturnal setting, indeed, represent more than one phase of a human plight: Gloucester victimizes and Edgar is victimized—he flees at night— because of the same kind of unseeingness. It is a meaningful, not merely a rhetorical, irony when Edmund calls, "Light, ho, here! / . . . Torches, torches! . . ." (33–34): those who want light least can call for it most loudly. Then Gloucester enters—how? ". . . with torches" (38)—the agent of light, but a kind of light—a physical reality like his eyes—that does him no good; it is inner illumination that he needs [pp. 45–46; Heilman's italics].

The "logic" Heilman discovers in the nocturnal setting for Edmund's next move is his, not Shakespeare's; for Edmund is surprised to learn that Cornwall is on his way to Gloucester's castle and decides on the spur of the moment to seize the opportunity thus presented for completing his design against Edgar. Edmund's call for torches is clearly part of his plan to appear to aid in

6. Act I, scene 2, ll. 30–45. All references to *King Lear* are to the Kittredge text.

the apprehension of Edgar; no one would have thought it merely rhetorical, but its meaning can scarcely be what Heilman says it is, for Edmund needs the lights very badly indeed—if there are none, no one will see his wound. That Gloucester in a scene laid at night and in answer to an urgent cry for torches should enter "with torches" seems to Heilman, intent upon his symbols, a veritable prodigy of metaphorical contrivance. The torches have shifted their symbolic allegiance in the space of four lines: when Edmund called for them, they were the kind of inner illumination he least wanted to have turned upon him; but now, when Gloucester carries them in, they are just ordinary physical lights, and the inner illumination has gone glimmering. Heilman goes on to attach a heavy symbolic weight to the references in the scene to the fact that Regan's visit to Gloucester's castle takes place at night (his count is wrong: there are four of these references in the scene, not just two); Regan, the point is, joins Edmund among those who must utilize the dark for their schemes. There are two excellent reasons for the references to darkness in the scene, neither very recondite: one is that it was customary, in plays acted in the afternoon, to aid the spectators' imaginations by verbal and spectacular identification of the physical scene—hence the references to night (and the torches);[7] second, that Regan uses the fact of their having traveled at night as proof of the importance of what she has to tell Gloucester, and thus she enhances our apprehensions about what is to come (ll. 120–31).

The examples I have so far given of Heilman's methods of interpretation have been limited to words and particular speeches. If we go to the other end of the metaphorical scale and consider the symbolic values attributed to the play as a whole, we will see the same arbitrariness in assigning such values, the same refusal to consider all the relevant evidence, and the same perverse ingenuity in avoiding the straightforward and direct.

In his preliminary discussion of the tragic structure of *King Lear*, Heilman writes as follows:

> In the latter part of the play Lear is reunited with Cordelia, and Gloucester with Edgar, just as in Act I the old men were enjoying close pseudo intimacies, respectively, with Goneril and Regan and with Edmund. It is, I think, not pushing the evidence too far to say that from the plot alone we may conclude that the change in associates has symbolic value. The reunion with the better children takes place after Lear and Gloucester have undergone a great deal of enlightenment; it may be read, then, as a kind of sign that there has taken place the achievement or recovery of insight which marks the experience of the tragic protagonists, just as their banishing of these children showed their fathers at their most obtuse. Thus Edgar and Cordelia symbolize a side of each of

---

7. See W. J. Lawrence, "Light and Darkness in the Elizabethan Theatre," *Englische Studien*, XLV (1912), 181–200, and *Pre-Restoration Stage Studies* (Cambridge, Mass., 1927), pp. 128–30; T. S. Graves, "Night Scenes in the Elizabethan Theatre," *Englische Studien*, XLVII (1914), 63–71; Chambers, *Elizabethan Stage* (1923), II, 543.

their parents, that side in which there lies the potentiality of salvation. But Edgar combats Edmund; Cordelia is on the opposite side from the sisters—those who once had parental confidence. By now the implication must be quite unmistakable: the children, like the Good and Evil Angels in Marlowe's *Faustus*, *represent the different elements which are in conflict in the fathers*. This is not true in a closely restrictive allegorical fashion, as we shall see; but it contains enough truth to indicate, together with what has already been said about the symbolic relationship between Lear and Gloucester, the essential tightness of structure of a play which has in it an unusual number of actions and characters. We see good and evil in conflict in the world, but by the structure we are reminded that the conflict is an emanation of that in the individual soul. Lear must recognize evil, must resolve his conflict—a conflict externalized in his attitudes to Goneril and Regan and Cordelia. By the fact of relationship the outer and inner evil become one, the two struggles are united. The children are not children for nothing; to be the father of Goneril is to create a symbol of the evil brought forth from oneself. The discerning reader of the play will hardly feel that he has done all his duty by hating Goneril [pp. 33–34; Heilman's italics].

This is a notable, but by no means uncharacteristic, example of Heilman's open-field running. First, we have a simple *post hoc, ergo propter hoc:* since the reunions take place *after* Lear and Gloucester have undergone enlightenment, they are signs of the enlightenment (*after*, not *because;* for Lear's reunion with Cordelia is in no way the effect of his discoveries about his daughters but is brought about by the actions of Gloucester, before he is enlightened, and of Kent and Cordelia, who are enlightened throughout; and Gloucester's reunion with Edgar is the effect not of Gloucester's discovery but of Edgar's late decision to reveal himself to his father). That fallacy is enough to negate what follows, but in the interest of familiarizing ourselves with our critic's technique we may go on. We have next an interesting, but illicit, substitution of terms: "enlightenment," which the innocent reader is likely to take as a somewhat hyperbolic reference to Lear's discovery about his daughters, becomes first "achievement or recovery of insight," which still seems harmless enough, and then "salvation." Where did salvation come from? To most people—and, as we later learn, to Heilman—salvation means much more than "enlightenment"; it suggests a religious context to which the familiar meanings of "enlightenment" are inappropriate. We hear no more of salvation at the moment, but, as I have said, it is a key term in Heilman's exegesis of *King Lear* as a drama of intellectual conquest, and it is instructive to note how it makes its way into his analysis. But why, to go on, should Edgar and Cordelia, because they are reunited with their fathers after the latter have recovered their capacities for insight, symbolize anything? Obviously, because they are in a work in which everything is metaphorical; it will not do for them merely to take their part in the action. But why, if they must be symbols, should their symbolic value be established only at so late a stage in the play, within a few scenes of the end?

What good is a crucial symbol if the author keeps it a secret, like the writer of a mediocre detective story? Shakespeare was clearly a novice, at least with symbols. But, assuming—as Heilman has no warrant to ask us to do—that we must read the play once to get the symbols fixed in our minds and at least once more to understand it, why should Edgar and Cordelia symbolize one side of their fathers' personalities? The author gives us the reason, on page 31, in his discussion of the tragic form: in the best tragedies the outer conflict is "symbolic of the movement of universal issues and is at the same time an objectification of the war within the protagonist" (cf. pp. 36–37). Now *King Lear* is one of the best tragedies; *ergo*, Edgar and Cordelia, who are part of the "outer" conflict, must symbolize an aspect of the "inner" conflict in the fathers. What is important here is not the obvious circularity of Heilman's reasoning but the derivation of symbolic connections, not from the text of Shakespeare's play, but from the critic's private theory of tragedy, which he asserts but never argues.

We are now in a position to grasp the curious logic by which Edmund, Goneril, and Regan come to symbolize the other side of their fathers' rather simple world. Edmund and Goneril and Regan are in conflict with Edgar and Cordelia; but, if one side of an outer conflict symbolizes the inner, so does the other; *ergo.* . . . But Goneril is also in conflict with Regan—indeed, she kills her, which seems a far more intense form of conflict than any action of Edmund toward Edgar. Why, then, doesn't the conflict between them symbolize some refinement or qualification of the trait in the father which they symbolize together? Perhaps to ask for such an obvious extension of the symbolism would lead to the "closely restrictive" allegorism of which Heilman says the play is innocent. But other questions are relevant. The conflict between Edmund and Edgar is obviously of a very different order from that between Goneril and Regan and Cordelia; what is the discerning reader, who gets as far as Heilman takes him, to make of this difference? Does it not, he is likely to ask, affect the symbolic value of Edmund or Goneril and Regan? Evidently not; but why would a careful workman, anxious to avoid the abstractionism of allegory, rely on so vague and abstract a relationship as mere "opposition" for the identification of his symbols? Again we must go back to Heilman's views about tragedy, as we must for an answer to the question of why there are only *two* elements in conflict in Lear and Gloucester. Why not three? Because, simply, good and evil are in conflict in tragedy; but it is Heilman, not Shakespeare, who makes this simple reduction of what is, in fact, a very complex organization of relationships in the play, whose moral implications are never so flatly represented.

Occasionally, Heilman attempts to justify his symbolic readings by showing their superiority over other readings, but his technique here is no less arbitrary than that which he employs in making the symbolic connections themselves. He is perfectly well aware that his readings are unusual; there are always immediate interpretations for a word or a speech other than the one he wishes us to accept. Though he feels obliged, naturally enough, to take account of these alternatives, the reading which he asks us to reject in favor of his own is always unlikely or absurd, and, doubtless because of this, he never attaches the name of a critic to the rejected reading but proffers it anonymously. A simple instance of this technique is in his remark that Lear's kneeling to Cordelia in Act V, scene 3, is so different from his mock kneeling to Goneril in Act II, scene 4, that "it has a reassuring rather than a horrifying quality" (p. 142). Again, Lear's madness is not "an isolated fact" but the center of a pattern of meanings (p. 174); the "simplest meaning" of Lear's request for an ounce of civet is that he wants to take away an evil smell, but "beneath the semantic surface" the significance is that once Lear had too sweet an imagination but now he has discovered unsweetness and stench (p. 205); Lear's final speeches in Act IV, scene 6, "instead of being a rant," are related to the play structurally by being held within the sight pattern (p. 208); in explaining the sources of the early errors of Lear and Gloucester, "the easiest way out" is to say that they merely make mistakes in identity, but the hardest way out is to follow Heilman (p. 33).[8]

We are repeatedly asked to shun a reading that is obvious, foolish, superficial, self-contradictory, or merely irrelevant and to accept Heilman's symbolism as the true alternative. Why? There are many more readings than he presents to us, and many of them make a kind of sense superior to that of the sophomore responsible for Heilman's rejected interpretations. Obviously, the critic cannot be expected to give a variorum of critical opinion, but it would have reassured the reader and strengthened our critic's case if he had cited the best of these and argued the superiority of his own interpretation. As it is, the author has an easy victory, but probably not over anyone familiar with the play.

Heilman's errors in interpretation are thus the inevitable consequences of his theory. He begins with a determinate structural scheme which, since the work must express meanings, must be embodied in the work if it is to have artistic value. He knows, in all important respects, what he is going to find out before he begins, and it is no wonder that, having begged all the important questions, he should find it. His interpretation is, moreover, in the proper sense, materialistic: form and structure are for him derivative from, and therefore strictly dependent on, the matter which the work expresses; the form of the

8. Cf. also Heilman, *op. cit.*, pp. 11, 45, 50, 73, 74, 104, 105, 134–35, 156–57, 160, 173, 198, 214, 220, 235, 265.

play, indeed, *is* its total meaning, and this is obviously not the characters, or their actions, or their thoughts, or even the language in which their thoughts are cast, but what these all represent. Were this not the case, Heilman's project would be meaningless; for these "more obvious" elements of the play, as he again and again points out, have been understood for a long time, while its "form" has not until now been apprehended. His theory, furthermore, is essentially a system of very simple dichotomies, which he attributes to the play itself.[9] And "meanings" are elaborated from a private and nonartistic theory of morality and religion, and then the necessary symbolic counterparts for the terms of the theory are "discovered" in the play.

A single example of this last influence of his theory upon his analysis of the play must suffice. In his final chapter Heilman tells us that *King Lear*, in addition to representing an eternal human problem, has also a historical relevance:

At an extraordinarily early time Shakespeare got hold of the modern problem, got hold of it when the Renaissance had, so to speak, barely started it on its way. Lear, in one sense, represents the old order, and the play becomes the tragedy of that order [pp. 278–79].

In what sense is it significant to speak of "the" modern problem? Who says, and on what evidence, that there is but one, or one more important than the rest? How do we know, if there is such a thing, that it is a modern problem only? Or, as some of Heilman's later remarks suggest, is it a problem that recurs in cyclical succession? What, in any case, is the evidence that this "problem" is the conflict between old and new orders rather than, say, between a search for security and a search for freedom common to all orders? Heilman goes on to say:

Given this clash of forces whose ramifications extend deep into the nature of man (Goneril, the representative of the new order, is of the flesh and blood of Lear, the representative of the old), Shakespeare outlines, in intense dramatic compactness, the overwhelming problems which beset both the individual and the age at the historical crisis [p. 280].

The children, indeed, are not children for nothing! It is in a way futile to ask why Goneril should symbolize the new order rather than Albany and Edgar, who are just as young, so far as we know, who identify themselves as the new generation (Act V, scene 3, ll. 325–26), and who survive—one to become king —and who might therefore be thought of as the "new" order. The reason, of course, is that Heilman believes all this nonsense about "the modern problem" and "the historical crisis" and knows what has to happen. Poor Bradley has been accused by modern critics of monumental crimes, chief among them

9. Cf., e.g., *ibid.*, pp. 28, 58, 91–92, 115–16, 127–28, 135, 178–79, 185, 222, 230, 277, and esp. 284–85.

being a habit of giving a psychological background for the characters in terms of his own, or his period's, conception of morality. The amplitude, privacy, and irrelevance of the moral, political, and religious theories by which Heilman supports—nay, determines—his reading of *King Lear* makes his distinguished predecessor seem like a beginner.

II

If Heilman's theory of the drama as metaphor forces him into arbitrary and hence often capricious interpretations of its symbolism, his conception of the function of imagery results in a construction that resembles a great play much less than it does an inferior philosophic dialogue. The critic lays it down that "in Shakespeare's language recurrency is an objective fact, not a figment of critics' enthusiasm" (p. 8), and everyone will probably agree. A word in a play, he continues, has "two kinds of meaningful relationship," explicit denotations, on the one hand, and, on the other, "latent meanings or dormant powers of suggestion that under certain circumstances may palpably modify or amplify the express meaning of the syntactical unit." *Hat*, to take his example, may refer to a man's headdress, or it "may contain, in unresolved form, the ideas, say, of formality or decency or protectedness" (p. 9). These implicative or suggestive powers are aroused when a word is repeated:

A recurrent word, as I have said, is found to exist in a dual relationship: one of its links is to the thing denoted, the other to the sum total of uses of the word. All these uses constitute a community which by its very existence calls our attention to it and which, once we are aware of it, sets up imaginative vibrations and thus imparts to us meanings beyond the level of explicitness. Repetition itself is a mode of meaning [p. 9].

In brief, "it is the recurrency of *hat* which calls *hatness* into the play, and *hatness* then is seen to have some thematic import in the work as a whole" (*ibid.*). Now, although Heilman goes on to say that the symbolic value of the word (e.g., the reference of *hatness* to *formality* or *decency* rather than, say, to *roguishness* or *avarice*) is "fairly likely" to be given an unequivocal statement at some time or other in the play and although, as I have said, he later speaks of such elements as character and action as providing the "most obvious" means of recognizing the recurrent patterns of imagery, these are not categorical requirements, and they sound very much like useful, but by no means essential, props for the less discerning.

It is evident that Heilman has not thought through, or has not given an adequate statement of, the mode of relationship between the patterns of poetic imagery and other elements of the play. If *hatness* in a given play means *formality*, how do we know this? The latent meanings and suggestive powers of a word are infinite apart from the play and, by Heilman's definition, not limited by the context in which they appear; unless interpretation is merely to display the linguistic virtuosity of the critic, some basis must be found on which the potentialities of signification in words can be realized in particular meanings appropriate to the play. It is fantastic to assert that the repetition of basic words "opens the consciousness to all the expressive possibilities of these words" (p. 18); for repetition could do this no more readily than could single occurrence, and, if it did, the play could obviously make no unified impression at all. What repetition, artistically handled, does is to open those possibilities, and those only, that are relevant to the play. But, clearly, Heilman is speaking loosely here; for he adds that the "resources" of the symbol are tapped differently according to "different contextual demands." And this is precisely the point; for it must be to the context, immediate or more remote, that the imagery is referred, and this necessity establishes the priority, both in the structure of the play and in critical analysis, of the primary determinants of the context—character, situation, antecedent action, intention, and the like, as all these are involved in the plot. If *hat* is to signify *formality* or a cognate concept throughout the play and if the play's effect is to be determined by the writer and not by the whim of the critic, then the connection between the two terms must be established in a metaphor or image in a context in which *formality* is clearly set forth as a basic term in the thought of a character, or in his mental or psychological makeup, or in the circumstances in which he acts, or in the standards of value employed by one or more of the characters, or in some similar manner. And I should think that this connection would have to be established early in the play if a pattern in any genuine sense is to be formed; for, in the absence of an explicit designation of the symbolic value of a word, no amount of repetition can produce anything except vagueness. Only when such a connection has been unequivocally established and when the symbol recurs in the same kind of context are we licensed to invoke "imaginatively" the earlier metaphorical attachment of *hat* to *formality*.

All this means, of course, that the verbal patterns are strictly relative to, and dependent for their value upon, those "larger and more conspicuous elements" of the drama of which Heilman takes so cavalier a view; and it means, further, that these verbal patterns cannot be the primary elements in the play's structure, as Heilman's procedure implies; for what is essentially derivative cannot provide the unifying principle for that from which it is derived. No one would suppose that the proper significance could be assigned to the thoughts expressed by the characters in a play except in relation to the characters expressing them and the circumstances and ends in relation to which they are expressed; a fortiori, therefore, the imagery, which is but one aspect of the expression of the thought, cannot be properly evaluated except in terms of a prior and controlling consideration of the thought, character, circumstances, etc. Heilman constantly reverses this order. For him the meanings expressed in the recurrent imagery are broader and more fundamental than those expressed in the action of *King Lear*; character and action are relative to the patterns, and their meanings exist for them. This inversion of the proper artistic relationships among the elements of the play can be seen in his assertion that from the plot of the play we can discern only "partial outlines" of its form, which must be "amplified and corrected" by the evidence of the symbolic language (p. 32), and in his contention that only the skeleton of the play can be derived from the plot, the flesh and blood from the poetic-dramatic patterns (p. 38; cf. also p. 25), but his whole analysis involves standing the play on its head.

The necessary consequence of this separation of the imagery from its proper artistic relation to the more important elements in the drama can be seen when Heilman comes to decide upon the order in which to consider the poetic patterns. By denying the relativity of the imagery, in any essential way, to character or action, Heilman has deprived himself of one principle of order among his patterns—the artistic order provided by the plot of *King Lear*. In place of this he has substituted an abstract order based on the implications which he discerns among the patterns. This we see when, in the "Critical Preliminaries," he tells us that his sequence of discussion is that "into which the different problems of meaning seem naturally to fall" (p. 27) and adds that the sight pattern is a "quite logical" place from which to work toward the "heart" of the drama because its chief figure is Gloucester, who is in a secondary tragic role. On artistic grounds it would seem that Gloucester's secondary role was the best possible reason for *not* starting with a pattern of imagery focused chiefly on him, but rather with the primary tragic figure in relation to whom his secondary function in the play is defined. But Heilman's order of procedure is not artistic but dialectical—from the outside in, from the secondary to the essential, from the surface to the heart—and the discussion is controlled by an extrinsic criterion, the "natural" order among the problems dealt with in the play. Thus he tells us that the sight pattern "prepares us for the study of evil that finds its main treatment in the madness pattern" (p. 51). Prepares us in what sense? Clearly not in the sense that the speeches of Goneril and Regan at the end of Act I, scene 1, prepare us for their later actions toward Lear, by forming our expectations through a statement of the ends for which they act and of the principles and physical means at their disposal; for the sight and madness patterns, developing simultaneously, have no proper temporal relation, and whatever expectations the imagery arouses cannot be in terms of character or action. The sight pattern prepares for the madness pattern through logical implication—what the sight pattern asserts, we are told, is that "to have eyes, and to see not, is to be at the mercy of evil, and thus to aid evil. Not to see is not to understand" (p. 51); and, since the madness pattern is concerned directly with the problem of understanding, the connection between the two is evident.[10] The connection is similar to that by which one level of discussion in a Platonic dialogue prepares for that above it, by formulating a paradoxical statement or question for resolution on the basis of truer or more inclusive principles. This movement back and forth, or up and down, between the various levels of significance in the play is the chief source of the countless paradoxes that Heilman finds in *King Lear;* their presence should surprise no one; for, given the assumptions that the critic makes about the kind of work it is, it is impossible that "paradoxes" of this kind should not be there.

As a final example of Heilman's dialectical manipulation of the problems with which he symbolically connects the play, we may consider the following, in which I have italicized the critic's intrusions:

The problem of the natural, we have seen, is elaborated by means of the imagery of injury and disease. *A comparable symbol of the vulnerability of human nature is age,* and of age there is significant awareness throughout the play. Further, the constant thinking in terms of what is natural and of the violation of the natural *would suggest, we might expect,* the subject of justice; and, as a matter of fact, the subject is a recurrent one in *King Lear.* Finally . . . in a world in which standards of justice differ and in which we must find methods of discrimination, *it is but a step* to the problem of values. *Through the problem of values we shall approach* what we have already said is the basic theme of the play—the problem of understanding [p. 134; cf. also pp. 64, 87, 133, 255].

Heilman's conception of the primacy of poetic imagery in the structure of the play leads necessarily to a view of *King Lear* as a logical or, better, a dialectical structure. The ultimate rationale of the parts is in their common bearing on a linked set of philosophic problems, the full significance of which the play, primarily through its imagery, progressively explores. The order of exploration and of understanding is a movement from the outer appearance to the inner reality, from the relatively simple to the more complex, from the particular to the universal, from the many to the one, in a sequence of levels

10. By similar expansion of the philosophic context, we move from the nature pattern as it defines man to the nature pattern as it defines nature: "This is what the patterns say about the nature of man. But man belongs to a universe; there are principles which operate both within him and outside him. From the nature of man it is a necessary step to the nature of nature" (Heilman, *op. cit.,* p. 112). Here we may ask why it is—assuming that we must proceed in the order given by the dialectical relations among the problems with which the play is said to deal—that this particular order is the necessary one; why, that is to say, must we go from man to the universe rather than from the universe to man, from the area of the more particular principles to that of the more general, rather than the reverse? This is obviously a philosophic rather than an artistic question, unanswerable from the evidence of Shakespeare's play, since it presents its meanings—if it does so at all—concurrently and by "interanimation"; the philosophy which makes this order necessary is Heilman's, not Shakespeare's, and he makes no effort to demonstrate its superior relevance.

of discussion in which what appears as complexities and paradoxes at one level is transformed, at the level next above, into a new paradox, embracing a larger area of meaning and approaching nearer to truth, until at last all the dialectical oppositions of the (logically) preceding levels are given a final translation in the apprehension of transcendental truth.[11] Whatever the philosophic merits of this procedure, it is not artistic in any distinguishable sense of that word; for it is a method of universal application, potential alike to the discovery of philosophic truth, the interpretation of dreams, the disclosure of religious mysteries, and, if one chooses, the implication of meanings by "plays."[12] Heilman reduces—or elevates, depending on one's preferences in art and philosophy—*King Lear* to an epistemological discourse in dialogue form. And this invites us to look at the epistemology.

III

The battles for physical and moral survival in *King Lear*, according to Heilman, are interpenetrated by "philosophic or quasi-philosophic struggles" (p. 281), and the problems about which these struggles revolve constitute an "amazingly inclusive anthropology" (p. 177). The play asks such questions as: What is man's nature? What is nature? (p. 26). What is reason? What is folly? What is wisdom? In what way of thinking about experience is man's

11. *King Lear* becomes, because of the logical rather than the temporal order of its principal parts, a static rather than a dynamic whole. Although the total meaning of the play is in process of complete formulation throughout the action of the play, it is the whole play considered as a complex metaphor which is the proper analogue of this meaning, and its parts are significant not so much in terms of how they are prepared for and how they, in turn, prepare for a later part as in terms of the symbolic relationships in which they participate, these symbolic relationships being as often to what has gone before as to what comes after. The play is a whole, therefore, more like a statue or a painting than like a drama in the usual sense: the critic can regard everything in it as existing and functioning simultaneously, without regard to its position in the temporal sequence. Thus, to take one example out of many, Heilman says, in discussing the sexual imagery used to characterize Goneril, Regan, and Edmund, most of which is drawn from the fourth and fifth acts: "This characterization of the sisters by the sex theme is aided by at least one careful contrast of them with Cordelia. Asking her father to make clear the cause of her disgrace, Cordelia insists that

'It is no vicious blot, murder or foulness,
No unchaste action, or dishonour'd step . . .' (Act I, scene 1, ll. 230–31).

Without the thematic context, *unchaste* might be merely part of a general catalogue; as it is, the word helps underline the sisters' animality" (*op. cit.*, p. 102; Heilman's italics). When Cordelia makes this speech, there is no context, sexual or otherwise; it is only through the kind of cross-reference permitted by a static conception of the play that Heilman's "aiding" and "underlining" become possible.

12. The applicability of the method, without essential change, to works "superficially" quite different, as well as the inner similarity which such different works come to have when exposed to treatment under Heilman's assumptions, can be observed by comparing his reading of *King Lear* with his reading of Henry James's *Turn of the Screw* (see "*The Turn of the Screw* as Poem" [the title reveals the reductive tendency of the method], *University of Kansas City Review*, summer, 1948, pp. 277–89; also in *Forms of Modern Fiction*, ed. William Van O'Connor [Minneapolis, 1948], pp. 211–28).

salvation? (p. 27). The play poses and suggests, if complexly, answers to the problems of seeing, of the uses and limits of rationalism, of innocence, of appearance and reality, of values, of the definition of "man's essential humanity," of the kinds of mental balance, of man's mode of understanding experience, of distributive justice, of man, and of The World. And, as we have seen, to the consideration of these eternal questions is joined Shakespeare's attack on "the modern problem."

From a play which "constantly labors" so many basic questions, which is "speculatively very active" in the realm of metaphysics, which "explores" such transcendental issues and aims at definitions of principles so fundamental,[13] we might expect, if the play deserves the reputation which three centuries have brought it, answers, or at least adumbrations of answers, of some intellectual distinction. But if we expect this we shall be disappointed. The philosophic yield from *King Lear* is pitifully meager—a poor thing by comparison, say, with that from the *Novum organum* or the *Laws of Ecclesiastical Polity.* Heilman's Shakespeare, it may be, labors, but he brings forth little more than platitudes. When the wonderful imagery of *King Lear* has been reduced to sense, and the doctrines of the play, disrobed of their ornaments, are left to the powers of their naked excellence, what shall we discover? That man, though he is liable to damnation, may yet achieve salvation (p. 91); that man is wholly evil when reason and animality work together (p. 105); and that there is, despite the horrifying chaos of phenomena, a substantial universal order upon which men may rely (p. 151). We may learn yet more—that man is a rational animal (pp. 98–100) and that man's weakness puts him in need of persuasion and that he is therefore subject to influence (p. 241). To these profound principles of natural knowledge are added some moral instructions equally new—that rational man is in danger of rationalizing essential values out of existence (p. 177); that real insight is apparently doomed to ill success in the world (p. 249); and that, while men may pray for justice because the gods will execute it, they cannot dictate the terms on which their prayers will be answered (pp. 255, 268). Surely a man of no very comprehensive search may venture to say that he has heard all this before. That these principles are profound and important no one is likely to question—so is the Golden Rule; but that the assertion of them, even through the details of a particular case, is likely to be powerfully moving, as the play has always been felt to be, is manifestly improbable. The grand irony of Heilman's interpretation of *King Lear* is that the more closely he approaches the play's total meaning—the more successful he is in suggesting the One which interpenetrates the Many—the more trivial the play becomes. As drama it is superb, original, inimitable; as philoso-

13. See, e.g., Heilman, *op. cit.*, pp. 28, 68, 92, 105, 133, 156, 284–85.

phy—or even "quasi-philosophy"—it is commonplace and undistinguished, amply justifying Shaw's protest against the "pretentious reduction of the subtlest problems of life to commonplaces, against which a Polytechnic debating club would revolt," and to platitudes "that even an American professor of ethics would blush to offer to his disciples."

So bald a restatement of some of the meanings of his *King Lear* may seem unfair to Heilman's analysis, if not to the play; for he points out on several occasions that the play does not assert or demonstrate its meanings as would a philosophic treatise: they are adumbrated or implied, usually in a paradoxical fusion of what normally appear to be incompatible areas of experience, so that what we have in the play is not didacticism or philosophy but embodiment and implication.[14] But a paradox is a mode of assertion; implications must be made explicit if we are not to surrender ourselves and the play to critical caprice. Despite his repeated emphasis on the method of paradox, Heilman emphatically denies that, in *King Lear*, Shakespeare is "resting in a detached presentation of the ambiguities of experience" (p. 189; cf. pp. 69, 91). Indeed, the mode of connection which we have observed Heilman establishing among the image patterns of the play is necessitated by the need to resolve, in the interests of a positive and not merely ambiguous significance, the paradoxes of each subordinate pattern of imagery in a supervening implication at a higher level. Thus the ironies of the good man's fate in the world suggested by the clothes and sight patterns are resolved in the nature pattern's implication of a higher realm in which the very qualities responsible for misfortune in the world become the conditions of salvation. And all the paradoxes of the play are resolved in the implications of the religion pattern, which suggests that the perception of eternal truth is the sanity of the mad, the dress of the naked, the sight of the blind, and the eternal life of the old (pp. 252–53, 255, 284–87).

Our author, evidently sensitive to the elementary quality of the meanings of *King Lear* when they are stated as such, attempts to save them from dismissal and to redeem the play by telling us that the meanings are "complexly," not simply, asserted. His chief instrument in this endeavor is the paradox, which avoids the obvious and encompasses the radically dissimilar; but he has more direct ways of arguing the "inordinately complex world," the "vast implications" that the play figures forth. What Heilman means by a "complex" as distinct from a "simple" view of things may be illustrated in his treatment of Lear's anguished comment on his evil daughters (Act IV, scene 6, ll. 126–29):

> Down from the waist they are Centaurs
> Though women all above;
> But to the girdle do the gods inherit,
> Beneath is all the fiend's.

14. See, e.g., *ibid.*, pp. 67, 89, 91, 108, 128, 177, 214, 253, 284–85.

The "complexity" of the attitude underlying these lines Heilman indicates as follows:

Man is equally capable of salvation or damnation. The Centaur is exactly the right image here, for it admits the possibility of high intellectual and spiritual attainment yet connotes primarily the proneness to violence and disorder which the play exhibits throughout. It exhibits man as a rational animal [p. 100].

Man, that is to say, is not entirely angelic or entirely bestial, but both! Again, in commenting on the treatment of the problem of justice, he says:

Indeed, not only Lear, but other characters, think repeatedly of justice; some ignore the subject entirely, but those who are conscious of it never lose faith that justice is being done or will at some time be done. Yet justice is treated complexly; human beings are not just at all times; and injustice is a fact, a fact which Shakespeare obviously treats with great fullness [p. 145].[15]

Complexity, it would appear, is a negative virtue—it really amounts only to the avoidance of the simple-minded; if an artist, even a mediocre one, represented man as entirely human or entirely animal, as always just or always unjust, we should be obliged to say that he was a simpleton and his work, if it purported to be serious, absurdly irrelevant to common experience. But is it meaningful to dignify as "complex" the mere avoidance of the ridiculous? If it is, then a host of hacks who are at least familiar with the facts of life are eligible for critical acclaim on the basis of their complexity; but it has been thought for a long time, and rightly, that Shakespeare's principal tragedies were wonderfully complex in some sense which makes them irreducible to the simplest axioms of human conduct.

The chief evidence of the "complexity" of attitude and implication in *King Lear*, however, is to be found in its paradoxes; and here, too, we find evidence of Heilman's simplism, for most of his paradoxes are merely puns, dependent rather on the ambiguities of words than on any genuine fusion of unlike things. The theory of the paradox was well developed in rhetorical literature in the Renaissance, and its practice extensively cultivated; a paradox in the fullest and most serious sense was taken to be a statement contrary to common opinion, yet true, such as Donne's assertion that "Nature is our worst Guide"; formally, it often, but by no means always, involved an opposition of contrary terms. The paradoxes of Heilman are rarely of this sort. One of the more important of them is that the blind may see, while those who see may be blind. But the paradox is only apparent: for *blindness* and *seeing* have different meanings on the two sides of both these assertions, and unless the *blindness* is in the organs or to the phenomena of which sight is said in the predicate to be possible, where is the paradox? Who would be surprised, or even illuminated

15. Cf. also *ibid.*, pp. 91–105, 124, 149, 176, 188, 189, 252, 267.

(and wondrous apprehension, as Puttenham's name for the figure surely indicates, is essential to the genuine paradox), by the assertion that blind men can apprehend spiritual truth?—surely no one in a religious, as well as verbally sophisticated, age, however plausible as paradox the pun may now seem. Similarly with the paradoxes that the naked may survive better than the well-protected and that age may endure: the naked in *King Lear* do not survive in terms of their nakedness, and age does not endure in any sense in which it is significant to speak of it as old. What we have in Heilman's *King Lear*, it would seem, is a body of platitude garbed in a merely verbal "complexity."

IV

Even if it were not true that the "meaning" of *King Lear* becomes, on Heilman's reading of it, a commonplace repetition of Christian parables, his theory and method have two further disadvantages. On the one hand, his conception of the "problems" of the play subverts its moral basis and consequently undermines its effect—by reducing character to an aspect of thought; and, on the other hand, he makes it impossible to read the play with understanding by converting into ultimate "implications" the ethical and philosophic assumptions on which it does in fact rest.

Important and difficult problems are unquestionably raised in *King Lear*—Lear, for example, is forced to deal with the problem posed by the impact of Cordelia's apparently unfilial behavior upon his love for her and his plans for the future; later he must cope with the problem raised by Goneril and Regan's refusal to carry out the terms of his gift of the kingdom to them. The important aspect of these problems for our present purpose is their quality: they are problems of specific characters (and, despite the mirror plot in the play, there are always important differences among the parallel problems of parallel characters); they are specifically defined by the character and his immediate circumstances, ceasing to be problems, or precisely the same problems, when character or circumstances are altered; they are dynamically related not only to character but to one another, the solution or failure of solution of one problem generating a further problem, and so on; they are fundamentally moral rather than intellectual problems—calling for action and involving deliberation and choice in terms of moral ends and ethical principles; and they are all definitively solved in one way or another before the end of the play. This is to say merely that a continuum of concrete moral problems provides the framework for the action of the play. It is not to suggest that intellectual or philosophic questions are not raised or are not important in the action, but it is to say that the relation of such questions—of which Lear's efforts in his madness to get at the nature of justice may serve as an example—to problems of the first sort must be kept clear: the intellectual problems arise from failures to deal satisfactorily with problems of a practical order, and the terms in which these intellectual problems are cast derive their meanings from the ethical context in which antecedent moral problems had been framed; the outcome of the solution of intellectual questions, in *King Lear* at least, is never repose in the abstract solution but a readjustment of character and thought to the circumstances and a renewal of the action on the practical level. In general, efforts of the characters to solve intellectual or philosophic questions function to supply the premises for action or discovery; but it is always for the sake of the latter that such problems are raised.

It is not in specific moral problems or even in contributory philosophic questions that Heilman finds the "meanings" of his *King Lear*. The problems of his *King Lear* are not so much problems of particular characters as problems of "the play"; once introduced, they remain unchanged, even if they are treated with increasing "complexity," throughout the play; they are related to one another not dynamically, through character, but logically, as we have seen; they are intellectual ("What is nature?" "In what way of thinking about experience is man's salvation?") rather than moral—directed, that is, not to action and happiness but to truth and salvation; and they are not solved before the end of the play but have their solutions metaphorically implied by the play as a whole.

The importance of these differences is in their consequences for the status of character and moral action in *King Lear*. The specific moral problems first mentioned are relative in each case to character: each is the problem of one character only, deriving its alternatives from the interrelation of his ends and moral principles and the possibilities available to him under the circumstances of the moment; the problem can never be understood apart from the character; and its artistic importance is in permitting a display of character (in deliberation, choice, or action) through which an ethical response is evoked and in engaging a character toward whom our feelings have thus been aroused in actions through which his happiness or misery is determined. The kind of problem with which Heilman conceives the play to be fundamentally concerned is not, thus, relative to character; character, rather, is relative to the problems; indeed character becomes for him merely the attitudes of the persons of the play to the leading problems with which it deals. "In one sense," we are told, "all the experiences of the major characters are a testing of ideas of theirs" (p. 128); and throughout the analysis it is clear that the characters take their places in the "structure" because of what and how they think or perceive—because of their mode of understanding, to use Heilman's phrase—for the unity of the play is in its "meanings," and these, so far as the characters are concerned, are expressed primarily in the attitudes, beliefs, and intellectual habits of the dramatis personae. Lear's tragic flaw is therefore intellectual rather than moral—he "endeavors to introduce quantitative norms where the questions are entirely qualitative" (pp. 217–18).[16] The effect of this conception of the play's problems is to dissolve or subvert the moral basis of the drama by making not what the characters are and do so much as what and how they think the cause of their happiness or misery.

But how, even if it were true that a work thus deprived of its moral basis could have the kind of emotional effect that *King Lear* has always been thought to have, could the play as Heilman interprets it be intelligible at any level? For his method necessitates treating the very premises on which the characterization and action of the play depend for their intelligibility as if they were not premises but unsolved problems.

Thus in his discussion of the nature pattern, Heilman tells us that the term "nature," in "the metaphorical usage of this play," besides signifying a normal ordered functioning of the physical world, "comes also to mean a normal, ordered functioning of the *moral* world, a final principle to which all moral phenomena are to be referred" (p. 119; Heilman's italics). "Comes also to mean" is inaccurate, for the conception of nature as moral order is evident from the first two scenes of the play and is obviously presupposed as a criterion for the assessment of Edmund's soliloquy at the opening of Act I, scene 2; Heilman himself retracts his phrase in going on to say of nature as a moral order that "many characters rely on this principle of order, they understand in terms of it; and they judge phenomena by it, as their language constantly shows." But perhaps this is only an apparent retraction, for Heilman's statements and his entire analysis suggest that in his view such fundamental questions as whether nature is a moral order in the universe are not determined until the end of the play; for Shakespeare, we are told, although "he does not choose sides in any obvious sense," finally implies the side that he is on:

Throughout the verbal and dramatic patterns of the play, throughout the structural dualities, there is a consistent and continual intimation: in the cosmos there is a justice (whatever the injustice in fact), there is an order (whatever the chaos in fact), there is an underlying reality (whatever the deceptiveness of appearance); in man there is a sight (whatever the blindness in fact) and an imaginative understanding (whatever the rationalistic obtuseness that may periodically dominate him) by which he may seize upon the realities necessary to his survival. These are the implications of the key words in the play [pp. 286–87; cf. also pp. 325–26].

16. Cf. *ibid.*, p. 171: "There are various ingredients in Lear's tragic flaw, but the most important is his failure to recognize what areas of value are not capable of rational formulation" (cf. also pp. 32–33, 164, 192–93, 225).

During the play the issue between these "structural dualities" is undecided, and it is the "tension" between these "contrapuntal oppositions" that gives the play its effect. A choral speech on nature is "not to be taken as dogmatic and final" but becomes "a hypothesis which the drama as a whole may reject or confirm" (p. 108); and concerning the opposition between Edmund's view of nature and that of certain other characters, Heilman writes:

The question is . . . whether he [Shakespeare] stops with a presentation of the complexities of definition—which is in itself no minor literary [sic] task or whether all the evidence of the play has the effect of making, in dramatic form, a judgment upon the problem of conflicting usages [p. 124].

To write thus about the indeterminacy of the key terms in the play is flatly inconsistent with the view that "the play as a whole proceeds on the assumption that nature is a principle of order—a principle subject to violation and apparently conquerable by chaos, and yet ultimately able to assert itself as the order of the whole and to bring into conformity with it that other 'nature' of Edmund's . . ." (p. 127); it is illogical to refer to an "assumption" as a "conflicting usage" upon which judgment is to be passed. Are we to convict Shakespeare of a circularity which will only intensify the low opinion of his philosophic powers that Heilman's statement of the play's meanings encourages us to entertain—the assumption of a premise which he then proceeds to "prove"? Or are we not rather to convict Heilman of reading the play in two quite different ways and of playing both ends against the middle? Surely, his instinct rather than his method is correct: the play as a whole presupposes—it asserts as a premise, it takes for granted, it includes among its *données*—that there is a justice, an order, an underlying reality, etc.; and the play as a whole "implies" these things, if it does so at all, only because they have already been built into the play as the basis of its probabilities, the ground for judgments of character, the conditions of immediate and over-all expectancy, and the terms for the statement of its particular moral problems. The reader knows from the outset, and does not have to wait for the ultimate dissolution of a system of dichotomies to learn, that the view of nature put forward by Edmund is, in all essential respects, wrong; that Gloucester, in the premises which he uses to judge Edgar, is correct; that Goneril and Regan's "case" against Lear's retainers is false. We know, in general, the fundamental answers to all Heilman's problems as soon as they become problems for the characters. For Shakespeare, unlike a good many modern novelists and unlike many dramatists of his own time, such as Beaumont and Fletcher, is an ironist in the proper sense—he supplies the audience with the premises and information withheld from, or wrongly interpreted by, the characters, in order that we may understand them, make judgments about them that will permit us to be emotionally affected by what happens to them, see their actions and sufferings as probable consequences of their knowledge and intentions, and—however surprised we may be at the turns of the action—recognize the inevitability of each and of the eventual outcome.

Heilman confuses "implication" and "presupposition," and he fails to distinguish between the problems of certain of the characters (e.g., Lear's uncertainty about nature as a moral order) and the problems of the play and its readers. If the solutions or implications of Heilman's problems emerge only when the play is complete, then there is no real basis for understanding it or for being affected by it; if, on the other hand, premises necessary to the intelligibility of the play are indeed provided, most or all of Heilman's problems disappear.

V

Even if it were not true, however, that *King Lear* is strictly unintelligible on Heilman's assumptions, the effect of the play suggested by his interpretation is one which no one has ever attributed to *King Lear*, which is, moreover, inappropriate to tragedy, and which, finally, Shakespeare's text does not support. On the whole, Heilman has very little to say about the way in which *Lear* affects the spectator and reader; and, while we may grant that the critic's main effort should be concentrated on the details of the text, this effort is likely to be undirected or misdirected unless it is controlled by a hypothesis—progressively confirmed or altered and, in any case, refined, as the analysis proceeds—concerning the precise quality of the power that the work exercises. Although Heilman acknowledges in his "Critical Preliminaries" a certain obligation to Aristotle, he finds no use for Aristotle's insistence that pity and fear are the emotions proper to tragedy and that from them as ends the specific properties of the form may be inferred. When Heilman mentions pity, it is usually reduced to pathos (or "mere pathos"), and his intention is to show the inadequacy of the emotions suggested by this word to *King Lear*, as in his judgment of the initial mistakes of Lear and Gloucester:

These errors may be fatal or merely pathetic; but we are not invited merely to condemn or to sympathize. Instead we are compelled to enter fully into perceptual experiences of distracting difficulty and hence to feel—if not to follow out to metaphysical conclusions—oppressive problems of personal identity [pp. 68–69].

Fear, so far as I am aware, he does not mention at all, not even to deny its relevance.[17] Although there are vague references to the force and power of

17. It is noteworthy, therefore, that Heilman has little to say about speeches and scenes in which impending action potentially dangerous or hopeful for Lear is deliberated, narrated, or enacted—such as Kent's speech at Act III, scene 1, ll. 17–55, and all of Act III, scenes 3 and 5; Act IV, scenes 3, 5, and 7; and Act V, scene 1. These, we may suppose, are more properly parts of the play's superficial aspect than of its inner reality; but that Shakespeare

the play as a whole and of certain of its scenes, nowhere are the specific emotional effects of the force and power made clear; when Heilman mentions an emotion it is always to deny that it is appropriate to the "inner reality" of the play.

We are not invited to condemn or sympathize; we are not to be horrified or cynical or sentimental. What state are we to be in? The answer should be apparent in the light of what has so far been said. We are to be enlightened, shown, convinced, or illuminated—we are to undergo, in short, the intellectual effect proper to one who perceives, after great difficulty, the One gleaming through the Many. Thus, in the passage just quoted, Heilman tells us that, instead of pity or antipathy, we are to feel "oppressive problems" of personal identity because we have entered into difficult "perceptual experiences"; later, denying that pathos alone, which is "too easy," could account for the powerful impression made by the scenes of Lear's madness, he insists that "beneath the superficial aspects of these scenes [those, that is, which make them shocking, terrible, and pathetic], there must be felt, by even a casual student, a reverberation of underlying meanings which constitute the inner reality of the scenes" (p. 173); and still later he points out that the play is bent, not upon giving final answers to the problems it raises, but "upon evoking a sense of their magnitude and of the well-nigh intolerable burden which they place upon the human mind" (pp. 177–78).

That the principal effect of the play must be some mode of intellectual activity, accompanied by appropriate but vague emotional overtones, could have been inferred from Heilman's early discussion of tragedy (pp. 30–32). Tragedy is not concerned, he tells us there, with "evil fortune that may lead to cynicism and despair" (p. 31). We gladly assent and look forward to a statement of the kind of emotion, if it is not cynicism and despair, that the evil fortune of tragedy does lead to; but we are rewarded with a different line altogether:

> Tragedy is concerned, not with evil fortune that may lead to cynicism and despair, but with evil that is understandable in terms of human character; a literary work that tells of destructive mischances may have its own excellence and validity, but its cosmos is a quite different one from that of tragedy. Tragedy records, eventually, victory rather than defeat; it asserts the authority of the spiritual scheme of things to which man, because of his flaw, does violence; and it presents man as understanding his deviation, undergoing a spiritual rehabilitation, recovering the insights by which he may endure. The suffering in tragedy is not an end, but a product and a means; through it

chose to present them, often at considerable length, encourages the supposition that they have some importance in the play as he wrote it. The evocation of fear by setting in motion or continuing contrary lines of development seems a reasonable hypothesis for their presence.

comes wisdom and, if not redemption, at least a renewed grasp upon the laws of redemption. The Eumenides exist only because man's soul is not corrupt [pp. 31–32].

"Understandable in terms of human character" replaces the designation of an emotion alternative to cynicism and despair, and we learn that the tragic protagonist has fundamentally intellectual ends, that his tragic error is intellectual, and that he is finally victorious. A tragedy, it would appear, traces the progress of a good man with an intellectual flaw from bad fortune to good (recovery of insights by which he may endure; redemption or renewed grasp upon the laws of redemption)—in other words, from rationalistic rags to imaginative riches. Since the "action" of the play is the paradoxical statement and enacted solution of philosophic problems arising from intellectual error and standing in the way of redemption or salvation and since redemption or salvation is a recovery of true insight, it obviously follows that the audience is to undergo an intellectual experience which parallels the spiritual progress of the protagonist (cf. p. 213).

If the play, in these terms, can have any emotional effect, it can be only a kind of awe (at the magnitude of the problems to be solved) combined with attenuated pity (because the sufferings of the protagonist are seen to be the necessary means to salvation), giving place to joy in the reversal (when insights are recovered and salvation achieved). It is not accidental that Heilman refers on several occasions to the similarities between his *King Lear* and *The Divine Comedy*, for the latter, though, as Dante said, quite opposite to tragedy, is precisely this kind of work. *King Lear*, so far as I am aware, has not been generally regarded, even by the more perceptive, as a joyful work; yet in the terms in which Heilman describes it I do not see how it can be anything else. The whole tendency of his analysis—with its emphasis on salvation as the goal of Lear's actions, with its Christian "transvaluation" of a pagan world, with its placement of the climax of the play in Lear's reachievement of insight, with its treatment of the reversal as a passage from bad fortune to good—all this and much more make it clear that Lear is a man who, after much suffering, which is expiatory and therefore in the proper sense deserved, achieves what he had all along been in search of—the vision in which is eternal life. That Lear dies, that he loses Cordelia at the moment of their reunion—these are incidental, parts of the play's superficial aspect, not of its inner reality, and serving at most to underscore paradoxically the magnitude of Lear's victory; for he that loseth his life shall find it. Only a person incapable, as Heilman says, of distinguishing between quality and quantity of life could feel anything but spiritual exaltation at Lear's triumph over himself and the world.

This interpretation is certainly original; for it has not been common among critics of *King Lear* to state its primary effect in terms of salvation or spiritual triumph and the emotional consequences of these. But Heilman's interpretation is not merely original, it is preposterous. It violates the unmistakable signs of the play's effect which appear in the text, and it is founded upon a radical confusion of the feelings which a sensitive and inquiring reader might have *after* the play is over with those he has *during* the action itself. That Lear recovers or achieves penetrating insights into himself and the world is a commonplace of critical discussion of this play, as is the observation that the action suggests— or more properly, presupposes—a morally ordered universe. But do the concrete language and action of *King Lear*, the particular details of its development as a drama, contain clear signs that Lear's career to the end of the play is to be thought of as having such insights and the affirmation of such a universe as its goal? Are we regularly reminded—indeed, are we reminded at all—that Lear's recovery of an imaginative synthesis, his earning the "realm of spirit," is what gives order and unity to the latter part of the play? Are we given in any way to understand that the attainment of "needful spiritual insight" is an ultimate end, or even a consolation? Why, if this is his end, does Lear cry out, over Cordelia's body:

> This feather stirs; she lives! If it be so,
> It is a chance which does redeem all sorrows
> That ever I have felt.

What, if some inner structure tending toward salvation is the unifying principle, is the sense of Kent's lines,

> That from your first of difference and decay
> Have followed your sad steps,

and his chilling words, "All's cheerless, dark, and deadly"? Why does Albany refer to Lear as "this great decay," and why does Kent, as Lear dies, say "Break, heart; I prithee break!"? And finally, not to prolong the list indefinitely, how is Heilman's etherealized conception of Lear's end compatible with the speech in which Kent adjures Edgar against attempting to revive the king:

> Vex not his ghost. O, let him pass! He hates him
> That would upon the rack of this tough world
> Stretch him out longer.

Our present business, says Albany, is "general woe." Could Shakespeare have written a final scene—let alone the rest of the play—in which the comments of all the characters so obviously contradicted the effect he wished to produce?[18] To suppose so is both to take a very low view of Shakespeare's

---

18. In comparison to the amplitude of his treatment of the first four acts, to Act IV, scene 6, which is for him the structural center of the play (*op. cit.*, pp. 173–222, *passim*), Heilman's discussion of the last four scenes is very sketchy indeed, perhaps because the inner reverberations of meaning sound so hollow there.

art and to disregard completely the necessities of popular dramaturgy.[19] Surely
it is more consistent—with the text, with what we know of tragedy and of the
conditions of Elizabethan theatrical practice, and with the mass of critical
opinion about *King Lear*—to regard Lear's imaginative insights as occasioned
by and directed toward his need for love and happiness with Cordelia, and
to be moved by the awful irony of Lear's return to his original majesty, to an
even greater majesty because it is now joined to a deep awareness of his humanity as well, precisely when it is too late for him to achieve that which alone
makes majesty, authority, even humanity, meaningful and valuable to him.
If, as we watch Lear's final agony over the body of Cordelia, we ascend to a
higher level, on which the general woe becomes ineffable joy and the surcease
of pain becomes the attainment of "the realities necessary to survival," what
happens to Shakespeare's play? It recedes into the background, becoming not
so much the concrete object which controls and dictates our emotions as the
occasion for reflections and feelings embracing it and much more besides.[20] It
may be that, in contemplation of the play as a whole, in mulling it over after
it has done its work and after our emotions have returned from their painful
excitement to an equilibrium, we shall decide, each according to his own philosophic or religious lights, that *King Lear* has for us a further significance, constitutes a spiritual affirmation, or even, as some have thought, is defective in
the distance at which it lies from a realization of man's spiritual possibilities.
But these are speculations occasioned by the reading of *King Lear* but in no way
the effects peculiar to it—interesting, perhaps even valuable if they come from

19. The interpretation of *King Lear*, for Heilman, to judge from the absence in his book
of any consideration of its status as a work of popular dramatic art, stands in no need of
guidance or control from a knowledge of its literary milieu. While we know too little about
Elizabethan audiences to justify any positive inferences as to the kinds of artistic structure
and effect possible, in works written for their immediate entertainment, one very important
negative inference can be drawn. We must conclude, surely, that the basic structure and
effect of a play written by a successful practicing dramatist for popular exhibition is of such
a sort as could be grasped during a performance by a possible audience—and the possible
can, for our present purpose, be drawn just as exclusively from among the judicious as Heilman wishes. That *King Lear* as he reads it does not meet this test can be shown most simply
from the fact that a large number of readers—not just spectators—of the most refined sensitivity—not just ordinary Elizabethan playgoers—have studied—not merely witnessed—*King
Lear* for three hundred years without perceiving the structure that Heilman now for the first
time discloses to us. No spectator could possibly hope to "follow" the play as Heilman, with
his leisure to trace evanescent coincidences of words, his note cards, his opportunity to
extract every last drop of ambiguity from a line, is able to do; who but a scholiast in his
study could notice that Albany's line at Act IV, scene 2, l. 62 "picks up" a couple of lines
uttered by Cordelia, all unsuspecting, at Act I, scene 1, ll. 283–84? The alternatives, when we
consider *King Lear* as a play written for an audience, seem to me clear: Shakespeare was
fooling his audience, or he was completely unsuccessful, or three centuries of readers and
critics have been in error, or Heilman is reading some other play.

20. For a general discussion of the effect of religious or abstract moral thought on
tragedy see E. E. Stoll, *Shakespeare and Other Masters* (Cambridge, Mass., 1940), pp. 75–78.

a sophisticated and philosophic mind—but not analyses of the play; for they base themselves on a reification of Lear and the others in a different and broader context, a context which, like Heilman's, is derived from the moral and philosophic assumptions of the speculator rather than from the limited— and hence more concentrated, more powerful—confines of Shakespeare's play.

And this leads to a final objection to Heilman's book, an objection which is logically prior to all the others but which I have reserved until now in order not to prejudice the discussion. It is that Heilman nowhere confronts—indeed, nowhere shows any explicit awareness of the need to confront—the logical responsibility imposed upon him by his basic assumption, that the proper reading of *King Lear* must be a symbolic reading. Nothing in the text of the play, nothing in Shakespeare's habits as a dramatist, nothing in the circumstances of its composition and production, nothing in Elizabethan dramatic practice in general, nothing in the dramatic criticism of Shakespeare's day—nothing, in short, internal or external, suggests, or has been thought until recent years to suggest, that a literal reading of *King Lear* will fail to account for essential features of the play and that the tragedy must be interpreted, therefore, as an organized body of symbols. Anyone who wishes to take this position is, of course, free to do so; but he must discharge the initial critical and logical responsibility of showing his assumption to be needful and relevant, by making it clear that an interpretation of the play as a literal action is inadequate to the author's intention as revealed in the details of the work. It is not enough to argue—as Heilman seems to do (p. 12, and by implication, throughout the book)—that a symbolic reading is justified if it is consistent or makes sense of the work or accounts for its principal features; this is to beg the question, for, given sufficient imagination and verbal ingenuity in the critic, any work can be given such a reading. The necessity of symbolic interpretation must be established independently of the interpretation itself. It has long been thought by scholars—who, whatever their critical deficiencies, have usually had some competence in logic and a broad enough reading to know that some works are symbolic and some not—a necessary preliminary to symbolic interpretation to demonstrate quite concretely the need for it for the full understanding of a particular work. The body of criticism on, for example, *Gulliver's Travels*, *Pilgrim's Progress*, and *A Game at Chesse* involves in a fundamental way such an analysis of the signs from which the inadequacy of a literal, and the resultant necessity for a symbolic, interpretation can be inferred. Heilman—save in the simple alternatives which he from time to time presents to us for rejection in favor of his own allegorism—shows no awareness of his obligations here. The tendency of much modern criticism—perhaps encouraged by the tendency of such modern writers as Kafka, Brecht, and Broch to write symbolic works—is to begin with the assumption, taken as self-evident or requiring only passing justification, that a symbolic reading is appropriate to any work. But it is obvious to anyone who knows anything of the comments of writers on their own work or of the history of criticism in general and the critical discusssion of allegory in particular that this assumption is not in all cases true. It must therefore be given fresh and particular justification as a preliminary to each application. When it is not given, we may respect the sincerity or marvel at the industry and ingenuity displayed in the analysis, but we need not take it seriously.

A SYMBOLIC READING OF THE *ANCIENT MARINER*[1]

ELDER OLSON

THE *Ancient Mariner* is one of those poems the interpretations of which have rather illustrated the different methods of interpretation than explained the poem itself. Mr. Warren's essay[2] seems to me to be valuable principally as exhibiting what happens to poetry in interpretation, and not particularly valuable as a comment upon the poem. His argument may be summarized as follows. The famous passage in the *Table Talk*, recording Mrs. Barbauld's criticism of the poem and the poet's response, may not be taken as evidence that the poem is without theme or moral. Warren is severe, thus, with Griggs and with Lowes. The former has, according to Warren, first "misread his text," since he interprets the passage as excluding a moral intention and, second, asserted that the poem is without theme or meaning. The latter asserts that the poem has a theme but "reverses his argument" in considering that it has no moral or, at any rate, none which will "hold water" outside the poem. Both men consequently make the poem "nothing more than a pleasant but meaningless dream." Yet dreams in Coleridge's view contain nothing absurd or nonsensical or causeless; and, similarly, the inferences of Griggs and Lowes from the remark that the poem was a work of "pure imagination" can be corrected by the restatement of Coleridge's concept of the imagination.

The *Ancient Mariner*, then, has a meaning—not a literal one, not an allegorical one, but a symbolic one. A symbol for Coleridge, says Warren, is "focal, massive, and not arbitrary"; that is, according to our critic, it combines idea and feeling, it implies a body of ideas and does not stand for a single idea, and "it is not a mere sign" but "contains within itself the appeal which makes it serviceable as a symbol." Read as a symbolic poem, the *Ancient Mariner* has two basic themes: the primary (not the more important but merely the more obvious) is that of the "One Life" or of "sacramental vision"; the secondary, the theme of the imagination. Discussion of the first turns on the nature of the Mariner's act: literally, he killed a bird; symbolically, he commits murder. Why is the crime unmotivated? It "symbolizes the Fall"; we are here "confronting the mystery of the corruption of the will." But the sin of the will is the expression of the essence of the will; the crime is the crime of pride.

1. Reprinted from *Modern Philology*, May, 1948.

2. Samuel Taylor Coleridge, *The Rime of the Ancient Mariner*, with an essay by Robert Penn Warren (New York: Reynal & Hitchcock, 1946).

The secondary theme is the theme of the imagination; in it the Mariner appears as one who is driven from a "world of comfortable familiarity" by a storm, which is "the creative urge," to a land of ice, which is "both beautiful and terrible, as is proper for the spot where the acquaintance with the imagination is to be made." Like the storm, it "shakes man from his routine of life"; but out of this apparent indifference to man "comes the first response to man—the Albatross." Wind and bird, according to Warren, are associated with the moon or the half-light, which is the symbol of the imagination; the sun, on the other hand, symbolizes the "light of the 'understanding.' " These symbols, we are told, are ambivalent, i.e., now hostile, now beneficial, to man. The crime is a crime against the imagination; the imagination obtains its terrible redress but also "heals" the Mariner; the wandering is also a blessing and a curse, for the Mariner is the *poète maudit* as well as the "prophet of universal charity."

I trust this much of summary will be sufficient—not perhaps to Warren, who, if he is like most authors, must feel that his best summary is his own work—but to most serious readers of his essay. On the supposition that it *is* sufficient, what can be said of his interpretations?

We may begin by noting how Warren so easily subverts the positions of Griggs and Lowes. "Obviously, only the reader who cannot enjoy this journey into the realm of the supernatural finds it necessary to seek out a moral," said Griggs; and Warren remarks: "I take it that Griggs uses the word *moral* in a broad, general sense, equating it with theme understood as a comment on human conduct and values. . . . And if this . . . is what he means, he is saying that the poem has no theme." Now, this "taking it" is precisely what Warren has no title to do, if, indeed, it be such sheer absurdity to assert that a poem has no theme,[3] especially since Griggs very obviously means something quite different, and something perfectly sensible. He means that the pleasure arising from the poem *as a poem* is so great that only one incapable of feeling that pleasure would ask for anything more. And this "equating" is a gratuity of Warren's, not of Griggs's; for, even granting that every poem must have a theme, it is by no means the case that every theme is a comment on human con-

---

3. We may indeed worry about whether, on the contrary, it is not an absurdity to conceive of a poem—i.e., any imitative poem—as *having* a theme or meaning. The words have a meaning; they mean the poem; but why should the poem itself have any further meaning? What sense is there in asking about the meaning of something which is itself a meaning? And, if there is any point to this asking, shall we not have a further meaning still, and so on *ad infinitum*, so that interpretation becomes impossible, as being an infinite process? Moreover, these "meanings of poems" are at best something very trivial, prosaic, and obvious: *Œdipus* means that man walks in darkness, *Hamlet* that man is utterly alone, the *Ancient Mariner* that life is one and that the imagination revenges itself, etc. Such interpretation springs from the use of a very arid grammatical apparatus and wholly blinks the question of how powerfully we are affected by the spectacle of human fortunes, as well as that of how the situation, character, passion, and thought of the poetic *personae* affect their speech.

duct and values; and even if that were the case, it would not follow that such comment would be *ethical* comment; and even if that, too, were granted, it would not follow that every ethical comment is a *moral*. The rout of Griggs, in short, is accomplished by incorrect interpretation followed by illicit inference. Even the passage of which Griggs has, according to Warren, "reversed the undebatable sense," suffers a similar fate; for, having just cited Coleridge's remark that the poem "ought to have had no more moral than the Arabian Nights tale," and so forth, Warren calmly says: "Nor did he [Coleridge] say or even imply that the poem would be better if there were *no* moral."

The refutation of Lowes is similarly facile. Lowes remarked that repentance, although it lightened the soul, did not absolve; this Warren takes as the "theme" and is astounded when Lowes goes on to say that this "law of life" appears merely to render the poem a more credible illusion, the moral being untenable outside the poem, because of the disproportion of cause to effect and of crime to punishment. This means, says Warren, that the moral is not to be taken seriously and, indeed, that it could not be; and this is unthinkable for Warren, for it means that poems are "in themselves meaningless and nothing but refined and ingenious toys for an idle hour." How Warren arrives at this conclusion is obvious; in his simple world poems either have a moral or they are mere toys, and no Puritan was ever so flat and dogmatic about the matter. Deny Warren's contention of a moral, and a trap opens to drop you into the abyss of absurdity. But, I protest, Griggs and Lowes are "refuted," not because of any absurdity in their statements or fallacy in their inferences; they are so only through Warren's introduction of a wholly untenable exclusive disjunction and through his complete distortion of their utterances.

Even so, how deep is this abyss of absurdity? Is it, after all, so utterly contemptible to regard poems as affording pleasure rather than truth? If so, Warren must contemn Coleridge as well; for, merely to quote Coleridge's famous definition of a poem:

A poem is that species of composition, which is opposed to works of science by proposing for its *immediate* object pleasure, not truth; and from all other species— (having *this* object in common with it)—it is discriminated by proposing to itself such delight from the *whole*, as is compatible with a distinct gratification from each component *part*.[4]

In other words, the differentia of the class *poem* is pleasure and the kinds and sources of pleasure; and, as Coleridge says, "The reader should be carried forward, not merely or chiefly by the mechanical impulse of curiosity, or by a restless desire to arrive at the final solution; but by the pleasurable activity of mind excited by the attractions of the journey itself." Nor is Warren's conten-

4. *Biographia literaria*, chap. xiv.

tion that imagination is cognitive pertinent here, for Coleridge sharply distinguished *poem* and *poetry;* it is to the latter that the imagination is relevant. The passage is well worth considering; having just defined "poem" as above, he continues:

> But if this should be admitted as a satisfactory character of a poem, we have still to seek for a definition of poetry. The writings of Plato and Jeremy Taylor, and Burnett's Theory of the Earth, furnish undeniable proofs that poetry of the highest kind may exist without metre, and even without the contra-distinguishing objects of a poem. The first chapter of Isaiah . . . is poetry in the most emphatic sense; yet it would be not less irrational than strange to assert that pleasure, and not truth, was the immediate object of the prophet. In short, whatever specific import we attach to the word, Poetry, there will be found involved in it, as a necessary consequence, that a poem of any length neither can be, nor ought to be, all poetry. Yet if an harmonious whole is to be produced, the remaining parts must be preserved in keeping with the poetry. . . .

And he continues, "What is poetry? . . . is so nearly the same question with, what is a poet?—that the answer to the one is involved in the solution of the other. . . . The poet, described in ideal perfection, brings the whole soul of man into activity." He unites and blends all the faculties "by that synthetic and magical power, to which I would exclusively appropriate the name of Imagination."

We may now ask: Was the action of the poem intended, as Warren seems to suppose, to be "real"? If so, in what sense? And how, since undoubtedly poems effect pleasure and since the *Ancient Mariner* is undoubtedly a poem, did Coleridge propose to effect pleasure by it? But again Coleridge answers these questions for us:

> In the one [series of poems], the incidents and agents were to be, in part at least, supernatural; and the excellence aimed at was to consist in the interesting of the affections by the dramatic truth of such emotions, as would naturally accompany such situations supposing them real. And real in this sense they have been to every human being who, from whatever source of delusion, has at any time believed himself under supernatural agency.

These persons and characters, "supernatural or at least romantic," were to be so treated "as to transfer from our inward nature a human interest and a semblance of truth sufficient to procure for these shadows of the imagination that willing suspension of disbelief for the moment which constitutes poetic faith."

Seldom has a poet so clearly indicated his intentions and method, and the case is clear: Griggs and Lowes have followed Coleridge, and it is Warren who has misread, or read with insufficient care, "his text." They have held that, as a poem, the *Ancient Mariner* proposed as its end pleasure and not truth and that the "reality" of the poem is a *reality by supposition*—something which, though unreal, we may suppose to be real by a "willing suspension of disbelief." Nor are they incorrect in calling the poem "dreamlike"; Coleridge himself could use the expression in precisely the same sense:

> You will take especial note of the marvellous independence and true imaginative absence of all particular space or time in the Faery Queene. It is in the domains neither of history nor of geography; it is ignorant of all artificial boundary, all material obstacles; it is truly in land of Faery, that is, of mental space. The poet has placed you in a dream, a charmed sleep, and you neither wish, nor have the power, to inquire where you are, or how you got there.[5]

Ignoring these *loci classici* of Coleridgeans, Warren in effect supposes (1) that the poem does not have the effect which Coleridge says it was to have and (2) that it has some other end which Coleridge denies it to have; and on this latter supposition his whole chimerical interpretation is predicated.

In the first place, despite the argument that the poem is symbolic and not allegorical, Warren's interpretation clearly makes the poem what Coleridge calls "allegory." The "true sense" of the word *allegory*, says Coleridge, "is this,—the employment of one set of agents and images to convey in disguise a moral meaning, with a likeness to the imagination, but with a difference to the understanding,—those agents and images being so combined as to form a homogeneous whole. . . ."[6] But, secondly, *is the Mariner a "symbolic" poem?* Here we must make a distinction. If by "symbolic" we refer to the imitative or participative relations of the One and the Many, familiar enough in the Platonic and Neo-Platonic philosophers with whom Coleridge associated himself, doubtless the poem is symbolic. It is this, in a Coleridgean sense, because in so far as it is also *poetry*, it reflects the particular activity of the imagination which produced that poetry; because that activity, in turn, images the imagination; and because the imagination, in turn, images the creative activity of God. Again, if by "symbolic" we mean merely the more particular as revealing the more universal, which is all that Coleridge seems to intend,[7] we need not quarrel. But if by any interpretation of the term we commit ourselves, as does Warren, to an exegesis of how one thing in Coleridge must always mean something else, we are exceeding our evidence. Coleridge's discussion of the origin of the *Lyrical Ballads*, already cited in part, offers no hint of symbolism

5. *Coleridge's Miscellaneous Criticism*, ed. T. M. Raysor (Cambridge, 1936), p. 36; from *Literary Remains*.

6. Raysor, *op. cit.*, pp. 32–33; cf. pp. 28–32, also pp. 98–103, where Coleridge discusses symbol and allegory, and *Don Quixote* in terms of them.

7. "I adopt with full faith, the principle of Aristotle, that poetry, as poetry, is essentially ideal, that it avoids and excludes all accident; that its apparent individualities of rank, character, or occupation must be representative of a class; and that the persons of poetry must be clothed with generic attributes, with the common attributes of the class: Not with such as one gifted individual might possibly possess, but such as from his situation it is most probable before-hand that he would possess" (*Biographia literaria*, chap. xvii).

in this sense. I can recall no use by Coleridge—certainly, no crucial use—of the term "symbol" as interpreted by Warren, even in such major critical flights as Coleridge's discussion of Wordsworth and of Shakespeare; nor, indeed, does the term "symbol" bear Warren's meaning even when it is central to the discussion, as in Coleridge's remarks on *Don Quixote*. Undoubtedly, Coleridge's conception of the imagination influenced his criticism and his creation; but it was a profoundly philosophical conception; and Warren's refusal to treat its profounder aspects is responsible, in part, for his interpretation of the term "symbol."

Thirdly, supposing the poem were symbolic, as it clearly is not, on what basis does Warren determine the referents of the symbols? How is the moon, for instance—the key-symbol according to him—equated with the imagination? We are told that the moon, or if not the moon, some sort of half-light, frequently appears in Coleridge's work; that it is sometimes symbolic; that it and sunset and other accidents of light and shade diffuse a sudden novelty over the familiar, not unlike "the modifying colors of the imagination," according to Coleridge. That is sufficient to make the moon the symbol of the imagination for Warren. The crime now is "a crime against the imagination." In vain we ask why. Warren simply says: "Of course." One should rather have supposed that, if the crime is one against the imagination, the Polar Spirit would have represented the imagination, for certainly it is the Polar Spirit, and not the moon, who loves the bird, who is offended by its slaughter, and who exacts revenge. Why is the wind the symbol of the creative urge? Why, particularly, is it a symbol of the necessary kind, "rooted in our universal natural experience," as are all phallic symbols? Does that mean that the wind can never symbolize anything else? All that Warren says here amounts to this: the wind is inimical, and so is the creative urge, to complacent man. Why is the sun the light of natural prudence? Because, says Warren, "the sun is, symbolically speaking, the cause of their [the other mariners'] acceptance of the crime . . . they repudiate the luminous haze, the other light, and consider it an evil, though we know that the fog and mist are associated with the moon in the wind-bird-moon cluster." And in their fortunes—Warren suggests—we have perhaps some fable of the Enlightenment which terminated in the blood-bath of the French Revolution. So amid generous assumptions, undistributed middles, inconsistencies, misinterpretations, ignorationes elenchi, post hoc ergo propter hoc's, etc., Warren makes his way by the light, or shall we say the half-light, of a vague supposition which he terms the "symbolic cluster"—a supposition that "symbols" simultaneously presented are henceforth linked (cf. p. 90). Here is an illustration of one of the crucial points in the interpretation:

The Albatross, the sacramental bird, is also, as it were, a moon-bird. For here, with the bird, the moon first enters the poem, and the two are intimately associated. . . . The sun is kept entirely out of the matter. The lighting is always indirect, for even in the day we have only "mist or cloud,"—the luminous haze, the symbolic equivalent of moonlight. But not only is the moon associated with the bird, but the wind also. Upon the bird's advent a "good south wind sprung up behind." And so we have the creative wind, the friendly bird, the moonlight of imagination all together in one symbolic cluster [p. 91].

Since Warren has been at pains to show a symbol to be, for Coleridge, "focal, massive, and not arbitrary," one would imagine that his demonstration would follow these lines; that, for example, he would argue that the moon is the symbol of the imagination because it is the focal, massive, and nonarbitrary representative of the imagination; but he does not—and, in fact, it is not. All such interpretation is really uncontrolled analogy; the double themes, their fusions, and the multivalent symbols permit anyone to make of the poem whatever he may choose.

In short, we may say to Warren what Coleridge himself once quoted. We shall not descend the dark cave of Trophonius with you, there to rub our own eyes, in order to make the sparks and figured flashes, which we are required to see. And more pertinently, perhaps, we may say, again with Coleridge:

Apollo be praised! Not a thought like it would ever enter of its own accord into any mortal mind; and what is an additional good feature, when put there, it will not stay, having the very opposite quality that snakes have—they come out of their holes into open view at the sound of sweet music, while the allegoric meaning slinks off at the very first notes and lurks in murkiest oblivion—an utter invisibility.

II

LITERARY CRITICISM AND THE CONCEPT OF IMITATION IN ANTIQUITY[1]

RICHARD McKEON

THE term "imitation" is not prominent in the vocabulary of criticism today. In such use as it still has, it serves to segregate the bad from the good in art rather more frequently than to set the boundaries of art. Yet as late as the eighteenth century imitation was the mark and differentia of the arts, or at least of some of them. To the critics of that century, literature and painting were imitative arts, and it was still important to debate whether or not music was an art of imitation.[2] The term had begun to slip into disrepute in writings on the philosophy of art even before critics of art found it cumbersome or inappropriate, and substitutes for it with more familiar philosophic justification have long since been found; if it does occasionally return to use, with the proper protection of a warning that it does not mean literal representation of its object, it is seldom extended to include music or literature.[3]

The defense, such as it is, of "imitation" as a term applicable to poetry or suited to apply to all of the arts, has in our times fallen largely into the hands of historians of aesthetics and criticism; and although the fortune varies in the

1. Reprinted, with minor alterations, from *Modern Philology*, August, 1936.

2. Thus James Harris, in the second of his *Three Treatises* (first published in 1744) entitled "A Discourse on Music, Painting, and Poetry," treats poetry, painting, and music as three types of imitation differing in their media and modes of imitation (2d. ed. [1765], pp. 55 ff.), although he goes on to say that poetry disposes of the charm of "numbers" as well as imitation (p. 92) and music possesses, besides the power of imitation, the power of raising affections (p. 99), "whereas Painting has pretence to no Charm, except that of Imitation" (p. 92). Thomas Twining, on the other hand, in the dissertation "On Poetry Considered as an Imitative Art," which he prefaced to his translation of Aristotle's *Poetics* (first published in 1789), distinguishes four senses of imitation as applied to poetry: imitation by the sounds of the words, by description, by fiction, and by dramatic imitation; and he argues (2d ed. [1812], I, 35) that, since the last is the proper sense of imitation, it is incorrect to say that all poetry is imitation; only dramatic poetry is properly imitative. Moreover, in the second dissertation prefaced to his translation, "On the Different Senses of the Word, Imitative, as Applied to Music by the Ancients, and by the Moderns," Twining concludes his argument by quoting with approbation from James Beattie's treatise *On Poetry and Music* the statement that music should be stricken off the list of the imitative arts (p. 91) and by maintaining further that painting, sculpture, and the arts of design in general are "the only arts that are obviously and essentially imitative" (p. 92).

3. Thus George Santayana, in *Reason in Art*, Vol. IV of *The Life of Reason* (New York, 1917), pp. 144 ff., discusses sculpture, acting, and painting as modes of imitation. Music, poetry, prose, and architecture had, however, been treated in earlier chapters before the concept of imitation was introduced.

debate, the discredit which the term has suffered in modern criticism tends to be found earlier and earlier. "That the 'Imitation' doctrine of the *Poetics* is in some respects disputable need not be denied," according to Saintsbury,[4] "and that it lent itself rather easily to serious misconstruction is certain. But let us remember also that it is an attempt—perhaps the first attempt, and one that has not been much bettered in all the improvements upon it—to adjust those proportions of nature and art which actually do exist in poetry." "It is natural," Bosanquet says,[5] "that the earliest formula adopted by reflection should be strained to the breaking point before it is abandoned." "Aristotle, as his manner was," according to Butcher,[6] "accepted the current phrase and interpreted it anew. True, he may sometimes have been misled by its guidance, and not infrequently his meaning is obscured by his adherence to the outworn formula." Atkins writes:

> Moreover the statement [i.e., Plato's statement of the relation of the arts to each other and to the universe in *Laws* 889B–D] helps to explain why "imitation" (and not "creation" or "expression") has been adopted as the process common to all the arts. To the Greeks before Plato, devoid of a mystical sense of an invisible order of realities, the plain and obvious fact was that the artist did not produce the objects of real life, but their appearances only; and it was therefore inevitable that the impression produced on their minds was rather that of imitative representation than of creation, interpretation, or the like.[7]

The practice of historians of literary criticism would be conclusive, even if their evidence from the writers of antiquity were not impressive, in establishing the variety of the meanings which the term "imitation" has assumed in the course of its history. Yet that diversity of meaning is seldom the direct object of critical attention: the term is vague, inadequate, primitive, and its use involves a play on words when it does not lead to self-contradiction. But when one returns to the ancient writers on which these historical labors are employed, it is difficult to retain a sense of the limitations and deficiencies with which scholarship has enriched the term. Instead, constant vigilance is required to discover the ineptitudes which should result from the use of so inept a word. For all the attempts that have been made to define "imitation" and for all the care that has been exercised in examining the statements in which it occurs, the philosophical contexts in which the word "imitation" is used and methodological questions as they apply to its use have received little scrutiny. Yet the meaning of a word will alter with a change in either context or peculiari-

4. George Saintsbury, *A History of Criticism and Literary Taste in Europe* (New York, 1900), I, 54.

5. Bernard Bosanquet, *A History of Aesthetics* (4th ed.; London, 1917), p. 13.

6. S. H. Butcher, *Aristotle's Theory of Poetry and Fine Art* (4th ed.; London, 1923), p. 122.

7. J. W. H. Atkins, *Literary Criticism in Antiquity* (Cambridge, 1934), I, 52.

ties of method, notwithstanding that the definition may be retained; and, if these remain unchanged, it is possible for the doctrine of imitation to persist in all essentials, even when the term has disappeared. If the critical views in which the word "imitation" appeared, no less than methodological devices peculiar to the systems in which the term was used, have survived the discredit of the term itself, the attempt to distinguish among the critical approaches of antiquity may not be without relevance to the modern analogues that have replaced them.

I

The word "imitation," as Plato uses it, is at no time established in a literal meaning or delimited to a specific subject matter. It is sometimes used to differentiate some human activities from others or some part of them from another part or some aspect of a single act from another; it is sometimes used in a broader sense to include all human activities; it is sometimes applied even more broadly to all processes—human, natural, cosmic, and divine. Like most of the terms that figure prominently in the dialogues, "imitation" as a term is left universal in scope and indeterminate in application. The dialectical method is used to determine its meaning in particular contexts, sometimes bringing out a meaning according to which any given statement in which it may occur is true, sometimes with equal force the meanings in which the statement is false; not infrequently both ends are accomplished in a single dialogue. Of existent objects, Plato says,[8] there are three things necessary for knowledge: the name (ὄνομα), the discourse or reason (λόγος), and the image (εἴδωλον); knowledge and the object itself are apart from these. Whether or not Plato wrote the epistle in which those distinctions are made, his practice seems to conform to it. "For as yet," the Stranger says at the beginning of the *Sophist*,[9] "we have in common concerning him only the name." He suggests that he and his interlocutor doubtless have the thing in mind as well; but they must come to an agreement concerning the thing by means of reason, not by the mere name without the reason. Somewhat later, in discussing angling, they arrive at agreement not only concerning the name but also concerning the reason or definition of the thing itself.[10] But when the search for the Sophist grows into an inquiry into being and non-being, pursued by way of word and reason, the Stranger remarks that in the case of being, as in that of every single thing which is supposed to be one, we call the single thing by many names and treat it as many.[11]

8. *Epist.* vii. 342A–B.

9. *Sophist* 218C.   10. *Ibid.* 221B.

11. *Ibid.* 251A–B. Consequent on this relation of names to things, Socrates frequently reproaches his respondents for finding many things where one is sought (as in *Meno* 72A or 77A), or again he is reproached by them for changing the meanings of his terms (as in

Not infrequently the speakers in the Platonic dialogues have reason to complain of the opposite difficulty, that many things are found to have the same name. It is probable that no small part of Plato's distrust of the written word is caused by the margin of independence which obtains between words, images, and reasons but which can be controlled in conversation by a skilled dialectician.

In any case, to require Plato to conform to an Aristotelian conception of definitions or terms, in which words are assigned univocal meanings, would be to distort his inquiry and make nonsense of much of his dialectic. It is invalid criticism to point out that a term like "imitation" has many meanings in Plato, and for the same reason it is questionable defense of the Platonic position to resolve the many meanings into one.[12] The word might be said to be defined in the course of the dialogues, but it receives no fixed meaning. The discussion proceeds by applying images and reasons to the elucidation of words, and in that process "imitation" and all like words suffer extensions and limitations. Unless the list is made indefinitely long to include infinite possible meanings, it is hardly accurate to say that the word has "several senses." From one point of view, "imitation" has only one meaning in Plato; from another, it has infinite meanings.

The methodological considerations which are so prominent in the use of words, and which control their meanings in what Plato would call a strange and wonderful fashion, may be stated in a way that has excellent Platonic precedent by setting forth the things to which Plato applied the word "imitation"and the other words which Plato applied to the same things—the many words which are applied to one thing, and the many things to which one word is applied. Without such considerations, on the other hand, inasmuch as they

---

Gorgias 483A); and, on the other hand, speakers are praised for reducing many or infinite things to one name and for finding appropriate names for each subdivision (as in *Theaetetus* 147C–148B).

12. J. Tate thus finds two kinds of imitation in the *Republic:* imitation in the literal sense, the mere copying of sensible objects, and imitation in an analogical sense, such that poetry in which imitation of this sort occurred could be considered nonimitative (" 'Imitation' in Plato's *Republic*," *Classical Quarterly*, XXII [1928], 23). In a later article ("Plato and 'Imitation,' " *ibid.*, XXVI [1932], 161–69), Tate refers to this as a distinction between a good and a bad sense of the term "imitation": poetry which is imitative in the bad sense is excluded from the ideal state, while poetry which is imitative in the good sense can be called nonimitative rather than imitative, depending on the sense in which the term "imitative" is used. In this second article Tate finds support in the remaining dialogues for his earlier interpretation of imitation in the *Republic*. W. C. Greene contrasts the "literal kind of imitation" implied in the tenth book of the *Republic* with the imitation in the second and third books of the *Republic*, which involves an attenuated form of the doctrine of ideas and which is criticized on ethical grounds in a not unfriendly spirit ("Plato's View of Poetry," in *Harvard Studies in Classical Philology*, XXIX [1918], 37–38). In Book x, according to Greene, Plato begs the question by assuming that the definition of imitation will cover the aim of poetry (p. 53). Imitation in its broadest sense was a metaphor to which Plato resorted, with evident dissatisfaction, to explain the relation of the world of sense to the world of ideas (p. 66).

underlie some of Plato's most esteemed devices for displaying the meanings of words, it is difficult to know how the Platonic doctrine of poetry (to mention only one application) can be stated, or how its relation to later theories can be estimated, or how the condemnations which Plato passed on poets can be judged. In one of its narrowest senses Plato used the word "imitation" to distinguish poetic styles into three kinds: pure narrative, in which the poet speaks in his own person without imitation, as in the dithyramb; narrative by means of imitation, in which the poet speaks in the person of his characters, as in comedy and tragedy; and mixed narrative, in which the poet speaks now in his own person and now by means of imitation.[13] In the *Republic* the preference among poets is for the unmixed imitator of the good, since the guardians of an ideal state should be educated to imitate only what is appropriate to them.[14] Even this discussion of style and the manner of imitation involves a distinction of objects of imitation into worthy and unworthy in terms of the scale of their perfection of being. Moreover, previous to the discussion of style, the examination of the tales themselves, limited to proper subjects among gods, heroes, and men, led to a distinction not between worthy and unworthy but between true and false. The truths of poetry are imitations of the good. Falsehoods in discourse are likewise imitations, but the objects of such imitations have no external existence. False tales are imitations (μίμημα) of a lie in the soul, an after-rising image (εἴδωλον) of it. Poetry, even false, is not an unmixed falsehood, but requires the antecedent lie for its explanation.[15]

The terms alternative to "imitation" (μίμησις) begin to make their appearance in the discussion of falsity. A lie occurs when one copies (εἰκάζειν) the true nature of gods and heroes badly; it is comparable to a portrait which bears no resemblance (ὅμοια) to the painter's model.[16] The argument concerning imitation may, moreover, be applied to the form in which it is itself stated, for the lie of the poet is explained by the image and likeness of the painter. Even at this early stage "imitation" may be applied to poetry in several senses; according to one, dramatic poetry is imitative of the speech of the characters; according to another, false poetry is imitative of a lie in the soul; according to a third, true poetry is imitative of the good. The lawgiver will lay down laws and patterns (τύπος) to which the poet will be required to conform,[17] and as soon as the philosopher is given his function in the perfect state, he too enters into the imitative process. He imitates the things which truly are and assimilates (ἀφομοιοῦσθαι) himself to them. He should, moreover, be compelled to mold (πλάττειν) human nature to his vision; no city is happy unless its

13. *Republic* iii. 392D–394C.
14. *Ibid*. iii. 397D.
15. *Ibid*. ii. 382B–C.
16. *Ibid*. 377E.
17. *Ibid*. 380C.

lineaments have been traced by artists who used the heavenly model (παρ-άδειγμα).[18] Through these varying applications the term "imitation" indicates a constant relation between something which is and something made like it: the likeness itself may be good or bad, real or apparent. When, consequently, poetry is examined again in the tenth book of the *Republic* and is found to be imitative, it is incorrect to suppose that the word "imitation" has been unduly extended or that it has been given a new literal sense. The imitator (μιμητής) is defined as a maker of images (εἰδώλου ποιητής) and is contrasted to the maker of realities; unlike the latter he has no knowledge of being but only of appearances.[19] Both varieties of maker, moreover, stand in contrast to an eternal reality. Like the painter who paints the picture of a couch, the imitator makes a product at three removes from nature, for he imitates not that which is but that which seems to be, not the truth but a phantasm.[20] Poetry, therefore, at that removal from truth, attains only a small part of the object, and the part it attains is not the object itself but an image (εἴδωλον) capable of deceiving. If the poet were able to produce the things he imitates instead of making only images, if he had knowledge of the truth, he would abandon imitation.[21] Truth and falsity, knowledge and opinion, reality and appearance delimit at each step the scope of "imitation"; but as its application has varied, it has marked consistently a contrast between the work of imitation and something else which is, in comparison with it, real.

Even when limited to poetry and analogous activities, then, the concept of imitation may expand and contract. It may embrace a part of poetry, or all poetry, or even philosophy as well. But it also extends to other human activities. All the arts are imitative. The painter is comparable to the poet in his imitative character;[22] a good picture is one which reproduces the colors and figures of its subject.[23] Music is an imitation (μίμησις), a representation (ἀπει-κασία), a copy (εἰκαστική); good music possesses a standard of rightness and is a likeness of the beautiful (ὁμοιότης τοῦ καλοῦ).[24] The entire art of dancing is the result of imitation of what is said in song or discourse.[25] Since values are determined either by the adequacy of the representation or the character of the object imitated, the standards in dance and song may be stated in moral terms: figures and melodies which are expressive of the virtues of body or soul, or of copies (εἰκών) of them, are good.[26] Or the term "imitation"

18. *Ibid.* vi. 500C–E.
19. *Ibid.* x. 601B–C.
20. *Ibid.* 597D–598B.
24. *Laws* ii. 668A–B; cf. vii. 798D–E; *Cratylus* 423D.
25. *Laws* vii. 816A.
26. *Ibid.* ii. 655B ff.; cf. vii. 812C.

21. *Ibid.* 599A–B.
22. *Ibid.* 596E; *Sophist* 234B.
23. *Cratylus* 431C.

may be expanded in another direction from poetry. All verbal accounts, including the dialogues themselves, are imitations. At the beginning of the dialogue which bears his name, Critias remarks that all discourse is imitation (μίμησις) and representation (ἀπεικασία); and he complains that his task is more difficult than the one that Timaeus performed, inasmuch as image-making (εἰδωλο-ποιία) is subjected to closer criticism when it represents well-known human subjects than when it represents divine things in which we are content with a small degree of likeness.[27] But in the *Timaeus* Socrates finds a difficulty in discourse almost the contrary to that of which Critias complained. To bring out the competence of the speakers in the succeeding dialogues, Socrates had been developing the contrast, in terms of the degree of their knowledge and the nature of their discourse, of philosophers and statesmen to the imitative tribe of poets and the wandering Sophists; the defects of his own presentation in the *Republic*, comparable to a defect he finds exemplified by the poets, arise from the fact that familiar things are easy to imitate, but what is unfamiliar is difficult to imitate in action and even more difficult in words.[28] Moreover, the component parts of poems, discourses, and dialogues are imitations. Words imitate things in a fashion distinct from that of music or design,[29] and the letters of which words are composed are themselves means of imitation. From letters and syllables, the lawgiver forms a sign (σημεῖον) and a name (ὄνομα) for each thing; and from names he compounds all the rest by imitation.[30] When the nature of things is imitated by letters and syllables, the copy (εἰκών) is good if it gives all that is appropriate, bad if it omits a little.[31]

Not only arts, philosophy, and discourse are imitation. Human institutions must be added to the list. All governments are imitations of the true government;[32] and the laws themselves, source of the true government, are imitations of particulars of the truth which are written down, so far as that is possible, from the dictation of those who know[33] But the expansion of the word "imitation" passes beyond human products, actions, virtues, and institutions; it extends to things themselves. All things change, imitating and following what happens to the entire universe; and the imitation conforms to its model even in conception, generation, and nutrition.[34] It extends finally to the first principles of things. The universe is distinguishable into three fundamental forms: the model

27. *Critias* 107B–C.

28. *Timaeus* 19D–20B.   30. *Ibid.* 426C–427C.

29. *Cratylus* 423C–424B.   31. *Ibid.* 431D.

32. *Statesman* 293E; cf. *ibid.* 297C. It is significant, once more, that the nature of that imitation of the true government is explained by recourse to an image or figure (εἰκών, σχῆμα) in which the king is represented (ἀπεικάζειν) as pilot and physician.

33. *Ibid.* 300B–C.   34. *Ibid.* 274A.

form (παραδείγματος εἶδος), the imitation of the model (μίμημα παραδεί-γματος), and the Space or Receptacle in which Becoming takes place. Figures enter and depart in the Receptacle, as in a lump of gold which is curiously manipulated, in imitation of eternal figures, stamped (τυποῦν) from them in a marvelous fashion.[35]

In its expansion and contraction, the word "imitation" indicates the lesser term of the proportion of being to appearance: if God is, the universe is an imitation; if all things are, shadows and reflections are imitations; if the products of man's handicraft are, his representations of them are imitations. If imitation is to be avoided, it is because of the danger of imitating, through error, ignorance, or falsehood, that which is not or that which is less than it might be or is less than that which imitates it. As confined to the arts, therefore, imitation is not coextensive with the productive arts; rather, it is a part of them, for they are divided into those which produce things which are and those which produce images (εἴδωλον); the latter is the imitative art. Even when art is contrasted to nature and chance, the arts are divided into those arts which produce images (εἴδωλον), related to each other but bearing little relation to truth, like music and painting, and those arts which co-operate with nature, like medicine, husbandry, and gymnastic.[36] The divine art suffers a like division, for in addition to natural objects which are the result of God's art, there are visions (φάντασμα) seen in dreams and waking, shadows (σκιά), and reflections seen in polished surfaces.[37]

Man likewise makes things which are, and he makes images. His imitative or image-making art (εἰδωλοποιικὴ τέχνη) is divided into two parts, the copymaking art (εἰκαστική), which follows its original in length, breadth, depth, and color, and the fantastic art (φανταστική), in which truth is abandoned and the images are given, not their actual proportions, but such proportions as seem beautiful. The products of the second branch of the imitative art are appearances or phantasms (φάντασμα), and they are no longer even like things which are.[38] The proportion of being to appearance may be pursued to even greater refinements: that portion of that fantastic art in which the artist uses his own person as his instrument, making his figure and voice seem similar to another's, is called imitation (μίμησις);[39] and the return is complete to the sense of imitation by which dramatic poetry was distinguished from other kinds

---

35. *Timaeus* 48E–49B; 50A–C.   36. *Laws* x. 889A–D.

37. *Sophist* 266B.

38. *Ibid.* 235B–236C. Cf. *Rep.* x. 598B, where painting is said to be an imitation, not of that which is as it is, but of appearance as it appears; it is an imitation of a phantasm, not of truth.

39. *Ibid.* 267A.

in the third book of the *Republic*. The proportion of truth to falsity, and the proportion of knowledge to opinion, as might be expected, play as constant a role in the discussion of imitation as the proportion of being to appearance. The art of midwifery which Socrates practices on Theaetetus to bring forth his ideas is employed to distinguish the image from the real offspring,[40] and it is unsuccessful when it produces mere lies and images (ψευδῆ καὶ εἴδωλα).[41] If statesmen had no knowledge of what they were doing, they would imitate the truth but would imitate it badly; if they had knowledge, the imitation would be the truth itself and no longer an imitation.[42] If a man had genuine knowledge of the things he imitated, he would abandon the fashioning of images and devote himself to real things and actions rather than to imitating them.[43] Yet, on the other hand, by imitation of the unvarying revolutions of the God, we may stabilize the variable revolutions within ourselves;[44] and there is intellectual delight in the imitation of the divine harmony manifested in mortal motions.[45]

Even in a hasty adumbration of the infinite gradations of meaning and application which the term "imitation" undergoes in the Platonic dialogues, it is apparent that a great many similar terms undergo similar variations and approximate similar meanings in the succession of subjects on which imitation is brought to play. Several such terms have been necessary for the preceding exposition. Imitation is the making of images (εἴδωλον). The art of image-making may produce copies (εἰκών) or phantasms (φάντασμα), the difference between the two being that a copy is like its object, a phantasm is not. Yet a copy, to be correct, must not reproduce all the qualities of that which it copies. The painter makes a copy when he represents (ἀπεικάζειν) the color and form of his subject.[46] The control of poetic copies was to be the specific object of the supervision of poets and other artisans in the third book of the *Republic*. They were to be compelled to embody in their work copies of the good and to be prohibited from setting forth copies of the evil.[47] Similarly, the competent critic in any of the arts must know, first, what the copy is; second, how correctly it has been presented; third, how well it has been executed in words, melodies, and rhythms.[48] Even philosophic arguments are copies, for the solution of the question whether injustice is profitable to the completely unjust man, in the *Republic*, is arrived at by fashioning a copy of the soul in discourse[49] (εἰκόνα πλάσαντες τῆς ψυχῆς λόγῳ) in order to show the propounder of that

40. *Theaetetus* 150A.

41. *Ibid.* 150E.

42. *Statesman* 300D–E.

43. *Rep.* x. 599A.

44. *Timaeus* 47C.

45. *Ibid.* 80B.

46. *Cratylus* 432B.

47. *Rep.* iii. 401B.

48. *Laws* ii. 669A.

49. *Rep.* ix. 588B.

view precisely what he is saying. There are copies (εἰκών) and likenesses (ὁμοίωμα) of ideas in which few, unfortunately, can see the nature which they copy;[50] and finally the universe itself is a copy of the intelligible (εἰκών τοῦ νοητοῦ).[51]

As these fundamental terms are expanded, others are added to the list. An image (εἴδωλον) is defined as a thing made in the likeness (ἀφομοιοῦν) of the true thing, but only after a preliminary skirmish in which images in water and in mirrors are invoked to explain images.[52] Reflection in mirrors and in water is a constant device by which Plato clarifies his use of images and copies: the images and phantasms of men and other things are seen in water preliminary to examining men and things in their true natures;[53] one's eyes would be ruined if one looked at the sun directly instead of at its copy in water or in something else of that sort;[54] one should make one's thought clear by means of verbs and nouns, modeling (ἐκτυποῦν) opinion in the stream that flows through the lips as in a mirror or in water;[55] the versatility of the imitative artist which produces the appearance, though not the reality, of all things is explained by comparison to a mirror;[56] the liver is so fashioned that the power of thought, proceeding from the mind, moves in the liver as in a mirror which receives impressions (τύπος) and provides images (εἴδωλον) and the spleen is like a wiper for the mirror.[57]

Images and copies, however, as the metaphor would suggest, provide no satisfactory substitute for reality, though they are a necessary stage in the approach to reality. To understand the image we must know the reality; but to know the reality we must dispose of images. If there are copies (εἰκών) of letters in water or in mirrors, we shall never know them until we know the originals, and we shall never be true musicians until we know the forms of temperance, courage, liberality, and the rest.[58] He who studies things that are in arguments and reasons (λόγος) is as distinct from him who looks at them in copies (εἰκών) as he is from him who considers them in their operations and works (ἔργον).[59] There are many variants to the figure. The mirror may even appear in a text in which the mind is like a block of wax,[60] on which perceptions and thoughts are impressed (ἀποτυποῦσθαι) like the imprint of signet rings (δακτυλίων σημεῖα);[61] these persist as memorial imprints in the soul (μνη-

50. *Phaedrus* 250B.

51. *Timaeus* 92C; cf. *ibid.* 29B ff.

52. *Sophist* 239D–240A.

53. *Rep.* vii. 516A–B.

54. *Phaedo* 99D.

55. *Theaet.* 206D.

56. *Rep.* x. 596D–E.

57. *Timaeus* 71B; 72C.

58. *Rep.* iii. 402B–C.

59. *Phaedo* 100A.

60. *Theaet.* 193C.

61. *Ibid.* 191D.

μεῖον ἐν τῇ ψυχῇ), impressions (τύπος), seals (σφραγίς),[62] imprints or signs (σημεῖον),[63] and even footprints (ἴχνος);[64] and we remember as long as the image (εἴδωλον) lasts.[65] The soul is likewise a book in which memory, perception, and feelings inscribe copies (εἰκών).[66] Analogies might be multiplied or the list of terms further extended; but in that development, even in an attenuated form, the discussion turns, as is inevitable if the thesis is correct, from the specific doctrine of imitation to embrace the entire philosophy of Plato and from the process of imitation to the devices of dialectic. Even the figure of the divided line is set forth in terms familiar to the doctrine of imitation, although the movement is from copies to reality rather than from reality to copies: all things are divided into the visible and the intelligible, and each of these parts in turn is divided into two classes. The first of the two classes of visible things is the class of copies (εἰκών), which includes shadows (σκιά) and reflections or phantasms in water (τὰ ἐν τοῖς ὕδασι φαντάσματα).[67] The second class of visible things is that of which the previous is a likeness or copy, that is, natural things, and the proportion between the likeness (ὁμοιωθέν) and that of which it is a likeness is the proportion between the objects of opinion and the objects of knowledge. But the soul, when it comes to investigate the first portion of the intelligible part of the line, must treat as copies the things which are imitated in the first part of the line; it is for that reason that the geometer draws squares and diagonals.[68] Once the discussion pursues this direction, it is only a step from "imitation" to the terms which guard the loftiest reaches of the Platonic dialectic, to recollection (ἀνάμνησις),[69] to presence in (παρουσία),[70] and participation (μέθεξις, κοινωνία).[71]

To elaborate the full significance of the term "imitation," consequently, more is required than the simple enumeration of the list of other words equivalent to it or used in its explication. Each of the terms of that lengthy list varies with the variation of "imitation." The set of significances employed in the dialogues may indeed be conceived as a huge matrix composed of all the words of a language, each possessed of an indefinite number of shades of meaning, the particular meaning of a word at any given time being determined by the meanings of other words drawn from that matrix in conjunction with which it is used. It is inevitable that the doctrine of imitation should invade the philosophic

---

62. *Ibid.* 192A.

63. *Ibid.* 192B.

64. *Ibid.* 193C.

65. *Ibid.* 191D.

66. *Philebus* 38E–39B.

67. *Rep.* vi. 509E–510A.

68. *Ibid.* 510B–511A.

69. *Phaedo* 72E, 92D; *Phaedrus* 249C; *Laws* v. 732B.

70. *Gorgias* 497E; *Phaedo* 100D.

71. *Sophist* 256A, 259A; *Parmenides* 132D.

enterprise and the dialectical method. All discourse is an imitation, and the interlocutors of the dialogues are constantly using, discussing, and complaining of images, likenesses, metaphors, and copies. " 'Your question,' I said, 'requires an answer expressed in an image [εἰκών].' 'And you,' he said, 'of course, are not accustomed to speak in images.' "[72] The image is frequently successful, frequently bad.[73] Even more important, the proportion of being to appearance, of truth to probability, obtains in discourse as in other things. It is proper to conceive all things as imitations; yet imitation should be avoided. All discourse deals in likenesses; yet one must be on one's guard against likenesses (ὁμοιότης).[74] Used with knowledge, however, there is no danger in imitation, whether the imitation be of lesser things or of greater; and so, too, dialectic may move in either direction, it may clarify the lesser by the greater, or the greater by the less.[75]

The criteria of good, true, and beautiful derive from the same proportion of being to appearance which operated throughout the doctrine of imitation. If the artificer of any object uses the uniform and eternal as his model, the object so executed must of necessity be beautiful; but if his model is a created object, his work so executed is not beautiful.[76] Discourse concerning the abiding and unshakable should be, as far as possible, irrefutable and invincible; but accounts of that which is copied after the likeness of the model are themselves copies and possess only likelihood, for as Being is to Becoming, Truth is to Belief.[77] In like manner and for like reason the Good gives truth to the objects of knowledge and the power of knowing, and is itself more beautiful even than they.[78]

The pursuit of beauty does not follow a different path from that which leads to truth and goodness. It is no accidental consequence, therefore, and it is no evidence of an inexplicable insensitivity to poetry in a great writer, that poetry should fall so low in Plato's analysis or that the poet should have no place in the perfect state. Criteria of truth and morality are applied as a natural course to the poet's work. He is permitted even in the ideal state to tell his tales, properly censored, as an incident of education and as a means of inculcating virtue. He may tell tales concerning the gods, to teach men "to honor the gods and their fathers and mothers, and not to hold their friendship with one another in

72. *Rep.* vi 487E. Cf. *Laws* 644C; *Gorgias* 517D; *Symposium* 215A, and *passim*.

73. *Phaedo* 99E.

74. *Sophist* 231A.

75. Thus, in the *Republic* ii. 369A, Socrates proposes first to treat of the state and then to seek the likeness (ὁμοιότης) of the greater in the lesser, whereas in the *Sophist* 218D the lesser is used as the model (παράδειγμα) of the greater. Cf. *ibid.* 221C, 226B.

76. *Timaeus* 28A–B.

77. *Ibid.* 29C.   78. *Rep.* vi. 508E.

light esteem";[79] he may tell tales concerning heroes to inspire the virtues of courage and self-control or temperance; but the discussion of the one remaining subject of his tales, men, is interrupted because justice would properly be inculcated by such tales, and, since the nature and value of justice has not yet been determined in the dialogue, instructions concerning the limitations of his poems are not yet ready for the poet.[80] Before that is possible the one remaining virtue, wisdom, which is left for expression to the scientist and the dialectician, since the poet can make no contribution to it, must be examined. If then one seeks tales about men, that is, tales by which men may learn justice, the *Republic* itself is such a tale, one long dialectical poem written for the elucidation of justice. In the *Laws*, where the concern is no longer with an ideal state but with one which is second best,[81] the function of the poet and the musician, still rigorously censored, is enlarged. In the *Republic* he found himself in competition with the dialectician, sadly handicapped by his lack of knowledge: in the *Laws* he is in competition with the lawgiver, for the whole state is an imitation of the best and noblest life, which is the very truth of poetry.[82] It is not its imitative character but its lack of truth and knowledge which brings poetry to its low estate. Homer and all the poetic tribe are imitators of images of virtue ($\mu\iota\mu\eta\tau\alpha\grave{\iota}$ $\epsilon\grave{\iota}\delta\acute{\omega}\lambda\omega\nu$ $\grave{\alpha}\rho\epsilon\tau\hat{\eta}s$) and of other things, but they do not lay hold on truth.[83] Poetry is a kind of madness comparable to the art of divination or prophecy, or to the art of purification by mysteries, or to that higher madness which seizes the soul when it contemplates in true knowledge, like that of the gods, essence, formless, colorless, intangible. But we are told that when the soul falls from such contemplation, it passes first into a philosopher or a lover; second, into a king or warrior; third, into a householder or moneymaker; fourth, into a gymnast; fifth, into a prophet or mystic; sixth, into a poet or imitator; and there are but nine stages in this progressive degradation of the soul.[84] The poet, like the interpreter of the poet, may be inspired by a divine gift;[85] but like the statesman, who is similarly inspired, he possesses at best only right opinion which is short of knowledge,[86] and like Ion, his interpreter, he is repeatedly given the rhapsode's final choice between inspiration and injustice.[87]

79. *Ibid.* iii. 386A.

80. *Ibid.* 392A–C.

81. *Laws* v. 739A; vii. 807B.

82. *Ibid.* vii. 817B: "You are poets and we are poets in the same things, your rivals as artists and actors in the fairest drama, which true law and that alone can carry out, as our hope is."

83. *Rep.* x. 600E.

84. *Phaedrus* 244A–245A; 248C–E.

85. *Ion* 533D–E.

86. *Meno* 99A–E.

87. *Ion* 542A.

II

In Aristotle's usage, not only does the term "imitation" have a different definition from that which it had for Plato but, much more important, Aristotle's method of defining terms and his manner of using them have nothing in common with the devices of the dialogues. There is a double consequence of these differences. Whereas for Plato the term "imitation" may undergo an infinite series of gradations of meaning, developed in a series of analogies, for Aristotle the term is restricted definitely to a single literal meaning. In the second place and as a consequence of the first difference, whereas for Plato an exposition of the word "imitation" involves an excursion through all the reaches of his philosophy, "imitation" for Aristotle is relevant only to one restricted portion of the domain of philosophy and never extends beyond it. For Plato dialectic is a device by which words, normally opaque, may be made translucent so that a truth and a beauty which are beyond words may shine through them. Though it is a device formulated in terms of words and conceived for the manipulation of words, it is the thing which is held constant; and it is the thing to which the attention of the mind is directed, while the word, on the other hand, varies and is to be discarded once it has served its function as a stage in the progress to truth. Things can be learned, Socrates says,[88] either through names or through themselves; but although one may learn from the name, which is a copy ($\epsilon\grave{\iota}\kappa\acute{\omega}\nu$), both whether it is a good copy and the truth of which it is a copy, it is better to learn from the truth both the truth itself and whether the copy is properly made. The end of the dialectical process may in a sense be said to be the definition of words, but any word may have many definitions. For Aristotle, on the contrary, the definition of terms and the establishment of principles are the beginnings of the scientific enterprise. Words may have many meanings, and Aristotle frequently enumerates divergent senses of a given word. But in science they must be terms and must therefore be univocal. A term is a word plus a meaning. Consequently, although the Aristotelian sciences are distinguished according to their subject matters, it is the term which is held constant; and a given object, under different aspects isolated by different terms, may move from science to science. As mind, man would be a subject for psychology; as animal, a subject for biology; as natural thing, a subject for physics; as moral agent, a subject for ethics; as tragic actor, a subject for poetics. There results from these two differences a third difference in the fashion in which Plato and Aristotle use words, among others the word "imitation." Plato may ask concerning a given thing in different contexts whether or not it is an imitation, and may arrive in two places, without inconsistency, at

---

88. *Cratylus* 439A–B.

two answers, that it is an imitation and that it is not an imitation; for Aristotle, if a given thing is an imitation, it cannot *not* be an imitation.

The method of Aristotle, then, proceeds by the literal definition of terms and by the division of the domain of knowledge into a number of sciences: the theoretical sciences—metaphysics, mathematics, and physics; the practical sciences or the sciences of action—ethics and politics; the "poetic" sciences or the sciences of making; each with its proper principles and, in the case of subordinate sciences, principles derived from superior sciences. Imitation functions in that system as the differentia by which the arts, useful and fine, are distinguished from nature. Art imitates nature, Aristotle was fond of repeating,[89] and, at least in the case of the useful arts, the deficiencies of nature are supplemented in the process of that imitation by art following the same methods as nature would have employed. "Generally, art partly completes what nature cannot bring to a finish, and partly imitates her."[90] Thus, if a house were a natural product, it would pass through the same stages that it in fact passes through when it is produced by art; and if natural products could also be produced by art, they would move along the same lines that the natural process actually takes. The fine arts differ from the useful in their means of imitation, and consequently in the end of their imitation, for they have no end beyond the perfection of their product as determined by their object and the means they employ. Apart from such differences they are imitations of nature in the same sense as the useful arts. The term, therefore, does not have the scope of application which it possesses in Plato; and such accidental coincidences of verbal expression as occur are in a limited region of philosophy, particularly in the discussion of poetry and most striking in the discussion of dramatic poetry. For Aristotle imitation is not, at one extreme, the imitation of ideas, such as philosophers and the Demiurge indulge in according to Plato; nor is it, at the other extreme, the imitation of appearances themselves imitations, such as satisfies the Platonic poet. Imitation, being peculiar to the processes of art, is not found in the processes of nature or of knowledge. For the natural is that which has an internal principle of motion, whereas the change which is effected in artificial objects is from an external principle. Moreover, for Aristotle imitation is not an imitation of an idea in the mind of the artist; such a statement would be meaningless in the context of the Aristotelian system, though one might properly point out that the forms of the things which proceed from art are in the mind of the artist.[91] Rather, imitation is of particular things; the ob-

89. *Physics* ii. 2. 194ª21–22; *Meteorol.* iv. 3. 381ᵇ6.

90. *Physics* ii. 8. 199ª15–17.

91. *Metaphysics* vii. 7. 1032ª31–ᵇ1.

ject of imitation, according to the statement of the *Poetics*[92] which seems to be intended to apply to all the fine arts, is the actions of men.

Aristotle says relatively little concerning the process of imitation, and that little has been subject to great differences of interpretation; yet what he says of natural objects and their production and of artificial objects and their making affords sound basis for reconstruction of his theory of imitation. The natural object, composite of form and matter, acts according to the natural principle of its being; in imitation the artist separates some form from the matter with which it is joined in nature—not, however, the "substantial" form, but some form perceptible by sensation—and joins it anew to the matter of his art, the medium which he uses. The action which he imitates may be "natural" to the agent, but the artist must attempt to convey not that natural appropriateness and rightness, but rather a "necessity or probability" suitably conveyed by the materials of his art. It is for this reason that "a likely impossibility is always preferable to an unconvincing possibility."[93] The analysis might be illustrated from the various arts. The man who sits for his portrait assumes a posture which is determined by the laws of gravitation, by the anatomy of the human body, and by the peculiarities of his habits; the painter must justify the line he chooses not in terms of physics or anatomy, but in terms of the composition which appears in the colors and lines on his canvas. A man performs an action as a consequence of his character, his heritage, his fate, or his past actions; the poet represents that action as necessary in his medium, which is words, by developing the man's character, by expressing his thoughts and those of men about him, by narrating incidents. For Aristotle, consequently, imitation may be said to be, in the fine arts, the presentation of an aspect of things in a matter other than its natural matter, rendered inevitable by reasons other than its natural reasons; in the useful arts it is the realization of a function in another matter or under other circumstances than those which are natural. It is no contradiction, consequently, that the artist should imitate natural things, and that he should none the less imitate them "either as they were or are, or as they are said or thought to be or to have been, or as they ought to be."[94] Art imitates nature; the form joined to matter in the physical world is the same form that is expressed in the matter of the art. Art does not abstract universal forms as science does, but imitates the forms of individual things. Yet, just as the form of man differs from man to man, so the actions of the historical Orestes differ from the actions presented as probable or necessary for Orestes in the plot of a play; and if Orestes had no historical counterpart, the play would still, in this sense of imitation, be an imitation of the actions of men.

92. *Poetics* 2. 1448[a]1.

93. *Ibid.* 24. 1460[a]26–27.   94. *Ibid.* 25. 1460[b]7–11.

Whereas the word "imitation" and related words appear in almost every dialogue of Plato, the incidence of the term "imitation" in Aristotle is limited, except for references to poetic problems in other works, almost entirely to the *Poetics*. It is the imitative element in his work that makes the poet a poet.[95] The various arts and the various kinds of poetry may be distinguished as modes of imitation; and therefore, approaching the problem in his accustomed scientific orderliness, Aristotle considers the arts according to the differences in the means, the objects, and the manners of their imitations. In the *Poetics* he has occasion to treat only of the arts which use rhythm, language, and harmony as their means of imitation, though color and form are mentioned as other means.[96] Flute-playing and lyre-playing use a combination of harmony and rhythm. The dance, with only rhythms and attitudes, can represent men's characters as well as what they do and suffer. The mime and the dialogue imitate by language alone without harmony. Other arts, including the dithyramb, the nome, tragedy, and comedy, combine all three means—rhythm, melody, and verse—differing from each other, however, in their manner of employment of these means. The object of imitation is the actions of men. With the differences of agents, the actions themselves are differentiated; and painters, musicians, and dancers can be distinguished and described according to the characters they represent. In this respect tragedy differs from comedy in that it makes its characters better rather than worse than the run of men. Given the same means and object of imitation, finally, two poems may differ in manner of imitation. One poet may speak at one moment in his own person, at another in the person of his characters, as Homer did; another poet may speak in a single person without change throughout; or in the third place the imitators may represent the whole story dramatically, as though they were actually doing the things described.[97] The familiar classification of the kinds of poetry thus recurs much as it appeared in Plato, and on this most concrete of the levels of Plato's dialectic Aristotle seems to come closest to the statement of his master. Yet, important distinctions must be made between the two statements. For Plato it is a classification of three kinds of poetry: that which is effected by pure narrative, that which is effected by imitation, and the mixed kind which is effected by both. The preference is for the "unmixed imitator of the good."[98] Aristotle's distinction is among the manners of imitation in poems whose object and means of imitation are the same; to the other aspects of poetic imitation one further imitative characteristic is added. The question of

95. *Ibid.* 9. 1451ᵇ28–29; 1. 1447ᵇ15.

96. *Ibid.* 1. 1447ᵃ18 ff.

97. *Ibid.* 3. 1448ᵃ19–25.   98. *Rep.* iii. 397D.

preference among the various types is reserved for a later place,[99] and takes the form of the question whether the epic or the tragic is the higher form of imitation, the unmixed form not being considered. Moreover, the choice is made, not on moral but on literary grounds, because tragedy attains the poetic effect better than the epic. Aristotle is engaged in making literal distinctions, within the field of imitative art, of imitative devices and characteristics; dramatic imitation is one further imitative device to be added to other aspects of poetic imitation; his terms do not change their meanings, and his criteria are derived from a restricted field of discussion without reference beyond. Plato, on the other hand, applies the word "imitation" by means of the proportion of the real to appearance; relative to the narrative, drama is imitation; relative to the good, narrative too is imitation. No restricted field of literature with criteria peculiar to itself is indicated; rather, the proportions mark off at each application portions of the whole of things, real and apparent, and the criteria, envisaging the perfection of being which man might attain in that whole, are moral.

These primary distinctions serve a function in Aristotle's analysis comparable to that of the first principles of a science, although poetics is not a theoretic science and, like ethics and politics, it has no first principles in the sense in which theoretic sciences do. These, however, are fundamental distinctions derived from the subject matter with which the inquiry is concerned, and they supply the apparatus about which the analysis of poetry is organized. There are six "parts" of tragedy: three—plot, character, and thought—determined by the object of imitation; two—diction and melody—determined by the means of imitation; one—spectacle—determined by the manner of imitation. For Aristotle, as for Plato, the object of imitation is of primary importance; but that statement has a different significance in the context of Aristotle's analysis. In the dialogues it directed our attention from earthly things to eternal objects of imitation; in the *Poetics* it focuses discussion on the plot as an imitation of the actions of men. The plot is "the principle and, as it were, the soul of Trage-dy."[100] The poet must be more the poet of his plots than of his verses, for he is a poet by virtue of the imitative element in his work, and it is actions that he imitates.[101] Character and thought follow in importance in the order named, and of the remaining three parts of the tragedy only diction is given extended discussion. The conditions of art, therefore, by which its representations are rendered necessary or probable are derived primarily from the object of imitation, and the discussion of tragedy in the *Poetics* is concerned largely with plot and character. Even the unity so essential to the work of art is not unrelated to

99. *Poet.* 26. 1461^b26 ff.

100. *Ibid.* 6. 1450^a38–39.   101. *Ibid.* 9. 1451^b27–29.

its object of imitation, since "one imitation is always of one thing."[102] Some of the conditions of art, as derived from the actions of men, pertain to the nature of art in general; some, derived from actions of a given kind, are specific to the art forms that are devoted to that kind; some conditions derived from the means of imitation, similarly, are generic to several kinds of art, as the devices of rhythm are used in poetry, music, and the dance; some are specific to particular arts, tone to music, words to poetry, color to painting.

In Plato it proved to be impossible to consider art without regard to its moral and political effects. Aristotle is no less aware of those effects and their implications; but in virtue of his method, whatever pertains to the subject of a particular science is reserved for treatment in that science. Tragedy may be used as a political instrumentality in the state or it may reflect political doctrines or motivations in its speeches: in either case, it does not function as a work of art but is properly treated among the problems of politics and rhetoric. Art in the state and thought in the drama are subjects which Aristotle apparently does not consider parts of the subject matter of the *Poetics*, for the first would need to be referred to the principles of political science, and the second, since thought is "the power of saying whatever is appropriate to the occasion,"[103] falls within the scope of rhetoric and is referred to the Art of Rhetoric for treatment. Aristotle adds dryly that the older poets make their characters discourse like statesmen, and the moderns like rhetoricians. In the *Politics*[104] he treats the arts as instruments of teaching virtue and forming character. His attention centers almost entirely on music in the portion of the discussion of education which survives in that book. Rhythm and melody supply likenesses (ὁμοίωμα) of anger, gentleness, courage, temperance, and other qualities of character as well as their contraries; and the feelings of pleasure and pain at mere representations are not far removed from the same feelings about realities. The objects of senses like taste or touch furnish no likenesses to the virtues. There are figures in visible objects which do have that characteristic, but only to a small degree; and all people do not share in the feeling they occasion, for they are signs (σημεῖον) rather than likenesses of moral habits, indications which the body gives of states of feeling. The connection of painting or sculpture with morals is therefore slight. But even in simple melodies there are imitations (μίμημα) of moral habits, and the same is true of rhythms. It is primarily music among the arts which has the power of forming character; and Aristotle urges, therefore, that it be introduced into the education of the young.

102. *Ibid.* 8. 1451ᵃ30–35.

103. *Ibid.* 6. 1450ᵇ4–8; cf. 19. 1456ᵃ34–36.

104. *Politics* viii. 5. 1339ᵇ42–1340ᵇ13.

If analogies are to be drawn between Plato's views on imitation and those of Aristotle and if the latter is to be assimilated to his master, as having effected either a distortion and retrogression or an advance and specification of the doctrines he learned in the Academy, the most fertile grounds for such comparison are found in the brief section in the *Politics*, for art is there discussed as a political force and politics is an architectonic science, limited by its practical character to the use of the analogical method. But even in the *Politics* the word and the method of its use falls short of the scope which it has in Plato's dialectic. Art, moreover, is there considered not as art but as a political device. To cite what is said concerning art in the *Politics* in refutation or in expansion of what is said on the same subject in the *Poetics*, without recognizing that the one is a political utterance, the other an aesthetic utterance, would be an error comparable to looking for evolution or refutation between the statements of the *Republic* and the *Laws*, without recognizing that the one has reference to a perfect state, the other to a state possible to men as they are. In the Aristotelian approach the aspects of things are distinguished from each other and treated independently; the major branches of the sciences are separated, and within each branch the major subdivisions; and since imitation is the differentia of art, and since the fine arts are further differentiated from the useful arts by their ends and their means, and since finally the fine arts are distinguished from each other by their respective means and the objects appropriate to those means, it follows not only that there is a branch of knowledge whose subject matter is the products of the arts, but also that each of the arts may be the subject properly for like investigation. The *Poetics* is such an examination of poetry in itself, not in its relation to education, morals, statesmanship, nature, or being. In Plato's analysis, on the other hand, poetry cannot be considered in isolation; it is one of the numerous strands of man's life and takes its importance and meaning from those strands; it bears analogies to all the other arts, to the phenomena of nature and the actions of the gods; distinctions in art parallel those of education, of science, of moral, social, and political life; in the dialectical examination of all these activities the same contraries are employed, the one and the many, being and becoming, the true and the false, knowledge and belief, the fair and the foul, and all of them involve imitation. Art is, therefore, never dissociated in the Platonic approach from the full context of life; and it is always subject to moral, political, educational, and scientific criticism, for there can be no other, no purely aesthetic, criticism of art.

The Platonic and the Aristotelian approaches to the consideration of art differ, therefore, not in the manner of two doctrines which contradict each other, but rather in the manner of two approaches to a subject which are mutually incommensurable. Even more, the differences of the two approaches and the peculiarities of the two methods indicate in themselves no superiority of the one over the other, nor are problems soluble by the one which are impervious to the analysis of the other. Although there is no place for distinct sciences, independent of each other, in Plato, there are none the less abundant devices by which to make distinctions; and likewise, although all problems are assigned to their proper scientific context in Aristotle and although each science has its proper domain, its proper scope, and frequently methodological devices peculiar to itself, knowledge is not hopelessly atomized, for there are devices by which to consider phenomena in the context of all the varieties of problems.

There are complementary dangers, moreover, in cross-references from one work of either of these philosophers to another. Plato never employs one dialectical strand alone: in the *Republic* and the *Laws* poetry is treated by means of analogies drawn successively from the numerous strands of political life; in the *Phaedrus* the analogies bind it to the other arts, particularly to the art of rhetoric; in the *Ion* it appears in connection with the divine gift of inspiration. Moreover, even between the *Republic* and the *Laws* the analogies have shifted—as indeed they shift from book to book within each of those works—for the context of one is the idea of a perfect state, the other the construction of a state short of perfection with specific social, economic, and political characteristics. What is said about poetry in one of these contexts cannot be taken to be literally the same or literally contradictory to what is said of poetry in any of the other contexts. Just as the meaning in each dialogue is brought out by a dialectical development, so the translation from dialogue to dialogue requires similar dialectical modification. The doctrine of Plato concerning poetry cannot be built up by collecting quotations in which the word "poetry" appears throughout his works; the result of such an enterprise indeed is no doctrine whatever but, as the history of criticism has abundantly illustrated, a collection of inconsistent statements. Contrariwise, whereas in Plato's treatment the concepts of art and imitation are generalized or particularized to various dialectical contexts, in Aristotle the treatment of art and imitation, considered in their own right and in their proper science, may be supplemented by a consideration of them as they impinge on the problems of other sciences, on grammar, rhetoric, logic, ethics, politics, physics, psychology, or metaphysics. But to collect from the works concerned with the various sciences quotations in which the words "imitation" or "poetry" or "art" appear, with the intention to place them one after the other and so find in them a coherent doctrine, results in an assemblage of statements as confused as the corresponding collections from the dialogues of Plato. As the statements of Plato require dialectical approximation to each other, the statements of Aristotle require the intrusion of

proper principles from the appropriate sciences to permit transition from one
to the other.

III

In Aristotle the term "imitation" is given a literal meaning and is limited in
application to works of human art; in Plato the meaning is developed and contracted in analogies so that the word cannot be said to have determined application but is sometimes more general, sometimes more restricted, than any
use in Aristotle. The word was used in still other senses by other writers in
antiquity, but considerations of method are not so important in the fashions
of their usage, and the systematic implications are not subtle. None of the
writers on literature employed the dialectical method of Plato in any but a
highly attenuated and faltering manner. Their definitions are literal like those
of Aristotle, but in their writings the term "imitation" does not appear in a
context of subject matters distributed in various scientific disciplines. Rather,
the meanings in which they use the term are derived for the most part from
one of the meanings which it assumed in Plato's dialogues, usually degraded
and rendered static or, what amounts to the same thing, in a meaning which
"imitation" might have had if Aristotle had used it in some other work than
the *Poetics*, as, for example, the *Rhetoric*.

A third variant to the meanings of Plato and Aristotle may therefore be said
to derive from the tradition of writers on rhetoric. In age, this view is at least
contemporary with the other two, and it has perhaps an even longer and certainly less distorted history since the age of Plato. "For the rest," Isocrates
says,[105] "he [the teacher] must in himself set such an example [παράδειγμα],
that the students who are molded [ἐκτυποῦν] by him and are able to imitate
[μιμήσασθαι] him will, from the outset, show in their speaking a degree of
grace and charm greater than that of others." Though Aristotle wrote a *Rhetoric*
(and, if Cicero and Quintilian are correct, justified himself in teaching rhetoric
by turning a scathing epigram against Isocrates), he confines his attention to
the analysis of the means of persuasion available to the orator and finds no
place for aphorisms concerning the imitation of past orators. He does say that
man is the most imitative of animals and learns at first by imitation;[106] he distinguishes repeatedly in his works between sciences, which are acquired by
learning; virtues, which are acquired by habituation; and arts, which are acquired by practice (ἄσκησις). It would be easier to find analogies in Plato for
Isocrates' use of the term; but for Plato it would have that meaning only as
applied to early education, for in maturity one would imitate, not the poet but
him who knows. Strictly even then imitation is of the virtues and the truth,

105. *Against the Sophists* 18.
106. *Poet.* 4. 1448[b]5–9.

not of the wise man. Yet imitation in this rhetorical sense, imitation of other artists, continued to be used in the writings of rhetoricians and orators. Cicero frequently recommends the imitation of good models, and Dionysius of Halicarnassus composed a treatise *On imitation*, preserved unfortunately only in fragments, which he tells us consisted of three parts, the first on imitation in general, the second on the choice of writers for imitation (including poets, philosophers, historians, and orators), the third on the proper methods of imitation. The last subject, which was never completed by Dionysius, is one to which Quintilian returns,[107] for to his mind there are three essentials in the formation of the ideal orator—power of speech, imitation, and diligence of writing.[108] Imitation alone, to be sure, is not enough,[109] for invention must precede imitation, and the greatest qualities of the orator, including invention, are beyond imitation.[110] One should consider, Quintilian says, first whom to imitate, second what to imitate in the authors chosen.[111] Imitation, he reminds us, should not be confined merely to words; one should consider also the appropriateness with which orators handle circumstances and persons, their judgment and their powers of arrangement, their concentration of all parts of the speech to the end of victory. Yet his own treatment of imitation is confined almost wholly to the question of style. According to Dionysius of Halicarnassus, imitation is "a copying of models with the help of certain principles," but it involves a kind of psychological elevation as well: it is an "activity of the soul inspired by the spectacle of the seemingly beautiful."[112] Longinus regards zealous imitation of the great historians and poets of the past as one of the roads which leads to sublimity.[113]

We, too, then, when we are working at some passage which demands sublimity of thought and expression, should do well to form in our hearts the question, "How perchance would Homer have said this, how would Plato or Demosthenes have made it sublime, or Thucydides in his history?" Emulation will bring those great characters before our eyes, and like pillars of fire they will lead our thoughts to the ideal standards of perfection. Still more will this be so, if we give our minds the further hint, "How would Homer or Demosthenes, had either been present, have listened to this passage of mine? How would it have affected them?"[114]

---

107. *Institutio oratoria* x. 2. 1–28.

108. *Ibid.* x. 1. 3. Cf. *Rhetorica ad Herennium* i. 2. 3 (ed. Marx), in which three aids to proficiency in oratory are enumerated: art, imitation, and exercise. "Art" is preception which gives a certain way and reason of speaking. "Imitation" is that by which we are impelled with diligent reason to be similar to some model in speaking. "Exercise" is assiduous use and custom in speaking. Cf. Cicero, *De oratore* ii. 22–23.

109. *Institutio oratoria* x. 2. 4.

110. *Ibid.* 2. 12.

111. *Ibid.* 2. 14. 27.

112. *On Imitation* A. iii (28).

113. *On the Sublime* 13.

114. *Ibid.* 14.

Imitation of past authors, however, though it may be useful as a device for training orators or as a touchstone for sublime passages of prose and poetry, will not supply an object of imitation or a subject matter for poetry. To be sure, as an English poet was later to suggest, to imitate Homer was to imitate nature, but nature has become too generalized to supply the function exercised in the object of imitation as conceived in Plato or Aristotle. In the Platonic usage, the object of imitation is consistently that which is, or being, through all the variations of the meaning of the word. For Aristotle the object of imitation in poetry is the actions of men, though some of the arts may imitate character and passion as well. According to Aristotle the plot, the soul of the tragedy, gives unity to the work. Plot is seldom discussed by the later writers; but instead character, thought, or even natural things become the chief object of imitation. According to Dionysius, poets and prose writers must keep their eye on each object and frame words to picture them or borrow from other writers words which imitate things. Nature, however, is the great originator and teacher in these matters and prompts us in the imitation of things by words, as when we speak of the bellowing of bulls,[115] or in the arrangement of words, as when Homer reflects the effort of Sisphyus rolling his rock uphill in the verses in which he describes it.[116] Plutarch marks this transition to the imitation of natural objects most explicitly. Imitation, he says, is of actions or works (ἔργον) or things (πρᾶγμα),[117] and apparently these terms are equivalent in his usage. One of the problems to concern him most is that imitations of ugly or even disgusting objects should be pleasing, a subject on which Aristotle touched for an opposite purpose in treating the origin of poetry, for he argued that imitation is natural to man since he finds even the imitation of disgusting objects pleasing.[118] The young should be taught to praise the genius and the art which imitates such subjects, according to Plutarch, but to censure the subjects and actions themselves, for the excellence of a thing and the excellence of its imitation are not the same. For him, as for Dionysius, the grunting of a hog, the noise of pulleys, the whistling of the wind, and the roaring of seas are the instances from which a discussion of imitation takes its natural beginning. But while poetry is based on imitation, in this sense, and employs embellishment and richness of diction suited to the actions and characters, Plutarch adds the warning, somewhat Aristotelian in language but Platonic in the development he gives it, that it does not give up the likeness of truth, since the charm of imitation is probability.[119] Imitation has the same significance for Longinus when he is not using the term

---

115. *On Literary Composition* 16.

116. *Ibid.* 22.

117. *Essay on Poetry* 3.

118. *How a Young Man Should Study Poetry* 3.   119. *Ibid.* 7.

to recommend the imitation of great writers: just as people who are really angry or frightened or worried or carried away by jealousy or some other feeling speak incoherently, "so, too, the best prose writers by use of inversions imitate nature and achieve the same effect. For art is only perfect when it looks like nature and nature succeeds only by concealing art about her person."[120] Demetrius cautions against crude imitation of the poets.[121] The dictum of Aristotle, that art imitates nature, has suffered a like degradation with the transformation of the word "imitation."

Although nature still supplies the object of imitation, imitation is no longer the central concept, either in the sense of Plato or in that of Aristotle, about which the analysis of poetry is organized. Occasionally, one of the later writers, like Plutarch, will take up the question of the truth of poetry and puzzle over the intentional and unintentional falsification of the poets; but although the men who followed Plato learned from him to worry concerning lies about the gods, the Platonic proportions of truth to falsity, of being to appearance, do not play upon poetry again in antiquity. Truth, if it is discussed, is usually measured in these later times by asking whether or not the event took place, and whether the object was such as it is represented. On the other hand, what later writers learned from Aristotle applicable to literature, they derived from the *Rhetoric* rather than from the *Poetics*, as indeed might be surmised, since it was a period which held rhetoric in high esteem and most of the writers in the tradition were professed rhetoricians. Yet that change marks them as significantly different from Aristotle, since to confuse rhetoric and poetics would in his system be a Platonizing error. He, himself, distinguished the two disciplines sharply: only two of the six "parts" of tragedy—thought and diction—are properly treated in rhetoric; and only one of them—thought—receives the same treatment in Aristotle's *Rhetoric* and *Poetics*. Aristotle's concern with action therefore and the emphasis he puts on plot, the soul of the composition, with its beginning, middle, and end, are not repeated in later writers.[122] With the gradual disappearance of plot, the Aristotelian scheme of the parts of the poem breaks down and the most prominent of his critical principles become irrelevant. Principles and criteria must be supplied from the tradition of rhetoric, and imitation moves to a place of comparative unimportance in the analysis of poetry. Rhetoric, according to Aristotle, is the faculty by which in any subject we are able to win belief in the hearer. That belief is produced by means of invention, disposing of three means: the character and behavior of

---

120. *On the Sublime* 22.   121. *On Style* ii. 112.

122. Horace's brief treatment of plot, which includes the enjoinder that the middle harmonize with beginning and end, is typical of the few remnants of the treatment of that aspect of the poem (see *Art of Poetry* ll. 119–52).

the speaker, the character and passions of the hearer, and the proofs which are alleged in the words of the speaker. If some other effect in the hearer is substituted for belief, as Longinus substituted ecstasy, such an analysis might be suited to any branch of literature. The time might even come when invention might take the place of imitation, as indeed Quintilian had recognized its greater importance while protesting it was not a subject of art. The "parts" with which the analysis deals gravitate about thought and diction, or some variant of the elements of rhetoric. According to Dionysius, two things require attention in all forms of composition: ideas and words, subject matter and expression.[123] According to Longinus, there are five sources of the sublime: power of thought and emotion, which proceed from natural genius; and figures, diction, and arrangement, which proceed from art.[124] According to Demetrius, each of the four kinds of style consists of thought, diction, and arrangement.[125]

IV

The consequences of these changes for the analysis of literature would be too long to enumerate. Whereas Plato considered poetry in the context of the total activity of man or in the context of the eternal ideas, poetry came to be considered more and more in isolation. On the other hand, the Aristotelian mode of analysis was not followed, for the work of art was not considered, in itself, objectively. Rather, it was the poets who were the subject of consideration in an environment of other poets whom they imitated and of audiences whom they pleased. The Hellenistic and Roman literary critic was sometimes a Platonist whose universe was limited to the literary world, sometimes an Aristotelian engaged in the rhetoric of poetry and prose. Since the plot had lost the central importance it had for Aristotle, imitation is of persons, actions, and things. Where Plato could be led by his dialectic to moral indignation at the imitation of the roll of thunder, the squeak of pulleys, the bleat of sheep,[126] or Aristotle could limit imitation to the actions of men and invoke aesthetic principles for the comparative judgment of kinds of poetry differentiated by the characters of the men imitated, later critics found occasion only to insist on the difference between the imitation and the object imitated and to separate admiration of the technique by which the one was produced from approbation of the other. Moreover, as criticism ceases to turn largely on action and the plot, the work of art as a whole passes out of the purview of the critic and attention is concentrated on analyzing the characteristics and determining the effectiveness of individual passages.

123. *On Literary Composition* 1.   125. *On Style* ii. 38, etc.

124. *On the Sublime* 8. 1.   126. *Rep.* iii. 397A–B.

The kinds of poetry, moreover, which Aristotle was careful to distinguish in terms of the means and object of imitation, are treated without distinction; and citations are drawn not only from poets of different kinds but from historians, orators, and philosophers as well. But most important of such differences, containing them as consequence, is the fact that after Plato and Aristotle, who judged literature primarily by reference to its object of imitation, there grew up a generation of critics, of numerous and long-lived progeny, who judged literature by considering its effect on the audience. Not that Plato or Aristotle was averse to considering the pleasure afforded by an object of art, but they subordinated such consideration to that of the object of imitation; and while the good work of art will be pleasurable to the mind prepared to understand it, pleasure as such, without consideration of person and object, would furnish no criterion for art. But the natural center of gravity in rhetoric is the audience, and the fourth variation of the meaning of imitation is marked by the disappearance of the term from its central place in criticism. For while a poet may imitate that which is, or the actions of men, or other poets, he pleases rather than imitates audiences. "It is not enough for poems to have beauty," Horace says,[127] "they must also be pleasing and lead the listener's soul whither they will. . . . If the speaker's words are inconsistent with his fortunes, a Roman audience, high and low will roar with laughter." The nature and origin of poetry is to please the mind.[128] "Poets desire either so improve or to please, or to unite the agreeable with the profitable. . . . The centuries of the elders reject plays without a moral; the haughty knights dislike dull poems."[129] Horace's criticism is directed in the main to instruct the poet how to keep his audience in their seats until the end, how to induce cheers and applause, how to please a Roman audience, and, by the same token, how to please all audiences and win immortality. But although imitation does not supply or illuminate these ends, it does help further them. The well-informed imitator is advised to take his models from life and custom and to derive from them a language faithful to life.[130] He should also study the Greek models;[131] the Socratic dialogues will supply matter, and words will follow quickly, once the matter is seen;[132] but the imitator is cautioned not to translate too literally lest his own style suffer.[133]

---

127. *Art of Poetry*, ll. 99–112.

128. *Ibid.*, l. 377.

129. *Ibid.* ll. 333–43. Cf. Plutarch, *How a Young Man Should Study Poetry* 1, 2, 3, 7, and 14 for another view in which pleasure and improvement vie; but for a contrasting view of the place of audience and pleasure in the judgment of art see Plato's *Laws* ii. 658A–659C and 668A–669B, or *Gorgias* 501D–502D.

130. *Art of Poetry* ll. 317–18.   131. *Ibid.* ll. 268–69.   132. *Ibid.* ll. 310–11.

133. *Ibid.* ll. 133–35; cf. his disdain for the servile herd of imitators and his statement of the fashion in which he followed Archilochus, *numeros animosque secutus Archilochi, non*

Imitation has been reduced to the imitation of other artists or to reflecting actual conditions or customs.

A fifth meaning for the term "imitation" of the same quixotic sort, that is to say, a meaning which, like the proportion of poet to audience, made the term unnecessary or impossible, remains to be indicated. Words may imitate thoughts, as Horace suggests; and if the analysis of poetry in terms of pleasure is an outgrowth of the rhetorical tradition, the analysis of poetry in terms of thought and diction is in a sense the lessened form which the Aristotelian poetic analysis took for later ages. Writers like Dionysius of Halicarnassus and Demetrius, when they limit themselves to relevant questions of words and their arrangements in relation to the thoughts they express, have in common with Aristotle the ideal of discussing the work of art in its own terms without reference to the universe, to authors, or to audience. But the object of imitation has been cut down to thought, and the subtlety of analysis is expended almost entirely on diction. Moreover, literature is considered in short passages, rather than whole works, and prose and poetry are treated together more or less indiscriminately. The problem of literature turns on propriety and the need to find distinguished thoughts and distinguished expressions and to clothe thoughts in appropriate words. These are problems which the term "imitation" was apparently not suited to embrace, and the writers in that tradition continued to speak only of the imitation of poets by poets and of things by words.[134]

Notwithstanding our changed attitude toward imitation, it requires no great alteration of terminology to recognize the tendencies of modern criticism in some of these five ancient attitudes, and there is much that is perhaps clearer in their example which might be considered with profit in the discussion of the nature of literature or the canons, tenets, or principles of criticism. Literature may be considered as a part of the social structure, and we have critics who engage in such social criticism today. It may be considered in terms purely of style, or in terms of the great writers and great works of the past, or in terms of the character and demands of audiences of the present and of posterity. It seems apparent that each of these approaches and each of their variants is distinct from the others. If its full intention is stated clearly, it is difficult to understand how one of them could be consituted the contradiction of the other, except in the sense

---

res et agentia verba Lycamben, and tempered the versification of Archilochus with Sappho and Alcaeus; the imitation was limited to measures and structure of verse and did not extend to subjects or arrangement (*Ep.* i. 19. 19–29).

134. Cf. nn. 112, 115, 116, 121, above. Demetrius returns frequently to the problem of onomatopoeia and the imitation of actions by words. Cf. *On Style* ii. 72. 94; iii. 176; iv. 221. Sometimes, however, he uses imitation in the sense of dramatic imitation in connection with the style of dialogues (*ibid.* iv. 226, 298).

that a given critic might prefer one to all the rest. Much that passes for differences of taste in literature consists in reality of differences of taste in criticism, of differences in the preferred approach to literature. A critic is seldom satisfied to make his own approach without having shut off all other roads. Such jealousy of one's own truth is not difficult to explain, for what I say, when I consider it my critical function to tell my experiences before works of art, may be expressed in words related to those you will use when you tell of art's social function; and those words will probably be used as in contradiction. What is needed is more than a definition of terms, for the terms used in definitions also vary in the context of the larger method and system in which criticism functions; ultimately contradictions and confusions are resolved by the exploration of the full philosophic implications of the attitude which the critic finds himself justified in assuming. It is not, perhaps, excessive to remark that the philosophic sweep in recent criticism has not been broad, nor has the interplay of implication been subtle. There have been few writers in the whole history of thought able to manipulate the Platonic dialectic; and of them, few have turned their attention to literature. There are few studies of literature in terms of its medium, the forms which are suited for expression in that medium, and the manner of such expression. It is hardly profitable or pertinent to regret that there have been few Platos and few Aristotles; but it is appropriate to remark on the misfortune, since there are so few, that we should neglect so signally to profit by their examples of method, but should be content in our studies and histories to find imperfections which they seem to possess only when their sentences are read without the logical and dialectical devices they supply to guide interpretation.

ARISTOTLE'S CONCEPTION OF LANGUAGE
AND THE ARTS OF LANGUAGE[1]

RICHARD McKEON

LANGUAGE, as a function of man, is a frequent subject of inquiry in the course of Aristotle's scientific investigations; for language not only has a natural basis in man's bodily organs and psychological powers but is, in turn, one of the natural bases of the virtues and of social and political relations, and it constitutes the natural means of imitation in the art of literature and the matter of which literary works are formed. In addition to such inquiries into the foundations of language in human organism, moral agent, and aesthetic object, Aristotle turns his attention to questions concerning the operations of language, for it can be put to various uses, and it can in any of them contravene as well as accomplish the purpose to which it is directed. Finally, on the background of these considerations of language as natural phenomenon and as rational instrument, Aristotle analyzes the arts of language in terms of symbolic properties and linguistic structures. Logic, rhetoric, and poetic are none of them purely "verbal arts" in Aristotle's philosophy: they are based on the natural properties of words, which are determined by physiological organs and physical medium, as well as on the conventional meanings which are determined by human reason and desire; they take into account the purposes for which men use language as reflected in the intentions of the speaker, the susceptibilities of the audience addressed, and the nature of the communications for which it serves as medium; and they treat, finally, of discourse in its various forms and relative to its proper parts. Language, as natural phenomenon, is part of the subject matter of the sciences—theoretic, practical, and productive. Language, as conventional medium adequate to, or at variance with, the purposes for which man uses it, is both an instrument and a problem in the formation of these sciences and in the development and acquisition of knowledge, virtues, and arts. Language, as artificial composition and symbolic structure, is the end of the numerous arts which are employed in scientific demonstrations, practical communications and regulations, and aesthetic compositions.

Since language is part of the subject matter in practical and productive as well as theoretic scientific investigations, the discussion of language and even the meanings of the basic terms of that discussion extend far beyond purely material

1. Reprinted from *Classical Philology*, October, 1946, and January, 1947.

or verbal problems. The physical sounds which man uses to convey meanings and the physiological organs by which the sounds are produced are objects of physical and biological inquiry. Aristotle was convinced, however, that meaning was no less an integral part of language than the sounds which bear the meaning and that language depends no less on the rational powers of man by which meanings are constructed than on the physiological organs by which sounds are formed. Language is therefore studied in psychology, for not only is the use of discourse one of the marks which differentiate the rational from the sensitive powers of the soul, but a "discourse of the mind" may be differentiated from the "outer discourse" expressed in words. Language is also part of the subject matter in the practical sciences, but in the communications of politics language is inseparable from considerations of the expedient and the inexpedient, the just and the unjust; and the "discourse" of ethics determines the guiding principles of actions. The word λόγος, since it signifies both linguistic and rational processes, may be extended in one direction to the forms which are signified in things and in another direction to the regulative principles which guide actions in men. Latin philosophers, in antiquity and the Middle Ages, tried to convey the interplay of linguistic and rational in the meanings of λόγος by a play on the words *ratio* and *oratio*,[2] and Stoics as well as Christians found the basis for the order of nature in the Λόγος or the Word. Modern scholars have recognized, without much dispute, the theoretic dimensions of the term which lead to its translation by words as various as "speech," "statement," "definition," "argument," "reasoning," and "reason"; but its practical extensions in ethics involve regulative aspects, and λόγος has seemed to some scholars to have lost in that context the significance of both "speech" and "reason" and to have come to mean "rule," "formula," "ratio," "rational principle," and "reasoning."[3] Language is, finally, a subject matter in the pro-

2. Cicero conceived logic or dialectic to consist *in ratione et in disserendo* or, more simply, as *disserendi ratio;* it consisted of two arts which covered the whole field of *ratio et oratio*—an art of discovery and an art of statement or judgment (cf. *De finibus* iv. 4. 8). Men are distinguished from other animals by the possession of reason and speech (*De officiis* i. 4. 11–12). Medieval writers learned from Isidore of Seville to associate speech and reason on Greek authority; cf. *Etymologiae* ii. 24. 7: "Λόγος enim apud Graecos et sermonem significat et rationem." Cf. also below, p. 279.

3. In his article, "On the Meaning of Λόγος in Certain Passages in Aristotle's *Nicomachean Ethics*" (*CR*, XXVII [1913], 113–17), J. Cook Wilson undertook to show from a survey of a large number of important passages that the word means neither "definition" nor "rule" but always "Reason" in Aristotle's use of it in ethics. "The conclusion then is that in all the passages reviewed λόγος means Reason in one of three senses; either (1) reason as the faculty of reason, or principle of reason in the soul, or (2) reason as reasoning, or (3) reason as what is reasonable, in the sense of the deliverance of reason—reason as ordaining the moral law, reasoning as inculcating it, or the moral law itself as a form of reason" (p. 117). The use of "Reason" to translate λόγος seems to J. L. Stocks to involve the term in such monstrous ambiguity as to suggest the desirability of eliminating it, if Wilson's thesis is well grounded, from our philosophical vocabulary. He argues ("On the Aristotelian Use of

ductive sciences, both in the sense that words and expression are the matter from which the concrete compositions of poetry, literature, and all varieties of communication and expression are formed and in the sense that the form in each variety of composition is found in the analysis of its proper λόγος or argument.

Language has many uses to which it has been put by man and many purposes which it may serve, and, although these uses have as natural basis the properties and effects of language, its meanings are determined by habit and convention. The criteria which are pertinent to the judgment of statements intended to serve the various purposes of linguistic use are themselves various, and, although any given statement may happen, in its various contexts, to achieve several purposes, it is possible to separate those purposes and indicate the considerations pertinent to judging their achievement. In the theoretic use of language the criteria are to be found in adequacy to the expression of a subject matter; in the practical use of language the criteria are to be found in the effect of language or reason in the moral control of desires and convictions, while the related criteria of rhetoric are in appropriateness to the effect intended to be produced in an audience or a particular character; in the poetic use of language the criteria are to be found in the qualities achieved in the work of art. A scientific composition may be considered in terms of its effect on an audience or in terms of its intrinsic beauty; or a poem may be treated in terms of its truth, its popularity, and its social effectiveness; but even such shifts of consideration depend on the possibility of differentiating those properties of a statement which make it theoretically significant, practically effective, and poetically beautiful.

The use of symbols as instruments of scientific inquiry and proof depends both on the nature of things, which the symbols must express translucently without distortion due to the peculiarities of the symbols or the passions or convictions of minds, and also on the properties of symbols by which such expres-

---

Λόγος: A Reply," *CQ*, VIII [1914], 9–12) that λόγος means the end of action, that is, the plan, ideal, or intention, or else the form of action, that is, its principle or soul, but never reason. Aristotle's use of λόγος in psychology, on the other hand, seems to Stocks evidence that Aristotle was saturated with Platonism: it is a matter of indifference whether the term be translated "form" or "ratio," provided form be understood to be separated or isolated from matter ("Λόγος and μεσότης in the *De anima*," *JP*, XXXIII [1914], 182–94). In 1915, when the Oxford translations of the *Great Morals*, the *Eudemian Ethics*, and *On Virtues and Vices* were published, W. D. Ross, general editor of the Oxford translation, prefixed to them a brief Preface in which he chided the translators for rendering λόγος, "in the traditional way, as 'reason.' Personally," he goes on, "I doubt whether this rendering is ever required, but the final choice in such a question rests with the translators." Ten years later he called attention, in another brief Preface set before his own translation of the *Nicomachean Ethics*, to the difficulty of translating terms like λόγος and ἀρχή "which are just crystallizing into technical meanings." He translated λόγος by expressions like "rational principle," "rational ground," "reasoning," "argument," "rule," "rule of life."

sion is possible. The end of scientific inquiry is to make the statement of principles and conclusions approximate accurately the nature and divisions of things: when this is done, according to Aristotle, "argument" (λόγος) and "form" (εἶδος) become equivalent expressions.[4] The achievement of truth, then, depends not only on knowledge of the form in things but also on awareness of the properties of language which make it possible to reproduce the form in argument: the characteristics of individual words and terms, their combinations in assertion and proposition, and the rules for their use as end and middle terms in argument and inference. This identity of form and statement can be achieved, not by measuring particular propositions against actual circumstances which they are meant to designate, but by discovering essential connections and causal laws and by relating particular propositions to the universal propositions which state such laws. The danger of error and fallacy in the search for scientific proofs arises from the obvious fact that the principles of an argument are not always statements adequately based on the nature of things; sometimes they are the expression of widely received opinion and sometimes distortions of received opinion, and sometimes, when the principles are true expressions of opinion, the conclusions only seem to follow from them as verbally plausible consequences. The use of language as a logical instrument can be differentiated into demonstrative, dialectical, and sophistical modes, each with its appropriate problems and canons. The analytic of demonstration or the use of language in the processes of scientific inquiry and proof is therefore concerned with the adequation of language to the nature of the classes of things appropriate to the various sciences. The topical analysis of statements and arguments or the use of language in the processes of dialectical question and answer is directed to clarify the implications of opinions more or less commonly held and to discover new propositions and principles, and it is not confined to a definite class of subjects but is universal. Sophistic differs from dialectic because of the moral intention of the sophist and the consequent differences of his use of language rather than because of a difference of the faculty or art, which he shares with the dialectician, of manipulating words and opinions.

The use of symbols as instruments of practical action depends on expressing the rule of rationality in individual action and on communication and control in communal action. Moral action depends on the rule of right reason (ὀρθὸς λόγος), and right reason differs from scientific truth, since it is concerned with the purposes, circumstances, and ends for which the prudent man may formulate the rule of what should be done, rather than with the natural causes or

4. *Metaphysics* iii. 2. 996^{b}5–8; viii. 4. 1044^{b}12–13; *On the Soul* i. 1. 403^{a}24–25, 403^{b}1–2; ii. 2. 414^{a}4–14.

universal propositions by which the scientist may formulate the law of what happens always or for the most part. Political action depends on communication, and community depends on the existence or formulation of right laws. Yet arguments may also be used as persuasion to any conviction or purpose without due concern with objective moral standard or political circumstance; and the rhetorical use of words is therefore distinct from ethics and dialectic although it has affinities with and likenesses to both, and it is sometimes wrongly confused with politics. Rhetoric is like dialectic and unlike the practical sciences of ethics and politics in not being limited to any one subject matter; but "rhetoric" is unlike "dialectic" in that it may refer not only to the knowledge of an art but also, like "sophistic," to the moral purpose with which the art is used. When principles are established by consulting opinions and probabilities rather than by direct inquiry into the nature of things, the proof is dialectical rather than demonstrative or scientific, and any argument may be applied dialectically to a variety of subject matters. When the consideration of justice and the good is based on commonplaces determined by the opinions of men, rather than on a consideration of moral habits or social institutions, the influence of discourse is rhetorical rather than moral or political, for arguments may be found by the use of rhetoric for and against any action or any end. The application of discourse to its subject matter is achieved differently in the theoretic and the practical sciences; and it is possible to shift from principles warranted by subject matter in either theory or practice to principles warranted by appeal to opinion—to a statement of probability dialectically grounded in the consensus of men or of scientists or to a statement of expediency, justice, or honor rhetorically grounded in the circumstances and the convictions and emotions of particular audiences and groups of men. In both dialectic and rhetoric, moreover, a further shift of argument is possible from the authority of widespread and well-grounded opinion to the distortion of opinion or the manipulation of consequences derived from opinion: this shift in the moral attitude toward the opinions and words used constitutes the difference between dialectic and sophistic and distinguishes one of the possible modes of rhetoric.

The use of symbols as matter and means of artistic production, finally, depends on the properties of symbols as such, their use symbolically for the presentation of thought and the representation of action, and the organization of symbols in the "argument" (λόγος) of a literary work. Language is the means of imitation in literature; it is the matter from which a poem is constructed; and the form of the poem, however much it may depend on the subject treated, is achieved by devices which may be recognized in the manner and organization of the expression. The characteristics of words as sounds, rhythms, and styles are the particular concern of this use of language; and, whereas they are also pertinent to achieving rhetorical ends, the prose of rhetoric is differentiated from poetic discourse by its closer approximation to ordinary speech. The characteristics of words as symbols, however, are no less important; and the poetic use of language is similar to the practical, since the element of thought in tragedy—to take the example on which Aristotle has stated his position most fully—may be defined as saying whatever can be said or what is appropriate to the occasion, and not only do the speeches in tragedy fall under the arts of politics and rhetoric, but language is the means of relating the thoughts of a character to his actions. Finally the action in a play, like the subject matter in a science, is presented by the argument (λόγος) or plot (μῦθος). The problems and faults, like the devices, of poetic composition are distinct from the similar difficulties encountered in the theoretic or practical uses of language. Impossibilities and improbabilities are faults in the poetic treatment of actions; but they may be justified if they serve the ends of poetry by making the action more astounding; and, in general, a convincing improbability is preferable, for the purposes of poetry, to an unconvincing possibility. Moreover, if the poet's description is not true in fact, it may be convincing as a representation of what the object ought to be; and if it is neither true nor a presentation of what ought to be, it may be defended if it is in accordance with opinion. Again, if what is said and done is not morally right, it may be defended as appropriate to persons and circumstances. Finally, other problems of aesthetic and literary criticism are found in the need of recognizing the strange words the poet may use, of understanding his metaphors, and, in general, of interpreting the language of his text, as well as in those problems of clarity, accuracy, and appropriateness for which analogues may be found in logic and rhetoric.

Once the nature of language and the variety of its uses have been recognized, it is possible to treat language in terms of the art of constructing "arguments." For any analysis of discourse, whatever the theory on which it proceeds, must ultimately treat the constitution of a body of words in terms of its structure and appropriate parts. Since Aristotle differentiates a great variety of "arguments," he seeks different structures and parts in the analysis of arguments, depending on the purpose for which the argument has been constructed. Demonstrative, dialectical, and sophistic "arguments" all have the ostensible purpose of formulating true or probable statements, and the criteria of their construction are in some reference to the facts. The parts of such arguments are univocal "terms" combined as nouns and verbs in "propositions," which are true or false, and "syllogisms," in which inference is made from the truth, necessity, or probability of certain propositions to that of others. In rhetorical "arguments" or speeches, it is possible to separate the consideration of arguments from that of style, that is, questions of what ought to be said from questions of how it ought to be said; but the criteria of both must be sought in reference to the audience, and only secondarily to the subject of discourse as determined by the audience. The parts of rhetorical arguments, like the parts of logical propositions, are nouns and verbs; but, since the connections in rhetorical argumentation are frequently verbal rather than inferential, conjunctions assume great importance; and, since metaphorical terms may be added to literal terms for purposes of persuasion, the construction of metaphors is of particular interest to prose writers. In the combination of statements into enthymemes and examples, proofs and apparent-proofs, and, finally, into speeches, the great stylistic virtues are clarity and appropriateness. Poetic "arguments" or plots are statements of action in narrative or dramatic form and are dependent, therefore, on the verbal expression of thought as representation of character. The criteria for the construction of the plot are to be found neither in the adequacy of the representation to what happens to be the case nor in the moral or practical responses of audiences, but in the structure which is achieved in the interplay of action, character, and thought pertinent to the poetic end. The parts of such "arguments," since they depend not only on connections demonstrated between facts or expressed between statements but also on connections perceived between the sounds and inflections of words, include the letter and the syllable as well as words—the conjunction, the article, the noun, and the verb— the cases of words and the speech (λόγος) itself; they go beyond the metaphorical expressions of rhetoric to the more unusual words proper to poetry, but not to prose, combined in more inclusive metaphorical statements, and the poem itself may be viewed as a speech resulting from conjunction of speeches.

Aristotle treated language, as subject matter, in the several sciences adapted to the investigation of the physical medium and organic production of sounds, the psychological bases of meanings, the practical use of discourse and communication, and the artistic production of literature. The variety of dimensions suggested in the scientific analysis of language as a physical, biological, psychological, moral, political, and poetic phenomenon indicates the variety of purposes to which language is put and the variety of sources from which criteria of its use may be sought for different purposes: from the subject matter of the discourse; the intentions, ideas, feelings, or purposes of the speaker; the susceptibilities or expectations of the hearer; the standards of excellence set by prudence for actions or discovered in the object of art. The nature and uses of language determine the three arts of language—logic, rhetoric, and poetic— which Aristotle, following the implications of his philosophy, organized as separate arts. In each he initiated manners of analysis which were long influential in the development of the art and meanings which were long attached to many of its fundamental technical terms. Aristotle did not, however, set up a philosophy of language or a science of symbols or signs. Significances are not natural, although both signs and what is signified may be; and there is no natural symbolic entity apart from the natural phenomena of language and its theoretic, practical, and productive uses. In the philosophy of Aristotle, sciences and arts are differentiated by their subject matters and purposes, and the several uses of language lead to the differentiation of logic, rhetoric, and poetic as the proper arts of language. The historical treatment of Aristotle's contributions to the linguistic and symbolic aspects of these arts has usually been conditioned by the supposition on the part of scholars and historians that there is a proper approach to language or a unified science of language—philology, grammar, psychology, logic, or semantics—and even in that history of reactions to Aristotle that goes by the name of "Aristotelianism" or "Aristotelian scholarship," Aristotle's treatment of language has been criticized both for separating language impossibly from its functions and for making it depend inseparably on commitments concerning things other than pure language. His logic has been censured as formal or verbal or even as restricted to the peculiarities of the Greek language and, not less frequently or more plausibly, as departing from linguistic or symbolic analyses in the interests of an irrelevant and stultifying anthropology, psychology, or metaphysics.

The criticisms of Aristotle's analyses of language depend on bringing together what Aristotle says in various contexts and sciences without consideration of the functional differentiations in the analyses. The treatments of many particular subjects, so assembled, seem confused and contradictory, and they have therefore been presented as evidence of stages of evolution to a more recent scientific truth or away from an earlier Platonic truth. Thus grammarians, when they examine the history of their subject, usually assign Aristotle an important place in the development of the "parts of speech"; but they are puzzled both because his enumeration of four parts (conjunction, article, noun, and verb) makes it difficult to explain how he could have observed so many parts of speech and no more and also because he expounded his views most extensively in the *Poetics*, as if he did not realize that the parts of speech belong to grammar or philology.[5] Yet a comparison of his enumerations of parts of speech—four in the *Poetics*, three (noun and verb, to which conjunction is added) in the *Rhetoric*, and two (noun and verb) in *On Interpretation*, to which

---

5. For a treatment of Aristotle's contributions to the theory of parts of speech cf. Viggo Brøndal, *Ordklasserne: Partes orationis* (Copenhagen, 1928), pp. 224–28. Ritter was so distressed by the treatment of "grammatical" subjects in chaps. 20–22 of the *Poetics* that he thought they could not be genuine; for a treatment of Ritter's arguments cf. H. Steinthal, *Geschichte der Sprachwissenschaft bei den Griechen und Römern* (Berlin, 1863), pp. 264–65. Cf. also I. Bywater, *Aristotle on the Art of Poetry* (Oxford, 1909), pp. 260–61; and J. Vahlen, *Beiträge zu Aristoteles' Poetik* (Berlin, 1914), pp. 125–26.

a third, the definite article, is added, but without great logical significance, in the *Prior Analytics*—suggests that the numbers depend on differences in the "parts" found in speech as it serves the ends of poetical construction, rhetorical persuasion, and logical demonstration and that none of these senses would be strictly pertinent to the analyses of formal grammar.

The problems of language have, however, been generalized in the history of philosophy to assume philosophic as well as philological universality. This may happen in either of two ways: the characteristics of language may be assimilated to some variety of things or processes, or the nature of things may be found to be basically linguistic or discursive. Discourse and symbols may be made into subjects to be treated in an independent science or in an architectonic science which takes the place of metaphysics in a system of speculation; or the investigation of metaphysical, psychological, and moral problems may disclose in the proper subject matters of those problems peculiarities of discourse dissociated from their original verbal connotations. These two tendencies have been prominent in the major philosophic controversies of the ages, and they have therefore, not unnaturally, contributed to the confusion of interpretations of Aristotle's method. The extension and analogizing of language transformed speculation concerning the nature of the Trinity and the implications of statement into disputes concerning the problem of the Logos in theology and the problem of the "universal" in logic during the Middle Ages; during the seventeenth and eighteenth centuries language was again an intrusive factor in the discussion of the development and nature of the human understanding, for Hobbes could conclude that understanding is nothing else than conception caused by speech and Berkeley that the proper objects of Vision are the Universal Language of Nature; and in modern discussions Behaviorists reduce thought to speech and Positivists undertake to resolve the fundamental problems of science by abandoning metaphysics and epistemology to construct a language of language.

It is tempting to suppose that highly elaborated doctrines of writers like Aristotle are treated adequately as stages toward distinctions and sciences which they did not express or describe and that their theories are lisping anticipations of later contradictory theories of the same matter. It is a supposition which has wide currency in the philosophic treatment of what other men say, and it has the authority of Aristotle's own practice in treating the scientific doctrines and philosophic theories of his predecessors. Unfortunately, it entails the disadvantages of distortion: the details of the doctrine must be ignored except as they fit another conception of science and other basic principles; and discrepancies between the doctrine analyzed and the criteria imposed must be interpreted as evidence of inconsistencies among the stages in the development of the author's position and as marks of the gradual crystallization of what later became technical terms and concepts. But if the philosophic use of history distorts earlier philosophies to purposes for which they were not conceived, the historical examination of philosophies may serve to reconstruct a past philosophy in its own terms, not as a stage to other philosophies, but as a rival to them and a source of theories which might be set in opposition to theories later current. Aristotle's analyses of language are worthy of such treatment precisely because his particular statements have in many cases been influential, but his theory has not been followed. He treated the phenomena of language in great detail, yet he did not construct a single science of language—a universal grammar, a symbolic logic, a semantics, or a physiological psychology. He did not construct a symbolic analysis based on formal rules of construction and operation without concern with actual content or historical usages, nor did he build a linguistic structure intended to duplicate the contextures of thought, concatenations of nervous system, or organizations of things. His theories are carefully drawn in opposition to these theories, which had currency later, and many of the confusions attributed to him result from reading his doctrines from the point of view of such theories, which are often modern forms of ancient positions which he thought to be erroneous. Aristotle's examination of the scientific basis of language serves both to prevent philosophic or semantic reductions of language to things, thoughts, or operations and also to discriminate among the arts those in which language is an instrument of knowledge and control relative to natural processes and things, those in which it is a medium of communication and understanding relative to men, and those in which it is a form of edification and pleasure relative to human products.

I. THE NATURE OF LANGUAGE: THE HUMAN ORGANISM AND ITS FUNCTIONS

The natural basis of "language" (λόγος) is "voice" or "articulate sound" (φωνή); and voice, in turn, is to be distinguished both from its articulation in "speech" (διάλεκτος) and from its natural basis in "sound" (ψόφος). The distinction is, in part, one of sounds and, in part, one of meanings. Voice is the matter of language, and man is peculiarly endowed among animals, since he alone makes use of voice in language.[6] Sounds are produced by anything which is capable of setting in motion a single mass of air which is continuous from the impinging body to the organ of hearing, and sounds are therefore studied in the psychological investigation of the sense of hearing,[7] but voice is a special kind of sound made by an animal, for it is a sound with meaning and is dependent, therefore, on the possession of special organs and on their operation, which is

6. *On the Generation of Animals* v. 7. 786^{b}19–22.

7. *On the Soul* ii. 8. 420^{a}3–19.

a function of the soul.[8] Teeth, lips, and tongue have, among other purposes, a function in the production of articulate sounds.[9] Language consists, on the material side, of the combination of sounds called "letters" (γράμματα) produced in voice by lips, teeth, tongue, and other organs; and, although other animals than man can utter indivisible sounds and have voices, man, and after man some birds, are peculiarly equipped to utter letters. The study of the mechanisms for the production of voice is part of biology; but the differences of letters, such as the distinctions between vowel, semi-vowel, and mute, as well as the nature and extent of these differences in syllabic combinations, are the subject of inquiry in the science of "metrics."[10] Inanimate things as well as some animals—insects, mollusks, crustaceans, fishes—produce sounds but no voice; and among animals which possess tongue and lungs, the voice varies with the species: oviparous quadrupeds have feeble voices; small birds are more vocal than the larger birds; viviparous quadrupeds utter vocal sounds of different kinds, but have no power of converse.[11] Voice is essential to speech, but not all animals who have voices have the power of speech; and, although the use of voice by animals and birds might be called a kind of speech, speech in a strict and full sense is peculiar to man.[12] Voice and speech differ, moreover, according to locality. Whereas voice strictly, as characterized by pitch and the kinds of sounds produced, is identical in the animals of the same species, that variety of articulated voice which might be called their "speech" differs according to differences in locality both among animals possessed of similar voices and even among animals of the same species. Men, as members of the same species, possess the same voice or range of vocal sounds, and they agree likewise in the possession of language or the use of vocal sounds to convey significances; yet they differ from each other in the multiplicity of their speeches and forms of language.[13]

"Voice" (φωνή), as it has been seen to be a kind of movement of the air or a kind of sound produced by an animal, may finally, since imagination as well as sound is required in voice, be defined as a kind of sound with meaning or a kind of significant *sound* (σημαντικός τις ψόφος).[14] The minimum unit of significance is therefore voice considered as individual word, possessed of

8. *Ibid.* 420^{b}4–421^{a}6.

9. *On the Parts of Animals* ii. 16–17. 659^{b}27—660^{b}11 and iii. 1. 661^{a}34–^{b}17; *Gen. Anim.* v. 8. 788^{b}3–9; *History of Animals* ii. 12. 504^{b}1–3; cf. *Problems* x. 39. 895^{a}7–14; xi. 57. 905^{a}30–34.

10. *Parts Anim.* ii. 16. 660^{a}2–8; and *Poetics* 20. 1456^{b}20–1457^{a}30.

11. *Hist. Anim.* iv. 9. 535^{a}26–536^{a}32.

12. *Ibid.* 536^{a}20–^{b}29; cf. also *Prob.* xi. 55. 905^{a}20–23.

13. *Hist. Anim.* iv. 9. 536^{b}8–20; cf. also *Prob.* x. 39. 895^{a}7–14 and xi. 1. 898^{b}30–899^{a}3.

14. *On the Soul* ii. 8. 420^{b}5–421^{a}5.

meaning itself but composed of parts which are meaningless, and it makes no assertion except in combination with other words, actual or understood. "Assertion" (λόγος)—phrase, sentence, or proposition—is therefore the minimum unit of significance in another sense, for the assertion relates one word to another, and an assertion may be considered true or false. The assertion (λόγος) is defined, therefore, as composite voice with meaning or significant composite *voice* (φωνὴ συνθετὴ σημαντική), some parts of which may have meaning by themselves, as the noun and the verb which are united in a single assertion are themselves composite significant *sounds;* but some parts of the assertion have no independent meaning.[15] The investigation of language is not exhausted, therefore, in the examination of sounds and marks or the rules for their combination; for the examination of meanings and their structures discloses the rationale of the rules for the combinations of words. The characteristics of language include those meanings which are set forth in arguments intended to express the nature of things, and rules for the scientific use of language reflect in this use a natural "discourse of the mind." Meanings are also disclosed in actions which show the influence of a "rational principle," and the reflections of the wise man and the communications of men are part, in this use, of a social discourse. Meanings depend, finally, on the arresting character and freshness of words and metaphors; and the artist imitates and constructs, in this use, thoughts, characters, and actions by devices of style and artificial discourse. The scientific, the practical, and the artistic uses of language all depend on characteristic significances which attach to language as much as on the properties of voice by which those significances are expressed and conveyed. The fact that Aristotle finds an extension beyond purely verbal materials and combinations in each of these three uses of language has proved puzzling to critics who are convinced that the "mature" Aristotle should have an "empirical" or nominalistic theory of language or that all his statements about language should form part of a single linguistic science. Moreover, in addition to these three uses, which find some anchorage for language in the nature of things, there are also the devices of dialectic, rhetoric, and sophistic, which depend on traits of language, tenets of opinion, and probabilities of occurrence and which advance, influence, and endanger science, action, and art.

In the scientific use of language, when propositions and arguments are properly constructed, they are symbolic of ideas in the mind; and those ideas flow in a discourse comparable to the verbal discourse in which they are expressed. When the purpose of discourse is to record and communicate knowledge, words express thoughts which image things, and knowledge is set forth in proofs whose principles are tested in things. Both thought and words are

15. *On Interpretation* 2. 16ᵃ19–20; cf. also *Poet.* 20. 1456ᵇ20–1457ᵃ30.

constituted into kinds of discourse. Yet it is possible to treat the two separately; and Aristotle occasionally notes, when he is using language as an example or refuting fallacious arguments, that the discourse which is said to be a discrete quantity is the discourse (λόγος) expressed in sound, or that those who argue for the sake of argument can be convinced only by refuting the argument (λόγος) as expressed in voice and words.[16] On the other hand, he argues, when it is a question of scientific proof, that demonstration is addressed not to the verbal discourse but to the discourse (λόγος) within the soul. No syllogism is addressed to the outer discourse, since we can always raise verbal objections to anything expressed in words, but we cannot always object to the inner discourse.[17] That inner discourse consists of mental experiences or, as Aristotle likes to put it, of what the soul undergoes, the passions of the soul. The discourse expressed in sound and voice is symbolic of these passions, much as written discourse is symbolic of spoken. There is, however, an important difference between the two discourses. The passions of the soul, which are symbolized in verbal discourse, are natural occurrences, for the reactions of the organism to stimuli in sensation and emotion follow natural laws and they are therefore the same for all men, as are the things of which our experiences are the images; verbal discourse, on the other hand, is significant only by convention, for no noun or verb has its meaning by nature.[18] The discourse of the soul not only is the source of the meanings attached to the articulations of verbal sounds but also gives verbal discourse, by supplying it with meanings, a kind of natural status in the things concerning which it may be true and in the minds on which it may be effective or informative. The discourse of the soul and verbal discourse are in a sense the same discourse, since words are symbolic directly only of thoughts, and therefore discourse—λόγος—may signify speech or thought, and there is no sharp line to separate the formula expressive of meaning from the meaning expressed in formula.

Language and thought are closely related, and linguistic meaning is not distinct from psychological meaning. Indeed, in some modern theories the closeness of the relation is taken to be an identity in the sense that there is no thought beyond verbal discourse and no meaning as such apart from the symbol and the thing signified. Aristotle, on the other hand, separated thought from perception because of consequences in thought of the operation of discourse. The perception of the proper objects of sense is always free from error, since an animal truly perceives what it perceives, and whether or not the object is as it is perceived is a further question dependent on judgment as well as on percep-

16. *Categories* 6. 4^{b}34–35; and *Metaph.* iv. 5. 1009^{a}18–22.

17. *Posterior Analytics* i. 10. 76^{b}24–27.

18. *Interpret.* 1. 16^{a}3–6 and 2. 16^{a}27–29.

tion. Thought, on the other hand, may be true or false, for thought is found only where there is discourse of reason (λόγος).[19] Imagination is shown to be distinct, in like fashion, from perception, discursive thought, and opinion, because, for one thing, opinion, unlike imagination, is accompanied by belief, belief by conviction, and conviction by discourse of reason, and there are animals which possess both sense and imagination without discourse of reason.[20] On the other hand, Aristotle queried the scientific basis of the division of the soul into parts or faculties, even by means of differences that take into account the rational or discursive powers of man; and he criticized Plato's division of the soul into the calculative (λογιστικόν), the passionate, and the desiderative, as well as the popular division into the rational (or that which possesses discourse, τὸ λόγον ἔχον) and the irrational (ἄλογον), since the possible and defensible bases of differentiation are infinite.[21] On functional grounds, however, powers and potentialities in general may be divided into two kinds, the rational (μετὰ λόγου) and the irrational (ἄλογον). All rational potentialities are capable of contrary effects, as the medical art can produce both disease and health; for the medical art is a science or formula pertinent, in different ways, both to the object proper to it and to its contrary or privation. A single irrational potentiality, on the other hand, produces only one effect, as the hot is capable only of heating.[22]

In the practical use of language, when actions are directed to an end or when standards are examined or promulgated, the rules of action are instances of "discourse" which might be translated into action or elaborated by verbal exposition or given force as social enactment. When the end of analysis and discourse is action, the standard for action is determined in thought and communicated in discourse. As the passions and thoughts of the mind are constituted a kind of discourse when examined in scientific inquiry, so discourse is made a kind of rational principle and rule when employed in practical action. It is important for the analysis of human actions in ethics, therefore, to recognize that man alone possesses discourse, reason, and science; and, consequently, the distinction, which Aristotle describes as one made in popular discussions, between the rational and the irrational parts of the soul, seems to him adequate to serve as foundation to the analysis of the virtues, however unsatisfactory it may be as a psychological theory. It supplies a functional interrelation of

---

19. *On the Soul* iii. 3. 427ᵇ8–16.

20. *Ibid.* 428ᵃ19–24.　　　　　21. *Ibid.* 9. 432ᵃ22–ᵇ8.

22. *Metaph.* ix. 2. 1046ᵃ36–ᵇ24 and 5. 1047ᵇ35–1048ᵃ15. Cf. also *Interpret.* 13. 22ᵇ36–23ᵃ6, where the question is not limited to internal powers or principles of change but is extended to logical possibilities in general, and some irrational potentialities are found also to admit of contrary actualizations, as, for example, a thing might either be cut or not be cut.

habits, inasmuch as the irrational part may be further subdivided into a vegetative part, which is not subject to habituation and in no way shares in the rational principle, and an appetitive part, which shares in the rational principle, in the sense of being amenable to it and obeying it.[23] The differentiation of intellectual from the moral virtues is based on this distinction. The irrational part of the soul is contrasted to the rational not only in cognitive but also in conative functions, and the prescription of rational rule is therefore opposed to the rule of passion, appetite, and desire,[24] while desire itself, like the irrational soul, may be differentiated into two kinds, one in accordance with reason and the other irrational.[25] The rule of reason in the irrational soul, moreover, implies a differentiation of the use of reason and discourse as they apply to changing things in action and production from their use as they apply to eternal things in inquiry into natures and causes; for that difference in subject matter and purpose constitutes the distinction both between the calculative and the scientific parts of the rational soul (τὰ λόγον ἔχοντα) and between practical and theoretic arguments (λόγοι).[26]

Politics and ethics are not independent sciences, according to Aristotle, but supplementary approaches to the common problems of the good life. Virtue in the individual is determined by the rule of reason, and the associations of men are made possible by discourse. The good man is the same as the good citizen only in the good state; and then the discourse which determines the institutions of the state embodies and transmits the rule of reason, which sets the standard for virtue. Three things make men good and virtuous: nature, habit, and reason (λόγος). Animals lead a life of nature, and, although some are also influenced to an extent by habit, man alone possesses reason. The moral as well as the political problem is to bring nature, habit, and reason into harmony, for men often act contrary to their habits and their nature because of their reason. The effectiveness of legislation is dependent on human nature; habit and reason, on the other hand, are affected by education.[27] Nature's part does not depend on us, and the direct influence of reason in teaching and argument is not great with all men.[28] Yet, directly or indirectly, reason is essential to the virtuous life. Happiness implies reason and cannot be without reason (λόγος);[29] and moral virtue is defined as a mean determined in accordance with a rational principle

---

23. *Nicomachean Ethics* i. 13. 1102ª23–1103ª3; and *Pol.* vii. 14. 1333ª16–19. Cf. *Nic. Eth.* vi. 1. 1138ᵇ35–1139ª6 and *Pol.* i. 13. 1260ª4–7.

24. *Pol.* i. 5. 1254ᵇ4–9 and 1254ᵇ20–24; iii. 4. 1277ª6–7; *On the Soul* iii. 10. 433ᵇ5–13.

25. *Rhetoric* i. 11. 1370ª18–27.

26. *Nic. Eth.* vi. 1. 1139ª6–15 and 5. 1140ᵇ25–30; and *Pol.* vii. 14. 1333ª21–25.

27. *Pol.* vii. 13. 1332ª39–ᵇ11.

28. *Nic. Eth.* x. 9. 1179ᵇ20–31.

29. *Ibid.* i. 7. 1098ª3–17.

(λόγος) or as a prudent man would determine it.[30] Therefore, to live as one should is to live according to reason, for the standard of virtue is right reason,[31] and the excesses of incontinence and of vice are both contrary to right reason.[32] Socrates had been in error when he identified the virtues with reason (λόγος), but in refuting that error Aristotle pointed out that, though not identical with it, virtues do involve or depend on reason.[33] The moral virtues are habits of acting in accordance with right reason; and the dictate of right reason about such matters, as distinguished from the habit of acting according to right reason, is prudence.[34]

Art and prudence, the intellectual virtues of the calculative part of the soul, which is concerned with processes of change, are defined, respectively, as a productive habit, in accordance with true reason (λόγος), and a practical habit, in accordance with reason (λόγος) and true, relative to human goods; and science is likewise a habit.[35] Science is one of the three intellectual virtues of the scientific part of the soul, whose objects are necessary and eternal: all sciences can be communicated by teaching and what is scientifically known must be learned, either inductively or deductively.[36] Learning depends on words, and even among the animals some are capable of receiving instruction from each other or from man, provided they possess the faculty of hearing or are at least able to distinguish the differences of sounds and signs.[37] Hearing makes the greatest contribution accidentally to prudence, for speech (λόγος), which is the cause of instruction, is heard, not in itself but accidentally, since speech is composed of words and words are symbols, while it is only the sound and the voice that are heard.[38] In the practical science of politics, on the other hand, discourse makes association possible by furnishing a means of communicating man's conceptions of expediency and justice:

> The reason why man is more of a political animal than bees or any other gregarious animal is clear. For nature, as we say, does nothing in vain, and man alone of the animals possesses speech [λόγος]. Mere voice [φωνή], to be sure, is a sign of pain and pleasure, and is therefore present in other animals (for their nature has been developed

30. *Ibid.* ii. 6. 1106ᵇ36–1107ᵃ2.

31. *Ibid.* i. 3. 1095ᵃ8–11; 13. 1102ᵇ14–25; ii. 2. 1103ᵇ31–34; iii. 5. 1114ᵇ26–30; 11. 1119ᵃ18–20; 12. 1119ᵇ12–17; iv. 5. 1125ᵇ33–1126ᵃ1; ix. 8. 1169ᵃ3–6.

32. *Ibid.* v. 11. 1138ᵃ9–11; vii. 3. 1147ᵃ31–ᵇ3; 4. 1147ᵇ31–35; 1148ᵃ28–32; 9. 1151ᵃ29–35 and 1151ᵇ32–1152ᵃ3.

33. *Ibid.* vi. 13. 1144ᵇ28–30.

34. *Ibid.* 1. 1138ᵇ18–34 and 13. 1144ᵇ21–28.

35. *Ibid.* 4. 1140ᵃ20–23 and 5. 1140ᵇ4–7, 20–21, 25–28; *Post. Anal.* i. 19. 100ᵃ6–13, ᵇ5–14

36. *Ibid.* 3. 1139ᵇ25–31.

37. *Hist. Anim.* ix. 1. 608ᵃ17–21.

38. *On Sense and the Sensed* 1. 437ᵃ3–18.

so far as to have perception of the painful and the pleasant and to make signs of those perceptions to one another), but speech is for the sake of making clear the expedient and the inexpedient, and therefore likewise the just and the unjust; for it is the peculiar property of man, distinguishing him from other animals, that he alone has perception of good and evil, of just and unjust, and the like, and it is the community in these things that makes a family and a state.[39]

Discourse is therefore essentially connected with the practical as well as the theoretic sciences: as it is an indispensable instrument in the acquisition of knowledge, so, too, as verbal means of communication, it is essential to the community of shared values and institutions, and, as rational principle, it is the standard of virtue and action.

In the artistic use of language, when words are used as matter for poetic composition, the forms of poetry may be viewed in terms of the plots which are the soul of poetry or of the arguments (λόγοι) in which the plots are developed. When the end of composition is the production of a poem, language both constitutes the parts and determines the whole; and thought is expressed, character is conveyed, and ultimately action is set forth or narrated by means of words. Voice (φωνή) and language (λόγος) are among the means of imitation used in the various arts, language with the pleasurable accessories of rhythm and harmony being proper to the art of tragedy.[40] The natural basis of poetry is therefore imitation, while the literary means of imitation, or the matter from which the poem is constructed, is expression in language (ἐν λόγῳ). The origin of poetry is due to two causes found in human nature. Imitation is natural to man from childhood, and one of his advantages over the lower animals is that he is the most imitative of all creatures and learns at first by imitation. It is also natural for man to delight in works of imitation. To be learning something is one of the greatest of pleasures not only to the philosopher but also to the rest of mankind, and the reason for the delight one takes in an imitation is that one is at the same time learning. Moreover, the sense of harmony and rhythm, like imitation, is natural to man.[41] The original differentiations into kinds of poetry, however, were determined by differences in the poets and their preferences among kinds of actions to be represented.[42] The origins of the poetic use of language are thus not unrelated to the inquiry and learning which motivate its scientific use; the differentiation into kinds is determined by considerations, not of genera of subject matter but of individual character; and character, in turn, is determined by discourse and thought in their practical use. Poetry is therefore distinguished from theory and practice

39. *Pol.* i. 2. 1253ᵃ7–18.

40. *Poet.* 1. 1447ᵃ18–23 and 6. 1449ᵇ24–31.

41. *Ibid.* 4. 1448ᵇ4–24.　　　　　　　　42. *Ibid.* 1448ᵇ24–27.

by the pleasure proper to the poem itself, in which the unity is constituted by argument and plot (λόγος καὶ μῦθος) expressed in language (λόγος) and in which the diction, in turn, may be viewed as a whole and analyzed into eight parts (among which assiduous grammarians have found four "parts of speech"), ranging from the letter which is the element of diction, through the syllable, the conjunction, the article, the noun, the verb, and the case to the speech itself, which is composite significant sound, so defined that the definition of a word or a simple assertion and the *Iliad* as a whole, as well as any intermediate unit of discourse, may be viewed as a single speech (λόγος).[43]

II. THE OPERATIONS OF LANGUAGE: HUMAN THOUGHT AND ITS EXPRESSION

Language is treated among the subject matters of the theoretic, practical, and productive sciences. It is related to its bases in the organism and the soul of man; its practical efficacy as rule of prudence and as instrument of communication is examined in determining the proportion which is sought in virtuous action and the bond of justice by which states are held together; its artistic realizations are discovered in the constructions of poetry. Yet in each of these sciences in which it is a subject matter language is also an instrument of inquiry and statement, and, in addition, it serves other functions beyond these scientific uses. The analysis of things is presented in language; and, when language is used scientifically, criteria by which to test statement and argument are sought in the subject matters which the sciences treat. Even the language of science, moreover, may be viewed not only in terms of its adaptation to the processes of inquiry and proof relative to the subject matter of the sciences but also in terms of its development in acquisition and use relative to processes in the mind of the inquirer and in terms of its elements and combinations relative to the symbolic system employed in stating and formulating the results of inquiry. The uses of language, however, do not all follow the model of scientific inquiry and proof, nor are they limited to the devices by which science is acquired and set forth. In its scientific uses, language, as well as the thought it expresses, is made to conform as closely as possible to a subject matter. Language may also express a normative rule for action which, if successfully performed, may alter the actual situation; and the criteria for such rules of action must be sought in potentialities that may or may not be actualized or in communities that may or may not be established or that may be preserved or destroyed. Language may, again, be determined by the relation between speaker and audience, and the criteria for expression no less than the

---

43. *Ibid.* 20. 1456[b]20–21 and 1457[a]23–30; cf. also *On Generation and Corruption* i. 4. 315[b]14–15.

conception of subject matter must then be sought in thoughts and emotions already possessed or to be conveyed. Language may, finally, find its efficacy primarily in the instrumentalities of words and style, even to the extent of making the improbable seem plausible and the unconventional acceptable; and the criteria for thought and the conception of nature must then be sought in the development of the argument and in the elements and combinations by which it is expressed. The development of an argument may thus be determined by science or by prudence or by art—or by dialectical, sophistical, or rhetorical supplements or approximations to such developments—and thoughts and oc-currences may be set forth in expressions determined by consideration, real or apparent, of truth and probability or of justice and expediency or of form and pleasure. Arguments (λόγοι) are used not only for proof and teaching but also for persuasion and regulation, for communication and artistic construction.

The variety of the uses of language and of criteria for the judgment of those uses depends on the same characteristics of language as make possible fallacy and error, vice and sophistry, artistic license and fault. Since language is the peculiar function of an animal who possesses a soul, that is, the imagination requisite for the imposition of meanings, as well as the special organs requisite for the production of voice, the marks of meaning may be found in the analysis of language as a symbolic structure or in the analysis of thought as expressed in language or in the analysis of things as signified by thought. The discourse of the mind, which is expressed in verbal discourse, may serve to organize thought, action, or production; but to do so it must discover a rational order in things or impose such an order. The characteristics of discourse are thus traced back to mental powers and physical processes, and, indeed, the significance of the word λόγος is extended from statements in language to include in its mean-ing thoughts in minds and forms in things. But if language may be identical with reason, it may also be used contrary to reason; statements may correspond with what is essential in things, and they may also be false and contrary to fact; and although art may be based on what has happened and although it has moral and political effects, the presentation of the improbable and the morally wrong may be artistically preferable to the true and the better. However lan-guage is used—to express the results of impartial inquiry, to communicate purposes or persuade to action, or to arouse the pleasure proper to discourses artistically contrived—the symbolic function is to be found in the relation of language to what is expressed, but the determination of that relation may turn on considerations of subject matter or of emotions and purposes or of form.

There is no simple equivalence between discourse and things. At each stage of the combination of words into statements and arguments or of the decomposition of arguments into their parts, language may be dissociated from any strict reference to things. Words may be ambiguous; assertions may be amphibolous; discussions and inquiry may be pursued for no other purpose than for the sake of the argument. The problem is, in part, a problem of the meanings of terms; in part, a problem of the combination of terms in assertions; in part, a problem of the grounds for the assertion of the principle or conclusion of an argument. A term may have a single meaning or several; a statement may be about a single thing or several; an argument may proceed from the reason, the fact, or simply from what was said. But even when a "single" word or a "single" statement is about "one" and the "same" thing, the words "one" and the "same," as used either in discourse or in the analysis of discourse, may have many meanings, and there are as many senses of "being" as there are of "one" and the "same." These differentiations of statement and being are essential preliminaries to discovering the respect in which the being or nature of a thing may be identical with the statement of its nature; and these essential differentiations—of meanings of statements and of kinds of being—can, in turn, be made only by examination of the uses of words.

In general, things may be one in four different ways: in number, in species, in genus, or by analogy. A thing is one in number whose matter is one; things are one in species or form (εἶδος) whose definition (λόγος) is one; things are one generically when they fall in the same category; and things are one analogically when they are related as a third thing is to a fourth. The latter forms of unity are always found when the former are, but the former are not always present in the latter: things that are one in number are all one in species, while not all things that are one in species are one in number; but things that are one in species are all one in genus, while things that are one in genus are not all one in species but are all one by analogy; and things that are one by analogy are not all one in genus.[44] Or, again, the senses in which a thing may be said to be "one" may be classified by consideration of indivisibility of motion, on the one hand, and indivisibility of thought and formula, on the other. There are, once more, on this basis of classification, four senses in which a thing may be one: (1) the naturally continuous, and in this sense those things have more unity and are prior, whose movement is more indivisible and simpler; (2) the whole, and in this sense a thing is one because its movement is one and indivisible in place and time; (3) what is one in number, and in this sense the individual is indivisible; and (4) what is one in form or species, and in this sense the universal is indivisible in comprehension and knowledge.[45] A thing may be the "same" if it is one in number, that is, in matter; or if it is one in both number

44. *Metaph.* v. 6. 1016ᵇ31–1017ᵃ3.
45. *Ibid.* x. 1. 1052ᵃ15–ᵇ1.

and formula, that is, in matter and in form; or if the formula or its primary essence is one.[46]

A thing is shown to be one in number when a variety of forms of appellation are substituted one for another in application to it. Those appellations may have an essential or an accidental relation to one another in the thing. An individual thing or a thing which is one in number is signified most strictly when the two words have the same definition, as "clothes" and "garment" may be applied to the same thing; or when a word and one of its definitions is used, as "animal that walks on two feet" is the same as "man." But a property may be used in the same fashion, as when "what can acquire knowledge" is called the same as "man"; and even an accident will serve to identify an individual, as when "the man who is sitting," or "who is musical," is called the same as "Socrates."[47] A distinction must be made, therefore, between "signifying one thing," as is done when the words applied to a single thing have the same meaning, and "signifying with respect to one thing," as is done when words like "white," "musical," and "Socrates" are used to signify the same person. Consequently, even when terms designate the same object, the connection between the terms must be investigated; and if a point has been proved about "clothes," the identity of "clothes" and "garment" must be demonstrated before the conclusion can be applied to "garment."[48] Indeed, one of the errors of philosophers like Heraclitus and Lycophron consisted in supposing that all things are one in the same sense as "clothes" and "garment," that is, in the sense of possessing a single definition.[49]

Individual things or things one in number are never predicable of a subject although some varieties of individual things may be present in a subject.[50] Terms which signify individuals, therefore, serve primarily as subjects of propositions; and the problem of scientific demonstration may be said to consist in relating such terms to predicates whose relation to them as subjects is established by inference from essential definitions and necessary premises. The problem must be viewed both in terms of the statement possible of an existent individual and in terms of the existence signified by a universal. What is one in number and in concrete existence is differentiated into what is many in formula, for any individual thing is subject to inquiry in many sciences; and what is one in formula is present in many existent things. What is one in formula is the

46. *Ibid.* 3. 1054ᵃ32–ᵇ3.

47. *Topics* i. 7. 103ᵃ6–39 and vi. 11. 149ᵃ3–4; cf. also *Metaph.* iv. 4. 1006ᵃ34–ᵇ5 and 1006ᵇ25–27.

48. *On Sophistical Refutations* 6. 168ᵃ23–33; *Metaph.* iv. 4. 1006ᵇ25–34; *Physics* iii. 2. 202ᵇ10–16.

49. *Phys.* i. 2. 185ᵇ19–25.　　　　　　50. *Cat.* 2. 1ᵇ3–9.

universal, and what is one in number is the individual. In the search for principles in science, either may be considered indivisible and prior to the other. The individual is prior as an element, that is, as matter in the composite, while the universal is prior as form. The individual or element is indivisible in time, while the universal is indivisible in formula.[51] The element is found by decomposing individual things into their ultimate parts; the universal states the unity which constitutes the form of the whole. The error of earlier philosophers in treating principles consisted, therefore, in their failure to distinguish what is one in formula from what is one in number or to treat either adequately.[52]

Things are one in form or species when they have a single formula or definition. A definition may serve to identify a thing which is one in number; it may

51. *Metaph.* xiii. 8. 1084^{b}2–23. W. D. Ross undertakes to explain away the distinction between indivisible in formula and indivisible in time, on the ground that it is unintelligible and unexampled in Aristotle's usage. Commenting on ll. 1084^{b}15–16, he argues that "an opposition of 'indivisible in λόγος' and 'indivisible in time' would be quite unparalleled in Aristotle, and no reasonable meaning can be attached to it"; and then, making use of Bekker's punctuation of the passage, he interprets it to say that the universal and the individual or element are both principles because they are both indivisible, but the manner of their priority as principles is of different kinds, one being prior in formula, the other in time (*Aristotle's Metaphysics: A Revised Text with Introduction and Commentary* [Oxford, 1924], II, 452–53). He does not avoid the difficulty by shifting from indivisibility in time and formula to priority in time and formula, since the universal and the element are prior in different senses precisely because they are indivisible in different senses. There is no difficulty in finding Aristotle's statement of this or of interpreting its meaning or even of recognizing the reasons for his changing modes of expressing the distinction. Aristotle's customary way of stating the general distinction is that in all cases the one is indivisible either in quality or in kind (*Metaph.* v. 6. 1016^{b}23–24) or that in all cases things are one either because the motion is indivisible or because the formula is indivisible (*ibid.* x. 1. 1052^{a}36–^{b}1). Depending on the context and the problem in hand, Aristotle treats the contrary of "divisible in formula or form" as "divisible in quantity" or, more particularly, in some variety of quantity, such as "number," "motion," "time," or "place." There is no inherent difficulty in interpreting the meaning of either "indivisible in formula" or "indivisible in time." Any formula is in itself, as formula, divisible, but a thing is one in formula when the formula states its essence; and therefore, in a process in which a thing changes in size, the thing may be said to be the same in formula at the beginning and end of the process (*ibid.* 1016^{a}32–^{b}3). A thing is one in time either in the sense that it is continuous, since the continuous has its own motion and the motion is one when it is indivisible in time, or in the sense that its substratum is one, as the various things that are melted have a single substratum, such as air or water (*ibid.* 1016^{a}5–24). Between these two extremes of form and matter, there are the cases of individuals which are one in form and number and of substrata which are one in form. Particular problems determine the selection of time or place as the discriminating quantity of that which is one in number. Thus, in treating common sense, when Aristotle is concerned to show that both the power and the time of its exercise are indivisible, he does so by differentiating "indivisible in being" from "indivisible in place and in number," for he concludes that common sense is divisible in being (inasmuch as it perceives two separate objects at once in discriminating between them) but in that perception it is undivided in place and in number (*On the Soul* iii. 2. 426^{b}24–427^{a}5). His problem in chap. 8 of Book xiii of the *Metaphysics*, where he is refuting the Platonists' conception of ideal numbers, on the contrary, is to show that they have failed to distinguish between the two varieties of principles and that the One would have to be a principle in both senses, as form or substance and as part or matter, and thus be indivisible both in formula and in time.

52. *Metaph.* xiv. 1. 1087^{b}9–18; i. 5. 986^{b}18–987^{a}2.

be applied to one or more members of a single species; and if it is the essential definition, it is not only the statement of the form and the formal cause but also the principle of all proof and change and, as such, is presupposed in the scientific use of efficient, final, and material causes.[53] The discovery of substance is therefore an essential part of the investigation of being, process, knowledge, and statement, for substance is prior in all senses: in formula, in knowledge, and in time.[54] To signify the achievement of this identity of the principles of proof, knowledge, and being—since the principles of things and processes must be knowable and stable in the degree that science is possible—Aristotle joins the term "formula" (λόγος) to terms like "definitory" (ὁριστικός),[55] or "substance" (οὐσία),[56] or "essence" (τὸ τί ἦν εἶναι),[57] or "essential" (τὸ τί ἐστι)[58] to signify "essential definition"; and he uses "formula" in juxtaposition with and as synonym for "substance," "essence," "form," "species," and "actuality."[59] The discovery of such definitions depends on the solution of problems of language and, even more, of problems of fact; for the unity of a definition is not merely a unity of continuity or conjunction of statements, like the *Iliad*, but of the essential inherence of a predicate in a subject because of the unity of the thing, and nothing which is not a species of a genus will have an essence.[60] The thing and the formula, however, are wholes; and the correspondence between them is such that parts of the formula correspond to parts of the thing, even though there are parts of the thing which are not repre-

53. In the enumeration of the kinds of causes λόγος is usually equated with the formal cause (cf. *Phys.* ii. 3. 194ᵃ26–29; *Metaph.* iii. 2. 996ᵇ1–14; viii. 4. 1044ᵃ36–ᵇ1; xii. 3. 1070ᵃ21– 22). On the other hand, the principle of all proof is substance (cf. *Metaph.* vii. 9. 1034ᵃ30–ᵇ1). Moreover, when causes are used as middle terms, the definition is implicated in each of the causes (cf. *Post. Anal.* ii. 11. 94ᵃ20–ᵇ26). The dependence of causal proof on form and λόγος is worked out in detail by L. Robin, "Sur la conception aristotélienne de la causalité," *Archiv für Geschichte der Philosophie*, XXIII (1909–10), 1–28 and 184–210.

54. *Metaph.* vii. 1. 1028ᵃ31–ᵇ2.

55. *Ibid.* viii. 4. 1043ᵇ31.

56. *Cat.* 1. 1ᵃ2, 4, 7, and 9–10; *Post. Anal.* ii. 13. 97ᵃ19; *Gen. and Corrup.* ii. 9. 335ᵇ7; *Parts Anim.* iv. 9. 685ᵇ16; 13. 695ᵇ18–19; *Gen. Anim.* i. 1. 715ᵃ5; ii. 1. 731ᵇ19–20; v. 1. 778ᵃ34–35; *Metaph.* v. 9. 1018ᵃ10–11; vii. 11. 1037ᵃ24; x. 3. 1054ᵃ35–ᵇ1; xi. 7. 1064ᵃ21–22.

57. *Phys.* ii. 3. 194ᵇ27; *Metaph.* v. 2. 1013ᵃ27; 6. 1016ᵃ33; 29. 1024ᵇ29; vii. 4. 1029ᵇ20; 5. 1031ᵃ12.

58. *Post. Anal.* i. 4. 73ᵃ36–37, 38.

59. For οὐσία, cf. *Meteorology* iv. 12. 389ᵇ29 and 390ᵃ6; *Parts Anim.* i. 1. 642ᵃ19–20; *Metaph.* vii. 10. 1035ᵇ26. For τὸ τί ἦν εἶναι, cf. *On the Soul* ii. 1. 412ᵇ15–16; *Metaph.* i. 10. 993ᵃ17–18; vi. 1. 1025ᵇ28–29. For εἶδος, cf. *Phys.* i. 1. 190ᵃ16; iv. 1. 209ᵃ21–22; *On the Soul* i. 1. 403ᵇ1–2; ii. 2. 414ᵃ13–14; *Gen. Anim.* ii. 1. 732ᵃ4–5; *Metaph.* iii. 2. 996ᵇ8; vii. 11. 1036ᵇ5; viii. 4. 1044ᵇ10; xii. 2. 1069ᵇ34; xiv. 5. 1092ᵇ24. For μορφή, cf. *Metaph.* vii. 1. 1042ᵃ28–29, and for ἐνέργεια, ibid. vii. 2. 1043ᵃ19.

60. *Metaph.* vii. 4. 1030ᵃ6–ᵇ13; viii. 6. 1045ᵃ12–14; v. 24. 1023ᵃ31–34; *Post. Anal.* ii. 7. 92ᵇ30–32; 10. 93ᵇ29–37; *Poet.* 20. 1457ᵃ28–30.

sented in the formula and parts of the formula which do not represent parts of the thing.

All scientific statements are either definitory or demonstrative, and the problems of scientific method turn on the relation of definition to demonstration,[61] for that relation has a bearing both on the relation of knowledge or statement to existence and on the relation of premises to conclusion. All the characteristics of discourse, including those which make possible the correspondence of statement to things, may be deduced from the possibility of relating statements about a thing to statements of what it is or that it exists. Since they are the principles of that inferential relation, the principle of contradiction—that the same attribute cannot at the same time belong and not belong to the same subject in the same respect—and the principle of excluded middle—that there cannot be an intermediate between two contradictories, but of one subject we must either affirm or deny any one predicate—are the most certain of all principles, both best known and nonhypothetical. They cannot be demonstrated, but the consequences of denying them can be shown by examining the implications of any statement which is made. Discourse and reasoning depend on definition or limitation: a starting-point of demonstration which is not itself demonstrated, for discussion and reasoning are destroyed if a reason is asked for everything;[62] a finite number of meanings for any given word, in order that a single meaning may be conveyed;[63] and a finite number of predications, which depend on differentiating the essential definition of a thing from accidental predications about it.[64]

The limitations set in discourse are, at the one extreme, individuals, to which discourse may be applied as subjects, and, at the other extreme, principles, which state the reasons for affirming predicates of subjects in the flow of discourse. There can be neither definition nor demonstration of sensible individual substances, because they have matter whose nature makes them capable of being or of not being. The individual is neither matter nor formula alone but matter and formula; and science therefore treats both of existing things in their universal aspects and of universal laws of being and process in their existential applications by treating the formula in its generality. The formula, however, may include matter, not the individual matter of the concrete things but the matter which is the potentiality of the processes proper to the thing, as the definition of "snub," as distinguished from "concave," includes "nose" without being dependent on reference to individual noses. The definitions of

61. *On the Soul* i. 3. 407^{a}25–31, and *Post. Anal.* ii. 1–10. 89^{b}23–94^{a}19.

62. *Metaph.* iv. 4. 1006^{a}5–11 and xi. 6. 1063^{b}7–14.

63. *Ibid.* iv. 4. 1006^{a}31–^{b}11.

64. *Ibid.* 1007^{a}21–^{b}17.

the physical sciences are of this sort. Or the formula may be independent of the matter in which the form must exist, as "concave" may be defined without reference to what is concave. The definitions of the mathematical sciences are of this sort.[65] The causes and principles of the different things studied in the different sciences are different. Even those principles which the sciences share are the "same" only universally and analogically, not literally; and therefore it is only analogically that there are three elements and four causes and principles of all things.[66] Yet for that very reason it is important that there is but one heaven, since the universe as a whole and the processes in it are one as a concrete thing as well as in form, and the unmovable first mover is one both in formula and in number.[67] The subject matter of metaphysics includes, and is determined by, forms which are and are known without matter, for the analysis of the first cause is based, in the investigation of the scientific grounds and principles of things, in the knowledge of things, and in the statement of that knowledge, not as they are, or are known, or are stated in their proper species and according to particular sciences, but universally and *qua* being. Many of the universal terms employed in metaphysical inquiry, like "being" and "unity," are the same and are one thing in the sense that they are implied in one another but not in the sense that they are explained by the same formula or definition.[68] If there were no forms which exist without matter or if there were eternal forms for all things that exist, there would be no need for metaphysics as a science distinct from physics. These opposite forms of the confusion of physics and metaphysics Aristotle attributed to Democritus and Plato, for both of whom reduction is possible because the distinction between mathematics and physics is ignored, in one case, by reducing bodies to mathematical forms and their combinations and, in the other, by making numbers independent existences.[69]

Both physics and mathematics require separation in thought and definition of what is inseparable in fact. Despite the differences between physical and mathematical definitions, to which Aristotle refers repeatedly and briefly in his numerous developments of the difference between "snub" and "concave," physics requires separation by thought or definition of the forms of changing things from the matter from which they are inseparable in number, and mathematics requires like separation by thought or definition of quantity from the

65. *Ibid.* vi. 10. 1039^{b}20–1040^{a}5; x. 9. 1058^{a}37–^{b}21; xi. 7. 1064^{a}10–28.

66. *Ibid.* xii. 4. 1070^{a}31–^{b}35.

67. *Ibid.* 8. 1074^{a}31–38.

68. *Ibid.* iv. 2. 1003^{b}19–1004^{a}9.

69. *Gen. and Corrup.* i. 2. 315^{b}24–33; *Metaph.* i. 9. 996^{a}24–^{b}1.

same matter from which it likewise is inseparable in number.[70] Moreover, the further inquiries in each require further separation by definition or formula of what is inseparable in fact or number. Thus motion may be one generically (in this sense any instance of "locomotion" is one generically with any other instance of locomotion, but generically different from "alteration," which is motion in quality rather than in place); or it may be one specifically (in this sense "whitening" is generically the same as "blackening" but differs from it specifically, and every instance of blackening is specifically the same with every other instance of blackening); or it may be one absolutely, that is, essentially and numerically (and it is in this sense that investigation is possible of "that which" is in motion, "that in which" the motion takes place, and "that during which" it occurs).[71] The analysis of motion and time, conceived in this absolute, that is, concrete, sense, requires a consideration of points and moments in which a differentiation must be made between what is one in number and what is one in thought or formula. A "point" marked off in the motion of any thing is a single point, although it is not single in formula, since it must be considered both as a finishing-point relative to what came before and as a starting-point relative to what is to come.[72] In like fashion, the "now" is the same in each of its instances and underlying all its relations; but, since it is the measure of time, it is in another sense different, for it is relative to the before and after, and in that respect differs in formula and in what is predicated of it.[73] Time is always at a beginning and at an end, and in much the same fashion the "convex" and the "concave" in the circumference of a circle can be separated in thought and formula, although they are inseparable in number.[74] Finally, the problem of whether the parts of the soul are separated, as are the parts of the body or any other divisible thing, or whether they are separable by definition but are by nature inseparable, like convex and concave in the circumference of a circle, may be put aside as irrelevant in ethics[75] and be taken up in psychology;[76] and the parts of the soul, which are differentiated by their powers, in turn, include an irrational part and are possessed of a rational principle or formula.[77]

As substance in the sense of the concrete individual is distinct from substance in the sense of the universal definition, so, too, the rational process by which universals are known is distinct from the sensitive processes by which particulars are experienced; and the same word, λόγος, is used to signify "definition"

70. *Gen. and Corrup.* i. 5. 320b17–25.

71. *Phys.* v. 4. 227b3–228a3.

72. *Ibid.* viii. 8. 262a19–21 and 263b12–14.

73. *Ibid.* iv. 11. 219b19–33.

74. *Ibid.* 3. 222a33–b5.

75. *Nic. Eth.* i. 13. 1102a28–32.

76. *On the Soul* iii. 4. 429a10–13; 9. 432a15–22; 10. 433b21–26.

77. *Metaph.* ix. 2. 1046a36–b2; *Nic. Eth.* i. 13. 1102a26–28.

as contrasted to concrete thing and "reason" as contrasted to sense. The universals of science are differentiated from the particulars of sense as that which is better known in nature in contrast to that which is better known to us; and the effort of science is therefore to bring the evidence of sense and the evidence of argument or reason into conformity and agreement. Aristotle's scientific works are dotted with passages in which he tries to supplement the results of experience and observation by arguments and definitions in an effort to base the credibility ($\pi i \sigma \tau \iota s$) of theory on both sense and reason ($\lambda o \gamma o s$).[78] Reason or argument, on the one hand, is a source of explanations not accessible to sense; and on the other hand, since it is concerned with universals, it is not held to the minuteness and precision of unrelated detail present to sense.[79] Aristotle's criticisms of his predecessors turn on the inadequacy of their arguments to treat of the data of experience or on their reliance on arguments without having collected all the information that can be gathered through sense or on the discrepancies between their arguments and the evidence of sense and experience; and he praises Democritus for the thoroughness of his reduction of all phenomena to a single argument.[80] He often shows, in particular, that the testimony of sight is in conformity with the consequences of his argument in questions of astronomy, meteorology, and anatomy; and there is evidence that he used illustrations for purposes of proof in his biological writings.[81]

Yet, in spite of the fact that reason and experience may be in agreement, what is prior in reason or formula is not prior according to sensation, and one and the same formula applies to many individual things, which are external to the soul (whereas universals are in a sense internal) and which are differentiated by matter or by place and time.[82] Argument or reason is therefore opposed to experience as knowledge of universal to knowledge of individual:[83] the inductive process, which begins from sense and the individual, or from what is confused but more observable to us, leads to reason and the universal, or to what is clearer according to argument;[84] and a demonstration which proceeds from the rational

78. Cf. *Phys.* viii. 8. 262ª17–19; *Gen. and Corrup.* ii. 10. 336ᵇ15–19; *On Youth and Old Age* 2. 468ª22–23; *Hist. Anim.* i. 6. 491ª23–25; *Parts Anim.* ii. 8. 653ᵇ22, 30; iii. 4. 666ª13, 19–20; *Gen. Anim.* i. 2. 716ª17–23; ii. 4. 740ª4–5.

79. *Meteorol.* i. 7. 344ª5–6; *Pol.* vii. 7. 1328ª19–21.

80. *Phys.* viii. 3. 253ª32–ᵇ2; *Gen. and Corrup.* i. 8. 324ᵇ32–325ª23; *Metaph.* i. 5. 986ᵇ31–987ª2.

81. *On the Heavens* i. 5. 272ª5–7; *Meteorol.* i. 6. 343ᵇ28–34; *Parts Anim.* iv. 5. 679ᵇ37–680ª3.

82. *Metaph.* v. 11. 1018ᵇ32–34; xii. 8. 1074ª33–35; *Post. Anal.* i. 31. 87ᵇ28–35; *On the Soul* ii. 5. 417ᵇ18–28.

83. *Metaph.* i. 1. 981ª12–24.

84. *Post. Anal.* ii. 19. 100ª1–3; *On the Soul* ii. 2. 413ª11–16.

principle or definition is contrary and supplementary to a demonstration by induction.[85] What is better known in the order of argument is contrasted to what is better known to sense, moreover, even in the case of scientists who have been led astray in their arguments and theories,[86] while the "appearances" or "phenomena" (φαινόμενα) which are observed by sensation or admitted by opinion are contrasted to arguments, sometimes as what appears to us even though it is contrary to fact and sometimes as what is verified as actually occurring.

The fashion in which Aristotle uses phenomena to supplement arguments, recognizing that the one may be illusory and the other fallacious, is well illustrated in his discussion of what we have come to call the "fifth element" and what Aristotle called the "first of the bodies." He remarks after his demonstration of the existence and qualities of this first and simple body that these conclusions will be clear to anyone who credits the assumptions he has made; and then he adds that his argument or theory (λόγος) seems to confirm phenomena and to be confirmed by them.[87] He goes for data concerning the phenomena to common opinion, to sense experience, and to common meanings of words. He appeals, first, in support of his theory of the "first body" to the common conceptions which all men, barbarians and Greeks, have of the existence and nature of the gods. Arguing, second, that the evidence of the senses is sufficient to convince us within the limits of human certainty, he points out that the record of astronomical observation shows no change in the scheme of the outermost heavens. Finally, the common name, *aether*, handed down from our distant ancestors, is evidence, since the name is derived from the fact that it "runs always" for an eternity of time, that they conceived of the first body in much the manner that Aristotle had expressed, for, he adds, the same manner of speaking has recurred in men's usage again and again. Phenomena, as generally accepted, are probable; they are known through the senses and can be checked in the scope and unanimity of recorded observations; and the history of beliefs and of language supplies information concerning what has appeared to be the case to men. The ideal of science, stated in terms of phenomena, is to have arguments and phenomena agree;[88] and theories are refuted either because they ignore the phenomena or are inconsistent with both phenomena impartially observed and valid contradictory arguments.[89] The test by

---

85. *Post. Anal.* i. 18. 81ª38–ᵇ9; 24. 86ª29–30; cf. also *Meteorol.* iv. 1. 378ᵇ13–14, 20–21.

86. *Phys.* i. 5. 188ᵇ30–189ª9.

87. *On the Heavens* i. 3. 270ᵇ1–25.

88. *On the Soul* ii. 2. 414ª25; *On Youth and Old Age* 4. 469ª23–29; *Metaph.* xiv. 1. 1087ᵇ2–3; *Rhet.* ii. 22. 1396ª3–7, 31–ᵇ11; *Pol.* i. 5. 1254ª20–21.

89. *Meteorol.* ii. 5. 362ᵇ12–14; *On the Soul* ii. 7. 418ᵇ23–24.

means of phenomena is used, moreover, in practical as well as in theoretical arguments, as when both occurrences and arguments are used to demonstrate that the legislator should direct all his military as well as his civil measures to the provision of leisure and the establishment of peace.[90] To possess an argument (λόγος) or to follow consequences in accordance with an argument, therefore, may be to have a reasonable and intelligible analysis pertinent to checking the facts, establishing scientific knowledge, and discovering grounds of sure belief;[91] it may simply signify the possession of a doctrine or opinion, more frequently false than true;[92] and, finally, it may refer to the subject matter or topic of inquiry,[93] or the form of disquisition or disputation consequent on inquiry and synonymous with syllogizing, reasoning, or conversing.[94]

The organization of propositions and the processes of reasoning cannot be made to duplicate in all details the structure of things and the phenomena of becoming, and it is easily possible to reason erroneously even from sound principles and to misinterpret accurate observations. Reasoning rests on statements, mental or verbal, and consists in following through to other assertions from what has been stated; refutation is reasoning which leads to the contradiction of a given proposition. There is no simple means of avoiding the danger in both reasoning and refutation that the principle may seem to be true and the inference may seem to follow in the words or even in the interpretation of the words, and yet principle and conclusion may reflect nothing in fact. We cannot exhibit the things themselves in argument or avoid recourse to symbolic devices, and undue skepticism concerning the discrepancies between the changing world and the generalities of statement reduces its proponent to the predicament of Cratylus, who did not think it right to say anything but confined himself to wiggling his finger in designation of things.[95]

Since it is impossible to discuss by bringing in the things themselves, and since we use names in the place of things as symbols for them, we suppose that what follows in the names, follows in the things as well, just as we suppose for calculators in the case of

90. *Pol.* vii. 14. 1334ᵃ2–6.

91. *Phys.* iii. 7. 207ᵃ33–ᵇ1; *On the Heavens* iii. 8. 306ᵇ15–16; *Gen. and Corrup.* ii. 3. 330ᵇ1–7; *On Respiration* 18. 476ᵇ13–16; *Parts Anim.* iv. 10. 689ᵃ14–16; *Gen. Anim.* i. 8. 718ᵇ4–5; iii. 5. 756ᵃ14–15; 11. 762ᵃ1–3; *Metaph.* xiii. 8. 1084ᵃ9–10; xiv. 1. 1088ᵃ4–6; *Pol.* vii. 7. 1328ᵃ10–15.

92. *Phys.* iv. 7. 214ᵇ3–5; viii. 8. 263ᵃ4–11; *On the Heavens* ii. 1. 284ᵇ5; iii. 6. 305ᵃ16–17; *Metaph.* iv. 5. 1009ᵃ6–7; v. 29. 1025ᵃ6–7; ix. 3. 1047ᵃ6–7, 14; 10. 1051ᵇ13–15; xiii. 4. 1078ᵇ12–16; 5. 1079ᵇ20–23; *Pol.* iii. 9. 1280ᵃ27–28.

93. *Post. Anal.* i. 2. 83ᵃ34; *Top.* viii. 6. 159ᵇ39; *Phys.* i. 2. 185ᵇ12; viii. 6. 258ᵇ13; *On the Heavens* i. 11. 280ᵇ3; *Metaph.* i. 5. 987ᵃ3.

94. *Pr. Anal.* ii. 13. 32ᵇ18–22; 27. 43ᵃ40–43; *Top.* i. 4. 101ᵇ11–16; *Metaph.* iii. 4. 999ᵃ24–26; xi. 6. 1063ᵇ7–11; xiii. 1. 1076ᵃ29–32; xiv. 3. 1090ᵇ11–13.

95. *Metaph.* iv. 5. 1010ᵃ7–15.

their counters. The two cases [of names and things], however, are not alike, for names are finite as is the sum-total of assertions, while things are infinite in number. It is necessary therefore that the same assertion and a single name have several meanings. Accordingly, just as those who are not clever in manipulating their counters in calculation are taken in by those who are expert, in the same fashion those who are unacquainted with the force of names in the case of arguments [λόγοι] commit paralogisms, both when they themselves discuss and when they listen to discussion of others. For this reason, then, as well as for others to be stated later, there are both syllogism and refutation which are apparent but not real.[96]

Just as the device of examining the opinions of men is a useful preliminary to discussing the principles of things, so, too, the examination of the senses in which words are used is an important preliminary to understanding the meanings of statements and the natures of things. The shift from science or demonstration to dialectic is from principles grounded in the nature of things to principles based on the authority of those who hold them; and the shift from dialectical to sophistical argument is from beliefs to deceptions which can be explained only by examining the psychological and linguistic processes of those who are deceived and the moral intentions of those who perpetrate the deception. There are good reasons which induce some people, like the Sophists, who make money from apparent but unreal wisdom, to take advantage of this appearance of reasoning and refuting.

Sophistical refutation may produce the false appearance of an argument either by means of language (and this may be done in six different ways: by the ambiguity of individual words or by an indeterminateness of phrase, such as amphiboly, combination, division of words, accent, or form of expression) or by fallacies that are independent of language (and these all depend on changing the interpretation of what is said, such as the use of an expression absolutely or with some qualification of respect or place or time or relation or on making more than one question one).[97] Deceptions which depend on the form of expression (λέξις) result from likeness in discourse, for it is difficult to distinguish what is signified by the same statement and what by different statements; and the man who can make those distinctions, Aristotle adds, is close to the understanding of truth. This kind of deception, which results from the use of an expression to denote what does not belong to an object or a class as if it did, occurs more readily when we are engaged in an inquiry with others than when we proceed alone, for common inquiry is conducted by means of language, while individual inquiry is carried on as much by means of the object itself. Yet a man is likely to be deceived, even when inquiring alone, when he takes language as the basis for his inquiry, for the deception arises from the

96. *Soph. Ref.* 1. 165ᵃ6–19.
97. *Ibid.* 4. 165ᵇ23–168ᵃ16.

likenesses suggested by the language used rather than from the things signified.[98]

The lists and analyses of different meanings of words, which form an integral part of Aristotle's arguments in the sciences, serve the purpose, not merely of conventional classification of usages or arbitrary selection of a definition to be employed, but of avoiding equivocation and determining the application of word to thing.[99] The thing signified may be single and the same in number, species, or genus, and there is a place even for analogical terms; the danger is in ambiguity or equivocation, in which the same word is used with two or more meanings or essential definitions. In its changed meanings the word applies to different things, and ambiguity may therefore occur by neglecting any of the important differentiations found in the examination of language as an instrument for stating the nature of things. One of the most frequent forms of ambiguity is the application of a word to things which have the same physical constitution or observable form but which differ, in that one lacks the power or function proper to a thing of such constitution or form: in this fashion a living and a dead or artificial hand, eye, or animal are the same only in name.[100] Similarly, a word may be applied to the abstract universal and the physical particular, as "circle" may mean circle in general or an individual circle involved in matter.[101] Or a word may be applied to matter and the passions which matter undergoes, as when bronze becomes hot or "fluid," and the hot and the fluid "bronze."[102] Or the equivocation may arise from applying a word to a whole and its part, as in the case of a blood vessel and a bit of blood vessel.[103] Again, a word may have a different meaning as applied to different things and a different contrary to each of those meanings, as "sharp" is the contrary to a "flat" note or a "dull" edge, and similar shifts are involved when it is applied to flavors and angles.[104] Finally, a word may be purely and completely equivocal, as when things happen wholly by chance to possess the same name.[105]

98. *Ibid.* 7. 169ª22–b2.

99. *Top.* i. 18. 108ª18–37; ii. 3. 110ª23–111ª7; v. 2. 129b30–130ª28; viii. 3. 158b8–15; *Phys.* iv. 3. 210ª14–27; *On the Heavens* i. 11. 280b1–281ª7; *Gen. and Corrup.* i. 6. 322b29–32; *Meteorol.* iv. 4. 380b3–4; *Parts Anim.* ii. 2. 648ª36–649b8; *Gen. Anim.* i. 18. 724ª20–35; *Metaph.* i. 9. 992b18–20; iv. 2. 1003ª33–b10; vi. 4. 1028ª4–6; vii. 1. 1028ª10–15; vii. 4. 1030ª17–b13; ix. 1. 1046ª4–9; x. 1. 1052ª15–b1; xi. 1. 1060b31–1061ª7; 8. 1064b15–17; xii. 5. 1071ª29; xiv. 2. 1089ª7–9; *Pol.* iii. 3. 1276ª22–24; *Rhet.* ii. 23. 1398ª28–29.

100. *Cat.* 1. 1ª1–6; *Meteorol.* iv. 12. 389b28–390b2; *On the Soul* ii. 1. 412b9–22; *Parts Anim.* i. 1. 640b29–641ª6; *Gen. Anim.* i. 19. 726b19–24; ii. 1. 734b24–31, 735ª4–8; *Metaph.* vii. 10. 1035b22–25; *Pol.* i. 2. 1253ª20–25.

101. *Metaph.* vii. 10. 1035ª34–b3.

102. *Phys.* vii. 3. 245b12–246ª1, or 245b26–246ª22.

103. *Parts Anim.* ii. 2. 647b17–20.

104. *Top.* i. 15. 106ª9–35, 107ª13–17, 107b13–26; *Phys.* vii. 4. 248b6–10.

105. *Nic. Eth.* i. 6. 1096b26–27.

These differentiations are of particular importance in establishing the property of a thing or in refuting statements of alleged properties[106] or in setting up a definition,[107] particularly in the physical and biological sciences, where a word may mean the composite substance or the actuality or form, as "animal" may be thought to mean "a soul in a body" or a "soul."[108] The fundamental errors of both Democritus and Plato may be specified by identifying the ambiguities on which they depend, for Democritus identified form with configuration without recognizing that a living and a dead hand possess the same configuration or that a physician in a painting and a flute in a sculpture, in spite of their names, cannot perform the functions proper to physician and flute,[109] while Plato separated the Form and the sensible so completely that, despite contentions of Platonists to the contrary, the Idea of a thing and a particular instance of it have in common only the name they share.[110]

Although discourse (λόγος) is, in one sense, synonymous with thought (διάνοια), it is also, in another sense, not only distinct from thought but even contrary to it. The same method of discussion, consequently, is not suited to all opponents, for some stand in need of persuasion and others of compulsion. In the one case, the thought rather than the expressed argument must be met, and the thought is often based on difficulties derived from observation of the sensible world: refutation in such discussions should be directed to removing the source of error or ignorance. In the other case, those who argue for the sake of argument (λόγος) can be convinced only by emending the argument as expressed in words;[111] for it is possible to speak rightly in a sense and still think wrongly or be ignorant in another sense, since one's words may have a defensible meaning if properly qualified.[112] Sometimes similar arguments are advanced by those who hold a conviction and those who merely assert the position without conviction;[113] sometimes it is utterly impossible to believe what is asserted, as, for example, in the case of the assertion that the same thing is and is not, which some people think Heraclitus made; and, in general, a man does not necessarily believe what he says.[114]

106. *Top.* v. 2. 129ᵇ30–130ᵃ28.

107. *Ibid.* vi. 1. 139ᵃ25–27; 7. 146ᵃ33–35.

108. *Metaph.* viii. 3. 1043ᵃ29–ᵇ4; cf. also *On the Soul* i. 1. 403ᵇ9–19; ii. 1. 412ᵇ25–413ᵃ3; *Parts Anim.* i. 1. 640ᵇ29–641ᵃ32.

109. *Parts Anim.* i. 1. 640ᵇ29–641ᵃ6.

110. *Metaph.* i. 9. 990ᵇ6–8, 991ᵃ5–8; xiii. 4. 1079ᵃ2–4, 35–ᵇ3; *Top.* vi. 10. 148ᵃ14–21. Plato and the Platonists, however, held that the name shared by an Idea and by the particular which participated in it was used univocally and not equivocally (cf. *Metaph.* i. 6. 987ᵇ7–10 and x. 10. 1059ᵃ10–14).

111. *Metaph.* iv. 5. 1009ᵃ18–25.   113. *Ibid.* 6. 1011ᵃ3–13.

112. *Ibid.* 1009ᵃ30–36.   114. *Ibid.* 3. 1005ᵇ23–26.

Aristotle finds many instances in the doctrines of earlier philosophers[115] in
which a position is held, not because it resolves a difficulty, but merely for the
sake of argument;[116] and, conversely, one of the signs which he adduces to show
that scientific demonstration must proceed from necessary premises is the objection which we raise against any professed demonstration, that its major
premise is not a necessary truth, either because we think it impossible absolutely or at least for the sake of argument.[117] When a point is a matter of indifference to the inquiry in hand, it may be assumed for the sake of argument;[118]
but some limitation must be put on such modes of argument because of their
effect, not on the argument, but on the hearer. It is dangerous, thus, to maintain
some positions—such as that pleasure is the good and that to do injustice is
better than to suffer it—because resentment is inspired if one is thought to
maintain them, not for the sake of argument, but because one really thinks
them to be true.[119] Even the use of language that flows from knowledge is no
guaranty of its meaning, for scientific proofs and the verses of Empedocles can
be uttered by men under the influence of the passions, and those who have just
begun to learn a science can string together scientific phrases without knowing
the science.[120] Indeed, one usually has recourse to a long story (λόγος), like
those which slaves tell, when one has nothing sound to say.[121] The rule in interpretation, conversely, is to seek meanings in content or intention rather than
in the accidents of words; and, even in the case of law, the rule of equity bids
us be merciful to the weaknesses of human nature, to think less about the laws
than about the man who framed them, and less about what he said (λόγος)
than about what he meant (διάνοια).[122]

It is useful, for dialectical purposes, to have examined the number of meanings of a term both for the sake of clarity and to insure that our reasoning be in
accordance with the actual facts and not addressed to the terms alone. Such
examination helps one also both to avoid being misled and to mislead by false
reasoning. The latter manner of verbal discussion, however, is not proper even
to dialectic, and dialecticians should resort to it only when the subject of discussion cannot be treated in any other way;[123] and it is justified then, under the
rule that against an objector who sticks at nothing the defense should stick at
nothing.[124] The demonstration of the ambiguity of their terms is not an effective
device against people who argue eristically, and they must be treated, not as
refuting but as merely appearing to refute, for arguments are solved in such

115. *Phys.* i. 2. 185ª5–12.

116. *Ibid.* 6. 1011ᵇ1–3; 7. 1012ª5–7.

117. *Post. Anal.* i. 6. 74ᵇ18–21.

118. *Nic. Eth.* vi. 13. 1144ᵇ28–33.

119. *Top.* viii. 9. 160ᵇ17–22.

120. *Nic. Eth.* vii. 3. 1147ª18–24.

121. *Metaph.* xiv. 3. 1091ª5–9.

122. *Rhet.* i. 14. 1374ᵇ10–16.

123. *Top.* i. 18. 108ª18–37.

124. *Ibid.* v. 4. 1343ª3–4.

discussions by appeal to general estimation rather than to truth; but ambiguities should be removed from definitions in most discussions, and even against Platonists the demonstration that some of Plato's definitions do not apply to the Ideas is a useful argument.[125] Nonetheless, even in the treatment of fallacies and sophistical refutations, where the argument which turns on words alone is the commonest and most usual source of fallacies,[126] the distinction between arguments directed against the expression and arguments directed against the thought is absurd, for any pertinent treatment of the expression, even when the words are used ambiguously, is directed against the thought;[127] and, conversely, in the fallacy of many questions, when several problems are made into one, the refutation is purely verbal and therefore no refutation.[128]

In scientific discourse the formula is considered in relation to its subject matter, and the adequacy or truth of statement is tested by reference to things. Statements, including scientific propositions, may also be considered in relation to men, and the adequacy or effectiveness of statement is measured by the conviction or belief produced. The conviction of one who has acquired scientific knowledge is unshakable;[129] but, even if what is said is based on the most exact knowledge, it does not always produce conviction, for scientific argument (ὁ κατὰ τὴν ἐπιστήμην λόγος) implies instruction, and there are audiences who are unaffected by scientific reasons as there are people whom one cannot instruct.[130] If discourse is used for the purposes of science and for the attainment of truth, the proposition is constructed to express a reason or an argument adequate to the form of the thing, and all three—statement, reason, and form— may be signified by the same word, λόγος. If discourse is used for the purposes of communication and for the inducement of conviction, the effectiveness of reasons and the conception of subject matter are both determined by the constitution and predisposition of the audience. Three kinds of persuasion are furnished by speech (λόγος): the first depends on the character of the speaker, the second on putting the hearer into a certain state of mind, and the third on the speech (λόγος) itself in so far as it proves or seems to prove.[131]

What is true and what is just have a natural tendency to prevail over their opposites and to be more persuasive; but, whereas the end of inquiry and proof is to bring formula, knowledge, and thing into coincidence, persuasion is produced if the speech is delivered in a manner which arouses confidence in the speaker or if the passions of the hearers are aroused by the speech or if a truth or apparent truth is established in the speech by means of arguments apparently

125. *Soph. Ref.* 17. 175ᵃ31–176ᵇ28; *Top.* vi. 10. 148ᵃ14–22.

126. *Soph. Ref.* 1. 165ᵃ3–6.

127. *Ibid.* 10. 170ᵇ12–171ᵇ2.

128. *Ibid.* 30. 181ᵇ19–24.

129. *Post. Anal.* i. 2. 72ᵃ32–ᵇ4.

130. *Rhet.* i. 1. 1355ᵃ24–29.

131. *Ibid.* 2. 1356ᵃ1–4.

suited to the subject matter. To employ these means of persuasion the speaker must be capable (1) of syllogizing or reasoning, (2) of understanding characters and virtues, and (3) of understanding the passions and how they are aroused. The art of rhetoric, which is the study of means of persuasion, is therefore closely related to ethics and politics; and the manner of their relation may be seen, as was true also of the relation of logic to the theoretic sciences, by the derivative meanings attached to the word λόγος by the extension of "discourse" to the rational processes pertinent to the functions of speech. In scientific discourse the effort is to discover a formula or reason or form; λόγος is contrasted as reason, in this enterprise, to both sensation and the concrete thing, in spite of the fact that verbal discourse may be in contradiction with reason. In practical discourse the effort is not to know virtue but to make men virtuous, and virtue is determined by the rule of right reason; λόγος is contrasted as reason, in this enterprise, to character and passion, in spite of the fact that words may be determined by passion and action may be determined by words or passions rather than by reason. Rhetoric is therefore not an instrument of ethics and politics, although it is useful; and its scope, like that of dialectic, which likewise derives its principles from opinions and common-places, is not limited to any one subject matter but is universal. The criterion for rhetorical performance is not found in right reason, which determines the virtues of men and their relations under law, but in the common-places by which arguments are selected appropriate to speaker, occasion, and audience. Logic is an instrument of the sciences, since it treats of the construction and demonstration of formulae which express the nature and processes of things. Rhetoric, as a faculty of persuasion, treats of the construction of arguments, plausible to the occasion, which fix opinions and may lead to action. The "argument" of rhetoric is adapted to the character of the audience; the "reason" of the practical sciences determines what the character of individual men and the laws of the association of groups of men ought to be.

Reason (λόγος) is related to nature differently in the discovery of truth and the achievement of good. Truth is found in nature, reason, and statement; men are good by nature, habit, or reason. Speech may be contrary to reason in both: it may be the statement of fallacious argument and false conclusion, and it may be the consequence or the cause of immoral habits and actions. Reason may persuade to actions contrary to both nature and habit, and the problems of ethics and politics are determined by the fact that the good is achieved when nature, habit, and reason are in harmony; and yet, although man alone possesses reason, teaching and argument are not effective with all men.[132] As a consequence, the problems of action must be treated in terms both of the moral

132. *Pol.* vii. 13. 1332ᵃ38–ᵇ11; 15. 1334ᵇ6–28; *Nic. Eth.* x. 9. 1179ᵇ2–31.

habits of individuals and of the political constitutions of states. Moral virtue is a habit determined relative both to the nature and to the circumstances of the individual and also to the rule of right reason.[133] Reason may rule the irrational impulses of anger, wishing, and desire by means of habit, although only the prudent man is able to discern the rule of reason. Reason and mind are the end toward which nature strives in men. The state is a community, not merely of living beings, but of like beings, aiming at the best life possible. The various kinds of states and the many forms of government are determined by the various qualities of men and the many ways in which they seek happiness. The state is a natural composition and not a mere mixture; and conditions which determine its nature and unity, therefore, are not necessarily its organic parts but, rather, their ratio (λόγος) relative to the functions of the state with respect to such things as food, the arts, arms, revenue, religion, and decisions with respect to what is for the public interest and what is just in men's dealings with each other.[134] Justice, which is the expression of that ratio or proportion, is a virtue in the individual and the bond of union of the state.[135]

Right reason (λόγος) as it influences the formation of character and the promulgation of law, therefore, has analogies both to the definition (λόγος) in which the nature of things is stated in the physical sciences and the formula (λόγος) in which the proportions of quantities are stated in the mathematical sciences:

What affirmation and negation are in thought [διάνοια], pursuit and avoidance are in desire; so that since moral virtue is a habit concerned with choice, and choice is deliberate desire, therefore both the reason [λόγος] must be true and the desire right, if the choice is to be good, and the desire must pursue just what the reason asserts. Now this kind of thought and truth is practical: the good and the bad functioning of the intellect which is theoretic, and not practical nor productive, are truth and falsity respectively (for this is the work of every intellectual power); but the good functioning of the power which is practical and intellectual is truth in accordance with right desire.[136]

Similar considerations are relevant to the consideration of political problems, for law is reason (νοῦς) unaffected by desire.[137] Consequently, one way of forming a virtuous character is by instruction and education; and the possibility of political organization is to be found in the possession of speech, which permits man to differentiate the expedient and the inexpedient, the just and the

133. *Nic. Eth.* ii. 2. 1103b26–1104a10; 6. 1106b36–1107a2; iii. 12. 1119b15–19; vi. 1. 1138b18–34; 13. 1144b27–30.

134. *Pol.* vii. 8. 1328a21–b23; cf. *Gen. and Corrup.* 1. 10. 328a5–17.

135. *Nic. Eth.* v. 1–5. 1129a3–1134a16; *Pol.* i. 2. 1253a29–38; ii. 9. 1280a7–b12; ii. 11. 1282b1–13; iii. 16. 1287a28–b5.

136. *Nic. Eth.* vi. 2. 1139a21–31.

137. *Pol.* iii. 16. 1287a32.

unjust. Moreover, among the virtues there are those concerned with the inter-change of words and deeds (λόγοι καὶ πράγματα) in social intercourse—friendliness, which turns on a calculus of pleasures and pains; truthfulness, which depends on neither belittling what one has nor claiming more than one has; and ready wit and tact[138]—as well as the virtues of the part of the soul which possesses reason (λόγος).[139] Similarly, as the state depends on speech and instruction for the formation of the virtues of its citizens and the promulgation of laws appropriate to its constitution, so the art of politics determines which of the sciences should be studied in a state, which sciences each class of citizens should learn, and up to what point they should be taught.[140] The art of rhetoric, as a final consequence, may use speech adapted for the purposes of persuasion to the characters of men as they are and to the passions which may be incited in them.

Discourse may be considered, finally, not only in relation to its subject matter or to men but in relation to the structure and unity which a work of literature possesses when viewed as a concrete whole (σύνολον) composed of form and matter. Poetry is an imitation of things as they are or ought to be, and each kind of poetry produces its proper pleasure; but it is also a whole, complete in itself, with a beginning, middle, and end and with all the organic unity of a living creature.[141] Aristotle therefore analyzes tragedy—and, by implication, the other forms of poetry and the fine arts in general would submit to similar analyses—in terms of a whole consisting of six parts: plot, character, diction, thought, spectacle, and melody, of which two are derived from the means, one from the manner, and three from the object of imitation. Discourse not only supplies the matter from which the tragedy is constructed, since it is expressed in language (λόγος) with pleasurable accessories, but also the form, since the argument of plot (λόγος καὶ μῦθος) is the end, the principle, and the soul of tragedy;[142] the poem itself, moreover, may be viewed in its unity as a single speech (λόγος). Four of the parts of tragedy, to which melody and spectacle are added, repeat thus in the new interrelations pertinent to the artistic use of speech the elements that went into the determination of its scientific and practical use. The things, thoughts, and formulae of scientific speech have become the plot (which is a combination of incidents or things—πράγματα),[143] the thought, and the diction; while the reason, habit, and actions of ethics have become the thought, character, and plot. These alterations are signs of a change in the criteria pertinent to the use of language in art; for, whereas in

---

138. *Nic. Eth.* iv. 6–8. 1126ᵇ11–1128ᵇ9.

139. *Ibid.* vi. 1. 1139ᵃ3–15.   141. *Poet.* 23. 1459ᵃ17–24.

140. *Ibid.* i. 2. 1094ᵃ27–ᵇ7.   142. *Ibid.* 6. 1450ᵃ22–23, 38–39.

143. *Ibid.* 1450ᵃ5, 22, 32–33, 37; 14. 1453ᵇ2–3.

science consideration of the attributes of things, one in number or in reason, furnished criteria for statement, and in action consideration of the proportions of habits and circumstances depended on the rule of reason in the determination of virtues and laws, in art considerations of plot, character, and thought may yield justification for the statement of the impossible and the portrayal of the immoral.

Tragedy is an imitation of action. In the natural order of things there are two causes of action: thought and character; and the agents of an action necessarily have distinctive qualities of character and thought, since it is from these that we ascribe certain qualities to their actions.[144] Tragedy is essentially, however, an imitation not of persons but of action and life, of happiness and misery. The action of a play, consequently, is not for the sake of the characters, but the characters are included for the sake of the action.[145] Statement and action, in turn, serve to differentiate thought and character. Thought is defined as saying whatever can be said or what is appropriate to the occasion. The speeches in tragedy, therefore, fall under the arts of politics and rhetoric; and the older poets are said to have made their personages discourse like statesmen, the moderns like rhetoricians. Thought carries with it in tragedy reflections of the traits observed in scientific inquiry, for thought is shown in all that the characters say when proving or disproving some particular point or enunciating some universal proposition. Character, on the other hand, carries with it the traits of moral decision, for it reveals choice by making clear the kind of thing a character chooses or avoids where the choice is not obvious, and consequently character is conveyed only in those speeches (λόγοι) which express choice or avoidance.[146] Character is therefore revealed by speech or action,[147] while thought includes all the effects of language, with the requirement only that it be shown to be consistent with action.

In thought are included whatever effects are to be produced by language. Some of these effects are proof and refutation, the arousing of emotions (such as pity, fear, anger, and the like), and again amplification and diminution. But it is clear that in the incidents also, when effects of pity or terror or amplification or probability are to be produced, the same rules must be used. The only difference is that the effects in action must be apparent without explanation, whereas the effects in language are produced by the speaker and arise from his language. For what would be the use of a speaker, if things were apparent in the fashion in which they should be and not because of the statement?[148]

Yet, in the construction of that combination of incidents or things which constitutes the plot, argument and plot (λόγος καὶ μῦθος) are used as synonymous

144. *Ibid.* 1449ᵇ36–1450ᵃ7.
145. *Ibid.* 1450ᵃ15–29.
146. *Ibid.* 1450ᵇ4–15.
147. *Ibid.* 15. 1454ᵃ17–19.
148. *Ibid.* 19. 1456ᵃ36–ᵇ8.

terms;[149] and, like the soul, in which the rational should rule the irrational part, the plot or story (λόγος), in the interests of probability, should never be made up of improbable or irrational parts (μέρη ἄλογα).[150] The speech (λόγος) is the most inclusive part of diction (λέξις), and the poem as a whole, in turn, is a single speech (λόγος), formed by the conjunction of many speeches.[151]

III. THE ARTS OF LANGUAGE: HUMAN STATEMENTS AND THEIR STRUCTURE

The differentiation of the scientific, practical, and artistic uses of language serves to isolate the criteria that are relevant to the consideration of statements as argument and proof, as incitation to action or influence to good, and as artistic form and aesthetic object. Such distinctions do not depend, however, on classifying statements in fixed genera, as if they had natural forms, definitions, and species. A work which is essentially poetic may be practical in its effects on the characters of men and scientific in its statement of incidental arguments; and it may therefore be considered, so long as attention is directed either to practical consequences or to theoretic precision, in terms of other criteria than those of poetry. Poetry is treated as such in the *Poetics*; its educational function is taken up in the *Politics*; the statements and arguments of poets and of characters in poetry are analyzed in the *Rhetoric*; the moral situations and moral aphorisms of poets are used in the *Nicomachean Ethics*; and poetry and mythology are quoted as evidence in the *Metaphysics*. In like fashion, ethics and politics, though practical in character, are dependent on the conclusions and distinctions of theoretic sciences like psychology, and arguments in the practical sciences are subject to the criteria of logical demonstration. Science, in turn, may be considered relative to man as virtue to be pursued in life rather than as knowledge to be acquired relative to a subject matter; and considerations of order and style are not irrelevant to the verbal and symbolic forms in which the theoretic and practical sciences are set forth. These interrelations may be recognized, once the differentiation of linguistic functions has been made; and, what is more important, the consequences of substituting one set of criteria for another may then be stated unambiguously.

A poem, thus, may be considered in terms of its own unity, its effect on audiences, or its imitation of actual things. To consider a poem in itself, however, is to consider what Aristotle calls its "proper pleasure," that is, its effect on an audience so constituted and informed that its reactions may be traced to causes proper to the work of art, but not necessarily on an audience taken at random, which might react to qualities accidental to a poem or its circum-

149. *Ibid.* 5. 1449^b7–9; 17. 1455^a34–^b2 and 16–17.

150. *Ibid.* 24. 1460^a26–32.

151. *Ibid.* 20. 1456^b20–21 and 1457^a28–30.

stances. The examination of such reactions without some control to relate the reactions of the audience to qualities in the poem would furnish information concerning audiences rather than insight into the work of art. To consider a poem in itself is likewise to consider it as an organization of incidents, a development of characters, and an expression of thoughts, and all of these are effective as imitations of nature and of life; but they are effective not as a literal report of what actually occurs but as an artistic representation which has a life of its own and a probability which does not depend on historical accuracy.

A scientific argument, similarly, may be considered in terms of its adequacy to the facts, its effect on those who examine it, and its own structure of development. To consider a demonstrative argument in terms of its adequacy to the facts, however, is to trace it to first principles, which are indemonstrable. Principles which are believed by all men or by a consensus of scientists competent in the field are taken as true; yet the arguments to justify the acceptance of the principle scientifically are derived from the nature of things rather than from the authority of scientists, although that may be sufficient grounds for the belief of laymen. To consider a demonstrative argument in terms of its adequacy to the facts is likewise to trace the steps of its proof and the meanings of its terms; but the structure of symbolic organization and the assumed definitions are determined neither by the nature of the symbols themselves nor by arbitrary conventions and modes of operation but by the structure of things examined in the inquiries of the sciences.

A rhetorical argument, finally, may be examined in terms of its probable effects on an audience, its adequacy to its subject matter, or its formal structure. To consider a rhetorical speech in terms of persuasion, however, is also to examine the subject matter treated, not as it is according to the conclusions of the most competent experts and scientists, but as it may be presented most effectively to a given kind of audience. To consider a rhetorical speech in terms of persuasion is likewise to consider its organization and structure, not as a work of art or as a demonstration of science, but in terms of the appropriateness of the style and arrangement to the audience and circumstances of the speech.

The various uses to which language is put are thus subject to three arts of language—logic, rhetoric, and poetic—in which different purposes and different criteria select different aspects of language to constitute different wholes from different parts. Poetry may be distinguished from prose, and the prose of rhetorical metaphor may be distinguished from the prose of literal logical proposition, by characteristics that can be found in the least parts of which statements are composed, as well as in the causes of unity which bind parts into organized wholes. Those characteristics of treatise, speech, and poem; of syllogism, enthymeme, and plot; of interpretation, communication, and style;

and of proposition, sentence, and verse reflect in the qualities and structure of language the uses to which language is put and the relation of language to the thought expressed and to the subject matter treated.

In the sciences the concern is with statements literally true of some subject matter, and the least part of the discourse with which the logician is concerned is therefore a "term" or a word with a definition. Words which are used univocally, that is, when both the word and the definition answering to the word are the same, are carefully differentiated from words which are used equivocally, that is, when a common name has different definitions, and from words which are related derivatively, that is, when words have different terminations but one is derived from the other. On the basis of those distinctions it is possible to enumerate ultimate categories of terms by considering their manner of definition, predication, derivation, contrariety, or variation in degree. Once nouns have been differentiated from verbs by considerations of predication and time, a sentence may be defined as a significant portion of speech, some parts of which have an independent meaning as an utterance, though not as the expression of a judgment. The concern of logic is limited to propositions, that is, sentences which are true or false; and all other sentences, such as prayers, commands, threats, or all statements considered in any function other than their expression of truth or falsity, are relegated to the study of rhetoric or poetic.[152] A premise is a sentence affirming or denying one thing of another, and a syllogism or an argument is constructed by so relating two premises that one term may be affirmed or denied of all or of some of another term because of the relations of those two terms to a third term. Moreover, the affirmation or denial in the premises and the conclusion may be merely stated or may be stated to be necessary or probable. A science, viewed in terms of the data of experience and the processes of inquiry, may be treated as a collection of terms and the interrelations among them: subjects of which attributes happen to be asserted, consequents which follow from their assertion, and attributes inconsistent with them. The principles of the science will be found in that collection of terms, but as argument and proof the science is dependent on the pre-existent knowledge from which the conclusion follows in teaching or demonstration. Since scientific knowledge cannot be other than it is, the truth obtained by demonstration will be necessary; and scientific demonstration must be an inference from necessary premises, that is, from premises in which the attribute is true in every instance of its subject, essential and not accidental to its subject, and universal. We may, to be sure, fall into error in supposing our conclusion to be primary and universal, but the search for scientific principles is an inquiry into essential definitions

152. *Interpret.* 4. 17ᵃ1–7; cf. *Poet.* 19. 1456ᵇ8–13.

of the various genera of things and into the causes of inherence of attributes in the subjects in which they are found.

The logician is concerned with the examination of the conditions of proof and definition, for, although demonstration and scientific knowledge treat of necessary laws and invariable connections in things, it is possible to state the origins from which principles are derived and the grounds on which they are tested as well as the ways in which conclusions are derived validly from them in any science; and, although the sciences are distinguished from each other by their subject matters, principles, and methods and although demonstration cannot move from one genus of things to another, the logic of propositions and proof is common to the sciences. The entire analysis, not only of premises and demonstrative syllogisms but also of terms, depends on the assumption of a difference between essential and accidental predication based on a difference between substance and accident in existence. The demonstration of the existence of substance is the task of the metaphysician, and the subject of his inquiry includes the relation of statement to things, not, however, as the logician considers that relation but as an inquiry into their relative status as two instances of existence and into the implications derived from the nature of statements which are valid for the conditions of being. Examination of the principles of the sciences, which are proper in each case to the genus of things studied in each science, leads the metaphysician to the examination of the most certain principles of all things, which are both best known and nonhypothetical—the principle of contradiction and the principle of excluded middle. These principles are strictly indemonstrable, but they are subject to negative demonstration by *reductio ad absurdum*, since any statement whatsoever, including statements about substance and accident, can be shown to depend on assuming them. The basic truths which are common to several sciences are one, not literally but by analogy, since they are used differently in application to the particular genera of the different sciences. A principle of limitation may therefore be applied in the mathematical and physical sciences, since it is not the function of a scientist to demonstrate the existence of his subject matter or to solve difficulties that do not arise, truly or falsely, from the principles of his science. The differentiation of the theoretic sciences, which have as their end simply to know, depends on differences found in the things which constitute their subject matter, but it can be stated in terms of differences in their principles and in the necessity of their conclusions.

One large class of things exists "by nature," and such natural or physical things are distinguished from the products of art by the possession of an internal principle of motion and rest. They move and remain stationary in place according to fixed principles; some of them increase or decrease in size as a result of biological processes; some change in the qualities they possess and are generated and pass away. These natural things include compound inorganic bodies and their constitutive elements, plants and their parts, animals and their parts; all such objects are studied in the sciences of physics, which are, in turn, differentiated into the various subdivisions of physical, biological, and psychological inquiry, according to kinds of natures and motions. In general, the concern of physics with "natures" is reflected in its definitions and principles, for they are never purely formal but always include consideration of matter and motion, and they are arrived at by induction from the changing things of experience. The surfaces and volumes, lines, points, and numbers, which are the subject matter of mathematics, are contained, like the properties studied by the physicist, in physical bodies; and, indeed, they are also treated as physical properties rather than as mathematical entities in the various branches of physics. The mathematician, however, treats them differently from the physicist, for, although they cannot exist apart from matter and motion in fact, they can be abstracted in thought and treated separately in science. The definitions of mathematics therefore involve no reference to matter but are related to physical definitions as "curved" is to "snub"; and the principles of mathematics depend on this peculiarity of quantity which makes it alone among the properties of things susceptible of abstract scientific development. Quantities, so understood, include not only numbers, points, lines, surfaces, and solids but speech, time, and space, and the mathematical proposition takes its most characteristic form as a formula which states a proportion or an equality. Things and their qualities may be arranged in serial order or in proportions; and, in addition to the inferential consequences which follow concerning quantities in mathematics, proportions may be found in the consideration of motions, the genera of animals, the nature of justice in the physical and practical sciences, in analogies which yield insight into the likenesses of things in metaphysics, and in metaphors which have both rhetorical and poetic uses. Finally, those forms which not only can be known but also can exist apart from matter and motion are studied in First Philosophy or metaphysics. The concern of metaphysics with being as such, therefore, involves inquiry not only into the ultimate principles of knowledge and the ultimate causes of existence and change but also into the principles of order, the unmoved movers, which, themselves exempt from the mutability of which they are the source and formulation, determine the interrelations of the universe, and among which God is supreme. The general differentiation of forms according to their existence and intelligibility in matter and apart from matter determines the differences among the definitions and principles, and therefore among the methods of inquiry and proof, in the three theoretic sciences—physics, mathematics, and metaphysics.

All three of the theoretic sciences, despite differences in their subject matter and, consequently, in their principles, treat of that which cannot be other than it is—that is, of the necessary rather than the contingent. Scientific propositions must be necessary, not merely probable; but necessity may be either "simple" or "hypothetical." Simple or absolute necessity is found in the relation of properties and definitions or essences, which imply each other and which are never found separate one from the other. Both the processes of physics and the inferences of mathematics require departure from this simple necessity to two varieties of hypothetical necessity. Both involve assumptions, which, if granted or satisfied, yield necessary conclusions; but the direction of the hypothetical reasoning is precisely opposite in the two sciences: in mathematics from antecedents to consequents, in physics from consequents to antecedents.[153] In mathematics if the premises are granted or are established, the argument can be shown to follow necessarily, but the premises are not necessarily true if the conclusion which is shown to follow from them is known to be true. In physics, if a process or motion has been completed, the antecedent steps can be shown to have occurred necessarily, but it does not follow from the existence of the antecedent stages that the effect must necessarily follow. The conclusions of mathematics are thus necessary and universal, even though its subject matter does not exist as it is known, for the antecedents may be shown to be necessary only if the relation is abstract; and the conclusions of physics are necessary and universal, even though they treat of that which happens always or for the most part, for the consequences follow necessarily only if the causes are unimpeded. Necessity in all three sciences depends on the discovery of essence: in metaphysics the discovery of essence is made in analogies, in mathematics it is stated in axioms, in physics it depends on matter; in all three the establishment of necessary propositions is a problem of definition and of the causes of the inherence of properties.

The subject matter of the practical and productive sciences does not permit as much precision as is possible in the theoretic sciences. The definitions of the virtues and of tragedy are not statements of the essences of "natural" things but rather of the formation of things which may be changed by human decision and choice, and the knowledge of either may be a means of generating them or of determining the characteristics they should have. Knowledge of falling bodies will not affect the law of their fall, but it may lead to the institution of an art for their utilization or control. Knowledge of the causes of appetites and passions will not affect the psychological laws of their incidence, but it may lead by action and habituation to a virtue which will control or suppress them. Definitions in the practical and productive sciences are therefore not strict

153. *Phys.* ii. 9. 199[b]34–200[b]8.

definitions by genera and differentia, since there are no precisely drawn or natural species of virtues, institutions, or art-forms, but definitions can be formed by consideration of causes in nature or man and of parts in the habit or artificial object. Principles cannot be formulated as necessary, but they can be found in the rule of right reason in action and in the forms suited to achieve ends in art. The method of the statesman in ethics and politics and the method of the critic in poetic depend on the use of a logical method analogous to that employed by the theoretic scientist, while differing from it as the method of one theoretic science differs from that of another, that is, in the manner in which principles are established and in the significances attached to terms in definitions. Both action and production lead to verbal arts, however, which are distinct from the practical and the productive sciences. Rhetoric has close connections with the subject matter of ethics and politics and with the method of dialectic; but it may construct arguments for either of two contrary positions, and it is without limitations to subject matter, being in this respect like dialectic and unlike the sciences; and it may employ means of persuasion which go beyond the formal limits of dialectical argumentation. Poetry may construct arguments similar to those of politics and rhetoric, but both are employed to make actions and characters plausible; and the use of diction in the construction of a poem is distinct from the use of inductive and deductive syllogisms, by which the nature of poetic devices is examined in the science of poetic.

Both dialectic and rhetoric employ "common-places" in the establishment and refutation of arguments. The common-places of dialectic, however, are used to set up or test definitions of terms, their genera, the properties asserted of them, and the accidents that may be connected with them. Dialectic explores defensible relations among terms as such; and in this function it may be a preliminary to, or even a part of, scientific inquiry. The common-places of rhetoric, on the other hand, serve to arrange subject matters as they might be presented and to prepare arguments as they might be effective, preliminary to inquiring into the styles and organizations of speeches appropriate to arguments chosen with reference to the circumstances and tendencies of particular kinds of hearers. The treatment of rhetoric, consequently, falls into three distinct, though related, parts, two concerned with what should be said as pertinent, first, to the relation of subject matter and audience and, second, to the relation of speaker and audience,[154] and one concerned with language conceived as the manner of presenting what should be said.[155]

Rhetoric is not bound to a single definite subject matter but is universal; and the better one succeeds in establishing propositions proper to a subject matter, the more one departs from the proper concern of rhetoric with words and forms

154. *Rhet.* ii. 22. 1395^{b}24–1396^{a}3.   155. *Ibid.* iii. 1. 1403^{b}15–22.

of reasoning suited to persuasion and enters one of the special sciences concerned with definite subjects. There are, nonetheless, three kinds of rhetoric determined by the three classes of listeners to speeches; and their subject matters are determined, in turn, not by intrinsic characteristics but by the operations of persuasion proper to such subject matters, the times of their occurrence, and the ends envisaged in persuasion. Political or deliberative oratory consists in urging us to do or not to do something; it is concerned with the future; its end is to establish the expediency or harmfulness of a proposed course of action. Forensic or legal oratory consists in attacking or defending somebody; it is concerned with the past; its end is to establish the justice or injustice of some action. Epideictic or ceremonial oratory consists in praising or censuring somebody; it is concerned with the present; its end is to prove a man worthy of honor or the reverse. In each of these fields the orator will equip himself with common-places from which to derive arguments for or against any pertinent position. When persuasion is achieved by proof or apparent proof, it makes use of two means: the enthymeme, which is like the syllogism in dialectic, and the example, which is like induction in dialectic. Since rhetoric is concerned with such matters as we deliberate upon without arts or systems to guide us, its arguments deal with what is, in the main, contingent. The materials of enthymemes are probabilities and signs, and probabilities are distinguished from signs in the field of contingent things in a fashion similar to the distinction of propositions that are generally true from those that are necessarily true in science. A probability is a statement of what usually happens, and it is related to any instance as a universal is related to a particular; signs are related to the statement of which they are signs as antecedent to consequent or cause to effect: the sign is infallible if the reasoning is from universal to particular (as when fever is taken as a sign of illness), but it is fallible if the reasoning is from particular to universal (as when fast breathing is taken as a sign of fever). Rhetorical reasoning is directed to a choice between alternatives for action, and it proceeds from signs and probabilities and from opinions accepted by our judges; dialectical reasoning is directed to the separation of essential from accidental predication, and it proceeds from opinions generally accepted; scientific demonstration depends on essential premises, since one does not have reasoned knowledge of conclusions derived from accidental premises even when they are invariable signs,[156] and on true and primary premises, which are believed on the strength not of anything else but of themselves.[157] Arguments in the physical sciences deal with the relations of antecedents and consequences. Although

156. *Rhet.* i. 2. 1356ᵃ35–1358ᵃ2; *Pr. Anal.* ii. 27. 70ᵃ3–ᵇ38; *Post. Anal.* i. 6. 75ᵃ28–37; *Soph. Ref.* 5. 167ᵇ8–20.

157. *Top.* i. 1. 100ᵃ25–ᵇ23.

these relations are found in occurrences which are not necessary but take place for the most part, as heavy bodies usually fall, they can be related to necessary laws by definitions which determine essential nature and by hypothetical propositions which bear on occurrences, as heavy bodies may be distinguished from light and the laws of falling bodies in the absence of restraining forces may be stated universally. In rhetoric, on the other hand, as well as in dialectic, the more correctly a particular subject is handled, the further the argument departs from rhetoric and dialectic.[158]

A statement or argument is persuasive and credible because there is somebody whom it persuades. In dialectic the principles of discussion are found in the distinctions between definition, genus, property, and accident; but in rhetoric they are derived from the view of the facts which the speaker can make acceptable to his audience, and the example, enthymeme, and maxim must therefore be considered in terms of a second group of common-places which bear, not on the plausibility of arguments relative to the alternatives presented, but on their plausibility relative to the persons addressed. In dialectic no separate consideration of the audience is required, but rather, since the opposition is between the consequences of the hypotheses entertained, the intrusion of a bias of opinion or a particular interpretation of statements can be exposed as fallacious reasoning. In rhetoric, on the contrary, the audience addressed determines both the subject matter appropriate to its interests in the particular common-places proper to the classification and treatment of the facts and also the principles that may be used effectively in the general common-places appropriate to the arguments.

Finally, and for much the same reason, the style and the arrangement of a rhetorical speech form a separate consideration in rhetoric, for, when language may be metaphorical as well as literal, words are an additional means of persuasion and their effective use depends on additional criteria found in the correctness, impressiveness, appropriateness, and rhythm of language. Scientific demonstration must be expressed in univocal terms and literal statement, and the criteria of expression, like those of thought, are determined by considerations of adequacy to the subject matter of the demonstration. Dialectical proof and refutation are directed to removing ambiguity, and the virtues of language are determined by the intellectual processes by which properties and definitions are separated from accidents. Rhetoric, however, has three separate problems in the use of language for persuasion, for the effects of argument depend not only on the plausibility derived from (1) adapting the argument to the issue and (2) making it acceptable to the audience but also on (3) the style in which the argument is set forth and the arrangement of the statement and proof.

158. *Rhet.* i. 2. 1358ª2–26.

The language of poetry is distinct from that of prose;[159] and, although oratorical prose at first took on a poetical color in writers like Gorgias, poetic may be distinguished from rhetoric by differences in the uses of the common resources of language and metaphor which distinguish poetic and rhetorical styles, in turn, from the literal predications and proofs of logic. The poetic use of language is not defined, however, by the use of verse and poetic rhythms but depends on the nature of poetry. A medical or physical theory does not become poetry by being stated in verse, but the nature of poetry is to be found in imitation,[160] while science consists in demonstration from necessary and primary principles. Nor is the distinction between history and poetry in the fact that one is written in prose and the other in verse; for history is not made poetry by being turned into verse, but history describes the thing that has been, while poetry describes the possible, and the statements of history are therefore singulars, while those of poetry are of the nature of universals.[161]

The possibility of science depends on argument which flows from definitions or formulae of what is essential in the nature of things; the possibility of poetry depends on a plot or argument which imitates what is possible of occurrence. Since questions of existence in general involve questions of unity and since to be is to be one, the differences in the constitution and existence of sciences and poems may be seen in the differences in the conditions of their being one. A single science deals with one genus of things,[162] and a single poem represents one action.[163] In short, the unity of a science is based on the nature of a kind of thing, while the unity of a poem reflects the completion of a kind of happening. The differences between these two sources of unity may be seen by contrasting the marks of unity found in the proofs of science with those found in the plot of poetry and by comparing the sources of necessity and probability on which each is grounded.

The unity of demonstrative proof is additive, that is, it is found in the parts and in the combinations of parts into wholes, by the opposition of terms, prior and posterior, and the interposition of middle terms; and for this reason Aristotle is careful to state the conditions which mark the single term,[164] the single proposition,[165] the single syllogism,[166] and the basic premises peculiar to each

159. *Ibid.* iii. 1. 1404^{a}19–38.

160. *Poet.* 1. 1447^{b}16–21.   161. *Ibid.* 9. 1451^{a}36–^{b}7.

162. *Post. Anal.* i. 7. 75^{a}38–^{b}20; 28. 87^{a}38–^{b}4; *Metaph.* iv. 2. 1003^{b}11–15; x. 4. 1055^{a}31–33.

163. *Poet.* 8. 1451^{a}31–35.

164. *Cat.* 2. 1^{a}16–19; 4. 1^{b}25–27; *Interpret.* 2. 16^{a}19–27; 3. 16^{b}6–8; *Pr. Anal.* i. 1. 24^{b}16–18, 26–30, 33–34; 47^{b}15–48^{a}28; *Post. Anal.* i. 19–22. 81^{b}10–84^{b}2; *Top.* i. 15. 106^{a}1–107^{b}37.

165. *Interpret.* 5. 17^{a}20–24; 8. 18^{a}13–27; *Pr. Anal.* i. 1. 24^{a}16–28.

166. *Pr. Anal.* i. 1. 24^{b}18–27.

science.[167] Science depends on the discovery of middle terms to account for properties of things or connections among things. A science may therefore grow without endangering its unity, not by the interposition of fresh middle terms, since the true cause of the connection is sought, but by the apposition of fresh extreme terms and, consequently, by the addition of new conclusions.[168] There may, however, be more than one demonstration of one connection, but in each case the true cause of a connection is the proximate and not the universal cause.[169] The unity of a poem, on the other hand, is organic, that is, it depends on the completeness of the work as a whole possessed of a beginning, middle, and end. The other parts of the poem—characters, thought, diction, melody, and spectacle—depend on the primary part, plot, which is the life and soul of a tragedy; and the incidents which make up the single action of the plot are so related to the whole that the transposition or omission of one of them will disjoin and dislocate the whole.[170] The other parts of a tragedy may be arranged serially after plot, according to their effectiveness in achieving the end of the poem: second after plot come the characters, and, indeed, some suppose erroneously that the unity of a plot consists in having one man as its subject; third comes thought; fourth, diction; and, of the remaining two, melody is the greatest of the pleasurable accessories of tragedy, and spectacle, though an attraction, has the least to do with the art of poetry. The unity sought in the practical sciences is achieved in the character of the individual man and the constitution of the state. Rhetoric has analogies to the methods of all sciences: theoretic, practical, and productive. It is similar to logic in that persuasion is effected by argument: the parts of a speech are the statement of the case and the proof, and these are comparable to the statement of a problem and the demonstration;[171] the relevant parts of speech in both rhetorical and logical argument are the noun and the verb; but the greater dependence of rhetoric on verbal connections gives the conjunction an importance for rhetoric which it does not have for logic;[172] and the unity is additive, in the sense that the speech has no natural definition or determination of unity, and the style of prose must be either free-running, in which the parts are united by nothing except the connecting words, or periodic, in which the speech is composed of periods, com-

167. *Post. Anal.* i. 9. 75^{b}37–76^{a}30.

168. *Ibid.* 12. 78^{a}14–21; 32. 88^{b}3–29.

169. *Ibid.* 29. 87^{b}15–18; ii. 18. 99^{b}9–14.

170. *Poet.* 6. 1450^{a}16–^{b}20; 8. 1451^{a}30–35; 23. 1459^{a}17–24.

171. *Rhet.* iii. 13. 1414^{a}30–36.

172. *Ibid.* 2. 1404^{a}26–27; 5. 1407^{a}19–30—^{b}11–14; 6. 1407^{b}37–1408^{a}1; 9. 1409^{a}24–27; 12. 1413^{b}31–34. Dionysius of Halicarnassus and Quintilian are authorities for the later tradition, built on these passages, that Aristotle enumerated three parts of speech: the noun, the verb, and the conjunction.

plete in themselves, and the periods may, in turn, be further divisible into members.[173] The criterion for determining the unity of the period is not derived, as the criterion for the unity of a proposition is, from consideration of its subject matter but rather resembles the marks of the unity of a poem; for a period is a portion of speech that has in itself a beginning and an end, being at the same time not too big to be taken in at a glance. But rhetoric differs from both logic and poetic in that a speech has no least parts comparable to the univocal terms of scientific demonstrations and no organic whole comparable to the plots of dramas; for the subject matter of oratory is not treated by scientific analysis and definition, in which terms acquire unique meanings, or by the devices of artistic imitation, in which plots acquire necessity or probability, but by the common-places of persuasion, in which the facts and their interpretation in argument and the use and manners of narration are all determined by reference to particular audiences.

In the theoretic sciences the truth obtained is necessary because of its dependence on knowledge of essential definitions and causes. A scientist occasionally makes use of arguments from probability or from signs, although neither provides demonstrative or scientific knowledge. Moreover, since a probability is a generally approved proposition—that is, what men know to happen or not to happen, to be or not to be, for the most part thus and thus—recourse to probability without other supporting evidence is usually an indication of a dubious extension of doctrine explicable only by taking into account the position or information of the scientist;[174] a sign, on the other hand, is a demonstrative proposition, necessary or generally approved, based on the coexistence and interrelation of things; and, although it is not necessary knowledge or based on causes, even when the connection is invariable and therefore necessary, it is a useful heuristic device preliminary to scientific inquiry or a substitute for scientific knowledge when causes are not to be found.[175]

Nature forms only part of the subject matter of the practical sciences, however, for men are good and virtuous by habit and reason as well as by nature, and art and education are designed to fill up the deficiencies of nature.[176] We deliberate about things that are in our power and subject to our choices and

---

173. *Ibid.* 9. 1409ª24–ᵇ32.

174. Cf. *Phys.* iv. 8. 214ᵇ23; *Meteorol.* i. 8. 346ª30; 14. 351ᵇ19; 352ª2; *Gen. Anim.* iv. 1. 765ª27–28; *Metaph.* iv. 3. 1005ª32.

175. *Pr. Anal.* i. 27. 70ª3–ᵇ38; cf. also *Interpret.* 1. 16ª16; *Post Anal.* i. 4. 73ª32; ii. 1. 89ᵇ27; *Phys.* iv. 11. 219ᵇ3; 12. 221ᵇ5–6; *Meteorol.* i. 8. 346ª23; 9. 346ᵇ34; 12. 348ª33–34; ii. 8. 367ᵇ8; iv. 2. 380ª1; *On Divination by Dreams* 1. 462ᵇ26–463ª3; 2. 463ᵇ22–31; *Hist. Anim.* i. 9. 491ᵇ15, 24; 10. 492ª4; 11. 492ᵇ1, 7; iii; 20. 522ª17; vi. 15. 569ᵇ4; 17. 570ᵇ28; ix. 7. 613ª30; *Gen. Anim.* iii. 10. 760ᵇ33; *Metaph.* i. 1. 980ª21, 981ᵇ7; ii. 1. 993ª31; iv. 2. 1004ᵇ17. For the combination of probability and sign cf. *Meteorol.* iii. 3. 372ᵇ22.

176. *Pol.* vii. 13, 1332ª38–ᵇ11; vii, 17. 1337ª1–3.

desires, not about things that happen by necessity or by nature or by chance; and therefore deliberation and action are concerned with things that happen in a certain way for the most part but in which the event is obscure, and with things in which it is indeterminate.[177] In such matters reason and habit, rather than nature, necessity, or chance, may be causes; and the end of ethics and politics is to bring character and reason to bear on matters of choice. Rhetoric is concerned with the same matters; but in ethics and politics action is influenced by reason through the formation of moral character and the institution of law, while in rhetoric action is influenced by persuasion suited to existing characters and conceptions of institutions. Since the persuasions have to do with contingent things, they are based not on universal laws but on probabilities and signs, on opinions held and coincidences observed.

The function of the poet, finally, is to describe, not what must happen or what has happened (and he will seek, therefore, neither scientific necessities and signs based on the nature of things nor historical probabilities and signs based on actual occurrences), but what might happen or what is possible, setting it forth as necessary and probable (and he is therefore, on the one hand, concerned, like the historian, with actions peculiar to individuals and their circumstances, while, on the other hand, his statements are universal, like those of the philosopher). The necessary statements of science are based on the discovery of a "universal" attribute, that is, an attribute which belongs to every instance of its subject and to every instance essentially and as such;[178] and necessity in the occurrences of nature is of two kinds: it may work in accordance with a thing's natural tendency or by constraint and in opposition to it.[179] In rhetoric, universals and common principles are less effective than the simple statement of what is known and near at hand;[180] and therefore the rhetorician uses probabilities, which are the judgment of what happens for the most part, and signs, which indicate interconnections, necessary or fallible, among things. In poetry, finally, a "universal" is defined as the sort of thing that a certain type of man will probably or necessarily say or do.[181] The incidents of a plot must not be impossible, and they must, in addition to their possibility, be credible. Possibility and credibility are interrelated, since the possible is credible; and, whereas we do not yet believe in the possibility of a thing which has not happened, that which has happened is obviously possible.[182] Possibility and credibility may, however, be in opposition, and in such a case a probable impossibility is preferable to an unconvincing possibility; but the ar-

---

177. *Nic. Eth.* iii. 3. 1112ª18–ᵇ11.

178. *Post. Anal.* i. 4. 73ᵇ26–33.

179. *Ibid.* ii. 11. 94ᵇ37–95ª3.

180. *Rhet.* ii. 22. 1395ᵇ27–1396ª3.

181. *Poet.* 9. 1451ᵇ8–11.

182. *Ibid.* 1451ᵇ16–19.

gument or story should have no irrational parts or improbable incidents.[183] Impossibilities may be justified by consideration of the nature of poetry or of the ideal or of opinion.[184] Improbabilities may be defended by showing that they are in accordance with opinion or that at times they are not improbable, for there is a probability of things happening against probability.[185] If the poet has succeeded in achieving necessity, his poem is probable, but he may achieve probability short of necessity.

Like the rhetorician, the poet must make what he says credible, and he is dependent, therefore, on probability in the sense of what would follow from opinions or information held. The rhetorician supplements his probabilities with signs, which mark interconnections and coincidences without specifying reasons, whereas the poet must seek the necessities and reasons for the interconnections; and, indeed, the use of signs is the least artistic kind of discovery, and the poet has recourse to it only through lack of invention.[186] The scientist, unlike the rhetorician, is unconcerned to make his theory credible on other grounds than on the evidence of its truth, and therefore the presentation in scientific discourse of a probability without necessity or at least signs expresses only the scientist's conviction in hypotheses entertained without factual support. The physical scientist may discover a hypothetical necessity in a process of change if he can show the dependence of an occurrence on causal antecedents; the necessity sought by the poet is determined by the beginning and the end of a sequence of events and depends on finding stages, necessary or probable, from one to the other. He can establish the necessity and probability in incidents,[187] in character,[188] in thought,[189] or in diction.[190] Where the scientist strives to abstract from inferences based on his own character (for mathematical discourses depict no character)[191] and to bring his thought into conformity with the facts, the dramatist makes use of characters and thought to supplement the necessity and probability of the facts and incidents.

One should always seek in characters just as in the organization of incidents [τῇ τῶν πραγμάτων συστάσει] the necessary or the probable, so that it is either necessary or probable for a person of such a description to say or do things of this description, and either necessary or probable for this thing to happen after that.[192]

183. *Ibid.* 24. 1460ᵃ26–32.

184. *Ibid.* 25. 1460ᵇ22–1461ᵃ4, ᵇ9–14.

185. *Ibid.* 1460ᵇ32–1461ᵃ9, ᵇ14–15; cf. also *ibid.* 18. 1456ᵃ23–25.

186. *Ibid.* 16. 1454ᵇ19–30, 1455ᵃ19–20.

187. *Ibid.* 7. 1451ᵃ9–15; 8. 1451ᵃ22–29; 9. 1451ᵃ36–1452ᵃ1; 10. 1452ᵃ12–21.

188. *Ibid.* 15. 1454ᵃ33–36.

189. *Ibid.* 19. 1456ᵇ2–4.

190. *Ibid.* 17. 1455ᵇ8–12.

191. *Rhet.* iii. 16. 1417ᵃ18–20.

192. *Poet.* 15. 1454ᵃ33–36.

The necessity or probability may be achieved, moreover, either by what happens or by what the character thinks or knows; and therefore necessity and probability are achieved better in complex plots than in simple plots in which the change in the hero's fortunes takes place without reversal or discovery; for reversal is a change in the state of things to its opposite in the probable or necessary sequence of events[193] and discovery is a change from ignorance to knowledge (and consequently to either love or hate in the persons marked for good or evil fortune), which is achieved best by means of a probable incident.[194]

The problem of thought is the same in rhetoric and poetic, and therefore the subject is referred in the *Poetics* to the treatment of thought which occupies the first two books of the *Rhetoric*.[195] In their respective uses of language, both poetic and rhetoric are related to, but distinct from, the art of elocution;[196] but rhetoric has a special problem of arrangement in the construction of a speech; and, although the styles of rhetoric and poetic make use of similar resources of language, the virtues and problems of rhetorical style are the converse of those of poetry. The organization of a drama is inseparable from the structure of its plot; but, since persuasion is a kind of proof, the arrangement of a speech has analogies with logic rather than with poetic, and the two essential parts of a speech are the statement of the case and the argument, which are similar to the statement of a problem and the proof.[197] The introduction, however, is comparable to the prologue in poetry and the prelude in music.[198] The perfection of style or diction in both rhetoric and poetic is achieved by choice of language at once clear and appropriate, without either meanness or undue elevation.[199] The difference between poetry and prose is therefore to be found not merely in the distinction between the meters of verse and the rhythms of prose[200] but in the fact that clarity is achieved easily in prose by the use of ordinary words, whereas meanness is avoided easily in poetry by the use of unfamiliar terms— such as strange words, metaphors, lengthened forms—which depart from the ordinary modes of speech.[201] The center of interest in both poetic and rhetoric is therefore the metaphor, but for opposite reasons. Prose writers must pay specially careful attention to metaphor, because their other resources are

193. *Ibid.* 11. 1452ª22–29.

194. *Ibid.* 1452ª29–37; 16. 1455ª16–19.

195. *Ibid.* 19. 1456ª33–ᵇ8; cf. *Rhet.* ii. 26. 1403ª34–ᵇ2.

196. *Poet.* 19. 1456ᵇ8–19; *Rhet.* iii. 1. 1403ᵇ21–1404ª19.

197. *Rhet.* iii. 13. 1414ª30–36.

198. *Ibid.* 14. 1414ᵇ19–21; 1415ª8–24.

199. *Ibid.* iii. 2. 1404ᵇ1–17; *Poet.* 22. 1458ª18–21.

200. *Rhet.* iii. 8. 1408ᵇ21–32.   201. *Ibid.* 2. 1404ᵇ1–26; *Poet.* 22. 1458ª21–ᵇ5.

scantier than those of poets,[202] whereas for poets it is the most effective of the numerous poetic forms designed to give diction a nonprosaic character. Mastery of metaphors cannot be learned from others, and it is also a sign of natural genius (εὐφυΐα), since a good metaphor implies an intuitive perception of the similarity in dissimilars.[203] It is comparable, therefore, to quick wit (ἀγχίνοια) or sagacity (εὐστοχία) in the perception of middle terms in demonstrations and similarities in things[204] and to excellence in deliberation (εὐβουλία) concerning alternative courses of action.[205]

The whole treatment of style in the two treatises reflects the tendency of prose to clarity and to the standards of ordinary speech and the tendency of poetry to distinction and the use of uncommon modes of expression. Special attention is given in the *Rhetoric* to current and ordinary words, nouns, and verbs; and strange words, inappropriate epithets, and poetic metaphors are censured as faults.[206] In the *Poetics*, on the other hand, style or diction is analyzed into eight parts, which include the characteristics, parts, and adornments of the word itself—the letter, the syllable, the conjunction, the article, the noun, the verb, the case, and the speech—as well as the ordinary meanings of nouns and verbs; and nouns are differentiated to include not only the ordinary word for the thing but strange words, metaphors, ornamental words, coined words, and words lengthened, curtailed, or altered in forms. The styles appropriate to the various kinds of rhetoric may be distinguished in terms of the qualities which make them suitable either to be read or to be heard, and the epideictic style is particularly suited to written prose, for it is meant to be read.[207] The styles of poetry, on the other hand, may be distinguished by the use of compounds in dithyrambs, strange words in heroic poetry, and metaphors in iambic poetry; and in the latter, which models itself on the spoken language, only those kinds of words are proper which are allowable also in an oration, that is, the ordinary word, the metaphor, and the ornamental equivalent.[208]

Aristotle's treatment of the arts of logic, rhetoric, and poetic was pioneer work—as he himself pointed out when he laid claims, directly and by implication, to originality in the analysis and formulation of these arts—not because

202. *Rhet.* iii. 2. 1405ª6–10.

203. *Poet.* 22. 1459ª4–8; cf. also *Top.* viii. 14. 163ᵇ9–16; *Nic. Eth.* iii. 7. 1114ª31–ᵇ12; *Rhet.* i. 6. 1362ᵇ23–25; *Poet.* 17. 1455ª32–34.

204. *Post. Anal.* i. 34. 89ᵇ10–20; cf. also *Nic. Eth.* vi. 9. 1142ª32–ᵇ6; *Rhet.* i. 6. 1362ᵇ23–25; iii. 11. 1412ª9–14.

205. *Nic. Eth.* vi. 7. 1141ᵇ12–14; 9. 1142ª31–ᵇ33.

206. *Rhet.* iii. 2. 1404ᵇ5–10, ᵇ26–1405ª2; 3. 1405ᵇ34–1406ᵇ19.

207. *Ibid.* iii. 12. 1413ᵇ3–1414ª18.

208. *Poet.* 22. 1459ª8–16.

he was the first to speculate on the uses of language but because he was the first to differentiate the ends for which language may be employed and to set forth the devices by which those ends may be achieved and the faults to which the devices are subject. The Pythagoreans, Socrates, Plato, and Democritus, in particular, had exemplified and analyzed the devices of inquiry, definition, and proof; but none of them had set forth the detailed requirements of scientific propositions, syllogisms, and principles; of dialectical proof and refutation; or of sophistical fallacies in a fashion adapted to the various requirements of the various sciences. There were handbooks of rhetoric before Aristotle wrote his treatise on that art; and the Sophists, Plato, and Isocrates had speculated on its philosophic ramifications; but none of them had had anything to say about the enthymeme, which Aristotle thought to be the substance of rhetorical persuasion, and what they wrote therefore concerned only the accidental accessories of the art. The poets and Plato had written about poetry with great insight; but what they had said bore usually on the truth, the political circumstances, or the psychological and moral effects of poetry rather than on its characteristics and standards.

In each of the arts of language Aristotle laid down lines of technical analysis and established basic terms in technical significances. His analysis of the arts and the meanings he gave to the terms depended, however, on the separation of the sciences and precise distinction of methods and arts. These basic distinctions have continued to operate in the history of Aristotle's influence; but criteria and methods have been scrambled, and revolutions have been worked in each of the arts by giving it functions and devices borrowed, usually without awareness of the derivation, from the other arts. When Aristotle's dictum that each science has its proper method has been forgotten and attention has been focused on the syllogism to the exclusion of the principles of the particular sciences, the "Aristotelian logic" has become "formal logic" or has become a science in which theory could be separated from practice, and its deficiencies were then to be remedied by investigating categories of things, discovering laws of thought, or establishing rules of symbolic operation. Or, following the lead of Cicero, who found a logic of discovery in Aristotle's rhetoric and dialectic, medieval philosophers were able to identify logic and dialectic; and the humanists and philosophers of the Renaissance, from Ramus to Bacon, found in the method of the common-places and the particular-places a remedy for the irrelevancies of formal logic in reconstituting the method of philosophy, literature, and the sciences. Historians could then discover the beginnings of anything peculiar to the Aristotelian logic in earlier writers; and pragmatists, denying the distinction between theoretic and practical, and between science and art, could seek the bases of all operations, not in the nature of the external world or in the structure of the mind, but in the processes of production. Rhetoric itself, even while it was being used as a source for new analyses in logic and poetic, was transformed, in turn, into a practical science conjoined with politics, a method for analyzing literature and Scripture, a technique for presenting legal arguments and for writing letters, and, finally, losing all connection with arguments, an analysis of figures of speech and style. Poetic, following the lead of Horace, was expressed in the remnants of Aristotelian language, interpreted rhetorically by reference to intentions of artists and effects on audiences; or, following the hint of Plato, it was used to trace moral and therapeutic consequences; or, using Platonic arguments to reverse Plato, it consisted in the discovery that poetry rather than philosophy is the architectonic discipline and the fullest expression of truth; or, it undertook to explain poetry by its social and psychological sources or to examine it as an instrument for social and economic revolution and counterrevolution. The influence of Aristotle can be found less surely in repetitions of his doctrines and conclusions than in the use to which his distinctions have been put to improve or undermine the arts as he conceived them. Yet such tangential influence is itself evidence of the vitality of the distinctions on which Aristotle's differentiation of methods and arts is based; and the disentanglement and restatement of that differentiation is useful, not only in throwing historical light on the complex evolution of the discussion of scientific, practical, and artistic problems since his time, but also in suggesting philosophic solutions to problems concerning which we have fuller information than he possessed but have forgotten the insights which are still interred in the discovery and arrangement of our information and which might be fruitful in restating and resolving the problems it presents.

THE ARGUMENT OF LONGINUS'
ON THE SUBLIME[1]

ELDER OLSON

THE brief and fragmentary treatise Περὶ Ὕψους presents the spectacle, not too uncommon in literature, of a major critical document which has gained assent—in this case almost universal assent—to its statements while the arguments which developed and guaranteed those statements have gone nearly unexamined. Since its publication at Basel by Robortello in 1554, and more particularly since Boileau's translation a hundred and twenty years later, the treatise has been frequently edited and translated, admired and eulogized, cited and discussed; but the quality of sensibility for which it has been chiefly esteemed, and which has won for it innumerable and illustrious admirers, seems unfortunately to have discouraged logical analysis. Twentieth-century commentators on the work, from Churton Collins[2] to J. W. H. Atkins,[3] seem to have written with Gibbon's famous remark in mind and consequently to have been occupied chiefly with the insight, the enthusiasm, and the originality displayed in the treatise; and while these preoccupations have in their turn produced eloquence and insight, as well as some excellent outlines and précis, they have as often led to the neglect and, in Saintsbury's case at least, even to the deprecation of the dialectical apparatus which underlies the work.[4]

Yet Longinus, if, indeed, he was the author of this treatise, exhibits on every page a concern with problems which could scarcely have arisen in a random discussion wherein literary enthusiasm was the solitary guiding principle of the critic; and even to grant, as numerous commentators have done, that the work presents clearly marked divisions, amid the ruins of which some fragments of an argument may still be discerned, is to offer insufficient explanation of the portions of the manuscript which are still extant. The eleven manuscripts of the work have been the object of much learned scrutiny from a philo-

---

1. Reprinted from *Modern Philology*, February, 1942. I have attempted a brief restatement of Longinus' position in comparison with that of Sir Joshua Reynolds in the Introduction to the "University Classics" edition of Longinus and Reynolds (Chicago: Packard & Co., 1945).

2. *Studies in Poetry and Criticism* (London, 1905).

3. *Literary Criticism in Antiquity* (Cambridge, 1934), II, 210 ff.

4. George Saintsbury, *A History of Criticism and Literary Taste in Europe* (New York, 1902), I, 159, 161–62.

logical point of view, but even in the collect they scarcely present, by the methods of consideration possible to grammarians, anything like an adequate representation of the whole treatise. As a consequence two courses, the pursuit of both of which has been sufficiently exemplified, have been open to the scholar operating on purely grammatical principles: either the lacunae might be made the subject of learned lamentation, in the absence of further manuscripts, or the text as we have it might be called in question on the basis of philological arguments of varying direction and cogency. To the literary historian yet another course is open: the topics with which Longinus is concerned may be treated as the conventional topics of Greek and Roman writers on rhetorical theory, and questions of their order and even of the manner of their discussion may be answered in terms of the practice of earlier, and not infrequently even of later, rhetoricians.[5] The objection to both the grammatical and the historical solutions is properly not that either approach is inferior or that distinguished efforts have been wanting in either but that, in terms of what Longinus himself says, many questions of importance remain unanswerable. The first page of the treatise, for example, presents to us an author who is preeminently concerned with method, for the criticism of Caecilius rests upon methodological grounds and the major preoccupation evinced by the introductory remarks is with the precepts according to which a technical treatise must be constructed. Again, the discussion of whether an art of sublimity is possible[6] becomes transformed, if we regard it as a matter of convention, into a servile and meaningless imitation of other and more philosophic inquiries; and, in like manner, topics of discussion throughout the treatise become unimportant and ineffectual—sometimes, indeed, wholly unintelligible—efforts to conform to a literary tradition. To such a place of unimportance, thus, we should have to consign the criticism of the *Odyssey*, the discussion of faultlessness versus faulty grandeur, the chapters on pettiness, and the discussion of literary decadence which closes the portion of the work which we have; and, similarly, numerous minor passages would become intrusions into a work which, in the judgment of many critics and scholars, would have been better without them. In the general disregard, then, of the logical schematism of the work, the *Peri Hypsous* has become an aggregation of fragments, important chiefly for the extraordinary "insights" which they contain; and those passages wherein the

5. Atkins' explication seems to me to be chiefly of this sort.

6. Sec. ii. For this essay I have chiefly used the text and Latin translation of Benjamin Weiske (Leipzig, 1809) and the text and English translation of W. Rhys Roberts (Cambridge, 1899). Most of the translated phrases which occur in the essay have been taken, however, from the translation of A. O. Prickard (Oxford, 1926). Since this essay does not depend upon genetic questions, such as that of the authorship of the treatise, I have chosen to refer to the author simply as "Longinus," whatever his actual name may have been.

power of insight seems to have failed, or wherein the author does not make his judgments intelligible, may be dismissed—by the author's own canon as expressed in sections xxxiii–xxxv—as faults which cannot dim the grandeur of the whole.

In opposition to these methods of consideration and as a possibly convenient auxiliary to them in the problems which they pose, a third approach might be suggested. While the treatise is doubtless of striking philological and historical interest, it is, nonetheless, as Longinus himself points out, a treatise on a certain kind of literary art, that is, it is a practical treatise expounding certain means as conducive to a certain end; as a consequence, unless the citation of means is to be regarded as purely arbitrary and dogmatic, the treatise might be exhibited as a reasoned structure, that is, as an argument, and considered wholly in that light.

The treatment of the work purely as a reasoned structure would turn, it goes without saying, on questions at most only equivocally connected with those ordering other methods. Indeed, it would be proper to lay down at once a series of postulates governing the procedure. In the first place, we may assume that any argument whatsoever—provided, of course, that it is strictly argument—comes about through the necessity of resolving some question and that the argument proper terminates, as having achieved its end, when that question is really or apparently resolved. Second, since the resolution of a question is the end of argument, it is clear that the question must be expounded solely from the text as from the only proper clue to the meaning and that the argument itself must be regarded at all times as the means by which, previous knowledge mediating, the end is achieved. In the third place, since in any extended inquiry a problem contains a series of subproblems, the argument must be divided according to these in its primary divisions, and into further subdivisions if these have subsidiaries. In the fourth place, we may assume that every device—distinction, definition, example, analogy, quotation, etc.—is used deliberately and that the use of every such device is to be explained in terms of the necessity of the end and to be noted as a sign of what the author considers to be demonstration. Finally, the order of the text as a whole is to be explained in terms of demonstration as the author conceives it, that is, in terms of his method.

It may be objected to such a proposal that the resultant analysis would depend wholly on the assumption that Longinus had indeed constructed the treatise with this particular end in view. The objection must, of course, be accepted; but the grounds of its acceptance would make it clear that it is acceptable not as an objection but as a general comment concerning any mode of consideration and interpretation of a work whatsoever. Any mode of grammatical analysis must depend on the assumption that the work in question was composed according to grammatical principles; any mode of historical consideration must rest, likewise, either on the assumption that the writer was to an extent shaped by his times and his admirations, consciously or unconsciously, or on the assumption that some relation, however tenuous, is traceable between the writer as a historical entity and certain other historical entities. Similarly, it is true, the philosophical analysis of a work must be based on some assumption appropriate to the mode of consideration, since no method proceeds *ex nihilo;* but it must be added that it can scarcely be dangerous or groundless to assume that philosophic works would be ordered to a philosophic end or that this treatise in particular is composed upon principles which alone—if we except sheer accident—could have given it the character which it is universally conceded to possess.

The treatise *On the Sublime* is an inquiry into the methods by which a certain quality of literary composition may be achieved. The question which it seeks primarily to answer, thus, is a question which neither Plato nor Aristotle nor the "scholastic" rhetoricians of Greece and Rome would have indicated as a principal question even in the study of literature. For Plato, rhetoric and poetics are arts which are occupied with the construction of semblances of the truth; and since the semblance is most perfect when its maker is one who knows what the truth is, the ultimate questions of poetic and rhetoric transcend the limitations of these arts and fall under dialectic, for they must involve knowledge—a problem which is properly to be treated by the dialectician alone. Thus in the *Ion* the true poet and in the *Phaedrus* the true rhetorician are ultimately the one who knows, i.e., the dialectician; and those who are rhetoricians and poets merely, like Lysias and Ion, are men in possession merely of the elements of their arts and, in sharper statement, indeed possess no art whatsoever. The question posed by Longinus is, therefore, for Plato, at best an elementary one; for Aristotle, on the other hand, it would have been an impossible one, since Aristotle's method entails a distinction between rhetoric and poetics and involves, even within these, a specialized treatment dependent upon a distinction into kinds. In such a method the question which Longinus poses as the primary question of his art consequently would not have been answerable as a generality; even in specific treatment, on the other hand, it would not have served as the subject matter even of an opusculum and in its reduction to the Aristotelian method would have been relegated, perhaps, only to the discussion of appropriate and impressive stylistic in the third book of the *Rhetoric.* Lastly, for the "scholastic" rhetoricians of Greece and Rome, the question of sublimity is posed never as an end but as a question relevant to the various means—

more specifically, to the different kinds of styles—of rhetoric; and, while for these rhetoricians the question would have been one of greater importance than for Plato or Aristotle, it would have been, nonetheless, specifically a rhetorical problem, and its solution would have consisted in the enumeration of stylistic devices—chiefly the "figures" of rhetoric—which are constitutive of the elevated style. Whereas Plato draws a distinction between literary kinds and transcends it, whereas Aristotle discriminates among kinds of works and uses this discrimination as a principle of his treatment of them, and whereas the scholastic rhetoricians find their primary distinctions among rhetorical ends rather than among kinds of means, Longinus obliterates ultimately all such distinctions of kinds and end and makes the focal point of his inquiry a certain quality discriminated from among other qualities of composition. A treatise so ordered is distinct in method from these other treatments; and the statements which are employed in the prosecution of that method cannot be compared directly, without a precarious shift of meanings, to the statements which arise out of such variously opposed treatments as those of Plato, Aristotle, and, let us say, the author of the *Ad Herennium*.

The criticism of Caecilius with which the treatise opens is significant of Longinus' awareness of the problems which a literary treatise, as a practical work, would involve. The criticism turns on two main issues: first, the earlier treatise had been too low and had failed especially in the omission of vital points; second, it had failed to give readers sufficient assistance in accordance with the proper first aim of every writer. While the generality of the statement of these censures allows a certain latitude of interpretation, the exemplification of Caecilius' errors, together with the positive precepts immediately laid down for a technical treatise—a treatise stating the various means to a practical end—perhaps makes the import of the criticism sufficiently clear. There are two main rules, Longinus tells us, for a practical treatise, the first dealing with the end aimed at, the second with the means toward that end: first, the end must be made evident, and, second, specific means to its achievement must be indicated; and it is a mark of Longinus' concern with the practical that the first question, which is a theoretical one, should be adjudged less important in the present treatise than the second, which is a practical one. By both these precepts, Caecilius has utterly failed. With respect to the first, he has sought to define the sublime by the mere collection of instances of sublimity; this is useless, either for a theoretical or for a practical inquiry, inasmuch as in the first consideration it does not provide a definition of sublimity and so affords no knowledge, and, in the second consideration, it does not afford such knowledge of the end as will permit the enumeration of the various means directed toward it. Sublimity is known instantially to all men of education and taste; and to write after the manner of Caecilius, thus, "as though we did not know," is to fail to construct an art of the sublime. With respect to the second precept, Caecilius, we are told, "unaccountably passed over" the indication of the means. Hence the earlier treatise has neither theoretical nor practical value.

Even from these earliest remarks, the ordering of the treatise, i.e., the principal division of its problems, can be seen clearly. Any art approached in this fashion must have three primary problems: clarification of the end aimed at, enumeration of the means to this end, and demonstration that the means are actually conducive to the proposed end. Since art involves purpose, the end must be known in some manner to the artist, or else his operations will be only vaguely purposive, if purposive at all; since any art affords instruments to its end and since not all instruments are appropriate to a given end, the appropriate means must be designated; and, since the efficacy of the art depends upon whether the instruments are actually efficient of the end, the connection of means and end must be demonstrated. The consideration of the end is clearly prior in a practical inquiry, since the means are determined by it; and we know the means when we know the causes of the end, so that what in a theoretical inquiry would be the causes would become in a practical inquiry the means; and to know the means as causes, third, of a given end is to know that the means are indeed efficacious of that end. The main body of Longinus' discussion, therefore, turns on these three problems: from the end of section ii to section viii he treats of the end of the practical inquiry, i.e., of sublimity and its opposites, together with the causes of all these; from section viii to the lacuna occurring in section ix, he deals with the demonstration of the means as conducive to sublimity; and the remainder of the work is given over to a discussion of the means and the divers problems which they entail.

Before these questions can be asked or answered, however, certain preliminary problems must be solved. Longinus has already treated, in his first paragraph, of the rules by which a technical treatise must be regulated; he must now ask, also, whether an art of the subject matter he proposes is in fact possible. To ask whether an art is possible is to pose two fundamental problems: it is, first, to ask whether the object produced by the art has existence (and Longinus is concerned with this question from sec. i. 3 to sec. ii) and, second, to ask whether there are modes of artificial production of that object (and this question occupies the extant whole of sec. ii). The object to be produced must first of all be something which can exist, for there could obviously be no production of what cannot exist; and in this proof of the existence of the object Longinus finds it necessary only to select from among admittedly existent psychological phenomena. These phenomena have as their immediate cause literary works; but it will be necessary to distinguish these from the phenomena caused by rhetoric, or the art of the sublime will not itself be distinct from rhetoric and, indeed, would be subsumed by it as a part under a whole, thereby precipitating the inquiry into an enumeration of the usual rhetorical devices. Consequently, to avert this danger, Longinus distinguishes his proposed art from rhetoric,[7] with which it might be so easily confused, and in his distinction he introduces the triad of terms—author, work, and audience—which constitutes the fundamental framework of his argument. With respect to the author, sublimity is that which has constituted the greatest poets and prose writers in their high place and given them their fame; with respect to the audience, the effect of sublimity is transport (ἔκστασις) and not persuasion (πείθω); and the former differs from the latter in that it is stronger than persuasion or the incidental pleasure attendant on persuasion, for the audience is powerless to resist ἔκστασις, although persuasion may be resisted; and, finally, with respect to the work, the excellences of rhetoric are contextual, that is, they emerge from the whole and are temporal, whereas the virtue of sublimity is that it emerges from the part and is instantaneous. Since there are psychological phenomena answering to this description, as, according to Longinus, all men of education and taste are aware, since there are productions of the kind described, and since there are men who are designated as the greatest writers, it is evident that sublimity has been proved to exist.

Next it is necessary to show that modes of artificial production exist by which sublimity may be generated, inasmuch as not every existent object is the product of art. Since Longinus assumes that man can produce literary works which have the quality of sublimity and that hence the quality exists, the argument[8] reduces to two questions which form the center of a dispute as to whether sublimity is produced, since produced it clearly is, by nature or by art and to a third question as to whether in any case its modes of acquisition are teachable. The import of these problems is clear: the first objection, that genius is innate, i.e., natural, and that the natural is spoiled by art, is countered by the statement that nature itself is systematic; were this not so, the present art would be impossible, since art must be an improvement upon nature; there are no arts of doing badly what nature can do well. The second objection, that nature is sufficient, elicits Longinus' response that even in genius it is insufficient, since genius falls into faults, exemplified fully in the later discussion, if left to itself without the controls of science; were this not so, again there would be no possibility of an art of the sublime, since there would be only a natural basis of sublimity and since there are no arts for doing what nature does adequately and infallibly. But, says Longinus, nature is to art as good fortune is to good counsel; and as good fortune is annulled where good counsel is wanting, so is

7. i. 3–4.　　　　　　　8. Sec. ii.

genius annulled by lack of art. The third objection, that production of the sublime is unteachable, is removed by an argument which turns on the very possibility of making the judgments which led to the first two objections: if those who argue against the possibility of an art of the sublime can make such objections, then, since these statements concerning sublimity themselves fall under art and not under nature, they serve to substantiate the existence of the art, and, since they are preceptual, the production of sublimity is teachable. Hence, by all considerations, there is possible an art of the sublime.

Since an art of sublimity is possible, Longinus now takes up the problems of the art itself; and the fundamental triad of terms signifying author, work, and audience makes possible an argument of considerable clarity and power. In the order of composition the genius (author) composes a work which has a certain literary quality of sublimity (work) and which effects ἔκστασις in hearers or readers (audience); the order of inquiry into the technique of composition, however, is the reverse of this; for we begin with a sensation in ourselves, as audience, which we recognize to be ἔκστασις. Inquiring into the cause of this sensation, we find it to be a certain quality of sublimity in the work; but, while this is perhaps explicative of our sensation, we can at this stage say nothing concerning the manner in which a work must be composed. Consequently, we must inquire beyond the work into the faculties of the author which permitted its composition; and when we have achieved a statement of these, we have only to ask how these may be acquired or cultivated to answer the question of how the sublimity of a work may be achieved or the ecstasy of an audience effected. The manner in which the terms of the triad may be employed is clear: the dialectic moves in the one direction or in the other across the triad, using a reaction of the audience to define a fault or virtue of a work, a quality of the work to illustrate a faculty of the author; and what warrants this motion, primarily, is that our sensibility distinguishes ἔκστασις from any other effect of discourse upon us and that we know ourselves to be moved to ecstasy by a literary work produced by a human agent. To argue in this manner, Longinus is well aware, is ultimately to analogize author, work, and reader; but the legitimacy of the procedure can hardly be called in doubt, particularly when we recall that the statements in the work which have gained most general assent—such statements as "the effect of sublimity is not persuasion but transport"[9] and "sublimity is the ring of a great soul"[10]—constitute the very foundations of the argument. So analogizing, however, Longinus has made it impossible to discuss separately the various literary kinds; there can be here no theory of tragedy, of comedy, epic, or comic-epic and no theory of rhetoric, since sublimity may be found in all these and in

9. ii. 4.   10. ix. 2.

philosophic and historical literature as well and since it results from the nature of neither one nor another of these kinds of literary production but from the faculties of the agent who produced these. So analogizing, too, it is impossible to escape the consequence that the foundations of the art must be stated in psychological terms; this, however, scarcely affords a foothold for objection, since it means merely that Longinus, in answering the question of how the sublime is produced, has chosen to answer it in terms of human character and faculties rather than in terms of the characteristics of a literary work or of the literary devices which must be employed. We may deny the analogy constituted by the triad, we may demand an answer in other terms; but the argument of the treatise itself could be called in question only if we insisted on affixing other significances to the terms which Longinus employs or on asserting that the study of literature involves totally different questions.

The text resumes, after a lacuna amounting to two pages of the Paris MS 2036, in the midst of a discussion of the faults into which unassisted genius may fall. Fragmentary as the whole treatise is, however, one perhaps need not despair of the intelligibility of the work; a careful consideration of the direction and method of argument and of the assumptions involved in the critical judgments affords excellent ground for some restoration of the lacunae, at least to the extent of reconstructing the argument. In the case of this—the first— lacuna, the missing argument can be reconstructed by an analysis of the most immediate problems of Longinus, and the reconstruction is supported by the resumption of the text itself. The argument has begun, let us remember, with an inquiry into ἔκστασις, a term falling under the audience-term of the triad; and the term itself has been defined, since a mere selection was intended, only by reference to a term in some way its opposite, persuasion, this term being taken also in the sense of an affection of the audience. This treatment by opposites is characteristic of the method of the entire treatise; sublimity itself is defined, at one stage, by contrast with opposite qualities of style, and the causes of sublimity are contrasted with the causes of these opposites; truth is held up against fiction, impeccability against sublimity, and the treatise closes, in fact, with an analysis of the mean style which parallels the analysis of the sublime and with an inquiry into the degeneration of contemporary writers. It is clear, therefore, that Longinus must have argued, from effects upon an audience contrary to that of ἔκστασις, toward qualities of style contrary to that of sublimity, since, indeed, we find him discussing, after the lacuna, exactly such qualities of style; and since the warrant for the existence of sublimity depended upon the audience's sensibility of a certain kind of passion, viz., ἔκστασις, it is clear that, if the treatise is consistent, the existence of the opposite qualities must have rested upon the same basis. For there are no topical terms (i.e., terms central to the discussion) which do not fall under one or another term of the triad of author, audience, and work; and since explication of qualities of style in terms of the author would be impossible, inasmuch as the argument has not yet reached that stage of development, and since explication of qualities in terms of kinds of works would likewise be impossible, inasmuch as no discrimination of kinds has been made—for, as we remarked, sublimity is a term predictable of any kind of work—therefore explication must have been made in terms of diverse effects upon the audience. And this is shown, furthermore, by the fact that the discussion, when it resumes, presupposes such discrimination of effects. On the grounds of these four arguments, then, such discrimination must have been made.

If this is so, we may attempt to reconstruct the discrimination; and this may be done either by considering the procedure of the previous argument or by asking what the resumption of the argument presupposes. First, in the former manner, we may note that since the discrimination is of effects upon the audience and since one known effect is that of ἔκστασις, which is defined as an irresistible moving of the souls of the audience, and since the other effects are the opposites of these, the opposites must therefore have in common the general characteristic of nonmovement in that special respect; and since ἔκστασις is literally a being-put-out-of-place so that, as Longinus later remarks, the audience is as one with the speaker, it follows that the opposite effects will differ specifically in that they are different kinds of movement away from that unity with the speaker. How they differ specifically may be discerned from examination of the text when it resumes:[11] Longinus is discussing three vices of style, two of which arise from certain relations of the passion of the speaker to the subject matter of the work, one of which arises from a lack of relation of his passion to the subject matter. Given a subject matter which lends itself to sublimity, the passion of the speaker may exceed the subject, and so the style will be turgid; or fall below it, and so the style will be frigid; or be unrelated to it, i.e., inappropriate to it, and so *parenthyrsus* results. If the classification of vices of style is on this principle, it is exhaustive; and there seems, consequently, no reason to suppose that parts of the classification are missing. The different opposites of ἔκστασις, therefore, would be effects upon an audience corresponding to each of these stylistic vices. In one sense, then, they are various kinds of indifference to the speaker; but they will be diversely attended, as special kinds of boredom, by risibility, mere contempt, and the confusion resulting from a display of unintelligible emotion.

It must be noted that Longinus has now moved in his discussion to a treatment of stylistic qualities; yet, from the resumption of the text at section iii, his

11. Sec. iii.

discussion of them is still in terms of sensibilities of the audience, and properly so: at this stage qualities of style can be discussed only through their effects, that is, either by naming the effect as contempt, risibility, etc., or by providing examples of stylistic viciousness which indicate the intended effect by actually inducing it in the cultivated and sensible reader. The author enters into the discussion not as one possessed or not possessed of the sources of sublimity but as one who aimed at sublimity and in some way missed in each case; and his introduction depends upon the necessity for illustrating his failure—a failure in art, in the strictest sense, since the intention of sublimity is actually present —to achieve that unification of author and audience which is ἔκστασις. The audience must feel what he feels—hence the statement of stylistic vices, in terms of passion as related to subject, becomes at this stage the only possible statement. When the vices of style are made clear in this manner, their cause can be stated, although not as yet with respect to the causes of sublimity, since sublimity itself has not yet been defined; and so Longinus remarks, in section v, that the general cause of these vices is a craving for intellectual novelties. The reason why no other vices of style have been treated becomes clear when we recognize that this is an exhaustive division, *given a sublime subject;* other vices would fall outside an art of the sublime, as not resulting from an intention of sublimity; but these may be confused with sublimity itself because, as he remarks, they are "thus intimately mingled with it," since sublimity is aimed at.[12]

Longinus has treated the opposites of sublimity in order to exhibit what constitutes failure in the art and what is to be avoided; and he has treated these vices before he has dealt with sublimity itself because sublimity is more readily located, as a kind of mean between these various extremes which are more easily apparent to sensibility—the latter being still his chief point of reference —than sublimity would be. Now, following his precedent treatment, he turns in section vi to a discussion of sublimity itself. For him sublimity permits neither a definition by example (as his criticism of the "instances of the sublime" provided by Caecilius would indicate) nor, on the other hand, of a purely theoretical statement; this is a practical problem, and hence discourse will not serve as a substitute for experience, for "judgment of style is the last and ripest fruit of much experience."[13] Now, if mere experience, on the one hand, or mere theoretical discussion, on the other, cannot provide knowledge of the sublime, there is a third way by which such knowledge may be achieved; and that is by means of an amalgamation of the two into touchstones for the sublime. Hence Longinus enumerates the signs or notes by which we may know whether or not a given work has true sublimity; drawing an analogy between

12. Sec. v.   13. Sec. vi.

true and false greatness in general, Longinus is enabled, first of all, to state his criteria in terms of proper and improper admiration and, proceeding thence, to adumbrate the sublime in terms of the character of admiration which it excites. The soul is elevated by sublimity to joy and exultation;[14] the reader feels an identification with the author, for the soul feels "as though itself had produced what it hears";[15] hence what does not elevate at all would not even be false sublimity, and that which elevates only temporarily and has a diminishing force forever after is false sublimity, while that which has a permanent force and which provides a perpetual nourishment for the soul is the sublime itself. Hence it is that transport which is impossible to resist and which establishes itself firmly in the memory and which always leaves material for fresh reflection. Since the sublime would have these characteristics, the most certain attestation of sublimity would be the discovery of its universal appreciation; thus the *consensus gentium* constitutes, for Longinus, an unquestionable test, since it abstracts from any possibility of individual error.[16]

The provision of these touchstones makes possible the recognition of individual works as instances of the sublime, on the one hand, and a knowledge of the nature of the sublime, on the other. Hence, since we now know what the sublime is, in something other than a merely instantial mode, we may know what its causes or sources are, and so state its nature causally. Thus Longinus, in secton viii, passes to a consideration of the sources of sublimity, to their enumeration and demonstration as exhaustive and discrete; and in so doing he completes his fundamental triad of terms by now stating sublimity in terms of characteristics of the author—that is, in terms of what the author must *be* in order to produce sublimity. That this is the case is clear; for Longinus is careful to use predicates which are strictly predicable only of a human subject: "having power of expression,"[17] "empowered with great (full-bodied) conception,"[18] "having passion,"[19] etc.; and his treatment of them, moreover, is precisely as human characteristics, for his preliminary classification of them is according to whether they are innate or acquired.[20]

The manner of derivation of the five sources is not explicit in the treatise; consequently, the enumeration of the sources has not infrequently been called in question, and sometimes, even, their importance for the treatise has been minimized. Saintsbury remarks:

> No nervous check or chill need be caused by the tolerably certain fact that more than one hole may be picked in the subsequent classification of the sources of ὕψος.

14. vii. 2.

15. *Ibid.*   18. *Ibid.*

16. vii. 4.   19. *Ibid.*

17. viii. 1.   20. *Ibid.*

These attempts at an over-methodical classification (it has been said before) are always full of snares and pitfalls to the critic. Especially do they tempt him to the sin of arguing in a circle. It cannot be denied that in every one of the five divisions (except, perhaps, the valuable vindication of the quality of Passion) there is some treacherous word or other, which is a mere synonym of "sublime." Thus in the first we have ἀδρεπήβολον, mastery of the ἄδρον, a curious word, the nearest equivalent to which in English is, perhaps, "stout" or "full-bodied," as we apply these terms to wine; in the fourth γενναία, "noble," which is only "sublime" in disguise; and in the fifth ἀξίωμα καί διαρσις, of which much the same may be said.[21]

If we may overlook in this statement what is merely dogmatic—as, for example, the curious carping that an art or method of achieving sublimity is somehow at fault for being methodical—we may concentrate on the principal issue of the objection, i.e., whether there is any circularity of argument. Longinus has been asking the causes of sublimity here, as in section v he discussed the causes of failures in sublimity. Since the fundamental triad of terms must be in alignment with a term signifying the subject matter which is sublime, the basis for an enumeration of five sources, and of only five, is fairly obvious. Sublimity of subject matter is not achieved by art, or there would be a fundamental tetrad rather than triad; since, given a sublime subject, an author must conceive it, secondly feel concerning it if it is excitative of passion, and thirdly express it, it is clear immediately that the sources would, at first sight, involve conception, passion, and expression. But the third factor is complex: since expression deals with words, words can be considered either as signs, simple or combined, or merely as sounds. If we consider words as signs in combination, we can regard them nonsyntactically, as constitutive of such modes of discourse as question, prayer, oath, etc. (in which case we have *figures of thought*, since such modes are prior to and independent of any syntactical consideration), or we may regard them syntactically, as constituted of certain grammatical elements (in which case we have *figures of language*, such as asyndeton, hyperbaton, polyptota, etc.); and Longinus groups these two under the head of figures, as his third source of the sublime. On the other hand, words may be regarded as simple, and here again there are two possibilities; all grammatical distinctions being dropped out, the problem is reduced to the imposition of signs for things and their qualities; and the imposition may be strict, i.e., literally stand for the thing, when the problem reduces to a choice of synonyms, or it may involve a comparison when the matter is one of a choice of tropes and metaphors. These problems are problems strictly of diction for Longinus, and their solution establishes the fourth source of the sublime. Finally, words may be regarded as sounds constitutive of rhythms and harmony; and he so treats of them under the head of σύνθεσις.

21. Saintsbury, *op. cit.*, I, 161–62.

If, indeed, there is a circularity here, the whole argument collapses; but Saintsbury's charge of paralogism falls a little oddly on our ears. It is difficult to see how an argument from effect to cause could involve a circularity, even though apparently synonymous adjectives be applied to both cause and effect; for example, there is nothing wrong with the statement that it takes a human being as cause to produce a human being as effect. In an alternative statement, we might simply say that Longinus' derivation of the sources depends upon the possibility of identifying the human faculties which make a literary work of a certain quality possible; and though for Longinus the soul of the great writer reflects the sublime subject and the work reflects the soul and the mind of the audience ultimately reflects the work, the similarities which the analogical argument discloses, and upon which, indeed, it depends, are not to be confused with such circularity as would vitiate syllogistic procedure.

The insistence of Longinus, in section viii, that Caecilius is in error in his enumeration of the πηγαί, or sources of sublimity, suggests, since the attack has a rational basis, that he regarded his own statement of them as defensible; and the nature of its defense may be reconstructed, perhaps, despite the length of the lacuna in section ix, without exceeding the evidences of that defense which the extant portions provide. The latter portion of section viii, for example, indicates through the objections posed to Caecilius the general character of the dialectic which would be used to establish any one of the five sources as actually distinct means conducive to sublimity. If Caecilius has omitted passion, Longinus argues, it is either because he has identified passion with sublimity or because he has not thought it conducive to sublimity. In the first case, he is in error because, if passion is inseparable from sublimity, then what is passionate must also always be sublime, and conversely; but both this consequence and its converse can be seen to be false, as well from an examination of works as from an examination of the faculties of orators.[22] In the second case, Caecilius is in error because "nothing attains the heights of eloquence so certainly as genuine passion in the right place."[23] The argument establishing the existence of any one source, thus, would turn on whether the "source" in question was distinct from any other and whether in fact it was a source at all. It is probable, therefore, that, since such questions have been raised, they will be answered; and undoubtedly the missing section in ix must have been devoted, in great part at least, to the settling of just these questions with respect to the remaining sources. The extant portion of section ix before the lacuna bears out this hypothesis: for Longinus proceeds to argue in it, first, that great conception is distinct from any of the linguistic sources, since "without any utterance a notion, unclothed and unsupported, often moves our wonder, because the

22. viii. 2–3.   23. viii. 4.

very thought is great"[24]—the example of Ajax' silence entering in as proof of this proposition—and, second, that greatness of conception is actually conducive to sublimity because "great words issue, and it cannot be otherwise, from those whose thoughts are weighty";[25] and the text is interrupted as Longinus is apparently proving this proposition also by example, in all likelihood the speech of Alexander to Parmenio which is reported in Arrian.[26] The third question which would be pertinent to each source—whether it permits of acquisition, since otherwise it could not fall under art—has likewise its answer in this section: even though, as Longinus has already remarked, great conception and passion are primarily natural, means for their development and cultivation may be indicated.[27]

In a similar manner, the missing portion must have treated of the remaining sources; and the character of the argument may be outlined. Once great conception and passion have been shown to be sources, Longinus has completed his treatment of those topics which would be common to all arts; the remaining discussion enters as resulting from the means. Since the treatise is concerned only with literary sublimity—although, as Longinus frequently remarks,[28] the ὕψος, in a wider sense, may be found in any of the other arts, painting, sculpture, architecture, music, etc.—and since conception and passion are independent of words,[29] it is necessary to consider how sublimity is achieved through the use of words, peculiarly; and, as we have seen, Longinus accomplishes this by considering words in connection with thought, the figures of thought resulting; next, by dropping out thought and considering words in relation to one another, the figures of language so resulting; next, by considering isolated words in their application to things, so that the problems of word choice emerge for solution; and, finally, by considering the word as a collocation of syllables, thus opening the questions of rhythm, and as an aggregation of letters, thus raising the problem of harmony, both rhythm and harmony being parts of the problem of *synthesis* or *compositio*. The power of expression, Longinus says, must be presupposed;[30] it is natural and does not fall under art; the latter three sources are not a substitute for it but grow out of it as special determinations of the exercise of that power. This presupposition made, however, it is impossible to attack Longinus' treatment of the verbal sources; since they arise from a consideration of the ways in which words may be employed, there must be a separate verbal faculty for each such employment; in the case of figures, mere use of figures does not constitute sublimity,[31] although a

24. ix. 2.

25. ix. 3.

26. *Exp. Alex.* ii. 25. 2.

27. ix. 1.

28. E.g., xvii. 3; xxxix. 3.

29. Secs. viii–ix.

30. viii. 1.

31. xvii. 1.

proper use of them is conducive to that end, so that a consideration of figures falls clearly within the art, but as a means; hence it falls among the sources, but it is a source distinct—on the one hand—from great conception and passion because these are primarily natural, whereas skill with figures is acquired, and because these are independent of words, whereas skill with figures is not, and—on the other hand—from diction and synthesis, although both of these involve words and are acquired faculties, because, as we have seen, different aspects of words are the object of each; and Longinus defends these distinctions by pointing out again and again[32] that works fall short of the sublime or achieve it by failures or successes in one of these respects or another and that authors who are skilful or inept in certain respects are not necessarily so in all. These matters are ascertainable by sensibility alone: "it is mere folly to raise problems over things which are so fully admitted, for experience is proof sufficient," but he does not therefore refrain from argument.[33]

The resumption of the text[34] reveals Longinus in the midst of a development of the means by which greatness of conception, as the first source of the sublime, may be achieved; and the first means, from various indications of the context, is by the direction of the author's mind toward great objects, so that, if true greatness be truly and completely ascertained, a commensurate greatness of conception must needs follow. The various indications of which I speak may be briefly stated. First, that this section falls within the means would be arguable, even if the problems of the treatise and their manner of treatment were less evident than they are, from Longinus' statement (x. 1) that we may pass on to consider any "further means"; and, second, that all this is relevant to greatness of conception may be seen from the close of section xv, in which he remarks that that topic may now be considered as closed. If this section is relative to μεγαλοφυές (or ἀδρεπήβολον) then, the quotations here must be taken, not as striking instances of hyperbole or other verbal devices, but as examples of noetic magnificence; it is the *conception*, here, which interests the critic and not the words. His first treatment of conception is in terms of the gods as its object; his second in terms of heroes; and conception is evidently subjected to two criteria: the first, truth; the second, completeness. Thus Homer is praised for his conceptions of Strife, of the horses of the gods, of theomachies, of Poseidon, and of Ares, in so far as he realizes the loftiness of deity, i.e., the truth about the gods; he is blamed, however, when the gods are conceived as in any way less than they actually are, as, for example, when "he presents to us woundings of the gods, their factions, revenges, tears, bonds, sufferings"; for then "he has made the gods men."[35] On similar grounds

---

32. See, e.g., x. 4. 5, 6; xvi. 2–3.

33. xxxix. 3.

34. ix. 4–5.

35. ix. 7.

Hesiod is condemned and Moses is praised;[36] and the assignment of the *Odyssey* to a lower place than that of the *Iliad* depends precisely on these considerations as well; and what we have here is no "instinctive, unreasoning terror" of the Greek at the "unknown Romance," as Saintsbury phrases it,[37] for the objection is not that these are myths but that they are myths which could not possibly be true of their subjects. The criticism which appears in this section has been frequently censured; but the censure is hardly justifiable on logical grounds. Longinus is saying that if you wish to nurture your soul to great conceptions you must contemplate great objects—gods, heroes, the majesty of nature, etc.—and that your conception will not be great if you fail to conceive the greatness of your object, i.e., if you fail to form a true and complete conception; for a true and complete conception of a great subject would necessarily be great. Thus the "dreams of Zeus" which occur in the *Odyssey*—"the stories of the wine-skin, of the companions turned by Circe into swine," and the many marvelous episodes of a similar nature—might well be the fantasies of the gods, they are certainly excellent literature; but they are hardly true and complete conceptions either of gods or of heroes, and they are therefore hardly sublime. Both the *Iliad* and the *Odyssey* are by Homer and are marks of his transcendent genius; but the former is "a throng of images all drawn from the truth," while the latter is "a wandering among the shallows of the fabulous and incredible."[38]

Next, according to Longinus (sec. x), "since with all things are associated certain elements, constituents which are essentially inherent in the substance of each," the writer who would gain greatness of conception must select and integrate these essentials. The meaning of this statement becomes clear if we consider the context. Greatness of conception is cultivated by the true apprehension of great objects, as we have seen; but, given a sublime subject matter of which the author has conceived, not all of its aspects are equally responsible for its sublimity, and hence it is the business of the writer to select those aspects which are most responsible and to integrate them in such fashion as that in which they are integrated in the object itself. Thus, for example, a storm is terrible, and hence sublime, inspiring fear and awe; however, not all its characteristics inspire these feelings, but only such as relate to its power and danger; hence the writer must choose those most relative and unite them in such manner, in his mind, that they are not scattered conceptions but "the form and features of that peril."[39] The integration must be present because it is the integration of the characteristics in the object itself which inspired such feelings as were peculiar to it; without such unification, the various concep-

36. ix. 5, 9.

37. Saintsbury, *op. cit.*, I, 163.

38. ix. 13.

39. x. 6.

tions would not induce a feeling comparable to that caused by the object. The *Ode to Anactoria* is praised for such selection and collocation; considering still the conception as opposed to the diction, Longinus remarks that the subject matter—"love-madness"—has been well treated, since Sappho has chosen to speak of those effects, physical as well as intellectual, which are the essential symptoms of love frenzy.[40] On the other hand, Aristeas of Proconnesus is blamed for the evident and just reason that the details of seafaring which he enumerates are hardly those by virtue of which the sea itself is sublime—sea-sickness, which forms the climax of his description, scarcely gives the impression of sublimity; and though Aristeas has talked around that painful subject by saying that the sailors' "inward parts, even, are tossed terribly to and fro," the trick is purely a verbal one, and so the description is more embroidery than sublimity.[41] Similarly, Aratus, in saying that "only a tiny plank keeps off bitter destruction," is not sublime[42] because he is merely verbalizing also; in all cases of sailing, a few planks keep off death, but there is no terror here because those planks are generally sufficient; the sea itself is not a source of terror at all times, but only when it rages; and so the device of Aratus constitutes an attempt to rhetoricize, to falsify a quite normal situation. One must understand Longinus as still speaking of *conception;* on that ground, the passage is bad; on a purely verbal ground he might have considered it excellent.

Again, the writer may achieve sublimity by the accumulation of vast detail, with the assurance that this multiplicity of detail will tend to give any subject importance and also to bring out whatever effects would be caused by that subject itself. The second mode—the mode of selection and integration—is conducive to sublimity in that the writer seeks those aspects upon which the effect of the subject depends; in this, the third mode, the effect depends, in so far as it is mere amplification, strictly upon number; as Longinus remarks, amplification always implies quantity and abundance. We may adumbrate a subject either by stating its essential characteristics or by enumerating at large its characteristics both essential and accidental; for in fact the thing itself so presents itself to us, as a mixture of the essential and accidental. It matters not how we effect this quantitative expansion, Longinus tells us; there are numberless varieties of amplification; we may either work through the topics or commonplaces or exaggerate (in the sense of forming a conception which exceeds the thing or fact or event) or emphasize, or do any one of ten thousand things; in any case, the writer must dwell upon the subject with accumulation and insistence, building always toward sublimity. If the subject contemplated is in truth a great subject, sublimity will be reached in this manner; if not, a merely rhetorical amplification will result; and Longinus is careful here, as

40. x. 1–3.   41. x. 4.   42. x. 5.

throughout the treatise, to discriminate between a device in its merely rhetorical use and the same device as a means of achieving sublimity; he finds it necessary, indeed, to redefine amplification, lest it be thought synonymous with the sublime itself and lest, consequently, the art of the sublime be collapsed into an art of rhetorical amplification. Like other modes of achieving sublimity, amplification is only conducive to sublimity, not identical with it; nor is Longinus so incautious as to omit a demonstration of this point. The comparatively brief lacuna which occurs at this place in the text interrupts both the demonstration and the exposition of its significance; but here, for once, the main lines of the discussion are not destroyed. When the text resumes,[43] Longinus is discussing, clearly enough, the proprieties of diffuseness (which would be achieved by amplification) and intensity.

So far, in his treatment of μεγαλοφυές, Longinus has considered the author as contemplating the great subject in order to formulate great conceptions; and, as we have seen, he has shown that the author may attempt either to formulate a conception commensurate with the sublime subject or to select and integrate those characteristics upon which its sublimity depends or to enumerate at large until the multiplicity of conceived detail approximates the real fulness of the thing. Following section xii, however, he suggests two other modes by which greatness of conception may be achieved. First, if the sublime authors, e.g., Homer, Plato, Demosthenes, etc., have attained sublimity by greatness of conception, so that their thoughts were commensurate with great subjects, it follows that, if an author can make his thoughts commensurate with their thoughts, he likewise will achieve greatness of conception; thus, greatness of thought can be attained by the imitation of great authors.[44] Longinus is not speaking of the reproduction exclusively of tricks of style; he says explicitly, "Therefore even we, when we are working out a theme which requires lofty speech and greatness of thought" must call to mind the performances of great authors;[45] and the analogy of this sort of literary inspiration to the Pythian vapors makes his meaning completely clear; if we are not able to achieve greatness of thought by contemplating the thing itself, we may contemplate instead those authors whose thoughts were stretched to its stature, as "even those not too highly susceptible to the god are possessed by the greatness which was in others."[46] And he gives the author touchstones again, formulating them in terms of the fundamental triad of author, work, and audience: in composing, the author is to consider Homer and the great ones as composing in his place, knowing them as he does through the medium of their works; in judging his work, he must regard them as his audience, and, further, he must ask how the ages to come will esteem his composition.[47]

43. xii. 3.   44. xiii. 2.   45. xiv. 1.   46. xiii. 2.   47. Sec. xiv.

Second, if we neither contemplate the object directly nor contemplate it through the contemplations of others, we may invent, we may imagine;[48] where our knowledge is partial and incomplete, we may piece out what is missing by imagination, and the examples which Longinus uses seem intended to illustrate invention out of whole cloth, as in the case of the sane Euripides imagining madness,[49] or of detail only, as in the ride of Phaëthon in *Iphigenia in Tauris*.[50] According to Longinus, there is a difference between the application of imagination in poetry and in rhetoric, the latter being limited by what is known to be true and what is thought to be probable. This much done, Longinus remarks that his treatment of the "sublime effects which belong to great thoughts, and which are produced by the greatness of man's soul, and secondarily by imitation or by imagination" has been adequate.

Longinus now[51] passes on to a discussion of the figures, postponing his treatment of passion for reasons which will be indicated later in this essay. As he remarks, there are infinite kinds of figures; dividing them into figures of thought and figures of language, he mentions in the former class adjuration (or apostrophe or oath), questions and interrogations, in the latter class, asyndeton, hyperbaton, polyptota (including all departures from the normal usage of case, tense, gender, person, and number), and periphrasis. Figures by themselves, Longinus tells us repeatedly, do not constitute sublimity; thus any merely rhetorical definitions of the figures are insufficient to indicate their use toward effecting sublimity, since such definitions are only recipes for the construction of the figures themselves, without consideration of the context of their use; consequently, in his treatment of the figures, Longinus is careful always to include some statement of the literary circumstances in which they would effect sublimity and of those in which they would not. Adjuration or apostrophe, for example, is an oath, discourse involving a solemn appeal to something sacred to witness that a statement is true or that a contract is binding; the rhetoricians tell us merely to swear by those names which are most sacred; "but," says Longinus, "it is not the mere swearing by a name which is great; place, manner, occasion, purpose are all essential";[52] and the rhetoricians have failed in their prescriptions because they have treated these variables of place, manner, occasion, and purpose as constants. Thus, though both Demosthenes and Eupolis swore by Marathon, so that in a sense their oath is the same, the apostrophe of the latter is merely that, whereas the apostrophe of the former is at once an assurance resting upon oaths, a demonstration, an example, a eulogy, and an exhortation.[53] His point, of course, is extremely well taken;

48. Sec. xv.
49. xv. 2–3.
50. xv. 4.

51. Sec. xvi.
52. xvi. 3.
53. *Ibid.*

indeed, any other statement would have been irrelevant or insufficient, since the sources stand related to sublimity as means to end.

While a formula of the constitution of a figure is necessary therefore, so that the orator may know what it is and hence be able to construct it at will, he must also know what effect it produces; consequently, throughout his treatment of the figures, Longinus states the effect of each figure, so that we may know whether it is conducive to the proper end. Questions and interrogations, thus, "reproduce the spontaneity of passion" and give intensity and vehemence and conviction to the discourse, "drawing the hearer off until he thinks that each point in the inquiry has been raised and put into words without preparation, and so it imposes upon him."[54] Asyndeton, wherein "the words drop unconnected and are, so to speak, poured forth almost too fast for the speaker himself," gives "the impression of a struggle, where the meaning is at once checked and hurried on."[55] Similarly, hyperbaton "is the surest impress of vehement passion"; the hearer fears that a failure of both syntax and logic is imminent, and, since this is a sign of vehement passion, he is persuaded that the discourse is an instance of vehement passion.[56] And thus Longinus treats also of the other figures. The principal determinant throughout is the tendency of the audience to reason from the consequent; and, although Longinus never makes such explicit reference to the tendency as Aristotle (*Poetics* 24), all the instances which he mentions are plainly arguments from signs.

Concerning the choice of words, next, Longinus clearly lays a basis for selection. Certain words are noble and beautiful, while others are inferior;[57] a similar distinction, as he remarks particularly in section xxxv, may be made among things and also among thoughts. Thus the primary determinant in the choice of words is the necessity of maintaining a correspondence between these hierarchies; and, while the choice of grand words is necessary for noble composition, the words must be accurate as well; and, like Quintilian, he likens the choice of a grand word for a thing of lesser stature to the fastening of a large tragic mask upon a little child.[58] An unfortunate lacuna occurs at this place, apparently just as Longinus was about to say that in poetry, however, which like fiction is less bound by probability than rhetoric or history, these restrictions do not always apply. Doubtless he proceeded to treat of the various possible permutations of the central terms of his discussion here; if we take only two elements—words and things—then two principles emerge; since the hierarchies, verbal and real, must correspond and since the effect is to be one of greatness, one must use the grand word as well as the right word, and the

54. Sec. xvii.

55. Sec. xix.

56. Sec. xxii.

57. Sec. xxx.

58. Cf. Quintilian vi. 1. 36.

choice of diction thus becomes merely a choice of objects of discourse. But this solution of the problem of word choice—one common enough in the history of rhetoric—is too simple for Longinus; it will do as a preliminary consideration, but one must also take into account the element of thought; and since it is possible that a low conception may be entertained by a great thing and conversely, several consequences emerge; in tragedy, for instance, Longinus would have been likely to argue, since the effect is to be one of grandeur, the characters are lofty, and their thoughts must consequently be lofty, even where the object of thought is common or mean; hence, too, their discourse must be lofty— even bombast is admissible in tragedy, he has said earlier, provided it does not degenerate into tasteless rant. On the other hand, vulgar words, as he is remarking when the text resumes,[59] may be preferable to ornamental language, may be used with an effect which is not vulgar when sheer accuracy and credibility are concerned.

Longinus' treatment of metaphor, trope, and simile under word choice, unconventional as it is, is consequent upon his careful separation of the sources. Since all grammatical collocations would fall under the figures, word choice deals with the selection of names for things, thought being an intermediary term: now words either stand for things strictly and literally or they do not, in which case they are either metaphors, paraboles, similes, or hyperboles. The differences obtaining between these (although they are in a sense akin) may be seen by an examination of the schematism which has developed them. On the one hand, Longinus clearly ranks words and things; on the other, within this hierarchy, words must either stand for what they strictly mean, and hence for what is like or different, or not. Hyperbole, thus, results, as he says,[60] when words exaggerate the thing in terms either of excess or of defect by likening it to what is more than it or less than it; the other tropes result when, although a comparison is involved, inasmuch as something is likened to what it is not, it is strict, i.e., is not of a greater to a less or of a less to a greater; and the distinctions between these are apparently that metaphor is absolute comparison, inasmuch as the name of the thing is actually substituted, whereas παραβολαὶ and εἰκόηες are not, these differing in turn from each other in that the former is in terms of difference, the latter in terms of likeness. Were the differences stated in grammatical terms—that is, in terms of the grammatical particles employed in the case of simile, for example—simile, parabole, and hyperbole would have fallen under the figures and would have been statable merely as formulas in consequence of this; but to state the problem as one of signification, as here, is to permit the choice of words to depend on the imposition of names and to introduce again the variable factors of place, manner, occasion, and pur-

59. Sec. xxxi.   60. xxxviii. 6.

pose—which again would appear as constants in a merely rhetorical formulation —as determinatives of the choice of diction. And in the problem of word selection, as elsewhere, Longinus is insistent that metaphor, simile, parabole, and hyperbole are always means, never ends; the device must be dependent upon the use, never the use upon the device; to provide mere recipes for the formulation of rhetorical devices, without clear indication of the variable literary circumstances in which they would be appropriate, is, in effect, to constitute them as ends not means, so that the work becomes not a final unity but an aggregation of ends; and since, for Longinus, the use is always statable in terms of the audience—a certain effect of ἔκστασις in the hearers—the unity of a work is properly stated not in terms of the work itself or of exclusively literary formulations but in terms of the unity of effect upon those reading or hearing. Consequently, Longinus remarks that there are no literary regulations as such governing the use of such devices as metaphor;[61] the proper determinant is the passion of the author, since whatever numbers and kinds of metaphors would appear appropriate to him in his passion would also appear appropriate to an audience to which that passion has been communicated; and Longinus is scornful, consequently, of the apparent decision of Caecilius that the number of metaphors to be applied to a single object should not exceed two or three.[62]

The treatment of synthesis,[63] finally, offers but little difficulty. In his first mention of this source of sublimity,[64] Longinus had remarked that synthesis included all the others; however, in his actual treatment of the source, it appears solely as a topic dealing with the arrangement of words into harmony and rhythm. While at first sight there seems to be a contradiction here, the contradiction is readily resolved from an examination of the contexts of the discussions. Synthesis—the arrangement of words—presupposes thought, passion, the figures, and the choice of words, and in a mere enumeration of the sources would be stated, therefore, as the consummation of all of them, as inclusive of all of them in the sense that any literary work may be ultimately regarded as a certain arrangement of words. If, on the other hand, one deals with the sources as means, expounding what is proper to each source, then synthesis appears only as the arrangement, rhythmic and harmonic, of words which have already been selected as a consequence of all the other artistic operations.

Longinus' argument concerning the importance of synthesis is a simple analogy; words considered merely as sound and incorporated into harmony and rhythm are to musical tones similarly incorporated as the effect of the former to the effect of the latter; then, if we recall what is superadded to words by their significance and recall also how tremendous is the effect of

61. xxxii. 4.

62. xxxii. 8.

63. Sec. xxxix.

64. Sec. viii.

music, we may gauge adequately the effect of the arrangement of words. Hence, section xl points out that synthesis is the ultimate collocation, in which all the sources meet.

The remainder of the extant treatise is given over, first, to a consideration of how literary works fall short of sublimity[65] and, second, to a consideration of the causes of the lack of sublimity among the authors of Longinus' time.[66] The first topic need scarcely be discussed; as Longinus remarks, "there is no present need to enumerate by their kinds the means of producing pettiness; when we have once shown what things make writings noble and sublime, it is clear that in most cases their opposites will make them low and uncouth"; and Longinus proceeds to treat them in reverse order to that of the sources of sublimity, going no further, however, than the choice of words. The second consideration enters into the topic importantly; if the times constrain the artist to the point where he cannot operate, then rhetorical tuition is useless; hence the artist must be demonstrated to be a free and independent agent. And, as he shows, in any failure of art it is the artist and not his time which is at fault, so that art remains a permanent possibility. At this point the extant treatise concludes, with a broken transition to the topic of the passions.

Unfortunate as the loss of the remaining discussion is, it cannot and need not be accepted as a permanent mutilation of the text. Since, as this essay has doubtless made clear, passion is one of the important determinants as well as a source in itself of literary operation, it follows that there must be some specification of the conception of passion if the *Peri Hypsous* is to appear as an intelligible technical treatise. And further, although we have no part of the promised treatise on the passions, we have in the text ample reference and comment on the subject of the passions from which Longinus' treatment of passion might be reconstructed, in sufficient part to render the technique of *Peri Hypsous* operable at least, although perhaps not sufficiently to permit a reconstruction of his entire theory of psychology.

Happily we have in section xx a definition of passion; it is a rush and commotion of the soul;[67] its contrary, calm, is a rest, a stasis of the soul;[68] and, although Longinus explicitly says that "passions are many, nay countless, past the power of many to reckon,"[69] so that an attempt to achieve their complete enumeration would clearly be useless, the text nevertheless furnishes us not only with many examples of the passions but with some indication of their causation and determination, their course, their symptoms, and their ordering. Pity, joy, fear, grief, pride, wonder, awe, hate, disgust, love, reverence, in-

---

65. Secs. xli–xliii.

66. Sec. xliv. 68. *Ibid.*

67. xx. 2. 69. *Ibid.*

spiration, madness, persuasion, ecstasy, suspicion, anger, indignation, jealousy, patience, shame, laughter, weeping, and envy constitute a partial list, and one more than adequate for our purposes; and Longinus' comments concerning those which are directly mentioned by him make it evident that, first of all, every passion has a cause—a cause which is its object. Since passion is a motion of the soul, then either the soul itself is the cause of motion or something external to the soul; but it is clear from Longinus' statements that something external to the soul is the cause, as peril of fear, safety of confidence, the gods of awe and reverence, the mean and vicious of disgust, etc. And it is clear, further, that passion admits of degree, since Longinus speaks frequently of vehement passion and since such statements constitute an admission of the possibility of degree. Further, it is clear that not every passion has the same object, since Longinus remarks that certain things excite terror, certain things disgust, and that not every object excites passion in the same degree, since he says also that one thing may be more terrible than another. It follows, therefore, that the object is by nature determinative both of the kind and of the degree of the passion which it excites. Hence, as he says, passions are infinite in number, since the objects are causative of unique effects. His remark concerning laughter, that "it is a passion, a passion which has its root in pleasure,"[70] provides the determination of the degree of passion; for, if pleasure is a root of passion, then pain must be a root also; and it follows from what has been discovered so far that every object is capable of inducing passion in so far as it is capable of inducing a motion of the soul attended either by pleasure or by pain and that the degree of passion which it induces would be proportional to the amount of attendant pain or pleasure. It would not be difficult, once this much is known, to construct definitions of at least the more familiar emotions, since the extant text provides ample illustration of Longinus' method of framing definitions; but perhaps this will be unnecessary if we remark that each such definition would state that the passion in question is an agitation of the soul, accompanied by pleasure or pain, and slight or great in proportion to that pleasure or pain, attended by such and such symptoms, the moving cause being something which in such and such a fashion is capable of inflicting pain or inducing pleasure.

Further, Longinus clearly ranks objects as high, common, or low; now, since passion is determined in kind and degree by the object, it follows that passions themselves must be capable of similar classification to that of objects; hence as high, common, or low; and this is borne out by his statement in section viii that wretchedness, annoyance, and fear are passions of a mean order. They are such because they cannot properly be caused by the highest objects; what is itself good in the highest degree must naturally cause, in the highest

70. xxxviii. 6.

degree, those passions which are highest; for example, love, reverence, and awe are passions which are properly excited in us to the highest degree by the gods; but disgust, pity, or annoyance they could not properly cause.

It is clear, furthermore, that for Longinus the soul has both an active and a passive principle, since the soul is capable of thought and since thought cannot here be passion, for if it were passion, it could not be reckoned as a distinct source of sublimity. And this is clear also from his statement that men have the power to be good and to think elevated thoughts;[71] for this would be impossible if the soul were passive only, and, indeed, it would be impossible for the soul to imitate any action whatsoever; hence, on the same grounds, an active principle of the soul is implied by the very possibility of an art of anything. If, then, there is this active principle, then either it governs the passive, or the passive governs it, or they govern reciprocally, or both are ruled together by some other thing. But this last is impossible; for if the active is governed by something further, there is no active principle; but we have seen that there is. Now passion can be known to be unseasonable or excessive or defective, while thought can be known to be false; and in whatever principle the criterion rests there must also be governance; but passion cannot know anything. It follows, then, that the active principle must be the ruling principle. Hence reason must rule appetite and passion, and, when it so rules with all propriety, virtue results. But in such cases as those in which passion and appetite gain the upper hand and either become dislocated from their proper objects or become excessive or defective, in these vice or madness must result.

The gods are passionless;[72] heroes are distinguished from common men in that they suffer a passion different either in kind or in degree from that which common men undergo, for the heroic passions have higher objects; thus the anger of Ajax arises from no common cause and exhibits itself in no common fashion, and similarly the fear of an Ajax is not of death but of a death which is unheroic.[73] Sublimity of passion, then, must be of this heroic order; but its evocation is ultimately dependent upon thought, noble passion resulting where thought itself is noble, and ignoble passion where thought is mean. The noble mind, if not passionless like the divine, is at least free of the meaner passions because it is averted from the objects which call these forth.

So much for the reconstruction of Longinus' theory of the passions; it remains to observe the consequences of such a theory for the Longinian art of the sublime. The method would now appear to be perfect and complete. Certain things are by nature sublime; by nature man is capable of recognizing them as sublime and of loving them with an eternal and invincible love, for nature determined man to be no low and ignoble animal; admitted into the universe in

71. Sec. xliv.   72. ix. 8.   73. ix. 10.

part as spectator, in part as participant, and driven by his love into rivalry and competition with the supremacy of the marvelous, the great, and the beautiful, he fulfils the function which these in a manner appoint him; and, although human understanding is limited and wonder results when marvels surpass human thought, in a sense also the mind grows beyond its ordinary bounds, so that "for the speculation and thought which are within the scope of human endeavor, not all the universe is sufficient."[74] The nobility of man's thought, then, finds its warrant in these sublimities, and thought itself is the warrant of all else; for it determines passion, and thought and passion together, in literary endeavor, determine the use of all literary devices and guarantee their success.

Consequently, the artist must himself be sublime in soul if he is to reflect the sublime; if he is led by the love of pleasure or the love of money, he becomes little and ignoble. Like a corrupted judge he mistakes his own interest for what is good and noble, he admires his mortal parts and neglects to improve the immortal, and he becomes eventually the prisoner of his passions.[75] And the ignoble man, the slave, cannot produce what is admirable; "the true Orator must have no low ungenerous spirit, for it is not possible that those who think small thoughts fit for slaves, and practise them in all their daily life, should put out anything to deserve wonder and immortality."[76] But "great words issue, and it cannot be otherwise, from those whose thoughts are weighty";[77] and literary greatness is to be estimated not by mere freedom from fault but by the greatness of the spirit reflected in the words as in a mirror. Art thus in a sense is a double discipline, being both moral and aesthetic; but its literary function is ultimately only to provide some suitable medium which the spirit of the writer transcends and illuminates. So the spirit of the writer be sublime and the mirror of words present an adequate image, hearers who are properly prepared cannot fail to be stirred, for words carry "the passion which is present to the speaker into the souls of the bystanders, bringing them into partnership with himself";[78] and the admiration of men for what is truly great is "as it were, a law of nature," failing only when men have sunk beneath their natural state or have not reached their proper development.[79]

The topic of the passions is not treated with the other sources because the passions are not, like them, open to voluntary acquisition; they are per se passive movements of the soul, hence cannot be initiated by the soul itself; but in the properly controlled spirit they are mastered by reason; and it is only then that, moving among higher objects which contemplation has discovered and

74. xxxv. 3.

75. xliv. 5.

76. ix. 3.

77. *Ibid.*

78. xxxix. 3.

79. Sec. xxxv.

provided, they form an important factor in sublimity. Passion alone, Longinus tells us, is not enough to effect sublimity, for not all passion is sublime; indeed, the soul wherein passion reigns deteriorates from its nobility. But, although reason must master passion for sublimity to obtain, the acquisition of that mastery is not an aesthetic, but an ethical, problem; there is no skill of the passions; and in so far as there are quasi-literary means for their control, the means must be found in elevated thought.

It should appear from this discussion that the term "sublimity" can scarcely be taken as referring to a mere elevation of diction, for to take it in this sense is to regard a literary work as a mere arrangement of words and to collapse all the sources of sublimity into those which are merely verbal, and perhaps all of these, even, into synthesis alone. The treatise of Longinus affords every evidence that he sought to avoid such a reduction and that hence the word should not be taken in its merely stylistic sense but should receive its definition in terms of that communication of nobility which is made possible by the perfection of the human soul and of art, and which receives its answer in the wonder and admiration of all men.

RHETORIC IN THE MIDDLE AGES[1]

RICHARD McKEON

EDIEVAL and Renaissance rhetoricians and philosophers, following the example of Cicero, seldom omit from their treatment of rhetoric some consideration of the subject matter, nature, and end of the art. Long before Cicero, rhetoric had become one of the focal points of the differences of philosophic schools, and the practice and application of the art had long wandered from field to field, reflecting and sometimes even affecting the complexities of philosophic discussions. Yet in histories which touch upon it, rhetoric is treated as a simple verbal discipline, as the art of speaking well, applied either as it was in Rome in forensic oratory and associated with the interpretation of laws or, more frequently, as it was in the Renaissance in the interpretation and use of the works of orators and poets and associated with, or even indistinguishable from, poetic and literary criticism. The history of rhetoric as it has been written since the Renaissance is therefore in part the distressing record of the obtuseness of writers who failed to study the classics and to apply rhetoric to literature, and in part the monotonous enumeration of doctrines, or preferably sentences, repeated from Cicero or commentators on Cicero. Scholarly labors have reconstructed only a brief and equivocal history for rhetoric during the Middle Ages. The development consists of slight and original increments of erudition in the compendia composed from the fourth to the ninth century—derived largely from the *De inventione* of Cicero and the *Ad Herennium*—and in later commentaries and treatises to the elaboration of coherent and complex doctrines in the twelfth century based on Quintilian and the later rhetorical works of Cicero, the *Orator*, the *De oratore*, and the *Topica*. The sequence of development is fortuitous and even implausible, for the treatment of rhetoric becomes more perfunctory as erudition in the works of rhetoricians increases, and rhetoric disappears abruptly when knowledge of it is at a maximum, particularly from the works of the authors who acknowledge the influence of Cicero and Quintilian. The translation of the *Rhetoric* of Aristotle, of the pseudo-Aristotelian *Rhetorica ad Alexandrum*, and of the *De elocutione* of Demetrius in the thirteenth century would seem to have had, by this account, no effect comparable to that of the other translations of the century in stimulating interest in its subject; and the return of rhetoric to promi-

1. Reprinted with alterations from *Speculum*, January, 1942.

nence during the Renaissance is explained only on the supposition that men's minds were turned once more, after a long interval, to literature and life.[2]

There is little reflection in the histories of rhetoric of the differences concerning the subject matter and purpose of rhetoric by which rhetoricians thought to distinguish and oppose their doctrines; and only occasionally and opaquely do some of the consequences of basic philosophic differences appear in the place given to rhetoric in the enumerations and classifications of the arts and sciences. The theoretic presuppositions which underlie the shifts and alterations of rhetorical doctrines are readily made to seem verbal and arbitrary preferences, for in the course of discussion all the terms are altered in meaning, and the contents and methods of each of the arts are transformed when grammar, rhetoric, poetic, dialectic, and logic change places or are identified one with another, or are distinguished from one another, or are subsumed one under another. Yet the confident readjustments of Renaissance

2. Valla, Vives, Ramus, and other Renaissance rhetoricians who treat the history of rhetoric pass over the intermediate period separating them from antiquity, to criticize, refute, and occasionally approve of the doctrines of Aristotle, Cicero, Quintilian, and Boethius. In early works of erudition and philology the scope of the history of rhetoric is no broader than the scope of contemporary controversy. D. G. Morhof makes the transition from Cicero, Quintilian and their predecessors, who are considered in the first nine of the thirty-two paragraphs headed *De scriptoribus rhetoricis* in his *Polyhistor, literarius, philosophicus et practicus* (vi. 1 [3d ed.; Lubecae, 1732], I, 941–56), to the Renaissance rhetoricians treated in the last twenty-three paragraphs with the remark, "Nos vero, missis nunc veteribus, ad recentiores sparsim enumerandos progredimur." J. Clericus carries the *Historia rhetorica* down to the Church Fathers in his *Ars critica* (Pars II, Sectio I, cap. 17 [Leipzig, 1713], I, 336–52). The history of rhetoric has more recently been extended to the Middle Ages, but it is always rhetoric in some particular sense, applied to some particular subject, and the history is usually negative or at least deprecatory. J. B. L. Crevier thus traces the history of rhetoric in education by noting the absence of any provision for rhetoric in the regulations of the University of Paris until the restoration of letters (*Histoire de l'Université de Paris* [Paris, 1761], I, 299, 307, 376, 479; II, 450; IV, 190, 243–44, 249, 330, 349, and *passim*). The pattern of rhetoric had, incidentally, not changed from the Renaissance to the eighteenth century in the important respect that Crevier found little use in his own writings on rhetoric for any authors between the ancients and his contemporaries, and the imperfections of Aristotle, Cicero, and Quintilian are his excuse for writing: "Aristote me paroit trop philosophe, Cicéron trop orateur, Quintilien trop scholastique" (*Rhétorique françoise* [Paris, 1808], I, xix). E. Norden treats rhetoric primarily in terms of style and is able, therefore, to dispose of the entire period from the ninth century to the time of Petrarch briefly in terms of the opposition of the study of authors to the study of the liberal arts, of classicism to scholasticism (*Die antike Kunstprosa vom vi. Jahrhundert v. Chr. bis in die Zeit der Renaissance* [4th ed.; Leipzig, 1923], II, 688–731); cf. the treatment of rhetoric and poetic (*ibid.*, pp. 894–98). According to C. S. Baldwin, the fate of rhetoric is determined by shifts in the interrelations of the arts of the trivium: rhetoric was dominant until the fall of Rome, grammar during the Carolingian period, dialectic during the Middle Ages (*Medieval Rhetoric and Poetic* [New York, 1928], p. 151). Rhetoric was crowded into medieval education between grammar for boys and dialectic for men, and Baldwin is therefore at pains to find reasons which explain "why there was no medieval rhetorician who really advanced the study" (*ibid.*, p. 182). The history of rhetoric during the Middle Ages is consequently the account of its misapplications and extensions: poetic is a misapplication of rhetoric to style (*ibid.*, pp. 185 ff., esp. 191–95); the dictamen is a development of rhetoric, but without need of perversion (*ibid.*, pp. 208 ff., esp. 214–15); and preaching in the absence of political and forensic oratory makes use of

rhetoricians, their redistribution of technical devices among the arts, and their correction of the confusions of the ancients seem no less whimsical and haphazard, if their reasons and criteria are ignored and only the repetition of enumerations of the disciplines and their parts is recorded. Rhetoricians from Cicero to Ramus have in common a persistent care in defining their art, and it seems plausible that a history of rhetoric traced in terms of its matter and function, as specified at each stage, might give significance and lively interest to the altering definitions, the differentiation of various conceptions of rhetoric itself, and the spread of the devices of rhetoric to subject matters far from those ordinarily ascribed to it. Such a history would not treat an art determined to a fixed subject matter (so conceived, rhetoric is usually found to have little or no history, despite much talk about rhetoric and even more use of it, during the Middle Ages), nor, on the other hand, would it treat an art determined arbitrarily and variously by its place in classifications of the sciences (so conceived, the schemes of the sciences would be arbitrary in their alterations and uncontrolled by philosophic principles or material content). The history of rhetoric should have as subject an art which, although it has no special subject matter according to most rhetoricians, nonetheless must be discussed in application to some subject matter: rhetoric has been applied to many incommensurate subject matters; it has borrowed devices from other arts, and its technical terms and methods have become, without trace of their origin, parts of other arts and sciences; its own devices have been bent back upon themselves in such a way that any part of rhetoric or any matter incidentally involved in it—words and style, character and passion, reason and imagination, the kinds of orations, civil philosophy, practical action—have been made basic to the definition of all technical terms and distinctions. Moreover, if the succession of subject matters and functions can be used to reduce the welter of changes in rhetoric to a

---

epideictic or occasional oratory, the third of Aristotle's genera (*ibid.*, pp. 229 ff.). According to P. Abelson (*The Seven Liberal Arts: A Study in Medieval Culture* [New York, 1906], pp. 52 ff.), rhetoric consisted of a practical training during the Roman period; then of the technical rules of a science; and, finally, when this theoretical and logical form of rhetoric fell into obsolescence, of the practical rules for writing letters and documents. In the account of N. Valois (*Guillaume d'Auvergne* [Paris, 1880], pp. 224 ff.) rhetoric was taught as a liberal art until the end of the twelfth century and then fell into discredit except as a practical discipline applied to preaching and prayer. The judgment of C. H. Haskins (*The Renaissance of the Twelfth Century* [Cambridge, Mass., 1928], p. 138) is no less concise in statement: "Ancient rhetoric was concerned with oratory, mediaeval rhetoric chiefly with letter-writing," and is illustrated with detailed evidence. More simply, if rhetoric is viewed as a form of literary criticism and associated with poetic, the decline of rhetoric is a symptom of the eclipse of the study of ancient literature (cf. L. J. Paetow, "The Arts Course at Mediaeval Universities with Special Reference to Grammar and Rhetoric," *University of Illinois Studies*, III (January, 1910), esp. 67 ff.; and D. L. Clark, *Rhetoric and Poetry in the Renaissance* (New York, 1922), pp. 43 ff.

significant historical sequence, the theories implicated in the shifts of its subject matter should emerge, not merely as philosophic or sophistic disputes, but
in concrete application, each at least defensible and each a challenge to the conception of intellectual history as the simple record of the development of a body
of knowledge by more or less adequate investigations of a constant subject
matter.

I

Three distinct lines of intellectual development during the Middle Ages were
decisively determined or strongly influenced in their initial stages by rhetoric:
first, and most properly, the tradition of rhetoricians themselves, who found
their problems assembled and typical answers discussed in the works of Cicero
and Quintilian; second, and less obviously, the tradition of philosophers and
theologians who found in Augustine a Platonism reconstructed from the Academic and Neo-Platonic philosophies (conscientiously reversing the process by
which they were derived from Plato's doctrines) and formulated in terms refurbished and simplified from Cicero's rhetorical distinctions; and, finally, the
tradition of logic which passed as "Aristotelian," yet which followed Aristotle
only in the treatment of terms and propositions and resorted to Cicero in the
treatment of definitions and principles. Whatever the estimate that critics and
historians are disposed to make of Cicero's achievement, originality, and consistency, his choices and emphases fixed the influence and oriented the interpretation of ancient thought, Greek as well as Latin, at the beginning of the Middle
Ages and again in the Renaissance; and we today are far from having freed ourselves from the consequences of that long tradition in scholarship, criticism, or
taste. During the Middle Ages and Renaissance many of the oppositions and
agreements of theology and dialectic, no less than problems internal to each,
were stated in language borrowed from or influenced by rhetoric and reflected
theories by which rhetoricians had in antiquity opposed philosophers and
logicians; surprising parallels were disclosed in theology and dialectic as well
as in other arts and sciences, and they were expressed in language familiar to
the rhetorician; innovations and discoveries were made which seem to follow
the dictation of nature if their pattern of statement is ignored; and mere equivo-
cations were pursued into interminable and recurrent verbal disputes.

The rhetoricians of the Middle Ages followed Cicero or suggestions found
in his works when they discussed civil philosophy as the subject matter of
rhetoric or divided that subject matter according to the three kinds of oratory—
deliberative, judicial, demonstrative—or when they sought to determine it more
generally by means of the distinction between *propositum* and *causa* (or *thesis*
and *hypothesis*, as the Greek terms were Latinized), or by consideration of the

characteristics of controversies and the constitutions (or *status*) of questions.[3]
Moreover, they could learn, even from the *De inventione*, that there had been
controversy on most of these points; and, in particular, the brief history of
three views concerning the matter of rhetoric—Gorgias holding that it is all
things, Aristotle dividing it into three kinds proper to the three kinds of oratory, and Hermagoras distinguishing "causes," which are specific to persons,
and "questions," which are without such specification—supplied the arguments by which to dissent from, as well as those to support, Cicero's version
of Aristotle's solution.[4] Major alterations in the contents and doctrines of
rhetoric attended these changes in subject matter, and they required for their
elaboration only a little erudition, such as might be derived from study of the
points of difference between the *Ad Herennium* and the *De inventione*, or from
the information supplied by Fortunatianus concerning figures and the Greek
technical terms of rhetoric, or, finally, from Quintilian's orderly enumerations
of divergent views and his statement and rectification of inconsistencies attributed to Cicero.[5] Even apart from the influence of theology and even before
the influence of dialectic was felt, the remnants of old and the seeds of new controversies were preserved in rhetoric itself.

Rhetoric influenced Augustine both in his reactions against it and in his as-
similation and use of devices borrowed from it; he differentiated two elo-
quences and two arts, much as Plato had proved rhetoric a pseudo-art in the

3. Cf. Cicero *De inventione* i. 4. 5: "Sed antequam de praeceptis oratoriis dicimus, videtur
dicendum de genere ipsius artis, de officio, de fine, de materia, de partibus." After determining that its *genus* is "civilis scientia," its *officium* "dicrere adposite ad persuasionem," and its
finis "persuadere dictione," Cicero defines the matter of all arts, including the art of rhetoric
(*ibid.* 5. 7): "Materiam artis eam dicimus, in qua omnis ars et ea facultas, quae conficitur ex
arte, versatur."

4. *Ibid.* 5. 7—7. 9. Cf. *ibid.* 9. 12 for illustration of the process by which basic terms are
altered and the distinctions of rhetoric are bent back on themselves: in this case the dispute
is concerning whether deliberation and demonstration are the genera of "causes" or are
themselves parts of a particular genus of "cause." Isidore's list of the "inventors" of the art
reflects the influence of Cicero's history of the matter of rhetoric, since the inventors are
clearly determined by this history, as is the testimony to the elusiveness of the distinctions;
cf. *Etymologiae* ii. 2: "Haec autem disciplina a Graecis inventa est, a Gorgia, Aristotele,
Hermagora, et translata in Latinum a Tullio videlicet et Quintiliano, sed ita copiose, ita
varie, ut eam lectori admirari in promptu sit, comprehendere impossibile. Nam membranis
retentis quasi adhaerescit memoriae series dictionis, ac mox repositis recordatio omnis
elabitur."

5. Cf. *Institutio oratoria* iii. 5. 4 ff. for an excellent statement of the problems involved in
rhetorical "questions," and the disputes concerning "thesis" and "hypothesis," and esp.
14–15 for the development of Cicero's doctrine. For a brief summary of some of the characteristic statements of the definition and end of rhetoric cf. *ibid.* ii. 15; for disputes concerning its matter, *ibid.* 21. Or again, in illustration of the bending-back of rhetorical distinctions,
what one man holds to be the "parts of rhetoric" another treats as the "work of the orator"
(*ibid* iii. 3. 11 ff.); the two positions are taken, respectively, by Cicero, *De inventione* i. 7. 9,
and Fortunatianus, *Ars rhetorica* i. 1 (Halm, *Rhetores Latini minores* [Leipzig, 1863], p. 81;
henceforth cited as "Halm").

Gorgias and yet had illustrated the method of the true rhetoric based on dialectic in the *Phaedrus*. Augustine was first attracted to philosophy by Cicero's *Hortensius*, which he encountered in the course of his rhetorical studies, and he was put off in his further attempt to combine philosophy with the name of Christ by the contrast of the scriptural and Ciceronian styles.[6] That stumbling block was finally removed in part by the aid of a rhetorical device which Augustine learned from Ambrose' preaching—the analogical method of interpreting Scripture[7]—and, although thereafter he refused to answer questions concerning Cicero's *Orator* and *De oratore*, on the grounds that it was a task unworthy of a bishop distracted with ecclesiastical cares,[8] his statement of Christian doctrine was, in the terms of Cicero, sublimated to new meanings and transformed to new uses. When he wishes to enumerate the questions basic to all inquiry, he resorts to Cicero's three "constitutions of causes"—whether a thing is, that it is, and what sort; and when he enumerates the methods to be used in treating scriptural questions, they turn out to be two of Cicero's five parts of rhetoric—discovery and statement; moreover, these two sets of questions seem to him exhaustive, and all problems and doctrines are concerned, as in the manuals of rhetoric, with "things" or with "signs."[9] This rhetorical language has, however, been adapted to the statement of a theology: discovery has been qualified as discovery of "what should be understood" and statement as statement of "what has been understood," with the result that the classification of signs and

6. *Confessions* iii. 3. 6—5. 9 (*Patrologia Latina*, XXXII, 685–86; henceforth cited as "*PL*").

7. *Confessions* v. 13. 23 and vi. 4. 5–6 (*PL*, XXXII, 717 and 721–22). Cf also the conversion of Victorinus the rhetorician and the effect of *salus* and *fides* on his rhetoric (*Confessions* viii. 2. 5 [*PL*, XXXII, 751]).

8. *Epistola CXVIII ad Dioscorum* i. 2 and v. 34 (*PL*, XXXIII, 432–33 and 448).

9. *Confessions* x. 9. 16—10. 17 (*PL*, XXXII, 786). Cf. Cicero *Orator* 14. 45: "Nam quoniam, quicquid est quod in controversia aut in contentione versetur, in eo aut sitne aut quid sit aut quale sit quaeritur: sitne, signis; quid sit, definitionibus; quale sit, recti pravique partibus—quibus ut uti possit orator, non ille volgaris sed hic excellens, a propriis personis et temporibus, si potest, avocat controversiam." The context and application of the questions are rhetorical in the *Confessions*, but cf. *De diversis quaestionibus LXXXIII* 18 (*PL*, XL, 15): "Ideoque etiam cum veritas quaeritur, plus quam tria genera questionum esse non possunt; utrum omnino sit, utrum hoc an aliud sit, utrum approbandum improbandumve sit." The tendency of these questions toward generalization beyond their specifically rhetorical meanings is assisted by some of the names attached to them: the pseudo-Augustine calls them "rational or logical" questions (*De rhetorica* 9 [Halm, p. 142]); Martianus Capella calls them "principal status" (*De rhetorica* 6 [Halm, p. 455]); Clodian names them "rational status" (*Ars rhetorica* [Halm, p. 590]). A fourth question or constitution or status is added by Hermagoras, is rejected by Cicero and Quintilian, and is mentioned by the pseudo-Augustine and Clodian. Concerning the variety and evolution of questions (or "status," as he prefers to call them), cf. Quintilian iii. 6. 29–85; his own decision is presented as one prescribed by nature and coincident with the doctrine of Cicero (*ibid.* 80): "Credendum est igitur his, quorum auctoritatem secutus est Cicero, tria esse, quae in omni disputatione quaerantur, an sit, quid sit, quale sit? quod ipsa nobis etiam natura praescribit." For Augustine's enumeration of scriptural methods and problems cf. *De doctrina Christiana* i. 1–2 (*PL*, XXXIV, 19–20).

their uses is dependent, as it had not been in rhetoric, on the classification of things. In the *De doctrina Christiana* the first three books are concerned with discovery, the fourth with statement. The treatment of discovery is based, in the first book, on the distinction of things into those which as final ends are loved or enjoyed (*frui*) and those which as intermediate ends are used (*uti*) for further ends; consideration of the former takes the form of a theological inquiry into the attributes of God and divine things; the treatment of the nature of things is supplemented, in the second book, by a philological inquiry into the nature of words in relation to the Scriptures and the arts and institutions of the pagans; and, finally, in the third book, the inquiry into means of removing verbal ambiguities requires appeal to two sets of rules—grammatical rules applied to the manner of statement and rhetorical rules to determine the circumstances of fact.[10] The treatment of statement in the final book is therefore concerned not so much with the *precepts* of rhetoric, although some precepts can be found from analysis of the fashion in which the three styles of Cicero are applied to their appropriate matters by "ecclesiastical orators," as with an eloquence in which the words are supplied by the things and by wisdom itself and the speaker is unlearnedly wise.[11] The judgment expressed by Cicero at the beginning of the *De inventione*, that wisdom without eloquence is of little benefit to the state and eloquence without wisdom a great danger, is transformed by Augustine's dialectic, and all the terms take on two meanings. The wisdom and eloquence of the world are to be contrasted to eternal wisdom and eloquence; for there are not only two kinds of things, temporal and divine, but two kinds of words, the external words instituted and used by men which have no correspondence to things except by designation and no controllable influence on our thought except by way of the context of other words, and the internal words, by which a master speaking within us teaches the truth.[12]

10. *De doctrina Christiana* iii. 4. 8, and 12. 18 (*PL*, XXXIV, 68 and 72–73).

11. *De doctrina Christiana* iv. 1. 1—7. 11 (*PL*, XXXIV, 89–94).

12. *De magistro* 3. 5–6 and 11. 36—12. 46 (*PL*, XXXII, 1197–98 and 1215–20). Cf. the excellent statement of the relation of language to thought by E. Gilson, *Introduction à l'étude de Saint Augustin* (Paris, 1929), pp. 87–103. Augustine's conception of rhetoric is developed most fully in the *De doctrina Christiana*, *De ordine*, *De catechizandis rudibus*, and *Contra Cresconium*. Cf. also J. Žůrek, "De S. Aurelii praeceptis rhetoricis," *Dissertationes philologae Vindobonenses* (Vienna, 1905), VIII, 69–109; M. Comeau, *La Rhétorique de Saint Augustin d'après le "Tractatus in Iohannem"* (Paris, 1930); G. Combès, *Saint Augustin et la culture classique* (Paris, 1927), esp. pp. 49–56, where true eloquence is distinguished from the oratorical art; H.-I. Marrou, *Saint Augustin et la fin de la culture antique* (Paris, 1938), esp. pp. 507–40 on Christian eloquence. The rhetoric of Cicero was moral and political in its applications, and the influence of rhetoric extended to political doctrine. The differentiation of things according to ends loved and means used had already entered Christian ethics in Ambrose' *De officiis ministrorum*, which was based on the distinctions of Cicero's *De officiis;* and Cicero's rhetorically conceived political theory supplies, by virtue of the same distinction, the terminology for Augustine's discussion of the City of God as well as the elements of the terrestrial city to which it is contrasted.

Whether things be treated as signs or signs as things, only the eternal meanings and realities are important; knowledge of temporal things and of the arts is chiefly useful for the interpretation of the language and symbolism of Scripture, and the Sacraments are signs adapted to the mutability of human sensibilities but immutable in their significance of the changeless things of God.[13] Once account is taken of the distinction of things and words into those which are temporal and those which are changeless, the influence of rhetoric is discernible in many traits of the Augustinian tradition: in the analogical interpretation of Scripture and in the numerous medieval encyclopedias prepared to facilitate such interpretation (for words are signs which are useful less to designate things than to express truths and persuade minds, and things therefore are useful to interpret signs, rather than signs to interpret things);[14] in the literal interpretation in which apparently contradictory texts were reconciled in canon law and theology by use of the rhetorician's "circumstances" of statement, that is, by consideration of "who" said it, "where, when, why, how, with what assistance";[15] in the organization of theological problems according to the distinction of things and signs; and in the place of rhetoric after dialectic in the enumeration of the liberal arts (since it supplies the means of stating truths, once they have been discovered) instead of before dialectic, as in the enumeration of an opposed tradition (since it achieves only probability and persuasion but falls short of truth).[16]

The discussion of logic during the Middle Ages may be divided into four periods. During the first period, the elements of logic were learned from simple treatises like the pseudo-Augustine's *Principia dialecticae* and *Categoriae decem* (which Alcuin recomended to Charlemagne as Augustine's translation of Aristotle's *Categories*) or the sections on dialectic in such handbooks as those of Martianus Capella, Cassiodorus, and Isidore of Seville. During the second period, after the curriculum instituted by Gerbert at the end of the tenth century the basis of instruction in dialectic was broadened to include the works and translations of Boethius, among them two of the six books of Aristotle's

---

13. *Epistola CXXXVIII ad Marcellinum* i. 7 (*PL*, XXXIII, 527): "Nimis autem longum est, convenienter disputare de varietate signorum, quae cum ad res divinas pertinent, Sacramenta appellantur. Sicut autem non ideo mutabilis homo, quia mane aliud, aliud vespere; illud hoc mense, illud alio; non hoc isto anno quod illo: ita non ideo mutabilis Deus, quia universi saeculi priore volumine aliud, aliud posteriore sibi iussit offerri, quo convenienter significationes ad doctrinam religionis saluberrimam pertinentes, per mutabilia tempora sine ulla sui mutatione disponeret."

14. Cf. Gilson, *op. cit.*, pp. 151–53.

15. *De doctrina Christiana* iii. 12. 18—29. 41 (*PL*, XXXIV, 72–81).

16. For the fashion in which rhetoric follows and supplements dialectic according to Augustine, cf. *De doctrina Christiana* ii. 35. 53—37. 55 (*PL*, XXXIV, 60–61); *De ordine* ii. 13. 38 (*PL*, XXXII, 1013).

Organon, which together acquired the traditional name of the "Old Logic." During the third period, the translation of the remaining four books in the twelfth century set up the New Logic, constituted of the *Introduction* of Porphyry, the *Organon* of Aristotle, and the *Six Principles* of Gilbert de la Porrée; but the authority of the Old Logic continued strong, since the contemporaries of John of Salisbury found the *Posterior Analytics*, which treats of the principles of scientific demonstration, difficult or even unintelligible[17] (and, indeed, the first important commentary on that work was written in the thirteenth century by Robert Grosseteste, while as late as the fourteenth century William of Ockham prepared an *Expositio aurea et admodum utilis super artem veterem*). Finally, during the fourth period, the discussion of logic is determined less by Aristotle's *Organon* than by the *Summulae*, written in the thirteenth century by Petrus Hispanus, Lambert of Auxerre, and William of Shyreswood. The extent of the influence of rhetoric on the development of logic may be judged from the fact that—although Aristotle's logic is characterized not merely by the schemata of terms, propositions, and syllogisms set forth in the first three books of the *Organon* but even more by the differentiation of proof, in accordance with the principles on which it depends, into three kinds: scientific or demonstrative, dialectical, and sophistical, which are expounded in the last three books, the *Posterior Analytics*, the *Topics*, and the *De sophisticis elenchis*— only the first three books had much influence until the thirteenth century, while principles were treated by devices which Aristotle used in rhetoric and dialectic, and, even after the thirteenth century, scientific method was in constant danger of being assimilated to dialectic, the *Posterior Analytics* to the *Topics*.

The early treatments of dialectic in the handbooks and encyclopedias run through a familiar sequence of subjects: the predicables of Porphyry; the categories of Aristotle; a brief treatment of propositions, in which the testimony of Aristotle's *De interpretatione* is mixed in small doses with that of the treatise by the same name attributed to Apuleius; an exposition of the categorical syllogism derived from the pseudo-Apuleius and of the hypothetical syllogism derived from the rhetorician Marius Victorinus; and, finally, in place of Aristotle's principles of demonstration, sections on definition and on "topics" or "commonplaces" derived from the Greek rhetoricians by way of Cicero and the lost works of Marius Victorinus. So direct is the descent of the principles

17. John of Salisbury *Metalogicon* iv. 6, ed. C. C. J. Webb (Oxford, 1929), p. 171: "Deinde hec utentium raritate iam fere in desuetudinem abiit, eo quod demonstrationis usus uix apud solos mathematicos est; et in his fere, apud geometras dumtaxat; sed et huius quoque discipline non est celebris usus apud nos, nisi forte in tractu Hibero uel confinio Affrice." In contrast to his brief and almost flippant treatment of the *Posterior Analytics*, John devotes more than half the third book (iii. 5–10; Webb, pp. 139–64) to praise of the utility of the *Topics*.

of demonstration from rhetoric that Cassiodorus closes his consideration of the art of dialectic, having treated of topics, with "atechnical" arguments (which form part of the *Topics* of Cicero but figure in the *Rhetoric* and not the *Topics* of Aristotle) and memory (which, although one of the traditional five parts of rhetoric, is common, according to Cassiodorus, to orators, dialecticians, poets, and jurists),[18] while Isidore supplements his statement of topics with a section on opposites derived from Cicero.[19] The basic pattern of this logic was not crucially altered by the return in the second period to the more extensive logical works of Boethius. "Dialectic" is not distinct from "logic" in the tradition of the Old Logic; rather, dialectic or logic is divided on the authority of Cicero into two parts, one (called "analytic" by the Greeks, according to Boethius) concerned with judgment, the other (called "topic" by the Greeks) concerned with discovery.[20] Boethius translated and wrote commentaries on Aristotle's *Categories* and *On Interpretation*, but he also translated and wrote two commentaries on the *Isagoge* or *Introduction* of the Neo-Platonist Porphyry, which expounds, as introduction to the *Categories*, the predicables treated by Aristotle in his *Topics*; and this dialectical treatment of "the five words" appeared thereafter, even when the influence of Boethius was slight, in medieval, Renaissance, and early modern treatments of Aristotle's logic and editions of his *Organon*. Instead of Aristotle's treatment of syllogism, medieval philosophers had, until the twelfth century, Boethius' essays *On the Categorical Syllogism* (in which the doctrine of Aristotle is modified by the doctrines of Theophrastus, Eudemus, and Porphyry),[21] *On the Hypothetical Syllogism* (in which the authority of Theophrastus and Eudemus is invoked for seeking necessary premises in the forms of propositions rather than in the nature of things),[22]

18. *Institutiones* ii. 3. 16–17, ed. R. A. B. Mynors (Oxford, 1937), pp. 127–28; cf. Cicero *Topica* 4. 24 and Aristotle *Rhetoric* i. 15. 1375ª22–1377ᵇ12. Mynors argues from the manuscripts that the *Institutiones* went through two recensions by other hands than Cassiodorus, and in them Boethius was substituted as authority in dialectic for Marius Victorinus (pp. xxviii and xxxvii). The closing sections of the later versions of the treatment of dialectic included, in addition to the rhetorical subjects of the earlier versions, a treatment of rhetorical places, discovery, and circumstances (*PL*, LXX, 1196–1202).

19. *Etymologiae* ii. 31.

20. *De differentiis topicis* i (*PL*, LXIV, 1173); *In Porphyrium commentaria* i (*PL*, LXIV, 73).

21. For references to Theophrastus, Eudemus, and Porphyry cf. *De syllogismo categorico* ii (*PL*, LXIV, 813, 814, 815, and esp. 829): "Haec de Categoricorum Syllogismorum introductione, Aristotelem plurimum sequens, et aliqua de Theophrasto et Porphyrio mutuatus, quantum parcitas introducendi permisit, expressi." The *Introductio ad syllogismos categoricos* (*PL*, LXIV, 761 ff.) seems clearly another recension of Book i of the *De syllogismo categorico*.

22. *De syllogismo hypothetico* i (*PL*, LXIV, 843): "Necessitas vero hypotheticae propositionis et ratio earum propositionum ex quibus junguntur inter se connexiones, consequentiam quaerit, ut cum dico: Si Socrates sedet et vivit, neque sedere eum, neque vivere necesse est; sed si sedet, necesse est vivere. . . . Necessitas enim propositionis in consequentiae immuta-

and *On Division* (which goes back to the "peripatetic" tradition, according to
the opening sentence of the essay, but cites explicitly only Andronicus, Plotinus, and Porphyry, for treatment of a "scientia dividendi" in which Aristotle
himself places little store).[23] The *De definitione* which went under Boethius'
name is by Marius Victorinus, and it supplies one more channel for the influence of Cicero and rhetoric.[24] Finally, instead of a treatment of the differences
of demonstrative, dialectical, and sophistical principles and proofs, Boethius
left two works which had the effect, during the Middle Ages and increasingly
during the Renaissance, of translating the problem of distinguishing principles
into the problem of discovering arguments or things: his *Commentary on the
Topics of Cicero* and his treatise in four books *On Topical Differences*, in which
the topical schemes or commonplaces of Themistius and Cicero are set forth
and reduced to a single classification.[25] With the advent of the New Logic in
the third period, during the twelfth century, however, logic was distinguished
from dialectic; and rhetoric became the counterpart of dialectic, although logic
continued to be divided into judgment and discovery. Finally, during the fourth
period, in the *Summulae* of the thirteenth century the emphasis is again on the
topics, as it is also in the reaction against logic during the Renaissance, when
the *Topics* of Cicero and of Boethius were once more used (as John the Scot
had used topics) as inspiration for a scientific method of discovering, not arguments, but things, and the scholastic logic was viewed as a verbal discipline
inferior in precision and practical effectiveness to these devices of rhetoric.

The effects of this extension of the devices of rhetoric to logic became apparent, in turn, in the treatment of rhetoric, and it became important to contrast
rhetoric and dialectic when both rhetoricians and dialecticians made use of
"places" for purposes of discovery. Paradoxically, in this tradition in which
the methods of rhetoric were similar to those of dialectic, rhetoric was subordinated to dialectic, while, in the tradition in which rhetoric was criticized
and then transformed to theological uses, dialectic was subordinated to rhetoric.

---

bilitate consistit." Cf. *De differentiis topicis* i (*PL*, LXIV, 1176), where such propositions are
called *per se nota*. For reference to Theophrastus and Eudemus cf. *De syllogismo hypothetico*
831.

23. *De divisione* (*PL*, LXIV, 875–76); cf. Aristotle *Prior Analytics* i. 31. 46ᵃ31–46ᵇ37.

24. On the question of the authenticity of the *De definitione*, cf. H. Usener, *Anecdoton
Holderi* (Bonn, 1877), pp. 59–66. For the effect of the *De definitione* in introducing rhetorical
distinctions into the medieval discussions of logic cf. C. Prantl, *Geschichte der Logik im
Abendlande* (Leipzig, 1855), I, 688–90.

25. Boethius refers to translations he has made of other books of the *Organon*, but no evidence has been found in medieval literature of their influence prior to the twelfth century;
cf. C. H. Haskins, "Versions of Aristotle's *Posterior Analytics*," in his *Studies in the History
of Mediaeval Science* (Cambridge, Mass., 1924), pp. 231 ff. For the rhetorical character and
effects of the *De differentiis topicis* cf. Prantl, *op. cit.*, I, 720–22.

The fourth book of Boethius' *On Topical Differences*, which treats of the differences between dialectical and rhetorical places, was used as a textbook of rhetoric in the twelfth and thirteenth centuries, and two short treatises devoted to rhetorical places passed under his name, the *Speculatio de rhetoricae cognatione* (which is more probably a compilation derived from Book iv of *De differentiis topicis* than an independent work by Boethius) and the *Locorum rhetoricorum distinctio*. Boethius finds the distinction between dialectic and rhetoric in their matter, use, and end: the matter of dialectic is "theses," that of rhetoric "hypotheses," and thesis and hypothesis are related as two kinds of "questions," the one universal, the other particularized to circumstances; dialectic uses interrogation and response, and its arguments are set forth in syllogisms; rhetoric uses continuous speech involving enthymemes; the end of dialectic is to force what one wishes from an adversary, that of rhetoric to persuade a judge.[26] Boethius takes over the early position of Cicero, as expressed in the *De inventione*, concerning the matter of rhetoric; but the whole question of end, function, and matter is raised in the context of a considerably longer list of questions, and in that context the other answers have changed. Boethius asks no fewer than nine questions about rhetoric: its genus, species, matter, parts, instrument, the parts of the instrument, the work and duty of the orator, and his end. The genus of rhetoric is no longer "civil science" (as it was for Cicero) but "faculty" (much as Aristotle had held it to be a δύναμις rather than a science). The matter of the faculty is all things suited to discourse, which, as Boethius puts it, is almost equivalent to the "civil question"; this matter of discourse is indeterminate until it is given specific form by the ends of rhetoric: the "civil question" is made into a judicial "cause" when the end considered is the just; into a deliberative "cause" when the end is the useful or the honorable; into a demonstrative "cause" when the end is the good. It is, as Isidore later observed, an elusive question, in which what one man considered the genus of an art can be transmuted by another into its matter; but that strange difference between the treatment of rhetoric as a faculty and as a social science is one of the slight remnants of the difference between Aristotle's conception of rhetoric and that of Cicero and the rhetoricians; and, from that remnant in Boethius' questions, medieval commentators were to reconstruct, with slowly increasing erudition, the full specifications of the old opposition.

II

These were not technical questions which were discussed by a few learned men, but distinctions which entered into all parts of medieval culture and life. Christianity had grown up in the environment of a culture which was pre-

26. *De differentiis topicis* iv (*PL*, LXIV, 1205–6). Cf. also *ibid.* i (*PL*, LXIV, 1177).

ponderantly rhetorical: indeed, the chief differences between Greek and Latin Christianity may be related to the differences between the Latin rhetoric of the Republic and early Empire (in which the arts and sciences had been put to the aid of rhetoric and civil philosophy had all but been reduced to the art of *forensic* pleading) and the Greek rhetoric of the Empire (in which philosophy itself had been displaced by display or *epideictic* rhetoric in the guise of sophistic, the rules of oratory had become the canons of literature, and Plato's and Aristotle's comparison of rhetoric and medicine had been made into a scientific method which rhetoric shared with medicine).[27] Since many of the early converts who first wrote on Christian doctrine had been professional rhetoricians before their conversions,[28] the rhetorical distinctions which they used in the statement of their problems and the organization of their works emerged often as doctrinal differences and empirical observations in later speculation on their statements. This emergence of rhetoric in the materials of discussion in all

27. For Greek doctrinal developments which led to the opposition of civil and sophistic rhetoric and to the advancement now of one, now of the other, as the preferred or unique manner of rhetoric cf. C. Brandstaetter, "De notionum πολιτικὸς et σοφιστής usu rhetorico," *Leipziger Studien zur classischen Philologie*, V (1893), 128–274. For the oppositions of sophistic, rhetoric, and philosophy cf. H. von Arnim, *Leben und Werke des Dio von Prusa* (Berlin, 1898), pp. 4–114; H. M. Hubbell, "The Rhetorica of Philodemus," *Transactions of the Connecticut Academy of Arts and Sciences*, XXIII (September, 1920), 276–84; J. F. d'Alton, *Roman Literary Theory and Criticism* (London, 1931), pp. 153 ff. For the interpenetration of rhetoric and dialectic and the transformation of dialectic by rhetoric in Hellenistic and Roman thought cf. Prantl, *op. cit.*, I, Abschnitt VIII, 505 ff. Philostratus includes in his *Lives of the Sophists* some of the ancient philosophers who approximated the rhetorical style of the Sophists, but he distinguished philosophy from sophistic (i. 481), since philosophers merely set snares for knowledge in their questioning but asserted that they had no sure knowledge, whereas Sophists of the old school professed knowledge of that whereof they spoke. Philostratus' enthusiastic account of the Sophists of the Empire is vivid indication of the spread and importance of epideictic rhetoric; its influence is likewise to be remarked in the Eastern church particularly among the Cappadocian fathers: cf. Norden, *op. cit.*, II, 529 ff. and 550 ff.; T. C. Burgess, "Epideictic Literature," *University of Chicago Studies in Classical Philology*, III (1902), 89–251; L. Méridier, *L'Influence de la séconde sophistique sur l'œuvre de Grégoire de Nysse* (Paris, 1906); M. Guignet, *Les Procédés épistolaires de St. Grégoire de Nazianze* (Paris, 1911); T. E. Ameringer, *The Stylistic Influence of the Second Sophistic on the Panegyrical Sermons of St. John Chrysostom* (Washington, 1921); J. M. Campbell, *The Influence of the Second Sophistic on the Style of the Sermons of St. Basil the Great* (Washington, 1922); A. Boulanger, *Aelius Aristide et la sophistique dans la province d'Asie au ii siècle de notre ère* (Paris, 1923). The crossing lines of rhetoric and medicine are apparent in Eunapius' *Lives of the Philosophers;* cf. particularly his accounts of Zeno of Cyprus, Magnus, Oribasius, and Ionicus (Secs. 497–99). Magnus made a happy combination of rhetoric and medicine by persuading the patients of other doctors that they had not been cured and then restoring them to health, apparently also by talk and questions; Ionicus was master of philosophy and medicine as well as the arts of rhetoric and poetry. Cf. P. H. and E. A. De Lacy, *Philodemus: On Methods of Inference* (Philadelphia, 1941), pp. 130 ff., where the relations between medicine and rhetoric are discussed in terms of an "empirical" or "conjectural" method.

28. Cyprian (cf. Jerome *De viris illustribus* 67 [*PL*, XXIII, 714]), Arnobius (cf. Jerome *Chronicon* ad annum 329 [*PL*, XXVII, 675–76]), Lactantius (Jerome *Chronicon* ad annum 319 [*PL*, XXVII, 669–70]), Augustine (*Confessions* iv. 2. 2 [*PL*, XXXII, 693–94]). Most of the other early Christian writers in the West, even those who had not been teachers of rhetoric, had studied the art as part of their education.

fields brought new questions into the technical disputes of the art. The numerous technical distinctions which had entered the apparatus and discussion of rhetoric took on applications which echo or anticipate many of the positions of philosophers, which vary according to three conceptions of rhetoric distinguishable and in shifting opposition in their treatment of the materials to which rhetoric is applied.

Until the coming of the New Logic in the twelfth century, the pattern of that opposition is relatively simple: the rhetorician who professed to treat of subject matters accessible to the "common notions" of the mind, without need of technical competence, found himself opposed, on the one hand, by theologians who had learned from Augustine to use the distinction between words and things to attack the rhetoric of the schools while practicing a rhetoric devoted to divine eloquence and divine things, and, on the other hand, by rhetoricians who had learned from Boethius to use the distinction between thesis and hypothesis to limit rhetoric to probable reasoning concerning specifically delimited questions subordinate to the general questions of dialectic. To the Augustinian, the excessive use or extension of rhetoric or of dialectic was suspect; to the peripatetic follower of Boethius, limitation or criticism of dialectic, whether from the point of view of theology or of rhetoric, was an attack on the use of reason; and to the rhetorician, as such, limitation of rhetoric by the laws of logic or theology was unwarranted restriction of the scope of reason and visionary neglect of the practical exigencies of the problems of law and morals. The simple lines of this opposition appear even in the early discussions of rhetoric, and they are preserved after the appearance of the New Logic, beneath the surface of the more intricate distinctions made necessary by the Aristotelian differentiation of logic from dialectic, poetic, sophistic, and rhetoric. These three main positions with respect to rhetoric may be marked off into four historical periods during the Middle Ages, sharply distinguished by the authorities on which the discussion of the arts was successively based: a first stage extending to about the end of the tenth century, when the chief authorities were the pseudo-Augustine, Martianus Capella, Cassiodorus, and Isidore; a second period extending through the eleventh and the first half of the twelfth century, dominated by Cicero, Boethius, and the Old Logic; a third period comprising the latter part of the twelfth century and the greater part of the thirteenth century, in which the New Logic became to some degree effective and was applied after a manner in the interpretation of the Aristotelian corpus; and, finally, the fourteenth century and the Renaissance, in which Aristotle and the Greek rhetoricians, Cicero, Quintilian, and Boethius all had increasing influence.

During the first period, rhetoric was concerned—on the authority of Hermagoras, Cicero, and Boethius, of Fortunatianus, Augustine, and Victorinus, and of all the even more derivative authorities that depended on them—with civil philosophy.[29] According to Cassiodorus, "The art of rhetoric is, as the masters of secular letters teach, the science of speaking well in civil questions"; and that definition is repeated in almost the same words by Isidore, Alcuin, and Rhabanus Maurus.[30] The occasion of the dialogue with Charlemagne in which Alcuin's doctrine is stated is a request made by the emperor for information concerning the art, since he thinks it ridiculous for one whose daily occupation is with civil questions to be ignorant of the precepts of the art; the dialogue, moreover, is frankly moral not only in its traditional title, *On Rhetoric and the Virtues*, but in purpose, since the transition from rhetoric to the virtues is accomplished by recognition that this "sermocinandi ratio" which is applied to civil cases and secular business must be supplemented by the other virtues. Yet, within this broad agreement among rhetoricians that rhetoric is concerned with civil questions, there are numerous differences of statement, which sometimes lead to changes in the devices thought proper to rhetoric and which seem often to entail major philosophic differences. The chief of these is the difference between the position (which seems to go back to Hermagoras and for which Fortunatianus is sometimes given as authority) which treats civil philosophy in terms of the "common notions" of mankind and therefore undertakes to differentiate the subject matter of rhetoric in terms of the questions treated, that is, the kinds of theses and hypotheses, and the position (which goes back to Cicero) which finds the subject matter of rhetoric in the three genera—deliberative, demonstrative, and judicial. The former has the effect of emphasizing the common bases of rhetoric in human knowledge while turning analyses

29. Cf. Cicero *De inventione* i. 5. 6; *Ad Herennium* i. 2. 2; Boethius *De differentiis topicis* iv (*PL*, LXIV, 1207); Fortunatianus i. 1 (Halm, p. 81); pseudo-Augustine, *De rhetorica* 3 (Halm, p. 138); Fabius Laurentius Victorinus, *Explanationes in rhetoricam M. Tullii Ciceronis* i. 5 (Halm, p. 171). The authenticity of the *De rhetorica* attributed to Augustine was questioned by his Benedictine editors in 1679 (cf. *PL*, XXXII, 1439) and by most authorities since that time; cf. M. Gibert, *Jugemens des savans sur les auteurs qui ont traité de la rhétorique* (Paris, 1716), II, 98: "Mais pour peu qu'on connoisse le style du Saint, il est aisé de voir que l'Ouvrage n'est pas de lui"; and G. Saintsbury, *A History of Criticism and Literary Taste in Europe* (New York, 1900), I, 377. Its authenticity has been defended on philological grounds by W. Crecilinus, *S. Aurelii Augustini de dialectica liber* (Elberfeld, 1857), and by A. Reuter, "Zu dem Augustinischen Fragment *De arte rhetorica*," in *Kirchengeschichtliche Studien Hermann Reuter . . . gewidmet* (Leipzig, 1888), pp. 324–41; but the arguments adduced have been answered by J. Žurek (*op. cit.*). The pseudo-Augustine attributes the position taken by Fortunatianus to Hermagoras.

30. Cassiodorus *Institutiones* ii. 2. 1 (Mynors, p. 97); cf. ii. Praef. 4 (Mynors, p. 91): "secundo de arte rhetorica, quae propter nitorem et copiam eloquentiae suae maxime in civilibus quaestionibus necessaria nimis et honorabilis aestimatur"; Isidore *Etymologiae* ii. 1 (Halm, p. 507); cf. i. 2. 1 and ii. 10, where law is treated as one of the subheads of rhetoric; Alcuin *De rhetorica et de virtutibus* 3 (Halm, p. 526); Rhabanus Maurus *De clericorum institutione* iii. 19 (*PL*, CVII, 396).

to the peculiarities of the questions that can be asked, the other the effect of centering on the common qualities of the subject matter and directing inquiry to the peculiarities and virtues of the orator. The problems of rhetoric arise largely in the mixtures of the two traditions. Cassiodorus, citing Fortunatianus, defines civil questions as those which fall within the common conception of the mind, that is, which anyone can understand when it is a question of the equitable and the good; Sulpitius Victor as those which are proper to no art but common to the opinion of all; Alcuin as those learned questions which can be conceived by the natural power of the mind.[31] Victorinus, on the other hand, divides the possible matter of rhetoric into two kinds: that with which the art operates (*ubi fit*)—namely, deliberative, demonstrative, judicial—and that from which the art is formed (*unde fit*)—namely, the arguments which contribute the matter of those three kinds—then limits the consideration of rhetoric to the former and refutes Hermagoras' doctrine of thesis and hypothesis in favor of the Aristotelian and Ciceronian doctrine of the three genera.[32] Martianus Capella repeats this differentiation of two kinds of matter but goes on to the exposition of theses and hypotheses, confining his disapproval to a remark concerning the extremely subtle reasons of some of the sectaries of rhetoric who hold that all rhetorical questions are general or theses.[33] The difference is between a tendency to make distinctions with reference to a subject matter and arguments suited to that subject matter and a tendency to make distinctions—often, ineeed, the same distinctions—with reference to the orator and his problems of discovering and stating arguments. The former emphasis tends to intellectualize the art and change its orientation to a subject matter and its peculiarities into problems of inquiry and understanding, as when Sulpitius Victor, having limited rhetoric to the civil question and having divided the civil question into two parts, thesis and hypothesis, finds three duties for the orator —understanding, discovery, and disposition (the first of which was neglected by Cicero but was adequately treated by the Greeks)—and then three genera of causes in the place of those long customary—the ethical, pathetic, and judicial. The latter emphasis leads to a series of questions, which were much discussed during the Middle Ages, concerning the relation of morals and eloquence, concerning the relation of art and wisdom, and concerning the definition of rhetoric as a virtue or an art or a discipline.[34] Rhetoric was to come into

31. *Institutiones* ii. 2. 1 (Mynors, p. 97); cf. Fortunatianus i. 1 (Halm, p. 81) and the pseudo-Augustine (*De rhetorica* 4 [Halm, p. 139]), who supplies the Greek term κοινὴ ἔννοια suggestive of Stoic origins. Sulpitius Victor *Institutiones oratoriae* (Halm, p. 314) and Alcuin *De rhetorica et de virtutibus* 3 (Halm, p. 526).

32. Fabius Laurentius Victorinus 5 (Halm, pp. 174–77).

33. Martianus Capella 5 (Halm, p. 454).

34. Sulpitius Victor *Institutiones oratoriae* 4 and 6 (Halm, pp. 315, 316). Cato's definition of the orator as *vir bonus dicendi peritus* (Quintilian xii. 1; Seneca *Controversiarum* i, Praef. 9)

conflict with dialectic as a consequence of this tendency, as it was to come into conflict with theology as a consequence of its tendency to annex the problems of morals and the interpretation of Scripture. Since its discipline was gradually limited by the transfer of the commonplaces, definition, and, finally, proof— even in the rhetorical formulations they had received from Cicero, Victorinus, and Boethius—to the domain of dialectic and since its subject matter was limited by the transfer of moral and political questions to theology, rhetoric developed during its second period along three separate lines: as a part of logic, or as the art of stating truths certified by theology, or as a simple art of words.

III

The subordination of rhetoric to logic was based usually on the greater particularity of its subject matter, that is, its concern with hypotheses rather than with theses. The terms of the discussion of the relation of rhetoric to dialectic were borrowed from Boethius. The doctrine is expressed, however, before the appearance of Boethius in the curriculum of the schools. According to Isidore of Seville, logic (Isidore adds that the Greek term λόγος means "rational") has two parts, dialectic and rhetoric.[35] John the Scot omits grammar and rhetoric from his treatise *On the Division of Nature*, first, because many philosophers think they are parts of dialectic; second, from considerations of brevity; and, finally, because, unlike dialectic, grammar and rhetoric do not treat of the nature of things but either of words significant by convention or of special causes and persons.[36] The pseudo-Rhabanus Maurus was one of the

was frequently repeated before the Carolingian period—by Fortunatianus, Victorinus, Cassiodorus, Isidore (Halm, pp. 81, 177, 495, 507)—and one of the favorite etymologies of "art" derived it from the Greek word for virtue. In the twelfth century Aristotle's authority (cited from the *Categories*) is used to deny that rhetoric is a virtue (cf. Abailard *Dialogus* [PL, CLXXVIII, 1652]; Hermannus *Epitome theologiae Christianae* [PL, CLXXVIII, 1750]; *Sententie Parisienses*, ed. A. Landgraf, *Écrits théologiques de l'école d'Abélard* [Louvain, 1934], p. 52). In the thirteenth century Aristotle's authority (cited from the *Nicomachean Ethics*) could be quoted to place it, together with the other arts, among the intellectual virtues. In the Renaissance, one of the chief grounds for Ramus' violent criticism of Quintilian is found in his tendency to identify rhetoric with morals (cf. P. Ramus, *Rhetoricae distinctiones in Quintilianum* [Paris, 1559]).

35. *De differentiis rerum* 39 (PL, LXXXIII, 93–94).

36. *De divisione naturae* v. 4 (PL, CXXII, 869–70): "Primum quidem, quia ipsae duae artes veluti quaedam membra Dialecticae multis philosophis non incongrue existimantur. Deinde brevitatis occasione. Postremo, quod non de rerum natura tractare videntur, sed vel de regulis humanae vocis, quam non secundum naturam, sed secundum consuetudinem loquentium subsistere Aristoteles cum suis sectatoribus approbat, vel de causis atque personis specialibus, quod longe a natura rerum distat. Nam dum Rhetorica de communibus locis, qui ad naturam rerum pertinent, tractare nititur, non suas, sed Dialecticae arripit partes." Rhetoric is limited to hypotheses or finite questions determined by the seven circumstances, while the common conceptions of the mind have become the property of dialectic; cf. *De divisione naturae* i. 27 (PL, CXXII, 475): "Rhetorica est finitam causam persona, materia, occasione, qualitate, loco, tempore, facultate discutiens copiose atque ornate disciplina;

philosophers who divided logic into three parts: grammar, rhetoric, and dialectic,[37] and Remigius of Auxerre divides philosophers into four kinds: dialecticians, rhetoricians, Sophists who always come to false conclusions, and jurists who dispute concerning the status of law.[38] Gerbert, who used all the dialectical works and translations of Boethius in his teaching at Rheims and Paris (including Cicero's *Topics*, which, like Cassiodorus, he thought Cicero had translated from the Greek, and the *On Definition* of Marius Victorinus), likewise considered dialectic and rhetoric parts of logic and taught rhetoric after dialectic.[39] Fulbert, finally, who restored studies at Chartres in the eleventh century and who knew, in addition to the *De inventione* and the *Ad Herennium*, Victorinus' commentary on Cicero and the two treatises on rhetorical places attributed to Boethius, has left twenty-one verses on the differences between rhetoric and dialectic: they are the three differences that Boethius found between the matters, uses, and ends of the arts.[40]

The transition to the third period in this tradition of rhetoric determined relatively to dialectic is accomplished when the increased influence, or at least the increased repute, of the New Logic led to separation of scientific or demonstrative proof from probable proof and to the location of rhetoric with dialectic under the latter. It is a gradual transition, dependent as much on increase of erudition in logic as in rhetoric. In the comprehensive collection of texts in the liberal arts prepared by Thierry of Chartres under the title *Heptateuchon* about 1141, all of Aristotle's *Organon* except the *Posterior Analytics* and the second book of the *Prior Analytics* appears, while under rhetoric are included (in addition to the traditional sources of rhetoric—the *De inventione*, the *Ad Herennium*, and Martianus Capella—and Cicero's *Topics*, which with Boethius' *De differentiis topicis* is classified under dialectic) only Cicero's *De partitione oratoria*

---

breviterque definiri potest, Rhetorica est finitae causae septem periochis sagax et copiosa disciplina. Dialectica est communium animi conceptionum rationabilium diligens investigatrixque disciplina."

37. V. Cousin, *Ouvrages inédits d'Abélard* (Paris, 1836), p. 614.

38. B. Hauréau, "Commentaire de Jean Scot Erigène sur Martianus Capella," *Notices et extraits des manuscrits de la Bibliothèque Impériale*, XX, No. 2 (1862), 11. Cf. *ibid.*, pp. 20–21, for his difference from the doctrine of John concerning the natural bases of rhetoric in human nature.

39. The sequence of studies, as directed by Gerbert, were: first, dialectic, which included the *Isagoge* of Porphyry (with Boethius' commentary), the *Categories* and *On Interpretation* of Aristotle, the *Topics* (translated by Cicero and with Boethius' commentary), Boethius' *On Topical Differences*, *On Categorical Syllogisms*, *On Hypothetical Syllogisms*, *On Definitions*, *On Divisions;* second, as preparation for rhetoric, the poets; third, rhetoric; finally, sophistic. He includes the entire program under the term "logic" (Richer, *Historiae*, III, 44 ff. (ed. G. H. Pertz, *Monumenta Germaniae historica*, Vol. V: *Scriptores*, III, 617).

40. A. Clerval, *Les Écoles de Chartres au moyen-âge* (Chartres, 1895), p. 115.

and Julius Severianus' *Precepts on the Art of Rhetoric*.[41] Yet Thierry of Chartres
wrote a commentary on the *De inventione* in which a history of rhetoric is reconstructed to explain the opening paragraph of Cicero's work as a refutation
of Plato and Aristotle: Plato had argued that rhetoric was no art, Aristotle
that it was an art but a bad art, while Cicero contends, against both, that it is
a good art.[42] A short Preface and an Introduction precede the fragment of the
Commentary which has been preserved. The Introduction is devoted to asking
ten questions concerning rhetoric—its genus, definition, matter, duty, end,
parts, species, instrument, who the orator is, and why the art is so called—to
which two specific questions are added—the intention of Tully in this work and
the utility of the work. The genus of rhetoric is still civil science, it is not a
part of logic, and its matter is hypothesis.[43] Nor is the position of Thierry an
anachronistic piece of conservatism, for one of the works which was most
influential in preparing the way for the new knowledge of the thirteenth century and which was eagerly consulted as a source of information concerning
the Arabic learning, the *De divisione philosophiae* of Gundissalinus, contains a
section on rhetoric which not merely asks the same ten questions as Thierry of
Chartres but is identical, apart from slight variations, with the Introduction to
his *Commentary*.[44] Gundissalinus differs slightly from Thierry in the classifica-

41. *Ibid.*, pp. 222–23; cf. R. McKeon, "Aristotelianism in Western Christianity," in J. T.
McNeill (ed.), *Environmental Factors in Christian History* (Chicago, 1939), pp. 215–19.

42. *Fragmentum scholiastae inediti ad Ciceronem De inventione rhetorica* (W. H. D. Suringar,
Historia critica scholiastarum Latinorum [Leyden, 1834], I, 213–53), pp. 224–36. Thierry's
reading in works of rhetoric was apparently more extensive than the contents of the *Heptateuchon*, since he quotes Quintilian (*ibid.*, p. 219).

43. *Ibid.*, p. 217: "Genus igitur artis rhetoricae est qualitas ipsius artificii secundum ejus
effectum: hoc autem est, quod ipsum artificium est, pars civilis scientiae major. Nam civilis
ratio dicitur quidquid civitas aut rationabiliter dicit aut agit; dicimus enim: ratio est hoc vel
illud facere vel dicere. Item civilis ratio dicitur, scientia dicendi aliquid rationabiliter et
faciendi. Et haec quidem ratio, scientia civilis dicitur, cujus quidem pars integra, vel etiam
major, rhetorica est. Nam sapientia i.e. rerum conceptio secundum earum naturam, et rhetorica civilem scientiam componunt. Et enim nisi quis sapiens et eloquens fuerit, civilem scientiam habere non dicitur. Major vero pars civilis scientiae dicitur rhetorica, quoniam magis
operatur in civilibus causis quam sapientia, etsi sine sapientia nihil prosit. Maximam enim
virtutem habet eloquentia in civitate, si sapientiae juncta sit." Thierry then goes on to
compare this solution with Boethius' doctrine that the genus of rhetoric is *facultas* and finds
the two doctrines in agreement, since the same science is an *art* in the master who teaches its
rules and a *faculty* in the orator. He is explicit in excluding rhetoric from logic: "Non est
autem dicendum, rhetoricam aut logicam esse aut ejus partem, idcirco quod logica circa thesin
solam i.e. circa genera agendi, tantummodo versatur." Cf. *ibid.*, p. 219 for *materia*. Cf.
Adelard of Bath, *De eodem et diverso* in *Beiträge zur Geschichte der Philosophie des Mittelalters*
(henceforth cited as "*BGPM*"), IV, No. 1, 19 ff.

44. Dominicus Gundissalinus *De divisione philosophiae*, ed. L. Baur (*BGPM*, IV, Nos.
2–3 [Münster, 1903], 63–69). For the strange history of scholarly inquiries into the commentary of Thierry cf. M. Grabmann, "Eine lateinische Übersetzung der pseudo-Aristotelischen Rhetorica ad Alexandrum aus dem 13. Jahrhundert," *Sitzungsberichte der Bayerischen Akademie der Wissenschaften, Phil.-hist. Abt.* (1931–32), No. 4, pp. 4–5. In spite of the
fact that it was published by Suringar in 1834, the fragmentary *Commentary* was discussed

tion of rhetoric; for, whereas Thierry would have it a part of civil science and not a part of logic, Gundissalinus classifies both rhetoric and poetic among the eight parts of logic, but he also classifies rhetoric and poetic as parts of civil science.[45]

Hugh of St. Victor, who was contemporary with Thierry of Chartres, follows the suggestion of the Aristotelian division of the sciences into theoretic, practical, and mechanical (which seems to be Hugh's substitute for Aristotle's productive science) : logic is a fourth branch and not a part of politics, which falls under the practical sciences. Moreover, his classification of logic makes an excellent transition from the customary classification according to the trivium of grammar, rhetoric, and dialectic to the "Aristotelian" classification as parts of logic and according to the kinds of proof. Following Isidore of Seville, Hugh points out the double etymology of λόγος, i.e., *sermo* and *ratio*, and argues that logic can be called either a verbal or a rational science (*sermocinalis sive rationalis scientia*) ; rational logic (which Hugh also calls *dissertiva*) is divided into dialectic and rhetoric, while verbal logic is the genus of grammar, dialectic, and rhetoric, and therefore rational logic is contained under it.[46]

---

as an unpublished document by Rohde in 1881, by Bücheler in 1883, and by Thomas in 1884; its author was supposed to have been a contemporary of Theodoric the Great until Thomas suggested that the document was medieval (and consequently of very little interest) ; finally, Manitius identified it as the work of Thierry or Theodoric of Chartres, and Klibansky pointed out its identity with the work published by Suringar. Grabmann does not notice that there is one further coincidence, viz., the identity of one of the three sections (Suringar, *op. cit.*, pp. 216–23) with the section on rhetoric in Gundissalinus. Short of examination of the manuscripts—unfortunately impossible at this time—the question of priority is difficult to decide: some of the sections contained in Thierry but omitted by Gundissalinus seem rather in the nature of additions to, than omissions from, an original text, and the references seem better suited to the *Commentary* than to the *De divisione philosophiae* (as, e.g., where Thierry says [p. 220]: "Sed quid sit circumstantia, in sequentibus melius dicetur," Gundissalinus says [p. 66]: "Set quid sit circumstancia in Tullio dicetur," although no further reference is made to Cicero on this point) ; on the other hand, the supposition that the work of Thierry was prior runs into the grave difficulty that all the sciences in the *De divisione philosophiae* are treated by means of the same ten questions here applied to rhetoric.

45. This section on the genus of rhetoric in Gundissalinus (p. 64) is the same as the statement quoted above (n. 43) from Thierry, but stops short before the discussion of Boethius and the statement that rhetoric is not a part of logic. In the section on logic, Gundissalinus cites Alfarabi for the eight parts of logic (p. 71): "Secundum Alfarabium octo sunt partes logice: cathegorie, perihermenias, analetica priora, analetica posteriora, thopica, sophistica, rhetorica, poetica." He need not have gone to the Arabs for this doctrine, for the equivalent of the six books of Aristotle's *Organon* plus rhetoric and poetic constituted the logic taught by Gerbert (cf. above, n. 39). Gundissalinus gives as the genus of logic that it is a part and instrument of philosophy (p. 69) and denies that its matter is "thesis," arguing that it is the second intention of the understanding (pp. 70–71). The genus of poetic is the same as rhetoric (p. 54): "Genus huius artis [*sc.* poeticae] est, quod ipsa est pars ciuilis sciencie, que est pars eloquencie. Non enim parum operatur in ciuilibus, quod delectat uel edificat in sciencia uel in moribus."

46. *Didascalicon* i. 11, ed. C. H. Buttimer (Washington, 1939), pp. 20–21; or i. 12 (*PL*, CLXXVI, 749–50). Cf. Isidore of Seville *Etymologiae* ii. 24. 7.

This treatment of the traditional trivium is supplemented, however, by another division of logic into grammar and *ratio disserendi* or "dissertive" logic, which is concerned with words as understood (*de vocibus secundum intellectus*). "Dissertive" or rational logic is, in turn, divided into integral parts, i.e., parts shared by its kinds, which turn out to be the Ciceronian distinction into discovery and judgment, and divisive parts, i.e., demonstrative, probable, and sophistic; the two parts of probable proof are dialectic and rhetoric.[47] John of Salisbury, one of the pupils of Thierry of Chartres, who had studied the whole of Aristotle's *Organon* and who was widely read in Cicero and Quintilian, attributes to Plato the division of logic into dialectic and rhetoric; but he prefers, as more philosophic, the division into demonstrative, probable, and sophistic, with the further division of probable into dialectic and rhetoric.[48] William of Conches, on the other hand, whom John calls the finest grammarian after Bernard of Chartres,[49] divides eloquence, which the ancients called "logic," into grammar, *ratio disserendi*, and rhetoric.[50]

IV

The translations of Aristotle affected the discussions of theology as well as philosophy, and the changes in rhetoric and in the relations of rhetoric to dialectic are reflected in the methods of theology. "Aristotelian" conceptions of the organization of logic with rhetoric as one of its parts were not, however, intruded into theology, since the opposition was between the Augustinian conception of a single body of theological and philosophic truth possessed of a single method and the conception of a philosophy independent in method and subject matter from theology; and therefore the simple organization of the trivium as three rational or verbal sciences continued in theology and even in

47. *Didascalicon* ii. 28–30; Buttimer, pp. 44–47; or ii. 29–31 (*PL*, CLXXVI, 763–66).

48. *Metalogicon* ii. 3, ed. C. C. J. Webb (Oxford, 1929), pp. 64–65. Baldwin complains (*op. cit.*, p. 157) that rhetoric is barely mentioned in the *Metalogicon* and seems "to have no distinctive composing function"; the few references which he finds indicate that he was looking for rhetoric before the treatment of logic, whereas John treats it under the *Topics*. Cf. *Metalogicon* iii. 5 (Webb, p. 139), and esp. 10 (Webb, pp. 154–55): "Quia ergo exercitatio dialectice ad alterum est; pares, quos producit et quos rationibus muniuit et locis, sua docet arma tractare et sermones potius conserere quam dexteras, et tanta cautela imbuit, ut totius eloquentie precepta hinc tracta principaliter, uelut a primitiuo fonte originis sue, manare perspicuum sit. Indubitanter enim uerum est, quod fatentur Cicero et Quintilianus, quia hinc non modo rethoricorum adiumentum, sed et principium rethores et scriptores artium assumpserunt; postmodum tamen propriis dilatata est institutis." The matter of dialectic is still the "question" as distinguished from the "hypothesis," which is the matter of rhetoric (*Metalogicon* ii. 12 [Webb, pp. 83–84]).

49. *Metalogicon* i. 5 (Webb, pp. 16–17): "Willelmus de Conchis, grammaticus post Bernardum Carnotensem opulentissimus."

50. C. Ottaviano, *Un Brano inedito della "Philosophia" di Guglielmo di Conches* (Naples, 1935), p. 28.

philosophy under the influence of Augustine long after it became obsolete in the philosophy influenced by Aristotle. Even as early as the sixth century, when Cassiodorus wrote his *Expositio in Psalterium*, he could appeal, in his introductory chapters, "On the Eloquence of the Whole Divine Law" and "On the Proper Eloquence of the Psalter," to an impressive list of learned Fathers—Augustine, Jerome, Ambrose, Hilary—who had studied both the figures which are common to sacred and secular letters and the proper modes of divine speech which are not touched by grammarians or rhetoricians.[51] Divine eloquence is not formed of human words or involved in human ambiguities, but, since its purpose is to spread divine law to all the corners of the world, it makes many uses of modes of speech, and it is "succinct with definitions, adorned with figures, marked by the propriety of words, expedited by the constructions of syllogisms"; and, while these devices are certain and clear in the Scriptures, they stand in need of the liberal arts when they come into contact with the opinions and disputes of men.[52] His commentary consists largely of such aids to understanding, dotted with identifications of kinds of definition, figures of speech, and forms of arguments.[53] The evolution of this use of rhetoric consists, primarily, in the increasing formalization of the methods of interpreting Scripture and the rules of divine eloquence and, secondarily, in the recurrent application of the secular art to Scripture and the recurrent expressions of concern at the excesses of the liberal arts in such application. In the one line of development, Augustine's simple suggestion that things as well as words are signs was elaborated until the spiritual sense, which balanced the literal sense, was divided into three kinds—the allegorical, the moral, and the anagogic; and this theological development of rhetoric eventually, in turn, influenced mundane

---

51. *Expositio in Psalterium*, Praef. xv (*PL*, CLXX, 21).

52. *Expositio in Psalterium* 19: "Eloquentia legis divinae humanis non est formata sermonibus, neque confusis incerta fertur ambagibus, ut aut a rebus praeteritis oblivione discedat, aut praesentium confusione turbetur, aut futurorum dubiis casibus eludatur; sed cordi, non corporalibus auribus loquens, magna veritate, magna praescientiae firmitate cuncta dijudicans, auctoris sui veritate consistit. . . . Eloquentia siquidem est ad unamquamque rem competens et decora locutio." Cf. *ibid.* 20: "Haec mundanarum artium periti, quos tamen multo posterius ab exordio divinorum librorum extitisse manifestum est, ad collectiones argumentorum, quae Graeci topica dicunt, et ad artem dialecticam et rhetoricam transtulerunt; ut cunctis evidenter appareat, prius ad exprimendam veritatem justis mentibus datum, quod postea gentiles humanae sapientiae aptandam esse putaverunt. Haec in lectionibus sacris tanquam clarissima sidera relucent, et significantias rerum utilissimis compendiis decenter illuminant."

53. Cf. *Expositio in Psalterium* i (*PL*, CLXX, 27), for identification of two kinds of definition according to the technical terms of Victorinus; (*PL*, CLXX, 33), where the figure is explained by means of the mathematical disciplines; vi. 1 (*PL*, CLXX, 61), where the fashion in which the divine eloquence has been enriched by the various arts and disciplines is illustrated by discussion of rhetorical *status*; xliii. 15 (*PL*, CLXX, 314), where the figure of *anaphora* is identified, and so *passim*.

or poetic rhetoric.[54] In the other line of development, more suspect of error and more frequently condemned in one form by conservative theologians who practiced it in another form, which they found indispensable to the understanding of Scripture, rhetoric supplied devices to clarify the meanings and remove the ambiguities of scriptural statements. Abailard begins his *Commentary on the Epistle of St. Paul to the Romans* with the statement: "The intention of all divine Scripture is to teach or to move in the manner of a rhetorical speech," and derives his triple division of the Old and New Testaments from these two purposes.[55] The divine pages cannot be read and appreciated without grammar and rhetoric.[56] An anonymous commentary on Romans repeats Abailard's statement of the twofold rhetorical purpose of the Old and New Testament, after having specified that all the arts are servants to divinity: grammar, which teaches constructions; dialectic, which expounds by arguments; and rhetoric, which consists in persuasion.[57] Even theologians who, like Robert of Melun,

54. Cf. Augustine *De utilitate credendi* 3, 5 (*PL*, XLII, 68) (historical, etiological, analogical, allegorical, senses); Gregory the Great *Moralia, epistola Missoria* (*PL*, LXXV, 510–15) (historical, allegorical, moral); Peter Abailard *Expositio in Hexaemeron* (*PL*, CLXXVIII, 731) (historical, moral, and mystic); Hugh of St. Victor *De sacramentis, Prologus* 4 (*PL*, CLXXVI, 184) (historical, allegorical, tropological); and Peter of Poitier *Allegoriae super Tabernaculum Moysi, Prologus*, ed. P. S. Moore and J. A. Corbett (Notre Dame, 1938), p. 1 (historical, allegorical, moral, anagogic); cf. P. S. Moore, *The Works of Peter of Poitiers* (Notre Dame, 1936), pp. 65–77. Cf. Thomas Aquinas *Summa theologica* i. q. 1, a. 10: "Respondeo dicendum quod auctor sacrae Scripturae est Deus, in cujus potestate est ut non solum voces ad significandum accommodet (quod etiam homo facere potest) sed etiam res ipsas. Et ideo, cum in omnibus scientiis voces significent, hoc habet proprium ista scientia quod ipsae res significatae per voces, etiam significant aliquid." The first of these significations is historical or literal, the second (in which things signify other things) spiritual, and the spiritual interpretation is further divided into allegorical, moral, and anagogic. Dante follows the division of Aquinas; cf. *Epistola X Domino Cani Grandi de Scala* vii. 98–116; *Convivio* ii. 1 (cf. *ibid.* 14 for rhetoric). The "four senses" are also used to explain the "form of wisdom" (cf. Bonaventura *In Hexaemeron, Collatio ii* [*Opera omnia*, ed. Quaracchi (1891), V, 336–42], i.e., uniform, multiform [allegorical, anagogic, tropological, each of which has two forms], omniform, and nulliform) and to classify the sciences (cf. M. Grabmann, *Die Geschichte der scholastischen Methode* [Freiburg i/Br., 1911], II, 43, n. 1, where a quotation is given from an unpublished manuscript, dated broadly as posterior to Hugh of St. Victor, in which the sciences are divided into theoretic, practical, and logical; practical science, in turn, is divided into actual [ethics, economics, and politics] and inspective, which is divided into *historia* and *spiritualis intelligentia;* history simply states the order of things without any hidden meaning apparent from that conveyed by the words; the spiritual understanding is divided into the tropological, allegorical, and anagogic. Rational logic is divided into dialectic, apodictic [or demonstrative], and sophistic). Bonaventura also uses these distinctions as the fourfold division in the "light of sacred Scripture" (*De reductione artium ad theologiam* 5 [*Opera omnia*, V, 321]).

55. *Commentaria super S. Pauli Epistolam ad Romanos*, Prologus (*PL*, CLXXVIII, 783–84).

56. *Introductio ad theologiam* ii. 2 (*PL*, CLXXVIII, 1044): "At jam profecto nec grammaticam a Christiano legi convenit, sine documentis cujus nec divina intelligi pagina, nec scriptura aliqua. Sic nec rhetoricam, quae omnis eloquentiae tradit ornamenta, quibus maxime sacra Scriptura est referta, nec ejus decor nisi his diligenter assignatis elucere poterit."

57. *Commentarius Cantabrigiensis in Epistolas Pauli e Schola Petri Abaelardi: In Epistolam ad Romanos*, ed. A. Landgraf (Notre Dame, 1937), pp. 1–2.

opposed the excessive use of rhetoric in secular as well as in divine letters, repeated the same judgment of the rhetorical purposes of Scripture.[58]

The method of rhetoric was, moreover, put to another and even more characteristic use in the interpretation of theological doctrine. The "scholastic method," as it came to be called, grew out of the assemblage of "sentences," which derived their name and their initial methods of treatment from rhetoric.[59] The early collections of canon law were collections of authorities—statements from Scripture, decisions of councils, decretals, opinions of the Fathers— which, because of the practical problems involved in direction of action, presented urgently the problem of bringing discordant or apparently discordant canons into concordance. When Peter Abailard assembled apparently contradictory texts in his *Sic et non*, the rules for interpreting them which he set forth in the Prologue are developments of the rules elaborated by a long line of canon lawyers—notably Hincmar of Rheims, Bernold of Constance, Ivo of Chartres—and involve such directions as careful consideration of context; comparison of texts; specification of time, place, and person; determination of original cause of statement; and differentiation of general measures from particular.[60] Although this method led to a further step in the dialectical resolution of the contradictions, the method at this stage is rhetorical rather than dialectical. The rules of interpretation of the Prologue of the *Sic et non*, thus, approximate the performance of Abailard's *Commentary on Romans*, which is grammatical and rhetorical; but the texts such as those assembled there serve him as a storehouse of quotations for his systematic works, the *Theologia "summi boni,"* the *Theologia Christiana*, and the *Introductio ad theologiam*, in which the method which Abailard calls "dialectical" is used to resolve their differences, not by consideration of contexts and circumstances, but by reduc-

58. Grabmann, *Die Geschichte der scholastischen Methode*, II, 349, n. 2. H. Denifle, *Die abendländischen Schriftausleger bis Luther über "Justitia" (Rom. 1. 17) und "Justificatio"* (Mainz, 1905), p. 76: "Ad erudicionem autem ipsius omnes scripture facte sunt, quarum partes sunt tam sacre scripture, quam ethnice. In ethnicis enim, id est gentilibus, scripturis et sermonum compositio et rerum proprietas docet. Sermonum composicio in trivio, rerum proprietas in mathematicis disciplinis secundum extrinseca et intrinseca. . . . Intencionem vero more rethorice oracionis docere et monere."

59. Cf. G. Paré, A. Burnet, and P. Tremblay, *La Renaissance du XIIe siècle: Les Écoles et l'enseignement* (Ottawa, 1933), pp. 267 ff., for an excellent statement of the rhetorical beginnings of the *sententiae*.

60. *Ibid.* 286 ff., where, however, the method is stated as dialectical. Cf. Grabmann, *Die Geschichte der scholastischen Methode*, I, 234 ff., and P. Fournier and G. Le Bras, *Histoire des collections canoniques en occident* (Paris, 1932), II, 334 ff. In the more orthodox tradition, theology derived its customary organization, indirectly from rhetoric, in Augustine's division of all doctrine into problems of things and problems of signs (cf. P. Lombard, *Sententiarum liber* i, dist. 1, cap. 1). The other distinction which Augustine makes at the beginning of the *De doctrina Christiana*, of all treatment of the Scriptures into the mode of discovery and the mode of statement, served as basis of organization of treatises on preaching (cf. Bonaventura *Ars concionandi* [*Opera omnia*, IX, 8]).

tion to an orderly body of true propositions. The difference, far from being slight, was to grow into one of the marks of differentiation between the line of Christian theology which adapted itself to the Aristotelian philosophy and made use of logic and dialectic and the line of Christian theology and philosophy which continued the distinction of the trivium and subordinated dialectic to rhetoric. One of the numerous admirers of Abailard, who tried to remove the taint of unorthodoxy from his doctrines, made that readjustment by shifting the functions of the arts, assigning to grammar a concern with meanings, to dialectic the production of conviction, and to rhetoric, finally, the motivation of the will.[61] This is a doctrine, moreover, which need suffer no opprobrium because of its connection with Abailard, since the same domination of the trivium by rhetoric is expressed, partly in the same words, by Bernard Sylvester, the friend of Thierry of Chartres, in his commentary on Virgil's *Aeneid*, a context which seems safe from the danger of heresy.[62]

61. [Anonymous] *Ysagoge in theologiam*, ed. A. Landgraf, *op. cit.*, p. 72: "Eloquentia vero est scientia ad congruam agnitorum prolationem suum formans artificem. Que, quia triplicem habet efficatiam, tres habet partes, respondentque efficatie partibus ut effectus causis. Est enim prima grammatica, que pertinet ad intellectum; secunda dialectica, que ad fidem; tertia rethorica, que ad persuasionem. Quod enim prima vocum attendit accidentia, ideo fit, ut secundum ea competens fiat earum contextus ad manifestandum conceptum loquentis vel ad constituendum consimilem in auditore. Sed quia, si pulsetur de veritate, intellectus, quem indicat et constituit, nequit fidem facere, succedit dialectica, que acceptis orationibus a prima componit ex eis argumentationem, qua fidem confert. Sed quia possumus intelligere et intellectum credere et tamen illud nolle, consummationem dat rethorica. Hec enim accipiens argumentaciones a logica, ut illa orationes a grammatica, ex eis per orationem [*read* perorationem] facit et, quod prima intelligere, secunda credere, ipsa facit velle."

62. *Commentum Bernardi Silvestris super sex libros Eneidos Virgilii* vi, ed. G. Riedel (Gryphiswaldae, 1924), p. 31: "Eloquentia est scientia formans suum lectorem ad congruam cognitorum prolationem. Haec autem Trivia dicitur quia [a] tribus artibus quasi tribus viis ad eam incedimus. Ut autem perfecte habeatur eloquentia, primo oportet scire loqui absque soloecismo et barbarismo quod per grammaticam habetur. Deinde sic loquendo oportet scire aliquid probare vel improbare quod fit per dialecticam. Adhuc necessarium [oportet] persuadere vel dissuadere: possunt enim auditores grammatica oratione aliquid intelligere, dialectica probatione de eodem certi esse et tamen illud nolle: ideo necessaria rethorica persuasio. Itaque est grammatica initium eloquentiae, dialectica dicitur provectus, rethorica perfectio. Atque adeo dicitur eloquentia Trivia." Cf. also *ibid.*, pp. 36, 38, 87–88. It would easily be possible to attach too much significance to the order in which the arts of the trivium are enumerated; yet many of the enumerations of the twelfth and thirteenth centuries underline the importance of the order; and even before that time authors tend to a consistency in their enumerations, which suggests that some degree of importance was attached to the enumeration. Dialectic appears third in the lists of Cassiodorus (*Institutiones* ii, Praef.; Mynors, p. 91), Isidore (*Etymologiae* i. 2), Alcuin (*Grammatica* [*PL*, CI, 853]: "Sunt igitur gradus, quos quaeritis, et utinam tam ardentes sitis semper ad ascendendum quam curiosi modo estis ad videndum: grammatica, rhetorica, dialectica . . ."), Rhabanus Maurus (*De clericorum institutione* iii. 18 [*PL*, CVII, 395]: "Prima ergo liberalium artium est grammatica, secunda rhetorica, tertia dialectica . . ."). Rhetoric is third in Augustine (*De ordine* ii. 13 [*PL*, XXXII, 1013]), Martianus Capella, and Gerbert. After the eleventh century the tendency is either to place the trivium, together with demonstration and sophistic, under logic or to list the three with rhetoric in the dominant position. The rule is far from being universal; e.g., Adelard of Bath, who was strongly influenced by the Platonism of Chartres, places dialectic third in his allegory (*De eodem et diuerso* [*BGPM*, IV, No. 1, 21]).

The two general tendencies which came to their culmination in the thirteenth century, that by which rhetoric was made part of logic and that by which rhetoric became an instrument of theology, are determined by the important methodological differences which separate the Aristotelians and the Augustinians. For Thomas Aquinas rhetoric is one of the parts of logic concerned with probable argumentation; for Bonaventura rhetoric is the culmination of the trivium. Thomas wrote a commentary on two books of Aristotle's *Organon*, and, since he separated the method and subject of the philosophic from those of the theological truth, he could use the devices of Aristotle in the a posteriori proofs of his systematic theology and those of Augustine in his commentaries on Scripture; Bonaventura wrote no work on logic but did compose an excellent *Art of Preaching*, which is useful for the interpretation of his theological treatises and commentaries as well as his sermons.

The translation of the whole of the *Nicomachean Ethics* (which was called the "New Ethics" in contrast to the truncated earlier translation) brought to further refinement the solution of questions concerning the relation of rhetoric to civil questions: according to Aquinas, the matter with which rhetoric is concerned is civil,[63] but rhetoric must not be confused with politics.[64] In much the same fashion the terminology and conclusions of the earlier rhetorical discussion enter into Thomas' classification of the parts of logic. The parts of logic or rational science or rational philosophy are determined by the diversity of the acts of reason: they are three of which the first is an act of immediate understanding and the last two are acts of reason. The first is the operation of the mind called (by Averroës) "information of understanding" or "imagination through understanding"; the doctrine which Aristotle treats in the *Categories* is ordered to this act of reason. The second is the operation of composition and division, which results in truth or falsity; the doctrine which Aristotle treats in the *De interpretatione* is concerned with this act of reason. Finally, the third act, which is the proper function of reason, is discursive movement from one thing to another, from something known to the unknown: the remaining four books of the *Organon* are concerned with this operation of reason. It may take any of three forms in conformity to a threefold diversity in nature: in some cases nature acts from necessity without the possibility of divergence; in some cases it operates for the most part in a certain way but with

---

63. *In decem libros ethicorum Aristotelis ad Nicomachum expositio* i, Lectio 3, ed. A. M. Pirotta (Turin, 1934), p. 12, n. 36. Infallible proof is impossible in human affairs, and therefore the conjectural probability of the rhetorician is adequate; cf. *Summa theologica*, i a, ii ae, q. 105, a. 2, ad 8: "Ad octavum dicendum, quod in negotiis humanis non potest haberi demonstrativa probatio et infallibilis, sed sufficit aliqua conjecturalis probabilitas secundum quam rhetor persuadet."

64. *In decem libros ethicorum Aristotelis* x, Lectio 16 (Pirotta, p. 689, n. 2173).

the possibility of deviation from its proper act; and there are therefore, in addition to necessary operations, two additional kinds of natural acts, those which occur for the most part and those in which nature deviates from what is proper to it. Corresponding to these there are three processes of reason: those by which scientific certitude is acquired and in which no deviation from truth is possible; those which come to conclusions true for the most part but not necessary; and those in which reason deviates from the true because of some defect of principle. The part of logic which treats the first of these processes is called "judicative," since its judgment is made with the certitude of science, and this part is treated in the *Analytics:* the *Prior Analytics* is concerned with the certitude of judgment which is based only on the *form* of the syllogism; the *Posterior Analytics* with the demonstrative syllogism, in which the certitude depends on *matter* or on the necessary propositions of which the syllogism is composed. The part of logic which is subject to the second process of reason is called inventive, for discovery is not always with certitude. *Topic* or *Dialectic* treats of this process when it leads to conviction or opinion (*fides vel opinio*); *Rhetoric* treats of it when it leads only to a kind of suspicion without total exclusion of the contrary possibility; *Poetic* treats of it when estimation inclines to one of the two parts of a contradiction only because of the manner of its representation. Finally, the third process of reason is called *sophistic* and is treated by Aristotle in the *De sophisticis elenchis.*[65]

Bonaventura's conception of rhetoric and logic, on the other hand, is quite unaffected by the Aristotelian philosophy: they are ordered in the trivium, dominated by rhetoric, and they are treated, with the other arts, by reduction to theology, or as parts of the first vision of God, which is by natural intelligence, or as part of the gift of science, which is one of the seven gifts of the Holy Spirit. There are four lights by which we are illuminated in knowledge: the exterior light of the mechanical arts, the inferior light of sensitive knowledge, the interior light of philosophic knowledge, and the superior light of grace and Sacred Scripture. The interior light by which we are illuminated to intelligible truths is of three kinds—rational, natural, and moral, corresponding to the traditional division of the philosophic sciences into logic, physics, and ethics. Rational truth or the truth of words is of three kinds—the expression of concepts (treated by grammar), the movement to belief (treated by logic), and the movement to love or hate (treated by rhetoric).[66] The actual

---

65. *In libros Posteriorum analyticorum expositio* i, Lectio 1 (Rome, 1882), I, 138–40.

66. *De reductione artium ad theologiam* 4 (*Opera omnia*, V, 321): "Et quoniam tripliciter potest aliquis per *sermonem* exprimere quod habet apud se, ut scilicet notum faciat mentis suae conceptum, vel ut amplius moveat ad credendum, vel ut moveat ad amorem, vel odium: ideo *sermocinalis* sive rationalis philosophia triplicatur, scilicet in *grammaticam, logicam* et

reduction of rational philosophy to theology is accomplished by consideration of the speaker (his expression of the conception of his mind is dependent on the eternal Word), his statement (in the congruity, truth, and adornment of which is seen the order of living, for actions by virtue of these have measure [*modus*], beauty [*species*], and order [*ordo*]), and the hearer (in whom the ends of speech are expressing, teaching, and moving, which are accomplished, as Augustine shows, only by the one true doctor who can impress species, infuse light, and give virtue to the heart of the hearer).[67] Or again, the first vision of God, which is by natural intelligence, is divided into three rays, since the light which is the truth of the soul illuminates the truth of things, of signs, and of morals: the second irradiation of truth is divided into three parts: grammar, logic, and rhetoric.[68] The consideration of general and special forms of argument in necessary matter as well as the consideration of "topical places" (in which induction proceeds by probable rather than necessary arguments) and sophistical places falls within logic, while rhetoric is concerned once more with civil utility and is divided into demonstrative, deliberative, and judicial.[69] Or again, the fifth gift of the Holy Spirit is science, comprising the three philosophic sciences (rational, natural, moral), in all of which, including rational philosophy or verbal science, Solomon was adept.[70]

It is in the platonizing Augustinian tradition, moreover, that music and poetry assume a broad sense and dominant importance: Roger Bacon assigns to music the function which Bonaventura ascribed to rhetoric, and then distinguishes both rhetoric and poetic into two kinds—a theoretic rhetoric and poetic (or *rhetorica docens* and *poetica docens*) which are parts of logic and an applied rhetoric and poetic (or *rhetorica utens* and *poetica utens*) which are parts of moral philosophy.[71] The opposed tendencies which led to the dominance of

---

rhetoricam; quarum prima est ad exprimendum, secunda ad docendum, tertia ad movendum. Prima respicit rationem ut *apprehensivam;* secunda, ut *iudicativam;* tertia, ut *motivam.* Et quia ratio apprehendit per sermonem *congruum,* iudicat per *verum,* movet per sermonem *ornatum:* hinc est, quod haec triplex scientia has tres passiones circa sermonem considerat."

67. *Ibid.* 15–18 (*Opera omnia,* V, 323–24).

68. *In hexaemeron,* Collatio iv. 18–25 (*Opera omnia,* V, 352–53).

69. *Ibid.* 20–21 (*Opera omnia,* V, 352–53).

70. *De septem donis Spiritus Sancti,* Collatio iv. 5–12 (*Opera omnia,* V, 474–75); esp. 8: "Impossible est, quod sapientia fiat doctrina nisi per sermonem. Sermo autem non est sufficiens ad docendum, nisi sit sententiosus. Et non loquitur homo sententiose, nisi sermo eius *discussivus, inquisitivus,* et *persuasivus,* scilicet quod habeat sermonem potentem ad loquendum omne illud, quod potest apprehendi vel nosci, vel ad quod affectus potest inclinari. Congrue autem exprimit quod dicit per *grammaticam,* rationabiliter investigat per scientiam *logicam* et efficaciter persuadet per *rhetoricam.* Ista igitur est pars philosophiae, scilicet scientia sermocinalis, quae triplex est, ut patet, quam adeptus est Salomon."

71. *Opus tertium,* cap. 75 (*Opera inedita,* ed. J. S. Brewer [London, 1859], pp. 303–8, esp. 306–7): "Nam moralis philosophus scit uti sermone suavi, et gestibus convenientibus

rhetoric in the Augustinian tradition and to the importance of logical demonstration in the Thomist tradition are integral with the total complexions of the
two theologies as evidenced in the conclusion of Bonaventura that theology is
neither theoretic nor practical but an affective habit midway between theory
and practice, as opposed to the argument of Thomas that theology subsumes
both theoretic and practical sciences and is itself more theoretic than practical.[72]
It is a distinction which later historians have treated crudely by trying to differentiate "voluntarism" from "rationalism."

V

Separate both from the tradition of the rhetoric assimilated to dialectic and
proof and from that of the rhetoric assimilated to theology and edification—
and the object of suspicion and attack by both—a third tradition of rhetoric
seems to have flourished, at least during the second and third periods of the
other two traditions, indifferent alike to the logical differentiation of necessary
and probable arguments and to the theological limitation of persuasion to profound or salubrious truths. Since the three traditions were engaged in a three-
cornered dispute, there is no single statement of the issue, for to logicians
the practitioners of this new art seemed sophists, while theologians lumped
them with the heretical dialecticians and garrulous ratiocinators; from the point
of view of the new art, which professed an exclusive concern with practical
issues and effective applications, that is, with actions or with words, the rules
of logic were themselves open to question, and visionary theories and inap-
plicable generalizations were devoid of moral attraction. For the most part we
know about the early members of this tradition from the violence of the attacks upon them and the bitterness of the satire in which they were portrayed,
but gradually in the course of the twelfth and thirteenth centuries they limited
their statements to figures and forms of words, accomplishing their practical
objectives by that device in a fashion which met with little effective opposition
from logicians or theologians; and, since they were unhampered by the need
to consider things or thoughts, they were prolific in production of the "new"
methods—they were fond of calling themselves *moderni*—which constituted

---

orationi delectabili conformandis. Similiter logicus et grammaticus. . . . Grammaticus igitur
utitur his pueriliter; sed logicus quantum ad formam arguendi quam constituit, in his procedit
viriliter, et causas et rationes assignat. Sed quantum ad decorem et ornatum et suavitatem
argumenti, certe non potest logicus, sicut nec grammaticus, causas et rationes assignare, sed
musicus; sicut geometer causas linearum, et angulorum, et figurarum, quibus utitur car-
pentator, habet dare." Cf. *Opus majus* iii and iv. 2, ed. J. H. Bridges (Oxford, 1897), pp. 71
and 99–102.

72. Bonaventura *Proemium in librum primum sententiarum* q. 3, concl.; i. 13; Thomas
Aquinas *Summa theologica* i, q. i, a. 4.

one of the important guises in which rhetoric entered the fourteenth century and the Renaissance.

A few fragments of the works of Anselm the Peripatetic are the only remains of the "Drogonic" sect—followers of the philosopher Drogo—which Anselm would have us believe was numerous and influential. He calls his art rhetoric; he professes allegiance to that art along with Hermagoras, Tully, Servius, Quintilian, Victorinus, Grillius, and Boethius and thought to illustrate it in his treatise *De materia artis* (now lost) and in the examples of rhetoric set forth in his *Rhetorimachia;* he specifies that rhetoric demonstrates, not truths, but verisimilitudes disguised as truths.[73] The *Rhetorimachia* is divided into three parts, one devoted to each of the genera—demonstrative, deliberative, and judicial—and each example takes the form of an attempt to turn the arguments of an opponent against him. The bearing of Anselm's performance on logic is not far to seek, since his approach permits him to deny the principle of excluded middle,[74] while its relation to theology is no less apparent from the allegory of the dream, related as part of his treatment of deliberative rhetoric, in which the embraces and arguments of three virgins named Dialectic, Rhetoric, and Grammar turn him from communion with the saints in Heaven.[75] A "sophist" named John seems in like fashion to have had a numerous following, of whom Roscelin of Compiègne alone is easily identifiable.[76] In the twelfth century John of Salisbury attacks the doctrine of a teacher whom he disguises under the name of "Cornificius" (allying with himself in the attack the most illustrious masters of the age—among others, Gilbert de la Porrée, Thierry of Chartres, William of Conches, Peter Abailard) who broke that union of wisdom and eloquence which is the foundation of philosophy, of society, and of morals and who made everything new in his teaching, innovating in grammar, modifying dialectic, despising rhetoric; his exclusive reliance on the precepts of eloquence apparently leads Cornificius to exploit the traditional puzzles of

---

73. *Epistola ad Drogonem phylosophum* (*Anselm der Peripatetiker, nebst andern Beiträgen zur Literaturgeschichte Italiens elften Jahrhundert*, ed. E. Dümmler [Halle, 1872], pp. 19–20).

74. *Rhetorimachia* i. p. 34; cf. *Epistola ad Drogonem magistrum et condiscipulos de logica disputatione in Gallia habita*, pp. 56–58.

75. *Rhetorimachia* ii, p. 42.

76. Cf. *Historia Francica* (quoted by J. Reiners, *Der Nominalismus in der Frühscholastik* [BGPM, VIII, No. 5], p. 33, n. 2): "In dialectica quoque hi potentes extiterunt sophistae: Joannes, qui eandem artem sophisticam vocalem esse disseruit, Rotbertus Parisiacensis, Roscelinus Compendiensis, Arnulfus Laudenensis. Hi Joannis fuerunt sectatores, qui etiam quamplures habuerunt auditores." Cf. J. A. Endres, *Forschungen zur Geschichte der frühmittelalterlichen Philosophie* (BGPM, XVII, Nos. 2–3), and *Petrus Damiani und die weltliche Wissenschaft* (BGPM, VIII, No. 3); also J. de Ghellinck, "Dialectique et dogme aux Xe–XIIe siècles," BGPM, Supplementband I, pp. 79–99.

the sophists, which turn on the confusion of word and thing or the application of a word or statement to itself.[77]

This tradition of rhetoric took form, for the most part, not in controversy or theory but in a vast number of textbooks which grew in three distinct groups, differentiated according to the subject matters once treated by rhetoric but now concerned with verbal forms employed in those three fields in lieu of direct treatment of subject matter. First, rhetoric had contributed to the method of studying law, but the substantive consideration of law had moved into theology and had taken with it most of the appurtenances which might have made the law a learned profession, leaving only the verbal rhetoric of the *dictamen*.[78] Second, the art of preaching, which had assumed in the Christian tradition an exhortative function approaching that of ancient deliberative oratory—once due allowance is made for differences between the terrestrial and celestial city—gradually moved to a formalism in which doctrine was left to theology and

77. John of Salisbury *Metalogicon* i. 1–6 (Webb, pp. 5–21, esp. 21): "Plane eloquentie precepta sapientiam non conferunt; sed nec amorem eius et sepissime quidem ei obtinende non conferunt. Res enim philosophia (aut finis eius, que est sapientia) querit, non uerba. Ex his itaque liquet quia precepta eloquentie ab operis suis philosophia eliminat." Cf. the confusion of the arts of the trivium reported by Hugh of St. Victor *Didascalicon* iii. 5; Buttimer, pp. 55–57. Cf. P. Mandonnet, *Siger de Brabant et l'Averroïsme latin au XIIIme siècle* (2d ed.; Louvain, 1911), I, 122–23.

78. For the voluminous literature on the *Ars dictaminis* and *Ars notaria*, cf. L. J. Paetow, *A Guide to the Study of Medieval History* (2d ed.; New York, 1931), pp. 448–52; for the relation of these arts to rhetoric, cf. N. Valois, *De arte scribendi epistolas apud Gallicos medii aevi scriptores rhetoresve* ("Bibliothèque de l'École de Chartres," Vol. XXII [1880]), pp. 161, 257; for the relation of rhetoric to the teaching of law, cf. Abelson, *op. cit.*, pp. 60–66. The manner of the change, no less than the pride in the novelty of it, may be judged from the contents of Boncompagni's two works, the *Rhetorica antiqua* (arranged in six books according to the character of the letter to be written) and the *Rhetorica novissima* (arranged in thirteen books: "Primus est de origine iuris. Secundus est de rhetoricae partibus et causarum generibus. Tertius est de diffinitionibus. Quartus est de naturis et consuetudinibus oratorum. Quintus de causarum exordiis. Sextus de principiis conuentorum. Septimus de rhetoricis argumentis. Octavus de memoria. Nonus de adornationibus. Decimus de invectivis. Undecimus de consiliis. Duodecimus de colloquiis. Tertius decimus de conditionibus"). Boncompagni professes in the Prologue to the former work not to remember ever having read Cicero, but he adds that he never dissuaded anyone who wanted to read him; and in the latter work he gives three reasons why he undertook to find a new rhetoric after Cicero had compiled a rhetoric from the infinite precepts of rhetoricians: (1) according to Boethius, the rhetoric edited by the ancients consists solely of precepts, without doctrine or utility; (2) students in civil and canon law would not get a solid foundation in the liberal arts, and (3) Cicero's rhetoric is rendered void, according to students of law, because it is never read in "ordinary" courses but is run through and taught like a mechanical art by stealth; to these he adds a fourth: that Cicero was mistaken about the origin of the law (cf. L. Rockinger, "Über die Ars dictandi und die Summae dictaminum in Italien," *Sitzungsberichte der Königl. Bayerischen Akademie der Wissenschaften zu München*, hist. Kl., I [1861], 135–45). For the closely related art of pleading, cf. A.Wilmart, "L'*Ars arengandi* de Jacques de Dinant avec un appendice sur ses ouvrages *De dictamine*," *Analecta Reginensia* (Vatican City, 1933), pp. 113–51. The relations of rhetoric to law and logic are reflected satirically in the "battle of seven arts"; cf. "*La Bataille des vii ars* of Henri d'Audeli," ed. L. J. Paetow, in *Two Medieval Satires on the University of Paris* (Berkeley, Calif., 1927), pp. 43 and 51. Cf. H. Kantorowicz, *Studies in the Glossators of the Roman Law* (Cambridge, 1938).

attention was centered on three problems: propriety of division of the subject stated in the theme of the sermon, brevity of distinction, and utility of expansion.[79] Finally, the art of poetry came to be considered, after the twelfth century, not a branch of grammar but alternately a kind of argumentation or persuasion (and, as such, subordinate to logic or morals) and a form of composition (and, as such, to be treated in terms of style, organization, and figures borrowed from rhetoric).[80] In common, these three tendencies continue the terms and some points of the organization of the *Ad Herennium* and of Cicero's *De inventione*, but the commonplaces which have been put to so many uses are

79. Cf. the anonymous *Art of Preaching*, portions of which are edited in the *Opera omnia S. Bonventurae* (IX, 6–7), in which four modes of preaching are distinguished: (1) that which concords really and verbally with the words of Scripture—used by "modern" doctors and expounded in this treatise; (2) that which employs only real concordance with Scripture—appropriate to those newly learned in theology; (3) that limited to verbal concordance; and (4) contrasted to the modern method, the ancient mode "quod observant antiqui Sancti, sicut Augustinus et Bernardus et multi alii, quorum sermones in Ecclesia recitantur, in quibus non proponitur aliquod thema, quod sit materia praedicandi, nec solent divisiones vel distinctiones fieri, quae postmodum concordentur, sed quasi narrative procedit." The modern doctors advise against following the ancient mode, for the curious reason that these Fathers were, in a manner, founders of the church (*quasi ecclesiae fundatores*), and therefore they avoided all curiosity concerning distinctions of themes, subdivisions of members, and concordances of both. Bonaventura likewise divides the problems of preaching into three parts, *divisiones*, *distinctiones*, *dilatationes* (cf. *Ars concionandi*, Prooemium, ix. 8). For an excellent exposition of the technique of the medieval sermon and review of the methods expounded in most important medieval handbooks, cf. E. Gilson, "Michel Menot et la technique du sermon mediéval," *Les Idées et les lettres* (Paris, 1932), pp. 93–154. Cf. H. Caplan, "Classical Rhetoric and the Mediaeval Theory of Preaching," *Classical Philology*, XXVIII (1933), 73–96; "Rhetorical Invention in Some Mediaeval Tractates on Preaching," *Speculum*, II (1927), 284–95; "Henry of Hesse on the Art of Preaching," *PMLA*, XLVIII (1933), 340–61. The treatises of Robert of Basevorn and Thomas of Wales are published in T.-M. Charland, *Artes praedicandi: Contribution à l'histoire de la rhétorique au moyen âge* (Ottawa, 1936), preceded by a survey of writers of *Arts* and the customary form of theory. Cf. the differentiation of the two modes most used by moderns, the French and the English (Robert of Basevorn, *Forma praedicandi* 7, p. 244). Cf. also M. M. Davy, *Les Sermons universitaires parisiens de 1230–1231* (Paris, 1931); G. R. Owst, *Preaching in Mediaeval England: An Introduction to Sermon Manuscripts of the Period c. 1350–1450* (Cambridge, 1926); and C. H. Haskins, *Studies in Mediaeval Culture* (Oxford, 1929), pp. 36–71.

80. In early treatments poetry, considered as metric, was a part of grammar, while as a form of argument it was a part of topic or dialectic. Thus Cassiodorus defines grammar (*Institutiones* ii. 1. 1; p. 94): "grammatica vero est peritia pulchre loquendi ex poetis illustribus auctoribusque collecta; officium eius est sine vitio dictionem prosalem metricamque componere," but he includes the poets among the artists to whom topical arguments are supplied by memory (*ibid.* 3. 17, p. 127; cf. *ibid.* 2. 2, p. 98, for the function of memory in discovery). Cf. Isidore of Seville *Etymologiae* i. 39; the Venerable Bede, *De arte metrica* (*PL*, XC, 149). John of Salisbury notes the tendency to make poetic an art by itself or to assimilate it to rhetoric rather than to grammar, but he is explicit in his own resolution of the problem; cf. *Metalogicon* i. 17, p. 43: "Profecto aut poeticam grammatica obtinebit, aut poetica a numero liberalium disciplinarum eliminabitur." Cf. C. Fierville, *Une Grammaire latine inédite du XIIIe siècle* (Paris, 1886), pp. 94–119. The transition is gradual from a consideration merely of the words, their character, and position to the consideration of the general conditions or places relevant to the choice and disposition of words; a further step is needed to carry it, during the Renaissance, from the figures of speech and the figures of doctrine to the rhetorical consideration of the thoughts of the author and the effects on the audience.

no longer devices for discovering arguments of things and their traits but devices for remembering, for amplifying, for describing, and for constructing figures.[81]

VI

Two translations of Aristotle's *Rhetoric* were produced during the thirteenth century, and there are also translations of the *Rhetorica ad Alexandrum*, Averroës' commentary on the *Rhetoric*, and Demetrius' *De elocutione*. The effect of the Aristotelian rhetoric and its variant interpretations (both Demetrius and Averroës passed as "Aristotelian") on philosophy may be judged from the fact that these works on rhetoric are frequently found in manuscripts which contain works on morals, politics, or economics, and, indeed, specific marks of the *Rhetoric* can be seen in Aquinas' analysis of the passions.[82] Yet there are relatively few early commentaries on the work itself: Aegidius Romanus in the thirteenth century and John of Jandun and John Buridan in the fourteenth century are the only outstanding scholastics to have left such commentaries.[83] The old problem of the genus of rhetoric, whether it is a part of civil philosophy or logic, is resolved by Aegidius into the difference between Aristotle (who placed it under dialectic) and Cicero (who made it a part of politics).[84] The position of this pupil of St. Thomas is indeed almost a parody of Bonaventura's doctrine that theology is midway between the practical and the speculative sciences, for he locates rhetoric midway between the moral and the rational sciences.[85] The readjustment is striking illustration of the fashion in which unchanged analyses may in the context of altered philosophies take on contrary significances, for the effort of rhetoricians from Quintilian through the early Middle Ages was to claim consideration of general or indefinite questions or theses and to resist efforts to restrict rhetoric to determinate questions or hypotheses, lest rhetoric yield its place and importance as a science to philosophy: the difference between politics and ethics, on the one hand, and rhetoric, on the other, according to Aegidius, consists in the fact that a science is deter-

---

81. Cf. E. Faral, *Les Arts poétiques du XIIe et du XIIIe siècle* (Paris, 1924), esp. pp. 52 ff. and 77 ff.

82. M. Grabmann, "Eine lateinische Übersetzung der pseudo-aristotelischen Rhetorica ad Alexandrum," pp. 6 ff.; G. Lacombe, A. Birkenmajer, M. Dulong, and A. Franceschini, *Aristoteles Latinus* (Rome, 1939), I, 77–79; B. V. Wall, *A Medieval Latin Version of Demetrius' "De elocutione"* (Washington, 1937).

83. The commentaries of Jandun and Buridan are unedited; that of Aegidius was published in 1515 in Venice, but I have been unable to consult a copy.

84. *De differentia rhetoricae, ethicae, et politicae*, ed. G. Bruni in *The New Scholasticism*, VI (1932), 5–8.

85. *Ibid.* (Bruni, p. 2). Cf. *Expositio in artem veterem* (Venice, 1507), 2v–3r, where speculative science is divided into *principalis* (concerned with things) and *adminiculativa* (the three arts of the trivium).

mined by its subject matter and that, whereas politics and ethics have a determinate genus, rhetoric is indeterminate, being concerned with knowledge of certain common notions which bear on moral questions. John Buridan divides all sciences into two kinds, the "principal" science, which deals with the proper things of the science, and the "instrumental" science, which is concerned with the mode of statement and teaching. The instrument of the theoretic sciences is logic or dialectic, but in moral science the problem involved concerns not only the doubtful and the true but also the need to stir desire as it bears on understanding, and a special moral logic or dialectic is required which is divided into two parts, rhetoric and poetic.[86] John of Jandun divides philosophy into nonorganic (practical and speculative) and organic, which includes grammar and logic, rhetoric being a subdivision of logic.[87]

The three main lines in which rhetoric developed during the Middle Ages—as they had grown out of philosophic oppositions in antiquity and as they had been continued by medieval writers under the compulsion of the circumstances and nature of the problems they treated—are extended through the discussions of the Renaissance, notwithstanding revolt against the scholasticism of the Middle Ages, alike by the weight of tradition and by the exigencies of the problems themselves. The tradition of rhetoric as a part of rational philosophy subordinate to logic had a long and honorable continuation, which included Zabarella, Campanella, Varchi, Robertelli, and many others.[88] The tradition in

86. *Questiones super decem libros ethicorum Aristotelis ad Nicomachum*, Prooemium (Paris, 1518), fol. 4r.

87. *Quaestiones subtilissimae super tres libros de anima*, Prohemium (Venice, 1519), fol. 2v.

88. According to Zabarella, *De natura logicae* ii. 13–23 (*Opera logica* [Cologne, 1597], pp. 78–100), rhetoric and poetic are instruments of civil discipline and parts of logic (the arts of demonstration, dialectic, and sophistic are also parts of logic); like logic, they are rational faculties, not verbal, like grammar. Logic is divided into two principal kinds, universal and particular; rhetoric and poetic are instances of particular logic. Campanella divided his *Philosophia rationalis* into four parts: grammar, dialectic, rhetoric, and poetic. Rhetoric is a part of rational philosophy, deriving its arguments from dialectic and its matter from morals; it does not treat of all questions but is limited to persuasion and dissuasion of good and evil; poetic has the same function, but it differs from rhetoric in its universality, since it presents all goods and all truths to all audiences (*Philosophia rationalis, pars tertia, rhetorica* 1. 1 [Paris, 1538], pp. 1–7; cf. *Pars quarta, poetica* 1. 1, pp. 89–93). B. Varchi follows the traditional division of philosophy into real, active, and rational; rhetoric and poetic are subdivisions of rational philosophy, although, strictly speaking, poetic is neither an art nor a science, but a faculty; dialectic, rhetoric, and poetic are essentially the same thing, differing only accidentally, and the dialectician, rhetorician, and poet can be put on the same level of nobility and honor; cf. "Della poetica in generale," *Opere di Benedetto Varchi* (Trieste, 1859), II, 684: "La filosofia razionale, la quale favellando di parole e non di cose, non è veramente parte della filosofia, ma strumento, comprende sotto sè non solo la loica (intendendo per loica la giudiziale) a la dialettica (intendendo per dialettica non tanto la topica, quanto eziandio la sofistica e la tentativa) ma ancora la rettorica, la poetica, la storica e la grammatica." Robertelli raises the question not in terms of the form of the art but in terms of its matter and end: poetic shares its matter, *oratio*, with four other disciplines: demonstration, dialectic, rhetoric, and sophistic; grammar is excluded from the list, since it does not involve the intel-

which rhetoric dominated the arts continued into the Renaissance not only in the methods and doctrines of theology but in a secular tradition which took one of two forms: either all philosophy and all subjects are assimilated to rhetoric, as in the doctrines of Majoragius and Nizolius,[89] or the method of discovery is refurbished and transferred from rhetoric to revitalize and revolutionize dialectic, as in the doctrines of Rudolph Agricola and Petrus Ramus.[90] The tradition in which rhetoric had become a discipline of words, independent alike of

---

lectual content of what is said. The five are easily and rapidly distinguished (*In librum Aristotelis de Arte poetica* [Basel, 1555], p. 1): "Ex his quaelibet facultas unum arripit genus. Demonstratoria verum. Dialectice probabile. Rhetorica suasorium. Sophistice id, quod probabilis, sed verisimilis habet speciem. Poetice falsum, seu fabulosum." The end of poetic (*ibid.* 2) is the "imitating word," as the end of rhetoric is the "persuading word,"; it is (borrowing from Cicero) the imitation of life, the mirror of custom, the image of truth. Cf. H. Cornacchinus, *Indagatio verae et perfectae definitionis logicae*, Pars V, cap. 21 (Padua, 1606), p. 247: poetic and rhetoric are parts or offshoots of logic, or rather aggregates composed from logic, grammar, and civil philosophy, and (*ibid.*, Pars IV, cap. 10, pp. 220–21) dialectic, sophistic, and rhetoric are midway between grammar and logic.

89. J. L. Vives (*De causis corruptarum artium*, Liber iv [Lugduni Batavorum, 1586], p. 239) reports the doctrine of philosophers who distinguish two rhetorics, one universal and applicable to all things, the other particular and suited to civil use; Vives interprets the position as being in opposition to the tendency to make rhetoric part of logic. The position is defended by M. A. Majoragius on the authority of Cicero (*De finibus* ii. 6. 17) against Aristotle (*Aristotelis Stagyritae De arte rhetorica libri tres cum M. Antonii Maioragii commentariis*, Liber i [Venice, 1591], p. 2). M. Nizolius holds, again on the authority of Cicero, that philosophy and oratory are not two separate faculties but one and the same art, composed of two arts which are imperfect when separated (*De veris principiis et vera ratione philosophandi contra pseudophilosophos* iii. 3 [Parma, 1553], p. 211); he quotes Laurentius Valla, with approval, when he argues that dialectic is a part of rhetoric, since it consists of only one of the five parts of rhetoric, namely, discovery (*ibid.* 5, p. 240); and, finally, he holds that rhetoric is a general art and science, under which are subsumed all other arts and sciences (*ibid.* iii. 8, p. 268). The distinction of the two rhetorics—the rhetoric of precepts and the rhetoric in use—is preserved by Riccoboni, who also adds "ecclesiastical" as a fourth genus to the traditional three, "deliberative," "demonstrative," and "judicial" (A. Riccobonus, *De usu artis rhetoricae Aristotelis commentarii vigintiquinque, quibus duplex, rhetorica strictim explicatus, altera, quae praecepta tradit persuadendi, altera, quae re ipsa persuadet*, etc. [Frankfurt, 1595]). The use of rhetoric in refurbishing scriptural interpretation is well illustrated in the *Heptaplus* of Pico della Mirandola (in which Moses emerges as the "Idea" of the writer, the exemplar of the prophet) and John Colet's *Enarrationes in Epistolas S. Pauli*.

90. Rudolph Agricola undertook to reinstate in dialectic the processes of discovery which had become part of rhetoric because civil philosophy came into prominence in Greece before the maturity of the other arts (*De inventione dialectica* ii. 18 [Cologne, 1538], pp. 538 ff.), and to correct the errors which Aristotle, Cicero, and Boethius had committed in treating and classifying the places. The function of rhetoric was limited to *ratio dicendi*. According to Petrus Ramus, logic or dialectic is a general art, the whole art of reason (*Scholae in liberales artes* [Basel, 1569], *scholae dialecticae* ii. 2, pp. 35–37). The parts of dialectic are discovery and judgment (*ibid.* 8, p. 53); the parts of rhetoric are elocution and action (*Scholae rhetoricae*, i, p. 238). The logic of Aristotle abounded in errors, confusions, vain precepts, and altercations: Ramus professed to have supplied the missing virtues, removed the errors, and made the art usable. The error of Cicero consisted in transferring all the Aristotelian devices of dialectic to rhetoric and of having made one art of two; and Quintilian mixed rhetoric with all the other arts; Ramus undertook to correct both errors (*Rhetoricae distinctiones in Quintilianum* [Paris, 1559], pp. 3–8).

philosophy and dialectic, finally established verbal distinctions which grew into doctrines of things: the long and subtle speculations of fourteenth-century philosophers on *insolubilia, obligatoria*, and sophisms laid the foundations for many of the early theories in physics and mathematics, and symbolic logic, though unconcerned with its past, still repeats the elements of this heritage; the analysis of the figures of the poet was made, without undue or violent altera-tion, into a theory of poetry, which dealt with imagination, passion, truth, and virtue; and political philosophy has never entirely lost the rhetorical turn from which its theories derived their modern concreteness and practicality.

Once the general movements in the arts, of which the variegated history of rhetoric is a symptom, have been set into some intelligible schema, the startling and revolutionary shifts of doctrines and of problems are more easily under-stood. Since the problems of the sciences and the arts are closely related and are often stated in almost identical language, a slight shift of theory or terminology may at a point bring an unsuspected richness from one art into the threadbare terminology of another. The three customary questions of rhetoric—*whether it is, what it is,* and *what sort*—merged readily with the questions of logic and influenced early modern attempts to formulate the scientific method. The customary rhetorical inquiry into the duty of the artist and into the matter and end of the art took on metaphysical generality when it was merged, in the thirteenth century, with the Aristotelian causes by the simple addition of questions of form to what were already questions concerning the efficient, ma-terial, and final causes; and, metaphysics apart, the four questions contributed to the foundations of philology in the inquiries into the four causes of books with which Aquinas and Bonaventura and other medieval writers opened their com-mentaries. The controversy concerning thesis and hypothesis merged with Plato's dialectical use of hypothesis and Aristotle's differentiation of thesis, hypothesis, and definition and contributed unsuspected commitments and im-plications in modern discussions of scientific method. Rhetoric is, at most, an unusually clear example among the arts and sciences of a tendency which ap-pears in the history of rhetoric only because it is universal in intellectual disciplines. In application, the art of rhetoric contributed during the period from the fourth to the fourteenth century not only to the methods of speaking and writing well, of composing letters and petitions, sermons and prayers, legal documents and briefs, poetry and prose, but to the canons of interpreting laws and Scripture, to the dialectical devices of discovery and proof, to the estab-lishment of the scholastic method, which was to come into universal use in philosophy and theology, and, finally, to the formulation of scientific inquiry, which was to separate philosophy from theology. In manner of application, the art of rhetoric was the source both of doctrines which have long since become the property of other sciences (such as the passions, which were considered in handbooks of rhetoric until Descartes proposed a "scientific" treatment of them different only in details) and of particular devices which have been applied to a variety of subjects (such as to the "commonplaces" which were sometimes techniques for inventing arguments, sometimes means for dilating statements, sometimes methods for discovering things, or to "definition" or "order," which may be determined entirely by consideration of the verbal conditions of expression, the psychological requirements of persuasion, or the circumstantial probabilities of fact). In theory or application, the art of rhetoric was now identified with, now distinguished from, the whole or part not only of grammar, logic, and dialectic (which were, in turn, distinguished from or identified with each other) but also of sophistic and science, of "civil philosophy," psychology, law, and literature and, finally, of philosophy as such. Yet, if rhetoric is defined in terms of a single subject matter—such as style or literature or discourse—it has no history during the Middle Ages; the many innovations which are recorded during that period in the arts with which it is related suggest that their histories might profitably be considered without unique attachment to the field in which their advances are celebrated.

POETRY AND PHILOSOPHY IN THE TWELFTH CENTURY: THE RENAISSANCE OF RHETORIC[1]

RICHARD McKEON

THE problems, the visions, and sometimes even the language of philosophy have served the purposes of poets; and philosophers have borrowed poetic modes of expression and have speculated on the nature and effects of poetry, on the criteria of poetic values, and on the fate deserved by poets. The variations of both poetry and philosophy have been so great, however, that no simple relation between them could continue long or in wide acceptance. At times and according to the precepts of some philosophies, poetry approximates closely to the subjects and problems of philosophy, and the relation of poetry and philosophy oscillates between identity and antithesis. The poet, who is often a philosopher, is then conceived as giving final expression to the fullest experience and the loftiest ideas that men have had about the actions and destiny of man and the nature and order of all things, while the philosopher, who is sometimes a poet, constructs an intellectual system in which the vain fictions of poets are among the chief sources of error and immorality. At other times and following the principles of other philosophies, the purest poetry is devoid of recognizable doctrine and often even of sense, and the investigations and conclusions of philosophy require distinctions and demonstrations for which the most ingenious critic would have had difficulty in finding poetic expression, if, indeed, there were any reason to undertake so unpromising an enterprise. It is a mistake to reduce this difference, as has been done,[2] to a distinction between the arduous methods of philosophic inquiry which are ill suited to poetic formulation and the sublime conclusions which the philosopher only touches by reason but which the poet grasps by passionate imagination. Despite the temptation to claim the scientific method for literary criticism, philosophy and poetry are not to be classified after the fashion of purely natural phenomena or things, precisely because they contain and are affected by the ideas used in defining and classifying them.

The period of the Middle Ages, which incloses within its limits examples of

---

1. Reprinted, with minor alterations, from *Modern Philology*, May, 1946.

2. Cf. G. Santayana, *Three Philosophical Poets: Lucretius, Dante, and Goethe* (Cambridge, 1910), pp. 10–11.

so many diverse things, affords an illustration of these two attitudes toward the relationships of poetry and philosophy, sharply separated in doctrine and yet closely related in time. During the twelfth century, philosophy reached a mature and characteristic form, Platonizing in manner and humanistic in tradition. Many of the major philosophers of the century expressed their philosophy in excellent poetry; and they continued in philosophy and poetry the paradox of Plato, who also used poetic devices and quotations from the poets to explore philosophic ideas and yet expelled poets from his second-best as well as his perfect state, retaining only carefully selected poetic forms for use in the education of the young. The poets and rhetoricians of the later Renaissance of the fifteenth and sixteenth centuries exemplified the same paradox when they borrowed philosophic problems from philosophers, not merely to seek more felicitous expression for solutions arrived at philosophically, but to attain to a fuller realization of truth than they thought possible by the technicalities and futilities of philosophic distinctions.

During the last half of the twelfth century and the first half of the thirteenth the translations of Aristotle and the Arabic philosophers changed the form and matter of philosophy. The tradition of the twelfth century was broken abruptly, and that break was accentuated by the fact that few of the philosophers who first struggled to assimilate the growing materials of the new translations were studied by their successors in the latter part of the thirteenth century or were recorded in later histories of philosophy. Great philosophers of the second half of the thirteenth century, as, for example, Thomas Aquinas and Bonaventura, continue to write excellent verse; but in their philosophies the ends and instruments of poetry are sharply distinguished from those of theory, and their poetry is not a device to express their basic or most characteristic philosophic doctrines, while Dante, the great philosophic poet of the period, is not a philosopher by the crucial test that, despite the philosophic doctrines that crowd his poem, scholars have been unable to agree concerning what his attitude toward the philosophers he uses is.

Bonaventura, seeking frankly to combine Plato and Aristotle after the fashion in which they had been combined by Plotinus and Augustine, assigns to Plato the realm of wisdom and the eternal and to Aristotle the realm of science and the changing. On the other hand, Aquinas, seeking to distinguish philosophy from theology, criticizes the Platonic method in philosophy and repeats Aristotelian refutations of the doctrine of Ideas, but retains Platonic devices in theology and even preserves Platonic Ideas by finding a place for them in the mind of God. Yet for both, as for Aristotle, poetry is distinct from philosophy, not an inferior but comparable discipline, rivaling the purposes of philosophy and endangering its ends. Dante, in like fashion, exhibits mingled traces of Platonism and Aristotelianism. His poetic use of the philosophic tendencies of his times is not in advocacy of a philosophic position or to sharpen philosophic differences but tends, rather, to reconcile the Aristotelianism of Aquinas with the Averroism of Siger of Brabant. His use of philosophy is not the expression of a philosophy, and it is difficult, if not impossible, to state his doctrines or place them among the schools of his time; yet, when he expounds the method by which his poem should be interpreted, he reverts to the devices of the twelfth century and requires, as had been customary, that his poem be placed under the proper part of philosophy, identifying that part as ethics.[3]

An examination of the relation of poetry and philosophy during the twelfth century has therefore more than merely historical interest, since light is thrown on the problems of criticism and of philosophy by the theory and practice of poetry in any period. The nature of poetry and the criteria for its evaluation as well as the techniques of expression and interpretation in literal statement and analogy, in proof and persuasion, are treated in detail by the Platonizing philosophers of the twelfth century, and, in the manner of Platonisms, the dialectical shifts in doctrines complete a circle in which the reasons used by philosophers in criticism of poetry suggest poetic reasons for the criticism of philosophy by theologians.

The Platonic tradition had attracted the Greek and Latin Church Fathers, but it had also set them the puzzling task of explaining how skepticism and idealism, no less than logic-chopping and mysticism, had all been derived from the teachings of Plato. Modern scholarship has given us fuller materials concerning the paradox of Socrates, but Augustine explored the full range of its implications. The conversations of Socrates have been the source of many and highly diversified inspirations. We have records of them in the plain common sense of Xenophon as well as in the philosophic subtleties of Plato; and we have constructed a Socratic problem, sometimes by seeking in internal evidence and external information touchstones to differentiate the Socratic from the Platonic strand in Plato's dialogues, sometimes by using the Platonic philosophy to suggest a missing level of communication in the account of Xenophon, hinted with enigmatic and parabolic intent or omitted because it went unobserved. Moreover, Socratic dialogues were written by Megareans and Elean-Eretrians, Cynics and Cyrenaics; and the Socratic method was invoked by hedonists, skeptics, dialecticians, cynics, idealists, and mystics, whose writings have

---

3. For the discussion of Dante's philosophy cf. B. Nardi, *Saggi di filosofia Dantesca* (Milan, 1930) and *Note critiche di filosofia Dantesca* (Florence, 1938); P. Mandonnet, *Dante le théologien: Introduction à l'intelligence de la vie, des œuvres et l'art de Dante Alighieri* (Paris, 1935); E. Gilson, *Dante et la philosophie* (Paris, 1939). For Aquinas and Bonaventura on the relation of poetry and philosophy, cf. below, nn. 30, 31, and 32; for Dante's critical method, cf. *Epistola X*, to Can Grande della Scala, and n. 35, below.

been lost and whose fragmentary history has been a puzzle to scholars and philosophers.

There is almost a consensus among the philosophers of the twelfth century that Plato was the greatest of philosophers, and he is frequently referred to, much as Aristotle was in the thirteenth and fourteenth centuries, as "The Philosopher."[4] Since little was known of Aristotle's philosophy, except a few books of his *Organon*, the materials for most of the philosophic controversies of the first half of the century may be found in the opposed elements of Platonism, learned also at second hand but developed with great philosophic sensitivity and skill. The philosophers of the twelfth century accepted from Augustine the judgment that Plato's philosophy was most nearly of all philosophies in accord with Christianity. Some of them made this the basis of their plea for the preservation of humanistic culture, while others found the homogeneity of Christianity and Platonism in Neo-Platonic doctrines, which Augustine had found in Plotinus and which had been blended with Christian doctrine

4. John of Salisbury calls Bernard of Chartres "perfectissimus inter Platonicos seculi nostri" (*Metalogicon* iv. 35, ed. C. C. I. Webb [Oxford, 1929]), p. 205; *Patrologia Latina* [cited henceforth as "*PL*"], CXCIX, 938C). Herman of Dalmatia dedicated his translation of Ptolemy's *Planisphere* to Thierry of Chartres, who was "the first and sovereign anchor of second philosophy [i.e., the quadrivium] in our times, the immobile support of studies tossed by every kind of storm, . . . in whom relives the soul of Plato descended from Heaven for the happiness of mortals, the true father of Latin studies" (A. Clerval, *Les Écoles de Chartres au moyen-âge* [Chartres, 1895], p. 190). Abailard calls Plato the greatest of philosophers: "Maximus omnium philosophorum Plato" (*Introductio ad theologiam* iii [*PL*, CLXXVIII, 1087D]); "ille maximus philosophorum Plato" (*Theologia Christiana* i [*PL*, CLXXVIII, 1144A]); "summum philosophorum Platonem- (*Th. Chr.* i [*PL*, CLXXVIII, 1155A]); "summus philosophus" (*Th. Chr.* i [*PL*, CLXXVIII, 1160D]); "Pluribus quoque sanctorum testimoniis didicimus Platonicam sectam catholicae fidei concordare. Unde non sine causa maximus Plato philosophorum prae caeteris commendatur ab omnibus, non solum a peritis saecularium artium, verum etiam a sanctis" (*Th. Chr.* i [*PL*, CLXXVIII, 1159C]); Augustine's praise of Plato is quoted with approval (*Th. Chr.* ii [*PL*, CLXXVIII, 1176B–1177C]); "maximus omnium philosophorum Plato" (*Th. Chr.* v [*PL*, CLXXVIII, 1317B]); "Novimus etiam ipsum Aristotelem et in aliis locis adversus eumdem magistrum suum et primum totius philosophiae ducem, ex fomite fortassis invidiae aut ex avaritia nominis, ex manifestatione scientiae insurrexisse, quibusdam et sophisticis argumentationibus adversus ejus sententias inhiantem dimicasse, ut in eo quod de motu animae Macrobius meminit" (*Dialectica* Pars i, lib. 2; *Ouvrages inédits d'Abélard*, ed. V. Cousin [Paris, 1836], pp. 205-6). Adelard of Bath refers to him in terms of esteem and familiarity: "a principe philosophorum" (*De eodem et diverso*, ed. H. Willner, in *Beiträge zur Geschichte der Philosophie des Mittelalters* [henceforth cited as "*BGPM*"], IV, No. 2, 4); "familiaris meus Plato" and "meus Plato" (*ibid.*, p. 13); "philosophus" (*ibid.*, p. 15); and his nephew, who is his interlocutor in the dialogue, *Natural Questions*, detects in him a complete acceptance of Platonic principles: "Cum enim et in philosophicis contemplationibus et in physicis causarum effectibus ethicisque etiam consultibus Platoni te penitus consentire perceperim . . ." (*Quaestiones naturales* 24, ed. M. Müller [*BGPM*, XXXI, No. 2, 31]); "auctor huius divinae rationis Plato simil cum suis celebretur et ametur" (*BGPM*, XXXI, No. 2, 34); and he is referred to throughout the *Natural Questions* as "The Philosopher" (cf. *BGPM*, XXXI, No. 2, 6, 9, 30, 31, and *passim*). John of Salisbury, despite his admiration for Aristotle and Cicero, ranks Plato above all other philosophers: "Totius etenim philosophiae princeps Plato (si tamen Aristotilici adquiescunt) . . ." (*Policraticus* i. 6; ed. C. C. J. Webb [Oxford, 1909], I, 40 [*PL*, CXCIX, 401C]);

through the influence of the pseudo-Donysius the Areopagite, and turned their speculations wholly to the return to God from the consideration of the world. Others learned from Cicero that both academic skepticism and stoic morality stem from Plato, and they found in Cicero's rhetoric a philosophic method and hints of a philosophic doctrine which harmonized with the logic and the logical realism taught by Porphyry and Boethius. Still others found the beginnings of science and cosmology in Chalcidius' translation of a portion of the *Timaeus* and his commentary on it, and in Apuleius and Marcobius.

The discussion of poetry during the twelfth century exemplifies the doctrinal diversity possible in the development of the tradition of Platonism. Four distinct, and even contradictory, positions concerning the relation of poetry and philosophy were developed in excellent literary and poetic form, and each

---

"Totius denique ueteris philosophiae princeps Plato . . ." (*Polic.* ii. 26 [Webb, I, 141; *PL*, CXCIX, 460A]); ". . . et in tantam eminentiam philosophiae et uigore ingenii et studii exercitio et omni morum uenustate eloquii quoque suauitate et copia subuectus est ut quasi in trono sapientiae residens praecepta quadam auctoritate uisus sit tam antecessoribus quam successoribus philosophis imperare. . . . Porro tantae multitudinis dissidentiam Plato qua praeminebat auctoritate cohibuit et in se attentionem omnium diutius prouocauit et tenuit" (*Polic.* vii. 5 [Webb, II, 105; *PL*, CXCIX, 644A–B]); "Sol e celo uisus est cecidisse qua die philosophorum princeps Plato rebus excessit humanis, et quasi lucernam mundi extinctam defleuerunt qui ad thronum sapientiae, cui ille diu praesederat, sua arbitrabantur studia referenda. Sed cum ei Aristotiles discipulus, uir excellentis ingenii et Platoni impar eloquio sed multos facile superans, in docendi officium successisset, . . ." (*Polic.* vii. 6 [Webb, II, 111–12; *PL*, CXCIX, 647C]); "Licet autem nominum et uerborum turbator habeatur, non modo subtilitate, qua cunctis celebris est, sed et mira suauitate dicendi eualuit, adeo quidem ut Platoni merito proximus fuisse uideatur" (Webb, II, 113; *PL*, CXCIX, 648B). William of Conches repeats the preference of Augustine: "Si gentilis adducenda est opinio, malo Platonis quam alterius inducatur; plus namque cum nostra fide concordat" (quoted from the *Dragmaticon philosophiae* by C. Prantl, *Geschichte der Logik im Abendlände* [reprint; Leipzig, 1927], II, 129, n. 96). Alan of Lille sets above Aristotle's logical inquiries Plato's more divine investigations of the nature of the things, of the heavens, and of God:

"Illic arma parat logico, logicaeque palaestram
Pingit Aristoteles; sed eo divinius ipsa
Somniat arcana rerum, coelique profunda
Mente Plato, sensumque Dei perquirere tentat"

(*Anticlaudianus* i [*PL*, CCX, 491B]); Plato is in philosophy what Croesus is in wealth, Cyrus in power, Narcissus in beauty, Turnus in courage, Hercules in strength, Hippolytus in chastity (*De planctu naturae* [*PL*, CCX, 468C]); "Plato ingenii splendore rutilabat sidereo. Illic stellata cauda Tulliani pavonis rutilabat. Illic Aristoteles sententias aenigmaticarum locutionum latibulis involvebat" (*De planc. nat.* [*PL*, CCX, 479D]); he is referred to, as he frequently is in the twelfth century, as "The Philosopher" (*Contra haereticos* i. 5 [*PL*, CCX, 311C]). Finally, Alan of Lille set for himself the task of translating or expanding Plato:

"His animadversis mens sese accingat ad illa,
Quae minime fiunt, sed sunt, velut ipsa Platonis
Verba canunt; . . ."

(*A deo semper incipiendum et in eumdem desinendum* [*PL*, CCX, 576B]). Cf. C. Baeumker, "Der Platonismus im Mittelalter," *Studien und Characteristiken zur Geschichte der Philosophie insbesondere des Mittelalters* (*BGPM*, XXV, Nos. 1–2, 139–79); and R. Klibansky, *The Continuity of the Platonic Tradition during the Middle Ages* (London, 1939).

reiterated Plato's love of poetry and his suspicion of its effects. All four positions reflect the Platonic statement of the problems in terms of the opposition of opinion and belief, on the one hand, to dialectic and philosophy, on the other. Poetry as a form of opinion and belief is opposed to philosophy and is full of dangers to the truth which those other poets, the lawgiver and dialectician, attain by means of knowledge; and yet it is possible for poetry to state right opinion and true belief, and, indeed, poetry and the interpretation of poetry may attain to truth by divine inspiration. Moreover, a further complexity had been introduced into Christian Platonism by the redefinition of belief or faith: for belief (πίστις), according to Plato, is that variety of knowledge which grasps *visible things*, and it is inferior, as empirical certitude, to the knowledge gained by understanding and reason, whereas medieval philosophers followed the Pauline definition of belief (*fides*) as the argument of things unseen, and belief or faith, defined as the knowledge of *invisible things*, assumed a place superior to reason in their classification of knowledge. The problem of the relation of poetry to philosophy or the liberal arts became, as a consequence, an extension or development of the problem of the relation of philosophy to religion or theology.

The position of Peter Abailard, renowned both as dialectician and as poet,[5] derives from Plato by way of Augustine. Abailard develops arguments borrowed from Augustine to defend the study of secular letters both for their utility and for themselves, since the liberal arts and philosophy are essential to Christian doctrine and the interpretation of Scripture. He also argues on Augustinian grounds that poetic figments are wholly forbidden to Christians,

---

5. Judgments concerning the poetic value of medieval poetry have undergone marked alterations during the last few decades. The prejudice against "didactic poetry" has not disappeared, but the present-day taste for speculative and metaphysical verse is reflected in the estimation of earlier poets. P. S. Allen (*Medieval Latin Lyrics* [Chicago, 1931], pp. 243–44) traces the history of the shift of his views in twenty-two years concerning Abailard's authorship of poems in the *Carmina Burana*. One reason for his hesitation in attributing poems from that collection to Abailard was his judgment of Abailard, revealed in his extant poetry as "the composer of a letter to Astrolabius, the author of cut-and-dried planctus on Old Testament subjects, the writer of ninety hymns and sequences that breathe but the lifeless excogitations of a theological wit." F. J. E. Raby, on the other hand, places Abailard high among the great hymn writers of the Middle Ages and is impressed particularly by the novelty and skilful development of his verse forms (*A History of Christian-Latin Poetry from the Beginnings to the Close of the Middle Ages* [Oxford, 1927], pp. 319–26); he praises the *planctus* for their "rich variety of rhythmical schemes and their sureness of execution"; and he finds even the poem to Astrolabe not wanting in facility, although the execution of verses is not above reproach (*A History of Secular Latin Poetry in the Middle Ages* [Oxford, 1934], II, 5–7). Helen Waddell judges the meters exquisite and the treatment poignant (*The Wandering Scholars* [7th ed.; London, 1934], p. 196); and F. A. Wright and T. A. Sinclair characterize Abailard as "a scholar, a philosopher, a theologian, an orator, and above all a poet" (*A History of Later Latin Literature* [London, 1931], p. 296). For a general survey and estimate of Abailard's poetry cf. M. Manitius, *Geschichte der lateinischen Literatur des Mittelalters* (Munich, 1931), III, 109–10.

not only because they expound errors and *a mouth that lieth destroyeth the soul* according to the Book of Wisdom (1:11) but also because the soul is enticed by cogitation on inane fables to desire the disgraceful things feigned in poetry and is abducted by them from the study of Sacred Scripture. Abailard is at pains, therefore, to interpret the numerous strictures against pagan letters, particularly those of Jerome, to show that they are directed exclusively against poetry and do not apply to the liberal arts or philosophy.[6] He defends the liberal arts strenuously on the ground that no knowledge, but only its improper use, can be evil, and no art should therefore be forbidden except on grounds of utility. But he can find no use for "poetic figments and inane fables." He refutes those who maintain that the study of the poets is essential to the arts of the trivium, arguing that Scripture supplies better material for grammar, rhetoric, and dialectic; and he points out that even Cicero, when he wished to set forth the art of discourse fully in his rhetoric, did not use poetic examples, but his own discourses, in which he said the art shone forth more fully. Will Christian bishops and doctors, Abailard asks, welcome to the city of God poets, whom Plato excluded from the city of the world? Yet misguided priests spend day and night on solemn feasts-days with troubadours and jongleurs—*joculatores, saltatores, incantatores,* and *contatores*—and reward them with recompenses stolen from ecclesiastical beneficies. Such actors (*histriones*) are a diabolical troup, and the devil himself has introduced theatrical obscenities (*scenicas turpitudines*) into the church of God.[7]

The position of the cosmological poets and philosophers, in the second place, derives from Plato by way of the *Timaeus* and the interpretations of Chalcidius and by way of the speculations of that mythical god and philosopher, Hermes Trismegistus, and the treatises of Macrobius and Apuleius. Poetry, in the allegorizing cosmological philosophy, may be joined with philosophy in the case of a poet like Virgil, and in the case of lesser poets it may be useful in education, although unsuited to mystical or allegorical interpretation, or it may be the statement of erroneous doctrines on questions concerning which the truth can be found only in the study of nature and God.

Bernard Sylvester, whose *De mundi universitate* is composed in prose alternating with poetry of great beauty,[8] takes the former of these alternatives.

6. *Introductio ad theologiam* ii. 2 (*PL*, CLXXVIII, 1040–46).

7. *Th. Chr.* ii (*PL*, CLXXVIII, 1209–12); cf. Abailard's citation of Augustine's statements in approval of the expulsion of poets by Plato (*Th. Chr.* ii [*PL*, CLXXVIII, 1182–83]).

8. *Bernardi Silvestris De mundi universitate libri duo sive megacosmus et microcosmus,* ed. C. S. Barach and J. Wrobel (Innsbruck, 1876). The critical estimate of Bernard's poetic abilities has varied between very widely separated extremes. He is compared to Dante in the account of his work in the *Histoire littéraire de la France* (XII, 272), and Hauréau summarizes that judgment without stating dissent (*Histoire de la philosophie scolastique* [Paris, 1872], I,

He finds occasion to discuss the nature and value of poetry when, in his allegorical interpretation of Virgil's *Aeneid*,[9] he expounds the pious hero's journey, at the beginning of the sixth book, to the temple of Apollo (interpreted as the philosophic or theoretic arts) near the vast cavern of the Sybil (interpreted as the profundity of philosophy) by way of a grove called Trivia (which suggests that the study of eloquence is preliminary to the theoretic arts). Science is divided according to Bernard into four parts: wisdom, eloquence, poetry, and mechanics. These are arranged in graded sequence: poetry is clearer and higher than mechanics, and eloquence has a like superiority over poetry, and wisdom or philosophy over eloquence. The study of eloquence, however, is pursued by instruction in authors, and the poets are therefore introductory to philosophy. But, although the amusing stories of authors and poets prepare for the arts of eloquence, and therefore for philosophy, they are not worthy to be interpreted mystically.[10] For this reason the priestess of Apollo and Trivia arouses Aeneas from the contemplation of the fables painted on the doors of the temple to invite him into the temple itself.

This judgment of poetry, however, is developed in a commentary on a poet; for Virgil in this form of the Platonic paradox is not merely a poet but a

---

417): "Il y a dans cet ouvrage, selon les auteurs de l'*Histoire littéraire*, des traits de génie. Il y a certainement de l'invention, et ce n'est pas trop louer certains passages du *Microcosme* que de les comparer à d'autres passages de la *Divine comédie*. Bernard n'avait pas seulement l'imagination ingénieuse et facile; il l'avait encore puissante: c'est vraiment un poëte." Gilson refers to the same authorities as prelude to his own more moderate praise (*La Philosophie au moyen âge* [2d ed.; Paris, 1944], p. 273: "Certains passages de cette œuvre ne sont pas sans beauté, mais il est vraiment excessif de rappeler à leur occasion, ainsi qu'on l'a fait, le grand nom de Dante et le souvenir de la *Divine comédie*." Charles Huit considers him the true philosopher-poet ("Le Platonisme au XIIe siècle," *Annales de philosophie chrétienne*, XXI [new ser., 1889–90], 169–70): "C'est un véritable poète philosophe, chez lequel l'éclat de l'imagination l'emporte sur la solidité du raisonnement, et qui a mérité de Charles Lenormant ce bien sincère éloge: 'J'étais attiré par un attrait irrésistible vers les écrits de Bernard: j'y trouvais un parfum littéraire, un sentiment de la belle antiquité, une intuition de la philosophie platonique (et pourtant Bernard n'avait à sa disposition que la traduction du *Timée*) qui ne pouvaient, il est vrai, arrêter un grand mouvement comme celui de la scolastique, mais qui du moins maintenaient la chaîne des traditions du goût.' Ses vers sont remplis de peintures riches et brillantes, attestant le progrès qu'avait fait entre tous les arts l'art d'écrire pendant ce demisiècle privilégié." Like Victor Cousin, Helen Waddell compares Bernard to Giordano Bruno (*op. cit.*, p. 115), and her praise of his *De mundi universitate* is enthusiastic (*ibid.*, p. 118): "His book has two sources, the *Timaeus* of Plato and the comment of Chalcidius; but the driest of the Platonic dialogues is only the fuel for his fire. The poet in him never sleeps; the sheer mechanism, the skeleton of philosophy, stuff like the theory of the four elements becomes a succession of visions. . . . The very baldness of his argument . . . is the dream of the *Faerie Queene*, of *The Tempest*, of *Hyperion*. And of the Providence, his prose is the prose of Shelley's *Defense of Poetry*." According to Raby (*op. cit.*, p. 297): "Bernard's verse, like his prose, is stiff and obscure, although he had read Horace, Virgil, and Ovid."

9. *Commentum Bernardi Silvestris super sex libros Eneidos Virgilii*, ed. G. Riedel (Gryphiswaldae, 1924), pp. 30–38.

10. *Ibid.*, p. 37; cf. Bernard's citation of Plato's *Timaeus* in support of the doctrine that poetry is imitation (*ibid.*, pp. 74–75).

philosopher, and, as Macrobius pointed out, he taught philosophic truth without neglecting poetic fiction.[11] The purposes of poets, which Bernard repeats from Horace, are utility and delight. Satirists aim at utility; writers of comedy, at delight; epic writers, at both. Virgil, as poet, pleases with adornment of words and with the situations and deeds narrated; and he serves likewise a double utility, as model for imitation in learning the art of writing and by exhortation to prudence by examples of right action. As philosopher he treats of the nature of human life according to a parabolic mode of demonstration proper to poetry.

In so far as he is a philosopher, he writes of the nature of human life. His mode of writing is this: he describes under concealment [*sub integumento*] what the human spirit does and suffers, situated temporally in the human body. And in writing thus he uses the natural order, and thus he observes both orders of narration, as a poet the artificial, as a philosopher the natural [i.e., the narrative begins literally *in medias res* and its temporal beginnings are supplied later in the tale related to Dido, but the six ages of man traced in the allegorical meaning follow their natural sequence through the first six books]. Concealment, moreover, is a genus of demonstration which enfolds the understanding of truth under a fabled narration, and therefore it is also called envelopment [*involucrum*]. Furthermore, man derives utility from this work according to his recognition of himself, inasmuch as it is of great utility to man, as Macrobius says, if he knows himself. Whence "From the heavens descends *notisheliton*," that is, *know thyself*.[12]

Poetry, though distinct from philosophy, may, nonetheless, coincide with it in a great poem; and together poetry and philosophy may deal in almost wholly pagan terms with a Christian theme, as the creation of the universe and man is treated in Bernard's *De mundi universitate*, to the confusion of later scholars who like to distinguish literally between pagan and Christian philosophy.

Alan of Lille, who also wrote excellent poetry on cosmological themes, took the second alternative of the cosmologists and argued in his poetry, with no less fidelity to the Platonic paradox, that poetry is committed to falsity. Cicero and Virgil are treated in sequence in the Alexandrian verses of the *Anticlaudianus*, and the poet suffers by comparison with the rhetorican: "Tully redeems his verbal poverty by the splendor of colors [i.e., figures] and gives lightning flashes of embellishment to his words. The muse of Virgil colors [i.e., glosses over] many falsehoods, and weaves cloaks for falsehood under the

---

11. *Ibid.*, pp. 1–3. The citation from Horace is of *Ars poetica* 333–34.

12. *Commentum Bernardi Silvestris*, p. 3; the citation is from Juvenal xi. 27, quoted from Macrobius *Commentaria in Somnium Scipionis* i. 9. 1–2; cf. also Macrobius *Saturnalia* i. 6. 6. The line from Juvenal is quoted also by John of Salisbury, *De septem septenis* 6 (*PL*, CXCIX, 956B). For other references to the allegorical interpretation of poets and particularly to the poetic mode of demonstration by *integumentum* or *involucrum*, cf. Alan of Lille, *De planctu naturae* (*PL*, CCX, 454C); John of Salisbury, *Polic.* viii. 24 (Webb, II, 415; *PL*, CXCIX, 816D–817A); and Honorius of Autun, *Selectorum Psalmorum expositio* (*PL*, CLXXII, 269C): "Ideo autem mysteria hujus libri sunt per involucra et aenigmata texta, ne vilescerent omnibus aperta."

guise of truth.''[13] In the *De planctu naturae*, the poet converses with Nature concerning such imperfections of man as sodomy and stirs his interlocutor to a truly Platonic outburst against poets by asking about their accounts of like ignominious deeds by the gods. The dreamy fancies of the poets deserve no credence, according to Nature, and philosophy's saner treatment files away and erases by means of higher understanding what was learned in the child's cradle of poetic teaching. Among the distortions of the poets, those concerning love are most of all in error.[14] When Alan persists in his interest in things poetic and asks concerning the nature of Cupid, which various authors have depicted under the concealing envelopment of enigmas (*sub integumentali involucro aenigmatum*) without leaving us any vestiges of certitude, Nature reproaches his inattention to her high discourse and promises in her prose argument to demonstrate the indemonstrable and to extricate the inextricable, as she puts it, by describing in certain description or defining in legitimate definition. "The artful exposition of her doctrine, the theory of the art of love" stated in a "chastened loftiness of style" is an artful lyric on the nature of love.[15]

13. *Antic*. i. 4 (*PL*, CCX, 491C). The judgments passed on Alan's verse are as various as those suffered by other poets of the century. Hauréau traces his transition from logical to poetical exposition of philosophic subjects and concludes (*op. cit.*, I, 522): "C'est, en effet, le philosophe des mystiques et des poëtes." Charles Huit counts him in the number of the most brilliant poets of the century (*op. cit.*, p. 178): "Si Jean de Salisbury est au premier range parmi les érudits du XIIe siècle, Alain de Lille compte au nombre de ses plus brillants poètes. Ses écrits attestent les progrès étonnants réalisés dès cette époque par la culture littéraire et le soin jaloux avec lequel, dans les classes lettrées, on étudiait pour les imiter les chefs-d'œuvre survivants de l'antiquité latine, à commencer par les vers de Virgile, d'Ovide, de Sénèque et de Claudien. La poésie didactique et allégorique, en si grand honneur au moyen âge, n'a rien produit de supérieur à l'*Anticlaudianus*, où Dante a puisé l'idée première de maint épisode célèbre de la *Divine Comédie*." Gilson finds little poetry in the *Anticlaudianus* but some grandeur in the *De planctu naturae* (*op. cit.*, p. 315). Raby finds Alan's philosophical poems less charming than his shorter *rhythmus* (*op. cit.*, p. 15). Allen quotes the same *rhythmus* (*Omnis mundi creatura*) that was praised by Raby, as evidence that "lyric song," which he seems to identify with "poetry in the modern sense, romantic poetry at least," is unknown among the products of the twelfth-century humanistic schools (*op. cit.*, p. 233). D. M. Moffat, who translated the *De planctu naturae*, has a particularly low opinion of the poetic quality of that work. After acknowledging the indebtedness of Chaucer and Jean de Meun to Alan, Moffat disposes of his poet in summary judgment (*The Complaint of Nature by Alain de Lille*, Preface [New York, 1908], p. 1): "The statement of Langlois that 'more than five thousand verses of the *Roman de la Rose* are translated, imitated, or inspired by the *De planctu naturae*'is excellent authority that this mysterious scholar of the Middle Ages, whose very identity is unascertained, was of those who beget kings in literature, though he himself were none." It would be difficult to gainsay Moffat's judgment on the basis of his prosy, though for the most part accurate, translation; but even Homer is not a poet in all translations. The differences of scholarly judgment indicate the need of a reanalysis of the intellectual poetry of the Middle Ages on other standards than those suggested by the romantic lyric.

14. *De planctu naturae* (*PL*, CCX, 451A–452A).

15. *Ibid.*, sexta quaestio (*PL*, CCX, 454C–456B). It should be observed that, since the purpose of the poem is demonstrative, it will naturally seem unpoetic to critics who dislike "allegorical" proof and the use of the "common-places." According to Raby (*op. cit.*, II, 20), "the 'descriptio Cupidinis' is a school-exercise."

The position of the humanists and the moderate skeptics, in the third place, derives from Plato by way of Cicero and the Roman rhetoricians and poets. The condemnation which Abailard brought against poetry itself is reserved in their criticism for the errors of poets, and the praise of poetry is reflected in its use and interpretations by philosophers. Moreover, in this analysis, poetry is not separated, as it is according to Abailard, Bernard, and Alan, from the liberal arts, but it may be a part of one of the liberal arts and a useful tool of theology.

John of Salisbury, whose urbane verses treat problems suggested by the history of philosophy and the errors of philosophers, wrote that he did not blush to acknowledge himself an academic skeptic, for he was content to doubt concerning things of which a wise man cannot be certain.[16] But this Ciceronian skepticism left him three sources of certain knowledge: the senses, reason, and faith. He is anxious to safeguard a modicum of culture from the ignorance of the illiterate masses, and he has no doubt that reading in the historians, orators, and mathematicians is essential to a liberal education. He can therefore repeat from Cicero both the condemnation of poets (since they are lauded in spite of the darkness they spread, the fears they engender, and the passions they inflame) and also the praise of poetry (since it is essential to education and philosophy).[17] John quotes Cicero's moral defense of poetry, probably from a portion of the *De re publica* which is no longer extant:

> He alone who does not fear to be the object of contempt makes the poets and the various writers of the arts and of history contemptible. For they both have the use of virtue and afford the material of philosophy; they note the vices, to be sure, but do not teach them, and they are attractive either because of utility or because of pleasure. They make their way thus through moral dangers only to establish a place for virtue.[18]

This journey through moral dangers to the pleasures of philosophy is to be found signified allegorically in the adventures of Ulysses; and John also repeats, in brief summary, Bernard Sylvester's allegorical interpretation of the first six books of the *Aeneid*.[19] According to John, Virgil intimates his philosophic conclusions under the cloak of his feigned invention (*sub involucro fictitii commenti*), and John quotes with approval the opinion of those expert in the

---

16. *Polic.*, Prologus (Webb, I, 17; *PL*, CXCIX, 388B–C); cf. *Metal.* ii. 20 (Webb, p. 106; *PL*, CXCIX, 882B). Since John is given to literal statement rather than to allegory, his poetry has fared better at the hands of modern critics. Raby admires his *Entheticus de dogmate philosophorum* as a medley of satire, philosophy, and moral counsel, and he exempts it from his favorite condemnation of intellectual poetry as school-exercises. Cf. *op. cit.*, II, 91: "The seriousness and the soundness of his outlook are abundantly clear; his poem is no mere *tour de force* or school-exercise. It has preserved its freshness because it bears the impress of his keen and judicial intelligence, of his grave irony and his deep seriousness."

17. *Polic.* vii. 9 (Webb, II, 126; *PL*, CXCIX, 655C–656A).

18. Webb, II, 127; *PL*, CXCIX, 656C.

19. *Polic.* viii. 24 (Webb, II, 415–18; *PL*, CXCIX, 816C–818B).

interpretation of authors that Virgil makes use of a twofold instruction, since he has enfolded the secrets of philosophic virtue in the vanity of poetic figment.[20]

The art of poetry, according to John of Salisbury, is to imitate nature, and poetic shares this function with grammar, the mother and nurse of the study of poetry. To be sure, grammar and rhetoric are not primarily natural; they are conventional, but nature has some control over them, since they imitate nature. He dismisses disdainfully the arguments of those who hold that poetic is a separate art and concludes that it must either be a part of grammar or have no place among the liberal arts.[21] Poetic is essential to philosophy, although, as Seneca pointed out, it is not sufficient to make a man good; but one who aspires to philosophy must lay hold of four things: reading, learning, meditation, and the practice of good works.[22] John states the relation of poetic to the liberal arts and the interrelations of the liberal arts in terms of an elaborate figure of speech derived from weaving, in which grammar and poetic furnish the background of the tapestry or brocatel.

Grammar and poetic, indeed, pour themselves out entirely and occupy the whole surface of what is expounded. Logic, bearing its colors [i.e., figures] of proof to this ground, as it is wont to be called, sets off its reasons in a blaze of gold; and rhetoric emulates the brightness of silver with its places of persuasions and brilliance of style. Mathematics is borne on the wheels of its quadrivium and, following on the tracks of the others, weaves its own colors and charms in manifold ways. Physics, having explored the counsels of nature, brings from its storehouse numerous charms of colors. Moreover, that which rises above the other parts of philosophy—I mean ethics, without which not even the name of philosopher subsists—surpasses all the others in the grace of ornament that it brings. Examine Virgil or Lucan, and you will find in them, whatever philosophy you profess, adornment for it.[23]

John of Salisbury is one of our chief sources of information concerning the methods of literary instruction and interpretation practiced by Bernard of Chartres—"the most perfect Platonist of our times," as John calls him—in which the identity of poetic and grammar and the fundamental contribution of grammar to philosophy are both apparent. John was convinced, moreover, that the liberal arts were all organically interrelated, both with each other and with philosophy; and the portrait of Gilbert de la Porrée which he draws in the *Historia pontificalis*, in careful balance to Gilbert's great antagonist, Bernard, is concrete manifestation of the possible contribution of poetry and philosophy to theology:

20. Webb, II, 415, 417; *PL*, CXCIX, 816D–817A, 818A.
21. *Metal*. i. 17 (Webb, pp. 42–43; *PL*, CXCIX, 847A–D).
22. *Metal*. i. 22–23 (Webb, pp. 51–53; *PL*, CXCIX, 852B–853C).
23. *Metal*. i. 24 (Webb, pp. 54–55; *PL*, CXCIX, 854B–C).

He used, as the matter required, the aid of all disciplines, for he knew that in these severally the whole rests upon mutual supports. He had connected the disciplines, and he made them serve theology, and he restricted the rules of all within the limits of the proper genera. For they are each adapted to their proper genera, and they are immediately vitiated when they have been transferred to another genus. He made clear the properties and figures of words even in theology by the examples not only of philosophers and orators, but also of poets.[24]

Within the interrelation of the arts, poetry has his proper place as part of one of the liberal arts and as support to philosophy and theology.

One final variant of the interpretation of poetry derives from Plato by way of mystical theology. Some of the great mystics of the twelfth century cultivated the liberal arts as one stage in the return of the soul from experience of things to self-knowledge and thence to God; and in their doctrine poetry is subordinate to the liberal arts and not wholly essential to them, while other great mystics were supicious alike of all secular arts—the liberal arts as well as poetry—and they expressed their adumbration of the truth missed by the liberal arts in poetry comparable for its force and imagery to the poetic statement other mystics gave to their suspicion of poetry.

Hugh of St. Victor, whose careful differentiation of the arts in the *Didascalion* presupposes the same kind of organic cohesion among them that John of Salisbury praised, finds only a secondary place for poetry.[25] There are two kinds of writings, one properly called "arts," such as grammar, dialectic, and rhetoric, which furnish subject matter to philosophy, the other only appendages to the arts, which look toward philosophy but have some subject matter outside philosophy. The latter include all the songs of the poets, such as tragedies, comedies, satires, heroic and lyrical poems, and iambics and certain didascalic poems, likewise fables and histories and even the writings of men usually called philosophers now, who are wont to extend a brief matter in long involutions of words and to obscure an easy meaning with confused words or even to bring together divers things at once as if to make a single picture from many colors and forms. The distance between the arts and the appendages to the arts, Hugh characteristically measures by a quotation from Virgil's *Eclogues*, for it is as great as that between the willow and the olive or the reed and the rose. Sometimes the appendages to the arts touch on bits torn here and there in disorder from the arts; or when they engage in simple narration, they may prepare for philosophy. One may, however, become perfect in reading without the appendages to the arts, whereas no perfection whatever can be conferred by the appendages without the arts.

24. *Historia pontificalis* 12, ed. R. L. Poole (Oxford, 1927), p. 28.

25. *Didascalion: de studio legendi* iii. 4, ed. C. H. Buttimer (Washington, 1939), pp. 54–55 (*PL*, CLXXVI, 768D–769C).

Honorius of Autun treats the liberal arts in a work entitled *On the Exile and the Homeland of the Soul*, for the exile of man is ignorance and the homeland, wisdom, to which he returns by a route which leads through the liberal arts as through cities. The first of these cities is grammar, in which there are certain subordinate *villae*, the books of the poets, which are divided into four kinds: tragedies, comedies, satires, and lyrics.[26] Tragedies are poems which treat of wars, as Lucan; comedies, those which sing nuptials, as Terence; satires, those which are concerned with reprehensible things, as Persius; lyrics, those which give voice to odes, that is, praises of gods and hymns to kings, as Horace.

Hildebert of Lavardin, finally, one of the great poets of the twelfth century, abandons philosophy as well as poetry as progressive stages in the return to Scripture. In one of his sermons he generalizes from what he has said about the Virgin to all interpretation of Scripture:

For we have, for the most part, passed by the fictions of poets, who are compared to croaking frogs. We have sailed over the pallid arguments of sophists, who are said to be hateful to God. We have bid farewell to the pompous opinions of philosophers, who have tried, while they were still among us, to raise their eyes above the heavens, among whom the more learned—I mean the academics—have confessed that truth is hidden in a bottomless well. We have given up magniloquent speech to follow veriloquent speech. For we sought wisdom, but behold it was not in the land of pleasantly speaking or living. *We heard of it in Ephrata*, that is, in a mirror or in a watchtower, that is, hidden in an image, but behold *we found it in the fields of the wood*, that is, in the manifestation of the New Testament and the obscurity of the Old Testament.[27]

26. *De animae exsilio et patria* (alias, *De artibus*) 2 (*PL*, CLXXII, 1243C–D).

27. *Sermo LX: in festo Assumptionis Beatae Mariae, et de laudibus, sermo secundus* (*PL*, CLXXI, 633A–B). For the reference to the Sophists cf. Ecclus. 37:23: "Qui sophistice loquitur, odibilis est." For the reference to "the land of pleasantly speaking or living" (*sauviter loquentium seu viventium*) cf. Job 28:13: "Nescit homo pretium eius [i.e., sapientiae], nec invenitur in terra suaviter viventium." Cf. Jerome *Comm. in Job* (*PL*, XXVI, 701A):"Et ideo suaviter dicti sunt vivere illi, qui nullo jugo disciplinae tenentur, et effrenes ac praecipites in labem prorumpunt vitiorum." Hildebert has apparently connected Jerome's reference to "disciplines" with the "disciplines" in the sense of the liberal arts and particularly the arts of speech. The Septuagint does not contain a term equivalent to "discipline" or, indeed, to the *terra suaviter viventium* which lacks discipline, but has merely οὐδὲ μὴ εὑρεθῇ ἐν ἀνθρώποις, and Jerome in his translation from the Greek (*Lib. Iob. Altera versio ex Graecis exemplaribus sive ex Originis Hexaplari editione* [*PL*, XXIX, 94B]) renders the passage "nex invenietur in hominibus." The interpretation of Ps. 132 (131):6, "Lo, we heard of it in Ephrata: we found it in the fields of the wood," which had taken a traditional form in the twelfth century, composed of elements which go back to Jerome and Augustine, is an excellent example of the allegorical and etymological interpretations. "Ephrata" is a name applied to the region of Bethlehem and to the town of Bethlehem itself (cf. Gen. 35:16 and 19, 48:7; Ruth 4:11; Mic. 5:2). Jerome was the source, for medieval writers, of both the literal explanation and some of the allegorical meanings. "Ephratha, regio Bethleem civitatis David, in qua natus est Christus. Est autem in tribu Juda (licet plerique male aestiment in tribu Benjamin), juxta viam ubi sepulta est Rachel quinto milliario ab Jerusalem, in eo loco qui a Septuaginta vocatur Hippodromus" (*De situ et nominibus locorum Hebraicorum* [*PL*, XXIII, 939]). Cf. *Commentaria in Jeremiam prophetam* vi. 21 (*PL*, XXIII, 877A–B) (this passage is repeated by Rhabanus Maurus, *PL*, CXI, 1035); *Commentaria in Abdiam* (*PL*, XXV, 1116C); *Commentaria in Micheam* v (*PL*, XXV, 1198B). Among the meanings attached to the word by

The language is close to that which Bernard and William of St. Thierry employed to condemn the intellectual audacity of Abailard, and the reasons are not unlike those which Abailard alleged to condemn the vain figments of the poets. The error of philosophers consists in raising their eyes to, or poking their noses into, things above the heavens[28] and in submitting faith to the manipulations of reason. Abailard had criticized the poets because of the discrepancies between their poetry and their faith, but he had held that reason and philosophy cannot be contrary to faith. Bernard criticized Abailard's dialectic because of the discrepancies between his philosophy and his faith, but in so doing he reproaches Abailard for trying to see all things face to face and for making no use in his philosophy of the device, familiar to poets, of seeing truth in a mirror and enigma. Bernard's criticism of philosophy and poetry thus accomplishes a

---

Jerome are *uberrima, ubertas, furorem videt.* "Ephratha vero et Bethlehem unius urbis vocabulum est, sub interpretatione consimili: siquidem in *frugiferam* et in *domum panis* vertitur propter eum panem qui de coelo descendisse se dicet" (*Liber Hebraicarum quaestionum in Genesim* [*PL*, XXIII, 1042B]). He interprets it *uberrima* (*Epistola* cviii [*PL*, XXII, 885]), *ubertas sive pulverulenta* (*Liber de nominibus Hebraicis* [*PL*, XXIII, 822]), *frugifera sive equidem (furorem?) vides* (*PL*, XXIII, 872). Augustine, however, seems to have been the source of the tradition in the Latin Middle Ages in which it is interpreted *speculum* (*Enarratio in Psalmum CXXXI* [*PL*, XXXVII, 1720]). Prosper of Aquitaine makes the two parts of the verse signify the mirror of the prophets and the lofty but erroneous achievement of the Gentiles: "Ephrata nomen Hebraeum interpretatur Latine speculum, in quo propheticae significationis imago precessit. Per speculum enim prophetiae, annuntiata haec sedes vel habitatio Dei, de qua dicitur, *Ecce audivimus eam in Ephrata,* id est, in eloquiis prophetarum. *Invenimus eam in campis silvae,* hoc est, in altitudine gentium, in quibus fuerunt vepres idololatriae, concretiones errorum, et silvestres incultarum mentium feritates" (*Expositio in Psalmum CXXXI* [*PL*, LI, 379A–B]). Much the same interpretation is put on the verse by Cassiodorus: "*Ephrata* lingua Latina significare memoratur speculum. *Campi* vero *silvae* indicant corda gentilium, quae ex peccatis quasi silvestribus ac dumosis, mundante Domino, campestri puritate patuerunt. *Campi* siquidem a capacitate et spatio diffuso dicti sunt. Facti sunt enim ex hispidis nitidi, ex agrestibus mansueti, ex sterilibus fructuosi, ex cubilibus daemonum templa Dominantis. Et ideo in campis silvae, id est, in gentibus dicit esse compertum, quod in imagine prophetiae Judaeis fuerat repromissum" (*Expositio in Psalterium* [*PL*, LXX, 949A–B]). Cf. Christianus Druthmarus *Expositio in Matthaeum* (*PL*, CVI, 1280D); Walafridus Strabus *Glossa ordinaria,* Genesis 35:16 and Ruth 1:2 (*PL*, CXIII, 162D, 533A–B); and Rupertus Tutiensis *De Trinitate et operibus ejus* xlii, *in Genesim* lib. ix (*PL*, CLXVII, 548B). Paschasius Radbertus emphasizes the interpretation *furorem videns,* which he reconciles with *frugifera* (*Expositio in Matthaeum* ii. 2 [*PL*, CXX, 131C–134B). Petrus Comestor has a plausible explanation to bring the three meanings together: "Ephrata, id est *furorem vidit,* id est experimento iram Dei cognovit. Vel interpretatur *speculum,* quia plaga ejus omnibus est posita in exemplum; sed tunc primo propter incredibilem ubertatem sibi [cibi?] reditam cepit vocari Bethlehem, quod est *domus panis*" (*Historia scholastica, historia libri Ruth* [*PL*, CXCVIII, 1293C]).

28. Hildebert describes philosophers in general with the characterization, "qui dum adhuc essent apud nos, conati sunt attollere oculos super coelos"; St. Bernard turns the same conception into an attack on Abailard in his letter to Innocent II: "Qui dum omnium quae sunt in coelo sursum, et quae in terra deorsum, nihil, praeter solum Nescio, nescire dignatur; ponit in coelum os suum, et scrutatur alta Dei, rediensque ad nos refert verba ineffabilia, quae non licet homini loqui: et dum paratus est de omnibus reddere rationem, etiam quae supra rationem, et contra rationem praesumit, et contra fidem" (*Contra quaedam capitula errorum Abaelardi, Epistola CXC seu Tractatus ad Innocentium II Pontificem* 1 [*PL*, CLXXXII, 1055A]).

complete reversal of literary criticism and philosophy; for it employs in defense of faith both the poetic devices of allegorical interpretation, which permit Bernard to criticize even the "profane novelties of words and senses" which Abailard introduced into his theological works, and also the philosophic arguments concerning self-knowledge and love, which echo the words of Socrates and prepare the matter, in prose and verse, of immortal poetry.[29]

All four of these conceptions of poetry, despite the oppositions among them, echo the judgment of Plato by which poets are condemned because philosophers are engaged on a more truly poetic enterprise. In the thirteenth century, poetry is no longer so close to philosophy or so dangerous a rival to it. Even after the translation of Aristotle's works, the influence of Platonism continued strong, particularly in the form in which the arts and philosophy serve as subordinate and preparatory stages to theology. Thus, for Bonaventura, poetry seems to

---

29. Cf. *Epistola CXCII ad Magistrum Guidonem de Castello* (PL, CLXXXII, 358C–D): "Magister Petrus in libris suis profanas vocum novitates inducit et sensuum: disputans de fide contra fidem, verbis legis legem impugnat. Nihil videt per speculum et in aenigmate; sed facie ad faciem omnia intuetur, ambulans in magnis et mirabilis super se. Melius illi erat, si juxta titulum libri sui, se ipsum cognosceret, nec agrederetur mensuram suam sed saperet ad sobrietatem." The last reproach refers to the title of Abailard's moral treatise, *Scito teipsum*. Abailard, on the other hand, accuses Bernard of introducing novelties, without authority and contrary to custom, into ecclesiastical matters, such as prayers, ritual, and the singing of hymns (cf. *Epistola X ad Bernardum Claraevallensem abbatem* [PL, CLXXVIII, 339]): "Si haec vestra novitas aut singularitas ab antiquitate recedat aliorum, quam rationi plurimum et tenori regulae creditis concordare: nec curatis quantacunque admiratione super hoc alii moveantur, ac murmurent, dummodo vestrae, quam putatis, rationi pareatis. Quorum ut pauca commemorem, pace vestra, hymnos solitos respuistis, et quosdam apud nos inauditos, et fere omnibus Ecclesiis incognitos, ac minus sufficientes, introduxistis. Unde et per totum annum in vigiliis tam feriarum quam festivitatum uno hymno et eodem contenti estis, cum Ecclesia pro diversitate feriarum vel festivitatum diversis utatur hymnis, sicut et psalmis, vel caeteris, quae his pertinere noscuntur: quod et manifesta ratio exigit. Unde et qui vos die Natalis, seu Paschae, vel Pentecostes, et caeteris solemnitatibus hymnum semper eumdem decantare audiunt, scilicet, *Aeterne rerum conditor*, summo stupore attoniti suspenduntur; nec tam admiratione quam derisione moventur." Despite his differences from Bernard's interpretation of its significance for philosophy, Abailard recognized the subordination of eloquence and philosophy to the wisdom of Christ (cf. *Hymnus LXV, Ad laudes et ad vesperas* [PL, CLXXVIII, 1805]):

> "Stulta seculi, mundi infima
> Christus eligens sapientia
> Quaeque conterit et sublimia.
>
> Nil urbanitas his rhetoricae,
> Nil verbositas [valet] logicae,
> Sed simplicitas fidei sacrae.
>
> Eloquentia cessit Tullü,
> 'Tace' dictum est Aristoteli;
> Leges proferunt mundo rustici.
>
> Perpes gloria."

For the discussion of the conceptions of love developed by Abailard and Bernard and their possible influences on the "courtly love" of poetic tradition, cf. E. Gilson, *La Théologie mystique de Saint Bernard* (Paris, 1934), pp. 183–89 and 193–215.

have become one of the mechanical arts. There are four lights by which the mind is illuminated: the exterior light of the mechanical arts, the inferior light of sensitive knowledge, the interior light of philosophic knowledge, and the superior light of grace and the Sacred Scriptures. The mechanical arts are concerned with the production of artificial things, which are classified, following the distinction made by Horace in the *Ars poetica*, as the useful and the delightful. Only one of the seven mechanical arts, the theater, is concerned with the delightful,[30] and under the theater Bonaventura includes all arts of play, whether of songs, instruments, figments, or gesticulations of the body. Grammar, logic, and rhetoric fall under the rational arts of philosophic knowledge, concerned, respectively, with apprehensive, judicative, and motive reason, and rhetoric therefore finds its function in moving to love or hate by means of ornate words. The treatment of the mechanical arts consists of three parts, which take account of the arts of the artificer, the quality of his effect, and the utility of his product or fruit; and Bonaventura concludes from such considerations that the illumination of the mechanical art is on the way to the illumination of Sacred Scripture and that nothing in it is not pertinent to true wisdom.[31]

The influence of Aristotle, on the other hand, had led in the thirteenth century to the establishment of a philosophy independent of theology in method and subject matter, and that philosophy likewise is not in opposition to poetry. Thomas Aquinas, thus, treats poetic not as the science of a product or process of production but as a subdivision of logic. Logic or rational science consists of eight parts, six of which correspond to the matter treated in the six books of Aristotle's *Organon*, to which rhetoric and poetic are added. Besides the parts of logic which treat of the certitudes of science and which are called Judicative, there are three parts which treat of the processes of discovery, often short of certitude, and which are called Inventive. Poetic is one of these. Dialectic treats of the process of discovery when it leads to conviction or opinion (*fides vel opinio*); rhetoric treats of it when it leads only to a kind of suspicion without total exclusion of the contrary possibility; poetic treats of it when estimation leads to one of the two parts of a contradiction only because of the manner of representation, as a man may be led to hold a certain food in abomination because it is represented to him under the likeness of something abominable. The specific function of the poet is to induce to virtue by fitting representation.[32]

30. *De reductione artium ad theologiam* 1–2 (*S. Bonaventurae opera omnia*, ed. Quaracchi, V [1891], 319–20).

31. *De reductione* 11–15 (*Opera omnia*, V, 322–23).

32. *In libros Posteriorum analyticorum expositio* i, Lectio 1 (*Opera omnia*, I [Rome, 1882], 138–40).

What philosophers say about poetry might have little bearing on the nature of poetry or of philosophy, if the grounds and consequences of their judgments were not clearly apparent in both. The repetitions in the twelfth century of Plato's moral criticisms of the poets, adapted to Christian theology and expressed with undiminished poetic force, suggest to the critic and the scholar several lines of inquiry in which the historical relations between poetry and philosophy may serve to elucidate some of the qualities and problems of poetry.

The approximation and rivalry of poetry and philosophy—one of the great commonplaces of Platonism which was, in its next recurrence during the Renaissance of the fifteenth and sixteenth centuries, to yield the victory to the poets—throws some light, in the first place, on the subject matters appropriate to poetry and philosophy. The twelfth century was a period in which poets and philosophers were engaged on the same themes, and the poetic expression of philosophy as well as the philosophic criticisms of poetry reflect the basic theological problem of the relation of reason and faith. This problem recurs in the great development of the liberal arts worked by philosophers like Bernard of Chartres, Thierry of Chartres, Abailard, Hugh of St. Victor, and John of Salisbury. But the liberal arts also furnished subject matter for poetry as various as the *Fons philosophiae* of Godefroy of St. Victor (in which the seven liberal arts are derived as streams from a single source, theology) and the numerous poems of Alan of Lille: the *De planctu naturae*, in which the arts of the trivium are considered in relation to the schools of Venus; the *Anticlaudianus*, in which the liberal arts construct a chariot for Prudence; and the mystic *rhythmus*, *On the Incarnation of Christ*, in which the seven liberal arts are applied to the Word of God. The methods of the liberal arts underlie the great cosmological speculations in which philosophers like Thierry of Chartres, Adelard of Bath, and William of Conches followed pagan inspirations related only occasionally to the account of Genesis. The same cosmological materials serve as subject matter for the poems of Bernard Sylvester and Alan of Lille, while enthusiasm concerning the creation of the world and of man is tempered by the recurrent theme *De contemptu mundi* in poets and philosophers like Bernard of Morlas, John of Salisbury, Hildebert of Lavardin, Alan of Lille, and Bernard. The same liberal arts are employed in the moral speculations to which twelfth-century philosophers returned, after the model of Socrates: the studies of passions and motives which Abailard develops in his ethical treatise *Scito teipsum* recur as poignant poetic subjects in his hymns and planctus; and Hildebert of Lavardin can turn from the collection of excerpts from moral philosophers, which constitute his *Moralis philosophia de honesto et utili*, to the vigorous verses in his *Libellus de quatuor virtutibus vitae honestae*.

The Platonic influence in the twelfth century, manifested in cosmological speculations inspired by the *Timaeus* and in Socratic inquiries into morals and method, runs through diversities which may be recapitulated in the interpretation of the Socratic dictum, "Know thyself." The concreteness of imaginative innovation and the richness of emotional antithesis developed in the interpretation of that dictum illustrate the use of philosophic issues by which they are made poetry, while the theoretic scope and opposition of the positions to which it was attached make it subject to numerous moral, cosmological, and mystic implications. Peter Abailard entitled his treatise on morals, *Know Thyself;* and for him self-knowledge is found in the specific analysis of actions, intentions, and sins, which constitute the abstract arguments of his ethics and are reflected in the concrete emotions of his lyrics and which lead, in turn, to his moral condemnation of poetry. Bernard Sylvester justified his allegorical interpretation of Virgil on the ground that it would assist man to know himself; and for him self-knowledge is attained through the analogies of literature, in which the career of a hero signifies the ages of man, and of nature, in which man is microcosm and the universe megacosm. "Know thyself" is the recurrent injunction of the mystics, of Bernard, William of St. Thierry, and Richard of St. Victor, for whom perfect self-knowledge was never attained by the philosophers, since man is the image of God, whom philosophers ignored. All these themes and issues are reflected finally in the philosophic analysis and poetic development of the concept of love, which is pervasively Platonic and persistently poetic, for it is the object of philosophical disputation and the source of poetry from the dialectical analyses and love songs of Abailard to the mystical developments of Bernard and William of St. Thierry and of Victorine and Cistercian poets.

The continuity of the subject matter of poetry and philosophy suggests a second inquiry into the methods and forms, which makes possible the transition from the interpretation of nature, art, and thought to the constructions of poetry and the demonstrations of philosophy. The common method is rhetoric, which assumes many forms and uses in the twelfth century. Abailard borrowed a method for philosophy from the procedures of canon law and laid the foundations of theological inquiry by assembling opposed authorities whose contradictions could be resolved by rhetorical devices, such as consideration of the circumstances under which the antithetical statements had been made; he was convinced, furthermore, that the intention of all divine Scripture is to teach and move in the manner of a rhetorical speech.[33] Matthew of Vendôme, in one of the earliest of the medieval treatises on the art of poetry, includes an analysis of

33. Cf. *Sic et non,* Prologus (*PL,* CLXXVIII, 1339–49), and *Commentaria super S. Pauli Epistolam ad Romanos,* Prologus (*PL,* CLXXVIII, 784).

poetry in a conversation between Philosophy and her four companions: Tragedy, Satire, Comedy, and Elegy. Elegy teaches Philosophy that the charm of poetry consists in three things: the content of the thought (*venustas interioris sententiae*), the form of the words (*superficialis ornatus verborum*), and the quality or rhetorical color of the expression (*modus dicendi* or *dicendi color*);[34] and the discussion of the "content of thought" consists in examining the verbal means of treating as subject matter of poetry such distinctions of character and emotion as might enter in their moral aspect into the philosophic discussions of virtue. Conrad of Hirschau, in one of the earliest histories of literature, the *Dialogus super auctores*, says that the treatment of ancient writers should consist of seven parts: author, title of work, quality of the poem, intention of the writer, order, number of books, and explanation, specifying that explanation is fourfold, with respect to letter, meaning, allegory, and morality. The explanation of modern writers, however, requires only four parts: the matter of the work, the intention of the writer, the final cause or fruit derived from reading the work, and the part of philosophy under which what is written falls; and the parts of philosophy are logic, physics, and ethics, the liberal arts being distributed under logic (the trivium) and physics (the quadrivium).[35]

The method of resolving differences in canon law, of posing theological and philosophical problems, and of interpreting poetry, finally, does not differ radically from the method expounded in the early treatises on the art of preaching; for Guibert of Nogent undertakes to justify the differentiation of the historical, allegorical, tropological, and anagogic modes of interpretation,[36] while Alan of Lille devotes himself to the consideration of the nature and subject matter of sermons, the quality of preachers, and the kinds of audiences; and he differentiates preaching from poetic composition by the fact that the preacher has no need for scurrilous or puerile words or melodies of rhythms and consonances of meters, such as might be suited to theatrical or mimic predication.[37]

34. *Ars versificatoria* ii. 4–11; iii. 1–2, ed. E. Faral, *Les Arts poétiques du XIIᵉ et du XIIIᵉ siècle* (Paris, 1924), pp. 152–54, 167–68.

35. *Conradi Hirsaugiensis Dialogus super auctores sive Didascalon*, ed. G. Schepss (Würzburg, 1889), pp. 27–28, 74–84. Dante follows a similar conception of criticism in the sixfold division which he makes of his Introduction to the *Paradiso* in his letter to Can Grande della Scala (*Epistola* X, 7): "Sex igitur sunt, quae in principio cujusque *doctrinalis Operis* inquirenda sunt, videlicet *Subjectum, Agens, Forma, Finis, libri Titulus*, et *Genus philosophiae*." The kind of philosophy under which the *Divine Comedy* falls is ethics; cf. *ibid.* 16: "*Genus* vero *philosophiae*, sub quo hic in Toto et Parte proceditur, est *morale Negotium*, sive *Ethica*, qui non ad speculandum, sed ad opus inceptum est Totum. Nam, etsi in aliquo loco vel passu pertractatur ad modum speculativi negotii, hoc non est gratia speculativi negotii, sed gratia operis; quia, ut ait Philosophus in secundo *Metaphysicorum*, 'ad aliquid et tunc speculantur practici aliquando.' "

36. *Liber quo ordine sermo fieri debeat* (*PL*, CLVI, 22–32, and esp. 25–26).

37. *Summa de arte praedicatoria* 1 and 39 (*PL*, CCX, 111–12, and 184). Chap. 39 states the threefold division of the treatise which reduces the fivefold scheme announced in the

In the art of preaching, subject matter is found and examined in the nature and origin of the virtues and vices, in the contempt of world and of self, and in the kinds of men and the means by which they are moved; and the fourfold method of reading is applied by the writers of the twelfth century to the interpretation of nature, which is an image of God, as well as of poetry and Scripture. Rhetoric is the connecting link not only among such divergent matters but also between Platonism and the increasing knowledge of the Aristotelian logic. The Aristotelian logic and the Platonic dialectic are at cross-purposes, but the Aristotelian and Platonic conceptions of rhetoric are homogeneous; for, according to Aristotle, rhetoric is characterized by its figurative language, while logic requires univocal terms and dialectic distinguishes among definitions, and, according to Plato, rhetoric, unless it is identified with dialectic, is imperfect dialectic based on insufficient knowledge of subject matter and expressed in language uncorrelated with fact. In the mystic theology, in which matters of faith are beyond the scope of reason and all things and all words have allegorical and mystical significances, the method which joins poetry to philosophy and Plato to Aristotle passes beyond all such matters to serve as surrogate for all techniques of inquiry or literal statement.

Questions of matter and form, however, suggest the third and basic question of poetic value. The philosophers of the twelfth century speculate about and write a kind of poetry whose subject matter—apart from love lyrics, drinking songs, and a few satires—has seemed by later standards unpoetic. Their poetry often employs allegorical devices of exposition and, whatever the style, is designed to be read according to an allegorical interpretation, whereas the modern reader, even when he can recognize allegorical meanings, seldom employs them as a means of discerning and appreciating poetic values. The poetry of the Middle Ages, like all great poetry, can be appreciated by other critical standards than those according to which it was conceived. Yet the poetic qualities on which the different interpretations fix seem to be the same, despite the differences of meaning attached to them. Modern readers find a literal trait of character or emotion or a concrete episode among unnoticed allegorical, moral, and anagogic significances, and they savor vague didactic allusions without feeling a temptation to determine what part of philosophy the poem falls under. What they find in medieval poetry is the ingenious and colored language, the concrete confrontation of emotion and intention which is the outer surface of the Socratic self-knowledge, the passionate moral aspiration, the partially understood didactic intention, and the grandiose mystic definition of

---

Praefatio along lines reminiscent of Aristotle and Cicero: "Dicto, quorum debeat esse praedicatio, et quales esse oporteant praedicatores, restat ostendere, quibus proponenda sit praedicatio."

the relation of man and God. The transformations of value and the continuities which make possible the discovery of values in related or identical qualities by different modes of analysis and criticism serve to isolate some of the basic problems of aesthetics. They are problems which are underscored for us by the poetry and philosophy of the twelfth century; for poetry is related to philosophy today in methods and matters as different as those of existentialism, Marxism, and pragmatism, and it has again returned to themes similar to those of medieval poetry and to echoes of philosophical and theological discussion which recall that man is in a grave predicament, that words are ambiguous, and that the church or its apostle is a hippopotamus and God is mysterious. A language which echoes folklore and religion has been constructed for poetry; subject matter is found in the motives and confusions of man set forth in simple unresolved oppositions; moral problems are made poetic by obscuring suggestions of resolution; and poetry may be didactic if its lessons are vague, or metaphysical if it is without commitment to a philosophy, or religious if religion furnishes a restraint to sentiment in the construction of figures. Philosophers and poets in the twelfth century were engaged on a single set of problems; poets in the twentieth century convey a sense of treating philosophic problems, but their philosophy has become little more than a play with the colors of language which medieval poets employed to express a philosophy.

ROBORTELLO ON THE *POETICS*

BERNARD WEINBERG

THE first full-scale exposition of the *Poetics* was contained in the commentary of Francesco Robortello published at Florence in 1548.[1] Of the various forms in which Aristotle's treatise had appeared earlier, Robortello knew only four: the Averroës paraphrase in the Latin translation (first printed in 1481), the Giorgio Valla translation into Latin of 1498, the *editio princeps* of the Greek text of 1508, and Alessandro de' Pazzi's Latin translation of 1536.[2] In none of these or in the other texts or translations had any attempt been made to expound the meaning of the document. After Robortello, however, major commentaries on the *Poetics* abound: Maggi and Lombardi's in 1550, Vettori's in 1560, Castelvetro's in 1570, Alessandro Piccolomini's in 1575, Riccoboni's in 1579 and 1587, to mention only the most extensive ones.[3] What these later commentators had to say about the text was closely related to Robortello's statements, either by acceptance or by rejection, and his name constantly recurs on their pages. Moreover, later theorists working in France and England in the seventeenth and eighteenth centuries continued to refer back to the 1548 text.[4] If Aristotle's work, through its transformations and deformations, is at the basis of the classical doctrine in European criticism, Robortello's lengthy interpretation of the work is the first step in the formation of that doctrine. What emerges from Robortello's study of the text will

1. This is the third of a series of analyses of important works on the poetic art written during the Italian Renaissance. The first, "The Poetic Theories of Minturno," appeared in *Studies in Honor of Frederick W. Shipley* ("Washington University Studies" [St. Louis, Mo., 1942]), pp. 101–29; the second, "Scaliger versus Aristotle on Poetics," in *Modern Philology*, XXXIX (1942), 337–60. A fourth, on Castelvetro's commentary on the *Poetics*, follows in this volume (pp. 349–71). In preparing the present analysis I have used a copy of the 1548 edition, graciously lent me by the University of Illinois libraries for an extended period: *Francisci Robortelli Utinensis in librum Aristotelis de Arte poetica explicationes* (Florence, 1548). I have also used, and in part collated, the copy of the 1555 Basel edition in the University of Chicago Library. For additional applications of the method of analysis used here, the reader is referred to the Introduction to my *Critical Prefaces of the French Renaissance* (Evanston, Ill.: Northwestern University Press, 1950).

2. For bibliographical indications see Cooper and Gudeman, *A Bibliography of the Poetics of Aristotle* (New Haven, 1928), items 108, 109, 1, and 4.

3. *Ibid.*, items 16, 20, 24, 200, 140, and 146.

4. E.g., Jean Chapelain, *Opuscules critiques* (Paris: Droz, 1936), p. 503; Thomas Twining, *Aristotle's Treatise on Poetry* (London, 1789), p. 324 n. Of course, Robortello's influence waned as first the late Italian critics (Castelvetro, Piccolomini, Riccoboni) and then the Dutch scholars (Heinsius, Vossius) became the accepted authorities.

in a significant way determine the general orientation of "Aristotelian" criticism during the following centuries.

If Robortello had no previous expositor of the *Poetics* to rely on, he was thoroughly familiar with a large body of relevant materials which he could bring to bear upon his commentary. He worked with one of the Medici manuscripts of the *Poetics* and with two other manuscripts in his own possession; these he used to correct the available printed texts. He knew Horace's *Ars poetica* word for word; he knew, especially, a large group of rhetorical documents: Aristotle's *Rhetoric*, Cicero, Quintilian, Dionysius of Halicarnassus, Demetrius, and other lesser texts. He knew, sufficiently to disdain it, the current notion of tragedy and comedy stemming from Donatus and Diomedes. Last of all, he was completely conversant with Greek poetry in all genres and with major works of Latin poetry which might serve as examples of his theories.

His commentary follows the traditional Renaissance form: a section of the Greek text (there are 270 such divisions), followed by the corresponding section of the Pazzi translation, reproduced almost verbatim, then by the commentary itself. It is in this last part that Robortello discusses textual matters, corrects the translation, expounds on the ideas, cites supporting texts and illustrative examples. Besides this central portion of the work, there is a dedication to Cosimo de' Medici, a Prologue entitled "De materie, et fine poeticae facultatis," a separate section at the end of the volume containing a *Paraphrasis in librum Horatio . . . De arte poetica* and several short treatises, *De satyra, De epigrammate, De comoedia, De salibus,* and *De elegia.*[5]

I

Much of the construction that Robortello puts upon passages in the *Poetics* results from his own conception of the end of the poetic art. This he states succinctly in his Prologue and develops later in the course of the commentary. The end seems to be triple. First, there is the dual Horatian end of pleasure and utility: "Poetry, if we consider it carefully, bends all its efforts toward delighting, although it also does profit."[6] Besides, there is the Aristotelian end of imitation: "And since this imitation or representation is produced by means of discourse, we may say that the end of poetry is language which imitates, just as that of rhetoric is language which persuades."[7] Those two kinds of end are

5. These shorter treatises have not been referred to, since their doctrine is essentially the same as that of the major commentary. In the text following, translations are my own. References to Aristotle's *Poetics* are to the edition of J. Hardy ("Association Guillaume Budé" [Paris, 1932]).

6. "Poëtice, siquis diligenter attendat, omnem suam vim confert ad oblectandum, & si prodest quoque" (p. 2).

7. "Et quoniam imitatio, & repręsentatio hęc per orationem fit; dicimus in poëtice finem esse, sermonem imitantem, sicut in rhetorice sermonem persuadentem" (p. 2).

brought together in such a passage as this (commenting on 1448ᵇ4): "Poetry thus sets a double end for itself, one of which is prior to the other; the prior end is to imitate, the other to delight."[8] If these three ends are present, several questions of primary importance for the analysis of Robortello's position at once arise: Can we discover, in the commentary, that one of these three ends is the essential and important one, to which the others are auxiliary? Is any one of the three the final end, to which the others are instrumental? Or are all three on an equal level, with the interrelationship among them ambiguous? To answer these questions, we must inquire further into the character of each end as it emerges in the course of the commentary.

The nature of the pleasure derived from poetry is further specified in the passage from the Prologue already cited:

> There is, indeed, for men no greater pleasure, truly worthy of a man of refinement, than that which is perceived by the mind and by thought; it frequently happens that things which arouse horror and terror in men as long as they are in their own nature, once they are taken out of nature and represented in some form resembling nature, give great pleasure. . . . What other end, therefore, can we say that the poetic faculty has than to delight through the representation, description, and imitation of every human action, every emotion, every thing animate as well as inanimate?[9]

Two salient features of this passage must be emphasized; first, that the pleasure is achieved *through* the imitation, which thus becomes an intermediate end; second, that the imitation is not only of human actions and passions (as in Aristotle) but of all kinds of objects as well. This will have later consequences. The pleasure involved is a natural one: "for men are born with a capacity for imitation, and in all men nature implants the ability to derive pleasure from imitation or from things expressed through imitation."[10]

The nature of the utility derived from poetry is much more explicitly and more frequently specified. Once again, the key passage is found in Robortello's Prologue:

> For, just as poetic readings and imitations are of various kinds, so they bring to men a multiple utility. If, on the one hand, the reading (or performance) and imitation consist in the virtue and the praise of some excellent man, people are incited to virtue; if, on the other hand, vices are represented, people are strongly deterred from those vices, and

8. "Finem enim duplicem habet sibi propositum poëtice, alterum altero priorem: Prior est imitari. Altero vero est, oblectare" (p. 30).

9. "Nulla verò inter homines maior voluptas, quae quidem liberali homine digna sit, quàm quae mente, & cogitatione percipitur; imò saepè contingit, vt quae horrorem, & terrorem incutiunt hominibus, dum in propria natura sunt, extrà naturam posita in quapiam similitudine, dum repraesentantur; multum oblectent. . . . Quem igitur alium finem poëtices facultatis esse dicemus, quàm oblectare per repraesentationem, descriptionem, & imitationem omnium actionum humanarum; omnium motionum; omnium rerum tùm animatarum, tùm inanimatarum?" (p. 2).

10. "nam homines apti nati sunt ad imitandum, & omnibus à natura insitum est, voluptatem percipere ex imitatione, seu ex rebus expressis per imitationem" (p. 30).

they are driven away from them with much greater force than if you were to use any other form of persuasion. If the imitation and performance on the stage is of horrible things and of perils, the temerity and the insane audacity of men is diminished; but if things worthy of pity should be represented, the minds of the auditors are bent toward gentleness and pity. What more need I say? Every imitation and every poetic perform-ance accompanied by action pulls, softens, drives, incites, touches, inflames the souls of men. . . . [Strabo] says that poets are the directors and the correctors of life, once called by the ancients the σωφρονιστάς. That great man makes it sufficiently clear that poetry was formerly a kind of philosophy which, through its fables, gradually suckled and nurtured men until the time when they would be more capable of understanding things in philosophy which are most difficult; for, since these things are troublesome and hard, men can easily be turned away from that most worthy study.[11]

In his commentary on that part of Aristotle's definition of tragedy relevant to purgation (1449[b]27), Robortello indicates in even greater detail how the spec-tators are benefited:

Thus when men are present at performances, and they hear and see people saying and doing things which very closely approach truth itself, they become accustomed to suffering, to fearing, to pitying; this, in turn, causes them, when they themselves un-dergo the common lot of all men, to suffer less and to fear less. Indeed, it is absolutely inevitable that one who has never grieved over any calamity whatsoever will afterward suffer exceedingly, should any misfortune befall him contrary to his expectation. Add to this the fact that men frequently are sorry and afraid inappropriately. But when the poets in the performance of their tragedies present persons and actions most worthy of pity and which any man, even a wise man, would rightfully dread, men learn what those things are which properly excite pity and sorrow, and which ones arouse fear. Finally, the auditors and spectators of tragedies gain this benefit, which is really the greatest one, that, since the fate of all mortal men is the same and since there is nobody who is not subject to disasters, men learn to bear more easily the befalling of misfortune, and surely they are most vigorously sustained by this consolation, that they remember the same thing to have happened to others.[12]

11. "Recitationes autem, & imitationes poëticae vt sunt multiplices, ita multiplicem af-ferunt hominibus vtilitatem; Nam si recitatio, atque imitatio virtutum fit, & laudum praeclari alicuius viri; incitantur homines ad virtutem: Si rursus vitia repraesentantur, ab his homines multum deterrentur; maioréque quadam ui repelluntur, quàm si alia quauis hortatione vtaris. Quòd si horribilium rerum, & periculorum imitatio, & recitatio in scena fiat; comminuitur hominum amens audacia, & temeritas. Sin autem commiseranda fuerint acta; eorum, qui audiunt mentes ad mansuetudinem, & commiserationem inflectuntur. Quid multis? imitatio omnis, & recitatio poëtica cum actione coniuncta hominum animos peruellit, emollit, vrget, incitat, frangit, inflammat. . . . [Strabo] poëtas ait esse vitae magistros, & correctores, appellatosque olim à veteribus σωφρονιστάς. Illud vnum certè satis constat poëticam olim fuisse quandam philosophiam, quae homines suis fabulis paulatim lactaret, & enutriret, donec aptiores essent ad percipienda ea, quae in philosophia difficillima habebantur; nam aspera, & dura cum essent, facilè à tam laudato studio homines deterreri potuissent" (pp. 3–4).

12. "Dum enim homines intersunt recitationibus; audiuntque & cernunt personas lo-quentes & agentes ea, quae multum accedunt ad veritatem ipsam; assuescunt dolere, timere; commiserari; quo fit, vt cum aliquid ipsis humanitus acciderit, minus doleant, & timeant, necesse est enim prorsus, vt qui nunquam indoluerit ob aliquam calamitatem, vehementius posteà doleat, siquid aduersi praeter spem acciderit. Adde quòd sepè homines perperàm dolent, ac timent; dum autem poëtae in recitationibus suarum tragoediarum offerunt per-

The utility is then essentially an ethical one, achieved through rhetorical means; men discover through poetry man's common fate, they learn what characters and events are worthy of dread and of commiseration, they achieve a capacity to moderate their own passions when adversity strikes. In this utility Robortello sees an exact agreement between Aristotle and Plato (as interpreted by Proclus):

> Aristotle approves of the opinion of Plato, in so far as he does not wish the imitation of the behavior of wicked men to be made in tragedy or in any other poems, except perhaps in comedy. . . . Plato does not approve of the mixture of good and bad persons; for, if poetry has always as its sole aim to make a useful contribution to the education of men, it must not imitate any kind of men except those who are good and wise. For, if there is a mixture of good and bad men in the poem, because of the fact that men by their very nature are more prone to pleasure than to virtue and wisdom, it is inevitable that their morals will be corrupted, since they will attempt to make themselves like the bad rather than like the good.[13]

Still another utility, perhaps of a more positive character, is found in such special forms as the *tragoedia morata:*

> An ethical tragedy is one in which many things are said relevant to the regulation of life and in which the poet undertakes this exceedingly difficult task of expressing the sacredness of moral standards and the probity of behavior in individual persons; and he sets forth precepts and certain common maxims by which men are admonished to follow virtue and to do those things which are honorable.[14]

In these passages on the various ends of poetry, it becomes clear that the end of imitation is an intermediate end, producing beyond itself either pleasure or utility of the moral kind so completely outlined. As to the primacy of either pleasure or utility, however, I find no specific indication in the text, no passage

---

sonas, ac res dignissimas commiseratione, quasque iure vnusquisque, vel sapiens, extimescat; discunt homines qualia sint ea, quae iure commiserationem cieant, & luctum, quaeque metum incutiant. Postremò auditores, & spectatores tragoediarum hanc capiunt vtilitatem, quae prorsus maxima est, cum enim communis sit omnium mortalium fortuna, nullusque sit, qui calamitatibus non sit subiectus; facilius ferunt homines, si quid aduersi acciderit, eoque se solatio planè firmissimo sustentant, quòd aliis etiam idem accidisse meminerint" (p. 53; cf. also p. 102).

13. "Probauit autem Platonis sententiam Aristoteles, quatenus improborum non vult morum imitationem fieri in tragoedia, neque aliis poëmatibus, nisi forte in comoedia. . . . Plato non probat hanc mistam varietatem, quia si poësis hoc sibi habet vnum propositum semper, vt vtilitatem afferat institutioni hominum; non est necesse imitari vllum hominum genus, praeter bonos, & sapientes; nam si varietas insit in poëmate, illa cum homines suapte natura propensiores ad voluptatem sint, quàm ad virtutem, & sapientiam, necesse est vt illorum mores corrumpantur; dum student illis similes esse" (pp. 166, 165–66). I have inverted the order of the two passages.

14. "Morata tragoedia est, in qua multa proferuntur, quae ad vitam instituendam spectant, isque potissimum labor est Poëtae propositus, vt sanctitatem morum exprimat, & probitatem in singulis personis; praeceptionesque tradat, & γνώμας quasdam communes, quibus admonentur homines; vt virtutem sequantur; & ea agant, quae honesta sunt" (p. 211).

which definitely affirms either to be the ultimate and important end. If we may take the amount of discussion devoted to each or the specificity of the discussion as a sign, then we may be led to believe that Robortello probably was more concerned with the end of utility. But this is by no means a proof of his position.

It becomes immediately apparent not only that the different ends of pleasure and utility are achieved by different means but that they result from different parts of the poem itself. Moreover, each separate kind of utility has its source in a separate poetic element. Neither is the pleasure a concomitant of the utility, nor is the utility a resultant of the total structure of the poem. Rather, Robortello proceeds by a fragmentation of the work and an analysis of what each fragment contributes toward one of the separate ends.

The case is especially clear with respect to utility. If we look back at the passages already cited, we discover that moral betterment derives from three separate sources: there are lessons from the fortunes of men, there are lessons from the characters of men, there are lessons from maxims or *sententiae*. Let us take the fortunes of men first. The conclusion that fate strikes all men equally, that men pass quickly from happiness to unhappiness, is deduced not from a study of men's characters but from the contemplation of the actions in which they are involved; hence it is related to the plot or the *fabula* of the play. The representation of such a plot on the stage is a powerful moral instrument:

> Indeed, the representation or action on the stage joins together with the mind and the imagination of men in, I know not what way, the image of the things which are represented, and acts upon the senses almost as if it were the thing itself. Furthermore, this representation is very powerful in moving and rousing the souls of men to anger and rage, on the one hand, or, on the other hand, in calling them back to gentleness and in softening them; now exciting them to pity, to sorrow, and tears, now to laughter and joy.[15]

But this effect is produced only if the representation is "as if it were the thing itself"; that is, the degree to which an action in a poem resembles an action in life will determine the degree of its moral effectiveness. Hence the criterion of truth to life and credibility enters as a fundamental consideration in any discussion of the actions of poems. The problem is a real one and a difficult one; for, essentially, poetry differs from the other arts of discourse in taking for its subject matter things which are not true. Again, the position is stated by Robortello in his Prologue:

15. "Repraesentatio enim, seu actio Scenica coniungit, nescio quo modo, cum cogitatione, & phantasia hominum imaginem rei, quę repręsentatur; & agitur quasi rem ipsam cum sensu. Magnam autem habet vim huiusmodi repręsentatio in commouendis, & inflammandis hominum animis, tum ad iram, & furorem; tum ad mansuetudinem reuocandis, & emolliendis, tum concitandis ad commiserationem, ad fletum & lacrymas; tum ad risum, & laetitiam" (p. 3).

Since, then, poetics has as its subject matter fictitious and fictional discourse, it is clear that the function of poetics is to invent in a proper way its fiction and its untruth; to no other art is it more fitting than to this one to intermingle lies. . . . In the lies used by the poetic art, false elements are taken as true, and from them true conclusions are derived.[16]

If from these fictional elements an impression of truth is to be obtained, the *plot* itself (episodes and decorations will fall into a special category) must contain actions belonging to one of three kinds: "For poetics speaks only of those actions which exist, or which can exist, or which have existed according to the ancient opinion of men"[17]—i.e., the true, the possible, the traditional. The true is the best: "we should try, if it is at all possible, to treat true actions."[18] The possible or probable is next best—"but, if not, we should invent new ones according to the probable."[19] This was the practice of ancient poets:

The ancient poets who wrote tragedies were accustomed not only to collect those calamities which actually happened and to express them in their plots in the same way in which they occurred but also to invent others out of other calamities according to the probable.[20]

In so far as a poet uses a true plot, he does not invent, and hence his work resembles the activity of a historian; his truly poetic activity, as we shall see, bears upon elements other than the plot. If he creates in accordance with probability, then he is an inventor on the level of plot as well. The whole range of possibilities is summarized by Robortello in his commentary on *Poetics* 1460ᵇ7:

The things, actions, and persons which a poet imitates are either true or invented. If true, they either exist now or did exist, or they are living or died long ago. If they exist and are living, the poet imitates them in two ways, either as they are commonly said to be or as they seem to be. If they are neither living nor exist, but died long ago, they are still imitated in these two ways, either as general opinion reports them to have been or as they seem to have been. If the persons are invented by the poet himself, he imitates and expresses them as it is fitting and proper that they should be.[21]

---

16. "Cum igitur poëtice subiectam sibi habeat pro materie orationem fictam, & fabulosam; patet ad poëticen pertinere, ut fabulam, & mendacium aptè confingat; nulliúsque alterius artis proprium. magis esse; mendacia comminisci, quàm huius. . . . in poëticis mendaciis principia falsa pro veris assumuntur. atque ex his verae eliciuntur conclusiones" (p. 2).

17. "Nam poëtice loquitur de iis tantum rebus, aut quę sunt, aut quae esse possunt. aut quas uetus est apud homines opinio, esse" (p. 2).

18. "danda est opera, vt si fieri possit, circa veras actiones versemur" (p. 219).

19. "Sin minus, nouas ex verisimili confingamus" (p. 219).

20. "Poëtae veteres, qui tragoedias scripserunt; non tantum ipsas calamitates, quae acciderant, colligere, eoque modo exprimere solitos in suis fabulis, quo acciderant, consueuisse; sed etiam ex aliis calamitates confingere secundum probabile" (p. 139).

21. "res, actiones, & personę quas imitatur, poëta, aut verae sunt, aut fictae. Si verae, aut sunt aut fuerunt, vel enim viuunt; vel iamdiu interierunt. Si sunt, ac viuunt duplici modo has imitatur poëta, aut quales aiunt vulgò esse, aut videntur esse. Si non viuunt, neq. sunt; sed iamdiu interierunt, imitatur etiam has duplici modo; aut quales rumor est fuisse, aut quales videntur fuisse. Si personae fictae sunt ab ipso poëta, eas imitatur; exprimitque, quales esse conuenit, & oportet" (p. 290).

It will be noted that, from this apparently exhaustive set of distinctions, Robortello omits the notion of imitation of things as they are. This is not accidental. "True" is equated with "said to be" and "seem to be" rather than with "are" for the simple reason that the realm of the poet is, after all, the fictitious. If he treats things as they are, then he trespasses upon the domain of the historian. The historian alone "narrat res gestas, vt gestae fuerint"; the poet, in so far as he imitates real things and does not invent, "narrat res, vt geri debuerint"; when he invents, "narrat res vt geri potuerint, secundum probabile, aut verisimile" (p. 89). The exclusion of the real or the actual is made specific in various places (cf. p. 89, "non quidem, vt acta fuerit," and p. 86, "patet igitur poëtam non insistere veritati").

It is by this line of reasoning that Robortello arrives at his interpretation of Aristotle's τὰ δυνατὰ κατὰ τὸ εἰκος, ἤ τὸ ἀναγκαῖον (1451ᵃ38); at his own theory of the possible, the probable, and the necessary; and at his central doctrine of credibility as determining the moral effect of the action. The true is credible, hence moving; the verisimilar is moving only in so far as it resembles the true. The whole argument is presented in the passage expounding 1451ᵇ15:

Tragedy has as its purpose to arouse two of the major passions of the soul—pity and fear. Now it is much more difficult to arouse these than others which agitate in a more pleasant way, such as hope, laughter, and others of this kind. For men by their very nature are prone to pleasant things but averse to unpleasant ones; they cannot, therefore, easily be impelled to sorrow. It is thus necessary for them first to know that the thing actually happened in that way. Thus if a tragic plot contained an action which did not really take place and was not true, but was represented by the poet himself in accordance with verisimilitude, it would perhaps move the souls of the auditors, but certainly less. For, if verisimilar things give us pleasure, all the pleasure derives from the fact that we know these things to be present in the truth; and, in general, to the extent that the verisimilar partakes of truth it has the power to move and to persuade. . . . If verisimilar things move us, the true will move us much more. Verisimilar things move us because we *believe* it to have been possible for the event to come about in this way. True things move us because we *know* that it did come about in this way. Whatever virtue is thus contained in verisimilitude is derived totally from its relationship to truth.[22]

22. "Habet sibi propositum tragoedia mouere duas maximas perturbationes animi commiserationem, & metum; multò verò difficilius est, has mouere, quàm reliquas, quae iucundius perturbant, qualis est spes, risus, & huiusmodi. sunt enim suaptè natura homines ad iucundas res proni; ab iniucundis autem alieni; non facilè igitur ad luctum possunt impelli. necesse est igitur, vt sciant prius rem ita cecidisse; quod si fabula tragica actionem contineat, quae non acta sit, neque sit vera; sed ab ipso poëta fuerit efficta secundum verisimile; commouebit fortasse animos audientium, at minus certè. nam verisimilia si nos oblectant, oblectatio omnis inde prouenit, quòd in veris inesse ea scimus; & omnino quatenus verisimile veritatis est particeps vim habet mouendi, ac persuadendi. . . . si nos verisimilia mouent, multo magis vera mouebunt. Verisimilia nos mouent, quia fieri potuisse credimus, ita rem accidisse. Vera nos mouent, quia scimus ita accidisse, quicquid igitur vis est in verisimili, id totum arripit à vero" (p. 93).

This passage relates credibility to verisimilitude and verisimilitude to truth. Other terms relevant to the action in a poem are treated elsewhere. The false and the impossible are never acceptable: "The poetic faculty rejects those things which are absolutely false"; "poetry errs in its imitation whenever it tries to express something which is impossible or completely unbelievable."[23] The necessary is the same as the true, consisting of those things which had happened or been done; as a critical term, it must then have the same meaning as the "true" and refer not to real existence but to possibility and opinion. The possible consists of those things which can be done (τὰ δυνατά) and subdivides into the necessary and the probable. If to this subdivision we add another one, that affecting unnatural and incredible objects (for these under certain circumstances are admissible into certain poems), we get another exhaustive distinction as follows:

Duplici modo fingere, & mentiri poëtas:
1. in rebus secundum naturam (the possible)
    a) τὸ ἀναγκαῖον (the necessary)
    b) τὸ εἰκός (the probable)
2. in rebus praeter naturam (the impossible)
    a) quae receptae iam sunt in opinionem vulgi (the traditional)
    b) non antè unquam auditis, aut narratis ab alio (the newly invented)

Even in the last two cases, however, a basis of credibility must be established, and this is done through sophistic persuasion ("ex paralogismo autem in primis deducuntur, quotiescunque falsa pro veris sumuntur").[24] Robortello in this way establishes a hierarchy of kinds of action susceptible of treatment in poems, with credibility as the criterion. At the top, the true, the real, the actual; but, although this is the most credible, it is not acceptable to poetry. Next, the various degrees of the possible: the necessary, which involves "true" actions as they should be or as they seem to be; the probable or verisimilar, which involves "invented" actions having the essential characteristics of "true" actions. The possible is the proper realm of the poet. Finally, there is the impossible or the false, which, because it is incredible, has no place in poetry, no persuasive power, no possible moral effect. But it is occasionally admitted when the poet can succeed in giving it a semblance of credibility.

In tragedy the special device for transforming credible action into moral utility is purgation. We have already seen (p. 326 above) the main passage in which the character of this utility is described. A further discussion is to be

---

23. "patet poëticen facultatem . . . reiicere ea, quae prorsus sunt falsa"; "quotiescunque poëtica in imitatione peccat; neque seruat, necessarium, ac verisimile, conaturque exprimere aliquid, quod impossibile sit; praeterq. omnem fidem" (pp. 284, 292).

24. P. 87.

found in the commentary on 1452ª1 ff. (pp. 99–100), where additional ideas are presented. First, and perhaps most important, is the notion that fear and pity are separable and independent effects; pity may appear alone in a given tragedy, in combination with fear in another. Second, either or both of these effects may be—indeed, must be—accompanied by the marvelous, which produces admiration in the spectators and results from recognition and reversal. Neither fear nor the marvelous may appear alone; but in combination with pity they produce the following possible types of plots:

1. Pity alone } simple plots
2. Pity and fear
3. Pity and the marvelous } complex plots
4. Pity, fear, and the marvelous

Third, certain types of actions, partaking of the marvelous, produce a religious or superstitious feeling which, in turn, produces fear and pity, "since they [the spectators] esteem that these things can happen to themselves and they fear lest at some time they might happen to them."[25]

If we now look back at the various passages on the action of poems in its relationship to utility, we shall discover the noteworthy fact that in many of these passages Robortello speaks of representation or performance (rather than merely of imitation) and of the effect upon spectators (rather than on readers). At several other points in his commentary he makes clear why this is done. The art of imitation is really two arts, a *poetic* art concerned with the writing of poems and a *histrionic* art concerned with their performance:

Representation, therefore, is not only poetic but also histrionic; yet the two are different one from the other in that actors have the faculty and the power of imitating and representing the characters, the passions, the persons, and the actions of men suitably for the belief and the persuasion of the auditors and the spectators. But the poet merely exercises all his power in expressing and describing the characters of men; so that the latter makes a kind of mute representation put in words, while the former, speaking and expressing through the voice, the mouth, the face, the gesture [creates] the very thing which is to be imitated.[26]

Note that the poetic art proper concerns itself only with character and has no effectiveness in the field of action. This division of functions is made even clearer in Robortello's commentary on *Poetics* 1449ᵇ31:

25. "quòd existimant ea quoque sibi posse accidere; metuuntque, ne eadem sibi aliquando accidant" (p. 102).

26. "Repręsentatio autem non tantum poëtica est, sed & histrionica; differunt tamen inter se; nam histriones habent facultatem, & vim imitandi, & repręsentandi mores; motiones, personas, & actiones hominum accommodatè ad fidem, & persuasionem audientium, & spectantium. Poëta verò vim suam omnem tantùm exercet in significandis, & describendis moribus hominum; vt hic mutam faciat veluti quandam repraesentationem in oratione positam; ille loquentem, & exprimentem voce, ore, vultu, gestu idipsum, quod est repraesentandum" (pp. 2–3).

It should be noted, in fact, that the imitation in tragedy may be considered in two ways, either in so far as it is scenic and is acted by the actors or in so far as it is made by the poet as he writes. If you think of it in terms of the poet who writes, then we may say that the principal end of tragedy is to imitate the nature of souls and the characters of men through written words; through which description it is possible to discern whether men are happy or unhappy. If you assume it to refer to the actor as he acts, then we may say that the greatest and most powerful end is that very action as a result of which men are judged to be happy or unhappy. In the writing and the imitation of the poets some such order as the following is established, if you follow nature: *character*, from which comes *happiness* or *unhappiness*. But in the action on the stage of the actor as he recites, in this way: *action*, from which comes *happiness* or *unhappiness*.[27]

Thus all that has previously been said about action belongs really to the histrionic art, and the moral utility deriving from the actions of certain poems is a product of the actor's art rather than of the poet's.

In the light of these ideas, one of Robortello's most puzzling statements about poetics becomes significant. In *Poetics* 1450ª10, Aristotle indicated that the six parts of tragedy (plot, character, thought, diction, song, and spectacle) might be distributed thus among the constitutive elements of poetry: three to the object, two to the means, and one to the manner of imitation. Robortello provides such a distribution, and in it plot (which in the Aristotelian text must be one of the objects of imitation) becomes the one part belonging to the manner of imitation; the manner is dramatic, what is acted is the action or plot, hence the plot is the part of tragedy belonging to the manner of imitation. He even goes on to demonstrate how that part of the means especially germane to stage presentation—spectacle or apparatus—is in a sense the end of tragedy and contains all the other parts inherent within itself.[28]

To recapitulate: one of the kinds of moral utility derived from poems—the lessons learned from the actions of men—is a result of the plot of the poem.

27. "Notandum verò . . . tragoediae imitationem duplici modo considerari; aut quatenus scenica est, & ab histrionibus agitur, aut quatenus à poëta fit scribente. Si quatenus à scribente poëta intelligas, dicimus primarium in tragoedia finem esse imitari, habitum animi, & mores hominum per orationem scriptam; ex qua descriptione homines cerni possunt an felices, an verò infelices sint. Si quatenus histrio agens eam refert, sumas . . . dicimus maximum, aç potissimum finem esse ipsam actionem, ex qua homines diiudicantur aut felices, aut infelices. In scriptione & imitatione poëtarum talis ordo constituitur, si naturam sequaris. MORES, ex quibus FELICITAS, aut INFELICITAS. In actione verò scenica recitantium histrionum, huiusmodi. ACTIO. ex qua FELICITAS, aut NFELICITAS" (p. 58; cf. also p. 240).

28. "Probat verò alia quadam ratione esse sex, per tres videlicet notas illas differentias, quae in principio libri appositae fuerunt, & declaratae. Sunt autem hae, οἶς. ὡς. ἄ. Per primam differentiam scilicet οἶς, quae instrumentum significat velut quoddam. Per secundam differentiam scilicet ὡς; quae modum significat, ex quo imitatio diuersitatem sumit. Per tertiam differentiam scilicet ἅ quae subiectam materiem significat, in qua versatur imitatio tragoediae. Ex prima differentia duae existunt partes, APPARATVS, MELODIA. Ex secunda vna pars tantum. FABVLA. Ex tertia; tres partes. DICTIO, MORES, SENTENTIA" (p. 57).

Since this plot is really the actor's, rather than the poet's, province, utility of this kind is essentially a product of the histrionic art.

These are not isolated distinctions and conclusions. They fit into the general pattern of Robortello's critical scheme. When we inquire into the nature of the second kind of moral utility—the lessons learned from the characters of men—we find a similar pattern. First, as is perhaps already clear from the passages cited, the depiction of character is the proper activity of the poetic art, paralleling the imitation of action in the histrionic art: note the formula in the text on page 58: "Mores, ex quibus Felicitas, aut Infelicitas," and, earlier in the same passage, "Si quatenus à scribente poëta intelligas, dicimus primarium in tragoedia finem esse imitari, habitum animi, & mores hominum per orationem scriptam." Any utility resulting therefrom would be a true product of the poetic art. Second, and with complete consistency, Robortello assigns to the object of imitation (in the distribution of parts already mentioned) the three parts of thought, character, and diction; the *subiecta materies* consists of *dictio, mores, sententia.*[29] The reason why these three should become the objects of imitation (in Aristotle, diction is one of the means) will be discovered as we investigate the whole problem of character and its moral utility.

If Aristotle agreed with Plato that no wicked characters should be depicted in poems, says Robortello, he disagreed with him on the broader problem of the utility of character:

> He did not agree with him in so far as Plato did not wish the passions and perturbations of the soul to abound in poems; for he thought of an imitation of this kind in entirely different terms than did Plato. Such passions do not at all corrupt the characters of men or become more abundant in their souls, but rather purge them of all kinds of perturbations.[30]

Indeed, although the "tragedy of character" is a special kind, it has a quality which should be present in all poems:

> Every poem must be provided with character, and tragedy, above all, which abounds in passions and emotions. . . . For all pity, terror, and admiration proceed from moral discourse, and this is made up of the mixture of characters.[31]

If from the spectacle of man's destiny as displayed in his actions the spectator may learn certain lessons, he will learn others merely from a study of the

29. *Ibid.*

30. "non probauit, quatenus Plato redundare affectionibus, & perturbationibus animi nolebat poëmata; nam tali imitatione putauit, longè aliter quàm sentiebat Plato; non modo corrumpi mores hominum; affluereque ipsorum animos talibus affectionibus, sed expurgari potius ab omni genere perturbationum" (p. 166).

31. "moratum oportet esse omne poëma; & tragoediam in primis, quae redundat affectionibus, ac perturbationibus. . . . Omnis autem commiseratio, terror & admiratio, ex oratione morata proficiscitur, haec autem ex mistione morum conficitur" (pp. 164–65).

characters. Thus tragedy arouses pity and fear "not so much by doleful and horrible words, or by frightful events and horrible action, but rather by the persons themselves with whom the tragedy is concerned."[32]

The fact that the characters as depicted do in a sense serve as examples to mankind makes it imperative that they be well chosen. Tragedy will present no wicked persons. Robortello explains what he means by "wicked" in his elucidation of *Poetics* 1448ª4, where Aristotle had distinguished between men like ourselves and men better or worse than ourselves. He takes "better" as meaning "superior to those who live in our times" and provides a gloss in these terms: "for it is an opinion of long standing that there was long ago a certain Age of Heroes, who were much wiser and more excellent than the men of our times."[33] These are the heroes of epic and gnomic poetry, the kings and heroes of tragedy. "Like" refers to characters who resemble men of our own times and who appear in dialogues and in epic poems. "Worse" means those who are morally base, "those who have the appearance of bad and dishonorable things." But it may also mean those who are of low station in life: "possunt etiam viles, & ignobiles intelligi."[34] As a matter of fact, as Robortello works with the distinction, it becomes more completely a social than an ethical one. When he comes to the characteristics of the tragic hero and to the explanation of the phrase ἐν μεγάλῃ δόξῃ, he concludes that it must signify "of high station." The argument runs as follows:

For Aristotle meant . . . that the tragic action is not drawn from the fault of just any man who might be of the people and of unknown origin. [For the poor and low are never happy and cannot fall into unhappiness.] Therefore, Aristotle very cleverly posited these two things: first, a grave and great fault, and then that the hero should fall from happiness to misery. For these things cannot happen at the same time to anybody unless he be a man of the highest authority and dignity and placed by fortune in the highest degree of happiness. . . . Nor was it ever necessary that Aristotle should · say outright that he was considering the nobility and the class of famous men; for, if tragedy receives heroic and royal personages, it did not belong to that special art to say so, since it derived as a consequence from another which was more primary. It is thus sufficiently clear that common men of low birth cannot sink to calamity from a happiness which they never have possessed.[35]

32. "non tàm verbis flebilibus, horribilibusque, aut rerum atrocium, horribiliumque actione; vel potius personis ipsis, circa quas versatur tragoedia" (pp. 129–30).

33. "nam est inueterata opinio, fuisse olim quandam Heróum aetatem, qui multò sapientiores erant, & praestantiores, quàm homines nostrae aetatis" (p. 20).

34. *Ibid.*

35. "significauit enim Arist. . . . tragicam actionem non duci à peccato cuiusúis hominis, qui è plebe sit, & filius terrae. . . . Ingeniosè igitur Aristo. duo haec sumpsit. Peccatum, graue, & magnum. Deinde. vt ex felicitate labatur in Miseriam; simul enim haec accidere nulli possunt, nisi qui summa dignitate sit, & authoritate vir; in altoque felicitatis gradu à fortuna collocatus. . . . neque enim vnquam necesse fuit, vt Aristoteles proferret, Nobilitatis, Illustriumque genere virorum esse habendam rationem; nam etiam si tragoedia personas

The "viles & ignobiles" would be acceptable only in comedy, where there is no passage from happiness to unhappiness or from fortune to misfortune and where the moral lessons are of a different kind.

Just as in the case of action no moral utility could be achieved unless the action itself were credible or were made credible, so in the case of character a basis of credibility must be established. The problem is perhaps more complicated than it was with action; indeed, all four of the requirements for character that Aristotle indicated in 1454ª15 ff. become, in the hands of Robortello, separate means to credibility. Here are the four terms in Aristotle with Pazzi's Latin equivalents, which are the first step in the direction of Robortello's interpretation:

1. τὸ χρηστόν—probitas
2. τὸ ἁρμόττον—conuenientia
3. τὸ ὅμοιον—similitudo
4. τὸ ὁμαλόν—aequabilitas

(1) *Probitas* (or goodness) requires, first, the elimination of wicked characters, as we have seen; this is *probitas per se*. But it may be considered as well relatively to the persons in whom it is found and, as such, becomes the first canon of propriety:

> For the same character which is praised in one person is not praiseworthy in another . . . so much difference and diversity are there in characters by reason of the persons to whom they are attributed . . . if the goodness of a woman is attributed to a man, it immediately becomes less good; if the character of a servant is ascribed to a king or to some illustrious man, it becomes not only less good, but it could even be considered bad; from which it is clear that what was goodness in a servant is vice in a king.[36]

Robortello goes on to describe the proper goodness of a king, of a woman, of a servant. This amounts to the establishment of type characteristics and brings with it the assumption that persons not conforming to these types would not be acceptable to an audience. (2) For an elucidation of *conuenientia*, Robortello turns to Horace's *Ars poetica*, verses 154 ff., 312–18, and to Book ii of Aristotle's *Rhetoric*, "where he describes how men are with respect to their characters, their passions, their habits, their age, and their fortune." He says that τὸ ἁρμόττον "refers to sex, age, and dignity [or rank?]."[37] Clearly, this

Regias Heroicasque recipit; non erat tamen artis idipsum proferre, cum consequatur ex altero; quod magis est primarium. Satis enim patet ad calamitatem ex felicitate, qua nulla vnquam potiti sunt, delabi non posse ignobiles homines, ac viles" (pp. 132–33).

36. "nam iidem mores, qui in aliqua persona laudantur; in alia iidem non fuerint laudabiles. . . . Tantum discrepantiae, ac diuersitatis est in moribus propter personas. . . . probitas vxoris si attribuatur viro iam deterior fit; Si serui mores attribuantur Regi, aut viro alicui insigni, non modò deterior, sed malus etiam videri poterit, ex quo patet, eam, quae in seruo erat probitas, iam in Rege esse vitium" (p. 167).

37. "vbi quales homines sint moribus, affectionibus, habitibus, aetate, fortunaque describit" (p. 168); "τὸ ἁρμόττον refertur ad sexum, aetatem, & dignitatem" (*ibid.*).

is the theory of decorum developed by the Latin rhetoricians, which derived, from the particular set of circumstances surrounding a given person, a complex of traits which must necessarily characterize him. Here, again, the audience is the repository of these expectations with respect to the person, and only if they are realized will the audience accept the character as credible. (3) The alternative translation to *similitudo* is "ut sibi constent"; but the kind of self-consistency designated is not, as one might expect, the constant displaying of the same traits or of similar actions. Instead, "it refers to any man, such as Socrates, or Plato, or Pericles, whose character must be expressed just as it was previously expressed by other poets who wrote before."[38] It means, in a word, that the traditional conception of the character must be observed: "it is deduced from the tradition already established and from the opinion accepted by men."[39] Horace is the authority (vss. 119–24), and the "accepted opinion" is held by the audience. (4) *Aequabilitas* is constancy of character. Since characters and actions spring from habit and since habit is constant, character must be portrayed as constant in all persons. But the precept refers, above all, to the characters of persons newly invented by the poet, for which he cannot have recourse to tradition: for traditional persons, the accepted characters; for new persons, constant characters, as provided and developed by the poet.[40]

This distinction between new and traditional characters is fundamental. We have already seen a similar distinction at work in connection with action: "true" actions, as they should be or seemed to be (note the traditional element), fall into the category of the necessary; "invented" actions into that of the probable or verisimilar. So for character:

> If, therefore, the persons are true and the actions in themselves and the outcome of the deeds related are true, then the characters of the persons must be expressed by the poet according to the necessary, that is (as Averroës correctly explains it), according to truth. If the persons are new, their characters will have to be expressed according to the verisimilar, that is (as the same Averroës interprets it), according to the opinion of the majority.[41]

There is some wavering and inconsistency here on the part of Robortello, since one would expect the opinion of the many to apply to traditional, not invented, persons; unless he means that the opinion of the many decides upon the

---

38. "refertur ad aliquem hominem, vt pote Socratem. Platonem. Periclem. cuius mores exprimi debent, sicuti antè ab aliis poëtis, qui antè scripserunt, expressi fuerunt" (*ibid.*).

39. "deducitur ex fama iam confirmata, & opinione ab hominibus recepta" (*ibid.*).

40. P. 169.

41. "Si igitur personae verae sunt, & facta ab ipsis, euentaque rerum, quae narrantur, vera sunt; debent tunc personarum mores exprimi à poëta, secundum necessarium. hoc est (vt aptè declarat Auerroës) secundum veritatem. Si nouae sint personae, illarum mores exprimendi erunt secundum verisimile. hoc est (vt idem interpretatur Auerroës) secundum plurimorum opinionem" (p. 175).

verisimilitude of the poet's creation, in which case, once again, the audience would be making a judgment of credibility. In any event, for both action and character we have this situation:

uerae: secundum necessarium
nouae: secundum verisimile

The way in which a "true" character may be different from its real prototype and may hence follow "necessity" is perhaps indicated in Robortello's statements about the universality of poetry. If the poet treats singular things, he asks, how, then, can Aristotle say that he is universal, more universal than the historian?

> I answer, then, that both of these are true and that the poet occupies himself with describing one action of a single person; but in describing it he occupies himself with the universal, which is nothing else than to consider what is general and common. So that, if he should wish to depict Ulysses "wise" in the performance of actions, he should not be considered as he actually was; but, the particular circumstances set aside, he should be transferred into the realm of the universal and depicted in the way in which the perfect "wise" and ingenious man is ordinarily described by the philosophers.[42]

In this way the poet, like the painter, does not portray the person or the object itself but the Platonic Idea of the person or the object.

These various statements about action and character assume that both truth and verisimilitude are within the jurisdiction of the audience; that the individual character or action is submitted to the judgment of the spectator or the auditor. The assumption is made more specific in connection with Robortello's treatment of the passages on the epic. He says:

> In epic poetry, just as in the others, this is the first thing that must be attended to: that the words used should have nothing about them that is incongruous or contradictory, but that they should in every respect agree among themselves and fit properly together. For, whenever either the period of time in which the action is done or the place or the person or the manner is not fitting, these things do not satisfy reason, nor are they acceptable to the mind of the readers or the hearers. If it is at all possible, therefore, one should see to it that nothing is incongruous or contradictory; but if this is not possible, one should at least arrange it so that these contradictions seem to be placed outside the action or the narration. . . . Thus one must perpetually watch carefully that nothing in the words be discordant, nothing inconsistent, but that all things agree in every respect and that they be suitable to the rational faculty of the auditors, who watch with utmost care the impending action.[43]

42. "Respondeo igitur, vtrunque verum esse, & poëtam versari in vna vnius personę actione describenda; in ea tamen describenda versari circa vniuersale, quod nihil aliud est, quàm respicere ad generale quoddam, & commune. vt si sit effingendus prudens in rebus agendis Vlysses, non qualis ipse sit esse considerandum; sed, relicta circunstantia, transeundum ad vniuersale, & effingendum esse, qualis prudens, callidusque ab omni parte absolutus describi solet à philosophis" (p. 91).

43. "In poësi Epica, sicuti etiam in aliis illud in primis videndum, ne sermones habiti absonum aliquid habeant, aut repugnans. Sed ab omni parte consentiant inter se, & quadrent;

The passage merits study; for it is one of those passages in which statements elsewhere made separately are suddenly collapsed together in a way that reveals what the author is thinking. What is disclosed here especially is that, for Robortello, the words expressing characters and actions are indistinguishable from the characters and actions themselves. You do not have to say that characters must fit actions or that actions must fit the circumstances; all you need say is that there must be agreement among the words. Moreover, there is essentially no internal mechanism by which characters are made to fit actions, actions circumstances, and so forth; we know that this takes place properly only when the audience says it does; if we are poets, all we can hope to do is to anticipate the reactions of the audience. All that remains in the nature of an internal criterion is a vague "fittingness" or "appropriateness" or "congruity" of the words, which seems to be not too dissimilar to the Horatian "Primo ne medium, medio ne discrepet imum."

It is perhaps in this sense that diction, along with *sententiae* and character, becomes for Robortello one of the objects of imitation; this is just as remarkable as that plot should be assigned to the manner. I have already called attention to the passage (p. 60) in which this division is made. I should add that certain other key passages seem not to be in complete consistency with the division. For example, in his commentary on 1447ª16 he notes that there are four things to be considered with respect to any imitation, "id quod agitur, spectator siue auditor, per quod agitur, agens"; "that which is represented" is then specified as "mores, actiones, sermones" (p. 10). Two of these reappear in a much later formulation (p. 292): "The poetic faculty . . . speaks of all things and produces ethical discourse [*orationem moratam*] which imitates the actions of men and various speeches."[44] With respect to actions, first, it is probable that he thought of these as different from the "action" of the play as acted by the actors on the stage and hence could see them as an object of imitation, whereas he saw the "action" as an appurtenance of the dramatic manner. There would thus be no correspondence, necessarily, between the "action" of the play and the actions imitated—a position impossible for Aristotle. As for the *sermones*, we must note that this is only one of three terms used; *oratio* is discourse in

---

Quotiescunque enim aut spatium temporis, quo res gesta fuit; aut locus, aut persona, aut modus, non constat; non quadrant rationi, neque cum legentium, aut audientium mente conueniunt; Si fieri igitur possit, danda opera, vt nequid repugnans sit, aut absonum; quòd si non possit, saltem efficiendum, vt extra narrationem & actionem repugnantia illa posita videantur. . . . Etiam igitur, atque etiam diligenter videndum; vt in sermonibus nihil discrepet; nihil repugnet; sed omnia ab omni parte quadrent, ratiocinationique auditorum qui in actione perpendenda euigilant, sint consentanea" (pp. 286–87).

44. "Poëtica facultas . . . de omnibus rebus loquitur, conficitque orationem moratam, quae imitatur hominum actiones, & sermones varios" (pp. 291–92).

general, *dictio* is language as the instrument of poetic expression, *sermo* is the speech assigned to a given person. But, unfortunately, no clear distinction is maintained among these terms, and *dictio* and *sermo* seem to possess ready interchangeability; so that, when either of these is used in a passage listing objects of imitation, it may mean speeches of persons in a quite understandable way. It could thus come to be equivalent to *sententiae*, as we shall see; in this fashion, the "mores, actiones, sermones" of the passage on page 10 would not be too far distant from the "plot, character, thought" of Aristotle.

Moreover, there is another sense in which diction (or *oratio* or *sermo*) very really becomes the end for which the imitation is made—an end with respect to the poem, of course, and not with respect to the audience. We have already seen that the poetic faculty "*produces* ethical discourse [*orationem moratam*]." Similarly, when Robortello finds himself obliged to distinguish between διάνοια and *mores* he does so in these terms: "For διάνοια is that which forms and produces the discourse, and the *mores* are that which, diffused throughout the discourse, makes it ethical and 'decorous'; but this ethical discourse is formed by means of the διάνοια itself."[45] Again, a little later, "the poetic faculty, in so far as it is concerned with tragedy . . . seizes upon character and produces an ethical discourse"; as for the epic, which does not have "action" as tragedy does, it fulfils one of its functions "when it expresses the ethical speeches [*sermones*, here] of different men; for its work resides in putting together ethical discourse with the greatest skill."[46] In all these passages, character and *sententiae* contribute to the production of a certain kind of discourse; in Aristotle, diction is merely the instrument for the expression of character and thought.

Since diction becomes in this way one of the objects of imitation, we are justified in asking whether, as in the other cases, (1) the object produces a given effect upon the audience, (2) a relationship is established between the object and "truth," and (3) a criterion of credibility is introduced. The answer to all three questions is an affirmative. As in rhetoric, so in poetic the *sententiae* must demonstrate, refute, arouse such passions as pity and fear, augment, and diminish (cf. *Poetics* 1456ᵃ37). Their general aim and that of speeches made by personages is to persuade and to move, and this they will do only if they appear true:

45. "διάνοια enim est, quae exprimit, & conficit orationem, mores igitur sunt qui diffusi per orationem eam moratam faciunt, & ἁρμόττουσαν, sed oratio exprimitur haec morata; per ipsam διάνοιαν" (p. 66).

46. "Facultas poëtica, quatenus versatur in tragoedia . . . arripit mores, & efficit orationem moratam" (p. 68); "cum moratos exprimit sermones diuersorum hominum; nam maximo opus est artificio in oratione morata conficienda" (p. 282).

Those speeches persuade and move most of all which are not invented by art but which are true and come from nature herself; or if they are from art, they must be represented as closely as possible according to nature; and if they are made in this way, they will not be different from the natural ones. Speeches are then said to be "natural" when they are spoken by those very men who are placed in calamitous circumstances and are moved by the passion itself.[47]

As for action and character, then, the most credible and persuasive speeches would be "true" ones; but, since these do not belong to the realm of poetry, the next best are those which most closely resemble "true" ones. The whole problem of the verisimilitude of speeches and their effect upon an audience is developed with respect to tragedy in the following passage:

Since tragedy particularly must be filled full of the weight of *sententiae*, and since these *sententiae* are different according to the matter of the things which are being treated, it is necessary for the poet to pay attention to the nature of the things, so that from them he may draw forth proper *sententiae*, all of which he will express beautifully, elegantly, and appropriately. . . . Since, then, the functions of *sententiae* are five in number . . . he must know how properly to derive all these from the quality and the nature of the things themselves of which the imitation is made. In tragedy . . . it is necessary to arouse pity and terror; but these cannot be aroused unless the things themselves are pitiable and terrible, and they will come to be such if they are expressed in suitable *sententiae*. . . . Nor is the fact to be overlooked that Aristotle in the text enumerates four things which are contained in the arguments or *sententiae* derived from tragic events; they are these: pitiable, horrible, great, and verisimilar things. If you consider these separately, you will see that they are appropriately included by Aristotle, since they belong to tragedy. We have already said that it was necessary to move pity and terror in it; next, it is necessary for tragic discourse to be full of majesty and great. . . . Lastly, the tragic poet will adhere to verisimilar events, since, from their number, all things in the action and in the episodes are represented, and, besides, if one must persuade and dissuade, prove or refute, all this is readily achieved through verisimilar things.[48]

47. "Ii sermones maximè persuadent, permouent, qui ab ipsa natura non ficti ab arte, sed veri proueniunt: aut si ab arte proximè secundum naturam fuerint effici; si tales enim fuerint, non differunt à naturalibus. Naturales autem sermones tunc dicuntur, cum proferuntur ab ipsismet hominibus, qui sunt in calamitate positi; & ea perturbatione agitantur" (p. 198).

48. "Cum sententiarum pondere refertam in primis oporteat esse tragoediam; Sententièque diuersae sint pro materie rerum, de quibus agitur; poëtam necesse est respicere ad naturam rerum; vt ex iis eliciat aptas sententias, quibus omnia explicet venustè, ornatè, & accommodatè. . . . Cum igitur sententiarum officia sint quinque . . . haec omnia sciendum est commode duci ex vi, & natura ipsarum rerum; quarum fit imitatio. In tragoedia . . . commiserationem, terroremque concitare oportet; at concitari haec non possunt, nisi res fuerint commiserabiles, & horribiles, fiunt autem huiusmodi, si aptis sententiis exprimantur. . . . Non est etiam illud praetermittendum, Aristotelem in contextu enumerare quatuor, quae continent. Argumentationes seu sententias ductas ex rebus tragicis, sunt autem haec. Commiserabilia; Horribilia; Magna; Verisimilia; quae si singillatim consideres, videas aptè ab Aristo. posita; quia ad tragoediam pertinent. Commiserationem, ac terrorem iam diximus in eo moueri oportere; grandem praeterea, ac maiestatis plenam orationem esse oportet tragicam. . . . Postremo verisimilia sectatur tragicus, quia ex iis omnia finguntur in actione, & in Episodiis, praeterea, siquid suadendum, dissuadendumúe est, probandum, aut refellendum; id commodè totum ducitur ex verisimilibus" (pp. 224–26).

The question arises here whether the actions and the characters themselves might not be chosen so as to make possible a certain kind of "thought" and a certain kind of diction; or, at least, whether the supreme function of art is not to produce that diction out of any materials whatsoever. This seems to be the sense of Robortello's remarks on 1456[b]4:

> For it is here that the skill of the speaker appears, here that one sees how much a clever poet is worth in his writing; for this, in short, is the greatest task, to make light things serious through the addition of the weight of the *sententiae*, to exalt small things, to enliven languid ones, to raise new ones from the soil, to add to those things which are not very sorrowful and mournful both mourning and sadness. For what, indeed, and of what nature are the virtue and the art of him who speaks or who writes, if things by their very own nature would appear serious, joyful, sorrowful, and great and not as a result of the knowledge and skill of that very one who either speaks or writes?[49]

The whole position is perhaps summarized in this formula: "For the use and abundance of good and proper words is like a certain foundation upon which the poet builds and to which he attaches his art."[50]

Once more, as for action and character, the realm of the poet in diction is not the "true" but the verisimilar and the probable: "he [Aristotle] means only that kind of speech which the poets use for the sake of amplification, in order to magnify the thing and make it more admirable, and departing, to be sure, from the true, they seize upon verisimilar and probable things."[51]

In summary, then, the various kinds of utility which men derive from poetry come separately from various parts of poems: from plot, the spectacle of man's happiness or unhappiness springing from his actions; from character, the example of man's happiness or unhappiness springing from his character; from *sententiae*, the statements which will persuade the spectator to action or dissuade him from it, which will demonstrate truths to him and move him to imitation or revulsion. These are not, perhaps, entirely separate, since the *sententiae* become the final expression of the lessons from both action and character. In all cases, utility will result only from a belief of the audience in the truthfulness of the poem, and that, in turn, will depend upon the degree to which the poem is made probable and verisimilar.

49. "hic enim dicentis artificium apparet, hic perspicitur; quantum scribendo valeat ingeniosus poëta, hic deniq. summus est labor, res leues, addito sententiarum pondere, graues efficere; paruas extollere; languentes excitare; repentes humi euehere; parum moestis ac luctuosis, luctum, moeroremq̄. adiungere; quae enim aut qualis esset scribentis aut dicentis virtus, & artificium; si res suapte natura graues, iucundae, luctuosae, & grandes apparerent, non peritia & ingenio ipsius; qui aut loquitur, aut scribit?" (p. 226).

50. "nam verborum propriorum, & bonorum vsus, ac copia est quasi solum quoddam, in quo aedificet poëta, et in quo adiungat artem" (p. 245).

51. "intelligit tantùm illud sermonis genus, quo poëtae vtuntur, amplificationis gratia, vt rem magis augeant, admirabilioremq̄. faciant; discedentes enim à vero, verisimilia captant, & probabilia" (p. 284). The reference in Aristotle is to 1460[a]20, where he speaks of paralogism.

Since Robortello's system is analytical in the sense that specific effects result from separate causes, we may expect that his treatment of pleasure will follow the same pattern. Pleasure itself will not be subdivided into a number of kinds, but separate parts of the poem will be distinguished as providing different aspects of the *voluptas* produced by poetry. Moreover, these will usually be different from the parts providing utility or will be special subdivisions of these parts. The whole problem of pleasure will be complicated by several considerations: (1) that it must be derived from subjects which are in themselves not pleasurable (in the case of tragedy); (2) that the audience will tend to prefer inartistic to artistic pleasures; (3) that the things done for the achievement of utility essentially militate against the achievement of pleasure.

Since the realm of poetry has been separated from that of truth, Robortello must establish a similar separation of pleasure from truth; otherwise no poetry could produce pleasure. This he does in the following passage:

> Aristotle answers that an equally great pleasure is experienced by those who do not know previously [that the plot is true] and by those who know it previously; from which it is clear that it makes no difference whether the plots of tragedies are drawn from true events or from fictional ones, provided that they be invented in accordance with the possible.[52]

The credible will thus be just as capable of producing pleasure as of achieving moral utility. However, credibility in itself is not enough (as it is for utility); some subjects will readily be "believed" by an audience, but they will not as readily be "liked." Hence there arises a distinction between genres such as comedy, where the subject matter itself is pleasurable, and tragedy, where it is not pleasurable; men will naturally prefer the former to the latter. Something special must be added to such a genre as tragedy, and in that special quality we perceive the true sources of poetic pleasure:

> The rough and ignorant crowd of men, led by the senses and by opinion rather than by prudence and knowledge and wisdom, almost always is at variance with what is right and with what is approved by the wise. Therefore, poets, trying to please it, once composed plots which they thought capable of gaining the approval of the mob, and, in so doing, they deviated from art, which hands down the norm for writing properly. Now art demands that tragic performances should purge those two major passions of the soul of which we spoke in the definition of tragedy—fear and pity. But men, who are more easily attracted by pleasures and joyful things, frequently flee doleful and tragic things because they are unpleasant. They therefore require a happy end to the action, so that they will not constantly be tormented and driven by terror and pity and so that they may return to their original gayety.[53]

52. "Respondet Aristoteles, aequè magnam percipi voluptatem ab iis, qui non norunt antè, ac ab iis, qui antè norunt; ex quo patet nihil referre, an ex rebus veris, an fictis, modo fictae sint secundum possibile, ac verisimile, tragoediarum argumenta ducantur" (pp. 95–96).

53. "Vulgus hominum rude, atque imperitum, quod sensu ducitur & opinione, magis quàm prudentia, & cognitione, aut peritia; semper ferè dissidet, ab eo, quod est rectum, et

And a little later, answering the question of how the unpleasant feelings of pity and terror can cause pleasure:

> But I reply that the pleasure which is obtained from tragedy is that which imitation provides. The power that this imitation has in delighting our souls may be sufficiently recognized from the fact that even horrible things, if they are expressed in some imitation, attract us to them and bring us delight and pleasure. . . . Such is therefore the pleasure that is derived from tragedy. Nor is that which comes from comedy unlike it, in so far as comedy contains imitation. The latter, therefore, pleases because it imitates in a joyous fashion the ridiculous actions of men; the former because it imitates in an artistic fashion the sorrow, the lamentation, and the calamity of mortal men. Now if you should ask which is the greater pleasure of the two, I should dare to affirm that the one deriving from tragedy is much greater, for it pervades our souls more deeply and touches us in a more unusual way, and that imitation is made with somewhat greater force. Therefore, to the extent that we know it to be more difficult to express that imitation, to that extent—if it be exact—we regard it with greater admiration, and we obtain from it a greater pleasure.[54]

I have cited these passages at length because they contain an elaboration of what essentially are the three bases of pleasure for Robortello: imitation, the *difficulté vaincue*, and admiration. Imitation, of course, has here the same status as in Aristotle, and Robortello does not expand much upon the statements of his text; we have already seen (n. 10) his statement that "à natura insitum est, voluptatem percipere ex imitatione." The *difficulté vaincue*, which commands our delight in seeing an almost impossible task well done, is offered as the final reason for the superiority of tragedy over other genres; men naturally prefer what is gay and pleasant, and the poet who succeeds in pleasing them through the presentation of what is sad and unpleasant attains the highest reaches of his art (p. 321). But it is in admiration that Robortello finds the most recurrent source of pleasure, and to it he devotes a great deal of discussion. He would define it as a feeling of wonder, of amazement, which comes from the spectacle

---

probatur à sapientibus; huic igitur poëtae inseruientes olim Fabulas conscribebant, quales vulgò probari posse putarent; discedebantque ab arte, quae normam tradit rectè scribendi; Ars enim postulat, vt tragicis recitationibus expurgentur duae maximae illę animi perturbationes, de quibus in definitione tragoediae locuti fuimus; metus, & commiseratio; homines verò, qui voluptatibus, rebusque iucundis facilius alliciuntur, saepe res lugubres, tragicasque, quòd iniucundę sunt, refugiunt. Felicem igitur postulant actionum exitum; ne perpetuò eos angant, vrgeantque & terror, & commiseratio. & redeant ad hilaritatem pristinam" (p. 142).

54. "Sed respondeo; voluptatem, quae capitur ex tragoedia, esse eam, quam parit imitatio. quantum verò habeat haec vim ad oblectandos animos, vel inde satis cognosci potest, quòd etiam horribilia, si imitatione aliqua expressa sese nobis obtulerint; delectationem, voluptatemque afferunt. . . . Talis est igitur voluptas quae ex tragoedia percipitur. Nec dissimilis huic est, quae ex comoedia prouenit quatenus imitationem continet. Haec igitur oblectat, quòd festiuè imitatur ridiculas actiones hominum, illa quòd artificiosè imitatur moerorem, luctum, calamitatemque mortalium. Quòd si quaeras vtra maior voluptas, ausim affirmare, quae ex tragoedia prouenit maiorem multò. altius enim peruadit animos, rariusque nobis contingit; maioreque quadam vi fit imitatio illa; quantò igitur difficilius exprimi eam posse scimus, tantò magis, si exacta fuerit, admiramur; maioremque capimus voluptatem" (p. 146).

of the unexpected, the extraordinary, the marvelous—of what Aristotle calls τὰ θαυμαστά. This immediately raises a crucial question: Is not the marvelous the exact contradictory of the credible, and would not the pleasure arising from it exclude the possibility of utility? Robortello works out the difficulty in a way entirely consistent with the previous *données* of his system. The marvelous is indeed in conflict with the credible. Hence it must be kept to a minimum in those genres where credibility is most essential (e.g., comedy) and may attain a maximum in other genres, where, because they are narrative rather than dramatic, credibility is of lesser importance (e.g., epic):

> . . . in tragedy and comedy the imitation is of men doing something in accordance with nature. The epic admits certain things, such as the stories told about Circe, the Sirens, the Cyclops. Tragedy does not receive these because it is not presented through narration, that is, a reporting of events, as is the epic. For in such reporting, many things, however marvelous [θαυμαστά] and against the belief of men, may be recounted, which cannot be acted by actors, on a stage, in the presence of spectators.[55]

The pleasure derived from admiration will thus be more appropriate to some genres than to others. But this does not mean that it will be excluded from tragedy; on the contrary, admiration is inseparable from pity and terror: "Therefore all pitiable and terrible things are at the same time admirable, nor does pity or terror ever lack admiration."[56] The problem for the poet is then to reconcile, within such a genre as tragedy, the credible with the marvelous; this is done in two ways. First, as we have already seen (p. 328 above), the marvelous in the form of recognition and reversal is added to pity alone or to pity and fear, in order to transform simple plots into complex plots. In a sense the pleasure becomes an adjunct to the utility and is associated with separate parts of the plot. The kind of man represented by the character is credible; the general action in which he engages is credible (the poetic and the histrionic aspects are thus both taken care of); but the particular circumstances by which the action is concluded—a discovery of the identity of persons accompanied by a turn in the fortunes of the hero—are extraordinary, hence essentially incredible, hence marvelous. It is these which produce the pleasure associated with plot. Second, whereas the central plot and the central personage must be "true" or possible in the ways already described, episodes and secondary personages will admit of a much freer "invention." Episodes are added "ad augendam fabulam, & amplificandum poëma" (p. 45); they expand a short

---

55. "in tragoedia, & comoedia imitatio est hominum agentium aliquid secundum naturam; Epopoeia aliqua admittit, quale illud, quod narratur de Circe, de Sirenibus, de Cyclopibus; tragoedia haec non recipit, quia non διάπαγγελίαν idest annunciationem fit, sicuti Epopoeia, in annunciatione autem, multa quàmlibet θαυμαστὰ, & praeter fidem hominum possunt narrari, quae alioqui agi ab agentibus coràm spectantibus non possunt in scena" (p. 87).

56. "Omnia igitur comiserabilia, & terribilia sunt etiam admirabilia, neque vnquam comiseratio, aut terror caret admiratione" (p. 99).

plot to the magnitude required for a long poem; they are the device for creating variety in the poem and suspense in the audience (p. 121). Once again, they will be most acceptable in the epic, of which they constitute one of the principal ornaments: "because of the variety of many things found in it, it removes satiety and distaste and over and over again relaxes and refreshes the souls of the listeners or the readers; finally, it can rightfully use dissimilar episodes, which makes it possible for it to grow constantly larger and larger."[57] As a matter of fact, the need for producing pleasure through admiration is so great that almost any artistic error may be excused if this need is satisfied: "He may be excused thus, provided that he achieve through these faults the end that he seeks. Now the end is to make the action more wonderful and of greater magnitude, so that it will affect the listeners with greater admiration."[58] Does this not, in the last analysis, make it possible for the poet to discard all concern for credibility in order to exploit all the available means of achieving the marvelous and the pleasure connected with it?

Finally, diction itself is a source of admiration. When things will not entertain the audience, words must. "Epic poets in long poems cannot constantly narrate actions which by their own virtue are capable of delighting the soul of the listeners; it is therefore necessary, above all, to introduce at such places ornate words and elaborate *sententiae*, so that the discourse will not drag."[59] In any genre, metaphorical language has the same function: "in any single word used metaphorically it is necessary that there be many things which stimulate and delight the soul of the listener, and at the same time produce admiration in it."[60] Both tragedy and epic must produce suspense and admiration; the epic poet has greater possibilities not only in the use of the marvelous and of episodes but in the description of innumerable objects: "The epic poet has another field through which he moves, in which he makes numerous descriptions of places, clothing, times, movements, gestures, and other things of this kind."[61] Such

57. "propter plurimarum rerum varietatem, quae in eo inest, satietatem fastidiumq. tollit; relaxatq̄. saepè, ac renouat animos audientium; seu legentium postremò pro suo iure vti potest dissimilibus Episodiis, quae res facit, vt magis, magisq̄. semper excrescat" (p. 276).

58. "poterit sic excusari, modò finem sibi propositum per illa consequatur; Finis vero est, vt rem admirabiliorem faciat; augeatq́ue magis, vt auditores maiore afficiat admiratione" (p. 294).

59. "Epici poëtae in longa poësi non semper narrare possunt res, quae sua vi auditoris animum oblectare possint; necesse est igitur tunc in primis ornata verba; elaboratasq́ue sententias afferre in medium, ne elanguescat oratio" (p. 289).

60. "in translato enim verbo vno multa insint oportet, quae audientis animum pungant, & oblectent, simulq́ue admiratione afficiant" (p. 249).

61. "Alterum campum, per quem excurrit, poëta epicus habet, in quo descriptiones locorum, vestium, temporum, motionum, gesticulationum, atque aliarum huiusmodi rerum quàmplurimarum descriptiones facit" (p. 282).

descriptions are essentially hors d'œuvre whose sole purpose is to add pleasurable decoration to the work.

The pleasures arising from imitation, the *difficulté vaincue*, and admiration are thus largely attached to parts of the poem different from those which produce utility; they come from episodes, from recognition and reversal rather than from the principal action of the plot, from secondary characters rather than from the hero, from elements of diction independent of the ethical speeches, from gratuitous descriptions. This does not mean that the other "essential" parts of the poem do not give pleasure. It merely means that, in keeping with his analytical tendency, Robortello seeks as much as possible to find separate causes for the pleasure and the utility derived by the audience. Pleasure will contribute to the achievement of the ultimate utilitarian goal of the work (if such a subordination indeed exists) only by making the poem as a whole enjoyable to the audience. The total effect upon the audience will be one of moral betterment accompanied by pleasurable sensations.

II

Persuasion, effect upon the audience, moral betterment, pleasurable sensations—I choose a few terms which seem to summarize the major tendencies of Robortello's system as we have seen it so far. If these be indeed the ends proposed for his system, then it becomes strikingly different from Aristotle's system in the text which Robortello is expounding. How different, and in what measure, will perhaps best be discovered by an investigation of this problem: To what extent is his system a rhetorical system rather than a poetic system in the Aristotelian sense? By "rhetorical system" I mean, of course, one in which a specific effect of persuasion is produced upon a specified audience by using the character of the audience, the character of the speaker, and the arguments of the speech as the means to persuasion.

Early in his Prologue, Robortello classifies poetics as one of the five arts of discourse. He establishes a descending hierarchy from the true to the false and places the five arts in it in the following order, each with its special matter:

demonstratoria:	verum
dialectice	: probabile
rhetorice	: suasorium
sophistice	: speciem probabilis, sed verisimilis
poëtice	: falsum, seu fabulosum [p. 1]

Such a classification as this explains why he elsewhere excludes the true from the subject matters of poetry; it also makes it necessary for him to clarify the sense of *falsum* (since the false would be incredible) as *fabulosum*, hence related to the traditions and the opinions of men. Indeed, poetics will have some points in common with all the other arts of discourse except the *demonstratoria*. It will produce a *sermonem imitantem*, just as rhetoric produces a *sermonem persuadentem* (p. 2). It will share with dialectic and rhetoric the quality of having no specific subject matter and will be distinguished from them only by the fact that it imitates (p. 291).

But these are largely distinctions of subject matter. When the effect is being discussed, the word *persuadentem* is just as applicable to poetic as to rhetoric. We have already seen some of the passages: "Sed prorsus poëta res exponit accomodatè ad persuasionem hominum, & fidem" (p. 66); "imitandi, & repręsentandi mores; motiones, personas, & actiones hominum accommodatè ad fidem, & persuasionem audientium, & spectantium" (p. 3). The really excellent poet "must possess every art of swaying the minds of the listeners in any direction whatsoever."[62] Moreover, this persuasion does not exist for its own sake; it must, as must rhetoric, move the listener to action of a given kind or to avoidance of certain actions. The kinds of character to be formed through this persuasion and the kinds of action to be sought or avoided have already been discussed. To this extent, then, Robortello's poetic is like rhetoric.

It is also like rhetoric in the specification of the audience; we do not have here a universal, uncharacterized audience but one specifically limited in several ways. First, it is an audience of the elite, not the *vulgus;* note his disdain (p. 339 above) for the demands made upon the poet by the "rough and ignorant crowd of men" and his indication that these demands must be ignored in favor of the requirements of the "wise," the *sapientes*. Similarly, the poet must reject the clamor of the crowd for the double ending:

> For these are delighted more by that kind of ending, because it is more gentle and has less terror in it and fills the soul with a certain pleasantness which is obtained from the punishment of the wicked and the happiness of the good. . . . But Aristotle affirms that this kind of pleasure is not to be sought in tragedy, since it is more proper to comedy.[63]

Second, it is an audience made up of good men only. The whole basis of the sympathy of an audience for character, of purgation and moral effect upon the audience, rests upon the assumption that the audience is so constituted. Robortello develops his idea at length in the commentary on 1453[a]5, "a man like ourselves":

> Fear is aroused, indeed, when we behold someone like ourselves who has fallen into misery. Aristotle means like the auditors themselves, almost all of whom are judged to

---

62. "omnem artem inflectendi mentes auditorum in quàmuis partem teneat oportet" (p. 213).

63. "Magis enim ii delectantur eiusmodi exitu, quia placidior est, ac minus terroris in se habet, et expletur animus suauitate quadam, quae ex vltione improborum, & felicitate bonorum percipitur. . . . Sed affirmat Aristoteles huiusmodi voluptatem non esse in tragoediis quaerendam; nam magis propria est comoediarum" (pp. 145–46).

be good; or else he speaks only of the good ones. For it is out of their souls that the rule for writing tragedy is derived, nor must any poet ever be mindful of the wicked, but he must adapt everything he writes to the nature of good men. Good men, then, when they see evil things happen to some good man, fear—since they understand that he is like themselves and that they are like him—lest the same thing at some time befall them, since they live in the same circumstances.[64]

For a corollary reason, the unhappiness of the good and the happiness of the wicked "would be repugnant to men and gods alike" (p. 110). Third, we know that the audience is possessed of a large amount of knowledge and a large number of expectations, all of which contribute to the constitution of its canon of credibility: what is true, what is traditional, what is a matter of opinion, what is probable and verisimilar—all these are known only by reference to the audience, and their achievement is to be discovered only by consulting the audience.

If this poetic system resembles a rhetorical system in its production of a specific effect of persuasion upon a specific audience, is also resembles such a system in considering the plot of a poem as a kind of argument. The parts of the plot must be related to one another as *praecedentia* and *consequentia;* the various modes of priority and posteriority are to be discovered in the *Categories* (pp. 104–5). The prologue and epilogue of a tragedy will have the same accessory relationship to the rest as the exordium of a speech: "Indeed, what else are the exordium and the epilogue but certain episodes of some forensic oration?"[65] In character, *hoc post hoc* relationships must obtain, taking into account cause, effect, and interval of time; in plot, *haec per haec*, providing mutual interdependence of causes; and the denouement is "deduced" (*deducitur*) from the characters of the persons and the preceding events (pp. 175–76).

In fact, the most frequent source of elucidations for the *Poetics* is in a multitude of rhetorical works, and the two arts are constantly compared by Robortello. He sees them as exactly similar in all things save one: "They agree in almost all things; they differ in this only, that the latter [poetic] uses meters, the former [rhetoric] prose discourse."[66] As a result of this difference, rhetoric

---

64. "Metus verò concitatur, cum intuemur aliquem nobis similem, in miseriam esse lapsum. Similem auditoribus ipsis intelligit Aristoteles; qui ferè omnes boni censendi sunt, vel de bonis tantum loquitur. nam ex eorum animis norma sumitur scribendę tragoediae; neque vllus debet poëta improbos vnquam respicere, sed totam suam scriptionem accommodare ad bonorum naturam. Viri igitur boni, cum immerenti alicui viro bono aliquid mali vident accidisse, metuunt, quòd similem illum sibi, séque illi esse intelligunt, ne idem sibi aliquando accidat, quia pari viuunt conditione" (p. 128).

65. "Exordium quippe, & Epilogus quid aliud sunt, quàm Episodia quaedam orationis forensis?" (p. 205).

66. "conueniunt enim fermè in omnibus rebus; hoc vno differunt, quod haec vtitur metris, illa soluta oratione" (p. 66). Cf. p. 229, "neque sanè quicquàm differt in hoc poëta ab oratore, vno excepto, quòd astrictior numeris, & rhythmo est Poëtae oratio."

will support a more ornate diction, whereas poetic (especially in the dramatic genres) must seek a simplicity approaching that of everyday speech (p. 45). The functions of διάνοια or *sententiae* will be the same in both (Aristotle had provided a basis for the comparison) (p. 223); both will operate in the realm of the probable: "conueniréque cum Rhetorice, quae ex probabilibus ducit argumentationes" (p. 284). There will, of course, be differences, but they will be of detail rather than of the essence of the two arts. For example, all the relationships of a tragic hero to his actions and circumstances will be strikingly different from those of a client being defended by an orator (pp. 113–14); the "fear" resulting from them in rhetoric will be of a purely human source, whereas, in poetic, supernatural and religious elements enter (p. 126).

All that is lacking, then, to make Robortello's approach a fully rhetorical one is the role of the character of the poet as an element of persuasion. There is no trace of any such role in his commentary. The poet, for Robortello, is merely a man capable of imitating, through gifts of nature and the acquired rules of art, the objects which he uses in his poems. He is not himself endowed with any moral character, and his personal characteristics (except in so far as the "good" poet will imitate good men) do not enter into the structure or the effectiveness of his poems. To this extent only is the rhetorical system of Robortello incomplete and the distinctly poetic orientation of Aristotle's system respected.

For it is now abundantly apparent that, in the course of this lengthy and painstaking commentary on the *Poetics*, much happens to the basic suppositions of the text and that what emerges is a poetic method essentially different from Aristotle's. The fundamental alteration comes in the passage from a poetic to a rhetorical position, from a position in which the essential consideration is the achievement of the internal and structural relationships which will make the poem beautiful to one in which the main problem is the discovery of those devices which will produce a desired effect upon a specified audience. I do not mean that in Aristotle no consideration is given to the effect of the poem upon the audience; indeed, at every crucial point in the *Poetics* the relationship of object of contemplation to contemplator is maintained constant.[67] Such concepts as the pleasure derived from imitation, the "effect" proper to a given species, the pity and fear of tragedy and their "purgation," the "likeness" of hero to audience among the requisites of character are integral to the argument; they are fundamental if the work of art is to fulfil its function of giving a certain kind of artistic pleasure to the men who see it or hear it. But herein lies the basic departure of Robortello: the effect produced is no longer one of artistic pleasure resulting from the formal qualities of the work, but one of moral persuasion to action or inaction, in which the pleasure involved is

67. For this interpretation of the *Poetics* see below, pp. 552 ff.

merely an accompaniment or an instrument; and the audience is composed of men capable of yielding to this persuasion rather than of men capable of enjoying this pleasure.

This means that the problem for the poet is no longer to compound out of the constitutive parts an artistic whole which, as a whole, will produce the desired aesthetic effect, but rather to insert into the works such parts as will, by themselves, produce multiple utilities and pleasures, each part producing a separate utility or a separate pleasure. The basis for the inclusion of any given part is its capacity, by itself, to awaken in a highly specified audience a given reaction of persuasion or of pleasure. This means, in turn, that the artistic unity and integrity of the work disappear as part of the problem: "plot" may be removed from among the poetic elements of a work and may be transferred to its specifically histrionic functions. Only the vaguest notions of a unifying and ordering structure for the work need be retained; these are not vital. On the other hand, such elements as diction and the means by which diction is made ornate assume great importance.

Moreover, since the sense of the total poetic structure is lost, there is no longer any possibility of deriving from such a structure the criteria for the appropriateness, for the goodness or badness, of individual parts. Instead, criteria for each separate part will be separately derived by a reference to the character of the audience as it specifically affects that part and in the light of the utility or the pleasure which that part should produce. At each step, there will be reference outside the poem. The poem becomes, as a result, a collection rather than a unit. From it the audience derives utility of a moral character and pleasure of a nonaesthetic kind, since it is not related to the structure or the form of the work as a whole.

Robortello, consequently, finds it possible to epitomize his conception of poetry in a definition which he takes over from Cicero and which Aristotle would regard as entirely inadequate: "imitationem uitẹ, speculum consuetudinis; imaginem ueritatis" (p. 2). The verb ποιεῖν, describing the process of writing poems, will not mean simply "facere," but "scribere versus, & poëmata pangere" (p. 28), thus making the inclusion of verse mandatory. He does, indeed, argue that verse is not of the essence of poetry (since he is commenting upon a text which states this to be true); but he still regards it as necessary: "You must know that poetry should properly be composed of two elements, namely, imitation and meter . . . that will be more truly and more properly called "poetry" which is composed of both imitation and meter."[68] From this

---

68. "Sciendum tamen poësin ex duobus propriè conflari debere: ex imitatione scilicet, & metro. . . . verius, magisque propriè appellatur poësis, quae & imitatione, & metro conflata fuerit" (p. 90).

definition, as from the concepts underlying it, all Aristotelian notions of the peculiar nature and the special characteristics of poetry are lacking.

We may appropriately ask, finally, how and why Robortello came to give this interpretation to the text of the *Poetics*. A full answer would require a history of the antecedent critical tradition and a description of the current intellectual approaches. This much may be said, briefly, by way of suggestion: With no earlier exegesis to rely upon, Robortello was obliged to turn to other texts and to long-standing habits of exposition for a method to be applied here. The texts to which he turned were largely rhetorical texts, or, if they were poetic texts, they were such—e.g., Horace—as presented an essentially rhetorical approach to problems of poetry. There is thus, throughout, a desire to equate what is said in the *Poetics* with Horace's *Ars poetica* and with all the principal rhetorical writings of antiquity. Through the equation, individual passages in the *Poetics* take on a rhetorical cast, which ultimately extends to the whole interpretation of the text. The habits of exposition which were applied may be characterized in the ensemble as the determination to reconcile all previous writers who might be regarded as "authorities." This is the method of the scholiasts. If Plato banishes poets and Aristotle admits them, a reconciliation must be discovered; it is found in an interpretation of purgation which provides poetry with the moral utility that Plato had failed to discover in it. And so on down the line. The difficulty with this method, of course, lies in its complete disregard of methodological considerations, in its wresting of passages from context, in its destroying of the systematic bases for the meaning of any statement or set of statements. If one is to apply it, one must fail—or refuse—to read texts as bodies of ideas having an organic interrelationship and be content with reading them merely as collections of passages. Robortello reads his source materials as collections of passages, and he reads Aristotle in much the same way. So it is that the fundamental conceptions of the *Poetics* escape him, and its component fragments are reassembled into a new system which has only rare points of contact with Aristotle's system. Unfortunately, this will be the procedure for all of Robortello's successors and will account for the progressive transformation and deformation of the idea of poetry contained in the *Poetics*.

CASTELVETRO'S THEORY OF POETICS

BERNARD WEINBERG

N THE history of modern literary criticism Lodovico Castelvetro figures as the man who invented the three pseudo-Aristotelian unities of time, place, and action. Or at least he is credited with having given the first complete expression to the time-place-action complex and with having thus exerted an important influence on the development of the classical doctrine. This is perhaps a correct estimate of his contribution. But it does not emphasize as fully as it should his real position in the movement away from the text of Aristotle and toward the theory of the French classicists. That position is not so much a matter of the incidental question of the unities as it is of his total philosophical approach, of his general treatment of poetic matters, of his method of analysis. For Castelvetro, whose *Poetica d'Aristotele vulgarizzata et sposta* dates from 1570,[1] represents in a sense a culmination of the tendencies already manifest in the first commentary on Aristotle's *Poetics*, Robortello's *In librum Aristotelis De arte poetica explicationes* of 1548.[2] He incorporates in his discussion the accretion of the intervening years; and what he produces, since it is more extreme, is much farther away from the text of Aristotle and much closer to the point of view of French classicism.

The first notable difference between Robortello and Castelvetro is to be found in their attitude toward Aristotle himself. For Robortello, the text which he is expounding is a masterpiece of clarity and logic. He pauses frequently to point out the excellence of its construction, to defend it against those who hold that it is fragmentary, imperfect, or erroneous. His intention is to justify and accept integrally the text of Aristotle; if he comes up with an essentially un-Aristotelian analysis, it is because of his incapacity to understand the text and because of long-standing habits of textual exposition, and not through any intention to disagree. With Castelvetro, the point of departure is a basic scorn for the text of the *Poetics*. The *Poetics* is not a complete work, but "a collection of poetic materials from which an art might be written";[3] it includes remarks

---

1. Vienna: Stainhofer, 1570. A second edition, posthumous, emended and corrected, appeared in 1576 (Basel: Pietro de Sedabonis); my analysis is based on this edition, from which all quotations are taken. I give page and line reference for the beginning of each quotation.

2. See my "Robortello on the *Poetics*" in this volume, pp. 319–48.

3. "vn raccoglimento di materie poetiche da comporre l'arte" (82. 23).

which Aristotle meant later to refute or reject;[4] many passages are out of place;[5] and there are obvious contradictions.[6] But these are merely matters of organization; Castelvetro's contempt goes farther. He does not hesitate to characterize certain ideas of Aristotle's as false: "Aristotle here and elsewhere is of the opinion that the same pleasure is derived from tragedy through reading it as through seeing it and hearing it recited in action; which thing I esteem to be false";[7] "Now, according to Aristotle, poetry always imitates one of the three things indicated by him. . . . This does not seem true to me, simply speaking";[8] "Now Aristotle assumes as simply true a thing which is not so at all."[9] He rejects Aristotle's ideas when they seem inadequately supported: "I should wish this to be shown to me otherwise than on his authority, since he seems to say and repeat several times this same thing without adducing a single reason of any value."[10] He goes so far as to ask the question, given the uselessness of Aristotle's precepts to the art of history: "What will prevent us, following the strength of this argument, from being constrained to say that these precepts are neither proper nor useful to poetry itself?"[11]

Nothing is farther from Castelvetro's mind, then, than to attempt a justification of the Aristotelian text. He tries to explain it when he can, to point out what he thinks Aristotle meant. But generally he uses it as a point of departure for the development of his own theories. His favorite device is to take a given passage in the *Poetics*, show how and why the distinctions made are incomplete and incorrect, and then proceed to his own set of distinctions on the same subject. We may take as an example his treatment of *Poetics* 1460[a]26, on the impossible probable:

Now, if I am not mistaken, this question would have been better understood, and greater light would have been shed upon the things which need to be said, if three divisions had been made, in each one of which would be the virtue to be followed and the vice to be avoided. And the first would be that of possibility and impossibility, and the

4. 35. 1, 111. 24.

5. 91. 36, 174. 8, 218. 16, 234. 30, 294. 33, 341. 24, 386. 30.

6. 275. 30.

7. "Aristotele qui, & altroue è di questa opinione, che quello diletto si tragga della tragedia in leggendola, che si fa in vedendola, & in vdendola recitare in atto. la qual cosa io reputo falsa" (297. 30).

8. "Hora secondo Aristotele la poesia rassomiglia sempre l'vna delle tre cose proposte da lui.... Il che non ci pare vero, simplicemente parlando" (583. 1).

9. "Hora presuppone Aristotele per cosa simplicemente vera quella, che non è cosi" (691. 15; cf. 315. 38, 386. 24, 491. 13, 694. 6, 697. 6).

10. "vorrei, che mi fosse mostrato per altro, che per autorita di lui, che pare dire, & ridire piu volte questo medesimo senza addurre ragione di niuno valore" (280. 29).

11. "che ci vetera, che seguendo noi il vigore di questo argomento non siamo costretti a dire, che non sieno ne conueneuoli, ne gioueuoli alla stessa poesia?" (7. 1).

second would be that of credibility and incredibility; these two divisions have been discussed so far. And the third would be that of usefulness and of uselessness to the constitution of the plot.

From this point he proceeds to a development of the distinction, to a subdivision into eight possible combinations, to the statement that the first and second divisions belong "to nature, or to civil and human reason," whereas the third is the proper province of the poet.[12] There are a score or more of similar passages. Castelvetro's real aim seems, then, to be the substitution of his own ideas for Aristotle's and the development of a set of statements which may properly be called "Castelvetro's theory of poetics."

I

Among those tendencies which, already in Robortello, marked a departure from the spirit of the *Poetics*, the most significant methodologically is the removal of the principal emphasis from the poem to the audience. Such a transformation means that all aspects of poetry are considered not in terms of the artistic exigencies of the poem itself but in terms of the needs or demands of a specifically characterized audience. Now in Castelvetro this tendency is pushed to the extreme: the audience is very carefully delimited and restricted, and every phase of the poetic art is considered in relationship to this audience. In the first place, Castelvetro assumes that Aristotle treats only such genres as were susceptible of public performance and that hence his audience is the "common people": "poetry was invented for the pleasure of the ignorant multitude and of the common people, and not for the pleasure of the educated";[13] "for purposes of the common people, and for the pleasure alone of the rough crowd, was invented the stage and the representative [or dramatic] manner."[14] Any audience of the elite is specifically excluded: "it is not true that in poetic imitations one must pay greater attention to the distaste of the intelligent spectators than to the joy of the ignorant spectators."[15] At times, special segments or special conditions of the audience will have to be taken into

12. "Hora, se io non m'inganno, questa materia si sarebbe intesa meglio, & sarebbe data maggiore luce alle cose, che s'hanno da dire, se si fossero fatti tre capi, in ciascuno de quali fosse la virtu, che si douesse seguire, e'l vitio, che si douesse fuggire. E'l primo fosse quello della possibilita, & della'mpossibilita e'l secondo fosse quello della credibilita & della'ncredibilita, de quali due capi in fino a qui s'è parlato. e'l terzo fosse quello del giouamento della constitutione della fauola, & del non giouamento" (564. 12).

13. "la poesia fu trouata per diletto della moltitudine ignorante, & del popolo commune, & non per diletto degli scientiati" (679. 35).

14. "per cagione del quale commune popolo, & per diletto solo della moltitudine rozza è stato trouato il palco, & la maniera rappresentatiua" (23. 1).

15. "non è vero, che nelle rassomiglianze poetiche si debba tenere piu conto della noia de veditori intendenti, che della gioia de veditori ignoranti" (679. 32; cf. 29. 38, 113. 26, 147. 16, 164. 11).

account: its political complexion will determine its reactions to given works,[16] and those members of the audience who are parents will have a peculiar attitude toward given plots.[17]

Since the elite and the educated are thus rigorously excluded, certain qualities of the mind will be denied the audience:

> poetry [was] invented exclusively to delight and give recreation, I say to delight and give recreation to the minds of the rough crowd and of the common people, which does not understand the reasons, or the distinctions, or the arguments—subtle and distant from the usage of the ignorant—which philosophers use in investigating the truth of things and artists in establishing the rules of the arts; and, since it does not understand them, it must, when someone speaks of them, feel annoyance and displeasure.[18]

"They are not, and cannot be capable of understanding scientific and artistic disputes, but they are able only to understand the events of the world which depend upon chance."[19] The audience will be almost completely lacking in imagination and will believe only the evidence of its senses: "Nor is it possible to make them believe that several days and nights have passed when they know through their senses that only a few hours have passed, *since no deception can take place in them which the senses recognize as such.*"[20] In matters not reducible to the senses, it will be incapable of going beyond what historical fact it knows— "We cannot imagine a king who did not exist, nor attribute any action to him"[21] —or beyond certain opinions which it holds as true; e.g., "the common people, which believes that God rules the world and has a knowledge of all particular things and a special care of them, also has the opinion that he does all things justly, and directs all things to his glory, and to the utility of his believers."[22] The consequences of this complete lack of imagination will be seen later; but it

16. 223. 2; cf. 61. 7.

17. 248. 8.

18. "la poesia sia stata trouata solamente per dilettare, & per ricreare, io dico per dilettare & per ricreare gli animi della rozza moltitudine, & del commune popolo, il quale non intende le ragioni, ne le diuisioni, ne gli argomenti sottili, & lontani dall'vso degl'idioti, quali adoperano i philosophi in inuestigare la verita delle cose, & gli artisti in ordinare le arti, & non gli'ntendendo conuiene, quando altri ne fauella, che egli ne senta noia, & dispiacere" (29. 36; cf. 25. 30).

19. "non sono, ne possono essere capaci, & intendenti di dispute di scienze, ne d'arti, ma solamente sono atti a comprendere gli auenimenti fortunosi del mondo" (23. 6).

20. "Ne è possible a dargli ad intendere, che sieno passati piu di, & notti, quando essi sensibilmente sanno, che non sono passate senon poche hore, non potendo lo'nganno in loro hauere luogo, il quale è tuttauia riconosciuto dal senso" (109. 27; italics mine).

21. "non ci possiamo imaginare vn re, che non sia stato, ne attribuirgli alcuna attione" (188. 25).

22. "il commune popolo, il quale crede dio reggere il mondo, & intendere tutte le cose particolari, & hauerne spetiale cura, porta anchora opinione, che egli faccia ogni cosa giustamente, & dirizzi ogni cosa a gloria sua, & ad vtile de suoi diuoti" (277. 34; cf. 278. 34, 337. 12).

is immediately apparent that the poet who must take it into account will be seriously restricted in his creative activity. In a similar way this audience will have a memory of limited capacity, and such technical devices as the division of tragedy into five acts will exist "to help the memory of the spectators to keep in mind an action which is not at all brief."[23] Conversely, an action which is related too succinctly will not be understood, and hence such a plot should be expanded.[24]

In addition to these limitations, the physical comfort and the convenience of the audience will need to be considered. We are speaking of poems presented before an assembled crowd; we must not ask the crowd to assemble for a poem so short that it would not be worth its while,[25] nor must we expect it to remain beyond a certain limit of physical endurance. Strangely enough, that limit is broadly conceived as extending up to twelve hours:

the restricted time is that during which the spectators can comfortably remain seated in the theater, which, as far as I can see, cannot exceed the revolution of the sun, as Aristotle says, that is, twelve hours; for because of the necessities of the body, such as eating, drinking, excreting the superfluous burdens of the belly and the bladder, sleeping, and because of other necessities, the people cannot continue its stay in the theater beyond the aforementioned time.[26]

Finally, this audience has as one of its characteristics the capacity to be pleased by certain things and to be displeased by others. Castelvetro studies this capacity in detail and finds several bases for pleasure and displeasure. One is knowledge: the audience takes pleasure in learning, "especially those things which it thought could not come about"; contrariwise, it dislikes stories from which it cannot learn anything, those which present commonplace events and rapidly lead to satiety.[27] Second, its hopes (or *volontà*): the audience is pleased by events which happen in accordance with its wishes, displeased by those which do not.[28] Third, the audience will relate the events of a poem to the fortunes of its own life; it will enjoy seeing the good happy and the wicked unhappy, since the case of the former will lead it to expect happiness from its own goodness and the case of the latter will give it a sense of security and of justice. On the other hand, if the good are unhappy, it will experience fear and

---

23. "per aiutare la memoria de veditori a tenersi a mente vna attione non miga brieue" (88. 31).

24. 164. 3.   25. 53. 27.

26. "il tempo stretto è quello, che i veditori possono a suo agio dimorare sedendo in theatro, il quale io non veggo, che possa passare il giro del sole, si come dice Aristotele, cio è hore dodici. conciosia cosa che per le necessita del corpo, come è mangiare, bere, diporre i superflui pesi del ventre, & della vesica, dormire, & per altre necessita non possa il popolo continuare oltre il predetto termino cosi fatta dimora in theatro" (109. 21; cf. 57. 11).

27. 553. 9.   28. *Ibid.*

pity, and if the wicked are happy, it will feel envy and scorn; but these will be only temporary displeasures, since they will give way to feelings of self-righteousness and of justice, which will be ultimately pleasurable.[29] With pleasure and displeasure will also be associated certain sentiments of a moral nature which will make the audience blush at "dishonest" actions, and hence reject them.[30]

Such is the audience for which Castelvetro's poet must write—ignorant, unlettered, lacking in imagination and memory, attentive to its creature comforts, bound by certain selfish considerations which limit its possibilities of pleasure.

What is more, the poet is not to attempt to improve this audience in any sense; Castelvetro specifically rejects any profit or utility as the end of poetry. The sole end of poetry, as far as the audience is concerned, is to delight, to give pleasure and recreation. Castelvetro summarizes his position in the following passage:

if we were to concede that the materials of the sciences and the arts could be the subject of poetry, we should also concede that poetry either was not invented to give pleasure, or that it was not invented for the uncultured crowd, but rather to teach and for persons initiated into letters and disputations; all of which will be seen to be false by the proofs that I shall now give. Now, since poetry was invented, as I say, to delight and give recreation to the common people, it must have as its subject those things which can be understood by the common people and, once understood, can make it joyous.[31]

The position is reiterated on several occasions, notably in his discussion of purgation in tragedy; he finds Aristotle in agreement with him on the matter of pleasure and sees the utilitarian notion of purgation (as he interprets it) as a contradiction on Aristotle's part:

For if poetry was invented principally for pleasure, and not for utility, as he demonstrated in the passage where he spoke of the origin of poetry in general, why should he now insist that tragedy, which is a part of poetry, should seek utility above all else? Why should it not seek mainly pleasure without paying attention to utility?[32]

Again, the contention of Plato or of his followers that poetry must serve the purposes of the state is attacked; no such end exists for it:

29. 121. 34, 122. 21.   30. 550. 8.

31. "se concedessimo, che la materia delle scienze, & dell'arti potesse essere soggetto della poesia, concederemmo anchora, che la poesia o non fosse stata trouata per dilettare, o non fosse stata trouata per le genti grosse, ma per insegnare, & per le persone assottigliate nelle lettere, & nelle dispute. il che anchora si conoscera essere falso per quello, che si prouera procedendo oltre. Hora perche la poesia è stata trouata, come dico, per dilettare, & ricreare il popolo commune, dee hauere per soggetto quelle cose, che possono essere intese dal popolo commune, & intese il possono rendere lieto" (30. 1).

32. "Percioche, se la poesia è stata trouata principalmente per diletto, & non per vtilita, come egli ha mostrato la, doue parlò dell'origine della poesia in generale, perche vuole egli, che nella tragedia, la quale è vna parte di poesia, si cerchi principalmente l'vtilita? Perche non si cerca principalmente il diletto senza hauer cura dell'vtilita?" (275. 30).

Moreover, the end of the government of the city is different from the end of poetry. For the end of the government of the city concerns living harmoniously together for the greater comfort and utility of the body and of the spirit, and the end of poetry concerns the mere pleasure and recreation of the auditors.[33]

In connection with pleasure, the question of purgation seems a very knotty one to Castelvetro. He explains it as an answer on the part of Aristotle to Plato's banishment of the poets on moral grounds; here, insists Aristotle, is a moral use for poetry.[34] The utility lies in the diminution of the passions of pity and fear in the audience or their expulsion.[35] But if it is admitted as a utility, this is only incidental to the real end of pleasure:

> Those who insist that poetry was invented mainly to profit, or to profit and delight together, let them beware lest they oppose the authority of Aristotle who here [*Poetics* 1459ᵃ21] and elsewhere seems to assign nothing but pleasure to it; and if, indeed, he concedes some utility to it, he concedes it accidentally, as is the case with the purgation of fear and of pity by means of tragedy.[36]

As a matter of fact, Castelvetro believes that purgation itself may be considered as a source of pleasure; thus he affirms that "Aristotle meant by the word ἡδονὴν [1453ᵇ11] the purgation and the expulsion of fear and of pity from human souls," and he goes on to explain how it can be pleasurable:

> it comes about when, feeling displeasure at the unhappiness of another unjustly suffered, we recognize that we ourselves are good, since unjust things displease us, which recognition—because of the natural love that we have for ourselves—is a source of great pleasure to us. To which pleasure is joined still another, not at all inconsiderable, that when we see the excessive tribulations which happen to others, and which could happen to us and to those like us, we learn in a quiet and hidden way how subject we are to many misfortunes, and how we should not put faith in the calm course of the events of this world; and this pleases us much more than if another, as a teacher and openly in words, should teach us the same thing.[37]

33. "Anchora il fine del reggimento della citta è diuerso dal fine della poetica. Percioche il fine del reggimento della citta riguarda al viuere concordeuole insieme per maggiore agio, & vtile del corpo, & dell'animo, e'l fine della poetica riguarda il diletto simplice, & la ricreatione degli ascoltanti" (592. 10). He does admit, however, that poetry is in a sense subordinate to politics, along with many other arts, and that it must not be allowed to violate the teachings of political expediency (592. 14). On pleasure as the end cf. also 35. 30, 158. 41, and 394. 13.

34. 9. 4, 116. 24, 272. 15, 697. 13.

35. 117. 16, 299. 12.

36. "Coloro, che vogliono, che la poesia sia trouata principalmente per giouare, o per giouare, & per dilettare insieme, veggano, che non s'oppongano all'autorita d'Aristotele, il quale qui, & altroue non par, che le assegni altro, che diletto. &, se pure le concede alcuno giouamento, gliele concede per accidente, come è la purgatione dello spauento, & della compassione per mezzo della tragedia" (505. 38).

37. "è quando noi, sentendo dispiacere della miseria altrui ingiustamente auenutagli, ci riconosciamo essere buoni, poi che le cose ingiuste ci dispiacciono, la quale riconoscenze per l'amore naturale, che noi portiamo a noi stessi ci è di piacere grandissimo. Al quale piacere s'aggiugne questo altro anchora, che non è miga picciolo, che, veggendo noi le tribolationi

Note that the pleasures involved fit into the pattern of the capacities of the audience for pleasure and displeasure: the act of learning, the sentiment of self-righteousness. The other sources of delight and sadness indicated for tragedy and comedy belong to the same categories; the "novelty of the case" contributes to knowledge,[38] and to the tendency to relate poetic actions to one's own life will belong such feelings as these: the joy, in tragedy, at the cessation of the danger of death and, in comedy, at the revenge for some insult; the sadness, in tragedy, at the coming of death and, in comedy, at the suffering of some such insult.[39] In each case the spectator will identify the hero with himself or with someone dear to him.

If the end of pleasure and its achievement are related to certain characteristics of the audience, the means by which the end is to be achieved are similarly related. Here the main consideration is the lack of imagination on the part of the audience. In sum, the argument runs as follows: the audience will derive pleasure only if it identifies itself with the characters and the events; this identification is possible only if the audience believes in their reality; its belief in their reality will depend upon the credibility—the verisimilitude—of the presentation. It is here that imagination enters. If the audience were endowed with great capacities of imagination, it would "believe" things far removed from the conditions of "real life"; since it is not, it will "believe" only what seems to it to be in the realm of its own experience, to be "true." Since the argument is complex and since the real crux of Castelvetro's poetic system resides here, I shall examine it in some detail.

For Castelvetro, all considerations of verisimilitude oscillate between two poles: the impossibility of pleasure, on one side, without credibility, and, on the other side, the inadequacy of credibility, by itself, to produce pleasure. Credibility is the *sine qua non*, but it is only a beginning. If the audience is to experience the pleasure to be derived from learning, what is merely credible must be supplemented by what is rare, extraordinary, marvelous—in a word, by the incredible. The precise point at which the "incredible" becomes "inverisimilar" is a matter of subtle and difficult determination by the poet. The demand for both credibility and the marvelous is insistently made by Castelvetro throughout the text. First, credibility:

all [the spectators] do not know whether the action or the names are true or invented, but those who do not know it believe that the action is true and that the royal names are

---

fuori di ragione auenute altrui, & possibili ad auenire a noi, & agli altri simili a noi, impariamo tacitamente, & di nascoso, come siamo soggetti a molte suenture, & come non è da porre fidanza nel tranquillo corso delle cose del mondo. il che ci diletta molto piu, che se altri come maestro, & apertamente con parole ci'nsegnasse questo medesimo" (299. 20).

38. 35. 30, 158. 41.

39. 221. 35.

true, and therefore these things give them pleasure; and if they knew that they were invented, they would feel displeasure in the same way as one who, having received a jewel and thinking it to be good, enjoys it, but, learning later that it is false, he becomes sad, and especially if it was sold to him for genuine.[40]

Just as in painting, so in poetry:

a monstrous thing, and which has never been, or is not, accepted by the common opinion of the people as possible to come about, or as probable—such a thing put into poetry cannot delight us, as far as the pleasure to be derived from resemblance is concerned.[41]

Whether the action be a true one or not, then, the spectator or the reader must believe it to be such, must see in it a resemblance to the reality which he believes exists. Next, the marvelous, which seems to be contained in the very definition of pleasure:

Now, since someone might ask for what reason the marvelous was required in tragedy, and was required in proportionately greater quantity in the epic, I answer that the end of poetry, as has been said, is pleasure and that the marvelous produces pleasure, and thus the marvelous is properly required in tragedy and in the epic, in order that the poem may achieve its own proper end in these types of poetry.[42]

The end of poetry, as has been said several times, is pleasure, and the marvelous especially produces pleasure; therefore, the tragic poet should, as much as he can, seek the marvelous, and the epic poet, because of the ease that he has in so doing, must produce it to a much greater extent.[43]

As a matter of fact, these two ingredients—the credible and the marvelous—are not entirely distinct; for the marvelous itself must be credible if it is to produce the proper pleasure:

And it is said [by Aristotle] that the invention of incredible things is permitted the poet if these incredible things bring about the end more marvelously than credible things would. And I myself say that incredible things cannot produce the marvelous. As, for example, if I hold it to be incredible that Daedalus should fly, I cannot marvel at the

40. "tutti non sanno, se l'attione, o i nomi sieno veri, o imaginati, ma quelli, che nol sanno, credono, che l'attione sia vera, ei nomi reali veri, & percio loro porgono diletto, &, se sapessono, che fossono imaginati, sentirebbono dispiacere non altramente, che alcuno, hauendo vna gioia, & reputandola buona, gode, ma risapendo, che è falsa, si contrista, & spetialmente, se gli è stata venduta per vera" (212. 34).

41. "cosa monstruosa, & non mai piu stata, o non riceuuta dal commune giudicio del popolo per possibile ad auenire, o per verisimile posta in poesia non ci puo dilettare, quanto è al diletto procedente dalla rassomiglianza" (73. 42).

42. "Poscia, perche altri poteua domandare, per qual cagione si richiedesse la marauiglia nella tragedia, & per proportione si richiedesse maggiore nell'epopea, si risponde, che il fine della poesia, secondo che è stato detto, è il diletto, & che la marauiglia opera diletto, adunque la marauiglia non senza ragione si richiede nella tragedia, & nell'epopea, accioche la poesia ottenga il debito fine suo in queste maniere di poesia" (549. 6).

43. "Il fine della poesia, come è stato detto piu volte, è il diletto, & la marauiglia spetialmente opera il diletto, adunque il poeta tragico dee, il piu che puo, procacciare la marauiglia, e'l poeta epopeico per l'agio, che n'ha, la dee procacciare molto maggiore" (552. 42).

fact that he is said to fly, since I do not believe that he does fly. . . . For it is absolutely necessary that we have credible things if the marvelous is to be produced.[44]

As a result, in various incidental definitions of poetry, both ingredients are included, directly or indirectly expressed: "the proper function of poetics consists in the imitation, through harmonious words, of a human action which could possibly happen, pleasurable through the novelty of the case"; plot is "a discovery of an action which has never yet happened, in whole or in part, but which could possibly happen and which is worthy of being remembered."[45]

If we would understand these distinctions of terms, we must examine Castelvetro's treatment of the general question of possibility. He divides the whole realm of possible actions according to the following schema:[46]

I. Possible actions, *which have actually happened*
   A. Natural
      1. According to the course of nature
      2. Contrary to the course of nature (i.e., monstrous or miraculous happenings)
   B. Accidental
      1. Resulting from chance or fortune
      2. Resulting from the will of men
II. Possible actions, *which have not yet happened*
   A. and B. as above

Now Category I, since it includes accomplished actions, is essentially the province of history; it corresponds to Aristole's τὰ γενόμενα and is limited to particular actions, performed by specific persons. Actions of this kind are essential in tragedy and epic, which, since they deal with royal persons, cannot dispense with a historical basis; we, the audience, are incapable of imagining kings who did not exist, etc. But no poem may be composed entirely of such actions, since then it would be a history and not a poem at all. Comedy, of course, needs no component of historical events, since its persons and their actions are private and obscure.

Category II, on the other hand, is coequal with Aristotle's τὰ δυνατά; it is the realm of the universal, since the actions are possible for many persons; it is thus the realm of poetry. All poems must possess some component of actions

---

44. "Et si dice, che si permette la fittione delle cose incredibili al poeta, se le cose incredibili operano il fine piu marauiglioso, che non fanno le credibili. Et io dico, che le cose incredibili non possono operare marauiglia. Come, per cagione d'essempio, se io ho per cosa incredibile, che Dedalo volasse, non mi posso marauigliare, che volasse, non credendo io, che volasse.... Perche fa mestiere di cose credibili, se la marauiglia dee nascere" (612. 6).

45. "la dirittura della poetica consiste in rassomigliare con parole harmonizzate vna attione humana, possibile ad auenire, diletteuole per la nouita dell'accidente" (592. 8); and "vn trouamento d'vna attione non mai piu auenuta ne in tutto, ne in parte, la quale sia possibile ad auenire, & degna, che sene faccia memoria" (150. 17).

46. For the full text see 184. 39 ff.

which have not actually happened. But whereas in the first category the question of credibility does not arise, in the second it is of primary importance. In order that credibility may be assured (and hence verisimilitude) and that the necessary ingredient of the marvelous may nevertheless be present, the following three requisites are established for possible actions:

a) They must be similar to those actions which have actually happened

b) They must be similar to those actions which had the least probability of happening, but which did actually happen

c) The parts or parcels of such actions must individually be similar to those parts of actions which happened in various cases to various people

The matter of verisimilitude is further clarified by a later distinction between possibility and credibility: possibility is a potential of the action itself, which contains no impediment that would prevent the action from coming to realization; credibility is a suitability (a *convenevolezza*) of the action to the expectations of the audience, "by which a person may be led to believe that that action was brought to realization."[47]

With respect to credibility, then, it may be assured by several means: first, by the use of a historical basis for the action in certain genres; second, by a close adherence, in invented actions, to the conditions of "real" or "true" actions. At this point, the expectations of the audience again impinge upon the poet in a very important way, for the audience is the touchstone of natural probability and it will believe whatever conforms to its conceptions of reality. The case is especially clear with the comic poet, who invents everything:

But let nobody believe for this reason that the creator of the comic plot has liberty to invent either new cities imagined by himself, or rivers, or mountains, or kingdoms, or customs, or laws, or to change the course of the things of nature, making it snow in summer and having men reap in winter, and so forth; for it is necessary for him to follow history and truth.[48]

The whole story of Oedipus runs against this natural probability, "for a private citizen who kills the legitimate king should be most sharply punished and not rewarded, nor should the queen be given him to wed and the kingdom as a dowry."[49] In the same way, certain apparitions of the ancient gods are unacceptable to the modern audience's conceptions:

47. 562. 30 ff.

48. "Ma non si creda percio alcuno, che il formatore della fauola della comedia habbia licentia di trouare o citta nuoue, & imaginate da lui, o fiumi, o monti, o regni, o costumi, o leggi, o di tramutare il corso delle cose della natura, facendo neuigare di state, & mietere d'inuerno, & simili. percioche gli conuiene seguire l'historia, & la verita" (189. 26; cf. 212. 15).

49. "percioche il priuato huomo, che vccide il re leggittimo, dee essere punito asprissimamente, & non premiato, ne gli dee essere data la reina a moglie, e'l regno in dota" (235. 10).

For you must know that the common people believe that God in the present day rules the world in a different way from what he did in ancient times. For the opinion is that in our times he rules it silently without showing himself in person through inspirations, through signs, or through visions, through admonitions to his servants, and through other means not understood nor considered by the coarse crowd; just as, on the other hand, the opinion is that in the first ancient centuries, in the time of the demigods, God intervened directly in the affairs of the world, by appearing personally and speaking with men.[50]

The natural probabilities so considered became a function of a given audience in a given time, losing any universal quality.

In this way the second means of assuring credibility comes to be very close to the third, which is the observance of decorum. A norm of *convenevolezza* is proposed. Again, the case of the comic poet is the most instructive. He may invent names for his personages: "But in so doing the poet must nevertheless pay attention to the usage of the place and the time when and where the action is supposed to have taken place, so that the names will not be exceptional for the given place and time."[51]

So for the conception of character:

For we know that the poet must follow what is appropriate [*il conueneuole*] in representing not only the persons under the sway of passions but the other persons, also, and the actions; which appropriateness is derived by the poet not from that which is in himself or from that which has happened to himself but rather from what is commonly found in that type of person similar to the one who is being represented, full attention being paid to the place, and the time, and the other circumstances; and from what usually happens to such a person.[52]

Such a notion of appropriateness is applied not only to persons of a given character (where it is related at once to the ἁρμόττοντα of Aristotle and to the Horatian decorum) but also to certain kinds of actions. If you speak of prophecy, for example, it must be in the light of invariable conventions. Vergil, here, has erred:

50. "Perche è da sapere, che la commune gente crede, che dio al presente regga altramente il mondo, che non reggeua anticamente. Percioche è opinione, che ne secoli presenti lo regga tacitamente senza dimostrarsi in persona con ispirationi, con segni, o con visioni, con ammonitioni de suoi serui, & con altri mezzi non intesi, ne considerati dalla gente grossa. si come dall'altra parte è opinione, che ne primi antichi secoli al tempo de semidei dio hauesse cura del mondo, apparendo personalmente, & ragionando con gli huomini" (337. 12).

51. "Ma dee non dimeno riguardare il poeta in far cio all'vsanza del luogo, & del tempo, doue, & quando finge l'attione essere auenuta, accioche i nomi non sieno fuori dell'vsanza del predetto luogo, & tempo" (192. 14; cf. 192. 41 for other genres).

52. "Percioche noi sappiamo, che il poeta dee seguire il conueneuole non pure nel rappresentare i passionati, ma l'altre persone anchora, & l'attioni. il quale conueneuole non si raccoglie dal poeta da quello, che è in lui, o da quello, che è auento a lui, ma da quello, che suole essere communemente in quella maniera di persone simile a quella, che noi rappresentiamo, hauendo rispetto al luogo, & al tempo, & all'altre circostanze, & da quello, che le suole auenire" (372. 9).

Vergil sins in the decorum of prophecy, which does not usually descend to the use of proper names, nor to things so clear and so particular; but, withholding names, it usually indicates the persons and their actions with somewhat obscure figures of speech, as we see observed in the prophecies of Holy Scripture and in the *Alexandra* of Lycophron.[53]

If restrictive conventions of this type are multiplied not only with respect to characters but also with respect to actions, the possibilities of "invention" on the part of the poet soon disappear; this is indeed the case with Castelvetro.

But the multiplication of these commonplaces and these conventions would also tend to make the poem completely uninteresting to the audience itself; the cause of credibility would be perfectly served, yet the resulting poem would be thoroughly dull. The antidote to this danger is the cultivation of the marvelous. Castelvetro, since he is unwilling to admit any improbability, conceives of the marvelous as a kind of infrequent probability:

There are two kinds of probabilities [*verisimili*], one of which represents the truths which most frequently occur according to the fixed course of nature, and the other of which represents the truths which occasionally depart from the usual course; as, for example, it is probable that a clever, wicked man should deceive and not be deceived, and that a powerful man should vanquish and not be vanquished, since truly we usually see things come to pass in this way. And it is, moreover, probable that a clever, wicked man, wishing to deceive, should on occasion be deceived, and that a powerful man, wishing to conquer, should at times be conquered. So that one of these probabilities concerns the "many times" of truth, and the other the "few times" of truth, and thus the one like the other is probable. But the second, because of its rarity, is more marvelous and is said to be probable outside of probability only because of its rarity and because it turns aside from the path of the first probability.[54]

On various occasions he points out that what happens more frequently is less marvelous, hence less desirable in poetry;[55] thus a recognition which could easily come about, through the will of the person recognized, is less to be sought than one which would be more difficult.[56] In a similar way, as regards

---

53. "peccando Virgilio nella conueneuolezza della profetia, la quale non suole condescendere a nomi propri, ne a cose tanto chiare, & particolari, ma, tacendo i nomi, suole manifestare le persone, & le loro attioni con figure di parlare alquanto oscure, si come si vede osseruare nelle profetie della scrittura sacra, & nell'Alessandra di Licofrone" (219. 37).

54. "Sono due maniere di verisimili, l'vna di quelli, che rappresentano le verita, le quali auengono per lo piu secondo certo corso, et l'altra di quelli, che rappresentano le verita, che alcuna volta trauiano dall'vsato corso. come, è verisimile, che vno astuto maluagio inganni, & non sia ingannato, & che vn possente vinca, & non sia vinto, percioche veramente noi veggiamo per lo piu auenire cosi. & è anchora verisimile, che vno astuto maluagio, volendo ingannare, sia ingannato alcuna volta, & che vn possente, volendo vincere, sia vinto alcuna volta. Si che l'vn verisimile riguarda l'assai volte della verita, & l'altro le poche volte della verita, & cosi l'vno, come l'altro è verisimile. ma il secondo per la rarita è piu marauiglioso, & è detto essere verisimile fuori del verisimile pure per la rarita, & perche si torce dalla strada del primo verisimile" (400. 17).

55. Cf. 248. 13.

56. Cf. 252. 13.

purgation, what happens less frequently is more pitiable and more horrible.[57] The admission of this kind of improbable probability makes way for the acceptance of certain brands of "impossibility" in poetry. Of the four varieties of impossibilities which he distinguishes,[58] two are forbidden the poet; these are actions impossible for God and for men and actions impossible for men alone. The other two may be used by the poets; they comprise actions not impossible to God, such as miracles, and actions which seem impossible to men because of their rarity. Both of these are recommended to the poet whenever he can find a justification for using them:

> And it is a sufficiently evident matter why poetic fiction can and should receive these two kinds of impossibilities used in this way and justified by reason, since the poet seeks to move the reader or the listener to admiration [*marauiglia*], which proceeds principally from miraculous doings and from those doings which happen only very rarely.[59]

I should insist at this point that all degrees of probability as Castelvetro conceives them are natural probability rather than aesthetic probability; that is, probability is established in a work not by reference to the conditions of the work itself or to preliminary statements within the work, but by reference outside of the work to the operations of nature. This is especially clear in the example he uses for distinguishing between necessity and verisimilitude. Actions of both kinds are possible, hence admissible into poetry. If a man is wounded on the head, it is "verisimilar" or probable that he will die; hence the poet may represent his death. If a man is wounded in the heart, it is "necessary" that he die; hence the poet may represent his death.[60] Similarly for actions springing from character, all of which are really matters of decorum: it is "necessary" that a mother who resolves to kill her innocent children (cf. Medea) do so only with great perturbation of her soul (this is presumably because of the eternal character of mothers as mothers); it is "probable" or verisimilar that a person who has been full of fear in the past will continue to be so (this is presumably a matter of consistency).[61]

In all such considerations of historical truth or natural probability or necessity and verisimilitude, the primary aim is not the imitation of nature for the

57. Cf. 305. 31, 306. 3.

58. 608. 1 ff.

59. "Et è cosa assai manifesta perche la fittione poetica possa, & debba riceuere queste due maniere d'impossibilita cosi fatte, & informate di ragione, cercando il poeta di commuouere il lettore, o l'ascoltatore a marauiglia, la quale procede massimamente dall'operationi miracolose, & da quelle operationi, che auengono radissime fiate" (608. 41).

60. 188. 1.

61. 330. 40.

sake of making the poem resemble nature but rather the resemblance to nature for the sake of obtaining the credence of the audience. Credibility remains the ultimate touchstone.

II

A poetics which in this way seeks to give pleasure to an audience of limited imaginative capacities presents a very special and a very difficult problem to the poet. The problem is not to produce a beautiful work of art through the ordering of all the parts to an artistically perfect structure. Questions of beauty rarely concern Castelvetro. Rather, it is the task of the poet to find some way of entertaining the audience while he keeps it convinced that what it sees (or reads) is true, that is, of striking a proper balance between the probable and the marvelous. "The greatest praise of a poet is that he makes the uncertain seem certain through every means of which he is capable."[62]

The first means to the achievement of this end is the proper selection and assorting of materials. In the tragic and epic genres this necessitates the choice of a historical subject, to assure credibility, and the addition to that subject of episodes or variations or developments that will make of it a new and interesting plot. This latter is the difficult part; for it is only in so far as he expands or embroiders upon his historical *données* that a poet is an inventor, hence a poet. "Invention is the most difficult thing that the poet has to do, and the thing from which it seems that he derives his name, that is ποιητής."[63] It is in connection with this demand for invention that Castelvetro introduces a criterion of originality:

> For a poet cannot compose a plot already composed by another poet, for this would either be history or a plagiarism. For example, if one should wish to arrange in a plot the events by which Orestes killed his mother, it would not be proper to follow any story of a son who killed his mother in the way in which she was killed in the plot composed on the subject by Aeschylus, or by Euripides, or by Sophocles. But it would be necessary that, setting aside all historical and poetical resemblances, he should give himself over to subtle searching and with his own wit to finding how that event might be made to come about in another way, which had not yet been narrated or written by anybody, just as those other poets had done.[64]

62. "al poeta, la cui sua maggiore lode è, che faccia la'ncertitudine parere certitudine per tutte quelle vie, che puo" (210. 35).

63. "la quale inuentione à la piu difficile cosa, che habbia il poeta da fare, & dalla qual parte pare, che egli prenda il nome, cio è ποιητής" (78. 2).

64. "Conciosia cosa che il poeta non possa comporre vna fauola composta da alcun poeta, percioche o sarebbe historia, o furto, come, se altri volesse ordinare in vna fauola, come Oreste vccise la madre, non conuerrebbe seguire historia alcuna d'vn figliuolo, che habbia vccisa la madre nella maniera d'vcciderla, ne la fauola composta di cio da Eschilo, o da Euripide, o da Sophocle, ma conuiene, che lasciate da parte tutte le rassomiglianze o historiche, o poetiche, si dea a sottigliare, & col suo ingegno a trouare, come possa essere auenuto quel fatto in altra maniera, che non è anchora stato narrato, o scritto da alcuno, si come fecero altresi que poeti" (67. 31).

Here, apparently, only the central action would be historical; the rest would be up to the poet. Put in another way,

the plot of tragedy and of the epic can be constituted only of things which have actually happened and are known, the royal estate upon which it is founded making this necessary. These historical events must nevertheless be known only summarily, so that the poet may exercise and demonstrate his own genius and find the particular things and the means by which that action was brought to its conclusion.[65]

Either the historical subject itself or the decorations provided by the poet must, in part at least, partake of the nature of the marvelous.

A second means to convincing and amusing the audience is the disposition of these materials in accordance with the unities of time, place, and action. We have already seen, early in the discussion, how the physical comforts of the audience and its lack of imagination have to be taken into account by the poet; these two factors lead, respectively, to the unities of time and of place. With respect to time, the clearest statement is found in the comparison of tragedy and the epic:

Now, just as the perceptible end of tragedy has found its proper compass within the revolution of the sun over the earth without going beyond this limit, in order to put an end to the discomfort of the audience and the expense of the actors, so the perceptible end of the epic has found its proper compass in being able to be extended over several days, since neither the discomfort of the listener nor harm or expense connected with the reciter took this possibility away from it.[66]

Essentially, then, the basic factor is that the audience can remain within the theater (for tragedy and comedy) only for a given time—maximum, twelve hours.[67] Besides, the action before its eyes will take place on a single spot, the stage. Hence two unities: "tragedy . . . must have as its subject an action accomplished in a small area of place and in a small space of time, that is, in that place and in that time where and when the actors remain engaged in acting, and not in any other place or in any other time."[68] For the imagination

---

65. "la fauola della tragedia, & dell'epopea non si puo constituire se non di cose auenute & conosciute, cosi richiedendo lo stato reale sopra il quale ella è fondata. Le quali cose auenute non dimeno non deono essere conosciute se non sommariamente, accioche il poeta possa essercitare, & far vedere il suo ingegno, & trouare le cose particolari, ei mezzi, per gli quali quella attione fu condotta al suo termine" (211. 18).

66. "Hora, si come il termine sensibile della tragedia ha trouata la sua misura d'vn giro del sole sopra la terra senza passare piu oltre, per cessare il disconcio de veditori, & la spesa de rappresentatori, cosi il termine sensibile dell'epopea ha trouata la sua misura di potere essere tirato in lungo per piu giornate, poi che ne disagio d'ascoltatore, ne danno, o spesa del recitatore non gliele toglieua" (534. 1).

67. 109. 23, 163. 26.

68. "la tragedia.... conuiene hauere per soggetto vn'attione auenuta in picciolo spatio di luogo, & in picciolo spatio di tempo, cio è in quel luogo, & in quel tempo, doue, & quando i rappresentatori dimorano occupati in operatione, & non altroue, ne in altro tempo" (109. 17).

of the audience, limited to the witness of its senses, will not permit it to believe that the action takes place in more than one locality—"restricted not only to a city, or a town, or a country place, or some such site, but even to that view which alone can present itself to the eyes of a person"[69]—or in a time in excess of that of the performance:

But as for the magnitude of the plot, which is subjected to the senses and is taken in by sight and hearing together, I must say that it should be as long as would be an actual event, depending upon fortune and worthy of being written down in history that might come to pass, it being necessary that this imagined event of the plot should occupy as much time . . . as was occupied or would be occupied by a similar event if it really happened or were to happen.[70]

Ideally, then, the invented action should occupy no more time than a real action, and this time should not exceed the time of performance; the place should remain unchanged and be contained within the space visible to a person who himself did not move.

The extent to which the senses, especially sight, are a governing factor in this theory of the unities is indicated by the change in requirements when the epic is considered. For the events of the epic do not actually appear before the eyes of the spectator. Instead, they are narrated to him. Since he does not see them, he can admit broad variations of place and a discrepancy between time of performance and time of action. Castelvetro draws a distinction between perceptible time (*il sensibile*, that distinguished by the senses) and intellectual time (*lo'ntellettuale*, that conceived of by the mind). In tragedy, the two must be identical; in epic, there may be a wide divergency between them.[71]

As for the unity of action, which for Aristotle is the only important one and which for him is of the very essence of the work of art, Castelvetro's treatment of it is highly revelatory of his general attitude toward poetics. To begin with, he denies any necessity—in the nature of things—for limitation of a poem to a single action; as so frequently, he takes issue sharply with Aristotle here:

For there is no doubt that, if in history one may relate in a single narrative several actions of a single person, . . . in poetry it will be possible in a single plot to narrate without being blamed for it several actions of a single person, just as similarly in poetry

69. "ristretto non solamente ad vna citta, o villa, o campagna, o simile sito, ma anchora a quella vista, che sola puo apparere a gli occhi d'vna persona" (535. 15).

70. "Ma della grandezza della fauola, che è sottoposta a sensi, & comprendesi con la vista, & con l'vdita insieme, è da dire, che sia tanta, quanta sarebbe quella d'vn caso fortunoso degno d'historia, che auenisse veramente, essendo di necessita, che corra tanto tempo in rappresentare questo caso della fauola imaginato.... quanto corse in simile caso, o correrebbe, mentre veramente auenne, o auenisse" (163. 13; cf. 381. 38, 533. 37).

71. 533. 23. The point of departure here is Aristotle's distinction (*Poetics* 1451ᵃ6) between τὴν αἴσθησιν and τὴν φύσιν.

one may relate without being blamed for it a single action of a whole people, for history does this with much praise. . . . And, indeed, in poetry not only a single action of a whole people may be narrated, but even several actions of a people. . . . And even if it were conceded to poetry to relate many actions of many persons or of many peoples, I do not see that any blame should come to it for this reason.[72]

Moreover, the presentation of a double or even a multiple plot would more readily serve the end of pleasure sought by the poet:

we should not marvel at all if several actions of one person or one action of a people or several actions of several persons delight us and make us attentive to listen, since such a plot carries with it, through the multitude of the actions, through the variety, through the new events, and through the multitude of persons and of the people, both pleasure and greatness and magnificence.[73]

Why, then, does Aristotle insist upon unity, and why does Castelvetro recommend it? The reason is different for the different genres. For tragedy and comedy, unity of action is a consequence of the unities of time and of place; it would not be possible to crowd, into a restricted space and into twelve hours, more than one action; indeed, sometimes one of these plays will contain only a part of an action.[74] For the epic, where this "necessity" does not exist, unity of action is sought for two other reasons: first, because such a unified plot is more "beautiful," less likely to satiate the spectator with an abundance of different things,[75] and, second, because such a plot demonstrates the ingenuity and the excellence of the poet:

In the narration of the single action of one person, which at first glance would not seem to have the capacity of keeping the minds of the auditors listening with delight, one discovers the judgment and the industry of the poet, who achieves that with one action of one person which others can hardly achieve with many actions and of many persons.[76]

72. "Perche non ha dubbio niuno, che, se nell'historia si narra sotto vn raccontamento piu attioni d'vna persona sola,... nella poesia si potra sotto vna fauola narrare senza biasimo piu attioni d'vna persona sola. si comme parimente nella poesia senza biasimo si potra narrare vna attione sola d'vna gente, percioche l'historia fa cio con molta lode.... Et non solamente pure nella poesia si potra narrare vna attione d'vna gente, ma anchora piu attioni d'vna gente.... Et, se le si concedera la narratione di molte attioni di molte persone, o di molte genti, non pero veggo, che biasimo alcuno le debba seguire" (178. 23). The argument rests upon an analogy between poetry and history which I shall indicate later.

73. "non sia punto da marauigliarsi se piu attioni d'vna persona, o vna attione d'vna gente, o piu attioni di piu persone ci dilettassono, & ci rendessono intenti ad ascoltarle, portando seco la fauola per la moltitudine dell'attioni, per la varieta, per gli nuoui auenimenti, & per la moltitudine delle persone, & della gente & piacere, & grandezza, & magnificenza" (179. 18; cf. 504. 36, 692. 31).

74. 179. 4; cf. 504. 19. Castelvetro thinks of the "action" as the whole of the traditional or historical story, not as the plot of the individual work of art.

75. 179. 16, 514, 29.

76. "in narrare vna attione sola d'vna persona, che in prima vista non pare hauer potere di ritenere gli animi ad ascoltare con diletto, si scopre il giudicio, & la'ndustria del poeta, operando quello con vna attione d'vna persona, che altri apena possono operare con molte attioni, & di molte persone" (179. 24; cf. 179. 16, 504. 23).

What is symptomatic about this position is its abandonment of any concern with the structural or formal beauties of the work and its insistence upon two such nonartistic considerations as the comfort and character of the audience and the glory of the poet.

A third means to the achievement of the ends with respect to the audience is what we might call, roughly, the total excellence of the work. This is in a way related to the unity of plot just discussed; a certain admiration, a certain sense of the marvelous, will result from the perfect execution of the poem. There might seem to be here an independent criterion of beauty, were it not for the fact that beauty is itself reduced to qualities already considered: "so that it [the plot] may turn out to be beautiful, that is, marvelous and probable."[77] Or, negatively, beauty is reduced to an absence of flaws from a form large enough to permit the perception of such flaws:

> For that thing is really beautiful in which no ugliness is discovered but in which, if there were any, it would be discovered; and that is really not beautiful which, being ugly, seems beautiful because for some reason its ugliness does not become apparent.[78]

The first consequence of this essentially negative criterion is that larger poems will be preferable to smaller; Dante is greater than Petrarch, since his poem is so "grande e magnifico" that, were there any errors in it, they would immediately be visible.[79] As far as the audience is concerned, such a poem shows the artifice of the poet and is a source of admiration. A second consequence is that magnitude of form will be accompanied by multiplicity of parts and by variety of developments, and that multiplicity and that variety, in turn, will be sources of pleasure.[80] These are major excellences of the poem, and they are to be sought in preference to such minor excellences as purity of diction, ornamentation through figures, and the sound of the verses. These latter may indeed supply pleasure, but it will be inferior to the pleasure derived from imitation.[81] Again with respect to total excellence, it should be noted that it is not an absolute quality but one discovered by comparison with other works: "for nothing reveals better the goodness or the badness of anything whatsoever than comparison."[82] The poet who would gain the admiration of his audience must

---

77. "accioche riesca piu bella, cio è marauigliosa, & verisimile" (140. 39).

78. "Perche quella cosa è veramente bella, nella quale non si scopre bruttezza, ma, se vi fosse, vi si scoprirebbe. & quella veramente non è bella, che essendo brutta, per alcuna cagione non apparendo la bruttezza, par bella" (162. 28).

79. 164. 21; cf. 673. 19 ff. on the errors of tragedy.

80. Cf. 536. 32 and n. 73 above.

81. 74. 2.

82. "conciosia cosa che nulla scopra piu il bene, o il male di che che sia, che il paragone" (290. 31).

therefore keep in mind all the precepts and "apply them so excellently that his poem will surpass in all things the poems of past poets."[83]

III

These indications of the ways by which the art of poetry achieves its ends—ends with respect to the audience and ends with respect to the poet—may be taken as preliminary steps toward a definition of the art itself. If we would further approach such a definition, the best means is to examine the relationships that Castelvetro establishes between poetry and the other arts.

The art to which poetry is most closely akin is the art of history. Indeed, their kinship is so intimate that, if we possessed an adequate art of history, it would be unnecessary to write an art of poetry, "since poetry derives all its light from the light of history." Such an art of history would tell us

what things were memorable in greater and in lesser degree and worthy of having a place in history, and, on the other hand, which ones were not memorable and unworthy of being touched upon by the historian. And then it would tell us what things should be narrated briefly and summarily and which ones at length and in particular; and afterward what order and disposition should be followed in recounting the events. And, besides, it would not fail to tell us when and where should be intercalated digressions, and descriptions of a place or of a person or of other things. And then it would decide whether it is permissible to the author of the history to offer a judgment on things that he relates, blaming or praising them, and adapting them to the instruction and utility of the reader and to his conduct as a citizen. And similarly it would decide if it is proper and possible for the historian to present some matters by narration, others by dramatic representation, as the poet does, or whether, indeed, this is a prerogative of poetry alone. And, finally, it would tell us what kinds of words suit history in general and what kinds do not, and which particularly in certain places and which not.[84]

Precepts of this kind, were they properly presented in an art of history, would not have to be repeated in an art of poetry, being common to both arts. Now if we examine in detail these precepts, we discover that they do, in fact, cover the primary preoccupations of Castelvetro throughout his treatment of poetry:

83. "metterle in opera cosi eccellentemente, che la poesia sua trapassi in tutte le cose le poesie de poeti passati" (393. 31).

84. "quali fossero le cose memoreuoli piu, & meno per gradi, & degne d'hauer luogo nell'historia, & quali dall'altra parte non fossero memoreuoli, ne meriteuoli d'essere tocche dall'historico. Et poi ci sarebbe stato detto, quali cose si douessono narrare breuemente, & sommariamente, & quali distesamente, & particolarmente. & appresso, quale ordine, & dispositione fosse da seguire in raccontare le cose. Et anchora non ci sarebbe stato taciuto, quando, & doue si douessono intramettere digressioni, & discrittioni di luogo, o di persona, o d'altra cosa. Et poscia si sarebbe determinato, se sia permesso all'autore dell'historia dar giudicio delle cose, che egli narra, biasimandole, o lodandole, & tirarle ad ammaestramento, & ad vtilita de lettori, & del viuer cittadinesco. Et parimente si sarebbe determinato, se si conuenga, & se si possa per l'historico far palese alcuna materia per via di racconto, & di rappresentamento, come si fa per lo poeta, o se pur cio sia priuilegio della poesia sola. Et vltimamente ci sarebbe stato detto, quali maniere di parole si confacessero generalmente all'historia tutta, & quali no. & quali particolarmente a certi luoghi, & quali no" (5. 28).

choice of subject matter (sufficiently noteworthy to be marvelous); distinction between central plot and episodes; ordering of the plot, digressions, moral conclusions from the plot; use of the *récit* in tragedy and of dramatic scenes in the epic; and the general problem of diction. The two arts differ in two respects only: history presents events which actually happened, poetry those which have not occurred but which might occur, and poetry uses verse whereas history uses prose.[85] Otherwise they are so much alike that poetry may be defined as "a resemblance or imitation of history."[86]

Aristotle's likening of poetry to painting, thinks Castelvetro, is essentially erroneous; for there are more dissimilarities than similarities between the two arts. They are unlike, first, in the kinds of things which they represent. Painting (like history) depicts true things—the "cosa certa & conosciuta"—whereas poetry imitates probable things—the "cosa incerta & sconosciuta." Moreover, whereas poetry represents actions, painting at its best represents objects (historical painting is a definitely inferior genre). They are unlike, second, in the relationship to be expected between the imitation and the object; in painting, exact resemblance is to be demanded: "the slightest dissimilarity between the image and the man depicted can be blamed and condemned as bad art"; in poetry, the imitation is an expansion, an embellishment, an idealization of whatever real events may have been taken as a starting point. Third, the sources of pleasure in the two are unlike. Painting, appealing to the eye, delights precisely through this exact resemblance, which in poetry is displeasing; on the other hand, the imitation in poetry of an unknown, probable action "delights us beyond all measure." This is explained on the basis of the difficulty involved for the artist. For the painter, faithful rendering is the hardest procedure, shows the greatest talent, evokes the most unlimited admiration. For the poet, such rendering makes him a simple historian; it is the introduction of the "unreal," of the "invented," of the "marvelous," that constitutes his greatest glory. Castelvetro himself sees only one basis of comparison between the two arts, and that is on the score of the *convenevole*, which here means the representation of things as they should be; but I see no attempt on his part to reconcile this with the requirement, for painting, that things be represented as they are.[87]

In the light of the close affinity which other theorists, such as Robortello, saw between poetry and rhetoric, we are compelled to ask whether Castelvetro also treats the two arts as cognate. We discover immediately that he does not. He makes a number of references to Aristotle's *Rhetoric*, largely on matters of

85. On the necessity of verse cf. 115. 41, 190. 1.
86. "similitudine, o rassomiglianza d'historia" (28. 19).
87. For the main discussions see 586. 9, 72. 4, 41. 11, 342. 28.

diction, the passions, and thought, but does not proceed from them to the indication of a general similitude between poetic and rhetoric.[88] This is all the more remarkable, since, as we have seen, in its broadest lines Castelvetro's system is essentially rhetorical. Perhaps the explanation may be found in his insistence on declaring the close relationship between poetry and history, on treating poetic as if it were a branch of the historical art, and on eliminating—by denial or by silence—any other art which might be set up as a contender to history. In the last analysis, this wedding of poetry to history may constitute one of the most original features of Castelvetro's system.

As a result of this likening of poetry to history, some of the usual preoccupations of Renaissance arts of poetry disappear. The poet himself does not need to be divinely inspired, to write under the influence of the *furor poeticus*, to feel himself the passions which he incorporates in his characters; these are superstitions fostered by the poets to improve their credit with the ignorant masses.[89] Instead, he is a careful and deliberate artisan, who follows the precepts of the art so as to achieve, immediately, the pleasure of his audience and, ultimately, his own glory.[90] We have already seen how these precepts relate to the choice, the disposition, and the embellishment of his materials. Castelvetro treats the moot question of the relationship of the poem to nature only summarily and indirectly. The notion of imitation as introducing differences between an object in nature and that object as represented in a work of art is completely absent; indeed, in a work which is a commentary on Aristotle, none of the implications of the Aristotelian concept of imitation are present. So completely are these implications lost that imitation (*rassomiglianza*) is said not to be present when true or historical events are treated and to be present only in the details and embellishments "invented" by the poet—in accordance with probability, of course.[91] Still, in relationship to imitation, the distinction between πράξεως and δρώντων is wrested from its meaning in such a way that the thing represented becomes the action of the poem and the person representing becomes the poet (e.g., the *Aeneid* and Vergil).[92]

With the popular conception of the poet as divinely inspired now discarded, with all notions of the poem as an imitation of nature either distorted or abandoned, with the resemblance to painting specifically denied, Castelvetro's poetic system becomes a very special system for his times. Poetics turns out to be a branch of history, but with the special feature of a history that attempts to please its audience and bring glory to its author. Whatever in a poem relates to

---

88. Cf., for example, 257. 43 on the qualitative and quantitative parts in poetic and rhetoric.

89. 65. 12, 180. 7, 372. 30, 374. 15.

90. 68. 38, 374. 37, 394. 17.

91. Cf. pp. 583–85.

92. 114. 40.

the necessities of credibility derives its characteristics and its criteria from the science of history; whatever relates to the necessities of pleasing an audience whose character is very carefully delimited derives its characteristics and its criteria from the art of rhetoric. If there is any proper role for an art of poetry—and at times this is practically denied—it is in the combination of the precepts supplied by these two parent-arts, in the filling of gaps where, as in the case of the unities, the other arts do not afford specific recommendations. Or, to state the case more accurately, the poet considers himself as a kind of historian and relies openly on the teachings of history to guide him in his writing of poems; but there are places where these teachings are inadequate, and here the poet—even though he may not recognize the fact—has recourse to the fundamental relationships existing between a work using language and the audience to which it is directed. This second kind of activity leads him to formulate for himself—or to take over from the previous formulations of such theorists as Castelvetro—a set of special conventions or rules or practices which, taken together, compose an art of poetry. But that art is never an independent art, bearing always the traces of its origins in history and rhetoric. It has, therefore, very little to do with the "art" of Aristotle. Anyone who would adopt it, theorist or poet, would thus be committing himself to an essentially un-Aristotelian system of poetics, one which was even farther removed from the presuppositions of the original text than had been the theory contained in the commentary of Robortello.

ENGLISH NEOCLASSICAL CRITICISM: AN OUTLINE SKETCH[1]

R. S. CRANE

RYDEN, declared Johnson in the *Lives of the Poets*, "may be properly considered as the father of English criticism, as the writer who first taught us to determine upon principles the merit of composition." Unfair to the efforts of earlier authors as this judgment may now seem, it points to the undoubted fact that it was in the period from Dryden to the end of the eighteenth century, and to some extent under the influence of Dryden's example, that criticism of poetry, painting, and the other fine arts became, for the first time in English literature, an important branch of learning, considered worthy of cultivation, for both practical and theoretical ends, by some of the most distinguished minds of the time. Beginning with the essays and prefaces of Dryden himself and the treatises of Thomas Rymer, the output of critical writings continued rapidly to increase in volume through the next two generations until, in the middle and later years of the following century, it is hard to name any author of consequence—poet, dramatist, novelist, philosopher, historian, or scholar—who did not attempt in some medium—treatise, essay, dialogue, lecture, preface, didactic poem, history—either to reformulate the principles of one or more of the arts or to pronounce on the merits of artists and works.

In terms of the scope or primary locus of their subject matter, the many products of this movement fall into at least six characteristic groups. There were many works, to begin with, in which the dominant concern was to reduce to some kind of method the rules or precepts peculiar either to one of the various arts considered as a whole or to some one of its branches or genres; e.g., Dryden's *Essay of Dramatic Poesy* (1668); the Earl of Mulgrave's verse *Essay upon Poetry* (1682); John Dennis' *The Grounds of Criticism in Poetry* (1704); Joseph Trapp's *Praelectiones poeticae*(1711–15); Jonathan Richardson's *Essay on the Theory of Painting* (1715); Charles Gildon's *The Complete Art of Poetry* (1718); Richard Hurd's commentary on Horace, with its annexed essays (1749–57), and his later dissertation on *The Idea of Universal Poetry* (1765); several of Johnson's contributions to the *Rambler* (1750–52); the *Art of Poetry*

1. Reprinted from *The Dictionary of World Literature*, edited by Joseph T. Shipley (New York: Philosophical Library, 1943).

on a New Plan (1762), sometimes attributed erroneously to Goldsmith; Sir Joshua Reynolds' *Fifteen Discourses Delivered in the Royal Academy* (1769–90); Percival Stockdale's *Inquiry into the Nature and Genuine Laws of Poetry* (1778).

With these, because of their common concern with the principles of art, may be associated a series of works, of which Dryden's *Parallel betwixt Poetry and Painting* (1695), James Harris' *Three Treatises* (1744), Daniel Webb's *Observations on the Correspondence between Poetry and Music* (1769), James Beattie's *Essays on Poetry and Music* (1776), and Thomas Twining's "Two Dissertations on Poetical and Musical Imitation" (1789) are characteristic examples, in which the major problem was the discovery of a basis both for clarifying the likenesses among the various arts and for making intelligible their differences. Something of the same interest in discovering unifying principles was present also in Hugh Blair's very popular *Lectures on Rhetoric and Belles Lettres* (1783), though Blair's mode of treatment lent itself more easily to an emphasis on the differences among the arts of language—oratory, history, philosophy, and poetry—than to an exhibition of their fundamental analogies.

In both these classes of writings, problems involving either the nature and functions of the creative artist in general or the genius and accomplishment of individual poets or painters were treated in subordination to a systematic exposition of the ends and rules of arts or genres. But a more specialized discussion was also possible and was, in fact, attempted, especially after the first quarter of the eighteenth century, in works which either, like Edward Young's *Conjectures on Original Composition* (1759) or the treatises on genius of William Duff (1767) and Alexander Gerard (1774), approached the question in general terms or, like Thomas Blackwell's *Enquiry into the Life and Writings of Homer* (1735), Joseph Warton's *Essay on the Genius and Writings of Pope* (1756), and Johnson's *Lives of the English Poets* (1779–81), introduced their principles in a context of biography and particularized critical evaluation.

In a fourth class of works, also more characteristic of the eighteenth century than of the seventeenth, the center of attention was shifted from the rules of art or the traits of artists to the qualities of individual productions or of particular, historically determined, styles of composition. Of this mode of criticism the most important early examples were Rymer's *Tragedies of the Last Age* (1678) and Dryden's *Dedication of the Aeneis* (1697); among many that followed after 1700 may be mentioned Addison's papers on *Paradise Lost* (1712), Pope's Preface to the *Iliad* (1715) and Postscript to the *Odyssey* (1726), Joseph Spence's *Essay on Mr. Pope's Odyssey* (1726–27), Johnson's essays in the *Rambler* on Milton's versification and on *Samson Agonistes*, Joseph Warton's appreciations of the *Odyssey* and of Shakespeare's *Tempest* and *King Lear* in the *Adventurer* (1753–54), Thomas Warton's *Observations on the Fairy Queen*

(1754, 1762), Hugh Blair's *Critical Dissertation on the Poems of Ossian* (1763), and John Scott's *Critical Essays on Some of the Poems of Several English Poets* (1785). Robert Lowth's *De sacra poesi Hebraeorum praelectiones* (1753), Richard Hurd's *Letters on Chivalry and Romance* (1762), and the critical portions of Thomas Warton's *History of English Poetry* (1774–81) differ from the others chiefly in that their writers chose to bring together in one context several or many works the qualities of which were dependent, at least in part, on common conditions of time or place.

The eighteenth century also saw the rise to popularity and importance of a species of criticism of which few models, in the form of extended works at any rate, are found earlier. Its distinguishing feature lay in the fact that it was concerned less with the rules of art (though these might enter by way of final deductions) or with the nature and achievements of artists (though these might be alluded to) than with the general qualities of art and their foundations in human nature. The earliest significant contribution to this kind of inquiry was Addison's series in the *Spectator* (1712) on the pleasures of the imagination; this was followed by Francis Hutcheson's *Inquiry into the Origin of Our Ideas of Beauty and Virtue* (1725), William Hogarth's *Analysis of Beauty* (1753), Hume's essays on tragedy and on the standard of taste (1757), Burke's *Philosophical Enquiry into the Origin of Our Ideas of the Sublime and Beautiful* (1757), Gerard's *Essay on Taste* (1759), Lord Kames's *Elements of Criticism* (1762), and Archibald Alison's *Essays on the Nature and Principles of Taste* (1790), to say nothing of a host of less distinguished or familiar attempts.

With these works, finally, may be grouped a number of writings that dealt with the question of criticism itself—its nature, its utility, its kinds, its history: the most notable of these were Pope's *Essay on Criticism* (1711), Goldsmith's *Enquiry into the Present State of Polite Learning in Europe* (1759), and Gibbon's *Essai sur l'étude de la littérature* (1761).

In spite of the diversity of interests reflected in these various classes of productions and in spite, also, of the many conflicts or apparent conflicts of doctrine and taste that separated their writers, it is nevertheless possible, without undue simplification, to tell the story of the development of criticism in England from Dryden to the death of Johnson in terms of a single dominant conception of the art, in relation to which even the more seemingly revolutionary changes in the latter part of the period can be interpreted as so many shifts of emphasis within the framework of a common conceptual scheme. The scheme was a sufficiently flexible one to permit the integration into it of terms, distinctions, topics of argument, and doctrines drawn from a great variety of earlier critical systems, ancient and modern. "Aristotle with his interpreters, and Horace, and Longinus," Dryden confessed, "are the authors to whom I

owe my lights"; but the list of preferred authorities, both for Dryden himself
and for his contemporaries and successors, included many more than these
three names: Plato and certain of the Neo-Platonists, Cicero, Dionysius of
Halicarnassus, Demetrius, and Quintilian from antiquity; Scaliger, Sidney,
and Ben Jonson from the Renaissance; Boileau, Rapin, Bossu, Bouhours from
the France of Louis XIV; and, as time went on, most of the distinguished
figures in the continental criticism of the eighteenth century—all these and
others, in varying proportions for different writers, were made to yield quotations or arguments, examples or schemes of analysis, suitable to the uses of
contemporary debate. The number of such borrowings, however, and the range
of philosophically very disparate sources from which they came should not be
allowed to obscure the fact that, if Restoration and eighteenth century English
criticism was highly eclectic in its choice of authorities, it was far from being
merely so in its selection of the ruling principles of method by which these
authorities were interpreted or its own original efforts controlled. With respect to such principles, at any rate, it constituted, from the beginning of the
period to the end, a distinct and fairly consistent school, which can be characterized most simply by saying that its basic historical affinities were Roman
rather than Greek, that its favorite masters were Horace rather than Aristotle
(for all its many debts to the *Poetics*) and Quintilian rather than Longinus (for
all the enthusiasm many of its adherents felt for the treatise *On the Sublime*),
and that its typical devices of analysis and evaluation owed more to the example of rhetoric, in at least one conception of that art, than they did either to
philosophy or to poetics in any senses of these terms that warranted a treatment of poetry or one of the other arts either in a context of universal human
values or as a distinct subject matter with principles of its own.

As determined by these influences and preoccupations, neoclassical criticism
may be described, in comparison with the Greek tradition, as being at once
broader in its scope than the criticism of Aristotle and more restricted than that
of Plato. Like Plato and unlike Aristotle, its invariable concern was with what
poets or artists ought to do, rather than with what they have done and hence
may do; but, unlike Plato, its characteristic appeal, on all issues that involved
the end or good of art, was not (as in the *Republic* or the *Phaedrus*) to the knowledge of the philosophers or (as in the *Laws*) to the sagacity of statesmen, but
rather to the trained taste and sensitive judgment of men expert in the enjoyment of poetry, painting, or music. Its frame of reference, in short, tended to
be not the republic but the republic of letters; and, although the larger context
of morals or civil philosophy was seldom left entirely out of view and although,
as we shall see, the statement of criteria for works of art involved the use
of terms applicable to values beyond the limited realm of taste, it still remains

true that the utility of criticism in this tradition was normally conceived in terms of the needs of men, not as moral beings or as seekers after truth, but as poets and artists, readers and spectators, listeners and connoisseurs. In the formula of Addison and of many others in the eighteenth century, its special domain was the pleasures of the imagination; but, though this was generally so, the result was never, on the other hand, any such concentration on the formal aspects of artistic products as had constituted, for Aristotle, the distinctive method of poetics as the science of imitation. Instead, both these extremes were avoided, in the arguments of the neoclassical critics, through the almost universal preference for a scheme of terms, inherited from such Romans as Horace and Quintilian, in which the problems of any of the fine arts, like those of rhetoric, could be treated in a fourfold context of the art itself, the artist, the work, and the audience, in such a way as at once to preserve its distinctness from other human activities or from things and to give to its peculiar aims and rules a clear justification in the nature of man.

Such was the flexibility of this scheme that any one of the four terms—art, artist, work, or audience—might be taken as a primary frame of reference for a particular discussion and the other terms subordinated to it; much of the variety of eighteenth-century criticism, as has been suggested, was due precisely to contextual shifts of this sort. No single statement, therefore, of the meanings or distinctions that might be attached to each of the four main topics can be expected to do exact justice to the structure of any one argument in which they appear. But, on the whole, it may be said that the special problems of art were those of ends and rules either for the art as a whole or for one or more of its distinctive species or genres; of the artist, those of the aims he ought to pursue and of the natural and acquired powers he must have in order to attain them; of the work, those of style or quality as determined by the art and the artist; of the audience, those of its particular composition or standards and of the demands it makes on the artists who would serve it. For each of these sets of problems an abundance of terms was available in the ancient traditions of rhetoric and poetics or in the more recent attempts to formulate, by analogy, the precepts of the other arts; and their use persisted, with relatively few additions from other sources, throughout the period, until in the early nineteenth century a new vocabulary of criticism, philosophical rather than rhetorical in origin, began to replace the old in the writings of Coleridge and others.

Thus in the analysis of an art the major terms were commonly derived from the rhetorical distinction of invention, arrangement, and expression—a distinction which, though signifying primarily the parts of the art, might also be applied in discussions of the artist, when invention was often referred to natural genius and the other parts to judgment, or in treatments of the work, when invention was correlated with the actions, thoughts, and images, expression with the style, and arrangement with both. The systematic statement of an art, however, was seldom considered complete without a section, usually a long one, on its various kinds; and here again the richness of the terminology bequeathed to the neoclassical critics by their predecessors in antiquity and the Renaissance for whom the question of genres was a central question of art, coupled with the possibility of obtaining criteria for definition and classification not only from distinctions of artistic matter and means but from differences in the natural faculties of artists and audiences, permitted a mode of analysis that was often (as in Boileau and Dryden) elaborate and subtle to a degree. The typical schematism for at least the major poetic kinds, such as drama and epic, came ultimately, though with many dialectical modifications, from the *Poetics;* but the influence of Roman rhetoric was also important, if not in determining the details of the discussions, at least in orienting them toward a conception of artistic genres as resting not so much on inductively ascertained differences among works as on distinctions of purpose, subject matter, and style that derived from the nature of the art itself. In general, the realm of art was the locus of differentiations: the final end was perfection or excellence or writing or painting well; but though, as Reynolds pointed out, there is only one beauty, the means by which beauty may be achieved are many, and, in consequence, the special pleasures that may be sought in an art are as numerous as the subjects that may be treated, the combinations of stylistic devices that may be employed, or the powers and disposition of the mind that may be appealed to.

For their discussions of the poet or artist, as distinct from the art, the neoclassical critics also drew, in the main, on topics long familiar in the tradition to which these critics belonged. Whether the immediate task of the argument was the statement of rules for an art or a genre or the appraisal of work already done, it was still appropriate to consider the comparative importance of nature, genius, or imagination, on the one hand, and of art, judgment, imitation, or culture, on the other, in the formation of the artist or in the determination of his success or rank; questions might be raised concerning the specific natural powers he must have or the knowledge he needs for the achievement of special effects, such as delineating character or moving the passions; and the particular ends of an art in relation to the audience might be stated, as in Quintilian and Horace, as so many interests or duties devolving on the artist—to instruct, to move, or (as in many eighteenth-century critics) simply to please. Again, all these terms and distinctions, as well as those pertaining to art as such, might be shifted from their original contexts and applied to the work considered as the product of both the art and the artist; apart from such considerations, discussion of the work tended to turn chiefly on distinctions of style relative to times and places or the tastes and ideals of individuals. The audience, finally, which functioned in this criticism as a distinct element related in various ways to all the others, was generally treated in terms either of propositions concerning the passions and temperaments of men (prominent in the tradition of rhetoric from the time of Aristotle) or of distinctions (such as Horace often introduced) of education or taste, nationality, social status, or, as in the frequent appeals to posterity, simply position in time.

Such, very briefly, was the apparatus for the analysis of poetry or painting inherited by seventeenth- and eighteenth-century critics from the Roman tradition of rhetoric as a fine art or of poetics rhetorically conceived. In the main and with due allowance for certain apparently radical variations in the middle of the eighteenth century, the four terms were related in much the same fashion as in Quintilian. In the first place, both the artist and the work were normally subordinated to the art; the artist as the agent by which excellence in art is achieved only if his natural powers are cultivated in conformity with the precepts and great examples given by the art itself; the work as the product of both art and artist and hence as something to be analyzed or judged primarily by reference to these two more inclusive topics. Art, in this tradition, was thus conceived as an impersonal ideal of excellence to which artists must subject themselves if their works are to be praiseworthy or useful to mankind; it was thought of, in short, as a species of virtue, and its standard was the universal criterion, common to art and morals alike, of the mean. In the second place, however, in spite of the fact that an art was treated commonly as more universal than the artist and as independent both of him and of any particular body of readers or spectators, it was nonetheless consistently subordinated to the audience in the triple sense that its origins and reason for existence are in the natural instincts of human beings to take pleasure in imitations or in eloquent and rhythmical language, that it achieves its effects, however artificial, by administering to the natural sources of pleasure in the mind of man, and that its value is necessarily measured, in the long run at any rate, by the approval of the public. Art was accordingly at the same time something distinct from nature and even superior to it—a set of particular rules and standards by which nature was to be imitated or improved—and something intimately dependent on nature as the "universal light," in Pope's phrase, that constituted at once its source, and end, and test.

The complications of the dialectic that resulted from the efforts of neoclassical critics to reconcile what Reynolds called the "demands of nature" and the "purposes of art" can be no more than indicated here. When the issue arose in a context of the rules of art or of the praise or blame to be bestowed on individual artists or works, a resolution could be effected by one or the other of two devices or (as more often happened) by their combination. On the one hand, the whole problem could be subsumed under art on the strength of the simple assumption that those things that have actually delighted all ages in the works of poets or painters must be proportioned to human nature and hence capable still of giving delight when they are imitated in modern productions: it was thus, according to Pope, that Virgil came to identify Nature and Homer; it was thus that the rules of Aristotle, founded, as they were, simply on observation of those traits in which Euripides, Sophocles, and Aeschylus pleased, acquire the authority which is rightfully theirs as "Nature still, but Nature methodiz'd." The appeals to example and precedent that this assumption seemed to warrant formed one of the distinctive marks of neoclassical criticism throughout its long history, even in critics, like Johnson or Blair, whose primary emphases were very different.

It was seldom, though, that the case for the harmony of artistic standards and the demands of nature was allowed to rest merely on a recourse to authority, however venerable. "He who is ambitious to enlarge the boundaries of his art," declared Reynolds, "must extend his views, beyond the precepts which are found in books or may be drawn from the practice of his predecessors, to a knowledge of those precepts in the mind, those operations of intellectual nature, to which everything that aspires to please must be proportioned and accommodated." This was written in 1778, but the expedient here recommended of basing the rules or verdicts of criticism on premises in which particular artistic techniques or qualities were referred directly to their natural effects on the minds of men had had a long and significant history in the tradition to which Reynolds belonged. It was in terms of such "natural reasons," stated sometimes as mere factual probabilities, sometimes as explicit deductions from psychological causes, that Horace had vindicated the importance of vivid sentiments and truthful characters, that Quintilian had urged the effectiveness of a temperate and timely use of metaphor, that Dryden had argued for the unities of time and place, that Hume had accounted for the delight we receive from tragedy in spite of its painful images, that Johnson explained why Butler's *Hudibras*, wanting that variety which is the great source of pleasure, is likely to weary modern readers. The principles thus brought into the criticism of a particular art, it was widely recognized, applied equally to all the arts and hence could be made the warrant of analogies between poetry and painting, or poetry and music, of a more than merely heuristic import: we have already noted the vogue of "parallels" of this kind between Dryden and the end of the eighteenth century. The importance, in short, of this direct appeal to nature, considered as the constant wants and desires of the mind to which artists must administer if their works are to give satisfaction, cannot be exaggerated; but the "demands of nature" in this sense could be reconciled with the "purposes of art" only by means of additional premises derived from a consideration, not of "what pleases most" in the productions of an art, but of "what ought to please." The function of artists, it is true, is to delight audiences; and to this end, both to avoid errors and to realize fresh opportunities, they need to know, if only instinctively, the "natural sources of pleasure in the mind of man." But, at the same time, if they are to achieve excellence, they must attempt to please on terms dictated not by the actual preferences or passions of particular men but by the proper standards of the art or genre—its ideals as reflected concretely in the great works of past artists or as expressed abstractly in the precepts of criticism.

When made explicit in writings on the theory of art or on the performances of artists, these standards could be formulated in terms either of the art itself or of the audience. Viewed in relation to the work, artistic excellence was invariably found to consist, like moral excellence, in a mean between two extremes or, what amounts to the same thing, in a just mixture, relative to the kind of work, or the nature of the audience addressed, of opposite qualities; and faults, conversely, were identified with excesses or defects in any of the traits determined as virtues or with an exclusive emphasis on one extreme of style or treatment to the neglect of its corresponding opposite. "It is allowed on all hands," wrote Hume, "that beauty, as well as virtue, always lies in a medium"; and the most superficial acquaintance with the writings of the neoclassical critics is sufficient to verify the truth of his generalization. The model again had been set by Horace and Quintilian (cf. the *Ars poetica, passim,* and the *Institutio oratoria,* esp. x. 1. 46–49, and xii. 10. 79–80); and both the form of the argument in the neoclassical writers and many of the particular terms they employed show how powerful still was the influence of the ancient tradition. "A play ought to be a just and lively image of human nature, representing its passions and humors, and the changes of fortune to which it is subject, for the delight and instruction of mankind"; "True Wit is Nature to advantage dress'd/What oft was thought, but ne'er so well express'd"; "Their thoughts are often new, but seldom natural; they are not obvious, but neither are they just"; "The skilful writer *irritat, mulcet,* makes a due distribution of the still and animated parts"; "In this work [*The Rape of the Lock*] are exhibited, in a very high degree, the two most engaging powers of an author. New things are made familiar, and familiar things are made new"; "The same just moderation must be observed in regard to ornaments; nothing will contribute more to destroy repose than profusion. . . . On the other hand, a work without ornament, instead of simplicity, to which it makes pretensions, has rather the appearance of poverty"—it was by such manipulations of contraries or of positive and privative terms that the critics of this school achieved their characteristic formulations of artistic ideals or applied them in the judgment of artists and works. In the best critics such statements were reinforced by constant appeals to examples and illustrations from the history of art and hence to the feelings of audiences whose natural love of truth or delight in liveliness and variety were, along with other passions and affections, the ultimate sources from which, as Reynolds said, "all rules arise, and to which they are all referable."

But the formulation of standards could also be made more directly in terms of the audience by means of devices designed to effect a qualitative separation between readers or spectators in general and those select minds whose judgment could be considered as in some degree equivalent to the reasoned verdict of true criticism itself, or at least as a confirmatory sign of the presence of merit. Frequently, when it was a question either of justifying traditional precepts or of assigning degrees of excellence to older artists, the "best" audience was identified with posterity, on the principle often quoted from Cicero that "time effaces the fictions of opinion, and confirms the determinations of Nature." Such, for instance, was Johnson's procedure at the beginning of the *Preface to Shakespeare*, though he hastened to buttress the judgment of time, which is never infallible, with arguments based on the critical premise that "nothing can please many, and please long, but just representations of general nature." Sometimes, again, the selection was made in terms of tastes, as evidenced in the preference of the chosen public for particular past artists, or in terms of a proper balance and cultivation of mental faculties, or simply of freedom from habits likely to interfere with a correct judgment. Examples of the three possibilities are, respectively, Dryden's definition of the best public as "those readers who have discernment enough to prefer Virgil before any other poet in the Latin tongue"; his remark that true comedy, as distinguished from farce, requires for its appreciation spectators "who can judge of men and manners" and who are moved by both fancy and reason; and Johnson's statement, in his critique of Gray's *Elegy*, that he rejoices "to concur with the common reader; for by the common sense of readers uncorrupted with literary prejudices, after all the refinements of subtilty and the dogmatism of learning, must be finally decided all claims to poetical honors."

By an easy transition, finally, warranted by the assumption that the public, as Blair said, is "the supreme judge to which the last appeal must be made in all works of taste," the focus of critical interest could be shifted from a preoccupation with guiding artists to a concern with educating the audience they address; and, when this was the case, as it was, for example, in Hume's essay on "The Standard of Taste" and in parts of Blair's *Lectures*, the problem of values was commonly solved by a dialectic that followed a reverse direction to that taken by the writers on the rules of composition. The issue was still the reconciliation of nature and art, but, whereas in the criticism of art the effort was to find principles for the artist which accorded with the highest or most permanent demands of audiences, the criticism of taste was characteristically oriented toward finding principles for audiences which accorded with the true purposes of the best achievements of art. The two inquiries, however, though opposed in aim, were yet closely related as complementary aspects of the same general question; and it is not strange, therefore, that in most critical writings of the eighteenth century the line separating them is somewhat hard to draw.

With this general view of neoclassical criticism as a background, it is possible to account for certain of the more striking changes in critical practice that took place especially after 1700 and that serve to distinguish the age of Johnson, Goldsmith, and Young from that of Rymer and Dryden. In particular, three main lines of development may be traced within the tradition, each of them involving a more or less pronounced shift of emphasis with respect to one of the major determinants of the tradition as a whole.

One important line of evolution had to do with the source and guaranty of the natural principles on which, it was universally admitted, the rules of art in general and of all particular arts are founded. Were they to be sought, whether by artist or critic, directly in the mind as known by common observation or philosophy, or indirectly through study of the great works of art which owed their permanent appeal to conformity with them? There were few, if any, writers on criticism from the beginning to the end of the period who did not, as we have seen, think it essential to combine the two approaches. In this respect, except for the distribution of their emphasis, Johnson and Reynolds, writing in the 1770's, were no different from Dryden writing a hundred years before, so that if Johnson could accuse Cowley, in 1779, of "not sufficiently enquiring by what means the ancients have continued to delight through all the changes of human manners," Dryden could, conversely, insist in 1679 that a dramatist who would move the passions must, in addition to possessing a lofty genius, be skilled "in the principles of Moral Philosophy." Nevertheless, between the two dates represented by these quotations, a significant change of emphasis did take place, and its character may be indicated by contrasting another statement of Dryden, written in 1677, with typical declarations of critics in the middle of the following century. It requires philosophy as well as poetry, Dryden had remarked in the Preface to his *State of Innocence*, "to sound the depth of all the passions: what they are in themselves, and how they are to be provoked." But, he added, "in this science the best poets have excelled," and their authority, as codified in the rules of critics like Aristotle, is, for the modern writer, "the best argument; for generally to have pleased, and through all ages, must bear the force of universal tradition." For Reynolds, on the other hand, writing in 1786, the ambition of criticism must be to rise from a study of the beauties and faults in the works of celebrated masters (a narrow and uncertain mode of investigation), through a comparison of the principles of painting with those of the other arts, to a comparison of all the arts with the nature of man—and this he says, "as it is the highest style of criticism, is at the same time the soundest: for it refers to the eternal and immutable nature of things." Burke, in 1757, had been even more critical of the position represented by Dryden. A consideration of the "rationale of our passions," he wrote, "seems to me very necessary for all who would affect them upon solid and sure principles." In this inquiry, however, we can learn little from the artists themselves, and, "as for those called cricticks, they have generally sought the rule of the arts in the wrong place; they sought it among poems, pictures, engravings, statues, and buildings. But art can never give the rules that make an art"—only the observation of nature can do that. To Lord Kames, again, whose *Elements of Criticism* (1762) was founded on an elaborate analysis of the emotions and passions in relation to various kinds of natural and artificial objects, the history of criticism in modern times stood in direct opposition to that of the other philosophical sciences. Whereas the latter had abandoned authority for reason, criticism "continues to be no less slavish in its principles, nor less submissive to authority, than it was originally." And he went on to speak of Bossu, "who gives many rules; but can discover no better foundation for any of them, than the practice merely of Homer and Virgil, supported by the authority of Aristotle." In spite of the somewhat exaggerated contrast these manifestoes draw between the new ideal of criticism and the old, they are indicative of an important shift of emphasis in the critical writing of the mid-eighteenth century— a shift that exalted the philosopher (in the current sense of an inquirer into the operations of the mind) over the artist or the mere critic as the expert best qualified to determine the rules of art and that served, hence, to bring about, within criticism, a sharper separation between criticism itself, considered as a codification of past artistic experience, and the "demands of nature," on which its precepts and judgments, if they are to be valid, must ultimately rest.

The consequences of the change were most marked in those writers from Addison to Hume, Burke, Gerard, Kames, and Alison who had acquired most completely what Hume called a "tincture of philosophy"; it was in them that the search for "natural reasons," which had been from antiquity an essential part of the critical tradition inherited by the eighteenth century, assumed most clearly the form of an explicit and systematic inquiry into causes. The majority of contemporary critics, including such figures as Johnson and Reynolds, were not "philosophical" in this strict sense but were content for the most part to rely on such knowledge of the operations of the mind as could be obtained by introspection or as was available in the common psychological wisdom of educated men. For both groups alike, however, the problem of the relation between the rules of art and nature presented itself in much the same light. It was no longer, as in the mid-seventeenth century, a question primarily of vindicating the great traditions of art against contemporary artists whose reliance on their own natural powers had seemed to lead only to irregularity or excess; what was at issue now was rather the authority of criticism itself as a body of rules, not all of which could be assumed, without examination, to be equally binding or essential. When Johnson remarked, in the *Preface to Shakespeare*, that "there is always an appeal open from criticism to nature," he stated a principle which would not, indeed, have been denied by any of his predecessors in the tradition but which led, in his own writings and in those of many contemporaries, to a new attempt, sometimes carried out with great shrewdness (as in his remarks on tragicomedy and on the unities of time and place) to distinguish between those established precepts of art that could be seen as necessary consequences of man's nature and those which, like Horace's rule of five acts, must be regarded as only "the arbitrary edicts of legislators," to be observed or not as the artist may choose. To appeal to nature in this sense was inevitably to give greater prominence to the generality of the audience than to the particularity of the art, and it is not surprising, accordingly, that in much of the criticism of the period the problem of genres became relatively less important than it had been for the critics of an earlier generation. It is noteworthy, for example, that Johnson tended to discuss pastoral, comedy, and tragicomedy chiefly in terms of reasons common to all poetry or even all discourse and derived from his characteristic distinction between general and particular nature and his insistence on resolving all poetic value, whatever its species, into a union of truth (in the meaning of "sentiments to which every bosom returns an echo") with novelty and variety. The same preoccupation with the universal psychological basis of artistic effects also accounts for the increased popularity of inquiries, like those of Harris, Webb, Beattie, and Twining, into the analogies between the arts and for the widely prevalent interest in the definition and distinction of such general qualities, peculiar to no art or species of art, as the sublime, the beautiful, the pathetic, the romantic, the picturesque. Finally, all these developments, in which the dependence of art upon the nature of readers and spectators and hence on philosophy became the starting point for new or at least more elaborate investigations, had their appropriate counterpart and completion, during the same period, in numerous attempts to bring the problems of the standard of taste and of the psychological principles operative in critical judgments within the context of one or another of the various contemporary sciences of human nature.

A second group of changes, running parallel to these, likewise involved considerations of the audience but from a point of view that emphasized its relation rather to the work of art than to the art itself. The question at issue was one that Quintilian had touched on briefly (xii. 10. 1–2) when, in speaking of the kind of style the orator should aim at in his discourses, he had remarked that the forms of style are many, "not merely because some qualities are more evident in some artists than in others, but because one single form will not satisfy all critics, a fact due in part to conditions of time or place, in part to the taste and ideals of individuals." The point, indeed, was sufficiently obvious not to have escaped the attention of many writers before the eighteenth century; but for the most part, except for incidental passages (such as Dryden's explanation of the differences between English and French plays in terms of the contrasting temperaments of the two peoples), the principle of relativity it implied was subordinated, in the earlier neoclassical critics, to an emphasis on the universal traits of audiences—witness the frequently reiterated assertion that "Nature is still the same in all ages"—and hence on the necessary obligation of the artist to the general rules of his art. In the eighteenth century, however, though this obligation was seldom, if ever, rejected entirely, the consequences drawn from it by critics like Rymer, or by Dryden himself in most of his statements, were often treated as of somewhat minor importance in comparison with the natural tendency or even duty of artists to produce works adapted to the peculiar tastes and manners of their own generation or country. There are only a few really universal rules, declared Goldsmith in 1759, and these few are likely to be obvious to all; what is needed, therefore, he insisted, is "a national system of criticism," which will take account of the differences between peoples and adjust its precepts and judgments accordingly.

As manifested in discussions of individual artistic monuments in the eighteenth century, the tendency to supplement an absolute consideration of works or styles in terms of the universal principles of the art of which they were products by a qualified or relative consideration in terms of the particular audience to which they were addressed owed its chief incentive to the need many writers felt of overcoming prejudices against certain productions of the past which had been conceived in an idiom different from the prevailing mode, or of doing fuller justice to esteemed poets or artists who, when viewed apart from circumstances of time and place, had been blamed for faults not properly theirs. This species of critical apologetics was a dominant, or at least an important motif in an increasing number of writings from the end of the seventeenth century on through the eighteenth: in various defenses of the Scriptures published before and after 1700, in which the "Oriental" style of the Sacred Books and, in general, their departure from the poetic and rhetorical canons of the ancients were both explained and justified by reference to the climate, manners, and peculiar genius of the Hebrew people; in several notable works on Homer, especially those of Thomas Blackwell (1735) and Robert Wood (1769), which attempt to explain historically those traits of the *Iliad* and *Odyssey* that had seemed to many earlier critics merely signs of Homer's artistic inferiority to Virgil or even to certain of the moderns; in the efforts of Thomas Warton (*Observations on the Fairy Queen* [1754 and 1762]), Richard Hurd (*Letters on Chivalry and Romance* [1762]), and others to account for the "Gothic" character of Spenser in the light of medieval manners and the vogue of chivalric romances in his time; in numerous discussions of Shakespeare, including the final section of Johnson's great *Preface* (1765), in which the admitted irregularities or stylistic faults of the plays were, if not entirely vindicated, at least made to appear consequences not so much of their author's failure in judgment as of the demands imposed on him by the audience of his age; lastly—not to prolong the list—in such writings as those of Hugh Blair on Ossian and of Thomas Percy on the romances, wherein the critical problem of winning favor or attention for works of supposed or undoubted antiquity that yet were written in an unfamiliar style was solved partly by insisting on their essential conformity to the rules of Aristotle and partly by relating them to the background of primitive manners and sentiments which they reflected. In many of these writings, critical argument or appraisal, based on the dictum that it is unfair to judge works by rules of which their authors were ignorant or which they did not intend to observe, was combined with erudition in such a way as to form a species of literary history much more common after the middle of the eighteenth century than before. Of this sort of history the most imposing monument was Thomas Warton's unfinished *History of English Poetry* (1774–81).

To complete the story of shifting emphases within neoclassical criticism, it is necessary, finally, to consider what happened after 1700 to the traditional conception of the artist. In the general scheme of this criticism, as we have seen, the work of art had been usually interpreted as the product at once of the artist and of the art, and the artist had been said to depend for such perfection as he might achieve on nature or genius, first of all, and then, as equally important conditions, on art (which included invention, arrangement, and expression), on exercise, and on imitation of models. The chief possibility of variant emphasis, therefore, had to do with the relative importance attached by critics to nature, on the one hand, and to the various terms associated with art, on the other.

For reasons that have been partly indicated, the disposition of most critics before 1700 or a little later was to place the main stress on art and hence on the judgment of the artist in contrast to his genius or imagination or natural powers of invention. The bias was particularly evident in Rymer, and it was never entirely absent even from Dryden, since both these critics were principally occupied with the problem of educating poets and playwrights to what seemed to them a more civilized standard of art. Even so, however, it would be an error to assume, because the improvement of art was the primary concern of writers like Dryden, Dennis, Addison, or Pope, that the natural sources of artistic perfection were regarded by them as of little moment. For the most part, their necessity was taken for granted, but no estimate of Dryden's critical system would be adequate that did not make clear his constant insistence on the need of imagination in poets and of "liveliness" as well as "justness" in works or that overlooked his assertion, in the *Parallel betwixt Poetry and Painting*, that no rules can be given for inventing, since that is the work of genius and "a happy genius is the gift of nature," without which, as all agree, nothing can be done; and equally it would be unfair to Pope not to recall his words about "a grace beyond the reach of art" or his enthusiastic praise of Homer's "invention" in the Preface to his version of the *Iliad*.

In the treatment of the problem of the artist the majority of critics after Pope and Addison in the eighteenth century differed from their predecessors, if at all, only in a somewhat more equal distribution of emphasis as between genius and art or imagination and judgment and (with notable exceptions, such as Hurd and Reynolds) in a somewhat more skeptical view of the importance of imitation. In many of them the influence of Longinus was evident; but, as in the criticism which Dryden wrote after his discovery of *On the Sublime*, the effects were apparent rather in incidental borrowings of passages, terms, and distinctions than in any serious dislocation of the traditional critical scheme. The same period, however, saw the publication of a series of writings in which, also in part under the stimulus of Longinus, the question of the relative importance of the natural and acquired qualities of the poet or creative artist was discussed in a considerably more radical spirit. The starting point of much of this literature was Addison's essay in the *Spectator* (No. 160 [1711]) in which he distinguished two classes of great geniuses, the one comprising those that have "formed themselves by rules, and submitted the greatness of their natural talents to the corrections and restraints of art," the other those that "by the mere strength of natural parts, and without any assistance of art or learning, have produced works that were the delight of their own times, and the wonder of posterity." The opposition of the two types continued to be a favorite topic throughout the century; but, whereas

Addison had been careful to leave their comparative rank undecided, many of the later writers did not hesitate to assert the necessary precedence of the "natural genius" over the genius formed by art and imitation. One of the most eloquent of these was Edward Young, whose *Conjectures on Original Composition* (1759) effected a fairly thoroughgoing reduction of all the traditional distinctions to a simple pattern of literary values in which everything in art is resolved into invention and invention is identified with a quasi-scientific discovery of new subject matter; in which imitation of the classics is at times denounced and at times recommended in the form of a reproduction of the creative activity of the artist chosen as model; and in which genius is exalted as a natural force whose operations need be checked by nothing external save the verities of the Christian religion. In other writings—for example, in William Duff's *Essay on Original Genius* (1767) and occasionally in Blair—support for a similar thesis was drawn from a consideration of the superiority of primitive society before the rise of arts, as a setting favorable to genius, to the modern state of enlightenment. It will not escape notice that, in sharp contrast with both the first and the second of the main lines of evolution in eighteenth-century criticism that have been sketched here, the inevitable effect of this increased stress on the natural powers of the artist was to minimize, rather than to enlarge, the significance of the audience as a determinant in the production and evaluation of art. The exaltation of the poet or painter as the chief, if not indeed the only, lawgiver for art was to be carried much further after 1800 than it had ever been before; but the extent to which the tendency had gone even by the middle of the eighteenth century may be seen by anyone who will compare Boileau's dictum, in the Preface to the 1701 edition of his works, that the poet achieves excellence by expressing justly the thoughts already possessed by a majority of his readers, with the statement of an anonymous writer for Dodsley's *Museum* in 1747 to the effect that the greatness of the major English poets, Chaucer, Spenser, Shakespeare, and Milton, lies precisely in their immense superiority to the times in which they lived.

THE THEORETICAL FOUNDATIONS OF
JOHNSON'S CRITICISM

W. R. KEAST

I

EVERY age, we are often told, rewrites Shakespeare in its own image. Perhaps each age performs the same service for other writers as well. At any rate Samuel Johnson, as he appears in modern discussions, seems often to reflect modern distinctions and modern preferences. Thus we find an American critic praising the English critic, F. R. Leavis, in these terms:

> Mr. Leavis is not a critic who works by elaborated theory. As between Coleridge, on the one hand, and Dr. Johnson and Matthew Arnold, on the other, he has declared his strong preference for the two latter—for the critic, that is, who requires no formulated first principles for his judgment but only the sensibility that is the whole response of his whole being.[1]

To distinguish so sharply between sensibility and principles as the guaranty of critical judgment is a modern habit, and it is common in our time, when this distinction is made, to prefer sensibility to principles. A somewhat similar view of Johnson appears in C. B. Tinker's essay, "Johnson as Monarch," but in terms of yet another distinction and preference. Despite the often outrageous injustice and inaccuracy of Johnson's critical statements, we rightly continue to read him, Tinker says, because he is a man "who can always be read with profit even when we dissent from the view set forth." "The explanation of this singular state of things lies, I think, in the fact that Johnson's criticism is not a *system*, every detail of which must be consistent with certain principles from which all casual expressions are supposed to derive." We read Johnson not to find out what to think about Milton or Pope, and not for any system, but "to enjoy the humor and the humors, the audacities and the prejudices of a man of genius"; in short, even when we concede that there are "frequently at work in his mind great fundamental convictions which are at the very heart and center of the man," it is "Johnson's tastes that we are eager to come at, his feelings about a given work of art and not that 'pomp of system and severity of science' (to use a phrase of his own) which he could bring to its praise or its destruction."[2] Here tastes and habits mirroring a distinctive personality are preferred

---

1. Lionel Trilling, "The Moral Tradition," *New Yorker*, September 24, 1949, p. 89.
2. Chauncey Brewster Tinker, *Essays in Retrospect: Collected Articles and Addresses* (New Haven, 1948), p. 28.

over principles and system. It is Johnson's practical criticism which it is now fashionable to praise, and his practice is customarily viewed as the product of sensibility or taste but seldom of reasoned views about the nature of art and criticism—save, in Tinker's phrase, as something Johnson could "bring to" a question after taste had made its determination. The common denominator of these modern estimates of Johnson's distinctive quality and value is the conviction evident in them that Johnson has or needs no principles, theory, or systematic view of literature and the belief that this absence of principles and theory from the conduct of practical criticism is a positive virtue.

But Johnson, we may recall, in his praise of Dryden as the father of English criticism spoke of him as the writer "who first taught us to determine upon principles the merit of composition"—and we may ask how this modern view of his own work as a critic would have struck Johnson. Or we may remember the definition of criticism he set forth as a preliminary to his *Rambler* papers on onomatopoeia:

It is . . . the task of criticism to establish principles; to improve opinion into knowledge; and to distinguish those means of pleasing which depend upon known causes and rational deduction, from the nameless and inexplicable elegancies which appeal wholly to the fancy, from which we feel delight, but know not how they produce it, and which may well be termed the enchantresses of the soul. Criticism reduces those regions of literature under the dominion of science, which have hitherto known only the anarchy of ignorance, the caprices of fancy, and the tyranny of prescription.[3]

Johnson would have been outraged by the current notion that he had and needed no reasoned view of literature as a foundation for his critical practice and that he was fortunate in the freedom of sensibility so secured. Critics of this sort he once characterized pungently: "The ambition of superior sensibility and superior eloquence disposes the lovers of arts to receive rapture at one time, and communicate it at another; and each labours first to impose upon himself, and then to propagate the imposture."[4] But students of criticism are familiar with the wide gulf that often separates a critic's statements about what criticism ought to be from what in his practice it actually is. The modern view of Johnson may be correct in spite of Johnson's repeated stress on the importance of principles and "rational deduction."

Several important characteristics of Johnson's criticism, indeed, give encouragement to this view. Certainly no other English critic of equal reputation has been known as little by his systematic thought, as contrasted to his particular judgments on books and writers. In his critical writings systematic in-

---

3. *Rambler*, No. 92, in *Works* (Oxford, 1825), II, 431–32. Subsequent references to Johnson's writings, except for the *Preface to Shakespeare* and the *Lives of the Poets*, will be to this edition.

4. *Idler*, No. 50 (*Works*, IV, 298).

quiry is rarely met with and, when present, is introduced sparingly into discussions prevailingly occupied with concrete questions of evaluation. Unlike many of his contemporaries—including several whose theoretical work he admired—Johnson composed no treatises. And this reluctance to engage in extended statements of theory reflects Johnson's profound suspicion of abstract speculation, a suspicion to which he gave repeated expression in his writings and which, as we shall presently see, is one of the cardinal tenets of his criticism.

But if Johnson, by nature and habit, distrusted systematic theorizing about literature, we shall nevertheless miss some of the most important characteristics of his criticism if we suppose him to have played entirely or even primarily by ear. The proportion between principle and sensibility involved in the production of critical judgment must always be difficult to settle, but the alternatives presented to us in attempting to understand Johnson's criticism are not so stark as this statement would imply or as the modern comments already quoted would suggest. Johnson, if he was not a systematic writer, had at any rate a systematic mind: the kinds of critical problems with which he deals, the particular doctrines and judgments he puts forward, the stands he takes on the leading critical issues of his day, and the methods of argument he habitually employs can all be traced in his criticism, early and late, to a coherent view of literature and a coherent body of assumptions concerning both its practice and its evaluation. That Johnson distrusted theory there can be no question, but such distrust can become, as we shall see it did for Johnson, in itself a theoretical commitment. If, after his fairly explicit early periodical essays, the exposition of the theory comes to be increasingly elliptical, discernible more in its effects on his practice than in extended statement, this is to be understood as a sign not of his emancipation from general views about literature and criticism but of his increasing maturity as a critic, of his habituation to the flexible employment of his dominant assumptions, and, above all, of the generality and adaptability of his principles.

The theoretical positions I have in mind lie somewhere between the "great fundamental convictions" to which Professor Tinker refers and the immediate premises of critical argument. Although this is a wide zone, Johnson, unlike some of his contemporaries, does not fill it with a regular scheme of analysis. He does not, indeed, fill this zone at all, for his basic assumptions about literature are relatively few—although they are not, for that reason, any less important—and they are in essential respects very similar to those which underlie his discussions of moral and political questions. Nor does he, given the more remote positions which shape his statement of critical problems and supply premises for their solution, operate in a predictable deductive fashion in deciding particular cases. Although one is seldom surprised by the general lines Johnson follows in any literary argument, the concrete substance of his remarks is often unexpected. This combination of predictable direction and unexpected event, so characteristic of Johnson's criticism, results from the relative generality of his principles, which permits the same general premise to be brought to bear on a wide variety of cases; from the important role he assigns to circumstantial accidents in critical judgment—an aspect of his theory about which I shall have more to say later on; and from an uncommonly rich assortment of subordinate terms and distinctions which he employs, in combination with general premises, to yield results that are always the same, yet always different.

To attempt a recovery and restatement of Johnson's theory of literature and criticism and of his critical method has more than a merely antiquarian interest. Isolated from the more remote principles from which they are derived, Johnson's verdicts on particular books and writers are exposed to those constant changes of regard with which the history of literary reputations is filled, and his criticism is likely to be praised or condemned on no more secure ground than that the authors he treats please or disgust the temporary fancy of the reading public. The decline of Johnson's reputation as a critic in the early nineteenth century illustrates this hazard. But there is a more important value in reconstructing his theory than the protection of his reputation from exposure to critical caprice. If we are to learn from the monuments of humanistic culture, we must understand them in such a way as to make them assimilable, in some degree at least, to modern use. It is very difficult to learn or to improve the art of criticism by a study of the particular judgments of past critics on authors and works. In the service of developing the art of criticism, the chief significance of such particular judgments is in helping us to ascertain the principles of more general import which underlie them and which may be instructive or useful in other contexts. What Johnson has to say about *Lycidas* tells us, of course, something about Johnson the man, something about the unconscious factors in reading poetry, as M. H. Abrams has shown, and perhaps something about eighteenth-century culture. But it does not, by itself, tell us much that would enable us to approach more justly T. S. Eliot's latest poem. But the strictures on *Lycidas* may have such a value if properly taken: they derive— with whatever superaddition of Tory prejudice—from positions capable of formulation, of confirmation or revision, and of application to works superficially very different from *Lycidas*.

II

With a writer whose theoretical statements are diffused through contexts predominantly practical, and so often determined by the requirements of the topic immediately at hand, perhaps the best strategy for examining the theoretical foundations of his work is to begin with his pronouncements on broad literary questions and to test the hypotheses thence derived against his practice in more restricted contexts. For Johnson, the papers on criticism and the rules of art in the *Rambler* (Nos. 37, 125, 156, and 158) and the discussions of tragicomedy and the unities in the *Preface to Shakespeare* offer an especially advantageous point of departure, for here not only does he address himself at some length and in considerable detail to large questions of critical theory, but he seems to be engaged in an attempt to summarize and evaluate an entire critical tradition and to define the alternative with which he would supplant it.

The substance of Johnson's attacks on the rules for pastoral poetry and comedy, on the prohibition of tragicomedy, and on the dramatic unities are familiar enough to need no restatement here. It is important to note that in each case Johnson seeks to subvert accepted critical dogmas and to deliver literature from the fetters of prescriptive criticism. The interest of these attacks for our present purpose is not so much in the content of Johnson's arguments as in the characterization of his own method that is afforded by his analysis of his opponents. The precepts he opposes are in general, he says,

the arbitrary edicts of legislators, authorized only by themselves, who, out of various means by which the same end may be attained, selected such as happened to occur to their own reflection, and then, by a law which idleness and timidity were too willing to obey, prohibited new experiments of wit, restrained fancy from the indulgence of her innate inclination to hazard and adventure, and condemned all future flights of genius to pursue the path of the Maeonian eagle.[5]

The established rules have a uniform characteristic: each specifies, for the genre to which it applies, a peculiar limitation of literary means—language, character, subject, manner of presentation, and the like—which alone can be regarded, in the opinion of the critics, as the proper or artistic way in which to achieve the effect aimed at. Comedy must deal with low characters, pastoral speakers must use rustic diction, tragedies must be divided into five acts, lyric poems may be disorderly, serious and comic actions must not be mingled in one composition, the time of a represented action must equal the time of the representation.

In each case Johnson contends that alternative means may equally well achieve the desired effects. Why does he find the limitation of means enforced by critical precepts to be arbitrary and partial? For three reasons, which form the bases on which, indifferently, Johnson rests his case against the critics. First, because the limitations proposed as universally valid have been derived from the practice of particular poets; second, because nature is the object of the

5. *Rambler*, No. 158 (*Works*, III, 248).

poet's activity; and, third, because literary works are designed to satisfy the general conditions of pleasure. We may examine each of these in turn.

Poets, exercising their essential faculty of choice, have selected such subjects, diction, modes of organization, and the like as fitted their peculiar interests, abilities, and circumstances; these choices, if made by early or honored poets, have been identified by critics with the art itself rather than with the special causes which produced them. Thus tragedy and comedy arose merely from the selection by the ancient poets, according to laws which "custom" had prescribed, of the crimes of men or their absurdities as subjects for drama; and the lack of methodical connection of thought which critics have erected into a principle of lyric poetry had its origin in the vehemence of imagination and the extensive knowledge of the first lyrists. But, when poetry is thus viewed in relation to the selective activity by which it is produced, it is apparent that the imagination—the faculty which predominates in the poet's selection—is limitless in its capacities and hence that other choices, determined by causes equally accidental or capricious, may be made. Precepts derived from the activity of poets are consequently partial and aribitrary.[6]

If the imaginative power distinguishing the poet is "licentious and vagrant, unsusceptible of limitations, and impatient of restraint,"[7] the subject matter over which the selective activity operates has an equivalent characteristic. The poetic imagination roves unconfined in the "boundless ocean of possibility"; nature, in Johnson's view, is limitless in the range of choices it presents to the artist. Critics who limit comedy to men of a certain social class run into absurdity because "the various methods of exhilarating their audience, not being limited by nature, cannot be comprised in precept."[8] Those who condemn the mingling of tragic and comic scenes in Shakespeare fail to realize that this mingling accurately reflects "the real state of sublunary nature,"

which partakes of good and evil, joy and sorrow, mingled with endless variety of proportion and innumerable modes of combination; and expressing the course of the world, in which the loss of one is the gain of another; in which, at the same time, the reveller is hasting to his wine, and the mourner burying his friend; in which the malignity of one is sometimes defeated by the frolick of another; and many mischiefs and many benefits are done and hindered without design.[9]

The real state of sublunary nature—"this chaos of mingled purposes and casualties"[10]—is the poet's object. That some poets, like the ancient writers

6. *Preface to Shakespeare*, in Sir Walter Raleigh (ed.), *Johnson on Shakespeare* (London, [1931]), p. 16; *Rambler*, No. 158 (*Works*, III, 249–50); cf. also Nos. 23 (*Works*, II, 116), 121 (*Works*, III, 76–77), 125 (*Works*, III, 93), and 156 (*Works*, III, 239).

7. *Rambler*, No. 125 (*Works*, III, 93).

8. *Ibid.*, p. 94.

9. *Preface to Shakespeare* (Raleigh, *op. cit.*, pp. 15–16).   10. *Ibid.*, p. 16.

of comedy and tragedy, have elected to restrict themselves to a part of the diversified whole cannot warrant the critic in imposing a similar restriction on others. Critical rules, Johnson says, have too often been derived from precedents rather than from reason, and hence "practice has introduced rules, rather than rules have directed practice."[11]

When he considers the readers of literature, Johnson finds that the critics have made an analogous error. They have assumed or argued that the demands of readers are for specific pleasures arising from specifically distinct types of works. Johnson, having examined the tastes of the common reader with some care, is convinced that this is not so, that, instead, readers demand the more general pleasures of recognition and novelty. Is it asserted that Shakespeare's plays fail to move because the intermingling of tragic and comic scenes interrupts the passions in their progress? Speculative principles do not serve the critic so well as perception, for what do we find when we submit the case to the test of experience?

The interchanges of mingled scenes seldom fail to produce the intended vicissitudes of passion. Fiction cannot move so much, but that the attention may be easily transferred; and though it must be allowed that pleasing melancholy be sometimes interrupted by unwelcome levity, yet let it be considered likewise, that melancholy is often not pleasing, and that the disturbance of one man may be the relief of another; that different auditors have different habitudes; and that, upon the whole, all pleasure consists in variety.[12]

Whichever of these three bases Johnson uses to ground his case against earlier critics—whether the activity of poets, the real state of nature, or the general conditions of pleasure—he is endeavoring to replace what he considers narrow principles with principles more commodious. And this endeavor regularly leads him to forsake the view of art as manifesting itself in distinct species, a view presented in great detail in the treatises of his predecessors, for the ampler domain of nature, in which, as he conceives of it, distinctions and definitions hitherto thought inviolable and "natural" can be shown to be rigidities, arbitrary constrictions, or, at best, ideal manifestoes. One of the chief distinctions of Johnson from his predecessors in criticism is in this careful reduction of the realm of art, and this habit of regarding literature as a natural process, set in the context of other natural processes such as social behavior, and thus amenable to treatment in relation to its psychological causes and effects, its natural materials, and its circumstantial determinants. Literary works, for Johnson, must be thought of not as specifically identifiable objects, instances of fixed classes of works, and embodying more or less perfectly

11. *Rambler*, No. 158 (*Works*, III, 248).
12. *Preface to Shakespeare* (Raleigh, *op. cit.*, p. 17).

an ideal form but as human acts to be judged in relation to the agency of their production and appreciation. They are, consequently, "things modified by human understandings, subject to varieties of complication, and changeable as experience advances knowledge, or accident influences caprice."[13] Literature, like morals, having life as its object, is not "prescribed and limited": "since life itself is uncertain, nothing which has life for its basis can boast much stability."[14] The "performances of art," in consequence of their implication with human action and natural models, are "too inconstant and uncertain, to be reduced to any determinate idea"; a poem is an object "so mutable that it is always changing under our eye, and has already lost its form while we are labouring to conceive it."

There is therefore scarcely any species of writing, of which we can tell what is its essence, and what are its constituents; every new genius produces some innovation, which, when invented and approved, subverts the rule which the practice of foregoing authors had established.[15]

It is important to notice an underlying paradox in Johnson's attack on earlier critics. He convicts them of fanciful prescription because they take an unwarrantably "scientific" view of literature; Johnson himself, intent as he says upon reducing under the dominion of "science" those regions of literature which have hitherto been under the influence of caprice, emphasizes the unpredictable, nonrational qualities in the process, materials, and effects of art. The importance of this point is not merely in the irony, of which Johnson was doubtless well aware, but in the fact that many of the characteristic features of his criticism grow out of his effort to find a secure ground for rational determination with regard to objects peculiarly unsuited to precise rational treatment. Johnson is known as a great rationalist, and in a sense he was: he sought to ground his statements on reason rather than on fancy or intuition, and he was convinced that such grounds could be discovered. But he was not a rationalist in the sense that he supposed all modes of existence to be equally amenable to rational treatment, or the human mind capable of arriving at certainty in all forms of discourse. In particular, he drew a sharp distinction between the operations of the mind in science and in the affairs and activities of men, including literature. The terms of this distinction help us to define the problems of the critic as Johnson saw them.

Johnson begins the *Preface to Shakespeare* with the observation that it has been charged, with some justice, that praises are without reason lavished on the

13. *Rambler*, No. 125 (*Works*, III, 93); cf. No. 23 (*Works*, II, 115) and *Lives of the Poets*, ed. G. B. Hill (Oxford, 1905), I, 18.

14. *Rambler*, No. 184 (*Works*, III, 361).

15. *Rambler*, No. 125 (*Works*, III, 93).

dead and that the honors due only to excellence are paid to antiquity. But the critic, Johnson points out, seeking to replace prejudice and caprice by reason, cannot disregard the opinion of mankind, liable though it is to error. He has no other criterion to use, for he deals not with objects having determinate natures, such as the objects of science, but with works of a different sort altogether:

> To works . . . of which the excellence is not absolute and definite, but gradual and comparative; to works not raised upon principles demonstrative and scientific, but appealing wholly to observation and experience, no other test can be applied than length of duration and continuance of esteem. . . . As among the works of nature no man can properly call a river deep, or a mountain high, without the knowledge of many mountains, and many rivers; so in the productions of genius, nothing can be stiled excellent till it has been compared with other works of the same kind.

"Demonstration," the work of the scientist, Johnson goes on to say, "immediately displays its power, and has nothing to hope or fear from the flux of years."[16] Science, he tells us elsewhere, pursues truth simply; and, since scientific statements bear a fixed and necessary relation to nature, their force is immediately evident to the rational mind.[17] But "works tentative and experimental," he continues, "must be estimated by their proportion to the general and collective ability of man, as it is discovered in a long succession of endeavours":

> Of the first building that was raised, it might be with certainty determined that it was round or square; but whether it was spacious or lofty must have been referred to time. The Pythagorean scale of numbers was at once discovered to be perfect; but the poems of *Homer* we yet know not to transcend the common limits of human intelligence, but by remarking, that nation after nation, and century after century, has been able to do little more than transpose his incidents, new-name his characters, and paraphrase his sentiments.[18]

Here again we see Johnson's conception of literature as a mode of activity, as one of the things men can do, and we observe the consequences of this conception: the limits of human ability cannot be specified; the relation of works of art to nature is not immediate but relative to the powers of poets and to the natural desires of readers; the excellence of literature is therefore "tentative," "gradual," and "comparative," and probability rather than demonstration is the utmost attainable by the critic.[19]

16. *Preface to Shakespeare* (Raleigh, *op. cit.*, pp. 9–10).

17. *Rambler*, Nos. 121 (*Works*, III, 76) and 184 (*Works*, III, 358–59); cf. Preface to John Payne's *New Tables of Interest* (1758), in *Samuel Johnson's Prefaces & Dedications*, ed. A. T. Hazen (New Haven, 1937), p. 144.

18. *Preface to Shakespeare* (Raleigh, *op. cit.*, p. 10).

19. *Rambler*, Nos. 92 (*Works*, II, 431), 93 (*Works*, II, 438–39), and 156 (*Works*, III, 239); *Adventurer*, No. 115 (*Works*, IV, 113); *Lives*, I, 14, 340, and II, 47.

The opposition between Johnson and the critics he attacks in the *Rambler* and the *Preface to Shakespeare* may be seen in terms of this distinction. The earlier critics, in his view of them, assumed for literary works a fixed relation to nature like that found in science; they therefore supposed it possible to deduce, from the objects represented or the effects proposed in works of different kinds, a determinate set of specifications for each literary genre. But Johnson, while not at all abandoning his effort to introduce into criticism as much certainty as the subject will permit, or his conviction that human nature and external nature possess certain common features which, when discovered or revealed by the passage of time, will provide the basis for reasoned statement, nevertheless abandons the pretense to certainty made by his predecessors and casts aside the principles and distinctions they have formulated.

The locus of principles for the evaluation of literature Johnson therefore transfers from art to nature. Given the relativity of art, which is a consequence of the view that it is a mode of activity rather than the perfection of objects having determinate characteristics, art itself cannot supply the principles for its own judgment, for, as we have seen, principles derived from the practice of poets or the traits of works are commonly arbitrary and accidental. The critic's recourse must be to nature. But here, too, difficulties arise. For Johnson, nature is infinitely complex and varied, and the human mind is incapable of encompassing it completely or of predicting its course in detail.[20] Hence Johnson's distrust of abstract speculation and the prominence, in his scheme, of time as a guaranty of opinion. But regardless of the difficulties involved in seeking natural principles which will permit the critic to give an account of literary excellence, the enterprise is sustained by the conviction that the common and general properties of nature are discoverable. Men are in essential respects everywhere the same. Experience tells us that the general conditions of pleasure are simple and fixed: all men take pleasure in the recognition of truth—the consonance of what is done or said to "the general sense or experience of mankind"[21]—and in the surprise of novelty or variety. No prediction can be made of the means by which these conditions may be satisfied, for Johnson will not, "like many hasty philosophers, search after the cause till . . . certain of the effect";[22] but the stability of the grounds on which literary ef-

---

20. *Rambler*, Nos. 13 (*Works*, II, 62), 70 (*Works*, II, 331–32), 63 (*Works*, II, 301), and 122 (*Works*, III, 80–81); *Adventurer*, Nos. 107 (*Works*, IV, 99), 108 (*Works*, IV, 101–2), and 131 (*Works*, IV, 135); Sermon XXIII (*Works*, IX, 500). Of Johnson's skeptical and empirical habit of mind, and of its consequences in his writings, J. H. Hagstrum has given an excellent account in "The Nature of Dr. Johnson's Rationalism," *ELH*, XVII (1950), 191–205.

21. *Lives*, III, 345.

22. *Rambler*, No. 61 (*Works*, II, 295).

fects may be produced affords a principle from which the critic can reason to their causes and hence from which he can argue questions of literary merit.

III

On the basis of these assumptions concerning the nature of literature and the task of criticism, Johnson develops the scheme of analysis which underlies his discussions of technical problems, works and genres, and individual authors. Of the four elements in the literary process—author, work, nature, and audience—the first and last are primary, and the other two are defined in relation to them. Literature is an activity or process directed to the pleasure and instruction of the common reader. Works succeed or fail—are excellent or poor—to the extent that they satisfy the general conditions of pleasure, namely, truth and novelty. Nature, being both regular and inexhaustibly varied, provides subject matter for art and, being external, a measure for judging it. The extent to which works embody truth and variety depends on the power of the author to discover these in nature, to select or invent matter which will embody them, and to represent it in words. All the steps in the process are relative to the last—the satisfaction of the general conditions of pleasure—not only because this is the aim of literature but because, as we have seen, these conditions, discovered by experience and guaranteed by the essential identity of men, provide the first principle of critical reasoning. But critical reasoning is with respect to the causes of literary pleasure; the critic's task is "to distinguish those means of pleasing which depend upon known causes and rational deduction, from the nameless and inexplicable elegancies which appeal wholly to the fancy." Among the causes of literary pleasure—and hence of literary excellence—the author is primary, not only because his selective activity initiates the process, but because the traits of works, the extent to which they exhibit general nature, and hence their capacity to excite pleasure are all grounded ultimately in the powers of the author. Works are treated by Johnson as "performances" manifesting the powers of the author, as compositions of materials which resemble—in themselves and in their conjunction—the traits of nature, and as the sources of recognition or surprise in the audience. Works figure in Johnson's scheme, consequently, as relative to all three, and the terms in which works are discussed are derived from a prior consideration of authors, nature, and readers. Nature also occupies a relative, rather than an independent, position in the scheme. Nature is the link between author and reader—the common elements that guarantee truth and the accidental variations that produce variety being the basis for selection by the one and for comparison and judgment by the other. For Johnson, nature is not an ontological, but a psychological, concept: it is defined, that is, not in terms of properties independent of the mind but in terms of its capacity to produce certain responses in men. General nature is thus what all men everywhere recognize as like themselves, and particular nature is what men in general recognize as present only at certain times, under certain conditions, or among certain men. Both truth and variety arise from the constant linkage between human passions and their effects: the regularity with which the same passions produce effects of the same kind permits recognition and hence truth; the infinite accidental modifications in the actual manner in which the passions do their uniform work afford novelty and variety.

The consequences of the general assumptions set out in the preceding section and of the theoretical scheme just described are everywhere apparent in Johnson's critical writings. Thus we see at once why Johnson's criticism is predominantly practical and why he developed no "art" of poetry nor engaged much in the literary theorizing so common in his day. His distrust of "inactive speculation" here co-operates with his conception of literature: an elaborated theory would necessarily involve, in Johnson's terms, an analysis or prescription of the possible or proper in art. But such an analysis or prescription must be arbitrary, for although the general conditions of pleasing may be specified, the aspects of nature and the traits of works which may conduce to this end cannot, since nature offers boundless possibilities to the poet and since there is no discoverable limit to human powers.

Not only does Johnson's theory of literature give his criticism its prevailingly practical cast, but his distribution of emphasis among the major terms of his scheme leads to the disappearance or revision of terms and distinctions that had received elaborate treatment at the hands of Johnson's predecessors and contemporaries. We have seen that in the literary process as he conceived of it the traits of works are relative to the effects they produce, the subject matter they represent, and the powers of the author from which they derive. The terms in which Johnson discusses works are consequently terms drawn from his analysis of these three; he has little use for traditional terms whose meanings seem to him to depend on an a priori analysis of art as a whole or of one of its species. The subordination of the work to the nexus of causes originating in the author and terminating in the audience may be seen in his treatment of the traditional literary genres. Early distinctions among the genres arise, in Johnson's view, as we have seen in his discussion of comedy, tragicomedy, and the unities, from attempts to discriminate effects peculiar to the different genres and to isolate, in relation to these, specific subject matters, styles, and manners appropriate to each. Johnson finds most such discriminations artificial: writers on pastoral, he says, "have entangled themselves with unnecessary difficulties by advancing principles, which, having no foundation in the nature of things, are to be wholly rejected from a species of composition, in which, above all others, mere nature is to be regarded." Thus critics, defining pastoral as a dialogue of men tending sheep, have required that the manners be those of the Golden Age, the diction rustic, and the persons uncouth and ignorant. Johnson's handling of the rules for pastoral is characteristic of his method of dealing with the other genres. Some of the rules—such as that requiring chaste sentiments—he retains, not on grounds specific to pastoral but in relation to the end of poetry in general. Others he refutes on the basis of a more generalized definition of the genre: pastoral is considered as "a representation of rural nature, and consequently as exhibiting the ideas and sentiments of those, whoever they are, to whom the country affords pleasure or employment." The specific properties of the form are consequently reduced: "pastoral being the representation of an action or passion, by its effects upon a country life, has nothing peculiar but its confinement to rural imagery, without which it ceases to be pastoral." Rural imagery he does not attempt to define, and, indeed, he broadens even this property of the form by insisting that rural imagery is compatible with dignity of sentiment and beauty of diction.[23] The effect of Johnson's operation upon the received analyses of pastoral is not to eliminate the concept of the genre, but to reduce its value and importance as a principle of criticism by stripping it of most of its peculiarities, and to throw the emphasis in criticism away from the analysis of the genre and toward the more general causes on which, in common with other forms of poetry, it depends.

The disappearance or reduction in importance of traditional distinctions based on peculiar traits of works and genres is paralleled in Johnson's criticism by a generalized method of dealing with poetic subjects. Poetry has a universal subject—nature and passion—but particular works have as their matter more or less specific subjects selected or dictated by choice, convention, or accident from the wide realm in which the imagination is free to rove. Such subjects always raise for Johnson the question of how far they approximate the universal subject of poetry, i.e., of the degree to which they are capable of satisfying the general conditions of pleasure—truth and novelty. This alone is the test applied to poetic subjects. Johnson does not classify or evaluate them in relation to more specific ends; for such ends could not, as we have seen, be inferred with any certainty from common human nature. Nor does he differentiate them in relation to the poetic powers to which they are adapted; for poetic power, as we shall see, is generalized rather than subdivided, and all the faculties are adapted to all sorts of subjects. Thus, although comments on the values of different subjects occur repeatedly in Johnson's criticism, subjects of the most diverse sorts are submitted to a common test. Religion and mythology are both

23. *Rambler*, No. 37 (*Works*, II, 182–84).

poor subjects for poetry; they differ, of course, in many respects, but the reason for their inadequacy is the same—neither is "level with common life," neither offers anything on which the imagination can rest while the mind compares the life represented with the life it knows.[24] Religious, pastoral, didactic, and descriptive subjects are defective in that they offer little, if any, opportunity for novelty and variety.[25] On the other hand, the excellence of the subjects of biographies and of works so diverse as the *Odyssey*, Gray's *Elegy*, and Rowe's *Fair Penitent* rests on a common principle—the presentation to the reader of "parallel circumstances and kindred images," which have the power of "gratifying every mind, by recalling its conceptions."[26] Subjects, like genres, are treated in terms not of their specific differences but of their common qualities, and these common qualities are, in turn, described not in terms of the substantial properties of nature but in terms of their capacity to evoke responses of a certain kind in the readers.

The audience to which the entire literary process is directed is the common reader. The importance of the reader in Johnson's scheme—and the reason, consequently, for his regular appeal from critics and authorities to "the common voice of the multitude"[27]—lies not merely in the fact that literature has a pleasurable end, for such an end has been stated by critics in whose work the reader plays a relatively unimportant role, but in the fact that Johnson is seeking a stable basis in nature on which to rest critical inquiry and judgment: the audience is the only fixed element in the process; for while nature has invariable features, they can be identified only through general recognition, and while poets may excel in the power to discover and represent nature, we become aware of this capacity only through its effect upon us. Johnson's reader is defined merely in human terms, and works of art are discussed in relation to his demands. This procedure is the reverse of that employed by Dryden, for whom the proper judge of literature is the man capable of understanding and appreciating the best works, his detailed qualifications emerging from an examination of such works. Thus the audience, for Dryden, though it establishes the final cause of art, is subordinated to the art over which it presides.[28]

---

24. *Lives*, I, 51, 147, 181, 182, 295; II, 16, 284, 311; III, 228, 438, 439.

25. On religious poetry see *Lives*, I, 182, 291; II, 263–64; III, 310; on pastoral, *Rambler*, No. 36 (*Works*, II, 178), *Lives*, I, 163; on didactic, *Lives*, I, 437; II, 295; III, 242–44; on descriptive poetry, *Rambler*, No. 143 (*Works*, III, 179).

26. *Rambler*, Nos. 60 (*Works*, II, 286), 36 (*Works*, II, 178); Boswell, *Life of Johnson*, ed. Hill-Powell (Oxford, 1934), IV, 219; *Lives*, II, 67; III, 441–42; cf. also Raleigh, *op. cit.*, pp. 162, 165; *Lives*, I, 245, 302, 360–61, 363; II, 69; III, 397.

27. *Rambler*, No. 52 (*Works*, II, 250); cf. also No. 23 (*Works*, II, 116), and *Adventurer*, No. 138 (*Works*, IV, 147).

28. Cf., e.g., Preface to *All for Love* and Dedication of the *Aeneis* (*Essays of John Dryden* ed. Ker [Oxford, 1926], I, 195–97; II, 223–26).

For Johnson, readers are antecedent to art, in the sense that the properties involved in his definition of the proper reader are derived from an examination of human nature and not from an examination of literature. The demands which readers make of literature are not confined to literature but are, indeed, the general causes of pleasure, operative in the affairs of life as well. The proper reader is the common reader, the reasonable man, no other traits being involved than rationality and common experience of the world. Johnson excludes from his description of the audience of art all traits merely variable, for these would introduce an element of uncertainty into the deductions made from the effects of literature. Hence he does not follow some earlier critics in differentiating readers by the times or places in which they live, by their nationalities or tempers, by their education or acquired knowledge. He does not appeal to the best readers, to the most experienced, or to an aristocracy of taste.[29] He looks rather to "the common voice of the multitude, uninstructed by precept, and unprejudiced by authority."[30] "Of things that terminate in human life," he says in the *Life of Pope*, "the world is the proper judge: to despise its sentence, if it were possible, is not just; and if it were just was not possible."[31] And the highest attainments of art are defined in relation to this broad conception of the proper audience. West's *Imitations of Spenser*, successful as they are with respect to meter, language, and fiction,

are not to be reckoned among the great achievements of intellect, because their effect is local and temporary; they appeal not to reason and passion, but to memory, and presuppose an accidental or artificial state of mind. . . .Works of this kind may deserve praise, as proofs of great industry and great nicety of observation; but the highest praise, the praise of genius, they cannot claim. The noblest beauties of art are those of which the effect is coextended with rational nature, or at least with the whole circle of polished life; what is less than this can be only pretty, the plaything of fashion and the amusement of a day.[32]

Although the audience supplies in Johnson's scheme the basis for critical inference, it is not about the effects of literature that the critic reasons but about the causes of those effects. The task of criticism is "to distinguish those means of pleasing which depend upon *known causes* and rational deduction, from the nameless and inexplicable elegancies which appeal wholly to the fancy, from

29. Except when, as in defending Pope's *Homer*, he argues that a writer's first obligation is to please his immediate audience. This is a prerequisite to a broader and more permanent effect—Johnson would not have thought well of writers who addressed themselves directly to the ages—but it is not equivalent to such an effect, and the greatest works rise above this minimum level of achievement.

30. *Rambler*, No. 52 (*Works*, II, 250); cf. *Lives*, III, 441.

31. *Lives*, III, 210; cf. also *ibid.*, I, 175, II, 16, 132; Boswell, *op. cit.*, I, 200.

32. *Lives*, III, 332–33.

which we feel delight, but know not *how they produce it*."[33] In his search for causes explanatory of the effects of literary works and hence permitting judgments of praise or blame, the critic addresses himself primarily to the author. The crucial position of the poet, for Johnson, arises from the fact that it is the poet's activity which imparts to literature its peculiarly tentative and experimental character and from the fact that the power of the author is the ultimate ground on which rests the capacity of works to evoke pleasure. Johnson's treatment of the poet reflects the fundamental orientation of his theory to the natural conditions of artistic activity, and it displays the tendency we have noticed in his treatment of works, subjects, and readers to avoid derivation of his basic terms from an analysis of the peculiar traits of art. To conceive of literature as a mode of activity essentially like activity of any other sort removes, for Johnson, the basis on which many earlier critics had isolated the faculties characteristic of the poet, assigned them to particular genres, and distinguished poets from other men. Johnson's reduction of art to nature has consequences here in two directions: it dissolves the basis for a separation between poets and men in general, and it collapses essential distinctions among kinds of poetic effects and materials. A definition of genius which made it distinctive of one class of men, adapted to one sort of material, or productive of one sort of effect would have to be founded on a classification or hierarchy of mental faculties, natural objects, literary genres, varieties of effects, or classes of readers; but we have seen why Johnson believes such classification to be untrustworthy. In any case such distinctions would assign but a part of literature or nature to genius, and this would constitute a limitation on the concept. Johnson therefore views the mental powers of the poet as determined to their objects accidentally, not essentially. Repeatedly we encounter his ridicule of the notion that genius is "a particular designation of mind and propensity for some certain science or employment."[34] The "true Genius," he observes in the *Life of Cowley*, "is a mind of large general powers, accidentally determined to some particular direction."[35] Genius is merely the sum of all the powers of the mind operating with maximum effect; the separate ingredients of reason, imagination, fancy, judgment, are less important than their combination; and the separate work or materials of each counts for less than the total vigor of mind which can discover and represent "the whole system of life" in both its regularity and variety, which can join novelty and credibility by penetrating

33. *Rambler*, No. 92 (*Works*, II, 431–32); my italics.

34. *Lives*, I, 2.

35. *Ibid*. Cf. *Rambler*, Nos. 25 (*Works*, II, 124–25), 43 (*Works*, II, 208–9), and 117 (*Works*, III, 54–60); *Idler*, No. 61 (*Works*, IV, 332); *Letters*, ed. G. B. Hill (Oxford, 1892), II, 184; *Miscellanies*, ed. G. B. Hill (New York, 1897), I, 314, II, 287; Boswell, *op. cit.*, V, 34–35; D'Arblay, *Diaries & Letters*, ed. Austin Dobson (London, 1904), II, 271–72.

far enough into the recesses of nature to uncover the causes of human passion from which life derives both its unvarying order and its manifold combinations.[36]

The measurement of genius thus defined is for Johnson an essential part of the critic's task, for "the enquiry, how far man may extend his designs, or how high he may rate his native force, is of far greater dignity than in what rank we shall place any particular performance."[37] The "silent reference of human works to human abilities" occasioned by Johnson's theory of literature as activity, together with the absence from his theory of any definition of genius which would permit a fixed standard of measurement, accounts for the care he displays in establishing an alternative measure. "All human excellence," he points out in *Rambler*, No. 127, "is comparative . . . no man performs much but in proportion to what others accomplish, or to the time and opportunities which have been allowed him."[38] The comparative criterion for the measurement of genius or power Johnson finds in his concept of the "general and collective ability of man."[39] The most notable property of this standard of excellence, by which he avoids both the absolutism of a fixed definition of genius and the relativism of judging each man's performances merely by his own abilities, is that it is itself not absolute and final but relative and alterable. The general level at which men may operate cannot be determined precisely and finally because a new genius may always appear to break through the levels previously established and force a revision of our conception of what human nature may accomplish.[40] Johnson's conception of the general and collective ability of man is accordingly a concept of the limit of human capacity, not deduced from a consideration of the ends or objects or forms of poetry, but derived empirically, "discovered in a long succession of endeavours." If the succession is long enough and inclusive enough, it will guarantee in an empirical way that the limit derived is stable; and in practice we see that the conception of the limit of human power provided by the work of Homer has never been revised, so that we can say that his poems "transcend the common limits of human intelligence."[41] But it is important for our judgment of Johnson's criti-

36. On comprehensiveness as the mark of genius see *Lives*, I, 48, 55, 56–57, 183, 212–13, 234–35, 245, 294, 320, 413, 417, 457; II, 54, 120–21, 207; III, 298–99, 324; 333, 337–38, 359, 416–17, 427, 432; on the difficulties of defining and distinguishing the mental faculties see *Lives*, I, 235, Boswell, *op. cit.*, V, 34; on genius as force or vigor of mind, see *Rambler*, No. 168 (*Works*, III, 293), *Lives*, I, 170, 185; II, 64, 177, 204; III, 222, 223.

37. *Preface to Shakespeare* (Raleigh, *op. cit.*, p. 31).

38. *Works*, III, 106.

39. *Preface to Shakespeare* (Raleigh, *op. cit.*, p. 10).

40. *Rambler*, No. 92 (*Works*, II, 431).

41. *Preface to Shakespeare* (Raleigh, *op. cit.*, pp. 9–10).

cism to observe that it provides for such revision by basing its inferences on an induction from past performances rather than on an absolute scheme of values.

A further consequence of Johnson's treatment of literature as a mode of activity—a consequence which accounts in a large measure for his most characteristic form of critical utterance—is the introduction into the process of poetry and hence into the purview of the critic of a variety of factors which influence the poet's work in one way or another. Johnson's aim is always to make as accurate a determination as possible of the native power of the artist, apart from all external assistance or obstruction; but, since power is displayed in activity and since every activity has a circumstantial setting which determines, in important respects, its form and outcome, these circumstances must be isolated and evaluated in order to arrive at a firm estimate of the poet's power. The native ability of the artist is only one of the causes of a work of art; it is modified by intention, diligence, time and opportunity, chance and good luck, the availability of suitable materials, education, criticism, models, and a wide range of other forces over which the poet has no control.[42] By viewing poetry in the setting of its production, therefore, Johnson has greatly complicated the problems of the critic and, at the same time, has greatly refined his analysis. When the critic looks at the poem as a sign of a writer's ability, he must be aware of the complex array of causal factors which mingled in its production, and he must avoid the easy but false expedient of inferring ability or excellence directly from the traits of the work. The process of disentanglement by which the critic sorts out the circumstances of a work, distinguishing those traits genuinely attributable to the poet's native power from those dependent on some external or accidental factor, is essential to criticism as Johnson conceived and practiced it. The circumstantial method, of which history and biography are the basic tools, is forecast in the *Miscellaneous Observations on the Tragedy of Macbeth* (1745): "In order to make a true estimate of the abilities and merit of a writer, it is always necessary to examine the genius of his age, and the opinions of his contemporaries";[43] it is a major element in the organization of the *Preface to Shakespeare*, one long section of which is justified on the ground that "every man's preformances, to be rightly estimated, must be compared with the state of the age in which he lived, and with his own particular opportunities";[44] and it provides the formal principle for Johnson's

42. See, e.g., *Lives*, I, 19, 21, 35, 413, 415–18, 423–24, 443, 447, 458–59, 464–65; II, 145–47, 228; III, 217–20, 337–38, 268.

43. *Works*, V, 55.

44. Raleigh, *op. cit.*, p. 30; cf. *Proposals* (Raleigh, *op. cit.*, pp. 1–8 *passim*, esp. 3, 4, and 8); Preface to Thomas Maurice, *Poems and Miscellaneous Pieces* ([1779]; Hazen, *op. cit.*, p. 142); *Lives*, I, 318, 411; II, 145–47, 338–39, 433; III, 238–40.

greatest critical work, the *Lives of the Poets*, in which his characteristic linkage of biography and criticism is brought to perfection. The threefold division of the fully developed *Lives*, in which external circumstances, the intellectual character of the writer, and the qualities of his works are successively treated (a mode of organization also used, though in a different sequence, in the *Preface to Shakespeare*), is the counterpart in practice of the theory traced above.

Johnson's shift of the emphasis in criticism from art to nature and his persistent substitution of a more generalized formulation of artistic genius, literary genres, and related questions for the more particularized definitions of his predecessors may be regarded as a blurring of useful distinctions, as a relinquishment of ground gained in the development of criticism during the preceding century. So to view it, however, is to neglect the abuses and rigidities of critical theory between Dryden and Johnson and to undervalue the reconstructive service performed by Johnson in focusing attention once again on the dominant obligation of art to please its readers and the duty of critics to ground their judgments on real distinctions. Johnson's work, on the other hand, owing to his effort to dispense with encumbrances of traditional theory which he finds unjustified by empirical test, may appear to involve a total abrogation of principle, leaving only sensibility or force of personal preference and statement as the armor of the critic. To view his work in this light, however, is to separate his effort to re-establish criticism from the essential theoretical foundations on which it is based and to obscure features of his critical practice whose value was by no means exhausted in the solution of the problems for which they were originally formulated.[45]

45. I have discussed some aspects of Johnson's critical practice in relation to its theoretical bases in "Johnson's Criticism of the Metaphysical Poets," *ELH*, XVII (1950), 59–70.

FROM ACTION TO IMAGE: THEORIES OF THE LYRIC IN THE EIGHTEENTH CENTURY

NORMAN MACLEAN

THE statement so often made that the neoclassical period was a "non-lyrical" age seems unambiguous, comprehensive, and, as a judgment upon the accomplishments of a hundred years, respectably close to the truth. Yet, as historical pronouncement, it lacks a good deal in respect to clarity, comprehensiveness, and exactness. For one thing, it does not include the tender act that should initiate all history—an understanding of what someone, usually beyond summons, thought of himself, and his reasons, if discernible, for thinking so. However low we may appraise the moments in which the neoclassical age felt it was lyrical, we should also realize that this "non-lyrical" age regarded the highest form of the lyric—the Great Ode[1]—as one of the supreme expressions of poetry and itself as a supreme epoch in the history of the lyric, with its first master, Cowley, at least rivaling Pindar, with Dryden secure among all competitors, and with Gray the last and the best. It is possible that our own estimate, so at variance with this, may be based upon an incomplete understanding of the neoclassical conception of the lyric art, although an increased understanding may add grounds to support our initial estimate of its lyric poets. Still, it is a higher form of justice—and, let us hope, of criticism—to arrange for another's future only after learning something about his past.

If, however, the whole history of lyric poetry and theory is kept in view, then the neoclassical age is a very important period. In its conception of what the lyric should be, it is antiquity turning toward the modern. It starts with a conception of lyric poetry which can be traced as far back as Plato and which

---

1. The word "ode" has a treacherous history. The word "lyric" was not used until Alexandrian times to designate the body of poetry that has since been so called; in Hellenic Greece these poems, when spoken of as one kind, were referred to either as odes (ᾠδαῖ) or melic poems (μέλη) (see Herbert Weir Smyth, *Greek Melic Poets* [London, 1900], pp. xvii-xx). From antiquity, then, the word "ode" had a meaning so general as to make it a synonym for lyric poetry, and it was so used until very recent times, when, however, its connotations have become specialized, the word "ode" now calling to mind only a particular kind of lyric—massive, public in its proclamations, and Pindaric in its classical prototype. Throughout the neoclassical period this massive lyric has many designations—the "Pindaric ode," the "Cowleyan ode," the "sublime ode." I have adopted a more neutral term—the "Great Ode"—with which to designate it when a neutral designation seems called for. The reader must also bear in mind that until recently all other kinds of lyrics were often referred to as "lesser odes."

had remained fairly constant during the intervening centuries. If we confine ourselves rigidly to a statement of Plato's opinions that enter into the early neoclassical conception of the lyric, the following four points emerge as perhaps most important. (1) Plato judged poetry, as he judged every other human accomplishment, by its relation to the good. Poetry has two possible relations to the good; it can celebrate the good and draw men to it, or it can expose error and evil and warn men of the consequences. (2) Poetry he divided by subject and style. There are three classes of poetical subject matter—gods, demigods and heroes, and men.[2] By dialectical subtlety, he equated these three classes of poetical subjects to his four (or five) cardinal virtues, poetry about the gods having as its proper function the promotion of wisdom (and holiness); poetry about heroes the furtherance of courage and temperance (since heroes should exhibit courage in war and temperance in peace); and poetry about men the promotion of justice, the all-supervisory virtue which, therefore, should be possessed by everyone.[3] (3) Under the large heading of style, he considered manner—the dramatic manner, in which the characters do all the speaking; the manner of the dithyramb (the most ambitious of Greek melic kinds), in which the poet most directly speaks in his own person; and the mixed or epic manner.[4] Of manner, he preferred (contrary to Aristotle) the manner which permits the good narrator to speak continuously, although the poet (presumed to be good in this point of his argument) could occasionally "imitate" the words and actions of men as good as himself.[5] (4) The poetical forms tolerated in his ideal state are hymns (ὕμνοι) and encomia (ἐγκώμια),[6] melic forms having the fol-

2. Long before Plato, this distinction must have been current in Greece. See, for instance, the opening lines of Pindar's second *Olympian Ode:* "Ye hymns that rule the lyre! what god, what hero, aye, and what man shall we loudly praise?" (trans. Sir John Sandys in the Loeb edition of *The Odes of Pindar*).

3. In Books ii and iii of the *Republic* Plato discusses the proper way in which poetry should represent first the gods, next "daemons" and heroes, and, finally, men (377E–392C). He then proceeds to discuss the style or "diction" of poetry, the subjects having been completely considered. The same division of the subjects proper for poetical imitation is used to discuss the function of poetry in the practical state governed by the *Laws* (vii. 801D–802).

4. *Republic* iii. 394B–C.

5. *Ibid.* 396B–E.

6. This is Plato's final pronouncement upon poetry in the last book of the *Republic*, where dialectic has lifted the state above those practical impulses of pleasure and pain to a level where reason is the law of a land that has never been inhabited, except speculatively. " 'Then, Glaucon,' said I, 'when you meet ecomiasts of Homer who tell us that this poet has been the educator of Hellas, and that for the conduct and refinement of human life he is worthy of our study and devotion, and that we should order our entire lives by the guidance of this poet, we must love and salute them as doing the best they can, and concede to them that Homer is the most poetic of poets and the first of tragedians, *but we must know the truth, that we can admit no poetry into our city save only hymns to the gods* [ὕμνοι] *and the praises of good men* [ἐγκώμια]. For if you grant admission to the honeyed muse in lyric or epic, pleasure and pain will be lords of your city instead of law and that which shall from time to time have

lowing characteristics: (*a*) they are celebrations of the good (evidently those forms exposing frailty are too negative and dangerous to be admitted to utopia); (*b*) they are celebrations of gods and famous men; (*c*) they are not in the dramatic manner but in the manner in which the poet can speak most directly himself; (*d*) they are choral, accompanied by music and performed by large companies.

The views of the eighteenth century concerning lyric poetry are thus at first those impacted in a tradition that extends back to the first literary critic, and of this tradition the following general statements can be made. (1) Lyric poetry is discussed in a critical context which postulates that its chief function is to move men to the "good." Plato's complex equation between the different poetical subject matters and the different virtues is ignored, but not his main formula—that the excellent poem is the "good" poem, although, by the time of Horace, Plato's third class of poetry, representing "men," is viewed as a celebration not of the universal virtue of justice but of the pleasures common to men, those of love and wine.[7] In respect to the two modes of moving men to the good, by celebrating it positively or by censuring transgression, lyric poetry is conceived of as being almost wholly of the higher order dedicated to praise (with occasional upbraidings of lovers as exceptions scarcely worth critical notation). (2) Lyric poetry is divided into subspecies by the threefold distinction in subject matters used in all other instances to separate species from one another. As a result, most of the discussion of the lyric is a discussion of the subspecies and their ingredients, and very little is said of lyric as a kind other than that it is poetry to be accompanied by music or, if only to be read, the most "musical" kind of poetry. To the early neoclassical period, however, as to Plato, the possibility of allying music with words was artistically and philosophically important. (3) Because the threefold distinction separating lyric kinds included the whole range of poetical excellence, there is a marked tendency to regard the subspecies of the lyric as separate species and to place the first two lyric kinds—the divine and the heroic—near the top of the poetical hierarchy (along with epic and tragedy) and the minor lyric near the bottom (generally somewhere between pastoral and epigram).

---

approved itself to the general reason as the best' " (x. 606E–607; italics mine). In the more lenient state governed by the *Laws*, a somewhat wider variety of poetical forms is permitted, but the great choruses, involving words, music, and dramatic presentation, are, if anything, more central to education. For an elaboration of the position that "choristry as a whole is identical with education as a whole," see *Laws* ii. 672E ff.; and for the organization and functions of the four state choruses, *ibid.* ii. 664B ff. The quoted passages are from the Loeb edition, the *Laws* translated by R. G. Bury and the *Republic* by Paul Shorey.

7. *Ars poetica* ll. 83–85: "To the lyre the Muse granted tales of gods and children of gods, of the victor in boxing, of the horse first in the race, of the loves of swains, and of freedom over wine" (translation from *Horace: Satires, Epistles, and "Ars poetica"* [Loeb ed.; London, 1936]).

By the end of the eighteenth century, however, a revolution was under way, but a revolution as yet without the inspiration of original creative genius or the direction of a great and original aesthetic theorist. Probably aesthetic inquiry was more general in the eighteenth century than in any earlier century; yet one would be partial to the age rather than to the inquiry if he judged any speculative critic of the period as a towering figure.[8] It was as yet a revolution in current opinion only. Whether it be true, as Matthew Arnold maintained, that great ages of poetry are preceded by great periods of criticism, it is certainly true that great theories are often erected after a geological disturbance in common opinion. In the closing decades of the eighteenth century—years in which Coleridge and Wordsworth lived and were shaping their theories and lyrical ballads—the following disturbing and "modern" opinions were not uncommonly expressed: poetry is essentially of two kinds, that which depends heavily upon material external to the poet, including plot, and that in which the poet's soul is its own source of materials and its own excuse for being; poetry is also divisible into two kinds in terms of the quality of soul that produces it, the higher kind being the product of the sublime imagination; short poems, hitherto judged minor, are often viewed as products of the sublime imagination; the essence of poetry is also assigned a linguistic equivalent, the striking image (a sign of the intense imagination), and, of striking images, none is so essentially poetical as the metaphor.

It is the purpose of this study to trace critical opinion as it changes from the one world to the other, from a conception of the lyric still shaped by the earliest expressions of classical poetry and literary criticism to a view of the lyric as an expression of the poet's soul, although it is not yet named "subjective" poetry.

What has just been said should suggest that literary criticism is here conceived of as a form of medial discourse and therefore, when isolated, seriously deficient in the power to explain itself. On the one hand, literary criticism has connections with philosophy and other forms of inquiry more abstract than itself. The critic furnishes insights, sensitive reactions, and workable distinctions to the speculative aesthetician who clarifies, rationalizes, amplifies, and systematizes; and, in turn, some part of these philosophical clarifications and amplifications seep back and become a part of critical tradition, somewhat altering the tradition, even if, as is often the case, the rationalization and systemization are blurred by common handling. On the other hand, literary criticism is in good part shaped by particular poems and groups of poems; and it, in turn, shapes to some extent subsequent creation. This study, then, primarily an explication of the theory of one kind of poetry, will involve secondary explica-

---

8. Kant certainly is a great exception, but this study is limited to English neoclassical critics and to those outside influences that seriously affected their views of lyric poetry.

tions of relevant aesthetics and of representative poems on the assumption that each of the three—general aesthetics, literary criticism, and poetry—will be illuminated by the involvement of the other two.[9]

I. THE SUBLIME AND THE BEAUTIFUL

Every period has its renaissances, if by "renaissance" is meant an excited rediscovery and a distinctive reinterpretation of some body of former knowledge, opinion, or creation. At the beginning of the neoclassical period there were two such rediscoveries that singly at first and then in combined force seriously altered the tradition of the English lyric. In 1656, Cowley published his *Pindarique Odes*.[10] These odes proved to be the literary sensation of the early neoclassical period in England and focused more attention upon the lyric of grandiose dimension than it had received since early Greece. An almost simultaneous sensation was created by the rediscovery of Longinus, a rediscovery of far larger import than the first, affecting not only lyric poetry but the whole field of aesthetic inquiry and literary creation. This section of our study will indicate how the critical opinions of Longinus entered into the general aesthetics of the period in ways that could affect the tradition of the lyric; and the following section will show the influences of Cowley and Longinus combining to affect every element involved in lyric creation.

It was not until 1652 that Longinus' treatise *On the Sublime* (*Peri hupsous*) was translated into English,[11] and it was later still before it had any appreciable effect in England.[12] Then, suddenly, Longinus became a vogue; edition after

9. I should add that this study of eighteenth-century theories of the lyric is only a part of a larger study, which, when completed, will follow the long discussion about lyric poetry from the time when it first becomes audible to the present. Accordingly, each period between the beginnings and the momentary end is viewed as a middle, having its own importance and complexity and also its connections with what was said before and afterward. I realize that certain difficulties are involved in a study that proposes to relate criticism to philosophy and poetry and, additively, to suggest the three dimensions of time. I can only hope that I have been more constantly aware of these difficulties than the reader will be.

10. Other odes by Cowley written in the same manner were published in *Verses Written on Several Occasions* (1663); and still others appeared in the complete edition of his works, published in 1668, a year after his death.

11. By John Hall.

12. It was not until after 1674 that Longinus was frequently quoted in England, according to Samuel H. Monk's *The Sublime: A Study of Critical Theories in XVIII-Century England* (New York, 1935), p. 20. This work should be consulted by anyone interested in the large question of the influence of Longinus in England during the neoclassical period. More recent —too recent, unfortunately, to have aided in the preparation of this study—is Gordon McKenzie's *Critical Responsiveness: A Study of the Psychological Current in Later Eighteenth-Century Criticism* (Berkeley, 1949), the broad subject of which includes important aspects of Longinus' influence. Indispensable to a study of Longinus' early influence on the continent is Bernard Weinberg's "Translations and Commentaries of Longinus, *On the Sublime*, to 1600: A Bibliography," *Modern Philology*, XLVII (February, 1950), 145–51.

edition appeared, and it became so universally the fashion to quote him that the fashion became the object of satire. According to Monk, Longinus "probably reached the height of his fame at about 1738"[13] and by bibliographical measurement this is probably true, for after that date there were fewer editions and probably he was less frequently quoted; but there can be a difference between a vogue and an influence, and the ideas of Longinus became more central to English criticism after he no longer seemed novel. In the second half of the eighteenth century "sublimity" is the term that dominates the aesthetic inquiries of English theorists (Burke, Kames, Alison, etc.), and it is then, rather than earlier, that a view of poetry emerges which is based on the most fundamental tenets of Longinus.

Of ancient critics, Longinus is the most committed to a psychological approach to literature. To him, literature occasionally reveals, as if by a flash of lightning, the presence of supermundane qualities—qualities that immediately "transport" the reader out of his normal senses and invest literary works with immortality. In the divinely sponsored universe of Longinus, nature itself in certain of its aspects gives visible embodiment to the supermundane and sublime, not in small streams but in the Nile, the Danube, the Rhine, and still more the ocean;[14] however, because Longinus is primarily interested in the sublime in literature and in the *art* of literary sublimity,[15] he places little emphasis upon natural objects as a source of the sublime (and hence differs, as we shall see, from many eighteenth-century "Longinian" critics). To Longinus, "sublimity is the ring of greatness in the soul,"[16] arising from five different "sources." The first two—"lofty enterprise in the thought" and "strong and inspired passion"—are the constituents of the "soul," and the last three are the verbal means of expressing the first two.[17] Longinus' literary interests, therefore, are in "thoughts that breathe, and words that burn." Two consequences of such a concentration of literary interests should be underlined, lest Longinus and "Romantic" criticism seem to have many attributes but no general characteristics. In the first place, the totality of an individual poem (unless it be short) and the differences among kinds of poems are aesthetic considerations of little significance. Literary qualities that "transport" must, almost of necessity, occur in short and blinding passages and may occur in any literary genre (poetic, historical, philosophical, or rhetorical). In more modern lan-

---

13. *Op. cit.*, p. 24.

14. *On the Sublime* Sec. 35. Unless otherwise specified, all quotations from Longinus are from the translation by Benedict Einarson in *Longinus, "On the Sublime," and Sir Joshua Reynolds, "Discourses on Art"* (Chicago, 1945). Cf. above, pp. 232–59.

15. *On the Sublime* Sec. 2.

16. *Ibid.* Sec. 9.   17. *Ibid.* Sec. 8.

guage, Longinus is concerned not with poems or kinds of poems but with "poetry," or "pure poetry," which is a rarity that can reveal itself only occasionally in a long poem but, because the great soul is not completely fettered by the forms of discourse, may appear in works that are not basically poetic in intention. In the second place, this concentration of literary interests reduces the number of elements fundamental to literature, with results that are important in the history of the theory of the lyric and in the larger history of criticism. In this view of literature, what is concentrated upon in individual works is what is common to all forms of elevated discourse, and forms as various as philosophy, poetry, and rhetoric have only these elements in common: thought, emotion, and language. To Longinus, therefore, plot and character delineation were subsidiary interests; plot to him was optional and was conceived of, not as what held a poem together, but as stirring incident that could serve as the occasion for lofty utterances, and the characters he approved of were only those capable of delivering such utterances. The criticism of the last two centuries, as it has shifted over to a psychological basis, has likewise been marked by a subsidiary interest in plot and its needful agents, so that long poems (and long poems generally involve a narrative) have the possibility of only here and there being "poetry." However, the reduction of "poetry" to the elements of thought, emotion, and language enhanced the value of one traditional poetic species that was a concentrated and pure expression of these elements, enhanced its value so much that often in "Romantic" criticism "lyric" is used as a synonym for "poetry." Indeed, in the case of Croce, who identifies art with the "intuitive" act of the "spirit," all of art is lyric, and lyric, he adds, is employed in this construction not as an adjective but as a synonym.[18]

It would be unfortunate to leave the impression that the rediscovery of Longinus was the sole cause of the emergence of "sublimity" as a central concept in eighteenth-century aesthetics. Success such as his is naturally reciprocal, involving both an arrival and a welcome. Let us consider three representative and influential discussions of sublimity in England during this century to see how they reflect the soul not only of Longinus but of this age—its religious, scientific, and psychological predispositions as well as its artistic tastes. Moreover, this seemingly turning road is the one that leads directly to the lyric. For, although most eighteenth-century inquiries into the sublime are more theoretical than *Peri hupsous*, more concerned with the natural causes of the sublime (the psychological interactions between the senses and their objects) and its final cause (God's manifestation of himself in his creations) than with the practical literary problem of how to "transport" audiences, nevertheless

18. *The Essence of Aesthetic* (London, 1921), pp. 32–33.

they are tightly connected with the theory and configuration of the lyric in this age and in the great lyric age that follows.

Even though Longinus is interested primarily in analyzing literary qualities, he makes clear, as we have said, that sublimity is a quality reflected by certain natural objects and that, in turn, sublime objects reflect the presence of a Divine Creator and his intentions in respect to man.[19] Varied and at times highly controversial though they are, eighteenth-century treatments of the sublime agree with one another and with Longinus concerning its final cause. Addison's *Spectator* papers "On the Pleasures of the Imagination"[20] reduce the fundamental aesthetic problem to two considerations: (1) the different classes of objects that arouse aesthetic pleasures and (2) the ultimate reason why man is delighted by these objects. The objects are of three kinds, the *"Great, Uncommon*, or *Beautiful."*[21] In respect to the pleasures aroused by these objects, it is impossible to trace out their "several necessary and efficient Causes," because "we know neither the Nature of an Idea, nor the Substance of a Human Soul"; on the other hand, *"Final Causes* lie more bare and open to our Observation," and for the pleasure aroused by each of the three classes of objects Addison assigns a final cause. Through the *Great*, God informs the soul of man "that nothing but himself can be its last, adequate, and proper Happiness"; by attaching pleasure to what is *New* and *Uncommon*, God instills in us a desire to pursue knowledge and "to search into the Wonders of his Creation"; and he has made what is *Beautiful* in our own species a source of pleasure so "that all Creatures might be tempted to multiply their Kind" and what is beautiful in other species pleasant to us in order that he "might render the whole Creation more gay and delightful."[22] Although Addison treats the aesthetic problem in terms fairly remote from literature and from the lyric in particular, yet actually this one form of poetry had from the beginning of criticism been subdivided into three or two kinds having close affinity to the classes of pleasures that Addison has raised to universal proportions, the Great Ode being *great* in its objects and *great* in its ultimate intention of celebrating the divine, and the Lesser Ode being, like the *beautiful*, "gay and delightful" and particularly concerned with the emotion that leads to the multiplication of species.

19. *On the Sublime* Sec. 35.

20. *Spectator*, Nos. 411–21. All references are to the "Everyman's Library" edition, edited by G. Gregory Smith.

21. *Spectator*, No. 412.

22. *Ibid.*, No. 413. Although Addison uses the term "great" rather than "sublime," it is clear from his argument that he is influenced by Longinus; also, see paper No. 409 for his statement that there is "something more essential to the art [than "Mechanical Rules"], something that elevates and astonishes the Fancy, and gives a Greatness of Mind to the Reader, which few of the criticks besides *Longinus* have considered."

Edmund Burke, in *A Philosophical Inquiry into the Origin of Our Ideas of the Sublime and the Beautiful* (1757),[23] reduces the aesthetic experience to two opposite states of mind closely approximating the distinctions that had long divided the lyric into major and minor forms. Thus Burke's inquiry has a practical bearing on our particular subject, even though it is, as its title indicates, a philosophical and psychological, rather than a critical, inquiry. What to Addison was the knowable cause of the aesthetic experience was to Burke an article of faith that could "never be unravelled by any industry of ours"; reverentially, therefore, he limits his inquiry to the efficient cause,[24] to the natural origin of our ideas of the sublime and the beautiful. The sublime and the beautiful arise from two opposite sets of passions in man—the passions for "*self-preservation*, and *society*,"[25] the first of which are aroused by danger—vastness, darkness, infinity, irregularity—and the second either by the "society of the *sexes*" or by "more *general society*."[26] Accordingly, the state of mind characterizing sublimity is terror (induced by a realization of danger), and beauty is characterized by two emotions closely allied—love (for the sexes) and sympathy rising in its highest form to pity (for mankind in general). Having traced the sublime and beautiful to antithetical psychological sources, Burke then discusses in detail and at great length the different kinds of objects that most effectively serve as stimuli, either by "association" or by "natural powers,"[27] to induce the two aesthetic experiences, which eventually he connects with opposite bodily states, the physiological concomitant of sublimity being "an unnatural tension of the nerves,"[28] and of beauty, a physiological state of "relaxation."[29]

Bishop Robert Lowth's treatment of the sublime has a different focal point from either Addison's or Burke's. Analyzing Hebrew poetry,[30] he nowhere

23. For a summary of the controversy over the date of the first edition see Monk, *op. cit.*, pp. 85–86. All references in this essay are to the second edition (London, 1759).

24. "That great chain of causes, which linking one to another even to the throne of God himself, can never be unravelled by any industry of ours. When we go but one step beyond the immediately sensible qualities of things, we go out of our depth. . . . So that when I speak of cause, and efficient cause, I only mean, certain affections of the mind, that cause certain changes in the body; or certain powers and properties in bodies, that work a change in the mind" (Burke, *Philosophical Inquiry*, Part IV, Sec. I, pp. 243–44).

25. *Ibid.*, Part I, Sec. VI, p. 57.

26. *Ibid.*, Part I, Sec. VIII, p. 60. Note the close resemblance between Addison and Burke in the passions they associate with aesthetic pleasures.

27. For an extended analysis of the influence of psychological associationalism upon English aesthetics during the late eighteenth century, see McKenzie, *op. cit.*, chapter on "Association and Emotion."

28. Burke, *op. cit.*, Part IV, Sec. III, pp. 246–49.

29. *Ibid.*, Sec. XIX, pp. 286–89.

30. "It may not be improper to apprise the Public, that although the following Lectures be entitled Lectures on the Hebrew Poetry, their utility is by no means confined to that

leaves a doubt as to its ultimately divine purposes, and he recognizes that sublimity is in part an exhibition of great objects,[31] but he is much closer to Longinus and to literature than are Addison and Burke. It is not his "intention to expound to the student of theology the oracles of Divine truth, but to recommend to the notice of youth who is addicted to politer sciences, and studious of the elegancies of composition, some of the first and choicest specimens of poetic taste."[32] The word "composition" completes the circle of primary interests in the sublime—the sublime as an effect of the Divine Creator (Addison), the sublime as an effect of natural objects upon the natural mechanisms of man (Burke), and the sublime as an effect of language (Lowth). How great an emphasis Lowth puts upon language can be seen from the outline of his lectures: the first set deals with versification, the second with "style" (there are three styles, and they are treated at great length—the "sententious," the "figurative," and the "sublime"), and the final set with "arrangement." And his general argument is reinforced by direct statements designating certain characteristics of language as the essential markings of poetry:

The poetry of every language has a style and form of expression peculiar to itself,—forcible, magnificent, and sonorous; the words pompous and energetic; the composition singular and artificial; the whole form and complexion different from what we meet with in common life, and frequently (as with a noble indignation) breaking down the boundaries by which the popular dialect is confined. The language of reason is cool, temperate, rather humble than elevated, well arranged and perspicuous, with an evident care and anxiety lest anything should escape which might appear perplexed or obscure. The language of the passions is totally different: the conceptions burst out into a turbid stream, expressive in a manner of the internal conflict; the more vehement break out in hasty confusion; they catch (without search or study) whatever is impetuous, vivid, or energetic. In a word, reason speaks literally, the passions poetically.[33]

---

single object: They embrace all the GREAT PRINCIPLES OF GENERAL CRITICISM, as delivered by the ancients, improved by the keen judgment and polished taste of their Author" ("The Translator's [G. Gregory's] Preface"). Lowth's lectures were first published in 1753 under the title *De sacra poesi Hebraeorum praelectiones academicae;* this work was translated in 1793. All quotations are from *Lectures on the Sacred Poetry of the Hebrews* (London, 1847).

31. "The word *sublimity* I wish, in this place, to be understood in its most extensive sense: I speak not merely of that sublimity which exhibits great objects with a magnificent display of imagery and diction; but that force of composition, whatever it be, which strikes and overpowers the mind. . . . In this use of the word I copy Longinus, the most accomplished author on this subject, whether we consider his precepts or his example" (*Lectures on the Sacred Poetry of the Hebrews*, Lecture XIV, "Of the Sublime in General, and of Sublimity of Expression in Particular," p. 155).

32. *Ibid.*, Lecture II, "The Design and Arrangement of These Lectures," p. 36.

33. *Ibid.*, Lecture XIV, "Of the Sublime in General, and of Sublimity of Expression in Particular," p. 156. Immediately after making this distinction, he gives a detailed description of Hebrew prose—grammatically "regular and uniform"; nonrhythmic; and in choice of words avoiding the unusual in meaning and application. He then uses this "normal" mode of expression reflecting a mind concerned with the matter-of-fact as that from which poetry is a deviation (compare with Longinus immediately below).

Bishop Lowth's view of poetic language looks backward and forward. It has a close connection with Longinus, whose discussion of the last three sources of the sublime—those relating to the verbal signs of sublimity—nearly always postulates a normal or "natural" mode of expression—straightforward and complete in its grammatical parts, mundane in its choice of words, and expository in its avoidance of emotional connotations—a mode of expression from which the sublime utterance is an abnormal divergence signifying that the author has been "transported" beyond the world of the matter-of-fact. On the other hand, Bishop Lowth's emphasis upon language as a characteristic of poetry would sound like the most recent criticism if only he had had the advantage of the adjective "semantic"; certainly, common and fundamental to both the bishop and the modern semantic critic is the distinction between the language of prose and poetry, the literal language of reason and the figurative language of the emotions, or, to speak with more modern connotations, between the language of "denotation" and the language of "connotation."

But Bishop Lowth is also a man of his century; and the eighteenth-century interest in sublimity and these representative, but somewhat speculative, ways of approaching it have a close, practical bearing upon the neoclassical lyric: (1) When the elements of sublimity are compounded, what emerges is an expression in *language* "elevated from common Language the most that is possible,"[34] reflecting a *soul* transported by the most magnificent of natural *objects*, such a soul and such natural objects being, in turn, creative expressions of the Divine Creator. Of artistic expressions, sublimity moves man to the supreme artistic pleasure. (2) During the eighteenth century and systematically during the latter part of it, a second aesthetic state of mind—beauty—is added to the sublime, so opposite in its qualities that the two are used by theorists as dialectical contraries, together including the total aesthetic experience (sometimes the sublime and beautiful are viewed as all-inclusive; sometimes intermediate states of mind are recognized and introduced between them).

One traditional species was shaped to exhibit fully these new critical specifications. Lyric poetry had long been viewed as dual in its nature, com-

---

34. Cf. Joseph Trapp, *Lectures on Poetry* (London, 1742), p. 204. This is a translation of *Praelectiones poeticae* (1711). The quotation above is part of his characterization of lyric poetry which is "of all Kinds of Poetry, the most poetical; and is as distinct, both in Style, and Thought, from the rest, as Poetry in general is from Prose" (p. 203). Trapp is an early-eighteenth-century critic who places great emphasis upon language as a differentiating mark of poetry. See, for instance, his comparison of oratory and poetry, which share so much in common that they "are Branches of Eloquence in general." The distinction between them is made in terms of language and an impassioned mind. "However, the Difference between them is very great; and Poetry has several other Characteristics besides that of Metre; a Style, for instance, peculiar to itself, Fiction, copious Descriptions, poetic Fire, and (to add no more) a certain Licence, denied to Orators, in the due Exercise of which the Poet's Art is chiefly conspicuous" (pp. 34–35).

prised of a major form dedicated to the divine and the heroic and of a minor form with love as its special province.

II. THE EARLY SUBLIME ODE

The popularity of Longinus merged quickly with that of the Cowleyan ode; and, almost as soon as the concept of sublimity became well known in England, it was regarded as peculiarly exemplified by the Great Ode. In 1677 Dryden used Longinus as authority and Cowley as example in arguing that bold imagery is a necessary ingredient of poetry;[35] and later (*ca.* March, 1693/94) he urged Dennis to attempt to bring the Cowleyan ode to perfection, because, as he said, "You have the Sublimity of Sense as well as Sound, and know how far the Boldness of a Poet may lawfully extend."[36] In 1706 Congreve, who shared the opinion that many followers of Cowley had degraded rather than perfected the Great Ode, nevertheless remarked that "nothing should be objected to the Latitude" Cowley himself had taken in rendering Pindar into English, since Cowley had often happily recaptured the "Sublimity of his Stile and Sentiments."[37] Before many years of the eighteenth century had passed, the connection seen by these earlier critics between sublimity and the major ode became fixed into a formula; the designation "the sublime ode" appeared more frequently than "the Cowleyan" or "the Pindaric ode"; and, whatever the designation, sublimity was regarded almost universally as the essential characteristic of the lofty lyric. In 1711 Trapp divided lyric poetry into two kinds, one the "Sublime," the other "of the lower Strain."[38] Of Lowth's three kinds of lyric poems (1753), one is sublime, one sweet, and one intermediate, combining both qualities.[39] Samuel Johnson's division, like Trapp's, is twofold; and, despite his many strictures against ode writers for their excesses, the lesser ode in his *Dictionary* "is characterised by sweetness and ease; the greater by sublimity, rapture, and quickness of transition." Hugh Blair's division (1783) is fourfold, but the two highest, "the Sacred Odes" and "the Heroic Odes," those like David's and Pindar's, "ought to have sublimity and elevation, for their reigning character."[40] And the testimony

35. "The Author's Apology for Heroic Poetry and Poetic Licence," *Essays of John Dryden*, ed. W. P. Ker (Oxford, 1926); I, 185–86.

36. *The Letters of John Dryden*, ed. Charles E. Ward (Durham, N.C., 1942), p. 72.

37. "A Discourse on the Pindarique Ode," prefixed to *A Pindarique Ode Humbly Offer'd to the Queen on the Victorious Progress of Her Majesty's Arms, under the Conduct of the Duke of Marlborough* (*The Complete Works of William Congreve*, ed. Montague Summers [1923], IV, 85).

38. Trapp, *op. cit.*, p. 214.

39. He has two lectures on the sublime ode and a lecture on each of the other two (Lowth, *op. cit.*, Lectures XXV–XXVIII).

40. *Lectures on Rhetoric and Belles Lettres* (London, 1783), II, 355.

of the closing decades of the eighteenth century makes it clear that the renowned lyric poets of the early nineteenth century grew up during years when the Great Ode, of which they were to produce truly great examples, was everywhere identified with sublimity. "Sublimity is the essential and characteristic perfection of the Ode," according to Robert Potter.[41] In 1785 John Pinkerton divided lyric poetry into two kinds, "the sublime," in which Pindar was unrivaled until Gray appeared, and "the beautiful," in which Anacreon and Sappho were still supreme.[42] In the same year Thomas Warton rebuked a critic for taking the position that "short compositions" can attain only neatness and elegance, because "Odes are short compositions, and they can often attain sublimity, which is even a characteristic of that species of poetry."[43] Two years later, William Preston closed his discussion of the irregular ode with the following remark: "I shall conclude with expressing a wish, that these hasty reflections may be the means of exciting some poetical genius to make trial of a species of composition, which, in my mind, is peculiarly susceptible of true sublimity."[44] And in the year of the *Lyrical Ballads* Nathan Drake divided lyric poetry into four kinds—the Sublime, the Pathetic, the Descriptive, and the Amatory, the first of which "demands a felicity and strength of genius that has seldom been attained."[45]

It is not difficult to understand why the Cowleyan ode became almost universally regarded as the purest exemplification of the Longinian precepts which, almost at the same time, were becoming the sensation of the critical world. In rendering Pindar into English and in writing original odes in the manner of Pindar, Cowley had introduced what was hailed as a new species of English poetry: a form attempting to give embodiment to a "lofty" and "inspired" soul in a state of transport; a form, therefore, admitting only the most elevated of subjects, the divine and the heroic; a form comparatively short in length, irregular in its verse form, abrupt and sudden in its transitions, and, in figurative language, "*bold*, even to *Temeritie*, and such as I [Cowley] durst not have to do withal in any other kind of *Poetry*. . . ."[46] The sublimity of Longinus is also brief, like lightning, a sudden insight, a burst of passion (his

41. *An Inquiry into Some Passages in Dr. Johnson's "Lives of the Poets": Particularly His Observations on Lyric Poetry, and the Odes of Gray* (London, 1783), p. 14.

42. *Letters of Literature. By Robert Heron, Esq.* (London, 1785), p. 33.

43. *Poems upon Several Occasions, English, Italian, and Latin, with Translations, by John Milton* (2d ed.; London, 1791), p. 282.

44. "Thoughts on Lyric Poetry," *Transactions of the Royal Irish Academy* (1787), section on "Polite Literature," p. 73.

45. *Literary Hours: Or Sketches Critical, Narrative, and Poetical* (3d ed.; London, 1804), II, 71.

46. *Poems*, ed A. R. Waller (Cambridge, 1905), p. 11.

examples are all short passages); the language of the sublime is an impassioned disruption of the normal mode of expression; and irregularity (even error) Longinus not only condones but views as a mark of writers with "more than human inspiration."[47] In other words, and not at all contrary to nature, shortly before there was a critical precept there was a poetical example of it.

Some indication should also be given of the impact of "sublimity" upon the whole theory of poetical genres, a theory extending back to Plato in which different classes of "subjects" and "styles" were used to divide poetry into kinds and to arrange them in a hierarchy with the epic generally at the top and the epigram or a miscellany of minor verse at the bottom. The outline of an answer to this larger question will give perspective to our view of lyric poetry, the changing fortunes of which may be measured by the company it keeps.

Longinus has been interpreted as a critic to whom the traditional distinctions among modes of discourse (history, philosophy, rhetoric, and poetry with its hierarchy of kinds) lacked fundamental aesthetic significance. To him, literary splendor was one, "the ring of greatness in the soul"; if literature were to be divided by considerations basic to a psychological approach, then the division would cut across the traditional classification. An example of a psychological classification would be Wordsworth's arrangement of his own poems according to the psychological faculty "predominant" in the composition of each. But the initial effect of Longinus upon English criticism produced no such fundamental revolution. The new was not substituted for the traditional but was added to it; that is, sublimity was taken as a quality distinguishing the three genres (epic, tragedy, and the Great Ode) which throughout most of the history of criticism had been placed at the top of the poetical hierarchy. The line between the greater and lesser species of poetry is drawn sharply by John Dennis, who characterizes the epic, tragedy, and "greater Ode" by "the Enthusiastick Passions" associated with sublimity.[48] Statistically, some such view as this was probably the prevalent one throughout the century, a view in which the sublime reinforced distinctions of relatively little aesthetic value to Longinus. But a fundamental revolution was not without its preparations in this century, and in these the influence of Longinus is clearly visible. Let us take as a striking example a mid-century classification of poetry based in good part upon psychological qualities, the highest of which is sublimity. In denying Pope a position

---

47. Longinus *op. cit.* Secs. 33–35.

48. *The Grounds of Criticism in Poetry* (1704), in *The Critical Works of John Dennis*, ed. Edward Niles Hooker (Baltimore, 1939), I, 339. The two sets of "Passions" used by Dennis to distinguish the major from the minor species are the "Vulgar Passions" and the "Enthusiastick Passions." The bases for the distinction between these two passions are stated later (see Sec. III) and should be compared with the bases used by Burke and others in distinguishing the sublime and the beautiful.

among the first flight of poets, Joseph Warton (1756) may have seemed inconsiderate of the recent dead, but he was judging literature by a canon of criticism which, if he were honest, could scarcely lead him to any other judgment. Poetry he divides into four classes, the first of which is distinguished by the sublime and the pathetic,[49] and these "are the two chief nerves of all genuine poesy"[50] or what he refers to a few pages earlier (p. iv), in even more modern phraseology, as "pure poetry." As for the second class of poetry, it consists of the moral, ethical, and panegyrical, in which there is "true poetical genius in a more moderate degree,"[51] and it is in this species of poetry that Pope, to whose memory and ability Warton pays reverential tribute, "is superior to all mankind: and I only say, that this species of poetry is not the most excellent one of the art."[52]

If we turn, finally, to the closing decade of the eighteenth century, we can find so revolutionary a point of view as that expressed by Anna Seward, who maintains that it makes little difference what traditional "order of composition" is chosen by the "sublimated imagination."[53] To her and other lyric enthusiasts of the closing years of the century, "imagination," "poetry," and "lyric" tend to be synonymous terms. Suggestions of this coming convergence will begin to appear as we examine the position commonly given the Sublime Ode in the traditional hierarchy of poetical species.

The position of the Great Ode in this hierarchy was ambivalent. On the one hand, the Great Ode was generally considered a major form of poetry, that is, it was grouped with the epic and tragedy, but placed below either or both of these. On the other hand, many of the same critics who gave it this ranking regarded it as being, in many of its fundamental qualities, the most "poetical" form of poetry. This ambivalence naturally disappears in a later view of poetry that sees little or nothing of value in the elements out of which epic and tragedy are chiefly constructed—the plot and its agents. In this later view, as Poe says, " 'a long poem' is simply a flat contradiction in terms";[54] he also says: "In regard to the Iliad, we have, if not positive proof, at least very good reason, for believing it intended as a series of lyrics; but, granting the epic intention, I can say only that the work is based in an imperfect sense of art."[55]

49. For a discussion of the "pathetic," Longinus' second source of the sublime, see below, n. 134.

50. Warton, *An Essay on the Genius and Writings of Pope* (2d ed.; London, 1762), p. x.

51. *Ibid.*, pp. xi–xii. The third class, describing familiar life, requires wit, elegant taste, and lively fancy; the fourth, smooth and mellifluous, is attractive largely because of its qualities of verse.

52. *Ibid.*, p. iv.   53. See below, p. 460.

54. "The Poetic Principle" (*The Complete Works of Edgar Allan Poe*, ed. James A. Harrison [New York, 1902], XIV, 266).

55. *Ibid.*, p. 267.

Although Dennis had listed the "greater Lyrick" as the third major species, he compares the Ode to the epic and concludes "that the Ode ought to have as much boldness, elevation and majesty, as Epic Poetry it self; but then it is certain that it ought to have more vehemence, more transport and more enthusiasm." The reason Dennis gives is that the ode has the same end as epic poetry, the arousing of "admiration," but, since it must achieve its effect in much shorter space, it must be more concentrated in its poetical display.[56] Later Lowth (1753)[57] and Potter (1783) make the same comparison, pointing out that the epic and longer poems in general must rise only to recede, whereas the ode strikes with immediate and sustained effect; hence, proper to it from the earliest times, according to Potter, have been "the highest flights of imagination to which even the Epic Muse dared not aspire."[58] Trapp (1711), as has already been observed, says that "it is, of all Kinds of Poetry, the most poetical";[59] Edward Young (1728) speaks of it as "more Spirituous, and more remote from Prose than any other, in *Sense, Sound, Expression*, and *Conduct*."[60] To Bishop Hurd, it is "enthusiasm, and stretch of genius, which is at once the characteristic and glory of the lyric composition."[61] And in the controversy over the "irregularity" of the Great Ode—a controversy presently to be outlined—both defender and critic of the ode acknowledge "liberty" to be one of its essential characteristics, since of all species of poetry it is the most direct expression of "genius" as distinguished from "art," and of "imagination" as distinguished from "judgment." It is not so very far from concepts such as these to Mrs. Barbauld's division of poetry into only two kinds, one of which is "pure Poetry," which is lyric poetry.[62] All these statements are closely allied in their impulsion: the higher branch of the lyric is of all poetry the farthest removed from prose; it is the most "spirituous" kind of poetry; more purely than any other poetical form, it is an expression of "genius" and "imagination." Dominating these statements is another—that sublimity is its reigning character—and they all clearly converge at a point just beyond the eighteenth century when poetry becomes one, radiated out of the soul of the poet.

It is true that there was widespread concern during the neoclassical period

---

56. "Preface to *The Court of Death*" (*The Critical Works of John Dennis*, I, 42).

57. Lecture I, "Of the Uses and Design of Poetry," *op. cit.*, pp. 21–22.

58. See below, p. 427.

59. *Op. cit.*, p. 203.

60. "On Lyrick Poetry," Preface to *Ocean: An Ode* (London, 1728), p. 18.

61. "Notes on the 'Art of poetry' " (*The Works of Richard Hurd, D.D.* [London, 1811], I, 272).

62. Anna Laetitia (Aiken), *The Poetical Works of Mr. William Collins* (London, 1797), pp. iii–v. This passage is quoted and discussed more fully in a later section of this essay.

over the "irregularity" and "liberty" of the Great Ode, but it is hard to see why later historians should imply that this concern was unjustifiable and a sign that the neoclassical period was the Age of Reason, in all its wakeful moments subordinating impulse to order, "genius" to "art," and imagination to reason. The Great Ode was "the free verse" of the neoclassical period and, like any loose form, attracted scores of writers who aspired to the heights of poetry because of the difficulties of prose.[63] Even the masters of prosody, after three hundred years of opportunity, have produced only a few "irregular odes" that memorably combine form with the illusion of being beyond it.

The first of these masters was one of the first to be concerned. Dryden regarded the Cowleyan ode as a great invention of his age, although even in the hands of its inventor "somewhat of the purity of English, somewhat of more equal thoughts, somewhat of sweetness in the numbers, in one word, somewhat of a finer turn, and more lyrical verse, is yet wanting," but, because "the seeming easiness of it has made it spread," it has been degraded rather than perfected.[64] Yet to labor to perfect it, as he himself did, was to Dryden not a task involving the elevation of reason over imagination, for in this same discussion he makes clear that his reservations concerning Cowley's ode are reservations concerning "the ornamental parts of it" and not of "the soul of it, which consists in the warmth and vigour of fancy, the masterly figures, and the copiousness of imagination."

Congreve's "A Discourse on the Pindarique Ode" (1706) is further evidence that the accomplished writers of the age regarded the perfection of the Cowleyan ode as one of their important tasks. Congreve's argument in outline follows Dryden's: it is based upon a respect for "the Sublimity" of Cowley's "Stile and Sentiments" coupled with a recognition that Cowley had assumed great "Latitude" in his practice;[65] the serious imperfections in the ode, however, are attributed primarily to Cowley's many uninspired and ignorant imitators, who lack any sense of prosodic pattern or intelligible sequence to their

---

63. Thomas Flatman probably differs from the flock only in openly stating his reasons for selecting "*The* Pindariqu' *strain*": the loose measures permit him liberty "*to correct the saucy forwardness of a* Rhime" and allow him, when his sense is too short for a stanza, "*to fill it up with a* Metaphor *little to the purpose, and (upon occasion) to run that* Metaphor *stark mad into an* Allegory" ("The Preface to the Reader," *Poems and Songs* [3d ed.; London, 1682]). A century later, William Preston also defends the irregular ode for reasons that are only justifications of technical ineptness (see below, n. 75).

64. "Preface to Sylvae: Or, the Second Part of Poetical Miscellanies," *Essays of John Dryden*, I, 267–68. Later (*ca.* 1693/4) he urged John Dennis to "cultivate this kind of Ode; and reduce it either to the same Measures which Pinder us'd, or give new Measures of your own. For, as it is, it looks like a vast Tract of Land newly discover'd. The Soil is wonderfully Fruitful, but unmanur'd, overstock'd with Inhabitants; but almost all Salvages, without Laws, Arts, Arms, or Policy" (*The Letters of John Dryden*, p. 72).

65. *The Complete Works of William Congreve*, IV, 85.

thoughts and feelings.[66] Upon the problem of versification Congreve concentrates his remarks, and these remarks give his "Discourse" its particular historical importance.

Congreve informs the English public that Pindar's stanzas have great variety and complexity but, within a given poem, form into triads which are regularly related, the antistrophe repeating the strophe, and the epodes concluding the triads paralleling one another but differing from the strophe and antistrophe. He does not insist that English ode writers follow this particular pattern, evidently because he judges it to be too closely associated with choral presentation to be universally adaptable; yet he does not see why some use "may not be made of Pindar's Example, to the great Improvement of the English Ode," and the ode to which his "Discourse" is a preface is triadic in its verse construction.

Cowley himself and at least certain others of the more distinguished men in letters and learning in the seventeenth century knew that Pindar's measures, unlike those of Cowley, were "regular," and even the intricacies of Pindar's regularity had already been described.[67] Nevertheless, Congreve's "Discourse" undoubtedly increased the circulation of this knowledge and must be regarded as a cause of some consequence in explaining these facts: the proportion of odes written in the irregular stanzas of Cowley declined during the eighteenth century,[68] a number were written in triadic structure, and the majority were written in a stanza, however varied internally, that was repeated throughout the poem. Anyone wishing to interpret these facts as a sign that the neoclassical period placed regularity, reason, and conformity above the powers of the

66. "The Character of these late Pindariques, is, a Bundle of rambling incoherent Thoughts, express'd in a like Parcel of irregular Stanzas, which also consist of such another Complication of disproportion'd, uncertain and perplex'd Verses and Rhimes. And I appeal to any Reader, if this is not the Condition in which these Titular Odes appear" (*ibid.*, IV, 82).

67. Robert Shafer and Arthur H. Nethercot have clearly demonstrated that earlier scholarship was mistaken in supposing that Cowley was unaware of the regularity of Pindar's measures (see Shafer's *The English Ode to 1660: An Essay in Literary History* [Princeton, 1918], pp. 149 ff., and Nethercot's *Abraham Cowley: The Muse's Hannibal* [Oxford, 1931], pp. 136 ff.).

Other literary men of the seventeenth century realized that Cowley's irregular verse did not follow Pindar's example. Edward Phillips in his *Theatrum poetarum, or a Compleat Collection of the Poets, Especially the Most Eminent, of All Ages* (London, 1675) is seemingly the first whose remarks distinguish the two (see the section entitled "Eminent Poets among the Moderns," p. 2). Dryden, as we have already seen, reveals that he is also aware of the difference (see above, n. 64). None of these writers makes any attempt to state with precision what the difference is; this was first done in England in the first English edition of Pindar (1697), edited by Richard West and Robert Welsted.

68. George N. Shuster, *The English Ode from Milton to Keats* (New York, 1940), pp. 222–23.

imagination, even in lyric poetry, should at the same time explain why approximately these same facts are true of the odes written by the Romantics.

When the new school of ode writers (Collins, Gray, and the Wartons) appeared in the second half of the eighteenth century, the ode again was criticized for its excesses, most severely by Dr. Johnson, a fact that did much to make him more noted for his certainty than his sensitivity. Johnson did not think highly of the ode writers of his day. Their fundamental difficulty was that they modeled themselves upon a primitive form of poetry written when the imagination "was vehement and rapid" and before science had been sufficiently developed to accustom the mind to close inspection and control. "From this accidental peculiarity of the ancient writers, the criticks deduce the rules of lyrick poetry, which they have set free from all the laws by which other compositions are confined, and allow to neglect the niceties of transition, to start into remote digressions, and to wander without restraint from one scene of imagery to another."[69] In his later criticism the irregular measures of Cowley are condemned,[70] even when practiced by such prosodic masters as Dryden and Pope;[71] ode writers are also condemned for failing to combine the "natural" and the "novel,"[72] for thinking their "language more poetical as it was more remote from common use," and, of course, for making overabundant employment of classical allusions and stale mythology.[73]

69. *Rambler*, No. 158 (September 21, 1751). John Ogilvie's "An Essay on the Lyric Poetry of the Ancients," published eleven years later, only amplifies Johnson's argument. The lyric poet, "more nearly than any other," is exposed to the danger of overemphasizing the "imagination" and neglecting the "reason" (*Poems on Several Subjects. To Which Is Prefix'd, an Essay on the Lyric Poetry of the Ancients; in Two Letters Inscribed to the Right Honourable James Lord Deskfoord* [London, 1762], pp. vi–vii). The earliest poetical productions were the lyric and pastoral, and, though it would seem natural for a species of poetry formed in a particular age for a particular purpose to change when the age did, "the Ode hath only been changed in a few external circumstances, and the enthusiasm, obscurity and exuberance, which characterised it when first introduced, continue to be ranked among its capital and discriminating excellencies" (p. xxiv). But, in a second letter, he warned the reader not to take his criticism of the lyric as a sign that he wished imagination to be subordinated to judgment, for only in didactic poetry should imagination play a secondary role (p. xlii). Because of the high degree of imagination required in lyric poetry, the ode is to be granted liberty in its transitions and digressions as long as connections are discernible (pp. lviii–lix).

70. "Cowley," in Johnson, *Lives of the English Poets*, ed. George Birkbeck Hill (Oxford, 1905), I, 47.

71. "Pope," *ibid.*, III, 227.

72. Much of his famous criticism of Cowley is based on the premise that Cowley sacrifices the natural to the novel and pursues "his thoughts to their last ramifications, by which he loses the grandeur of generality . . ." ("Cowley," *ibid.*, I, 45). On the other hand, Gray's "Ode on Spring" exhibits the opposite fault: "the thoughts have nothing new" and the "morality is natural, but too stale . . ." ("Gray," *ibid.*, III, 434).

73. Gray especially is criticized on both these scores. Again and again his language is condemned because it is "too luxuriant" ("Gray," *ibid.*, III, 434, 435, 437–39), and because it is weakened by the "puerilities of obsolete mythology" (*ibid.*, p. 439). Parts of Pope's "Ode for Music on St. Cecilia's Day" also detain us "in the dark and dismal regions of mythology" (*ibid.*, p. 228).

This is fairly comprehensive condemnation of poets who had been accustomed to comparison with Pindar; yet, in context, Johnson is a successor to Dryden and Congreve, concerned in perfecting the ode. He certainly thought it farther from perfection than they did, a judgment for which his shade should not have to continue to beg forgiveness. His taste also should be distinguished from his theory. The main charges that he brought against the Great Ode were not new, and his historical account of its origin and the perpetuation of its defects indicates only that he believed uncontrolled imagination should not be its sole property. Correctly defined, the Great Ode is characterized by "sublimity, rapture, and quickness of transition."[74]

Nevertheless, devotees of the lyric were naturally aroused by Johnson's criticisms. In *An Inquiry into Some Passages in Dr. Johnson's "Lives of the Poets"; Particularly His Observations on Lyric Poetry, and the Odes of Gray* (1783),[75] Robert Potter dismisses Johnson's historical account of the origins of lyric poetry as "unscholarlike," insisting that the earliest of surviving lyric poets wrote in a period of enlightenment, not barbarousness, and were fully conscious of their artistic obligations. They "knew that rapture, not argumentation, was the constituent part of that species of poetry which they cultivated" because it is dedicated to gods and demigods:

Hence it appears that this composition not only allowed, but even required sudden and bold transitions, and the highest flights of imagination to which even the Epic Muse dared not aspire: she prescribed laws to herself, which confined her to one great action; and she pursues her plan with grave dignity: but the Lyric is a Muse of fire that rises on the wings of Extasy, and follows her Hero or her God from one glorious action to another, from earth to heaven.[76]

74. See above, p. 419. What Johnson thought was possible in lyric poetry as distinct from what he thought of most lyric poets is implied in this remark about Akenside: "It is not easy to guess why he addicted himself so diligently to lyrick poetry, having neither the ease and airiness of the lighter, nor the vehemence and elevation of the grander ode" ("Akenside," Johnson, *op. cit.*, III, 419).

75. Gray's odes occasioned a less noteworthy difference of opinion over the irregularity of the ode, one confined to its versification. In his edition of *The Poems of Mr. Gray. To Which Are Prefixed Memoirs of His Writings* (London, 1775), Mason excused the irregular verse structure of the "Ode for Music—Irregular," because this particular ode was occasional and intended for music—but he urged that only the "regular" ode be regarded as "legitimate" (p. 98 of *The Poems*). This brief note produced a full-length refutation, William Preston's "Thoughts on Lyric Poetry" (published in *Transactions of the Royal Irish Academy* in 1787). Several of Preston's arguments for the irregular ode sound as if they were made by a man who had experienced some difficulties in writing verse. For, besides quoting classical authority (pp. 67–69) and urging that separate stanzas can be "made light and airy, slow and plaintive, or swelling and sonorous, according to the subject matter" (pp. 71–72), he points out that the poet unrestrained by the irregular ode need not be checked by technical details or bring in superfluous words to eke out a stanza (pp. 69–70), and he speaks with considerateness of the ear of the reader which would be relieved by irregular stanzas, especially if the poet lacked prosodic skill and was obliged to repeat his discords (p. 70).

76. Potter, *op. cit.*, p. 14.

Potter's rhetorical emphasis is upon the imagination; yet theoretically he, no more than Johnson, allows lyric imagination to be beyond the restraint of judgment:

> Sublimity is the essential and characteristic perfection of the Ode; where this can be attained by "the placid beauties of methodical deduction," that artful course is pursued; but it is more often seized by a rapid and impetuous transition; yet this is always under the controul of some nice connexion, is never vague and wanton, never loses sight of its important object. The Ode is daring, but not licentious; though it is great, it disclaims "the proud irregularity of greatness."[77]

Even the pressure of controversy (and the weight of Johnson's prose) should not obliterate the fact that neoclassical critics, whatever their differences, agreed upon a formula for the Great Ode: its essential quality is sublimity; more completely than any other poetic form, it is governed by imagination, rapture, and genius; intrinsic to it, therefore, are a liberty and a boldness (in verse pattern, diction, and design) that would elsewhere be excessive; nevertheless, like any artistic creation, it should be, in part, a product of "art" and "judgment"—the "art" and "judgment" in the case of the Great Ode, however, revealing themselves in concealment, since otherwise they would contradict the nature of a soul "transported."

An account of the eighteenth-century theory of the highest branch of the lyric would stop short of theory if it stopped with a formula, and it would probably stop short of history if its conclusion suggested that no changes of consequence took place in a hundred years of discussion of the same subject. So far, this study has been concerned primarily with the elements in the discussion which were continuous; but, despite the formula verbally agreed upon, there were general shifts in shadings and meanings which signified great shifts in theory. For, after all, later-eighteenth-century theory of the lyric was part of the early environment of Coleridge and Wordsworth, who wrote lyrics before the nineteenth century. In the Introduction to this study, we stated that literary criticism would be viewed as a form of medial discourse, entangled with at least the fringes of philosophy and, more obviously, shaped by and shaping this or that group of poems. We began our explication of the theory of the lyric by relating it to the more abstract aesthetics of the period; and we turn now to neoclassical odes, believing that, if they are also involved in the explication, certain subtleties and changes in all three of the related factors—general aesthetic theory, criticism of the lyric, and the lyric itself—may be more easily observed.

The later eighteenth century agreed that with Collins and Gray (and such

77. *Ibid.*, p. 14.

lesser figures as Joseph Warton and Akenside) a new school of ode writers had arrived, their creations marking a renaissance in a form that in the previous decade or two had fallen into considerable disrepute. Let us accept this contemporary distinction between the odes that were fashionable before 1740 and those of Collins and Gray and their school on the presupposition, not necessarily that the latter are better but that they are different in ways reflecting changes in the conception of what lyric poetry—possibly even of what poetry itself— should be. The Great Odes of the first three decades of the eighteenth century are, in most of their salient features, like those of more remote dates. They are, to take only one step backward, very similar to the Great Odes written by the immediate followers of Cowley (if we set aside as not of salient importance the fact that an increased proportion of eighteenth-century odes were written in "regular" stanzaic patterns). Actually, the Great Odes of the late seventeenth and early eighteenth centuries show a close affinity to the earliest recorded traditions of the ode, those that determined Greek melic poetry, and the choruses praising gods and men which, alone of all forms of poetry, were not debarred from Plato's ideal state.[78] Both in ultimate intention and in outward show the major lyrics of the early neoclassical period are neoclassical and are closer to the ancient dithyramb than they are to the odes of Keats written only a century later. Indeed, to us they seem not so much the poetic representations of moving human experience as specimens of epideictic rhetoric aiming at the exaltation of what is worthy of admiration (or, negatively, the exposure of folly or more serious transgression).

Rhetoric, classically distinguished, has three branches. The deliberative is directed toward future action, is concerned ultimately with what is expedient, and employs the example as its most convincing mode of argument. The forensic is directed toward what has happened in the past, is concerned ultimately with what is just or lawful, and relies heavily upon the enthymeme. Epideictic rhetoric is that of the compliment, the commemorative address, the patriotic speech, the funeral oration. It deals with what the present is willing to believe is the case (that an event, personage, or institution deserves commendation—or condemnation), and the epideictic art is to make this object more magnificent (or more faulty) than it is commonly thought to be. Its chief mode of argument, therefore, is amplification, and treatises on rhetoric from antiquity had devoted long sections to listing different devices for adding luster to what in itself was already illustrious. The Great Odes of the early neoclassical period are specimens of the art of adding magnificence to objects already splendid in attribute and accomplishment.

78. See above, pp. 409–10.

The neoclassical period also followed Plato[79] in dividing the ode according to the "subjects" that it praised, the Great Ode being of two kinds, one celebrating the divine attributes and the other heroic events and personages (the "minor" lyric, as we shall see later, being confined to the third of Plato's classes of poetical subject matters). Cowley himself had furnished models for what came to be commonly designated as the religious or sacred ode.[80] Behind his authority extended two compelling traditions, each exalting the power of the sacred lyric. Besides the classical, there was the Christian tradition, and, in English eyes, the "poetry" of the Bible seemed strangely similar to the verse that Cowley had used in rendering Pindar into English—loose in its measures; bold, congested, and rapturous in its imagery; and puzzling to common sense in its transitions. No sacred ode written during the neoclassical period has survived in common and profane memory; the simpler hymns of the age evidently were more suited to its poetical gifts, and many of them are still cherished, although it should be remembered that the line between a sacred ode and a hymn cannot always be clearly drawn and that so famous a poem as Addison's "The Spacious Firmament on High" was first published as an "ode." But, although none of the more pretentious sacred odes of the period has proved memorable as poetry, history should record, in deference to the piety of the past, that many were written, and should perhaps add a note to the effect that the most interesting specimens of the seventeenth century were those of John Norris and of the early eighteenth century those of Isaac Watts.

Following Pindar's example, the early neoclassical period dedicated a large proportion of its odes to the praise of public accomplishment, especially the accomplishment of the nobility and the royal family, although the illustrious in letters and learning were occasionally regarded as worthy of the massive encomium.[81] Moreover, English odes during this period, like the higher melic kinds of early Greece, were often formally attached to political and social institutions and civic occasions. Royal birthday odes in Pindaric "measures" became an "established institution," inaugurated in 1689 by Thomas Shadwell;[82] and the New Year was another appointed time for public compositions

79. Aristotle also specifies hymns and economia (ὕμνους κὰι ἐγκόμμια), melic forms celebrating gods and heroes, as the two earliest forms of serious poetical utterance (*Poetics* 4. 1448^{b}24 ff.).

80. In irregular ode form are "The Resurrection," "The Plagues of Egypt," and "The 34. Chapter of the Prophet Isaiah."

81. Perhaps the only enduring ode of this last type is also one of the earliest, Dryden's "To the Pious Memory of the Accomplisht Young Lady Mrs. Ann Killigrew. Excellent in the Two Sister-Arts of Poesie, and Painting. An Ode" (1686). But Cowley himself had written Pindaric odes celebrating the learned (see "To Mr. Hobs," "To Dr. Scarborough," and "To the Royal Society").

82. Shuster, *op. cit.*, p. 134.

in Pindaric strain.[83] By 1730 encomiastic odes were so numerous and in tone so subservient that the Great Ode acquired a reputation from which it has never completely freed itself—that of being the natural form for aspiring laureates to attempt to conceal servility with pomposity.

But we must turn to the musical ode in order to realize how in respects other than epideictic intention and subject matter the massive lyric of the early neoclassical period resembled the choral expressions of early Greece. In 1683 a group called the London Musical Society established the institution of annually performing an ode celebrating the power of music, especially Christian music symbolized by St. Cecilia. These musical odes were presented by a chorus of some sixty voices, and the total number of participants was between eighty and ninety.[84] The form naturally was evolutionary and remained somewhat varied but, in general, sought after the parts clearly discerned by Dryden in "Alexander's Feast"—recitative, air, and chorus (the chorus in "Alexander's Feast" being a repetition of the air).[85] In addition, the individual voices were accompanied by different musical instruments, a fact often used to justify the irregular Cowleyan verse form, since the irregularity permitted stanzas to differ for special instrumental effects. We must also realize that, through the influence of the St. Cecilia odes, many of the sacred and heroic odes were composed for dramatic presentation and musical accompaniment, and thus the Great Odes of the early neoclassical period were often all that Plato said poetry should be—they were choruses in praise of gods and heroes, and, as such, supported the most lofty of intentions with the combined effects of all the arts: words, bodily presentation of the words, and musical accompaniment, instrumental and vocal.[86] Obviously, a form such as this was too top-heavy and alien to English taste to be more than a temporary fashion,[87] a fact certainly account-

83. *Ibid.*, pp. 173–74.

84. Robert M. Myers, "Neo-classical Criticism of the Ode for Music," *PMLA*, XLII (June, 1947), 404–5. This article should be consulted for a much more detailed discussion of the musical ode than can be given here.

85. *Ibid.*, pp. 419–20.

86. John Brown's *A Dissertation on the Rise, Union, and Power, the Progressions, Separations, and Corruptions, of Poetry and Music* (London, 1763) shows how completely the early neoclassical ode was modeled upon the practice and theory of the Greeks. Writing after the ode for music had fallen into considerable disrepute, Brown argues for the restoration of an art form that would combine words, action, and "*choral Song,*" a form that he describes as "the *Narrative* or *Epic Ode*" (p. 234). His defense of this form is based in part upon the practice of the primitive Greeks; his theoretical defense is Platonic. He laments that the arts cannot be completely reunited but urges that, so far as possible, a reunion be effected and be made central to basic education, as Plato's choruses had been.

87. The annual performance of the St. Cecilia ode was discontinued after 1703, although there were occasional performances after that (Myers, *op. cit.*, p. 405) and although the most famous of the later neoclassical ode writers occasionally composed odes for music (see Collins' *The Passions: An Ode for Music* [1747], which attempts to refresh the St. Cecilia

ing in part for the alterations made in the ode by the school of ode writers of the later eighteenth century.

These changes that occurred during the eighteenth century in the theory and creation of lyric poetry will appear more clearly if we examine briefly two representative odes of the early neoclassical period, when major lyric poems were shaped by epideictic intentions and were constructed, block by block, out of rhetorical "amplifications." Let us take two odes already referred to— Congreve's "A Pindarique Ode, Humbly Offer'd to the Queen, on the Victorious Progress of Her Majesty's Arms, under the Conduct of the Duke of Marlborough," and Dryden's "Alexander's Feast: Or, the Power of Music; an Ode, in Honor of St. Cecilia's Day"—the first an ode directly extolling illustrious personages and events by weighting them with rhetorical additions and amplifications, and the other an ode for musical accompaniment,[88] celebrating the power of music but celebrating it brilliantly and indirectly through dramatic incident.

In verse pattern, Congreve's ode exemplifies the comments prefaced to it. It is written in five triads, each composed of strophe, antistrophe, and epode, with the stanzaic constructions used to mark shifts in epideictic "arguments." The first triad is an invocation to Calliope, without whose aid no poet is adequate to sing of Anna (certainly a conventional mode of amplification—to assert that divine inspiration is necessary to do justice to the splendor of this mortal). In the second triad the lyre is struck, and immediately the inspiration is again magnified because it is the same as that which "kindled *Mantuan* Fire" and Spenser and Milton (another common mode of amplification—to magnify the present by attributing to it a genealogy important in myth or history). But, going upward, the triad asserts that the object of the present song transcends even Virgil's Augusta, for the country ruled over by Anna is free and enjoys plenty and internal repose. The fortunate condition of England is used in the third triad as "proof" that the "honor" motivating the queen has no impurity and therefore is most worthy of encomium; only mercy and sorrow in purest form (Anna's subjects being free from suffering) could have prompted her to unsheath her sword (the Duke of Marlborough) to free Europe from tyranny. In the fourth triad, the poet exalts the duke by confessing that his muse cannot

---

tradition by condemning the complexity of her music and pleading for a return to the simple designs of the Greeks; see also Gray's ode "For Music. Irregular" [1768]). Nevertheless, in the decades just preceding this new school of ode writers, both the encomiastic and the musical odes were subject to a great deal of ridicule (for fuller discussions of this attack see Myers, *op. cit.*, pp. 409–11 and Shuster, *op. cit.*, pp. 172 ff.).

88. "Dryden's *Alexander's Feast* was twice ill set to music [by Jeremiah Clarke and Thomas Clayton] before Handel enhanced the beauties of that ode with his brilliant setting" (Myers, *op. cit.*, p. 407). ,

rise to the sublime heights reached by this commander and that, even if it could, the praise should not end there, since the duke's triumphs are "incessant" (the amplification more colloquially expressed by "you haven't seen anything yet"). Accordingly, in the concluding triad, the poet warns his muse not to attempt to sing deeds surpassing such historical (and rhetorical) commonplaces as Cannae and Pharsalia. Poetry, the poet asserts, can do justice to middle virtues but not to "deeds sublime." And, as deeds of great scope are known epideictically by the magnitude of their just rewards, the ode comes to a close by urging the "Great Chief" to continue until he has achieved universal peace, when he will receive, not merely a poem, but the queen's favor and his country's love. The reader should himself look to see whether this ode does much more than rhetorically "ornament" these rhetorical "arguments"—and thereby confirm a nonconvertible premise upon which this portion of the discussion is based. The premise: many poems praise, exhort, console, or compliment; but most praises, exhortations, consolations, and compliments are not poems.

Cowley's reputation waned, and, in the later eighteenth century (in certain circles at least), Gray was regarded as the greatest of ode writers, ancient or English, but the beginning, middle, and end of this century agreed that one ode was a classic, "Alexander's Feast,"[89] and even in the briefest of our anthologies it has its established place. But, although its greatness has become undated by the test of time, it is doubtful whether we feel moved by it as we are by Wordsworth's "Ode on Intimations of Immortality," Shelley's "Ode to the West Wind," or Keats's "Ode to a Nightingale"; it is even doubtful whether we feel that it is the same kind of thing that they are (barring the fact that they are all called "odes"). The dramatic inventiveness and prosodic virtuosity for which it was admired in its own age[90] certainly distinguish it qualitatively

89. Dryden evidently agreed with the judgment of his own age about his own ode. "I am glad to heare from all Hands," he wrote Jacob Tonson, "that my Ode is esteemed the best of all my poetry, by all the Town: I thought so my self when I writ it but being old, I mistrusted my own Judgment" (*The Letters of John Dryden*, p. 98). Speaking more universally, he is reported to have said, "A nobler Ode never *was* produced, nor ever *will*" (Edmond Malone, *The Critical and Miscellaneous Prose Works of John Dryden* [London, 1800], I, Part I, 477).

90. The analysis of "Alexander's Feast" that follows is concerned in showing how the ode is constructed to the epideictic end of glorifying the power of music, especially Christian music as symbolized by St. Cecilia. It touches only indirectly the problem of the suitability of the ode to musical accompaniment, although no one can form an adequate estimate of the artistic skill displayed in this ode unless he reads the analysis of this aspect of it by Ernest Brennecke, Jr. ("Dryden's Odes and Draghi's Music," *PMLA*, XLIX [1934], 1–36). Brennecke points out, for instance, the suitability of the words for such musical devices as "*vocal polyphony*, in which one or two lines may be assigned to voices that enter successively and whose sense may survive being thus scrambled" and "*antiphony*, by which two lines may be hurled back and forth alternately between two groups of singers without distortion of meaning or poetic effect" (the lines, "Assumes the god, Affects to nod," he gives as an example of the first device, and the lines "On the bare earth expos'd he lies, With not a

from other early neoclassical odes but do not distinguish it from them in kind; those just mentioned by Wordsworth, Shelley, and Keats, however, are not artistic constructions designed to the end of amplifying the wonders, respectively, of immortality, wind, and nightingales.

"Alexander's Feast" is controlled by the purpose implied in its title, that of glorifying "the power of musique" which has been most completely realized by Christian music. Its two most discernible major parts are parts because they are parts of what is basically one epideictic "argument." In this "argument," the object of praise is first shown performing wonders that seem to exceed all human expectation; the conclusion announces that the wonders just viewed are only rudimentary, since they were performed by the object before it reached the full development of its power. The first part, which includes all but the last stanza, displays the power of pagan music by exhibiting its effects upon Alexander and his company; the last stanza proclaims that these incredible effects were produced before the coming of St. Cecilia, who "enlarg'd the former narrow bounds" of music with "sacred store," the invention of the organ, and the addition of "length to solemn sounds." The first part raises "a mortal to the skies"; the last draws "an angel down."[91]

But "Alexander's Feast" is not epideictic in panoramic outline only, and closer examination of the construction and development of the first part, so justly praised for its dramatic inventiveness, will show how its dramatic inventiveness is bent toward the end of praise. The first part, and therefore all but the last stanza, are praise by indirection, happy chance or Dryden's own capacities as an artist leading him to observe a well-tested epideictic precept—that direct praise is not improved by length. Quantitatively, the part indirectly praising music is out of all proportion to the last stanza; psychologically and artistically the two parts are in balance. The mode of indirect praise selected

---

friend to close his eyes," as illustrative of the second). These are only details from his analysis, which is concerned in showing that "Alexander's Feast" "demands the use of almost every musical device then current" and "marks the climax of Cecilian poetry."

91. Compare the closing lines of "Alexander's Feast" ("He [Timotheus, the pagan musician] rais'd a mortal to the skies;/ She [St. Cecilia] drew an angel down") with the closing lines of Pope's "Ode for Music on St. Cecilia's Day" ("His numbers [those of Orpheus, the pagan musician] rais'd a shade from hell,/ Hers lift the soul to heav'n"). Despite the statement attributed to Pope, that he wrote this ode at the request of Steele and "not with any thought of rivalling that great man [Dryden], whose memory I do, and have always reverenced" (Joseph Spence, *Observations, Anecdotes, and Characters, of Books and Men* [London, 1820], p. 12), he nevertheless paralleled Dryden's ode in major and minor aspects and, therefore, seemed to be inviting comparison. Pope's ode is constructed on the same major epideictic argument that gave Dryden's ode its two parts, the second part announcing the coming of St. Cecilia and the organ (the last stanzas in both odes) and the first part being in the form of a dramatic exemplum, with Orpheus substituted for Timotheus as the pagan musician working wonders. The two odes have even the same number of stanzas.

by Dryden is also one anciently recommended—that of showing the power of an object (in this case, music) by exhibiting the magnitude of its effects, of which none is more convincing than human actions and reactions. The particular action chosen is commended by Johnson (in his comparison of "Alexander's Feast" with Pope's "Ode for Music on St. Cecilia's Day") for being drawn from history (and hence for being more credible than the mythological material utilized by Pope) and for being highly concentrated, since the varied effects of music are revealed in a single action (whereas Pope can show the varied effects of music only by an episodic selection from the whole Orpheus legend). The interior of the poem is also rhetorical in its construction. In epideictic rhetoric, as in science, great effects are signs of great causes. In "Alexander's Feast," music conquers the first conqueror of the world at that moment when the world lay vanquished before him and Thais and his court sat beside him for the triumph, only to be themselves triumphed over by music. Moreover, the development of the action involving these personages is rhetorical "proof" that the power of music is perfect power, its effects being varied, complete, and climactic; for less than complete power would be revealed in effects that are limited or diminishing. Stanza by stanza, Timotheus sings a different song to Alexander, arousing in him a different set of passions, and, with one exception, each stanza is connected to the next by the principle of psychological contrariety; that is, the set of passions aroused in Alexander by a given song is the opposite to the set of passions aroused in him by the preceding or following stanza, and thus the emotional progression is startling in its variety and suggests, after a time, a completeness of emotional effect (a succession of opposites having the quality of suggesting all-inclusiveness). This principle controls the progression of many other neoclassical odes, and undoubtedly the sudden and abrupt transitions always specified as characteristic of Great Odes were startling shifts in feeling as well as in thought.

Timotheus' first song, which "began from Jove," so convinces Alexander of his divine origins that he "assumes the god," but the next song is of Bacchus and of wine, "the soldier's pleasure" (the psychological opposites long used in literary theory to separate the maximum lyric celebrating gods and demigods from the minimum lyric, the drinking song). The third song is juxtaposed to the first two, which combined to arouse in Alexander an unchecked pride alarmingly verging on madness; when "the master" sees "the madness rise," he changes his tune to one infused with soft pity for "Darius great and good, / By too severe a fate, / Fallen, fallen, fallen, fallen." The next stanza is the only one linked to its predecessor by similarity rather than by contrariety of passion: "The mighty master smil'd, to see / That love was in the next degree: / 'Twas but a kindred-sound to move, / For pity melts the mind to love." But these two stanzas are linked together by two kindred and tender emotions only to heighten the terror to be portrayed in the last stanza—and we have already seen that, later in the eighteenth century, aestheticians such as Burke regarded love and pity (the beautiful) as psychologically and physiologically the opposites of terror (the sublime). The final stanza is final and climactic, in that it inspires the whole Greek assembly (Thais and the Greek army as well as Alexander); in that it produces not merely a state of mind but an overt action; in that the action is mass destruction of the Persians; in that the state of mind motivating the action is most startlingly juxtaposed to the previous stanza in which Alexander has sunk upon his lover's breast, vanquished by pity and love. " 'Revenge, revenge!' Timotheus cries," and, remembering the unburied dead, "the king seiz'd a flambeau," and "Thais led the way, To light him to his prey, / And, like another Helen, fir'd another Troy."

III. THE LATER SUBLIME ODE

Two creations distinctive of the new school of ode writers of the middle and later eighteenth century are the allegorical and descriptive odes (1746 is the date of publication of Collins' *Odes on Several Descriptive and Allegorical Subjects*). Somewhat later in the century, especially after the publication of Gray's "The Bard. A Pindaric Ode" (1757), "The Descent of Odin. An Ode" (1768), "The Fatal Sisters. An Ode" (1768), etc., a third kind of ode was recognized as a product of the times—the ode of terror. These three "kinds" may at first seem like a haphazard trio, but they are interrelated in their theoretical background; and an attempt to relate them and their reception to this background involves a consideration of the main topics about which much criticism of the time was centered—the subjects, language, and emotions most proper for poetry. For an explanation of the allegorical and descriptive odes in terms of prevailing theory will direct us primarily to changing conceptions of poetical subjects and language, and the ode of terror reflects changes in the emotions felt to be most moving poetically. Indeed, the theory surrounding these odes in many of its aspects is more revolutionary, more "Romantic," and "newer" than the odes themselves, which, with few exceptions, soon lost the appearance of freshness.[92]

The "new" odes, all three kinds, were traditional, in that they usually had an epideictic intention. In the tradition extending back to Pindar, the panegyrical ode celebrated some particular person, occasion, or accomplishment and

92. In "The Reviewers and the New Trends in Poetry, 1754–1770" (*MLN*, LI [1936], 214) E. N. Hooker maintains that the prevailing taste of the period, as reflected by the comment of critical journals, was "romantic" and that "the new poetry, harbinger of later romantic feeling, cannot accurately be said to have been in advance of public taste—at least in so far as public taste is reflected in the reviews."

eventually the general attributes, moral or intellectual, manifested by the particular person in his accomplishments. The allegorical ode is the panegyrical ode without personal investiture; it is a laudation of abstractions, abstractions such as art or any of its several kinds, science (even inoculation, not to forget the ode that Coleridge immortalized by remembering[93]), adversity and its opposite, and, of course, all the virtues and commendable states of mind—benevolence, hope, simplicity, pity, etc. The descriptive ode and the ode of terror also were often panegyric and not of particular living persons. Undoubtedly, the practices of ode writers of the early eighteenth century were in part responsible for this change, for the countless birthday, prenatal, and New Year offerings of the professionals soon appeared tired and mercenary. No doubt, too, changes in a society ceasing to be dominated by the court brought changes in the attitude toward the professional compliment and hence toward the most complimentary form of poetry; but the social changes affecting literature are beyond the boundaries set for this study, and besides, although social changes often give literature its impulse, literary causes give it its shape.

Although these new odes generally retain a panegyric intention, they are designed ultimately to display not so much the power of the subject addressed as the power of the poet's imagination. Joseph Warton in the "Advertisement" to his *Odes on Various Subjects* (London, 1746) makes very clear the heretical intention of his odes. "The Public," he says, "has been so much accustom'd of late to didactic Poetry alone, and Essays on moral Subjects, that any work where the imagination is much indulged, will perhaps not be relished or regarded." And he concludes his manifesto with the assertion that "as he is convinced that the fashion of moralizing in verse has been carried too far, and as he looks upon Invention and Imagination to be the chief faculties of a Poet, so he will be happy if the following Odes may be look'd upon as an attempt to bring back Poetry into its right channel." The imagination of the poet, then, is a general conception to keep in mind as we proceed to a more detailed discussion of the new odes.

The distinction separating the allegorical from the descriptive ode is central to many of the general aesthetic discussions of sublimity in the eighteenth century, especially in the later part of it.[94] Of more importance is the fact that this distinction is genetically related to the distinction between "subjective" and "objective" poetry, the Romantic distinction that revolutionized the theory of artistic kinds and made the lyric a theoretical half (the subjective) of poetry. No doubt the influence of the metaphysics of the German Idealists (to

93. *Biographia literaria*, ed. J. Shawcross (Oxford, 1907), II, 66.

94. I am interested in tracing this distinction, not the terms "allegorical" and "descriptive," which had many meanings in the eighteenth century.

whom the terms "subject" and "object" were central) explains in good part the extent and contours of its appearance in nineteenth-century criticism, but Coleridge himself points out that as a philosophical distinction it can be traced back to the Greeks. Here, however, we can only indicate its rudimentary appearance in English criticism of the eighteenth century, its relation to discussions of the sublime, and its particular connection with the lyric, especially the allegorical and descriptive odes.

The distinction which Dennis drew in 1704 between "Vulgar" and "Enthustiastick Passions" in terms of which he separated major from minor species of poetry is partly a distinction between passions stimulated by "Objects themselves" and passions aroused by "Ideas in Contemplation."[95] The first set, with a lower common appeal, has the advantage of moving more men, but the "Enthustiastick" passions are more subtle and lofty, being aroused by what to Dennis (and, for that matter, to Coleridge and Wordsworth) were man's loftiest ideas, his religious contemplations. In 1753 Bishop Lowth distinguished between two kinds of sublimity in preparation for his analysis of Hebrew poetry, the crowning glory of which was its sublimity, especially as manifested in its "odes." The first kind is that "which exhibits great objects"; and the material for the second is internally derived, derived, as he points out, from the two "sources" of the sublime that Longinus had designated as most innate—the concepts and passions of the poet.[96] Bishop Lowth's preference for the internal sublime is clearly marked throughout his whole analysis as well as by explicit statement: poetry, he says, consists "in imitation" and may imitate "whatever the human mind is able to conceive," such as "things, places, appearances natural and artificial, actions, passions, manners, and customs"; but that species of poetry which is an image of the inflections and secrecies of the mind is superior, since "whatever is exhibited to it from without, may well be supposed to move and agitate it less than what it internally perceives, of the magnitude and force of which it is previously conscious."[97]

The distinction between "external" and "internal" poetry is already be-

95. Two variables are involved in Dennis' distinction. The "Vulgar Passions" are aroused either by "the Objects themselves, or by the Ideas in the ordinary Course of Life"; the "Enthustiastick" by "Ideas in Contemplation, or the Meditation of things that belong not to common Life." Ideas from common life are very different from "Ideas in Meditation"; for example, the sun, if mentioned in common conversation, gives the idea of a round, flat body about two feet in diameter, but "in Meditation, gives the Idea of a vast and glorious Body, and the top of all the visible Creation, and the brightest material Image of the Divinity." The "Enthustiastick Passions," he adds, are most purely expressed in those parts of epic poetry "where the Poet speaks himself" and in "the greater Ode" (*The Grounds of Criticism in Poetry*, in *The Critical Works of John Dennis*, I, 338–39).

96. Lowth, *op. cit.*, Lecture XIV, "Of the Sublime in General, and of Sublimity of Expression in Particular," p. 155.

97. *Ibid.*, Lecture XVII, "Of the Sublime of Passion," pp. 184–85.

ginning to carry with it a corollary important in determining the history of criticism and the shape of poetical creations to come. For, included among "external" poetical materials are not only natural objects external to man but man's manners and actions, constituents of the poetic element of plot. Aristotle had designated the plot as the end or "soul as it were" of poetry; and, although most critics after him viewed poetry as ethical in its final intention and therefore reduced plot to a subservient role (that of an *exemplum* or "fable"), it remained in a place of high esteem, being consistently regarded as the most powerful of poetic devices in "moving" men toward virtue and warning them away from vice, grossness, or comical exhibitions of human frailties. As long as this esteem for plot continued, epic and tragedy were generally placed at the top of the poetical hierarchy because they conveyed the most weighty matter in the most moving of devices by language the most embellished. Also, as long as plot was the most esteemed element of poetry, lyric poetry could not come to be regarded as it was in the nineteenth century—either as synonymous with poetry or at least as its most "poetical" part. Moreover, the place given to plot not only affected the place given to the lyric but altered its nature. The Great Ode had been a fragmentary plot, involving a leading character and a single act or selection of acts to reveal his attributes. The later allegorical ode was a creation of the "imagination," substituting the poet's personifications for external persons and events.

Bishop Lowth had been traditional in designating all poetry as "imitation" but had divided its sources into the internal and the external (actions being one of the materials outside the poet) and had elevated the former; for "when a passion is expressed, the object is clear and distinct at once; the mind is immediately conscious of itself and its own emotions," whereas, when the subjects are without, the mind must work less vividly by memory, comparing the objects described with their archetypes.[98] To Sir William Jones, also, "the finest parts of poetry, musick, and painting, are expressive of the *passions*, and operate on our minds by *sympathy*"; the other parts are based upon another principle, the principle of imitation and "are descriptive of natural *objects*, and affect us chiefly by *substitution*."[99] Thus Jones's poetics rests upon two derogations of a critical order long honored, for it is a poetics that detracts from the importance of plot material and from the conception of imitation. His major argument is designed to show that the history of literature supports these detractions; poetry, he insists, did not have its origins, as Aristotle had maintained, in the desire to imitate, but in an impulse for expressing the passions. And when we

98. *Ibid.*

99. "On the Arts, Commonly Called Imitative" in *Poems Consisting Chiefly of Translations from the Asiatick Languages* (Oxford, 1772), pp. 216–17.

get to "expression," we are getting up-to-date; we are also getting close to the notion that lyric poetry is the original poetical ingredient, both historically and analytically, in the dramatic and narrative forms, and to the notion that these forms are "poetical" only to the extent that the "lyrical" element is present in them, either in passages that transport or in a "poetical" tone that pervades the whole. The most ancient of poetry, Jones argues, sprang from joy and resulted in praise of the deity; even dramatic poetry, which is the only species with the exception of epic that can be called imitative, sprang from a song in praise of Bacchus.[100] Thus Jones inverts the architecture of Aristotle's history of poetry, although incorporating much of the same material, for Aristotle in tracing the origins of poetry from the early hymns and encomia to the dramatic[101] is tracing a development that to him resulted in more complicated and moving forms of art, whereas Sir William regards the later dramatic forms as top-heavy superstructures reared upon a base of pure poetry, the direct expression of passion.

This part of our discussion closes with a statement made just a year before the Romantic date of 1798, and one focused upon the later neoclassical odes. It is a statement explicitly dividing all poetry into two kinds, one of which depends upon material "external" to the poet and the other of which has the poet's mind as its central source. It is a statement, moreover, explicitly designating the latter kind as lyric, and lyric as pure poetry. In her Preface to *The Poetical Works of Mr. William Collins* (London, 1797), Mrs. Barbauld wrote that the "different species of Poetry may be reduced under two comprehensive classes." The first includes "all in which the charms of verse are made use of, to illustrate subjects which in their own nature are affecting or interesting"— epic, dramatic, descriptive, didactic, etc.

The other class consists of what may be called pure Poetry, or Poetry in the abstract. It is conversant with an imaginary world, peopled with beings of its own creation. It deals in splendid imagery, bold fiction, and allegorical personages. It is necessarily obscure to a certain degree; because, having to do chiefly with ideas generated within the mind, it cannot be at all comprehended by any whose intellect has not been exercised in similar contemplations; while the conceptions of the Poet (often highly metaphysical) are rendered still more remote from common apprehension by the figurative phrase in which they are clothed. All that is properly *Lyric Poetry* is of this kind.[102]

If we narrow our focus again to the allegorical ode, we see that only one element of it has been located—a configuration of the poet's mind or, in terms of the five sources of the sublime, a lofty conception (of mercy, adversity,

100. *Ibid.*, pp. 203–4.

101. *Poetics* 4.   102. Pp. iii–v.

simplicity, peace, pity, etc.). What is missing becomes apparent when we ask how the poet is to objectify his conception, especially when he wishes to avoid the anciently established practice of ode writers—that of embodying the conception in an agent and his actions. What many writers of allegorical odes did to solve this problem can be simply stated; they turned from action and agent to a device of language. For persons they substituted the extended personification.[103] To later generations the particular linguistic device that "carries" the allegorical odes has seemed inadequate and artificial; but the decision to rely upon image instead of upon action is significant and is reflective of great changes that were then occurring in the theory and creation of poetry, when the theory, formulated in antiquity, of the poet as a maker of plots was being replaced by the modern theory of the poet as a maker of images.

How the allegorical ode substituted the linguistic devices of personification for action can be illustrated quickly by a comparison of "Alexander's Feast" (and Pope's "Ode for Music on St. Cecilia's Day") with Collins' *The Passions: An Ode for Music*. The comparison can be restricted to a comparison of means, since the intention of the odes is the same—that of praising the power of music. In the odes of Dryden and Pope, incident is the main device used to exemplify this power, an incident in which a particular musician singing various songs sways his listeners to various passions and actions. But in Collins' allegorical ode, the Passions (capitalized) gather around the early Greek abode of Music (also capitalized and a "Heav'nly Maid") and, as persons, are swept into action by her divine fury. In succession, each Passion (fear and anger, despair and hope, revenge, etc.) seizes its appropriate instrument and plays in verse that fluctuates with the passion and the instrument accompanying it.

The allegorical ode undoubtedly includes a variety of creations, but there is one clear formula that governs many of them, and many others are only modi-

---

103. For a general discussion of this subject, with many useful references, see Earl R. Wasserman, "The Inherent Values of Eighteenth-Century Personification," *PMLA*, LXV (1950), 435–63. Prototypes of nearly all the types of odes discussed can be found in the English "inventor" of the Pindaric ode. Cowley's odes "Upon Liberty" and "Destinie" (and "Of Wit," although this ode is written in a regular verse pattern) are obviously addressed to abstractions, but their resemblance to the allegorical odes of Collins and Gray is not very close, and especially in respect to the linguistic characteristic just mentioned. The odes "Upon Liberty" and "Of Wit" are more like versified essays on their respective subjects. "Upon Liberty," for instance, is a discourse on the problem of what class of mankind can possess freedom combined with virtue. The answer is immediately given—only those whose life is bounded by the Golden Mean. Then both extremes are explored. The great are found to be fettered by aspirations and possessions; the poor are riveted to "the laborious task of Bread." At the end of the discourse, the poet announces his preference for a life which "should a well-order'd Poem be / (In which he only hits the white / Who joyns true Profit with the best Delight)." "Destinie" is a little closer to the formula evolved by Collins and others, but it is clearly not a poem governed by this formula.

fications of this linguistic ritual.[104] The poem generally opens with a "Thou" or "O thou," the "thou" invoked being a lofty conception central to the poem (simplicity, pity, liberty), but the conception is already a person (female and a nymph if exemplifying a soft or tender quality), who at this stage of the poem is a child, descended from some appropriate pagan god or brought forth from the mind of some appropriate Greek poet or statesman. The child is clothed in suitable color (sky-blue, black, bloody, etc.) and is located in an appropriate "haunt," in deep shade or on mountains wild or in a golden car or on the "deathful field" of battle. This person has relatives, also personified; sometimes one is a husband or wife (mercy married to valor), sometimes a sister, in which case there are several, who are naturally personifications of qualities allied to the main one. Also, there are enemies, "a horrid train" of abstract vices or undesirable states of mind. The poet indirectly or explicitly indicates that he and Great Britain are sorely beset.

The historical "haunt" of the personification then changes, always ultimately to England, where "The *British* Lion, Goddess sweet, / Lies stretch'd on Earth to kiss thy Feet," although frequently there are intermediate stops, such as Rome. The first stop in Great Britain usually is during the time of Spenser, Shakespeare, and Milton, but, if the quality being celebrated is valor or liberty or an allied virtue, the first visit to England is much earlier.

The conclusion varies according to the mood of the poet, and the mood of the poet is determined by the chances the poet believes he and his country have of again possessing the quality being celebrated. And different prospects for the present and the future naturally make for different views of the past and therefore introduce variations in the formula just given. In Collins' "Ode to Liberty" the poet speaks in pride and joy, the shrine erected to liberty in Britain being partly "Doric" and partly "Gothic" in its architecture and more solid than either. The "Ode on the Poetical Character" is at the other extreme, the poet concluding that "Heaven, and *Fancy*, kindred Pow'rs, / Have now o'erturn'd th' inspiring Bow'rs, / Or curtain'd close such Scene from ev'ry future View." More frequently the poem ends in an intermediate mood, in which the poet feels that the quality he is contemplating was possessed more fully in former times and by writers superior to himself, but nevertheless hopes that the quality will make its power felt again in him and his countrymen. In this mood the poet either exhorts the personification to make his country and

---

104. The formula governs such poems as Collins' "Ode to Fear," "Ode to Liberty," "Ode to Peace," "Ode to Pity," and, to a degree, his "Ode on the Poetical Character." Gray's "Hymn to Adversity" and "The Progress of Poesy" also fall under it; but, on the whole, Gray was the more diversified ode writer. Odes by Gray will be used to illustrate all three types of odes—the allegorical ode, the descriptive ode, and the ode of terror.

his own breast her next "haunt" or expresses a determination himself to return in fancy to one of her previous "haunts."[105]

The descriptive ode may be treated with comparative briefness, since it has been characterized in good part indirectly by what has been said of the allegorical ode. The initial distinction characterizing the allegorical ode is also initial to a discussion of the descriptive ode, but it is initial only, for, as George Dyer pointed out, the poet who is content with "a picture of *mere nature*" to which little or nothing is added from his own mind "will have too much reason, after all, to exclaim,

> Ah! silly I, more silly than my sheep,
> Which on the flow'ry plains I once did keep!"[106]

And certainly most of the descriptive odes are not merely descriptive but rather move from a description of some natural object or set of objects to a lofty concept abstracted from the scene. The distinction, then, between poetry in which the poet's mind furnishes its own material and poetry in which the material is external to the poet is not an exclusive distinction and probably no one ever used it as such, but it marks off certain poems from others and the allegorical from the descriptive ode, although the allegorical ode, in externalizing the concept, nearly always uses descriptive elements, and the descriptive ode, to be of human concern, suggests thought or feeling.

Let us begin with the natural objects that serve in the descriptive ode as

105. A history of the theory of lyric poetry would lose track of itself if it entered into the labyrinthian immensity of a history of the theory of language, but the linguistic characteristics of lyric poetry just discussed have certain large and clear relations with contemporary philosophical inquiry, which should be summarized here: (1) Central to the philosophical inquiry of the period, given its psychological bias, is the problem of the relation of sensory experiences (impressions) to their higher compounds (ideas or concepts). (2) Viewed as having the dual obligation of instruction and pleasure, poetry, unlike intellectual inquiry, has the task of arousing both particular impressions and ideas. (3) Central to discussions of the language of poetry is the problem of how to objectify concepts or ideas so that the senses will be aroused, particularly sight, which was regarded by nearly all critics as the dominant sense. Cf. the basic theory underlying Erasmus Darwin's conception of poetry as a personification of the loves of plants: "And as our ideas derived from visible objects are more distinct than those derived from the objects of our other senses, the words expressive of these ideas belonging to vision make up the principal part of poetic language. That is, the Poet writes principally to the eye, the Prose-writer uses more abstracted terms" (*The Botanic Garden* [London, 1791], Part II, p. 48). (4) Psychological associationalism, centering the problem of apprehension upon the awareness of relations between impressions, also emphasized the poetic power of metaphor, especially personification, with its human reference. The metaphor is everywhere regarded as a sign of the sensitive and the impassioned mind. (5) As poetry more and more comes to be viewed as the expression of such a mind, so the metaphor is more and more frequently taken as the essential verbal characteristic of poetry. (6) And, to attach these points to the lyric, we need only recall that the Great Ode had always been viewed as that form of poetry in which figurative and impassioned language could be used most abundantly.

106. *Poems* (London, 1802), I, lix–lx.

stimuli to feelings and thoughts. In eighteenth-century aesthetics there was one essential distinction between natural objects: there were sublime and there were beautiful natural objects—one group, massive, irregular, elevated, gloomy, and awesome, arousing the turbulent and transporting emotions; the other inducing the opposite emotional state, one of "relaxation." This distinction is just as visible in the descriptive poems of the period as in the general aesthetic theory and clearly served as a principle determining the poet's selection of detail. In Gray's "The Bard," which will be scrutinized more closely later, every descriptive detail can be found in nearly all the many neoclassical lists of sublime objects. Furthermore, many descriptive lyrics of the closing years of the eighteenth century parallel in their choice of detail the philosopher's list of beautiful objects, but lyrics so confined are, by definition, lesser lyrics, and, conversely, there are few odes approaching the stature of the Great Ode that do not suggest the sublime. This is true even of Collins' "Ode to Evening," although its prevailing mood is determined by the "quiet rule" of evening, and although the immediate evening of the opening stanzas is hushed, and small objects (the bat and beetle) are used to describe it. But this particular evening fades into a contemplation of other evenings, of which there are two kinds—the mild and cheerful evenings of spring and summer and those of autumn and winter, "yelling thro' the troublous Air." In the final stanza the poet's feelings return to the first evening, and the "gentlest Influence" of the object of contemplation gives it its final and "fav'rite Name." Certainly, the choice of the poet in this ode is for the quiet and the beautiful, but wild and "awful" aspects of the object are used structurally to indicate a choice of aspects in natural objects and of moods aroused by them.

But the descriptive ode, as pointed out before, also involves a progression from a highly selected description of natural objects to some great concept supposedly inhering in the objects selected. The ending of Gray's mock-ode "On the Death of a Favourite Cat" satirizes this formalized progression: "From hence, ye Beauties, undeceiv'd, / Know, one false step is ne'er retriev'd," etc. And Gray's serious odes that most closely approach the descriptive type, "Ode on the Spring" and "Ode on a Distant Prospect of Eton College," could well be objects of his own satire. After describing spring, the poet reclines "in rustic state" so that with him "the Muse shall sit, and think," and think of "insect youth" which is on the wing, until in fancy the "sportive kind" replies to his reveries: "Poor moralist! and what art thou? / A solitary fly!" etc. Similarly constructed is the close of the "Ode on a Distant Prospect of Eton College": "No more; where ignorance is bliss, / 'Tis folly to be wise." At the end of Collins' "Ode to Evening" the poet announces that the following abstract qualities inhere in evening—"*Fancy, Friendship, Science*, smiling *Peace*"—

although this announcement seems somewhat startling, and one has difficulty in seeing, for instance, how just *"Science"* got into the poem.

Before turning from the descriptive ode, let us remind ourselves of its connection both with the general aesthetics of the eighteenth century and with the poems of succeeding poets, such as Wordsworth. As these eighteenth-century descriptive poems move from a perception of natural objects to a contemplation of their immanent powers (powers ranging from the humanly commendable to the divine), they only parallel poetically the prevailing theory, which held that sublime and beautiful natural objects were God's manifestation of his attributes and of those lesser glories which he had bestowed on man. Wordsworth was a revolutionary poet and a better poet than any eighteenth-century lyrist, but many of his poems were descriptive, and descriptive in the sense already defined, the poet being stirred initially by the natural aspects of an object such as a quiet evening, and then, as the silence increases and the poem progresses, he has a glimpse into the incorporeal and finds there, not just genial human qualities, but the mighty Being and a "sound like thunder—everlastingly."

When the "ode of terror" is detached from its setting, it is little more than a literary curiosity; but the fact that many of the new school of the later eighteenth century regarded "The Bard" as the finest lyric written in any language and placed Gray above Pindar, Cowley, and Dryden[107] should indicate that it is an embodiment of concepts and prescriptions fundamental to the time. Beneath these surface prescriptions are the emotions that, by their different tones, give ultimate identity to particular poems, poets, and schools of poets. Yet even the emotions of a poet are in some measure prescribed and

107. For Potter's statement (1783) that "The Bard" is "the finest Ode in the world," see below, p. 447. Pinkerton (1785) said: "Gray is the first and greatest of modern lyric writers; nay, I will venture to say, of all lyric writers" (*op. cit.*, p. 131); of writers of the sublime ode, he said that "Pindar stood without a rival till Gray appeared" (*ibid.*, p. 33). In a letter written in 1788, Anna Seward spoke indignantly of Mason, because of "his silence over Johnson's malignant injustice to the greatest lyric poet the world ever produced, not excepting Pindar himself . . ." (*Letters of Anna Seward* [Edinburgh, 1811], II, 42); this opinion is expressed in other letters: *ibid.*, IV, 159–60, 364; V, 189–90. For the reasons that led Drake (1798) "without any exception to place it ['The Bard'] at the head of lyric poetry," see below, p. 447. These opinions are widespread during the closing decades of the eighteenth century, but it should be pointed out that, throughout the neoclassical period, the lyric was involved in the "ancient-modern" controversy and that some maintained that the moderns were inferior to the ancients only in the lyric. The most surprising eighteenth-century figure to side with the ancients is Joseph Warton (see *An Essay on the Genius and Writings of Pope*, pp. 62 ff.); Drake's comments on the lyric are in part an answer to Warton. Since the argument is centered chiefly on the question whether the English language is sufficiently mellifluous to respond to the lyric impulses, only passing reference is made to it in this study of theory. In *An Essay on the Genius and Writings of Pope*, Warton places "Alexander's Feast" at "the head of modern lyric compositions" (pp. 50–51), and in his edition of *The Works of Alexander Pope, Esq.* (London, 1797) he again places it at "the head of modern Lyric compositions" but adds significantly, "always excepting The Bard of Gray" (I, 143–44).

publicly bestowed, and the poet "feels" in part as some theory of poetry says a poet should "feel," or as his favorite poets "feel," or as this or that political journal "feels" about current events and the proximity of the Day of Judgment —he also "feels" by anathema, in present times oppositely to "Romanticism" and especially Rossetti. Matthew Arnold again and again lamented the fact that a strange disease of his own time made it impossible for him to feel the calm tranquillity that Wordsworth felt, and the poet of the last twenty years has been confronted with this same emotional impossibility but, conversely, has found it much too easy to "feel" the "dry, hard" feelings advocat :d by T. E. Hulme and expressed by T. S. Eliot.

Eighteenth-century aesthetics increasingly focused upon the problem of aesthetic pleasures, which were reduced to two inclusive sets—one that was physiologically turbulent and soul-searing (the sublime), and another that was "relaxed," aroused by what was usually designated as "the beautiful." As a general aesthetic distinction, this classification naturally applied to many artistic species; and in the final section of this essay we shall observe how it divided lyric poetry into emotionally different kinds. Here, however, we are concerned with the sublime ode and the fact that terror was everywhere treated either as the emotional equivalent of sublimity or as one of its most characteristic signs. This fact, in turn, is connected with the coming history of literature, which includes an important chapter usually entitled "Romantic Terror."[108]

Burke had erected the sublime and beautiful upon opposite sets of passions, those directed toward self-preservation and those aroused by social impulses. To him, sublimity, involving prospects that endanger the beholder, necessarily arouses terror or emotions analogous to it.

Whatever is fitted in any sort to excite the ideas of pain, and danger, that is to say, whatever is in any sort terrible, or is conversant about terrible objects, or operates in a manner analogous to terror, is a source of the *sublime*; that is, it is productive of the strongest emotion which the mind is capable of feeling. I say the strongest emotion, because I am satisfied the ideas of pain are much more powerful than those which enter on the part of pleasure.[109]

A variant treatment of the relation between terror and the sublime has an important bearing upon lyric poetry. Many critics of the neoclassical period look upon terror as a necessarily frequent ingredient of the sublime, but not as its sole emotional sign. According to Bishop Lowth, "That sensation of sublimity

---

108. For a detailed analysis of the vogue during this period for melancholy poetry (in good part, lyric) see Eleanor M. Sickels, *The Gloomy Egoist: Moods and Themes of Melancholy from Gray to Keats* (New York, 1932). The following remarks are intended to relate the literary phenomenon which is the subject of her study to the general aesthetics of the period.

109. *Op. cit..* Part I, Sec. VII, pp. 58–59.

which arises from the greatness of the thoughts and imagery, has admiration for its basis, and that for the most part connected with joy, love, hatred, or fear"; but these emotions he immediately subdivides by associating them with the dual epideictic ends of poetry, praise of the good and censure of transgression. Love and joy accompany "the pursuit of the supreme good"; and grief, hatred, and fear should be detached from the usual trivial objects that arouse them and be reserved for "the supreme evil."[110] Thus religious exaltation and its opposite, dread, are emotional complements constituting the sublime and are here as close together in analysis as Coleridge and Wordsworth were later in companionship and authorship, the one writing most characteristically in joy and love and most memorably in the ode on "Intimations of Immortality," and the other in the grief and fear reflected in *The Ancient Mariner*, "The Ode on the Departing Year," and "Dejection: An Ode."

The Great Ode was so closely identified with sublimity that one should not have to look far for statements to the effect that terror, regarded as integral to the sublime, was essential to the loftiest of lyric expressions. Of "The Bard," Potter wrote: "The wild and romantic scenery, the strength of conception, the boldness of the figures, the terrible sublimity, the solemn spirit of prophecy, and the animated glow of visions of glory render this 'the finest Ode in the world.' "[111] Among many others, Drake shared this opinion, for "over this inimitable ode a tinge so wildly awful, so gloomily terrific, is thrown, as without any exception to place it at the head of lyric poetry."[112] And of the Sublime Ode which constitutes the first of his four classes of lyric poetry (the others being the Pathetic, the Descriptive, and the Amatory), he wrote:

To excel in this species of Ode demands a felicity and strength of genius that has seldom been attained; all the higher beauties of poetry, vastness of conception, brilliancy of colouring, grandeur of sentiment, the terrible and the appalling, must combine, and with mysterious energy alarm and elevate the imagination. A lightning of phrase should pervade the more empassioned parts, and an awful and even dreadful obscurity, from prophetic, or superhuman agency, diffuse its influence over the whole.[113]

110. Lowth, *op. cit.*, Lecture XVII, "Of the Sublime of Passion," pp. 187 ff. Cowley himself wrote Pindaric odes depicting this kind of terror (see "The 34. Chapter of the Prophet Isaiah" and "The Plagues of Egypt"). On the other hand, in G. Gregory, the translator of Bishop Lowth (see his footnote to Lecture XIV, "Of the Sublime in General, and of Sublimity of Expression in Particular," p. 153), and in Sir William Jones (*op. cit.*, p. 217) the influence of Burke is admitted or clear, and, in particular, they treat terror as always involved in the sublime.

111. *Op. cit.*, p. 37.

112. Drake, *op. cit.*, II, 72–73.

113. *Ibid.*, pp. 71–72. Attack as well as defense often indicates the presence of a position. "All that we find new in this collection [*Poems by Mr. Gray*] is, The Fatal Sisters, an ode, the Descent of Odin, an ode, and the Triumphs of Owen, a fragment. These turn chiefly on the dark *diableries* of the Gothic times; and if to be mysterious and to be sublime be the same thing, these deep-wrought performances must undoubtedly be deemed so. For our part, we

Let us conclude our discussion of the neoclassical Great Ode with a closer scrutiny of "The Bard," since it must embody many of the critical preferences of an age that ended by placing it at the apex of lyric accomplishment.

Different as "The Bard" is from earlier neoclassical odes, it is nevertheless traditional in at least two important respects. In the first place, it is based upon an action (as is "Alexander's Feast," for which Gray had the greatest admiration). Furthermore, as in "Alexander's Feast," the incident is taken from historical legend—in the case of "The Bard," from the Welsh legend that Edward I, after conquering Wales, ordered all bards to be captured and put to death. The ode is largely the speech of an imaginary Welsh bard as he contemplates the scene of carnage; and the poem ends with the suicide of the bard, whose choice is limited to honorable or dishonorable death. The ode is also traditional in its epideictic intention, that of celebrating the powers of poetry.[114] It is both negative and positive epideictic. In the first and longer section of the ode the Welsh bard prophesies doom, death, and final loss of succession to the line of Edward I, and it is this part of the poem that seemed to contemporary admirers the essence of sublime terror. In the final part the bard prophesies the poetically just coronation of an English queen, Welsh in her lineage, the immediate flowering of great poets (among them Shakespeare moving "Pale Grief, and pleasing Pain, / With Horrour, Tyrant of the throbbing breast"), and a future of limitless splendor.

Although "The Bard" in these two important respects is within the long tradition of the Great Ode, it is a synthesis of other features, some of them equally fundamental, that are distinctive of the middle and later eighteenth century. Its basis in fact was shadowy; it was, to contemporary admirers, essentially a "fiction," a creation of the imagination, a transformation of whatever was external into an image of the soul of a poet. The dramatic situation is an imaginary objectification of a lofty concept, to use the language of Longinus; and the character is also a "fiction." The poem is largely a dramatic monologue, the speech of an imaginary Celtic poet, who, perched on the terrible sublime ("On a rock, whose haughty brow / Frowns o'er old Conway's foaming flood"), contemplates the terror engulfing his country and his profession before he himself plunges "headlong from the mountain's height / Deep in the roaring tide." The soul of the poet speaking is conceived of as the soul of poetry. The bard is a primitive, Ossian-like poet, an original *vates*, hav-

---

shall for ever regret the departure of Mr. Gray's muse from that elegantly-moral simplicity she assumed in the Country Church-yard" (*Monthly Review*, XXXVIII [May, 1768], 408). In his Index to the first series of the *Monthly Review*, Benjamin Christie Nangle attributes this review to John Langhorne.

114. Gray's companion ode, "The Progress of Poesy. A Pindaric Ode," is a completely allegorical celebration of the powers of poetry.

ing not only the power of words and music but a prophetic power more accurate than that ascribed to the poet by Shelley, who thought the poet could "foreknow the spirit of events" but not "the form," which Gray's bard predicts to the next-to-last detail, omitting only the exact dates. Shelley was also minimal in his conception of the force of poetry in history, for he said only that there was a constant conjunction between the state of poetry in an age and the age's general cultural level, and waived the question of cause and effect, whereas Edward's extermination of the Welsh poets is treated as the causal force determining the future of England, including a Welsh ascension to the throne. This conception of the power of poetry is fundamental to the "superhuman" quality so frequently ascribed to this ode, and it also transforms this ode of terror into something approximating an allegorical ode, for the abstraction celebrated is personified or superpersonified into the dramatic agent determining the whole narrative of human affairs.

Turning from lofty thought to the second source of the sublime—passion— we can immediately see the signs of terror, see them more clearly, perhaps, because they fail to move us. The ode is an undisguised collection of all the current prescriptions for inducing terror in the patient. There are the obvious deaths and dooms of kings prophesied for Edward's line—the premature death of Edward's gallant son, the Black Prince; the butchery of Edward II in Berkeley castle; the machinations of his adulterous queen; and, of course, Richard III ("The bristled Boar in infant gore") and civil war. There are also the final two lines of the poem in which the bard, completing his prophecy, leaps from the top of a mountain into the roaring Conway. As for the descriptive details, all are to be found in eighteenth-century lists of sublime objects—the wild, the irregular, the vast, the high, those suggesting great power and approximating the infinite. The bard is stationed on a high cliff and "each giant-oak, and desert cave, / Sighs to the torrent's aweful voice beneath!" The height above him is also filled in with objects long prescribed for suggesting the terror that abides in "elevation": "Far, far aloof th'affrighted ravens sail; / The famish'd Eagle screams, and passes by." Sublimity was also thought to involve masses of time as well as space, vast spans extending from remoteness to the infinite future. And we have already observed how this poem is located in the romantically remote and, by the device of prophecy, joins this remote past to the sweep of succeeding history and to visions of poetical glory in times yet to come.

IV. THE LESSER LYRIC: THE BEAUTIFUL AND THE SUBLIME

Throughout the long history of poetic theory, lyric poetry had been spoken of sometimes as three, sometimes as two, in kind, although there is no critical conflict between the numbers. The threefold distinction, stressed by Plato, among the "subjects" of poetry (gods, heroes, and men) underlies both divisions; and the universal veneration for Pindar's lofty odes, which at the same time celebrated both gods and heroes, accounts in good part for the tendency to view the lyric as constituted of a major and a minor kind. This tendency became much more marked after Cowley's renditions of Pindar into English. The Cowleyan ode, divine and heroic, was viewed as "a vast *Species alone*,"[115] alone above rules and defiant of order, regularity, and moderation, since it was trying to imitate the essence and height of abnormality—a soul in the state of transport. The force of this new form acted as a magnet to attract together and place as a polar opposite to itself many "forms" that the Renaissance only to some extent had thought of as one kind and a kind called the "lyric." These "forms" were distinct largely because of differences in verse patterns, but such differences had seemed basic to English writers in the sixteenth and early seventeenth centuries, when the limited native prosodic tradition was suddenly enriched and confused by the metrical creations of the Continental poets and the humanistic rediscovery of the classical lyrists. But the critical importance of verse distinctions had diminished as English poets mastered their technique, assimilating or rejecting foreign patterns and inventing many of their own. And, tending always to attract them together was the force of classical tradition that placed near the bottom of the poetical hierarchy a group of poems, various in their verse forms but united because of an alliance (real or legendary) with music and with the subjects of love and wine. By the end of the seventeenth century, the lyric was generally spoken of as of two kinds, the "Ode" and the "Song," or the "Greater Ode" and the "Lesser Ode."[116] The "Song" or "Lesser Ode" was viewed as a creation contrary in nearly all its aspects to the "invention" of Cowley—not impassioned but graceful and "natural" in its spiritual impulsion and, therefore, requiring not so much "genius" as "art"; conversant not with the divine or the heroic but chiefly with the most general and moving of human affections, love; satisfactory in final accomplishment if pleasure be given without moral offense; and in diction and versification, regular, smooth, "natural," and simple. Subspecies

115. Cowley, "The Praise of Pindar."

116. Charles Gildon notes that Sheffield "has divided his Precepts relating to Songs from those of *Odes*, as if of a different Kind, interposing his Remarks on the Elegy between them" (*The Complete Art of Poetry* [London, 1718], I, 175). Perhaps Sheffield's order of discussion indicates that, like certain Renaissance critics, he views them of a different kind; more likely, however, his order is his order of merit, with the elegy interposed between the two lyric kinds because it is superior to the minor lyric but inferior to the ode. Gildon surmises that Sheffield separated the Song from the Ode because of "the weak Performances of this sort in our Language" and graciously unites them with the suggestion that when songs are "improv'd by his Grace's admirable Precepts, I presume they will be admitted without difficulty into the lesser *Ode*."

so antithetical naturally acquired the status of somewhat separate species and were placed at almost extreme ends of the poetical hierarchy, the lesser lyric so close to the epigram that early-eighteenth-century critics were troubled with the problem of distinguishing the two.

This is where we begin, with a view of the minor lyric as indeed minor. Before the end of the eighteenth century, however, even the sonnet was regarded as relatively unlimited in its power to produce aesthetic pleasure.

Although many minor lyrics of the complimentary sort were written during the eighteenth century, it is not surprising that, regarded so casually, they drew comparatively little critical comment or that the comment is meager, prescriptive, and repetitious. In 1713 Ambrose Philips prefaced his remarks upon the song with the statement that he did "not remember ever to have met with any Piece of Criticism upon this Subject."[117] The casual nature of his remarks is emphasized by his ascription of them to a gentleman of good taste and skill in writing, especially concerning love, who the previous day at a tea-party had been asked by a Mrs. Annabella Lizard what his opinion was concerning songs in general. His reply is that there has always been in every nation a tribe of song writers immortalizing their bottles or mistresses, but they have not realized the proper nature of songs: "It is true, they do not require an Elevation of Thought, nor any extraordinary Capacity, nor an extensive Knowledge; but then they demand great Regularity, and the utmost Nicety; an exact Purity of Stile, with the most easie and flowing Numbers; an elegant and unaffected Turn of Wit, with one uniform and simple Design." He then goes on to say that the smallest blemish in a song is ruinous, unlike blemishes in a large poem; and he criticizes Donne and Cowley for trying to cram so much material into a song that a new design is started with almost every line: "A Song should be conducted like an Epigram; and the only Difference between them is, that the one does not require the Lyrick Numbers, and is usually employed upon Satyrical Occasions; whereas the Business of the other, for the most part, is to express (as my Lord *Roscommon* translates it from *Horace*)

> *Love's pleasing Cares, and the free Joys of Wine.*"[118]

But Phillips' remarks were not the first on this subject, nor are they in any way original. For instance, Sheffield, in *An Essay upon Poetry* (1682) says of the

---

117. *Guardian*, No. 16 (March 30, 1713).

118. William Oldys reports that critics distinguish between a song and an epigram in this fashion: ". . . indeed it sometimes happens, that more than one thought is pursu'd in a Song; but, if the criticks be right, that's as much a fault there, as in an Epigram; and the difference they make is, that a Song consists of one thought, without a point; and, if it extends farther, becomes a Ballad; while an Epigram has a right to a point." He himself regards this difference as a critical nicety and maintains that length is the distinguishing factor (*A Collection of Epigrams* [2d ed.; London, 1735], p. v).

song that "no part of Poetry requires a nicer Art," for a defect that would escape attention in rows of "richest Pearl" would plainly appear in a small ring; he insists that the diction seem smooth and natural, as if the effect of chance, but he cautions the expression not to "creep" and the "fancy" animating the poem not to "fly"; he indicates that warm and chaste love is its province and then attacks the Restoration writers (especially "the late Convert") for their "nauseous Songs."[119] But it is William Walsh, Pope's early critical guide, who gives the most practical, if not the most convincing, reason for adhering to "natural" language and "natural" sentiments in writing love lyrics, the purpose of which should be, not "the getting Fame or Admiration from the World, but the obtaining the Love of their Mistresses"; hence love-poets should write about thoughts that are natural to everyone in love (i.e., tender and passionate) and should not fill their verses with surprising and glittering thoughts or far-fetched conceits, similes, and "*Shining Points*" that are clearly evidences of insincerity.[120]

In 1772 John Aikin published an anthology of songs with long introductions for the various sections and claimed that there had been only one previous critical discussion of this branch of poetry, that by Ambrose Phillips.[121] But, despite this claim, Aikin's essay gives little evidence of critical originality. Lyric poetry is divided into the "ode" and the "song." The ode is character-ized by sublimity and "the boldest flights of poetical enthusiasm"; the song "is confined to gaiety and tenderness, or, to express it classically, the Sapphic and Anacreontic."[122] The subject matter of the song is not restricted, but, because the song is tender or gay by nature, custom has confined it almost solely "to love and wine."[123] The lower key of the emotions and the fact that the song,

119. *Op. cit.*, pp. 5–6.

120. *Letters and Poems, Amorous and Gallant* (London, 1692), Preface.

121. *Essays on Song-writing: With a Collection of Such English Songs as Are Most Eminent for Poetical Merit* (2d ed.; Warrington, 1774), pp. 2–3. Criticism of minor lyric forms was admittedly slight, but it was not so rare as its producers claimed. For instance, there is John Newberry's *Poetry Made Familiar and Easy to Young Gentlemen and Ladies, and Embellished with a Great Variety of the Most Shining Epigrams, Epitaphs, Songs, Odes, Pastorals, &c. from the Best Authors*, a work first appearing in 1746. Newberry divides English lyric poetry into the "Ode" and the "Song." "Yes, with us they are different Things, the *Ode* being seldom sung, except upon solemn Occasions, and being usually employed in grave and lofty Subjects, such as the Praises of Heroes and great Exploits, and even of GOD himself (*The Circle of the Sciences* [3d ed.; London, 1769], IV, 88). Of the song, he says: "The *Song* admits of almost any Subject, but the greatest Part of them turn either upon *Love* or *Drinking*. Be the Subject, however, what it will, the Verses should be easy, natural, and flowing, and contain a certain Harmony, so that Poetry and Music may be agreeably united. In these Compositions, as in all others, obscene and profane Expressions should be carefully avoided, and indeed every Thing that tends to take off the Respect which is due to Religion and Virtue, and to en-courage Vice and Immorality" (*ibid.*, IV, 116–17). Then nearly twenty pages of examples follow.

122. Aikin, *op. cit.*, pp. 19–20.   123. *Ibid.*, pp. 12–13.

unlike the ode, is closely associated with music make regularity an essential characteristic of its verse.[124] In grouping his poems, Aikin has three rather than two (the tender and the gay) classes of songs, but the first group, "Ballads and Pastoral Songs," is included probably because of its musical connections. The other two groups are easily recognized under their titles, "Passionate and Descriptive Songs" (tender) and "Ingenious and Witty Songs" (gay).[125]

To establish the continuity of this view of the minor lyric, we shall discuss two more critical statements, one from each of the remaining decades of the eighteenth century. Hugh Blair's division of lyric poetry is fourfold—sacred odes, heroic odes, moral and philosophical odes, and festive and amorous odes.[126] The four, however, are the two polar lyric states of mind (the sublime and the gay), with a slight rearrangement of the temperate zones. The sacred and heroic odes have sublimity as their "reigning character"; the moral and philosophical odes, occupying the "middle region," are inspired by virtue, friendship, and humanity and are exemplified by Horace; Anacreon and some of Horace set the pattern for the festive and amorous odes, the reigning character of which "ought to be elegance, smoothness, and gaiety."[127] Blair's fourfold division of the lyric is essentially not much different from Aikin's division into ode and song, both divisions reflecting three states of mind—the sublime and the gay and, in between, the tender. As close to "the Romantic age" as 1795, the *Encyclopaedia Britannica* divided lyric poetry into three kinds: the Sublime ode, the Lesser ode, and the Song.[128] The Sublime ode receives the customary characterization. Songs generally "turn either upon *love, contentment*, or the *pleasures* of a *country life*, and *drinking*," with the result that obscenity is a constant risk to be guarded against; and, as for the verse, it "should be easy, natural, and flowing, and contain a certain harmony, so that poetry and music may be agreeably united." The lesser ode has sweetness as

124. *Ibid.*, p. 21; also pp. 12–13.

125. In 1811 Aikin published another anthology of songs, entitled *Vocal Poetry, or a Select Collection of English Songs*, in which he says that he has "revised his notions respecting the character and distinctions of these compositions" (p. v). This anthology has some noticeable differences from the earlier one, reflective of shifts to be discussed shortly in the critical outlook of the last part of the eighteenth century. The general elevation of sentiments is reflected by the fact that, in *Vocal Poetry*, songs are considered expressive of only "emotions and sentiments," and hence "Ballads and Pastoral Songs" are no longer regarded as songs, properly speaking, but only as a kindred kind, since they are narrative (p. 22), although a few examples are included in the anthology. The change in the approved sentiments is reflected in his attitude toward "Ingenious and Witty Songs," which in *Vocal Poetry* are much subordinated to natural songs on love depicting real feeling (pp. 35–37).

126. See above, p. 419.

127. Blair, *op. cit.*, II, 355.

128. Moore's Dublin edition, *s.v.* "Poetry."

its distinguishing character, its diction should be easy (although at times it may rise to the figurative and the florid), and it affects and soothes the passions.

On the other hand, the number and nature of short lyrics written during the neoclassical period significantly did not remain constant. R. D. Havens can find only thirteen persons who used the sonnet form between 1660 and 1740[129] and less than twenty quatorzains published in periodicals before 1777, but in 1789 the *Gentleman's Magazine* printed fifty-nine. "In the last two decades of the century the same periodical and the *European magazine* published between them nearly six hundred, the sonnet having by that time become perhaps the most popular kind of magazine verse."[130] And the revival of other lyric types hitherto regarded as minor had begun even earlier in the century.[131]

Important as this revival is historically, it can boast of writers no more il-

129. *The Influence of Milton on English Poetry* (Cambridge, 1922), p. 488.

130. *Ibid.*, p. 499. The question should be raised whether the sonnet was consistently viewed at this time as a lyric form. Not infrequently it is discussed as if it were a somewhat distinct class of poetry, and at other times it is spoken of as "elegiac." A history of the criticism of the sonnet cannot be cramped into a footnote, but these facts are relevant to the present question: (1) Since its introduction into England, the sonnet has frequently been treated as if it were a somewhat independent form, a tendency still observable in modern anthologies of poetry, which often have a class of poems entitled "Lyrics" followed by one entitled "Sonnets." The independence of its early history and the precision with which its verse patterns and conventions can be described (although this clarity succeeded early confusion over the term "sonnet"; see Sidney Lee's *Elizabethan Sonnets* [Westminster, 1904], I, xxxiii) have encouraged the independent treatment which it has frequently received, but it is doubtful whether many critics who treated it separately thought it fundamentally unallied to any of the larger and older species of poetry. (2) An explanation of the occasional identification of the sonnet with the elegy would naturally also involve a history of the theory of the elegy, which from antiquity until modern times had been viewed as a species of poetry on the same level of division as epic, drama, lyric, etc. From the long history of the elegy, these facts have a particular bearing on our problem. The first fact deals with versification; the classical elegy was associated with alternate lines of hexameter and pentameter, and this alternateness was soon thought to be best suggested in English poetry by variation, not in line length, but in rhyme scheme. The generally recognized English "elegiac measure" was iambic pentameter rhymed a, b, a, b ("Elegy Written in a Country Church-Yard" and the English sonnet). The second fact is that the elegy was associated in the minds of Renaissance and neoclassical critics with the subjects of love and grief. These facts should help to explain why the elegy lost its status as a species in English criticism and became regarded as a lyric expression; in English poetry the elegy possessed no real critical grounds upon which it could be distinguished as a species from the lyric. But, from the sixteenth century on and therefore before the elegy was subsumed by the lyric, the sonnet was grouped among the minor lyric forms far more frequently than it was treated independently or allied with the elegy. The fact that the vogues of the sonnet and of the minor lyric were simultaneous during the late eighteenth century is also evidence that the sonnet then was generally thought to be lyric.

131. These are the results of Havens' comparison of the several volumes of Dodsley's *Collection of Poems:* "In the first three volumes (published in 1748) there are 57 pages devoted to blank verse, 132 to octosyllabics, 205 to stanzas, and 404, or nearly half, to couplets; in the last three (the fourth published in 1755, the fifth and sixth in 1758) 73 pages are given to blank verse, 146 to octosyllabics, 427 to stanzas, and 246 (practically a quarter) to couplets. It will be noticed that in the ten-year interval the stanzaic poems have exchanged places with those in couplets" (*op. cit.*, p. 434).

lustrious than Bowles, Brydges, the Della Cruscans, Hayley, Anna Seward, and Charlotte Smith. But their creative mediocrity raises a critical problem, for they did not acknowledge the slightness of their endowments and attempt only "the lower flights" of poetry. They were "poets" aspiring to more than a graceful pen with which to ask courtly favors. Their revival of "minor" lyric forms at the close of the century signifies that these forms were no longer regarded as "minor." The change in estimate is clearly suggested by Nathan Drake in his comments upon the sonnets of Bowles and Charlotte Smith. "In unaffected elegance of style, and in that pleasing melancholy which irresistibly steals upon and captivates the heart, they have excelled all other writers of the sonnet, and have shown how erroneous are the opinions of those who deem this species of composition beneath the attention of genius."[132]

Before the close of the eighteenth century the "minor" lyric forms were no longer beneath the attention of genius because they were viewed either as "beautiful" or as "sublime."

The Great Ode had been identified with the sublime almost as soon as England was aware of both; toward the end of the eighteenth century, after the beautiful came to be commonly viewed as an aesthetic completion of the sublime, the lesser lyric was identified with the lesser aesthetic pleasure, both originating primarily out of love. Thus the traditional scheme of the lyric was matched to the scheme of the new aesthetics. But, as the conjunction of the Great Ode with the concept of sublimity was not a mere matching of an example with a precept, affecting no alteration in either, so the completion of the proportion coupling the lesser aesthetic state of mind (the beautiful) with the lesser lyric was accompanied by changes in both critical concept and poetic form. Those "tender" emotions that in the late eighteenth century attached themselves to the "minor" lyric forms and raised them far above the level of the epigram and the "point" are emotions that take on "Romantic" hues when their shadings are added to their outlines. Nathan Drake has already been quoted, extolling the sonnets of Charlotte Smith and Bowles for "that pleasing melancholy which irresistibly steals upon and captivates the heart," and we shall see from other statements that before the end of the century tender melancholy had marked the lesser lyric as its own.[133] There was also a tendency to refine melancholy further to a kind having loneliness as a characteristic ingredient. Let us attempt a partial explanation of how emotional shadowings such as these fell across the outline of the beautiful and the "beautiful" or

132. Drake, *op. cit.*, I, 113–14.

133. Chapters v and vi of Eleanor Sickels' *The Gloomy Egoist* treat in detail the close relation between the vogue of melancholy and the revival of the sonnet and the shorter lyric forms.

"pathetic"[134] lyric during the eighteenth century. That we are dealing with no ultimate oddity should be evident from the fact that in the history of the succeeding period the chapter entitled "Romantic Terror" is no more extended than the chapter on "Romantic Melancholy." Viewed in terms of the past, Burke's distinction between the sublime and the beautiful is a separation of the two emotions which Aristotle thought were most powerful when combined in a single form—fear and pity. The eighteenth-century identification of sublimity with terror has been discussed. As for the beautiful, it was derived by both Addison and Burke from love, the personal and amatory, and, above that, from the love of general society, which culminates in pity.[135] The beautiful aspects of nature are those that are emotionally compatible and hence are gentle and "relaxing." It should not be too difficult, therefore, to penetrate the shadows that fall across Bowles's sonnets, remembered with such tenderness by Coleridge, or Gray's *Elegy*, which is better remembered by us. The poet places himself in some natural scene of beauty and hence among objects that are quiet, relaxing, and suggestive of the peace that the soul longs for. But amid this scene, often a quiet evening, the poet finds his thoughts turning to the objects that constitute the human half of beauty—to "general society," to use Burke's phrase, and to those aspects that arouse pity, and hence to the undeserved misfortunes that befall mankind as a whole: to countless Miltons unfulfilled, and to "hands, that the rod of empire might have sway'd." The poet's original loneliness now becomes a heightened fact—a hope, although admittedly an illusory one, that he is detached in this scene from the inexorable outside it. Or, not permitting the illusion, he may write, as Gray does, his own epitaph, commemorating the melancholy fact that as a lonely individual he awaits the fate of mankind.

But melancholy and loneliness are not the only "Romantic" hues that color the lesser lyric of the late eighteenth century; they are also characterized by such "Romantic" adjectives as "personal" and "spontaneous." When psychological considerations such as the "personal" and the "spontaneous" are used to bring together poems that tradition had classified primarily by their association with the subjects of love and wine, a new tradition of criticism is on the

---

134. Late-eighteenth-century critics of the lyric frequently use the term "pathetic" to indicate the range of "tender" emotions that is the higher component of the beautiful. It is in this sense that the word has continued to be commonly used. But this is a greatly restricted and altered meaning of the "pathetic" (πάθος) as used by Longinus, to whom it is the second source of the sublime and, as such, signifies "passions" as distinct from "thought," the first source of sublimity. In the neoclassical period it is also used in the large sense generally assigned to it by antiquity, and then it signifies the passionate content of poetry.

135. That the beautiful could be viewed as one or two is correlated with the fact that the lyric is sometimes divided into the sublime and the beautiful, and sometimes into the sublime, the pathetic, and the amatory.

way. The late eighteenth century turned the minor lyric to the tender, and the tender is generally personal, as the personal is generally contradicted by any sign of premeditation. These are new hues and modulations, and the life of poetry and, to a lesser extent, of criticism is in its hues rather than its outlines; but it should be a matter of record that the outline of the first literary criticism is discernible among these new modulations. Plato's poetry about gods and heroes is ancestral to the sublime, and, as for his poetry about "men," we should remember that to Addison and Burke the beautiful originated in the relationships between sexes and culminated in enlarged sympathies for men in general. But the new reappears if we recall that poetry about "men" to Plato ideally should represent "justice" and not melancholy or loneliness.

All these changes in the neoclassical conception of the lyric are clearly reflected, although not always in combination, by the following statements made before 1798. In 1785 John Pinkerton dismissed as ignorant most of those who had previously written on the subject of lyric poetry and asserted that a study of Greek models was necessary before any just distinctions concerning it could be made. "If we examine these models with care, we shall perceive that this species of poetry divides itself, in resemblance of the works of nature, into two kinds, the sublime, and the beautiful. In the first class Pindar stood without a rival till Gray appeared. In the second Anacreon and Sappho still remain without equal competitors."[136] In the same year Richard Polwhele in the "Advertisement" to his sonnets declared that sonnets were peculiarly suited to a depiction of the beautiful,[137] a restriction significantly not accepted by one of his reviewers, as we shall observe later. In the Preface to his "Sonnets, Love Elegies, and Amatory Poems," William Preston viewed the sonnet as essentially an expression of sentiments pathetic, mournful, genuine, and spontaneous:

> The sonnet will ever be cultivated, by those who write on tender and pathetic subjects. It is peculiarly adapted to the situation, of a man violently agitated, by a real passion, and wanting composure and vigour of mind, to methodize his thoughts, and undertake a work of length. The sonnet, from its shortness, and its dwelling simply on a single thought, is fitted to express a momentary burst of passion, and its tender and plaintive melody is calculated to accompany affecting and mournful sentiments, by congenial sounds.[138]

Whatever the English Romantic movement was or became, it began with men who lived before 1798, and whose early critical opinions could not have been influenced by their final performances. The critical opinions expressed

136. Pinkerton, *op. cit.*, p. 33.

137. "The Sonnet seems peculiarly turned to the Beautiful; and perhaps (in the Province of the Beautiful) the more pictoresque Objects of still Life" (*Pictures from Nature* [2d ed.; Exeter, 1786]).

138. *The Poetical Works of William Preston, Esq.* (Dublin, 1793), I, 268.

in this passage published posthumously in 1793 are much closer to the opinions of the young Romantics than to those propounded in the *Biographia literaria* (although it, too, is not a discontinuity from the past that we are tracing). In 1796 Lamb refused to accept any of Coleridge's corrections to his sonnets on the ground that the sonnet was too personal and tender a poetical form to be altered by anyone except the author himself: " 'Thinking on divers things foredone,' I charge you, Col., spare my ewe lambs, and tho' a Gentleman may borrow six lines in an epic poem (I should have no objection to borrow 500 and without acknowledging) still in a Sonnet—a personal poem—I do not 'ask my friend the aiding verse.' "[139] In this same year Coleridge wrote a Preface to a pamphlet of sonnets by himself, Lamb, Lloyd, and Southey. Detached from history, the critical opinions expressed in this preface seem eerie. Even though a poem be in the conventional sonnet scheme of fourteen lines, it is not a "sonnet," he declared, unless it develop "a lonely feeling."[140] He also opposed the Italian rhyme scheme, since it defeats the sonnet's purpose of expressing a momentary burst of passion.[141] History cannot possibly make this into a bright critical observation, but perhaps enough history has been given to make it believable.

The identification of the concept of the beautiful with the lesser lyric, while elevating that lyric group which early in the century puzzled critics by its affinities with the epigram, still left it a "lesser" class of poetry, the beautiful being the lesser component of the aesthetic experience. The beautiful, however, does not have sufficient dimension to match the aspirations of at least some of those late-eighteenth-century writers who passed over Shakespeare and took the sonnets of Milton for models. And the beautiful does not have the shading or scope to match a sonnet soon to be written opening with the line, "Milton! thou should'st be living at this hour." Nor is plaintive melancholy or loneliness the essential quality of many other memorable fourteen-line compositions by Wordsworth. But, before Wordsworth wrote sublime sonnets, others believed that they could.

In 1785 a reviewer refused to accept the limitations placed upon the sonnet by Richard Polwhele: "The 'Beautiful,' he observes, is characteristical of this 'miniature painting,' but that the 'Sublime' is incompatible with it. But in this we cannot agree with him when we recollect Mr. Edward's Sonnet 'On a Family Picture,' in Dodsley's Collection, vol. II."[142] Two years later, in the

---

139. *The Letters of Charles Lamb: To Which Are Added Those of His Sister, Mary Lamb*, ed. E. V. Lucas (London, 1935), I, 19.

140. *Poems by S. T. Coleridge* (2d ed.; London, 1797), p. 72.

141. *Ibid.*, pp. 73–74.

142. *Gentleman's Magazine*, LV (June, 1785), 461.

same magazine, a contributor signing himself "H. White" viewed the sonnet as suited to either the tender or the sublime.

The style of the sonnet should be nervous; and, where the subject will with propriety bear elevation, *sublime;* with which simplicity of language is by no means incompatible. If the subject is familiar and domestic, the style should, though affectionate, be vigorous, though plain, be energetic. The great models of perfection for the sublime and domestic sonnet are those of Milton's "To the Soldier to spare his Dwelling-place," and "To Mr. Laurence."[143]

And in "An Essay on the English Sonnet" this characterization of the sonnet is quoted and approved by a critic who, however, is indignant because the author of it could not find the quality of sublimity in Charlotte Smith's sonnets.[144]

Few of the late-eighteenth-century writers who deluged the printing facilities with lyric stanzas and sonnets left much in the way of critical opinion, and this is unfortunate. Not that great critical systems abounded then which perished for want of a publisher. But before there are new systems of thought, erected by the few who are able to penetrate and then systematize thought, there are generally new currents of opinions, dogmas, slogans, claims, and counterclaims. Both Plato and Aristotle recognized that the substructure of their philosophic wisdom was made out of the stones and straw of contemporary opinions. Undoubtedly, the minds of these late-eighteenth-century devotees of the lyric did not conceive of a universe in which, as to Coleridge, all apprehension and creation were fused together by the *"imagination, or esemplastic power,"* which in its primary aspect was "a repetition in the finite mind of the eternal act of creation in the infinite I AM." But, in the finite minds of at least some of these later-eighteenth-century poets, poetry had fused together into one and was an expression of the sublime imagination, even if the fusion was of very nebulous matter. The revaluation of such small particles as lyric stanzas came about as the result of a conjunctive change—one altering these little poems, and the other, of far greater significance, re-evaluating poetical values. For the principles which had long served to divide poetry into kinds and to arrange them in a hierarchy, extending from epic and tragedy down to epigram (which could not always be distinguished from the lesser lyric) were not first principles to the Romantics. By the principles fundamental to the Romantics, poetry in the highest sense was one as the soul is; it was constituted, as is the soul, of the elements of thought and feeling; if divisible into important kinds, it was divisible by some such system as Wordsworth used in arranging his poems according to the psychological faculty predominant

143. *Ibid.*, LVI ("Supplement for the year 1786"), 1110.

144. *Universal Magazine of Knowledge and Pleasure*, XCI (December, 1792), 410.

in the composition of each; and it was so indifferent to labor that a single sentence, a single image even, could be poetry with nothing essential omitted.

Fortunately, the letters of Anna Seward are voluminous and full of literary discussion. As one of the most admired zealots of the new school, she expresses opinions concerning the traditional hierarchy of poetical species that should give an insight into the minds of others like herself who believed, more correctly than they knew, that they were engaged in a creative and critical revolution. She angrily summarizes Mrs. Piozzi's ranking of poetical species: "You say Mr. M. [Merry] having only written odes and love verses, is neither an epic, a dramatic, nor a preceptive poet, and must therefore aspire only to a fame of a far lower kind, such as an *odist* may pretend to."[145] As far as "orders of composition" are concerned, she replies that she has always understood that the lyric ranks next to the epic, and she asserts that Shakespeare is the only dramatist whose fame exceeds that of Pindar, Horace, Dryden, and Gray. But her argument elevating the lyric to such a place in the traditional hierarchy of poetical kinds is not based upon premises that fundamentally interest her; her conclusion rests on the premise that "it matters little what order of composition is chosen by an highly sublimated imagination." This is also the position she took earlier in just as angry a letter to Miss Weston, who did not take as self-evident the proposition that the true qualities of poetic imagination "may be almost equally well conveyed in one form of composition as in another."[146] To demonstrate this proposition, Miss Seward turns an elegy by Lord Lyttleton, for which Miss Weston had declared a special affection, into three sonnets, and toward sonnets Miss Weston had expressed an outdated aversion.

We have several times observed that psychological criticism, whether Longinian or modern, views poetry from a perspective that elevates its lyric elements, the impassioned soul of the poet, and its verbal sign, of which none is more concentrated than the metaphor. Miss Seward, to whom little mattered but the highly sublimated imagination, thus without contradiction could say: "Our very peasants show that the seeds of poetry exist in the rude soil of their minds. Awaken their passions or excite their wonder, and you will often hear them speaking in metaphor, which is the poetic essence."[147]

145. *Letters of Anna Seward*, II, 376.
146. *Ibid.*, I, 259. 147. *Ibid.*, III, 320.

III

THE PHILOSOPHIC BASES OF ART
AND CRITICISM[1]

RICHARD McKEON

REFERENCE back to philosophic principles to expose erroneous assumptions and to establish common grounds for judgments of fact or value could not be justified easily by the record of its success in producing agreement. Philosophers have frequently expressed the expectation that philosophic disagreements would be resolved by applying scientific principles to a subject matter for the first time or that doctrinal disagreements in particular fields of inquiry or action would be removed by discovering and expounding philosophic principles. Yet doctrinal differences seem to have persisted, after each such effort at resolution, translated into more inclusive and more obstinate philosophic oppositions, and the differences of philosophers have disappeared because they have been forgotten more frequently than because they have been resolved. Long before the formulation of such convictions in present-day varieties of pragmatisms and positivisms, the practical man, the artist, the scientist, and the theologian expressed impatience with philosophic considerations because they were impertinent to operations considered urgent, or incompatible with attitudes defended as realistic, or inadequate for ends assumed to be ultimate. The pragmatic impatience with theory and the positivistic exposure of "unreal" problems, however, even in their abbreviated expressions, are philosophies; and the dialectical consequences of principles are particularly apparent, though unexamined, in those minimal philosophies which are expressions of conviction concerning the subject of an inquiry or concerning the method by which the inquiry must be pursued. For general principles, which may seem arbitrary or indefinite in theoretic formulation, have precise significances and consequences in particular applications; while particular things, which may be assumed to have an obvious and simple guise in the beliefs unchallenged in habitual practical operations, possess, without trace of inconsistency, other specifications and characteristics in scientific theory. The significances of all philosophies, even those which are satirized as remote from reality and indifferent to experience, are tested in application to particular subjects; but convictions concerning the nature of things, even those of unwilling philosophers who acknowledge only one dogma of reality, are tested by the

1. Reprinted from *Modern Philology*, November, 1943, and February, 1944.

persistent differences which are the outstanding fact of intellectual history. Whether or not certainty is thought to be possible in human and natural investigations, it is no less true that the nature of things, in so far as it is known, is determined by philosophic principles than that philosophic principles are determined, in so far as they are verified, by the nature of things.

Any general discussion expounds at once the principles of philosophy which it employs and the subject with which it is concerned; but, of all discussions in which philosophy finds an application, the criticism of art is influenced in a peculiarly nice balance by commitment to principle, determination by subject, and use of method. As viewed in its application to the practices or objects of art, the problems of criticism seem to be determined in any one theory by concrete and empirically ascertainable facts and to depend on principles which are determined by the same facts. As viewed in the statements of critics and philosophers, however, the problems of criticism seem to have been determined by a vast diversity of principles used in almost countless approaches, each applied to phenomena irrelevant to other critical precepts and criteria. There is as much disagreement concerning the nature of art or concerning what a poem is— whether it is what is seen on the page or what is heard, whether it is what is imagined by the poet or felt by his reader, or what is judged by the competent or what lies behind or above the expression of any poet[2]—as there is concerning the nature of being or concerning what may be said to be—whether only things in time and space exist, or whether existence can be attributed only to operations and relations, or whether to be is to be perceived, or whether true being is Ideal or God alone truly is; nor is there any more disagreement concerning beauty, form, imagination, or judgment than concerning truth, virtue, knowledge, or law, and much the same indeterminacy is found in the terms and principles chosen as appropriate in any of these discussions. Yet examination of discussions in the philosophy of art affords clearer insight into the nature of philosophic problems and principles than would other applications of philosophy, since its subject matter no less than its history renders improbable the supposition that the resolution of philosophic differences depends on preliminary agreement concerning the character or even the identity of objects treated in rival theories. For agreement concerning an object usually conceals principles, both those employed to arrive at agreement and those ignored lest they forestall it; and the multiplicity and subtle shadings of theories of art adumbrate the general patterns which reappear in philosophic discussions with less distortion than speculations in those branches of philosophy in which dog-

---

2. Cf. S. C. Pepper, "The Esthetic Object," *Journal of Philosophy*, XL (1943), 477–82; R. Wellek, "The Mode of Existence of a Literary Work of Art," *Southern Review*, VII (1942), 735–54.

matism is more plausible concerning the things which terms point to or designate. The subject matter of the philosophy of art is, whatever its technical definition, a human process and production, and it is therefore influenced by theory as is the subject matter of no other branch of philosophy. Natural philosophers may suggest operations according to the laws they discover, but the "nature" of things is not directly affected by physics, and even moral philosophers must find means by which to make their intellectual analyses indirectly effective by habituation or will, apathy or passions. Notwithstanding the tendency of idealists to argue that all things are thoughts, or of materialists to reduce thought to the motion of matter, or of dialecticians to repeat some form of Socrates' identification of virtue with knowledge, there is no real danger of confusing the other branches of philosophy with their subject matters, whereas the discussion of art is itself an art, and is, in many analyses, possessed of the same characteristics and directed to the same end as the arts it treats.

What men have said about art may be examined and interpreted for philosophic purposes to elucidate the operation of philosophic discussions in general; but such a use of statements will achieve its philosophic purpose only in the measure that the analysis clarifies the interpretation of theories of art, their oppositions, and their histories. Things and principles are not independent, since principles are employed in any statement of things and things are involved in any statement of principles. Consequently, the examination of theories that have been stated or employed, if it introduces order into the principles applied to things, will also indicate the nature of things which determine principles. Three kinds of data may be differentiated in approaching the problems of art by way of what has been said as a preliminary or as a check to treating ascertainable facts or to following the implications of defensible theories; for facts, principles, and judgments are not always separate in the statement of a critical judgment or even the formulation of a philosophic argument, but they are readily separated in the oppositions and controversies of philosophers. The philosophic principles and the methods of criticism are usually treated indirectly by arguing in detail, after the relevant objects of discussion have been chosen without argument, concerning the "real" nature of those objects. The nature of art, the appropriate methods of criticism, and the true principles of aesthetics are all in a sense determined by the facts and the phenomena; but we are dependent on the testimony of critics, sophisticated or naïve, for the report of phenomena and on the principles of philosophers, deliberate or haphazard, for the criteria of their choice and evaluation. The facts may therefore vary or be approached in different ways; the evaluation of the facts may depend on different principles or on principles differently interpreted; the statements of the critics and the principles of the philosophers, finally, become in their expression themselves "things" subject to evaluation and explanation, and they are not exempt from the relativity of art objects and evaluations.

The consequences of these variabilities in art and philosophy, as well as in criticism, are apparent in the difficulties which impede efforts to achieve common designation, mutual intelligibility, and objective evaluation. Since there is little relation between the subjects, the terms, or the principles of the various analyses of art, it is seldom easy to translate the statement of one analysis into an equivalent statement in another; or, if the translation is possible, to relate the two theories to the same subject; or, if they do bear on the same kind of data, to derive comparable evaluations of any given object. In the consequent relativity of criteria of truth and relevance, any thing may be identified as a work of art and any characteristic may make it good or bad of its kind; any judgment may seem as valid or as true as any other; and any theory may be set forth plausibly as the unique and absolute truth or, at least, as more probable than other theories. These difficulties are not to be solved, if what has been said of the nature of the discussion of art is correct, by referring the problem to irreducible and stubborn facts or (what is the same thing) to indisputable and appropriate theories, but by examining the meanings of the various explanations and their relations to one another and by formulating criteria for the truth and utility possible to such theories. For such purposes consideration of the nature of art and of the philosophy of art may properly be focused in the statements of the critic and philosopher, since those statements can be treated, without prejudice to fact or principles, first, in their relations to the various subjects to which their principles make them relevant; second, in their relations to other forms of judgment, like science, history, philosophy in general, and art itself; and, third, in their relations to the various terms in which they are stated and which in turn derive varying significances from the ends and criteria proper to criticism in its various modes.

I

The subject matter and meaning of statements about art—what art is and what one discusses when one discusses art—are determined by the principles of discussion and the things discussed, for the choice of things and of aspects of things relevant to a question is a way of choosing and determining their scope and use. Both the things which are the subject matter and the principles which determine the discussion must be discovered from examination of the terms in which the theories are stated. The words of the statements are themselves ambiguous, and the things which they designate or to which they refer in different theories are too numerous and unorganized to reveal interrelations or system in meanings unless they are arranged according to principles, either principles employed in the statements or principles borrowed for their interpretation from theories concerning references of signs, forms of judgment, ways of being. The latter adjustment occurs constantly in philosophic discussion and critical evaluation, for any theory can be stated in terms of any other theory, usually at considerable expense to its sense and cogency, and every theoretic statement involves, in so far as it is presented as true, as adequate, or simply as different, a judgment passed on other theories, usually removing the need for further consideration of them, since they turn out to be irrelevant to the facts, unscientific, an earlier stage in what has been a progressive march toward a truth which will never be absolute, impractical, or abstract. Yet for all the differences in their subject matters and in judgments about them, the principles which theoretic statements invoke seem to bear a simple relation to one another, at least definite enough to bring them into some contact with other theories and to make them echo or oppose statements of other philosophers. Principles which are independent or contradictory determine a meaning for the statements of opposed theories as definitely as the consistent and fruitful principles of a single system determine the meanings of statements within that system; and it should be possible, therefore, to elucidate controversies and oppositions, much as the meaning of any system is reconstructed and understood, by means of the principles involved.

The words which are used to state the principles and to determine the subject matter of modern discussions of art emerge fairly clearly in the statements of their oppositions. The basic question among present-day oppositions is, perhaps, whether one discusses art adequately by discussing something else or by discussing art, for, in the former case, other oppositions turn on what precise subject other than art should be discussed and, in the latter case, on what art itself is. The theories which have been based on the assumption that the meaning of art is explained best, or solely, by means of other phenomena have recently, as in the past, borrowed the principles and terminology of aesthetics and criticism from some fashionable science, from semantics, psychoanalysis, or economics, from sociology, morals, or theology. The art object and the art experience are then nothing in themselves, since they are determined by circumstances[3] and require, like the circumstances which determine them, bio-

3. Cf. John Dewey, *Art as Experience* (New York, 1934), p. 4: "In order to understand the meaning of artistic products, we have to forget them for a time, to turn aside from them and have recourse to the ordinary forces and conditions of experience that we do not usually regard as esthetic." For Dewey the relevant phenomena are basically biological; cf. *ibid.*, p. 18: "In life that is truly life, everything overlaps and merges. . . . To grasp the sources of esthetic experience it is, therefore, necessary to have recourse to animal life below the human scale." The work of art is treated, finally, in terms of experience; cf. *ibid.*, p. 64: "The real work of art is the building up of an integral experience out of the interaction of organic and environmental conditions and energies." It is not to be identified, except potentially, with a physical object; cf. *ibid.*, p. 162: "It has been repeatedly intimated that there

logical, social, psychological, or historical principles of explanation.[4] The theories which have been based on the assumption that aesthetic phenomena should be analyzed separately, whatever the complexities of the relations in which the aesthetic object or experience is involved, have sought principles in the construction and unity of the art object viewed in terms of expression (in which experience and intention are matched to form), composition (in which details are organized in form), or communication (in which emotion is evoked by form). The art object may then be isolated by a variety of devices. It may

---

is a difference between the art product (statute, painting, or whatever), and the *work* of art. The first is physical and potential; the latter is active and experienced." A similar endeavor animated by similar purposes may lead to the eventual separation of art from experience; thus, e.g., T. C. Pollock states as his purpose (*The Nature of Literature* [Princeton, 1942], p. xiii) "to lay a theoretical basis for the investigation of literature as a social phenomenon in terms which are consonant both with our contemporary knowledge of language and with the development of modern science"; and in pursuit of that purpose he finds it necessary to differentiate "experience" from "literature" and to define literature in terms of uses of language (*ibid.*, pp. 55–56). This is no theoretic distinction, since Dewey's inquiry would give importance to the continuity of the aesthetic with other experiences and to the problem of conferring an aesthetic quality on all modes of production (*op. cit.*, pp. 80–81), while Pollock's problem is one of differentiating the use of language from other parts of human experience and the literary from other uses of language. Or, again, the consideration of other phenomena and other problems seems sometimes to lead to the conclusion that all aesthetic considerations are in comparison abstract and false; cf. M. Lifshitz, *The Philosophy of Art of Karl Marx*, trans. R. B. Winn (New York, 1938), p. 5: "Even the eighteenth century, the classic age of aesthetics, could not remain confined to abstractions such as 'the beautiful' and 'the sublime.' In the background of purely aesthetic discussions concerning the role of genius, the value of art, the imitation of nature, practical problems of the bourgeois-democratic movement intruded themselves with increasing insistence." Theories themselves, finally, are sometimes refuted by reference not to what they state but to the conditions under which they are stated. Dewey, thus (*op. cit.*, p. 10), disavows the intention of engaging in an economic interpretation of the history of art but states his purpose "to indicate that *theories* which isolate art and its appreciation by placing them in a realm of their own, disconnected from other modes of experiencing, are not inherent in the subject-matter but arise because of specifiable extraneous conditions." Cf. Dewey, *Reconstruction in Philosophy* (New York, 1920), p. 24: "It seems to me that this genetic method of approach is a more effective way of undermining this type of philosophic theorizing than any attempt at logical refutation could be." The variety of ways in which earlier or other theories have been discovered to be impertinent, inadequate, or false would supply a significant schematism for the history of thought. Modern philosophic disputes are usually tangential: positions are most frequently attacked because they are not scientific or fail to treat the facts; they are defended usually, not as scientific and factual, but as indicating work to be done, the progress of science, and the impossibility of certainty.

4. The explanation sometimes involves the reduction of art to the laws of some other science; cf. N. Bukharin, "Poetry, Poetics and the Problems of Poetry in the U.S.S.R.," *Problems of Soviet Literature*, ed. H. G. Scott (New York, n.d.), p. 195: "Poetic creation and its product—poetry—represent a definite form of social activity, and are governed in their development, regardless of the specific nature of poetic creation, by the laws of social development." The explanation sometimes involves the abandonment of older analytical techniques and the use of science in preparation for specifically aesthetic questions; cf. Y. Hirn, *The Origins of Art: A Psychological and Sociological Inquiry* (London, 1900), p. 5: "Modern aesthetic, therefore, has still its own ends, which, if not so ambitious as those of the former speculative science of beauty, are nevertheless of no small importance. These ends, however, can no longer be attained by the procedure of the old aesthetic systems. As the problems have

be isolated by making criticism itself an art, as Spingarn did when he prescribed as the only possible method of criticism the question, "What has the
poet tried to express and how has he expressed it?"

All criticism tends to shift the interest from the work of art to something else. The
other critics give us history, politics, biography, erudition, metaphysics. As for me, I
re-dream the poet's dream, and if I seem to write lightly, it is because I have awakened,
and smile to think I have mistaken a dream for reality. I at least strive to replace one
work of art by another, and art can only find its *alter ego* in art.[5]

It may be isolated in relation to the artistic problem of creating art[6] or in relation to the aesthetic experience of perceiving art.[7] It may be isolated by the

---

changed with changing conditions, so too the methods must be brought into line with the
general scientific development. Historical and psychological investigation must replace the
dialectic treatment of the subject. Art can no longer be deduced from general philosophical
and metaphysical principles; it must be studied—by the methods of inductive psychology—as
a human activity. Beauty cannot be considered as a semi-transcendental reality; it must be
interpreted as an object of human longing and a source of human enjoyment. In aesthetic
proper, as well as in the philosophy of art, every research must start, not from theoretical
assumptions, but from the psychological and sociological data of the aesthetic life." It is impossible to deal with concrete works of art or to explain artistic activity in relation to them.
The tendency to engage in artistic production and artistic enjoyment for their own sake can be
explained only by studying the psychology of artists and their public; and, in this study of
the "art-impulse" and the "art-sense," the "art object" becomes an abstract and ideal datum.
Yet such a study will be relevant to problems of aesthetics and criticism; cf. *ibid.*, p. 17:
"Thus a theory of the psychological and sociological origins of art may furnish suggestions
for those which have been considered as distinctive of aesthetic proper, such as the critical
estimation of works of art, or the derivation of laws which govern artistic production." The
explanation is sometimes distinct from the purely artistic concerns to which it is nonetheless
pertinent; cf. H.Wölfflin, who finds that, of the three terms which he uses to analyze "style,"
one—"quality"—is artistically determined, while two—"expression" (which is the material
element of style) and "mode of expression" (which is vision)—are historically determined
(*Principles of Art History*, trans. M. D. Hottinger [New York, 1932], p. 11): "It is hardly
necessary here to take up the cudgels for the art historian and defend his work before a
dubious public. The artist quite naturally places the general canon of art in the foreground,
but we must not carp at the historical observer with his interest in the variety of forms
in which art appears, and it remains no mean problem to discover the conditions which, as
material element—call it temperament, *zeitgeist*, or racial character—determine the style of
individuals, periods, and peoples. Yet an analysis with quality and expression as its objects
by no means exhausts the facts. There is a third factor—and here we arrive at the crux of this
enquiry—the mode of representation as such. Every artist finds certain visual possibilities
before him, to which he is bound. Not everything is possible at all times. Vision itself has
its history, and the revelation of these visual strata must be regarded as the primary task of
art history."

5. J. E. Spingarn, "The New Criticism," *Criticism in America: Its Function and Status* (New
York, 1910), p. 14.

6. Cf. C. Bell, *Since Cézanne* (New York, 1922), p. 41: "In the pre-natal history of a
work of art I seem to detect at any rate three factors—a state of peculiar and intense sensibility, the creative impulse, and the artistic problem." *Ibid.*, p. 43: "The artistic problem is
the problem of making a match between an emotional experience and a form that has been
conceived but not created."

7. Cf. the statement of Matisse quoted by H. Read (*Art Now* [London, 1933], pp. 72–73):
"Expression for me is not to be found in the passion which blazes from a face or which is made

effort of the scientist to separate from extraneous considerations the form which determines the parts as well as the whole in a work of art.[8]

The echoes and apparent similarities which can be detected in modern discussions of art are due in part to the terms which emerge in them—"form" and "matter," "expression" and "content," or similar pairs of terms—differentiating principles of criticism bearing on organization or unity and materials organized or unified. Moreover, these principles of criticism are given content and precision by use of what seem to be comparable philosophic principles expressed in terms of "processes" and "relations," "symbols" and "effects." Yet, even within the broad modern orthodoxy in which problems are solved by operations and words, there are many warring sects who differ concerning the nature of operations and the analysis of symbols; and for each philosophic doctrine and substitute for metaphysics there is a variant interpretation of artistic form and aesthetic expression and of the material which is formed or expressed. The problem in each case is to locate the art object between artist and audience and in so doing to explain characteristics of the art object in terms suggested by that relation.

The opposition between those who examine the art object and those who examine the art object qua experience or act or symbol flows from two interpretations which can be put on those principles of criticism in view of opposed

---

evident by some violent gesture. It is in the whole disposition of my picture—the place occupied by the figures, the empty space around them, the proportions—everything plays its part. Composition is the art of arranging in a decorative manner the various elements which the painter uses to express his sentiments. In a picture every separate part will be visible and will take up that position, principal or secondary, which suits it best. Everything which has no utility in the picture is for that reason harmful. A work of art implies a harmony of everything together [*une harmonie d'ensemble*] : every superfluous detail will occupy, in the mind of the spectator, the place of some other detail which is essential."

8. Cf. K. Koffka, "Problems in the Psychology of Art," *Bryn Mawr Notes and Monographs*, IX (1940), 243–44: "We shall derive from this relationship a rule for the purity, or sincerity, of art. If, as we said, the artist wants to externalize a significant part of his own world with its particular ego-world relationship, then, if he is successful, the object which he creates will be such as to comply with the demanded relationship; and that means, looked at from the other side, that the way in which the Ego is drawn into the situation must be demanded by the art-object and not by any outside factors which, however they may be suggested by the art-object, are not part of it. And so we have arrived at what we call purity of art: demands on the Ego must not issue from sources that are extraneous to the art-object." Cf. also *ibid.*, pp. 246–47: "Thus what is 'extraneous' to a work of art, in the sense used in defining the purity of art, is determined by the subject and its self-limitation. We saw before that a work of art is a strongly coherent whole, a powerful *gestalt* and such self-limitation is a definite *gestalt*-property. But this determination of the term extraneous is still too narrow: a demand issuing from a part of an art object is extraneous, and, therefore, an effect produced by it artistically impure, if it is not itself demanded by the total pattern of the work. For a *gestalt* not only makes its own boundaries, but also within its boundaries rules and determines its parts in a sort of hierarchy, giving this a central position, this the rôle of a mere decorative detail, that the function of contrast, and so forth."

philosophic principles, for the structure of the object of art may be found in traits that it shares with the artist and his audience or in traits which distinguish the artist from the effects of his action and the audience from the stimulus to which it responds. The two interpretations of what seem similar or identical principles of criticism—"form" and "matter," "expression" and "content"— result from differences of analysis; they are not opposed in the sense that one is right and the other wrong (although either may be employed well or poorly by the critic), nor is the difference between them one that need be "resolved" or in which an appeal to the "facts" would embarrass either disputant. They are differences to be explained by the philosophic principles which underlie the use of the terms in criticism; and those philosophic principles, in turn, are expressed in similar terms of "process" and "symbol" interpreted either analogically in a dialectic of being and becoming[9] or literally in a logic of cause

9. Cf. K. Burke, *The Philosophy of Literary Form: Studies in Symbolic Action* (Baton Rouge, La., 1941), p. 124: "It is, then, my contention, that if we approach poetry from the standpoint of situations and strategies, we can make the most relevant observations about both the content and the form of poems. By starting from a concern with the various tactics and deployments involved in ritualistic acts of membership, purification, and opposition, we can most accurately discover 'what is going on' in poetry." *Ibid.*, pp. 89–90: "The general approach to the poem might be called 'pragmatic' in this sense: It assumes that a poem's structure is to be described most accurately by thinking always of the poem's function. It assumes that the poem is designed to 'do something' for the poet and his readers, and that we can make the most relevant observations about its design by considering the poem as the embodiment of this act. In the poet, we might say, the poetizing existed as a physiological function. The poem is its corresponding anatomic structure. And the reader, in participating in the poem, breathes into this anatomic structure a new physiological vitality that resembles, though with a difference, the act of its maker, the resemblance being in the overlap between writer's and reader's situation, the difference being in the fact that these two situations are far from identical." *Ibid.*, p. 102: "At every point, the content is functional—hence, statements about a poem's 'subject,' as we conceive it, will be also statements about the poem's 'form' " (cf. also *ibid.*, pp. 73–74). The dialectic of being and becoming is apparent in one of its most competent employments in Dewey's use of such terms as "form" and "expression" in the sense both of a process and of a product and in his treatment of "matter" in both connections. Cf. *Art as Experience*, p. 134: "Form as something that organizes material into the matter of art has been considered in the previous chapter. The definition that was given tells what form is when it is achieved, when it is there in a work of art. It does not tell how it comes to be, the conditions of its generation." *Ibid.*, p. 64: "An act of expression always employs natural material, though it may be natural in the sense of habitual as well as in that of primitive or native. It becomes a medium when it is employed in view of its place and rôle, in its relations, an[d] inclusive situation—as tones become music when ordered in a melody." *Ibid.*, p. 82: "Expression, like construction, signifies both an action and its result. The last chapter considered it as an act. We are now concerned with the product, the object that is expressive, that says something to us." Separation of these two meanings would in each instance be an error, and for this reason Dewey regrets the absence in English of a word that includes unambiguously what is signified by "artistic"—the act of production—and "aesthetic"—the act of perception and enjoyment (cf. *ibid.*, p. 46). Nor should artist and audience be separated, since "to perceive, a beholder must *create* his own experience" (*ibid.*, p. 54), nor matter from form, since "the truth of the matter is that what is form in one connection is matter in another and vice-versa" (*ibid.*, p. 128); and if one makes a conscious distinction of sense and thought, of matter and form, one does "not read or hear esthetically, for the esthetic value of the stanzas lies in the integration of the two" (*ibid.*, p. 132).

and effect.[10] This is a philosophic opposition, and the broad disputes concerning the possibility of conceiving or analyzing individual substances, natural or artificial, and concerning the reality of causes are only slightly transformed, in the discussion of artistic form and content, into disputes concerning the possibility or error of treating the form of the work of art independently of experience or strategies, the reality of the distinction of form and matter, and, most striking of all, the nature of matter—whether it is to be sought, on the one hand, in experience, tactics, emotions, temperament, *Zeitgeist*, racial characteristics or, on the other hand, in the "parts" of the work of art—and the nature of form appropriate to such matters.

When terms are defined by the method of analogy, the principles of the discussion are found in the fundamental metaphor or metaphors.[11] Poetry may be conceived as vision, contriving, or imitation, experience, imagination, or emotion, symbol, action, or relation. Any one of these may be generalized or specified to determine a sense in which all men, or the best of men, or the best of some peculiarly fortunate kind of men, are poets or poems,[12] since the traits of the poet or the structure or contents of the poem are universally those of mankind or even of the Deity and the universe or since the poem or its expression or the emotion it embodies is universally intelligible or universally moving or corresponds with and reflects aspects of the universe or since its effects are homogeneous with the common experience or aspirations of mankind. When terms are defined literally, the principles of the discussion are to be found in the causes by which an object is to be isolated in its essential nature. If poetry is to be treated as poetry, it must be differentiated by its qualities as a thing or by the nature of the judgment appropriate to it or by its effects. Such distinc-

10. Cf. Koffka, *op. cit.*, pp. 209–10: "Perhaps the reader is somewhat baffled as to the kind of object-characteristics we are speaking about. They are to be such as to affect the Selves directly, to play on their emotions; but where are such characteristics to be found in psychology? Indeed there was a time when psychology did not contain any place for such characteristics, when psychological data were reduced to sensations and their attributes, the secondary and some of the primary qualities of Locke. But psychology has changed a great deal since such a statement was true. Now it derives some of its most important explanatory concepts and principles from such perceptual qualities as round, angular, symmetrical, open; fast and slow, rough and smooth, graceful and clumsy; cheerful, glowering, radiant, gloomy —a list that could be continued through many pages. Let us add a few words about it. The examples in the first group, which the reader will be willing to accept at their face-value, show us a feature characteristic of all our samples: they are features that belong to extended wholes, not to atomic parts or points."

11. Burke (*op. cit.*, p. 26) recognizes in the synecdoche the " 'basic' figure of speech" for "both the structure of poetry and the structure of human relations outside poetry."

12. Cf. Coleridge, *Biographia literaria*, chap. xiv (*The Complete Works of Samuel Taylor Coleridge*, ed. Shedd [New York, 1853], III, 373): "My own conclusions on the nature of poetry, in the strictest use of the word, have been in part anticipated in some of the remarks on the Fancy and Imagination in the first part of this work. What is poetry?—is so nearly the same question with, what is a poet?—that the answer to the one is involved in the solution of the other" (cf. above, n. 9).

tions are possible only in the context of a philosophy, consciously or unconsciously employed, in which sciences are distinguished from one another by principles and subject matter and in which the same object, undefined but identified in time and space, is properly treated in the variety of subject matters relevant to its characteristics—physical, psychological, moral, political, and aesthetic. By the use of the analogical method a trait or some traits suggested by the poem, by the poet, or by the audience are used to explain all three—as life is explained by synecdoche, poems by actions, and poets by qualities intended to distinguish man from the brute and assimilate him to God—and all aspects of poetry are included in one analysis. By the use of the literal method the aesthetic analysis of poetry is concentrated on characteristics properly attributed to the poem, and other problems are treated in other sciences—the ideas and emotions which the poet sought to express or those which a given audience experienced are treated in psychology, if it is a question of the thought of the poet or the reaction of the audience, or in rhetoric, if it is a question of means and medium, while the moral and political consequences of the poem, if they are considered, require analysis in terms of virtues, actions, and institutions; and the poem as conceived in terms of its various causes and effects is distinct from the poem conceived in terms of structure and form. Properly executed and understood, a complete analysis by the one method should treat all characteristics considered by the other and should even result in comparable judgments: aesthetic, moral, psychological, and practical. But even in that happy coincidence, the statements of the two analyses would clash on every point. There is doubtless but one truth in aesthetics as in other disciplines, but many statements of it are found to be adequate, more are partially satisfactory, and even more have been defended.

Such differences in the philosophic principles which determine the force and application of principles of criticism indicate a second dimension of variation, for even the discussion of the meaning of "process," "relation," and "symbol" —whether they are to be interpreted analogically and organistically or literally and causally—involves the recognition, if only by gestures and asides to discredited and obsolete opponents, that other principles have sometimes been used. In the literal discussion of principles it is a problem of fundamental qualities, sequence of causes, and order of discrimination. The *poem* may be fundamental in the sense that poetic effects can be identified for examination and poets can be recognized for description only if the stimulus of the one and the product of the other possess a distinguishable poetic quality. The *poet* may be fundamental in the sense that poetic composition can be treated as a poem, and its proper poetic effects can be differentiated from the accidental associations of an uninitiated audience, only by appreciating the intent of the poet.[13] The *effects* may be fundamental in the sense that an unexperienced poem is no aesthetic object, whatever the virtues of its form and structure, and the poem variously understood is not one but many objects.

In the analogical discussion of principles the same shifts of emphasis may be detected in the fundamental metaphor which is derived originally from poet, poem, or audience and is then applied to all three (as when experience, symbolic act, or creation characterize all three)[14] or restricted to two (as when poet and poem are conceived on a different level of experience or imagination from those which characterize even the prepared reader)[15] or restricted to one (as

13. This process may apparently be carried through a series of steps if one is asked to consider the writer (say, of this paper) who considers the critic who considers the artist (who might conceivably consider, as Peacock did, the intellectual ancestors of the writer who considered the critic). Cf. D. A. Stauffer, Introduction, *The Intent of the Critic* (Princeton, 1941), p. 5: "His opinion is a safe guide, therefore, only if we know Coleridge the critic as well as we know *Hamlet*, the play criticized. Such examples of the necessity of rectifying a critical pronouncement by some inquiry into the critic's character and bias and intention might be multiplied. They show the question, 'What is the intent of the critic?' may be as important to the reading public as the prior question, 'What is the intent of the artist?' is to the critic himself.'"

14. Cf. above, n. 9, for Burke's differentiation of poet, poem, and reader in terms of physiology and anatomy. Poetry, so conceived, is part of our natures, and all men are poets. The symbol of this may be found in men's lives and their susceptibilities to the universal poetry of nature; cf. R. W. Emerson, "The Poet" (*Works* [Boston, 1929], II, 15–17): "Every man is so far a poet as to be susceptible of these enchantments of nature; for all men have the thoughts whereof the universe is the celebration. I find that the fascination resides in the symbol. Who loves nature? Who does not? Is it only poets, and men of leisure and cultivation, who live with her? No; but also hunters, farmers, grooms and butchers, though they express their affection in their choice of life and not in their choice of words. . . . The people fancy they hate poetry, and they are all poets and mystics!" Sometimes the poetry of nature may take narrow, or even geographic, boundaries in the special sensibilities of a people; cf. W. Whitman, *Leaves of Grass*, Preface to the original edition (1855) (London, 1881), pp. 1–2, 4–5: "The Americans of all nations at any time upon the earth, have probably the fullest poetical nature. The United States themselves are essentially the greatest poem. In the history of the earth hitherto the largest and most stirring appear tame and orderly to their ampler largeness and stir. Here at last is something in the doings of man that corresponds with the broadcast doings of the day and night. . . . Their manners, speech, dress, friendships —the freshness and candour of their physiognomy—the picturesque looseness of their carriage . . . —the terrible significance of their elections—the President's taking off his hat to them, not they to him—these, too, are unrhymed poetry." Or, again, the poetic nature, although essential to mankind, may be possessed in varying degrees; cf. W. C. Bryant, *Prose Writings*, ed. Parke Godwin (New York, 1884), I, 13–14: "In conclusion, I will observe that the elements of poetry make a part of our natures, and that every individual is more or less a poet. In this 'bank-note world,' as it has been happily denominated, we sometimes meet with individuals who declare that they have no taste for poetry. But by their leave I will assert they are mistaken; they have it, although they may have never cultivated it."

15. If all men are poets, it is then imperative either to introduce a distinction of degree, completeness, or kind to distinguish the poets from other men or to distinguish the poetic from the appreciative or critical processes. Emerson, following the first of these alternatives, makes the poet representative among partial men and finds half of man in his expression; cf. *op. cit.*, II, 5: "The breadth of the problem is great, for the poet is representative. He stands among partial men for the complete man, and apprises us not of his wealth, but of the common wealth. The young man reveres men of genius, because, to speak truly, they are more himself than he is. They receive of the soul as he also receives, but they more." Lowell distinguishes two lives, one of which the poet nourishes; cf. "The Function of the Poet,"

when poets are said to aspire to express a vision which cannot be stated adequately in any poem or be experienced fully by any audience).[16]

Literally or analogically conceived, therefore, the philosophic principles which lie behind the discussions of the critic select for him, by defining his terms, a subject matter and principles from the vast diversity which those terms

Century, XLVII (1894), 437: "Every man is conscious that he leads two lives, the one trivial and ordinary, the other sacred and recluse; the one which he carries to the dinner-table and to his daily work, which grows old with his body and dies with it, the other that which is made up of the few inspiring moments of his higher aspiration and attainment, and in which his youth survives for him, his dreams, his unquenchable longings for something nobler than success. It is this life which the poets nourish for him and sustain with their immortalizing nectar." Lowell emphasizes the likenesses which makes poets men intelligible to other men rather than the differences in the poet's observation which set him apart; cf. "The Life and Letters of James Gates Percival" (*Works* [Boston and New York, 1891], II, 156–57): "The theory that the poet is a being above the world and apart from it is true of him as an observer only who applies to the phenomena about him the test of a finer and more spiritual sense. That he is a creature divinely set apart from his fellow-men by a mental organization that makes them mutually unintelligible to each other is in flat contradiction with the lives of those poets universally acknowledged as greatest." The second of the two alternatives is involved in definitions of poetry which derive from the genius of the poet or the differentiation of the poem relative to creator and to critic. Coleridge thus relates his definition of poetry to genius; cf. *Shakespeare: With Introductory Matter on Poetry, the Drama, and the Stage* (*Works*, IV, 21–22): "To return, however, to the previous definition, this most general and distinctive character of a poem originates in the poetic genius itself; and though it comprises whatever can with any propriety be called a poem (unless that word be a mere lazy synonyme for a composition in metre), it yet becomes a just, and not merely discriminative, but full and adequate, definition of poetry in its highest and most peculiar sense, only so far as the distinction still results from the poetic genius, which sustains and modifies the emotions, thoughts, and vivid representations of the poem by the energy without effort of the poet's own mind,—by the spontaneous activity of his imagination and fancy, and by whatever else with these reveals itself in the balancing and reconciling of opposite or discordant qualities, sameness with difference, a sense of novelty and freshness with old or customary objects, a more than usual state of emotion with more than usual order, self-possession and judgment with enthusiasm and vehement feeling,—and which, while it blends and harmonizes the natural and the artificial, still subordinates art to nature, the manner to the matter, and our admiration of the poet to our sympathy with the images, passions, characters, and incidents of the poem. . . ." Samuel Johnson accounts for the changes of judgment and taste by distinguishing the poetry based on nature and truth from that of fanciful invention; cf. "Preface to Shakespeare," in *Johnson on Shakespeare*, ed. Raleigh (London, 1929), p. 11: "But because human judgment, though it be gradually gaining upon certainty, never becomes infallible; and approbation, though long continued, may yet be only the approbation of prejudice or fashion; it is proper to inquire, by what peculiarities of excellence *Shakespeare* has gained and kept the favour of his countrymen. Nothing can please many, and please long, but just representations of general nature. Particular manners can be known to few, and therefore few only can judge how nearly they are copied." According to Matthew Arnold, the critical power is of a lower rank than the creative; cf. "The Function of Criticism at the Present Time," *Essays in Criticism: First Series* (London, 1910), p. 4: "The critical power is of lower rank than the creative. True; but in assenting to this proposition one or two things are to be kept in mind. It is undeniable that the exercise of the creative power, that a free creative activity, is the highest function of man; it is proved to be so by man's finding in it his true happiness. But it is undeniable, also, that men may have the sense of exercising this free creative activity in other ways than in producing great works of literature or art; if it were not so, all but a very few men would be shut out from the true happiness of all men."

16. The content and aspiration of poetry are so lofty that in the fullest sense they may exceed not merely the appreciation of the audience but the powers of the poet, and therefore Emerson concludes that we have no poems, although we do have poets; cf. "Poetry and

might encompass. If the poet is the source of distinctions or analogies, the discussion may be of character, knowledge, or technique; or of imagination, taste, or genius; or of beauty, truth, or moral goodness. If the poem is fundamental, all problems may be translated into those of form and content; or of imitation and object; or of thought, imagination, and emotions; or of activity and effects. The effects finally, if they are fundamental, may be treated in terms of expression and communication; or of context and moral, social, economic, or semantic determination; or of influence and emotion.

The critic's discrimination of poet, poem, and effect, like the philosopher's preoccupation with process and relation, is only one part or possibility selected from a larger intellectual pattern which extends beyond, and is constantly intruded into, the more limited vocabularies of the conversations and disputes about art which are expressed in terms of operations and symbols. The principles of art have been sought in the nature of things and in the faculties of man as well as in the circumstances of artistic production or the effects of aesthetic contemplation. The "things" which have been considered have been various—the products of human activities or the materials from which they have been worked, the activities or the ideas and emotions from which they originated, and the poet or man himself. Philosophers who treat art in terms of things may seek poetic or dialectical principles, in the former case differentiating the artificial things which are made by man from the natural things which are the subject matter of physics, and in the latter case discovering the qualities of art in nature, which is a "poem" or a "book" or a "creation" or an "imitation." The "faculties" have been used as causes of the production of art objects or as means of their appreciation, and philosophers who seek epistemological or psychological principles in the human faculties either distinguish the visions, powers, and performances of artists from those of other men or treat scientists, moralists, politicians, and even mankind as essentially, though in varying de-

---

Imagination," *Letters and Social Aims* (Boston, 1883), p. 74: "Poems!—we have no poem. Whenever that angel shall be organized and appear on earth, the Iliad will be reckoned a poor ballad-grinding. I doubt never the riches of Nature, the gifts of the future, the immense wealth of the mind. O yes, poets we shall have, mythology, symbols, religion, of our own." Lowell, on the other hand, distinguishes two functions which are united in the poet—the function of the seer and that of the maker—and which facilitate the distinction between what he sees and what he expresses; cf. *op. cit.*, pp. 432-33: "And however far we go back, we shall find this also—that the poet and the priest were united originally in the same person; which means that the poet was he who was conscious of the world of spirit as well as that of sense, and was the ambassador of the gods to men. This was his highest function, and hence his name of 'seer.' . . . Gradually, however, the poet as the 'seer' became secondary to the 'maker.' His office became that of entertainer rather than teacher. But always something of the old tradition was kept alive. And if he has now come to be looked upon merely as the best expresser, the gift of seeing is implied as necessarily antecedent to that, and of seeing very deep too."

grees, poets. The "processes" have been the actions and operations, causes and effects, relations and wholes by which men have been prepared to produce objects or to be affected by them; and operational or semantic principles are sought either by distinguishing the symbols or effects of art from those of science, practical affairs, and nature or by stating all human concerns and all knowledge in terms of pragmatic and symbolic analyses. The discrimination of such principles and systems is to be found, not in differences in the gross scope of possible statement, but in what is taken as fundamental and in the precision or effectiveness with which details can be treated. A discussion which is primarily concerned with the effects of art will entail consequences which bear on the nature of works of art and on the nature or intention of the artist; and all schools of philosophers, whether they talk realistically about the work of art or idealistically about the imagination or the conditions of aesthetic judgment or pragmatically about the experience of art, will be able to state and defend metaphysical and psychological, moral, and aesthetic judgments appropriate to their principles and approaches.

The contemporary writers whose statements concerning art and criticism have been used to illustrate a pattern in modern discussions, therefore, exemplify the "philosophic temper of the present" in the sense that they talk in terms of operations and consequent relations, and the dogma is widespread among those who use this vocabulary—among philosophers as well as others who profess an interest in philosophic principles, among physicists who write on the freedom of the will and God, sociologists who write about ideologies and "stages" of knowledge, educators who reform curricula with a view to the "circumstances" of the world today or tomorrow—that there are no independent things or "substances" and that the "faculties" of the mind—and the mind itself—are fictions. Within that terminological agreement, however, all the old disputes concerning principles seem to have survived in methodological oppositions which have introduced splits between pragmatists who would choose significant questions by the criterion of operations and logicians who talk of operations but find it desirable to distinguish operations concerned with things from operations concerned with words or, further, to distinguish words which designate things from words which designate other words; and between linguists for whom things and words are sufficient to explain the phenomena of communication and proof and semanticists who require, in addition, some treatment of meanings or even emotions and motives. These differences of content in the principles signified by the same words are clarified in the broader discussion of principles signified by other words, for the ancient problems involved, though unrecognized, in the oppositions of contemporary doctrines, are only gradually uncovered in the progress of disputes; and verbally different statements of similar conceptions serve to set apart the different conceptions contained in statements that are verbally similar.

The subject matter of discussions of art is determined by three considerations which bear on things and which depend on principles: first, the determination of the kind of things appropriate to the discussion is stated in general philosophic principles; second, the determination of the mode of classifying such things depends on the methodological definition of principles; third, the determination of the characteristics relevant to the evaluation of such things is stated in the principles of criticism. The meaning and the subject of any critical judgment depend on all three considerations, although writers who use the same or similar terms may agree on one or more, while differing on other determinations of their meanings. Plato and Aristotle, thus, seek general philosophic principles in the nature of things, while Bacon and Kant seek them in the human understanding, and Horace and Tolstoy seek them in operations. Yet each of these pairs, although associated in the choice of philosophic principles, is divided both by the methodological determination and use of those principles and by the principles of criticism determined by them. For all the similarities of their statements, therefore, the six philosophers treat six distinct, though intricately related, subject matters in their analyses of art.

Plato and Aristotle both discuss the nature of art in terms of imitation. Plato, however, uses the distinction of poet (or maker), model (or object of imitation), and imitation (or construction) to state the principles of his physics as well as his aesthetics and so to account for all things,[17] while for Aristotle those principles are the means of differentiating artificial from natural things; but, although human nature, in the poet and in his audience, is used in his analysis to account for the natural causes and origin of poetry, the principles of Aristotle's aesthetics, as derived from imitation, are the object, the means, and the manner of imitation.[18] As a consequence, although Plato and Aristotle both talk about imitation and about things, they talk about different things. Plato's discussion of poetry is about men, or men and gods, those imitated in the poem, those influenced by the poem, the poets who write the poems and find themselves in competition with lawgivers, rhetoricians, and dialecticians—inferior to all who know the truth and sixth among the lovers of beauty—and

17. *Timaeus* 28C ff.; *Republic* x. 596A ff.; *Sophist* 234A–B. For a fuller discussion of the point treated in this paragraph, see above, pp. 149–68. These passages and the others from Plato, as well as those from Aristotle, Longinus, and Vico quoted in this essay, are translated by the author.

18. The arts are differentiated according to differences of their means, objects, and manners in the first three chapters of the *Poetics*; the natural causes and origin of poetry are then taken up in chapter 4. 1448b4 ff. Once the definition of tragedy has been given, the six parts of tragedy are discriminated as means, objects, and manner of imitation (cf. *Poet.* 6. 1450a7 ff.).

the universe which is also a living creature and an imitation; whereas Aristotle's discussion of poetry is about tragedy and epic poetry, their plots which are their end or their soul, and their parts.[19]

Kant and Bacon, similarly, both discuss the nature of art in terms of imagination. Kant, however, differentiates the faculties of understanding, reason, and judgment in order to treat the representations of imagination and the judgments of taste; like Aristotle, who distinguishes theoretic, practical, and poetic sciences, he differentiates theoretic and practical knowledge from aesthetic judgment; but, like Plato, whose analysis of art applies equally well to nature, he finds the principles of his analysis, not in the arts or their products, but in the judgment of beauty which applies to nature as well as to art and which has affinities with the judgment of the sublime as well as with the understanding of the purposiveness of nature.[20] Bacon, on the other hand, differentiates poesy from history and philosophy by relating them to the three parts of man's understanding—imagination, memory, and reason—respectively; like Aristotle, he treats poetry in particular rather than the conditions of art in general, he distinguishes it from history, and he divides it into kinds (narrative, representative, and allusive); but, like Plato, he merges aesthetic with moral judgments.[21]

19. The early treatment of music in the *Republic* is in terms of its subject matter, under which is considered the adequacy of tales to the gods, heroes, and men portrayed (*Rep*. ii. 376E—iii. 392C); its diction, under which is considered the effect of imitative speech on character (*ibid*. 392C–398B); and its manner, under which is considered the effect of modes and rhythms (*ibid*. 398C–403C). We shall be true musicians only when we recognize temperance, courage, liberality, high-mindedness, and the other virtues and their contraries in their various combinations and images (*ibid*. 402C; cf. also *ibid*. viii. 568A–B; x. 607A). Poets, rhetoricians, and lawgivers who write with knowledge of the truth are to be called "philosophers" (*Phaedrus* 278C–D; cf. also *Laws* vii. 811C–E); poets are in competition with lawgivers (*Rep*. iii. 398A–B; *Laws* vii. 817A–D; ix. 858D). For the low place of the poet in the hierarchy of lovers cf. *Phaedrus* 248C ff.; and for the universe as a creation of divine art cf. *Soph*. 265C ff. According to Aristotle, the plot is the principle and, as it were, the soul of tragedy (cf. *Poet*. 6. 1450ª38); it is the end and purpose of tragedy (*ibid*. 1450ª22); it is the first and most important thing in tragedy (*ibid*. 7. 1450ᵇ21). The analysis treats of tragedy in terms of the unity and the parts of tragedies.

20. Kant, *Critique of Judgement*, trans. J. H. Bernard (London, 1914), Introduction, pp. 7 ff.: Part I, Div. I, Book II, "Analytic of the Sublime," § 23, "Transition from the Faculty Which Judges of the Beautiful to That Which Judges of the Sublime," pp. 101 ff.; Part II, "Critique of the Teleological Judgement," pp. 259 ff. The nature and the analysis of the Beautiful is distinct from the nature and analysis of the moral, yet the Beautiful may be a symbol of the morally Good; cf. Part I, Div. I, Book I, § 42, pp. 176–77: "Thus it would seem that the feeling for the Beautiful is not only (as actually is the case) specifically different from the Moral feeling; but that the interest which can be bound up with it is hardly compatible with moral interest, and certainly has no inner affinity therewith"; and Div. II, § 59, pp. 250–51: "Now I say the Beautiful is the symbol of the morally Good, and that it is only in this respect (a reference which is natural to every man and which every man postulates in others as a duty) that it gives pleasure with a claim for the agreement of every one else" (cf. also *ibid*., § 52, pp. 214–15).

21. *Of the Proficience and Advancement of Learning*, Book II (*The Works of Francis Bacon*, ed. Spedding, Ellis, and Heath, III [London, 1857], 329, 343 ff.); *De augmentis scientiarum*, Book II, chap. xiii (*Works*, IV [London, 1858], 314 ff.). Aristotle's distinction is that poetry

As a consequence, although Bacon and Kant both talk about the imagination and the human understanding, the "imagination" of Bacon is a cognitive faculty, whereas the "imagination" of Kant is a faculty of presentation. Bacon's discussion of poetry is, therefore, about a branch of learning considered as form and matter, whereas Kant's discussion of art is about a form of judgment which relates the presentations of imagination to the concepts of reason and understanding and which applies to natural and artistic beauty.[22]

Horace and Tolstoy, finally, both discuss the nature of art in terms of operations. Tolstoy, however, defines art as a human activity which serves as a means of bringing about a community among men and of furthering their welfare.

Art is a human activity consisting in this, that one man consciously, by means of certain external signs, hands on to others feelings he has lived through, and that others are infected by these feelings and also experience them.

Art is not as the metaphysicians say, the manifestation of some mysterious Idea of beauty or God; it is not, as the esthetical physiologists say, a game in which man lets off his excess of stored-up energy; it is not the expression of man's emotions by external signs; it is not the production of pleasing objects; and, above all, it is not pleasure; but it is a means of union among men, joining them together in the same feelings and indispensable for the life and progress towards well-being of individuals and of humanity.[23]

is more philosophic and graver than history, since its statements are rather of the nature of universals, whereas those of history are singulars (*Poet.* 9. 1451ᵇ5). Bacon draws his distinction from the matter of poetry and therefore makes the difference between poetry and history more nearly analogous to Plato's distinction between knowledge and opinion than to Aristotle's formal distinction between kinds of probability; and, as a consequence, he excludes, as parts of philosophy and parts of speech, all forms of poetry (satires, elegies, epigrams, odes, and the like) except the three which are treated as forms of feigned history, and he derives the moral judgment of poetry from this difference between it and history; cf. *De augmentis scientiarum*, Book II, chap. xiii, pp. 315–16: "As for Narrative Poesy,—or Heroical, if you like so to call it (understanding it of the matter, not of the verse)—the foundation of it is truly noble, and has a special relation to the dignity of human nature. For as the sensible world is inferior in dignity to the rational soul, Poesy seems to bestow upon human nature those things which history denies to it; and to satisfy the mind with the shadows of things when the substance cannot be obtained. For if the matter be attentively considered, a sound argument may be drawn from Poesy, to show that there is agreeable to the spirit of man a more ample greatness, a more perfect order, and a more beautiful variety than it can anywhere (since the Fall) find in nature. And therefore, since the acts and events which are the subjects of real history are not of sufficient grandeur to satisfy the human mind, Poesy is at hand to feign acts more heroical; since the successes and issues of actions as related in true history are far from being agreeable to the merits of virtue and vice, Poesy corrects it, exhibiting events and fortunes according to merit and the laws of providence; since true history wearies the mind with satiety of ordinary events, one like another, Poetry refreshes it, by reciting things unexpected and various and full of vicissitudes. So that this Poesy conduces not only to delight but also to magnanimity and morality. Whence it may be fairly thought to partake somewhat of a divine nature; because it raises the mind and carries it aloft, accommodating the shows of things to the desires of the mind, not (like reason and history) buckling and bowing down the mind to the nature of things." Cf. also *Of the Proficience and Advancement of Learning*, p. 343.

22. Kant, *op. cit.*, Part I, Div. I, Book I, § 23, pp. 101 ff., and § 45, pp. 187 ff.

23. *What is Art?* trans. A. Maude, in *Tolstoy on Art* (Oxford, 1924), p. 173.

Tolstoy's judgment of art, like Plato's, is predominantly moral, and, like Kant, he would attribute to art an important function in uniting theoretical knowledge and practical precepts. Horace, on the other hand, is concerned with the effects of poetry, not as they might be manifested in a moral, social, and religious union of mankind, but as they might be formulated in an "art" of poetry as practical precepts to instruct poets in their function, resources, and ends,[24] and in view of those ends to set forth the means poets should employ if they wish to please Roman audiences and to attain lasting fame. Wisdom is the principle and fountain of good writing, in the sense that moral philosophy and the Socratic pages will furnish the poet material;[25] and poets aim to teach or to please or to profit and amuse at the same time, in the sense that they attract the applause of the elderly by utility, of the young by amusement, and of all if they can blend the two.[26] Like Aristotle, Horace treats of poetry and its kinds, of the parts and the essential unity of the poem; and his analysis of poetry, like Bacon's, consists in treating the various kinds of subjects and the words and meters in which they can be adorned. As a consequence, although Horace and Tolstoy both consider the processes by which a poet fashions a work and the work influences an audience, the processes are entirely different in their respective treatments. For Horace they are external and causal: the poet uses any appropriate materials, old or new, in appropriate verbal form to win the approval of a select, though heterogeneous, audience. For Tolstoy the processes are internal and organic to mankind as a whole: the artist finds his material in feelings, and he makes that material intelligible to all by the form of his statement, in which the feelings are made infectious and by which mankind is united and improved.

If critics and philosophers sometimes find their subject matter in "beauty" and the "sublime," or "taste" and the "imagination," or "action" and "experience," whereas other critics and philosophers treat of poetry, or even of tragedy, the epic, and the lyric, or painting, sculpture, and music, the choice is not arbitrary or without consequences, but follows the methodological devices by which they employ their principles. Aristotle, Bacon, and Horace make use of different philosophic principles, since Aristotle treats of poetry by considering the poem as an artificial object, Bacon by considering it as a branch of learning subject to imagination, and Horace by considering it as a product of the poetic processes of composition; yet they agree methodologically, since they all begin their analyses with, and seek their principles in, a specifically human product, faculty, or activity for the purpose of discovering what is peculiar, in their respective approaches, to poetry or to some kind of poetry. Plato, Kant, and Tolstoy likewise make use of different philosophic principles, since

24. *Ars poetica* 304–8.
25. *Ibid.* 309–11.   26. *Ibid.* 333–44.

Plato treats of beauty and art in terms of an eternal pattern for imitation, Kant in terms of the a priori conditions of judgment, and Tolstoy in terms of an achievable perfection in human relations; yet they agree methodologically, since they all begin their analyses with, and seek their principles in, something fundamental in the nature of things, or the human faculties, or the community of feelings, which conditions in varying degrees all things, all imaginations, or all actions. What is essential in the one approach is accidental in the other. The philosopher who begins with beauty seldom has difficulty in discriminating or treating various kinds of art or even various kinds of poetry, although, to be sure, he frequently finds nothing real in the arts to correspond to the distinctions of "genres"; and the philosopher who begins with kinds of art objects usually has something to say of beauty, if only to identify it with some aspect of structure, or perception, or pleasure. The evaluation of the facts, so defined by principles and methods appropriate to them, requires a third step—the choice of the principles of criticism. The judgment of art as art may be separated from the consideration of its effects in education, morals, politics, and all the other relations which art may have to human institutions and activities; and thus Aristotle, Kant, and Horace separate the moral from the specifically aesthetic problem, while making provision, each in his way, for the indirect relation of the two problems—Aristotle by treating the moral and social effects of art in the *Politics*, Kant by relating the beautiful and the good while separating judgment and practical reason, Horace by using the moral precepts among the material to be transformed by the poet. The same facts about the objects of art may be evaluated, on the other hand, in such fashion that there is no separation of the aesthetic from other aspects of human activities, social institutions, or natural processes, except possibly for a tendency in such organic judgments to develop a fundamentally moral, economic, sociological, or religious bias, and thus Plato, Bacon, and Tolstoy each makes use of a moral criterion appropriate to his approach to the criticism of poetry and art—Plato requiring a knowledge of the Good, Bacon requiring the imagination of acts and events more agreeable to the merits of virtue and vice, Tolstoy requiring the perfecting of mankind. Differences which seem inconsequential or insoluble—such as those involved in the long discussions concerning whether painting, music, and poetry are the same essentially but different in detail, or different essentially though similar in some respects, or concerning whether art should be considered in itself or in its contexts, or whether the good, the beautiful, and the true mutually condition one another or are mutually independent—become significant if the varying meanings which critical terms assume in the context of philosophic principles are permitted to determine the meaning of the statements and are related to the subject matter of the criticism.

The changes in the subject matter of criticism may be seen compactly in the different applications of relevant criteria which such terms as "matter" and "form," "content" and "expression," have had in different philosophic and critical orientations. Thus Plato, Kant, and Tolstoy treat of the conditions of art rather than of the products of art, but Plato's critical judgments are based primarily on the nature of the object imitated, and the "matter" of art is man or more generally living creatues; Kant's critical judgments are based primarily on the subjective form of judgment, and the object of the judgment of taste is either nature or art, which follows the rule of nature;[27] Tolstoy's critical judgments are based on the feelings expressed and communicated, and not only is the "matter" of art feelings, but the sign distinguishing real art, apart from consideration of its subject matter, is the infectiousness and the quality of the feelings it transmits.[28] The content of "matter" and the relative importance of "form" and "matter" have shifted in the systematic context of these three kinds of criticism; and yet there is a continuity in the relevant traits of the "object" of art, for in Plato's doctrine it is found in the virtues portrayed, in Kant's doctrine it is found in the purposiveness of the representation, and in Tolstoy's doctrine it is found in the moral and religious feelings transmitted. Or, to reverse the order of comparison, the social community which is to be effected by art, according to Tolstoy, is present in the recognition of the empirical interest in the beautiful by Kant[29] and in the strenuous measures taken against poets by Plato to safeguard the perfect community of the *Republic* and the second-best community of the *Laws* from the dangers consequent on poetry. In general, these three modes of criticism have in common an appeal to criteria exterior to the work of art by which a comparison of arts with one another results in the discrimination of true art from spurious art or better art from worse: in Plato it is the criterion of truth and the moral effects of falsity

27. On the superiority of natural to artificial beauty cf. Kant, *op. cit.*, Part I, Div. I, § 42, pp. 178 ff.; on the relation of art and nature, *ibid.*, § 43, pp. 183 ff.; on the relation of the characteristics of the object in the judgment of natural beauty and the judgment of a product of art, cf. *ibid.*, § 33, p. 158; § 46, p. 188; and § 48, p. 194. Of the subjectivity of the judgment of taste, cf. *ibid.*, § 1, pp. 45–46: "The judgement of taste is therefore not a judgement of cognition, and is consequently not logical but aesthetical, by which we understand that whose determining ground can be *no other than subjective*" (cf. also *ibid.*, § 25, p. 161). The critique of taste, however, is subjective only with respect to the representation by which an object is given to it; it may also be an act or a science of reducing to rules the reciprocal relation between the understanding and imagination (cf. *ibid.* § 34, p. 160).

28. Tolstoy, *op. cit.*, chaps. xv and xvi, pp. 274–96.

29. Kant, *op. cit.*, Part I, Div. I, § 41, p. 174: "Empirically the Beautiful interests only in *society*. If we admit the impulse to society as natural to man, and his fitness for it, and his propension towards it, *i.e. sociability*, as a requisite for man as a being destined for society, and so as a property belonging to *humanity*, we cannot escape from regarding taste as a faculty for judging everything in respect of which we can communicate our *feeling* to all other men, and so as a means of furthering that which every one's natural inclination desires."

which justifies the condemnation of poetry in opposition to the art of the
statesman; in Kant it is the criterion of genius and the free play of imagination
which places music in a place inferior to poetry;[30] in Tolstoy it is the criterion
of religion and the infectiousness of feelings that brands modern art as spurious in contrast to true religious art. The fundamental differences between them
go back to the differences to be found in philosophic principles of processes,
faculties, and things. Tolstoy, emphasizing the process of communication, finds
art supplementing theory by making science intelligible and accomplishing the
ends of practice by removing the need of external political control.[31] Kant,
emphasizing the judgment, finds *criticism* the indispensable preliminary, not
only to the appreciation of art and nature, but to theoretic knowledge and moral
decision. Plato, emphasizing the nature of being, finds *philosophy* the necessary
source of criticism and the basis of art.

Aristotle, Bacon, and Horace, on the other hand, treat of poetry rather than
of beauty or nature or feeling. Yet for Aristotle the plot is the soul of the
tragedy and the source of its unity, and words are the means of imitation,
while for Bacon words are the form, and the content of the words is the matter
which constitutes poesy a branch of learning analogous to history.[32] Like

30. *Ibid.*, § 53, pp. 215–18. Contrast Aristotle *Poet.* 26. 1461^b26, in which the comparison
of tragedy and epic in terms of their respective audiences is refuted and a comparison in
terms of the unities achieved by their respective imitations and the pleasure appropriate to
them is substituted.

31. Tolstoy, *op. cit.*, chap. x, p. 225: "The business of art lies just in this: to make that
understood and felt which in form of an argument might be incomprehensible and inacces-
sible." *Ibid.*, chap. xx, p. 322: "True science investigates and brings to human perception
such truths and such knowledge as the people of a given time and society consider most important. Art transmits these truths from the region of perception to the region of emotion."
Ibid., p. 331: "Art is not a pleasure, a solace, or an amusement; art is a great matter. Art is
an organ of human life transmitting man's reasonable perception into feeling. In our age the
common religious perception of men is the consciousness of the brotherhood of man—we
know that the well-being of man lies in union with his fellow-men. True science should indicate the various methods of applying this consciousness to life. Art should transform this
perception into feeling. The task of art is enormous. Through the influence of real art,
aided by science, guided by religion, that peaceful cooperation of man which is now maintained by external means,—by our law-courts, police, charitable institutions, factory inspection, and so forth,—should be obtained by man's free and joyous activity. Art should cause
violence to be set aside."

32. When Aristotle argues (*Poet.* 9. 1451^a36) that the work of Herodotus would still
be history if written in verse, the argument proceeds on the principle that the poet is concerned with the probability and necessity essential to the plot, which is the "first and most
important thing in Tragedy" (*ibid.*, 7. 1450^b21, 1451^a9 ff.; 8. 1451^a22 ff.), and on the principle that the poet is not distinguished by his use of verse as a means. When Bacon argues
for the same conclusion, the argument proceeds on the principle that the difference between
verse and prose is a difference in form and on the principle that the difference between history and poesy is a difference in matter. Cf. *De augmentis scientiarum*, Book II, chap. xiii,
p. 315: "Now Poesy (as I have already observed) is taken in two senses; in respect of words
or matter. In the first sense it is but a character of speech; for verse is only a kind of style
and a certain form of elocution, and has nothing to do with the matter; for both true history
may be written in verse and feigned history in prose. But in the latter sense, I have set it

Bacon, Horace analyzes poetry by treating subject matter and expression; but, unlike either Aristotle or Bacon, he recommends, as a device of imitation, the use of life and customs as an exemplar from which to draw living words; he is convinced that, if the matter is given, the words will follow, and he thinks of the problem of pleasing an audience in terms of decorum of subject and style.[33] Once again the content of "matter" and the relative importance of "form" and "matter" have shifted in the systematic context of the three kinds of criticism, and yet there is again a continuity in the relevant trait of the object of art which is for these critics the poem, the statue, or some like concrete object which requires some mark or measure of unity. In Aristotle's doctrine, unity is found in the plot, which has a beginning, middle, and end, and the relevant verbal unity depends on the unity of subject;[34] in Bacon's doctrine poetry is restrained with respect to words but quite unrestrained by matter;[35] and in Horace's doctrine unity has become a matter of decorum which depends on consistency in the relations of the parts of the poem to one another and appropriateness of the language to the matter, but it is otherwise unrestricted except in view of the reactions of audiences.[36] Or, again, the order of the comparison may be reversed, and the instruction, utility, and delight which are prominent in Horace's analysis may all be found in their appropriate functions in Bacon and Aristotle: in Bacon service to magnanimity, morality, and delectation are the mark of all poesy, while the clarification, or concealment, of a point of reason to make it intelligible or mysterious is the special function of one kind, parabolical poetry;[37] whereas in Aristotle tragedy has its appropriate

---

down from the first as one of the principal branches of learning, and placed it by the side of history; being indeed nothing else but an imitation of history at pleasure." Cf. *ibid.*, Book VI, chap. i. p. 443: "The Measure of words has produced a vast body of art; namely Poesy, considered with reference not to the matter of it (of which I have spoken above) but to the style and form of words: that is to say metre or verse."

33. Horace *op. cit.* 317–18; 311; 1–23; 86–118; 153–78 and *passim*.

34. *Poet.* 7 and 8, 1450^{b}21 ff.; for the unity of the epic cf. *ibid.* 23. 1459^{a}17; for unity of diction cf. *ibid.* 20. 1457^{a}28.

35. *Of the Proficience and Advancement of Learning*, Book II, p. 343: "Poesy is a part of learning in measure of words for the most part restrained, but in all other points extremely licensed, and doth truly refer to the Imagination; which, being not tied to the laws of matter, may at pleasure join that which nature hath severed, and sever that which nature hath joined, and so make unlawful matches and divorces of things: *Pictoribus atque poetis*, etc."

36. Horace *op. cit.* 23: "Denique sit quod vis, simplex dumtaxat et unum." The difference between Horace and Bacon is indicated by the fact that Bacon's quotation *Pictoribus atque poetis*—"poets and painters have always had an equal power of hazarding anything"—is, in the context of Horace's poem (*ibid.* 9–10), an injected anonymous objection which Horace grants only with restrictions on the kind of things that may properly be combined.

37. *Of the Proficience and Advancement of Learning*, Book II, p. 343: "So as it appeareth that poesy serveth and conferreth to magnanimity, morality, and to delectation." In parabolical poetry, ideas which are objects of the intellect are represented in forms that are objects

pleasure, which is that of pity and fear, and the effectiveness of plot structure depends on an element of astonishment, but the moral effects of poetry are reserved for treatment in politics, and poets are quoted for their doctrine in the sciences.[38] In general, the three modes of criticism have in common a concern with characteristics that can be found in the poem: Aristotle seeks a unity in the plot which organizes the parts as material and has its appropriate effect in pleasure; Bacon is concerned with the distinctive matter of poesy, and therefore he does not raise the question of unity but does find effects in pleasure, edification, and parabolic instruction; Horace is concerned with effects, and he is therefore indifferent to matter as such but finds unity in the interrelations of parts with one another and their relations to the manner of their expression. This, again, is a fundamental difference which goes back to differences of philosophic principles, for the first is an organic unity appropriate to a thing; the second is the free organization of matter appropriate to the imagination; the third is a union of content and expression suited to achieve a specified result.

The intricate interrelations of consequences in statement and doctrine which can be traced to the interplay of philosophic principles and methods make it possible to detect similarities and differences in the various modes of criticism and to trace the transformations which a rule or generalization undergoes as it passes from one intellectual context to another. On the basis of such systematic interrelations the canons of criticism can be compared in terms of the criteria appropriate to each philosophic doctrine. Tolstoy, thus, states three criteria which bear, respectively, on the importance of the content of the work of art to its audience, on its beauty of form, and on the relation of its author to it.

The value of every poetical work depends on three qualities:

1) The content of the work: the more important the content, that is to say, the more important it is for the life of man, the greater is the work.

---

of the sense; cf. *ibid.*, p. 344: "And the cause was, for that it was then of necessity to express any point of reason which was more sharp or subtile than the vulgar in that manner; because men in those times wanted both variety of examples and subtilty of conceit; and as hieroglyphics were before letters, so parables were before arguments: and nevertheless now and at all times they do retain much life and vigour, because reason cannot be so sensible, nor examples so fit. But there remaineth another use of Poesy Parabolical, opposite to that which we last mentioned: for that tendeth to demonstrate and illustrate that which is taught or delivered, and this other to retire and obscure it: that is when the secrets and mysteries of religion, policy, or philosophy are involved in fables or parables."

38. The tragic pleasure is that of pity and fear (*Poet.* 14. 1453^{b}11); it is peculiar to tragedy (*ibid.* 13. 1453^{a}35; 23. 1459^{a}17; 26. 1462^{b}12); it depends on the unexpected, the marvelous, and the astounding (*ibid.* 9. 1452^{a}2; 14. 1454^{a}2; 16. 1455^{a}16; 24. 1460^{a}11; 25. 1460^{b}24). For the consideration of the moral effects of art cf. *Politics* vii. 17. 1336^{b}12 ff.; viii. 5–7. 1339^{b}10–1342^{b}34. For the use of poets for theoretic purposes cf. the quotation of Homer, Hesiod, and myths in *Metaphysics* i. 3. 983^{b}27; 4. 984^{b}23; 8. 989^{a}10; ii. 4. 1000^{a}9; iv. 5. 1009^{b}28; xii. 8. 1074^{a}38; 10. 1076^{a}4; and *passim*.

2) The external beauty achieved by the technical methods proper to the particular kind of art. Thus in dramatic art the technical method will be: that the characters should have a true individuality of their own, a natural and at the same time a touching plot, a correct presentation on the stage of the manifestation and development of feelings, and a sense of proportion in all that is presented.

3) Sincerity, that is to say that the author should himself vividly feel what he expresses. Without this condition there can be no work of art, as the essence of art consists in the infection of the contemplator of a work by the author's feeling. If the author has not felt what he is expressing, the recipient cannot become infected by the author's feeling, and the production cannot be classified as a work of art.[39]

For Kant there are two problems in art which require critical criteria—the problem of the judgment of the beautiful in art and the problem of the production of beautiful objects of art. Criteria are supplied in both, not by the artificial object, but by the faculties of the mind in their mutual interrelations or as guided by nature. There is no objective principle of taste, but the product of beautiful art must resemble, and yet be distinguishable from, nature;[40] there is no rule to govern the production of art, but genius is an innate mental disposition through which nature gives the rule to art.[41] Plato considers the problem of criticism in terms which reflect the influence of the same three variables—audience, work of art, and artist; but in the orientation of his analysis to truth the criterion of effectiveness is found in the object of imitation instead of the audience; the quality of the art object in the correctness of the imitation; and the virtue of the artist in the excellence of the execution of the copy.

Then must not the judicious critic of any representation—whether in painting, music, or any other art—have these three qualifications? He must know, first, what the object reproduced is, next, how correctly it has been reproduced, and third, how well a given representation has been executed in language, melody, or rhythm.[42]

39. "Shakespeare and the Drama" (*Tolstoy on Art*, pp. 445–46). Cf. "On Art" (*ibid.*, p. 82): "Therefore, though a work of art must always include something new, yet the revelation of something new will not always be a work of art. That it should be a work of art, it is necessary: (1) That the new idea, the content of the work, should be of importance to mankind. (2) That this content should be expressed so clearly that people may understand it. (3) That what incites the author to work at his production should be an inner need and not an external inducement." *Ibid.*, p. 84: "A perfect work of art will be one in which the content is important and significant to all men, and therefore it will be *moral*. The expression will be quite clear, intelligible to all, and therefore *beautiful;* the author's relation to his work will be altogether sincere, and heartfelt, and therefore *true.*"

40. Kant, *op. cit.*, Part I, Div. I, § 45, p. 187: "In a product of beautiful art we must become conscious that it is Art and not Nature; but yet the purposiveness of its form must seem to be as free from all constraint of arbitrary rules as if it were a product of mere nature. . . . Nature is beautiful because it looks like Art; and Art can only be called beautiful if we are conscious of it as Art while yet it looks like Nature."

41. *Ibid.*, § 46, p. 189: "Therefore, beautiful art cannot itself devise the rule according to which it can bring about its product. But since at the same time a product can never be called Art without some precedent rule, Nature in the subject must (by the harmony of its faculties) give the rule to Art; i.e., beautiful Art is only possible as a product of Genius."

42. *Laws* ii. 669A–B.

Whereas Kant had considered questions which involved the same three variables in terms of two problems concerned with the faculties of the mind and
nature, Plato's formulation of the questions leads to the reduction of them all to
problems which can be solved only by reference to the nature of the object.

For Aristotle, on the other hand, critical questions bear fundamentally, not
on something external to the work of art, but on the poem itself, and questions
of fault no less than of excellence are determined in view of the end of poetry
and the use of devices within the framework of the plot which is the end of
poetry. Questions concerning the artist, the work of art, and the audience,
therefore, appear in his criticism, as in Plato's, transformed so as to be related
to an object; but for Aristotle, unlike Plato, the orientation is to an artificial, not
an eternal or even a natural, object, and the faults, alleged by critics, based on
external criteria may be justified by consideration of the work of art itself.
Criticism of the poet's art takes the form of alleged impossibilities; criticism
of the faithfulness of the work to fact depends on alleged improbabilities;
criticism of expression or meaning depends on alleged contradictions and improprieties of language. The dialectic of criticism as developed by the philosophers who argue analogically is in terms which depend on the criteria relevant
to poet-poem-audience, or making-judging, or object; but the same problems
appear in the tradition of literal criticism in terms which bear on the criteria
relevant to organization-content-language, or making-judging, or language.
Aristotle holds that faults in respect to impossibility, improbability, and contradiction may be justified if they contribute to the end of art. Impossibilities
are faults in the poet's art, but they may be justified by reference to the requirements of *art*, if they contribute to the plot by making it, or some portion
of it, more astounding.[43] Improbabilities are errors in the representation of fact,
but they may be justified by reference to the *better* or to *opinion*, for the artist
should portray men better than they are or he should take account of circumstances, of what men are thought to be and of the probability of things happening
against probability.[44] Inconsistencies or contradictions of language may be

43. *Poet.* 25. 1460^{b}22: "First, with respect to critical problems relating to the poet's art
itself, if he has set forth impossibilities he has committed an error; but the error may be justified, if the poet thereby achieves the end of poetry itself—for the end has already been
stated—if, that is, he thus makes this or some other part of the poem more astounding. . . .
Again, is the error with respect to something essential to the art or only accidental to it? For
it is less of an error not to know that the hind has no horns than to make an unrecognizable
picture of one." *Ibid.* 1461^{b}9: "In general the 'impossible' must be justified relative to the
requirements of poetry, or to the *better*, or to *opinion*. Relative to the *requirements of poetry* a
convincing impossibility is preferable to an unconvincing possibility."

44. *Ibid.* 1060^{b}32: "If the objection is that the poet's narration is not true, the answer
should be that perhaps it ought to be, just as Sophocles said that he made men as they ought
to be, while Euripides made them as they are. . . . Again, relative to the question whether
what has been said or done by someone has been well or badly said or done, we must examine not only what has been done or said, inquiring concerning it whether it is noble or base,

solved by consideration of usage, metaphor, punctuation, and the like.[45] By holding to the conception and standard of the unity of the work, the critic is able to follow Aristotle's dialectic in playing the technique of the artist against the opinions of the audience and both against the probabilities of the matter. Bacon, on the other hand, approaches poetry in terms of the matter accessible to and organized by imagination, and therefore treats of two problems of criticism in his characteristic effort to advance human learning: the estimation of existing poetry—and in this, unlike other branches of learning, he finds no deficiency—and recommendations for improvement—for which he finds no means.[46] Bacon has no criterion of organic unity, and he has little patience with questions of poetic language; his criticism, therefore, is almost entirely in terms of matter as object or product of imagination. Horace, finally, since he approaches poetry in terms of the technique of the poet, uses the terms suggested by *poeta-poesis-poema;* and, since the audience is pleased by a familiar or a consistent matter well expressed, and since words are fitted to matter, the problems of criticism consist—even those which bear on the unity of the poem and the choice of content—largely in questions for which the relevant criteria are found in terms of words.[47]

In application and precept, therefore, modes of criticism thus differently oriented will select different points of excellence in the work of the artist and indicate different objectives to be urged on his attention. The same traits will

---

but also who did it or said it, to whom, when, by what means, and for what end—whether, for example, he does it to secure greater good, or to avoid a greater evil." *Ibid.* 1461b12: "Such men as Zeuxis painted may be impossible but may be justified by the *better,* for the model ought to improve on the actual. The improbable must be justified by *what is commonly said,* and also by showing that at times it is not improbable, for there is a probability also of things happening contrary to probability."

45. *Ibid.* 1461a9 and 1461b16.

46. *Of the Proficience and Advancement of Learning,* Book II, p. 343: "The use of this Feigned History hath been to give some shadow of satisfaction to the mind of man in those points wherein the nature of things doth deny it; the world being in proportion inferior to the soul; by reason whereof there is agreeable to the spirit of man a more ample greatness, a more exact goodness, and a more absolute variety, than can be found in the nature of things." *Ibid.,* p. 346: "In this third part of learning, which is poesy, I can report no deficience. For being as a plant that cometh to the lust of the earth, without a formal seed, it hath sprung up and spread abroad more than any other kind." Cf. *De augmentis scientiarum,* Book VI, chap. i, pp. 443–44: "But for poesy (whether we speak of stories or metre) it is (as I said before) like a luxuriant plant, that comes of the lust of the earth, without any formal seed. Wherefore it spreads everywhere and is scattered far and wide,—so that it would be vain to take thought about the defects of it. With this therefore we need not trouble ourselves."

47. Horace *op. cit.* 408–53, esp. 445–40: "A good and prudent man will censure lifeless verses, he will find fault with harsh ones; if they are inelegant he will blot them out with a black line by drawing his pen across them; he will cut out pretentious ornaments; he will force you to turn light on things not sufficiently clear; he will argue against what has been said ambiguously; he will mark what should be changed; he will become an Aristarchus"; cf. also *Epistles* ii. 2. 106–25.

be given not merely a different importance but a different meaning and locus in the statements of different critics, and they will become in one view the points of highest excellence and in another faults. Tolstoy insists on the essential importance of novelty in a work of art—it cannot be a work of art without something new in it—and he seeks the novelty in the content. Horace is indifferent to a novelty of content—he recommends a tale newly invented if it is consistent, while urging the traditional subjects even more strongly, particularly the themes drawn from Homer—but he defends with vigor the right of the poet to invent new words or to put old words to new uses.[48] For Kant novelty is translated into the originality of genius and is reflected in the freedom of imagination essential to the judgment of beauty.[49] For Bacon, who is concerned, not with the forms of judgment, but with the parts of learning, novelty is found in the lush and uncontrolled growth of poetry which makes useless and unnecessary any plans for its advancement. If the operation of novelty as a criterion is sought in Aristotle, it is found to have shifted once again, from judgment and learning to the object of art as it had shifted from the processes of composition to the faculties of the mind, and to have become the novel and marvelous element which contributes to the structure of the plot, while in Plato it is criticized as the fickle changeableness which is incompatible with the contemplation and imitation of an eternal model of beauty.[50] The choice of principles may seem a matter of initial indifference or of basic dogma, and the development of statement and determination of method may seem, in the critic who fits what he says to the instances he adduces, to depend on the facts of nature or art or experience, but the judgments of the critic may have a double effect on the facts by influencing the purposes of the artist and the taste of the audience; and therefore it is no less true that the nature and purposes of art depend on what the critic, broadly conceived, thinks his function to be than that the function of criticism is to judge the products and achievements of art.

II

Philosophic principles determine the meaning and subject matter of statements about art, and, conversely, the explication and application of statements

48. Horace *Ars poetica* 46–72.

49. Kant, *op. cit.*, Part I, Div. I, § 47, pp. 192–93: "Now since the originality of the talent constitutes an essential (though not the only) element in the character of genius, shallow heads believe that they cannot better show themselves to be full-blown geniuses than by throwing off the constraint of all rules; they believe, in effect, that one could make a braver show on the back of a wild horse than on the back of a trained animal. Genius can only furnish rich *material* for products of beautiful art; its execution and its *form* require talent cultivated in the schools, in order to make such a use of this material as will stand examination by the Judgement."

50. *Rep.* iv. 424B–C.

determine principles, for a single statement—an identical combination of words —may express or follow from different philosophic principles as it is variously defined and applied to various subject matters. Moreover, statements which seem explicitly to express the same or comparable philosophic principles may, as a result of methodological determination in use, apply now to a broad, now to a limited, subject matter, and in so doing they may unite the objects of art with those of nature or separate them, and they may analogize the products of the different arts to each other or differentiate them. Such differences in the application of principles to subject matter—involving questions concerning whether the same principles apply to nature and art or to moral action and artistic production—reflect changes in meaning which can be set forth in terms of method as well as of subject matter, for they result from separating theoretic, practical, and poetic judgments or in turn from merging (in varying manners of identification and varying degrees of mixture) considerations of knowing, doing, and making. The same differences in the determination and use of principles may therefore be seen in the functions attributed to artist, critic, and philosopher and in their relations to each other, for when subject matters and methods are distinct, the critic is distinguished from the artist and the philosopher, but when they merge the poet is critic, the critic is poet, or both are philosophers or—in lieu of philosophy for those philosophers who hold philosophy in disrepute—historians, sociologists, psychologists, semanticists, or scientists.

To discuss the function of the critic, therefore, is to discuss the function of the poet and philosopher. Indeed, the varying conceptions of the critic are illustrated historically in a dispute, which has been continuous since it was first formulated by the Greek philosophers and rhetoricians, between artist, critic, and philosopher. In the course of that dispute, the function of the critic has sometimes been limited to tasks less constructive or imaginative than those of the artist and less theoretic or intellectual than those of the philosopher; it has sometimes been broadened to include the functions exercised by both, while each of the disputants has claimed the functions of the others and the three have been collapsed repeatedly and again separated. The function of the critic may be identical with the functions of the artist and the philosopher either because criticism is conceived to be creative or intellectual or because art and philosophy are conceived to depend fundamentally on critical judgment; and if the functions of artist, critic, and philosopher are distinguished, it is because the critic operates in accordance with some form of philosophy which will permit him to seek causes and effects in the materials and forms of the artist. The function of the critic is determined alike in the fundamental assumptions of the philosopher, the critic, and the artist. It is determined in the principles from which the philosopher derives not only his system but the criteria by which to judge it and the rules of art by which to develop it, and even short of the development of a philosophy, the function of the critic is determined in the philosophic principles assumed in the critical judgments and criteria which artists and critics, as well as philosophers, evolve and apply. It is determined, likewise, in the conception of art which is the critic's minimum philosophy as well as the grounds of his judgments of art. It is determined, finally, in the conception of artistic purpose which is the artist's minimum critical theory and philosophy as well as the implicit formulation of his processes of production. The different conceptions of the functions of criticism, and the consequent variability of critical judgments, flow from assumptions and involve consequences which extend beyond variations in the functions of the critic to variations in art and philosophy, and the examination of criticism may fruitfully proceed through the consideration of (1) variations in the conception of art and the artist, which reflect consequences of criticism, and (2) variations in the conception of philosophy and philosophic method, which involve the grounds of judgments of value, to (3) variations in the conceptions of criticism itself and its applications.

Artists are necessarily critics in the act of artistic construction or composition. They sometimes, in addition to this active and illustrative criticism, explain what they have tried to do and relate it to the productions of other artists or the statements of other critics. Poets in particular have entered not only into that competition with other poets which is involved in the production of new poetic effects but also into competition with critics in defense of a conception of art and criticism, and with philosophers in justification of a view of life consonant with such critical values. They have frequently written as critics, expressing in their verses judgments of other poets, as Aristophanes did, or of poets and critics too, as Byron did. They have developed theories of criticism and poetics, both in verse—as did Horace, Vida, Boileau, Pope, and Browning —and in prose—as did Sidney, Dryden, Wordsworth, Coleridge, Shelley, Emerson, Bryant, and Newman. All the functions which the philosopher and the rhetorician have assigned to the poet reappear in the theories of poets: he is maker, contriver, and imitator; he is engaged in pleasing, instructing, and edifying; his poetry is a source of, as it is derived from, inspiration, enchantment, and imagination. In addition, however, the poet is assigned all the functions which any philosopher has sought to contrast to poetry in a more limited conception of the domain of art, and poets as critics have made converts of other critics and other historians and have taught them to present the poet eloquently not only as maker, but as seer, prophet, scientist, philosopher, moralist, and legislator, and to trace the history of all human knowledge and accomplishment from poetic beginnings or to poetic fulfilments. What the poet is conceived to be—since it determines how poetry will be read, for scientific truth and moral precept, for imaginative construction and emotional stimulation, for enrichment of experience and impetus to action, for pleasure and edification—becomes in itself the statement of a history, a morality, a politics, and a philosophy.[51] All sciences are dominated and perfected by poetry;[52] man and human

51. George Puttenham, *The Arte of English Poesie*, ed. G. D. Willcock and A. Walker (Cambridge, 1936), Book I, chaps. iii and iv, pp. 6–9: "The profession and use of Poesie is most ancient from the beginning and not, as manie erroniously suppose, after, but before, any civil society among men. . . . Then forasmuch as they were the first that entended to the observation of nature and her works, and specially of the Celestiall courses, by reason of the continuall motion of the heavens, searching after the first mover, and from thence by degrees comming to know and consider of the substances separate and abstract, which we call the divine intelligences or good Angels (*Demones*) they were the first that instituted sacrifices of placation, with invocations and worship to them, as to Gods: and invented and stablished all the rest of the observances and ceremonies of religion, and so were the first Priests and ministers of the holy misteries. . . . So also were they the first Prophetes or seears, *Videntes*. . . . So as the Poets were also from the beginning the best perswaders and their eloquence the first Rethoricke of the world. Even so it became that the high mysteries of the gods should be revealed and taught, by a maner of utterance and language of extraordinarie phrase, and briefe and compendious, and above al others sweet and civill as the Metricall is . . . so as the Poet was also the first historiographer . . . they were the first Astronomers and Philosophists and Metaphisicks." The sum of all wisdom is frequently found in a single poet; cf. Sir Thomas Elyot, *The Gouernour*, ed. Henry Croft (London, 1880), I, 58–59: "I coulde reherce diuers other poetis whiche for mater and eloquence be very necessary, but I feare me to be to longe from noble Homere: from whom as from a fountaine proceded all eloquence and lernyng. For in his bokes be contained, and most perfectly expressed, nat only the documentes marciall and discipline of armes, but also incomparable wisedomes, and instructions for politike gouernaunce of people: with the worthy commendation and laude of noble princis: where with the reders shall be so all inflamed, that they most fervently shall desire and coveite, by the imitation of their vertues, to acquire semblable glorie." According to Sidney, *The Defence of Poesie* (*The Complete Works of Sir Philip Sidney*, ed. Feuillerat [Cambridge, 1923], III, 5), poetry is the origin of all learning and the passport by which philosophers and historiographers first "entered the gates of populer judgements"; cf. *ibid.*, pp. 4–5: "This did so notably shew it selfe, that the Philosophers of Greece durst not a long time appear to the world, but under the masks of poets. So Thales, Empedocles, and Parmenides, sang their naturall Philosophie in verses. So did Pithagoras and Phocillides, their morall Councels. So did Tirteus in warre matters, and Solon in matters of pollicie, or rather they being Poets, did exercise their delightfull vaine in those points of highest knowledge, which before them laie hidden to the world." Or, again, poetry may be made to embrace all the higher activities of man, including the other arts; cf. Shelley, *A Defence of Poetry* (*The Prose Works of P. B. Shelley*, ed. H. B. Forman [London, 1880], III, 104): "But poets, or those who imagine and express this indestructible order, are not only the authors of language and of music, of the dance, and architecture, and statuary, and painting; they are the institutors of laws and the founders of civil society, and the inventors of the arts of life, and the teachers, who draw into a certain propinquity with the beautiful and the true, that partial apprehension of the agencies of the invisible world which is called religion." Or similar convictions may be expressed in terms of an evolution in which poets gradually fell from a high estate; cf. Lowell, *op. cit.*, pp. 432–33: "And however far we go back, we shall find this also—that the poet and the priest were united originally in the same person; which means that the poet was he who was conscious of the world of spirit as well as that of sense, and was the ambassador of the gods to men. This was his highest function, and hence his name of 'seer.' . . . Gradually, however, the poet as the 'seer' became secondary to the 'maker.' His office became that of

life are by nature poetical;[53] the universe itself is the creation, or at least the re-creation of poetic art.[54]

---

entertainer rather than teacher. But always something of the old tradition was kept alive. And if he has now come to be looked upon merely as the best expresser, the gift of seeing is implied as necessarily antecedent to that, and of seeing very deep, too. . . . Now, under all these names—praiser, seer, soothsayer—we find the same idea lurking. The poet is he who can best see and best say what is ideal—what belongs to the world of soul and of beauty."

52. Sidney, *op. cit.*, p. 19: "Now therein of all Sciences (I speak still of humane and according to the humane conceit) is our Poet the Monarch. For hee doth not onely shew the way, but giveth so sweete a prospect into the way, as will entice anie man to enter into it." Wordsworth, "Preface to the *Lyrical Ballads*" (*The Prose Works of William Wordsworth*, ed. A. B. Grosart [London, 1876], II, 91): "Poetry is the breath and finer spirit of all knowledge; it is the impassioned expression which is in the countenance of all science. . . . Poetry is the first and last of all knowledge—it is as immortal as the heart of man." These contentions concerning the nature of poetry are made in the face of opposition; cf. Peacock, "The Four Ages of Poetry" (*The Works of Thomas Love Peacock*, ed. H. F. B. Brett-Smith and C. E. Jones [London, 1934], VIII, 21): "The highest inspirations of poetry are resolvable into three ingredients: the rant of unregulated passion, the whine of exaggerated feeling, and the cant of factitious sentiment; and can therefore serve only to ripen a splendid lunatic like Alexander, a puling driveller like Werter, or a morbid dreamer like Wordsworth. It can never make a philosopher, nor a statesman, nor in any class of life a useful or rational man." Even in this estimate of poetry the function of the poet is conceived to extend to philosophy, politics, and the practical problems of life, and Shelley's reply to Peacock's criticisms merely asserts what Peacock denies. Shelley includes among poets, not only the authors of language and music, but also the institutors of laws, the founders of civil society, the inventors of the arts of life, and the teachers of religion (*op. cit.*, p. 104), and he denies the distinction between poets and prose writers, philosophers and historians, holding, indeed, that all authors of revolutions in opinion are necessarily poets (*ibid.*, p. 107). "Poetry is indeed something divine. It is at once the centre and circumference of knowledge; it is that which comprehends all science, and that to which all science must be referred" (*ibid.*, p. 136). "Poets are the hierophants of an unapprehended inspiration; the mirrors of the gigantic shadows which futurity casts upon the present; the words which express what they understand not; the trumpets which sing to battle and feel not what they inspire; the influence which is moved not, but moves. Poets are the unacknowledged legislators of the world" (*ibid.*, p. 144).

53. Hazlitt, "On Poetry in General" (*The Complete Works of William Hazlitt*, ed. P. P. Howe [London, 1930], V, 2): "It is not a branch of authorship: it is 'the stuff of which our life is made.' The rest is 'mere oblivion,' a dead letter: for all that is worth remembering in life, is the poetry of it. Fear is poetry, hope is poetry, love is poetry, hatred is poetry; contempt, jealousy, remorse, admiration, wonder, pity, despair, or madness are all poetry. Poetry is that fine particle within us, that expands, rarefies, refines, raises our whole being: without it 'man's life is poor as beast's.' Man is a poetical animal; and those of us who do not study the principles of poetry, act upon them all our lives, like Molière's *Bourgeois Gentilhomme*, who had always spoken prose without knowing it." Or, again, the poetic nature of mankind is at the background of the poet's direction of man and poetry's dominance of the sciences; cf. Whitman, *op. cit.*, pp. iv, vii: "Of all nations the United States with veins full of poetical stuff most need poets and will doubtless have the greatest and use them the greatest. Their Presidents shall not be their common referee so much as their poets shall. Of all mankind the greatest poet is the equable man. Not in him but off from him things are grotesque or eccentric or fail of their sanity. Nothing out of its place is good and nothing in its place is bad. He bestows on every object or quality its fit proportions neither more nor less. He is the arbiter of the diverse and he is the key. . . . Exact science and its practical movements are no checks on the greatest poet but always his encouragement and support. . . . In the beauty of poems are the tuft and final applause of science."

54. Augustine *De civitate Dei* xi. 21: "What else indeed is to be understood by that which is said through all things: 'God saw that it was good,' but the approbation of work done

To determine the function of the poet is to mark the scope of the other arts, of criticism, and of philosophy; and whatever poetry is distinguished from or opposed to, in one account, may be viewed as essentially poetical in another: music, painting, and the rest of the arts may be instances of poetry; the true critic may be poetic and creative; and Plato may be made a poet by the same processes as made Homer and Shakespeare philosophers. Poetry is expanded and contracted both with respect to the arts conceived as poetic and with respect to the practices thought proper to them. The critic and philosopher— or the poet and amateur functioning as critic and philosopher—may affect the practices and the interrelations of the arts. It is only a recent instance of an old complaint that Lessing expresses when he reproves "modern critics" for having crudely misconceived the relation of painting and poetry, sometimes compressing poetry within the narrow limits of painting, sometimes making painting fill the whole wide sphere of poetry, and for having generated by their spurious criticism a mania for pictorial description in poetry and for allegorical style in painting.[55] As criticism, operating through the activity of

according to the art which is the wisdom of God." Shelley, *op. cit.*, p. 140: "It reproduces the common universe of which we are portions and percipients, and it purges from our inward sight the film of familiarity which obscures from us the wonder of our being. It compels us to feel that which we perceive, and to imagine that which we know. It creates anew the universe, after it has been annihilated in our minds by the recurrence of impressions blunted by reiteration. It justifies the bold and true word of Tasso: *Non merita nome di creatore, se non Iddio ed il Poeta* [None deserves the name of creator except God and the Poet]."

55. G. E. Lessing, *Laocoön*, Introd. (*Werke*, ed. J. Petersen [Leipzig, n.d.], IV, 292). The discussion of the relation of poetry and painting goes back to ancient beginnings, to Horace, Plutarch, and Pliny, and by way of them to Simonides' conception of painting as silent poetry and poetry as speaking painting. Cf. also John Dryden, *Parallel of Poetry and Painting* (1695); Abbé du Bos, *Réflexions critiques sur la poésie et sur la peinture* (1719); Charles Lamotte, *An Essay upon Painting and Poetry* (1730); James Harris, "Concerning Music, Painting, and Poetry," *Three Treatises* (1744); Joseph Spence, *Polymetis; or, an Inquiry concerning the Agreement between the Works of the Roman Poets and the Remains of the Ancient Artists, Being an Attempt To Illustrate Them Mutually from One Another* (1747); G. E. Lessing, *Laocoön* (1766); Daniel Webb, *Observations on the Correspondence between Poetry and Music* (1769). Poetry may be conceived as the essential nature or the definition of painting and music, or it may merely share with them some common characteristics or effect some common responses. Cf. S. T. Coleridge, *Shakespeare: With Introductory Matter on Poetry, the Drama, and the Stage* (*Works*, IV, 39): "In my last address I defined poetry to be the art, or whatever better term our language may afford, of representing external nature and human thoughts, both relatively to human affections, so as to cause the production of as great immediate pleasure in each part as is compatible with the largest possible sum of pleasure on the whole. Now this definition applies equally to painting and music as to poetry; and in truth the term poetry is alike applicable to all three." Cf. also John Stuart Mill, "Thoughts on Poetry and Its Varieties," *Dissertations and Discussions: Political, Philosophical, and Historical* (New York, 1882), I, 89: "That, however, the word 'poetry' imports something quite peculiar in its nature; something which may exist in what is called prose as well as in verse; something which does not even require the instrument of words, but can speak through the other audible symbols called musical sounds, and even through the visible ones which are the language of sculpture, painting, and architecture,—all this, we believe, is and must be felt, though perhaps indistinctly, by all upon whom poetry in any of its shapes produces any impression beyond that of tickling

artists, affects art, those immanent critical processes in turn affect criticism and the philosophic ideas it embodies; and criticism and philosophy undergo like changes with the variations in art. The discussion of the function of the poet is a philosophic discussion, and its progress through the ages reflects the differences between those philosophers who find poetry and philosophy essentially the same and therefore seek only to determine whether poetry is perfect or deficient philosophy and whether philosophy is supreme or partial poetry and those philosophers who distinguish artistic constructions from philosophic speculations and therefore make use of art or criticism or philosophy to prevent the confusion of disciplines.

There is a rivalry between poetry and philosophy in so far as they are pertinent to the same ends and in so far as the same standards may be applied to both. The quarrel was ancient in the time of Plato,[56] and it has continued to the present because the tradition of discussion sets poetry to be judged against a standard of truth and reason, and philosophy to be criticized for its ineffectiveness and uncouthness. Plato banished the poets from the perfect state, not despite but because of the charm he acknowledges in their art, for it endangers the highest ends of man and the most vital functions of the state. The danger of poetry lies precisely in the fact that the poet, with all his art, may speak well and badly according to the standard of philosophic truth; and in the dialectic of Plato the indeterminacy for which poetry is criticized is removed only when the poet writes with knowledge, and then the poet is rightly called "philosopher." The standard applied to the poet is the same as that of the lawgiver, and therefore in the perfect state the philosopher is poet as well as ruler. Even in the second-best state delineated in the *Laws*, the principles of art are inseparable from those of morals, legislation, and philosophy; and, when a model is sought in that dialogue to indicate what is wrong and what is right in poetry, it is found in the discourse itself, which the interlocutor finds is framed exactly like a poem.[57] Moreover, the poet is under suspicion in that state as well as in the perfect republic, and writers of tragedies are viewed as rivals of lawgivers who are not philosophers as well as of those who are.

Best of strangers, we will say to them, we ourselves are poets, to the best of our ability, of the fairest and best tragedy, for our whole state is composed as an imitation of the fairest and best life, which we assert to be in reality the truest tragedy. Thus you

---

the ear." The three seem to overlap, without being identified essentially, according to Leigh Hunt; cf. "An Answer to the Question What Is Poetry?" (*Critical Essays of the Early Nineteenth Century*, ed. R. M. Alden [New York, 1921], p. 378): "Poetry includes whatsoever of painting can be made visible to the mind's eye, and whatsoever of music can be conveyed by sound and proportion without singing or instrumentation."

56. *Rep.* 607B.
57. *Laws* vii. 811C–D.

are poets and we likewise are poets of the same poems, opposed to you as artists and actors in the fairest drama, which true law alone, as our hope is, is suited to perfect. Do not imagine therefore that we will easily permit you to erect your stage among us in the market place and to introduce your actors, endowed with fair voices and louder than our own, and allow you to harangue women and children and all the people, saying concerning the same questions, not the same things as we do, but commonly and on most things the very opposite.[58]

This is a tradition of discussion and opposition which the poets were to continue, reversing the dialectic to find poetry in Plato's works while puzzling over his antagonism to poetry, to criticize the cold insensitivity of philosophy while claiming for poetry high philosophic insight, and to seek a truth in poetry while revising according to its standard the canon of true poets. All of the terms shift their meanings in the dialectic of this discussion. Plato is sometimes a poet, although philosophy is distinct from poetry, since, as Sidney argues, "who so ever well considereth, shall finde that in the body of his worke, though the inside and strength were Philosophie, the skin as it were and beautie, depended most of Poetrie."[59] He is sometimes an instance of the highest kind of poetry,[60] and philosophy is indispensable to poetry, since "no man," as Coleridge presents the case, "was ever yet a great poet, without being at the same time a profound philosopher."[61] He is sometimes essentially a poet, and Shakespeare is a philosopher, despite differences, such as Shelley emphasizes, in literary forms.[62] He is sometimes a true poet; and, since, as Emerson formulates the nature of poetry, poets are scientists and logicians, inspirers and lawgivers, some reservations must be made concerning the poetic quality of Shakespeare.[63]

58. *Ibid.* 817B–C.   59. Sidney, *op. cit.*, p. 5.

60. Coleridge, *Biographia literaria* (*Works*, III, 373): "The writings of Plato and Jeremy Taylor, and Burnet's *Theory of the Earth*, furnish undeniable proofs that poetry of the highest kind may exist without metre, and even without the contradistinguishing objects of a poem."

61. *Ibid.*, p. 381. The statement is applied in a discussion of Shakespeare and Milton.

62. *Op. cit.*, pp. 107–8: "Plato was essentially a poet—the truth and splendour of his imagery, and the melody of his language, are the most intense that it is possible to conceive. He rejected the harmony of the epic, dramatic, and lyrical forms, because he sought to kindle a harmony in thoughts divested of shape and action, and he forbore to invent any regular plan of rhythm which would include, under determinate forms, the varied pauses of his style. Cicero sought to imitate the cadence of his periods, but with little success. Lord Bacon was a poet. . . . Nor are those supreme poets, who have employed traditional forms of rhythm on account of the form and action of their subjects, less capable of perceiving and teaching the truth of things, than those who have omitted that form. Shakespeare, Dante, and Milton (to confine ourselves to modern writers) are philosophers of the very loftiest power."

63. Emerson, "Poetry and Imagination," *Letters and Social Aims* (Boston, 1883), p. 42: "For poetry is science, and the poet a truer logician," from whence it follows (*ibid.*, pp. 66, 68): "The poet who shall use nature as his hieroglyphic must have an adequate message to convey thereby. Therefore, when we speak of the Poet in any high sense, we are driven to such examples as Zoroaster and Plato, St. John and Menu, with their moral burdens. The Muse shall be the counterpart of Nature, and equally rich. . . . But in current literature I do not find her. Literature warps away from life, though at first it seems to bind it. In the world of

This rivalry of poetry and philosophy seems to disappear in the tradition of discussion in which poetry is contrasted literally to philosophy on all the points which served for their analogical comparison. Yet in the mixture of the traditions of literal and analogical discussion which constitutes the greater part of the history of thought, the effect of such distinctions is to supply points to serve as bases for later analogizing. The Platonic analogy of poetry and philosophy, thus, is combated in Aristotle's philosophy by distinguishing the kind of knowledge required for poetic constructions from other kinds of knowledge by its purpose; for theoretic knowledge is pursued for its own sake and for truth, practical knowledge for the sake of conduct, and poetic knowledge for the sake of making something useful or beautiful. The distinction having been made, however, the analogizing technique may be applied to it, and philosophers since the time of Aristotle have stated their basic principles by determining whether philosophy is essentially theoretic, or practical, or poetic. The conception of philosophy, therefore, is affected, no less than that of poetry, each time it is decided that philosophy is or is not poetry and that poetry is or is not philosophy: so long as the principles of philosophy are sought in the nature of things, philosophy may pretend to be fundamentally theoretic and speculative for all its practical implications and consequences;[64] when principles are sought in the nature of the human faculties or the development of human knowledge, practical knowledge tends to assume ascendancy in the hierarchy of the sciences;[65] and, finally, when principles are sought in operations and in the relations of symbols and when we seek substitutes for cer-

---

letters how few commanding oracles! Homer did what he could; Pindar, Aeschylus, and the Greek Gnomic poets and the tragedians. Dante was faithful when not carried away by his fierce hatreds. But in so many alcoves of English poetry I can count only nine or ten authors who are still inspirers and lawgivers to their race. . . . We are a little civil, it must be owned, to Homer and Aeschylus, to Dante and Shakespeare, and give them the benefit of the largest interpretation." Cf., also, Montesquieu, *Pensées diverses* (*Œuvres complètes de Montesquieu* [Paris, 1866], p. 626): "Les quatres grands poètes, Platon, Malebranche, Shaftesbury, Montaigne!"

64. Plato *Statesman* 259E, 285E–286A; *Rep.* vii. 518B–519D. Aristotle *Metaph.* i. 1. 981ᵇ25–982ᵃ3.

65. Kant, *Critique of Pure Reason*, trans. F. M. Müller (2d ed.; New York, 1919), Part II, "Transcendental Doctrine of Method," chap. ii, "The Canon of Pure Reason," pp. 647–48: "Pure reason, therefore, contains, not indeed in its speculative, yet in its practical, or, more accurately, its moral employment, principles of the *possibility of experience*, namely, of such actions as *might* be met with in the *history* of man according to moral precepts. For as reason commands that such actions should take place, they must be possible, and a certain kind of systematical unity also, namely, the moral, must be possible; while it was impossible to prove the systematical unity *according to the speculative principles of reason*. For reason, no doubt, possesses causality with respect to freedom in general, but not with respect to the whole of nature, and moral principles of reason may indeed produce free actions, but not laws of nature. Consequently, the principles of pure reason possess objective reality in their practical and more particularly in their moral employment" (cf. "Introduction to the Second edition," pp. 695–96).

tainty in the precisions of measurement, philosophy becomes an art again, since art takes precedence over the practical and the theoretic and man ceases to be *homo sapiens* and finds his best characterization in the functions of *homo faber*.[66]

The Platonic analogy of poetry and philosophy based on their common ends is closely related to the analogy of art and nature as imitation and exemplar. Aristotle countered that analogy with the distinction of natural objects, in which the principle of motion is internal, and artificial objects, whose cause must be sought in the idea and intention of artist or artisan. Like the analogy of poetry and philosophy, the analogy of art and nature was continued either in its original terms as a likeness found in things or in terms (derived from Aristotle's literal distinctions) which connect art and nature in characteristics found in the judgments of man or in his actions. Hobbes, thus, like Plato, not only treats art as an imitation of nature but conceives nature as a kind of art:

Nature, the art whereby God hath made and governs the world, is by the *art* of man, as in many other things, so in this also imitated, that it can make an artificial animal. For seeing life is but a motion of limbs, the beginning whereof is in some principal part within; why may we not say, that all *automata* (engines that move themselves by springs and wheels as doth a watch) have an artificial life? For what is the *heart*, but a *spring*; and the *nerves*, but so many *strings;* and the *joints*, but so many *wheels*, giving motion to the whole body, such as was intended by the artificer? *Art* goes yet further, imitating that rational and most excellent work of nature, *man*. For by art is created that great LEVIATHAN called a COMMONWEALTH, or STATE, in Latin CIVITAS, which is but an artificial man.[67]

That analogy of God's creation in nature to man's creations in art lent itself easily to the terminology of Christian theology and, during the Middle Ages,

66. H. Bergson, *L'Évolution créatrice* (34th ed.; Paris, 1929), p. 151: "Si nous pouvions nous dépouiller de tout orgueil, si, pour définir nôtre espèce, nous nous en tenions strictement à ce que l'histoire et la préhistoire nous présentent comme la caractéristique constante de l'homme et de l'intelligence, nous ne dirions peut-être pas *Homo sapiens*, mais *Homo faber*." Cf. Dewey, *Reconstruction in Philosophy*, p. 71. Kant's emphasis on the conditions of thought and on *possible experience* leads to a philosophy in which practical rather than theoretical reason occupies the central place; Dewey's emphasis on the conditions of action and on *experience* yields a philosophy in which theory and practice are both arts; cf. *Experience and Nature* (New York, 1929), pp. 357–58: "But if modern tendencies are justified in putting art and creation first, then the implications of this position should be avowed and carried through. It would then be seen that science is an art, that art is practice, and that the only distinction worth drawing is not between practice and theory, but between those modes of practice that are not intelligent, not inherently and immediately enjoyable, and those which are full of enjoyed meanings. When this perception dawns, it will be a commonplace that art—the mode of activity that is charged with the meanings capable of immediately enjoyed possession—is the complete culmination of nature, and that 'science' is properly a handmaiden that conducts natural events to this happy issue. Thus would disappear the separations that trouble present thinking: division of everything into nature *and* experience, of experience into practice *and* theory, art *and* science, of art into useful *and* fine, menial *and* free."

67. *Leviathan* (*The English Works of Thomas Hobbes*, ed. W. Molesworth [London, 1808], III, ix).

bent even the Aristotelian view of God as First Mover and First Cause to its services. When, however, a philosophic basis was sought for our judgments of things by examination of the nature of our knowledge, art was analogized to nature by means of the human faculties which bring together traits by which Aristotle had distinguished them, as judgment, for Kant, bears on the perception of purpose in nature and the perception of beauty in nature and art and so serves as link between the practical and the theoretical:

The concept formed by Judgement of a purposiveness of Nature belongs to natural concepts, but only as a regulative principle of the cognitive faculty; although the aesthetical judgement upon certain objects (of Nature or Art) which occasions it is, in respect of the feeling of pleasure or pain, a constitutive principle. The spontaneity in the play of the cognitive faculties, the harmony of which contains the ground of this pleasure, makes the above concept [of the purposiveness of nature] fit to be the mediating link between the realm of the natural concept and that of the concept of freedom in its effects; whilst at the same time it promotes the sensibility of the mind for moral feeling.⁶⁸

When, finally, a philosophic basis for our concept of nature and our judgment of values was sought in the examination of experience, purposiveness disappeared from nature as such and value from things as such, and art was analogized to nature by bringing together traits by which Aristotle had distinguished them, as all objects, for Dewey—the objects of the sciences and the objects of the arts—are tools, and art is natural, since it originates in natural tendencies in man and employs natural means to further natural ends.

In experience, human relations, institutions, and traditions are as much a part of the nature in which and by which we live as is the physical world. Nature in this meaning is not "outside." It is in us and we are in and of it. But there are multitudes of ways of participating in it, and these ways are characteristic not only of various experiences of the same individual, but of attitudes of aspiration, need and achievement that belong to civilizations in their collective aspect. Works of art are means by which we enter, through imagination and the emotions they evoke, into other forms of relationship and participation than our own.⁶⁹

68. Kant, *Critique of Judgement*, Introd., pp. 41–42. E. A. Poe makes similar, though more simple, use of the faculties of the mind to put Aristotelian distinctions to un-Aristotelian uses; cf. "The Poetic Principle" (*Works*, ed. Stedman and Woodberry [New York, 1914], VI, 11): "Dividing the world of mind into its three most obvious distinctions, we have the Pure Intellect, Taste, and the Moral Sense. I place Taste in the middle, because it is just this position which in the mind it occupies. It holds intimate relations with either extreme, but from the Moral Sense is separated by so faint a difference that Aristotle has not hesitated to place some of its operations among the virtues themselves. Nevertheless, we find the *offices* of the trio marked with a sufficient distinction. Just as tl.e Intellect concerns itself with Truth, so Taste informs us of the Beautiful, while the Moral Sense is regardful of Duty."

69. *Art as Experience*, p. 333; cf. also p. 79: "In other words, art is not nature, but it is nature transformed by entering into new relationships where it evokes a new emotional response." Cf. also *Experience and Nature*, pp. 136, 150–51, and esp. 358: "Thus the issue involved in experience as art in its pregnant sense and in art as processes and materials of

Nature is art because the universe, like the objects of art, is created, or because the judgment of purpose in nature, like the judgment of beauty, involves the free interplay of our faculties, or because our experience of things permits no sharp separation of our use, our knowledge, and our enjoyment of them; and each of these reasonable analogies is also reduced to literal-minded statements and criticized because it involves fictitious suppositions of eternal patterns of things, universal principles of thought, or collective aspects of epochs and civilizations.

The form in which Plato expressed his philosophy is indistinguishable from other forms of communication in his philosophy; for the subject matters of philosophy, poetry, rhetoric, and history are analogous, and the ends of the various forms of human activity are ultimately the same. It is no dramatic accident that Socrates spent part of the last hours of his life experimenting by divine direction with a poetic form; and there is no sharp line, in Plato's employment, between dialectic, myth, and history. Aristotle could therefore commend his recording of the Socratic method as the discovery of the universal in science and philosophy, and could deprecate his separation of the universal from the particular.[70] Aristotle's favorite means of differentiating the arts from one another is, in his sense, formal; and he therefore separated philosophy from poetry in terms, not of metrical forms, but of comparative universality, illustrating the distinction by placing poetry between philosophy and history.[71] So long as the principles of philosophy are sought in the nature of things, science is of universals, since it must apply to more than the particular instance; but, when the principles of philosophy are based on a preliminary examination of the nature of thought, the virtue of science may be found either in its universality (since scientific laws must be shown to be necessary, while their objectivity may be assured by the laws of thought) or in its particularity (since scientific laws must be shown to be objective, while their universality may be assured by the uniformity of nature). Poetry may in this stage of the discussion

---

nature continued by direction into achieved and enjoyed meanings, sums up in itself all the issues which have been previously considered. Thought, intelligence, science is the intentional direction of natural events to meanings capable of immediate possession and enjoyment; this direction—which is operative art—is itself a natural event in which nature otherwise partial and incomplete comes fully to itself; so that objects of conscious experience when reflectively chosen, form the 'end' of nature."

70. *Metaph.* xiii. 1078^{b}27–32.

71. *Poet.* 1. 1447^{a}16–20: "Even if statements concerning medicine or natural philosophy be set forth in metrical form, it is customary to call the author a poet. Yet there is nothing in common between Homer and Empedocles except the meter, and therefore it is right to call the one poet, but the other physicist rather than poet." *Ibid.* 9. 1451^{b}5–7: "Wherefore poetry is more philosophic and more serious than history, for poetry is expressive more of universals, while history states singulars."

be analogized to philosophy or to history; and the poetic quality, since it is midway between the general and the particular, may combine the two, or indeed it may be the source of the generality of philosophy or the particularity of history. Sidney borrows Aristotle's example to discover Empedocles a poet[72] and to assign to poetry the performance of moral tasks at which philosophy and history fail.[73] According to Bacon, on the other hand, poetry is nothing else than an imitation of history for the giving of pleasure,[74] while Newman can quote Bacon to illustrate Aristotle's doctrine that poetry is more general than history and can follow Aristotle's judgment that Empedocles was no poet but a natural historian writing in verse in support of the doctrine that natural history and philosophy are proper materials for poetry.[75] Wordsworth, on the other hand, makes use of vague echoes of Aristotle to support the position that poetry is the most philosophical of all writing and to contrast poetry to matter of fact or science.[76] Like "philosophy," which may be taken either as identical

72. Sidney, *op. cit.*, p. 4.

73. *Ibid.*, pp. 13–14: "The Philosopher therefore, and the Historian, are they which would win the goale, the one by precept, the other by example: but both, not having both, doo both halt. For the Philosopher setting downe with thornie arguments, the bare rule, is so hard of utterance, and so mistie to be conceived, that one that hath no other guide but him, shall wade in him till he be old, before he shall find sufficient cause to be honest. For his knowledge standeth so upon the abstract and generall, that happie is that man who may understand him, and more happie, that can apply what he doth understand. On the other side, the Historian wanting the precept, is so tied, not to what should be, but to what is, to the particular truth of things, and not to the general reason of things, that his example draweth no necessarie consequence, and therefore a lesse fruitfull doctrine. Now doth the peerlesse Poet performe both, for whatsoever the Philosopher saith should be done, he gives a perfect picture of it by some one, by whom he presupposeth it was done, so as he coupleth the generall notion with the particuler example."

74. *De augmentis scientiarum*, Book II, chap. xiii (*Works*, IV, 315); *Of the Proficience and Advancement of Learning*, Book II (*Works*, III, 343). Cf. above, n. 21.

75. Newman, "Poetry, with Reference to Aristotle's 'Poetics,'" *Essays Critical and Historical* (London, 1890), I, 12: "Empedocles wrote his physics in verse, and Oppian his history of animals. Neither were poets—the one was an historian of nature, the other a sort of biographer of brutes. Yet a poet may make natural history or philosophy the material of his composition."

76. Wordsworth, *op. cit.*, p. 89: "Aristotle, I have been told, has said, that Poetry is the most philosophic of all writing: it is so: its object is truth, not individual and local, but general, and operative; not standing upon external testimony, but carried alive into the heart by passion; truth which is its own testimony, which gives competence and confidence to the tribunal to which it appeals, and receives them from the same tribunal. Poetry is the image of man and nature. The obstacles which stand in the way of the fidelity of the Biographer and Historian, and of their consequent utility, are incalculably greater than those which are to be encountered by the Poet who comprehends the dignity of his art." Cf. *ibid.*, p. 86 n.: "I here use the word 'Poetry' (though against my own judgment) as opposed to the word Prose, and synonymous with metrical composition. But much confusion has been introduced into criticism by this contradistinction of Poetry and Prose, instead of the more philosophical one of Poetry and Matter of Fact, or Science." Cf. J. R. Lowell, "Shakespeare Once More," *Literary Essays* (Boston, 1894), III, 70–71: "The aim of the artist is psychologic, not historic truth. It is comparatively easy for an author to *get up* any period with tolerable minuteness in externals, but readers and audiences find more difficulty in getting them down, though

with poetry or as an imperfect truth perfected by poetry, "history" takes on two senses in this Platonic opposition of a complete and partial truth. Shelley contrasts history to poetry:

A poem is the very image of life expressed in its eternal truth. There is this difference between a story and a poem, that a story is a catalogue of detached facts, which have no other connexion than time, place, circumstance, cause, and effect; the other is the creation of actions according to the unchangeable forms of human nature, as existing in the mind of the creator, which is itself the image of all other minds. The one is partial, and applies only to a definite period of time, and a certain combination of events which can never again recur; the other is universal, and contains within itself the germ of a relation to whatever motives or actions have place in the possible varieties of human nature.[77]

Froude, on the other hand, finds the universality in that which is better and genuine in man and contrasts prose and verse but identifies the highest history with the highest poetry:

The prose historian may give us facts and names; he may catalogue the successions, and tell us long stories of battles, and of factions, and of political intrigues; he may draw characters for us of the sort which figure commonly in such features of human affairs, men of the unheroic, unpoetic kind—the Cleons, the Sejanuses, the Tiberiuses, a Philip the Second or a Louis Quatorze, in whom the noble element died out into selfishness and vulgarity. But great men—all MEN properly so called (whatever is genuine and natural in them)—lie beyond prose, and can only be really represented by the poet.[78]

Finally, if the principles of our knowledge and the nature of things are sought in the processes of experience, history may assume dominance among sciences and things, either in the sense of accounting for the historical succession of poetry and philosophy as forms of wisdom and explanation—as Vico finds the "Aristotelian" aphorism that nothing is in understanding that was not prior in sense exemplified in the sequence after an age of poets, whose wisdom is of the sense, of an age of philosophers, whose wisdom is of the understanding[79]—or in the sense that all things are histories—as Dewey finds

oblivion swallows scores of them at a gulp. The saving truth in such matters is a truth to essential and permanent characteristics." Lowell, moreover, appreciated the fashion in which Wordsworth's doctrine that *poetry* is *philosophy* involved the further identification of philosophy with a kind of *history*, the history of the poet's mind; cf. "Wordsworth" (*Writings* [Boston, 1898], IV, 397–98): "He was theoretically determined not only to be a philosophic poet, but to be a *great* philosophic poet, and to this end he must produce an epic. Leaving aside the question whether the epic be obsolete or not, it may be doubted whether the history of a single man's mind is universal enough in its interest to furnish all the requirements of the epic machinery, and it may be more than doubted whether a poet's philosophy be ordinary metaphysics, divisible into chapter and section."

77. Shelley, *op. cit.*, p. 108.

78. "Homer," *Short Studies on Great Subjects*, 1st ser. (New York, 1873), p. 410; cf. also "The Science of History," *ibid.*, pp. 32–35.

79. G. B. Vico, *Principii di scienza nuova*, Book II (3d ed.; Naples, 1744), I, 129 and 376. The relation between poetry and philosophy is conceived in terms of particularity and gen-

history basic to all knowledge and histories more truly known than mathematical and physical objects.[80] Aristotle's distinction of philosophy, poetry,
and history has been made the basis for assigning to poetry or history functions
and characteristics which Aristotle conceived as philosophic, and, as a final
irony, historians of philosophy have reproached him for mistaking poets for
philosophers, misled in his humorless literal-mindedness by Plato's gentle
irony.[81]

While poets dispute the authority of philosophers, supplementing scientific
inquiries, rectifying metaphysical reflections, and expounding lofty and enigmatic visions, and philosophers in their turn borrow the devices of the poet to
expound the nature, function, and place of the arts and use the arguments of
the moralist or the economist to banish poets from their perfect states or to instruct them in their tasks as educators or propagandists, the critic sometimes
conceives his function to be distinct from that of the artist and dialectician and

---

erality (cf. *ibid.*, Book I, pp. 90–91): "Axiom 53. Men first perceive without noticing; then
they notice with perturbed and agitated soul; finally they reflect with a pure mind. This
axiom is the principle of poetic judgments, which are formed by the perception of the passions
and emotions, unlike philosophic judgments which are formed through reflection by reason.
Wherefore the latter approximate more closely to truth the more they are raised to universality, and the former are more certain the more they descend to particularity." The
poetic truth may be true metaphysically when the physical truth is false (*ibid.*, p. 88). The
history of mankind is analogized to the life of a man, and the infancy of the race is an age of
poetry, prior to the formation of philosophy; the relation of art to nature is therefore complex—men supplement nature by the attentive study of art, but in poetry no one succeeds by
art who has not the advantages of nature, and therefore, if poetry founded pagan civilization,
from which in turn followed all the arts, the first poets were by nature. The people of the
infant world were poets, and the arts are imitations of nature, a kind of *real poetry* (*ibid.*,
p. 90). From this poetic wisdom derive on one branch a poetic logic, a poetic morality, a
poetic economics, and a poetic politics, and on the other branch a poetic physics, from which
proceed a poetic cosmography, astronomy, chronology, and geography (*ibid.*, p. 132).

80. *Experience and Nature*, p. 163: "And yet if all natural existences *are* histories, divorce
between history and the logical mathematical schemes which are the appropriate objects of
pure science, terminates in the conclusion that of existences there is no science, no adequate
knowledge. Aside from mathematics, all knowledge is historic; chemistry, geology, physiology, as well as anthropology and those human events to which, arrogantly, we usually restrict the title of history. Only as science is seen to be fulfilled and brought to itself in intelligent management of historical processes in their continuity can man be envisaged as within
nature, and not as a supernatural extrapolation. Just because nature is what it is, history is
capable of being more truly known—understood, intellectually realized—than are mathematical and physical objects."

81. J. Burnet (*Early Greek Philosophy* [3d ed.; London, 1920], p. 127) argues that Aristotle
is mistaken in treating Xenophanes as the founder of the Eleatic school and that this mistake
originated in his misinterpretation of Plato. "Just as he [Plato] called the Herakleiteans
'followers of Homer and still more ancient teachers,' so he attached the Eleatics to Xenophanes and still earlier authorities. We have seen before how these playful and ironical remarks
of Plato were taken seriously by his successors, and we must not make too much of this fresh
instance of Aristotle's literalness." Cf. *ibid.*, p. 32: "It is often forgotten that Aristotle
derived much of his information from Plato, and we must specially observe that he more than
once takes Plato's humorous remarks too literally."

sometimes enters into competition with both, assuming the role of poet among poets and dialectician among dialecticians. The functions assigned to criticism reflect all the analogies and distinctions found in the ends of poetry and philosophy, the objects of art and nature, and the forms of history, poetry, and philosophy. For criticism may be conceived as a technique applied only to works of art, if the literal distinctions are maintained; or it may be implied in any knowledge, involved in any activity, and applied to any object. The history of criticism can be traced and understood, therefore, in part by differentiating kinds of criticism applied to art, and in part by finding the manners in which criticism, conceived more broadly in a variety of ways, applies to art in particular. In the analogical tradition the effort is to avoid unreal distinctions between the emotional and the intellectual, the moral and the aesthetic, the artistic and the practical; and the development of the tradition is therefore the evolution of a single dialectic in which opposed devices for achieving critical universality jostle one another: criticism is sometimes the application of a theory in the judgment of objects and actions; it is sometimes the technique which determines both theories and arts; it is sometimes, like theory, itself an art. In the literal tradition the effort is to find a technique proper to each subject matter and therefore to separate, for the purposes of accuracy and clarity, considerations of moral, political, scientific, metaphysical, and aesthetic characteristics even in the judgment of a single object; and the development of the tradition is therefore a succession of analyses which achieve critical particularity in application to objects of art, canons of taste, or means of production and manners of social use. Echoes of the one effort emerge from the mingling of the two traditions as speculations concerning the Good, the True, and the Beautiful; and the other effort leaves its mark in discussions of the individual arts.

For Plato, "criticism" was a general term applied to all processes of judgment, those involved in the common distinctions made by the interlocutors in the dialogues as well as the technical distinctions of reason, but used particularly for the judgments pronounced in law-courts in application of the law; the judgment of art is usually treated by Plato in the context of broader political and judiciary functions. There are two intellectual arts or sciences—the science of commanding, which is the proper art of the statesman, and the art of judging, which, since it pronounces on what falls under or is disclosed by the art of commanding, is also part of the statesman's art.[82] Judgment is a decision between better and worse in all fields: between the unjust and the just man,[83]

---

82. *Statesman* 259E–260A, 292B, 305B.

83. *Rep.* ii. 360D.

between possible kinds of lives and pleasures,[84] between pleasure and wisdom,[85] between true and false.[86] The criteria by which judgment pronounces on its subject matter to determine the comparative value of things among gods and men, and the degree of their approximation to the eternal good, are three: experience, intelligence, and discussion (λόγος), the latter being the "instrument" of judgment; in all three the philosopher has the advantage over other men.[87] The lawgiver, therefore, combats an erroneous doctrine—such as the separation of the pleasant from the just—by habituation, commendation, and discussion; and in the opposition of two judgments the character of the judge is reflected in the soundness of the judgment, for the judgment of the better man is more authoritative.[88] One might even concede the opinion of the majority of men that pleasure is the proper criterion of music and poetry, not the pleasure of any chance person, but of that man or those men who excel in virtue and education, for the critic should be a teacher; and when poets adapt their works to the criterion of the pleasure of their judges (so that their audiences become the teachers of the poets), they corrupt themselves as well as their audiences, whose criteria of pleasure ought to be improved by the judgments of better men rather than degraded to the common level.[89] The charm which causes pleasure, however, is usually accompanied by correctness or utility; and consequently the arts which are imitative and produce likenesses are not to be judged by pleasure or untrue opinion but by the proportion and equality they possess: to judge a poem, one must know its essence, for one must know what its intention is and what original it represents, if one is to decide whether it succeeds or fails in achieving its intention.[90] The critic of music, poetry, and the other arts is therefore the philosopher in the perfect state, or, failing that, the lawgiver and the educator.[91]

There are numerous ingredients of later criticism in Plato's philosophy—the moral emphasis; the use of the criteria of experience, intelligence, and words or discussion (any one of which might assume a dominant position in derivative forms of criticism); the prominence of pleasure balanced by various forms of rightness or utility; and, finally, the background of an eternal beauty, which things imitate, which philosophers and poets seek in their manipulations of words, and which cannot itself be expressed without recourse to eternal standards of truth and goodness. The influence of Plato on later criticism is to be found for the most part in the emphasis given to one or another

84. *Ibid.* ix. 580B–C; *Philebus* 27C.

85. *Philebus* 65A.

86. *Theaetetus* 150B.

87. *Rep.* ix. 581E–583A.

88. *Laws* ii. 663A–C.

89. *Ibid.* 658E–659C.

90. *Ibid.* 667B–668B.

91. *Ibid.* viii. 829D; xii. 948E–949A; vi. 765B.

of these critical criteria or aesthetic traits rather than in the dialectical association of them and the interplay among them which are essential to Plato's conception of criticism. In particular, criticism is reduced to narrower limits and the dialectic of its discussion is restricted and frozen in either of two ways: by limiting its application to works of art or literature, or by assigning to criticism the role of applying theory to practice in specific subject matters. The first restriction was accomplished, probably under Stoic and Epicurean influences, in Hellenistic Greece. The word "critic" is used in counterdistinction to "grammarian" in the "Platonic" *Axiochos* (366E), which may show Epicurean influences; and Crates, the Stoic philosopher, is credited with having first distinguished "critic" and "grammarian," the former being learned in all the erudite sciences, the latter being equipped to interpret unusual words and to treat of accents and similar properties of words; the critic thus is related to the grammarian as the architect to the craftsman.[92] It is probable that this literal distinction of critic concerned with meanings from grammarian concerned with words reflects the influence of Aristotle's restriction of the word "grammarian" to the treatment of words as sounds and symbols apart from significances, while the second manner of restricting "criticism" was developed from a like analogizing and fitting of the meaning of the term "criticism" to his division of the sciences. Aristotle held that every theory and every method admitted of two kinds of proficiency: scientific knowledge of the thing and a kind of broad educational acquaintance with the science, so that it is the mark of a well-educated man to be able to criticize and judge with some probability whether a thing is well or badly expounded.[93] In later writers Aristotle's conception of the theoretic and practical is confused with Plato's conception of the intellectual and practical, and every science (contrary to Aristotle's supposition) is made to have a theory and an application between which criticism mediates. Clausewitz, thus, in his treatise *On War*, devotes a chapter to criticism so conceived:

The influence of theoretical truths upon practical life is always exerted more through criticism than through rules for practice. Criticism is the application to actual events of

92. Sextus Empiricus *Adversus grammaticos* i. 79. For the evolution of κριτικός, γραμματικός, and φιλόλογος cf. Gudeman's article κριτικός, Pauly-Wissowa-Kroll, *Real-Encyclopädie der classischen Altertumswissenschaft* (Stuttgart, 1921), XI, 1912–15. In the course of the discussion "grammarian" is analogized to, or made synonymous with, "critic," and the identification as well as the discrimination of meanings is continued even into modern discussion. This discussion of the relation of grammarian and critic is frequently associated with the second manner of fixing and restricting the meaning of "critic" by consideration of the boundaries of the sciences. Both processes are illustrated, for example, by Octavius Ferrarius (*Prolusiones et epistolae: accesserunt formulae ad petenda doctoris insignia* [Padua, 1650], p. 116): "Sed Criticos nostros sive Grammaticos duplici crimine arcessis, altero quod ineptias sectantur acerrimo, altero quod non contenti finibus suis, audent etiam vestros limites revellere, et in scientiarum campum audacter transcendere."

93. *De partibus animalium* i. 1. 639ª1–6.

theoretical truth, and so not only brings the latter nearer to life but also accustoms the intelligence more to these truths through the constant repetition of their applications.[94]

The "critical narration" which Clausewitz employs in his treatment of war consists of three parts, each of which has its special pertinence and history in the development of criticism: (1) the historical discovery and establishment of doubtful facts; (2) critical investigation proper, which consists in tracing the effect from its causes; and (3) criticism proper, which consists in testing the means employed. These two particularizations of Platonic criticism divide between them the text of the poet (which may be interpreted analogically to apply to any subject) and the truths or significances of the sciences (which may be brought analogically to apply to any text).

The Platonic criticism may, on the other hand, be used to resist such particularization, for it may be made to apply to the whole of philosophy to become a preliminary to or substitute for dialectic. Protagoras and the other Sophists are prominent in the philosophy of Plato because they are the dramatic representation of the consequences which follow from denying objective Truth and Beauty: philosophy then becomes critical; I am the judge of the existence of things that are to me and of the nonexistence of things that are not to me;[95] we all sit in judgment on the judgment of everyone else;[96] the criteria by which we judge things are internal, as, for example, the coincidence of thought and sensation;[97] and each is his own best judge concerning what is future.[98] Yet those same relativistic devices are used by philosophers to avoid relativism and skepticism, for the certainty of knowledge of things and the universality of moral standards may be based on judgment, either in the sense of making criticism of human faculties a preliminary to philosophy or of making judgment the basis of first principles in each of the branches of philosophy. "Our age," Kant said, "is, in every sense of the word, the age of criticism, and everything must submit to it."[99] Criticism becomes a necessary prelude to the task of philosophy:

It will now be seen how there can be a special science serving as a critique of pure reason. Reason is the faculty which supplies the principles of knowledge *a priori*. Pure reason therefore is that faculty which supplies the principles of knowing anything entirely *a priori*. An Organum of pure reason ought to comprehend all the principles by which pure knowledge *a priori* can be acquired and fully established. A complete application of such an Organum would give us a System of Pure Reason. But as that would be a difficult task, and as at present it is still doubtful whether and when such an expansion

94. *On War*, trans. O. J. M. Jolles (New York, 1943), Book II, chap. v, p. 92.

95. *Theaet.* 160C.

96. *Ibid.* 170D.   98. *Ibid.* 187E.

97. *Ibid.* 178B.   99. *Critique of Pure Reason*, p. xix, n. 1.

of our knowledge is here possible, we may look on a mere criticism of pure reason, its sources and limits, as a kind of preparation for a complete system of pure reason. It should be called a critique, not a doctrine, of pure reason. Its usefulness would be negative only, serving for a purging rather than for an expansion of our reason, and, what after all is a considerable gain, guarding reason against errors.[100]

Aesthetic judgment, which bears on beauty in art or in nature, requires no inference, theoretic or practical, to external things, but depends wholly on the free interplay of imagination and understanding. Judgment may, on the other hand, be the basis of philosophy, because judgment and common sense are equally distributed among men, unlike apprehension or conception of the things we judge, and truth and falsity are qualities which belong only to judgment.[101] Since judgment may be either intuitive or grounded on argument, the chief problems of philosophy center about the judgment of first principles, among others the first principles of taste:

I think there are axioms, even in matters of *taste*. . . . The fundamental rules of poetry and music, and painting, and dramatic action and eloquence, have been always the same, and will be so to the end of the world. . . . I do not maintain that taste, so far as it is acquired, or so far as it is merely animal, can be reduced to principles. But, as far as it is founded on judgment, it certainly may. The virtues, the graces, the muses, have a beauty that is intrinsic. It lies not in the feelings of the spectator, but in the real excellence of the object. If we do not perceive their beauty, it is owing to the defect or to the perversion of our faculties.[102]

In either sense the critic discovers the fundamental rules of philosophy and art, of the perception of truth and the apprehension or construction of beauty. Lessing remarks that the first person who compared painting and poetry was a man of taste, an amateur who observed that they both produced pleasure in him, and that the second person, who investigated the inner cause of this pleasure and found that it flowed from the same source, was a philosopher; these two could not easily make a wrong use of their feeling or their reason, but the third person, the critic, who reflected on the value and distribution of these rules, might misapply them and so affect art and taste.[103]

100. *Ibid.*, pp. 8–9.

101. Cf. Thomas Reid, *Essays on the Intellectual Powers of Man* (*The Works of Thomas Reid, D.D.*, ed. Sir William Hamilton [8th ed.; Edinburgh, 1895], I, 366). Reid cites Descartes in support of his position: "Nothing is so equally distributed among men as judgment. Wherefore, it seems reasonable to believe, that the power of distinguishing what is true from what is false (which we properly call judgment or right reason) is by nature equal in all men; and therefore that the diversity of our opinions does not arise from one person being endowed with a greater power of reason than another, but only from this, that we do not lead our thought in the same track, nor attend to the same things." He quotes Cicero to the same effect: "It is wonderful when the learned and unlearned differ so much in art, how little they differ in judgment. For art being derived from Nature, is good for nothing, unless it move and delight Nature." Cf. also *ibid.*, p. 243.

102. *Ibid.*, p. 453.   103. Lessing, *op. cit.*, p. 292.

If, finally, the hope of examining the conditions of all possible experience by criticism or of arriving at common principles of taste by judgment is thought to be as illusory as the appeal to eternal ideas, then principles are sought in actual experience, and criticism, as well as philosophy itself, becomes an art. Viewed in terms of the activity of man, according to Spingarn, critical judgment and artistic creation are fundamentally the same:

> The identity of genius and taste is the final achievement of modern thought on the subject of art, and it means that fundamentally, in their most significant moments, the creative and the critical instincts are one and the same. From Goethe to Carlyle, from Carlyle to Arnold, from Arnold to Symons, there has been much talk of the "creative function" of Criticism. For each of these men the phrase held a different content; for Arnold it meant merely that Criticism creates the intellectual atmosphere of the age, a social function of high importance, perhaps, yet wholly independent of aesthetic significance. But the ultimate truth toward which these men were tending was more radical than that, and plays havoc with all the old platitudes about the sterility of taste. Criticism at last can free itself of its age-long self-contempt, now that it may realize that aesthetic judgment and artistic creation are instinct with the same vital life.[104]

Or criticism may be conceived to be properly neither impressionistic nor judicial, but to consist, as Dewey holds, in reliving the processes the artist went through to the end of deepening the appreciation of others:

> For critical judgment not only grows out of the critic's experience of objective matter, and not only depends upon that for validity, but has for its office the deepening of just such experience in others. Scientific judgments not only end in increased control but for those who understand they add enlarged meanings to the things perceived and dealt with in daily contact with the world. The function of criticism is the reëducation of perception of works of art; it is an auxiliary in the process, a difficult process, of learning to see and hear. The conception that its business is to appraise, to judge in the legal and moral sense, arrests the perception of those who are influenced by the criticism that assumes this task. The moral office of criticism is performed indirectly. . . . We lay hold of the full import of a work of art only as we go through in our own vital processes the processes the artist went through in producing the work. It is the critic's privilege to share in the promotion of this active process. His condemnation is that he so often arrests it.[105]

Or, finally, criticism may be conceived, as it was by Tolstoy, as one of the conditions which lead to the production of counterfeit art in our society, since art criticism is impossible in societies in which art is undivided and appraised by the religious conception of life common to the whole people, but it grows on the art of the upper classes, who do not acknowledge the religious perception of their time.[106]

---

104. *Op. cit.*, pp. 42–43.　　　　105. *Art as Experience*, pp. 324–25.

106. Tolstoy, *What Is Art?* pp. 241–43. The analogy of Dewey's basic principles to those of Tolstoy may be seen in his condemnation of the separation of art from the conditions of life consequent on the growth of capitalism and the *nouveaux riches* and his condemnation of

The literal separation of the arts and the sciences requires the differentiation of subject matters and methods, for the difference between the analogical and the literal is not to be found in any difference in the ease with which arts may be separated or compared by the two methods, but in the priority given to the differences or the likenesses, so that either differences are worked dialectically from basic similarities or similarities are found among things whose differences have been stated. "Criticism" and the related terms (κρίνειν, κρίσις, κριτικός), which for Plato are general terms, are restricted in Aristotle's usage to one of the three kinds of sciences; and some of the peculiarities of the history of criticism are to be attributed to the fact that they belong properly not to the theoretic, or the poetic, but to the practical sciences or to the practical treatment of any science which is possible since politics is an architectonic science: they do not appear in the *Poetics* (except as part of the title of a tragedy), but they are used extensively in the *Nicomachean Ethics*, the *Politics*, and the *Rhetoric*, and their other appearances in the works of Aristotle can be explained by the primarily practical sense given to them there. There are two sources of movement in man, appetite and mind,[107] imagination being a kind of thinking. The moral problem consists in a sense in submitting the appetitive part of the soul to the rational.[108] The problem of art, on the other hand, turns primarily on the application of knowledge to the organization of external materials, and therefore, unlike the moral virtues, the arts consist in the possession of knowledge, and their products are themselves capable of excellence or virtue.

Moreover, the case of the arts is not similar to that of the virtues, for works of art have their merit in themselves, so that it is sufficient if they are produced having a certain quality, but acts performed in accordance with the virtues are not done justly or temperately if they have a certain quality, but only if the one who performs them has a certain quality when he performs them: first, he must act knowingly; second, he must act by choice and by choice of the act for its own sake; and third, he must act from a firm and constant character. These are not numbered among the essentials for the possession of the arts, except only knowledge; but for the possession of the virtues knowledge has little or no weight, whereas the other conditions have, not a little force, but all,

---

the criticism which results from these conditions (*Art as Experience*, pp. 8–11). Conversely, Tolstoy pleads the importance of the proper kind of criticism, modeled on Matthew Arnold's view of the purpose of criticism to find among all that has been written that which is most important and best and to direct attention to it—unlike the actual criticism of the time, which set itself the task of praising such works as have obtained notoriety, devising foggy philosophic-aesthetic theories to justify them, or of ridiculing bad work or works of another camp more or less wittily, or of deducing the direction of the movement of our whole society from types depicted by writers and, in general, expressing economic and political opinions under the guise of discussing literary productions ("Der Büttnerbauer," in *Tolstoy on Art*, pp. 382, 386–87).

107. *De anima* iii. 10. 433ᵃ9.

108. *Nicomachean Ethics* i. 13. 1102ᵇ28; iii. 12. 1119ᵇ11.

since it is the very nature of the virtues to be acquired from the repeated performance of just and temperate acts.[109]

Art and the virtues are both related to knowledge, but in different and characteristic fashions. The arts, since they are external principles of change, are productive (that is, poetic) powers which are rational or (which is the same thing) sciences which are productive; they are themselves intellectual virtues.[110] The virtues, since they are habits of action, involve knowledge, but they are distinct from prudence, which is the intellectual virtue concerned with action.[111] The arts share with the sciences the peculiarity that they may deal with opposite things and may have opposite effects, as medicine may produce either health or disease, while the virtue or habit which produces a certain result does not also produce the contrary.[112] It is possible, therefore, to speak of a virtue of art; and, indeed, wisdom, the highest of the intellectual virtues, may be detected in the virtue or excellence of art, but there is no virtue of prudence; in art, moreover, voluntary error is preferable to involuntary, but in matters of prudence and the moral virtues the reverse is true.[113] An intellectual process which is not the same as opinion or any particular science is therefore involved in the virtues: intelligence (σύνεσις) is either the use of *opinion* in *judging* (κρίνειν) of what is said about matters which fall under prudence or the use of *science* in *learning* about matters proper to science, and consideration (γνώμη) is right judgment (κρίσις ὀρθή) of the equitable. Intelligence differs from prudence in that prudence determines what ought to be done or not to be done, that is, it commands, whereas the function of intelligence is limited to making judgments, that is, it is merely critical.[114] There are, in all, four faculties which treat of ultimate and particular things: intuitive reason (νοῦς) perceives principles and the particulars which fall under them in the context of science; prudence (φρόνησις) is concerned with action in the context of the right principles; while intelliegence (σύνεσις) and consideration (γνώμη) are concerned with judgment (κρίσις) of contingent particulars.[115] In an important

109. *Ibid.* ii. 4. 1105ª26–1105ᵇ5.

110. *Ibid.* vi. 4. 1140ª1–23; *Metaph.* ix. 2. 1046ª36.

111. *Nic. Eth.* ii. 6. 1106ᵇ36 ff.; vi. 13. 1144ᵇ1–1145ª2.

112. *Ibid.* v. 1. 1129ª13; *Metaph.* ix. 2. 1046ª36 and 5. 1048ª8; *De interpretatione* 13. 22ᵇ36.

113. *Nic. Eth.* vi. 5. 1140ᵇ21–25; 7. 1141ª9–12.

114. *Ibid.* vi. 10–11. 1142ᵇ34–1143ᵇ17; esp. 1143ª10, 14, 15, 20, 23, 30.

115. *Ibid.* 1143ª25–1143ᵇ7. This differentiation is of the utmost importance, not only for the discrimination of the sciences from one another, but for the separation of knowledge from virtue in Aristotle's philosophy and in the literal tradition in general. The modern revolt against what passed for Aristotelianism may be stated succinctly as the reduction of these four processes or "habits" to judgment. When first principles are known by "judgment" or "common sense" or *bon sens*, and when that ability to judge the true and the false is attributed

sense, therefore, actions require *judgment*, while objects of art are *known*. Or, to state the conclusion paradoxically in the modern cognates of the terms Aristotle used: "criticism" is essential in ethics and politics, while art is understood and explained in its proper "science."

The arts and the sciences are therefore associated and distinguished from actions and practical affairs in the manner in which they are subject to knowledge and criticism. We are in general good judges or critics of those matters with which we are acquainted, of a particular subject if we are trained in that or universally if we have a general education. Therefore the scientist is a judge of any matter that falls under his science, but his judgment does not differ from his scientific knowledge; and a well-educated man is a good judge of any matter pertinent to the scope of his interest, but his judgment is the application of the arts he has learned to the argument or the construction. In questions bearing on the moral virtues or political actions, however, the application of reason is less direct, for it is not easy to determine such questions by reasoning or to state the resolution in words, since judgment depends on the particular fact and is based on perception; this is the reason why the young are educated in the arts and the sciences but are improper auditors of lectures on politics.[116] On the other hand, judgment and criticism have a peculiar place in ethics, since the moral virtues are habits of choice, and choice involves judgments.[117] Pleasure attends both the operation of the contemplative faculty on intelligible, and that

---

in general to all mankind, the distinction between theoretic and practical, between moral criticism and artistic knowledge, disappears. The line that runs back from the modern *bon sens* to the Stoic tradition, which Gilson traces, is therefore mediated by the Aristotelian *synesis* and *eusynesia;* and Gilson overemphasizes the exclusive importance of the one element when he says, "La traduction latine de *bon sens* n'est possible qu'au moyen du gallicisme *bona mens*" (René Descartes, *Discours de la méthode*, ed. E. Gilson [Paris, 1925], pp. 81–83). Cf. Thomas Aquinas, *In decem libros ethicorum Aristotelis ad Nicomachum expositio*, ed. A. M. Pirotta and M. S. Gillet (Turin, 1934), Lib. VI, lect. 9, par. 1240, p. 409: "Unde dicit quod prudentia est praeceptiva, inquantum scilicet est finis ipsius determinare quid oporteat agere. Sed synesis est solum judicativa. Et pro eodem accipitur synesis et eusynesia, id est, bonus sensus, sicut et iidem dicuntur syneti et eusyneti, id est sensati et bene sensati, quorum est bene judicare." Cf., for *bonus sensus, Summa theologica* IIa, IIae, qu. 51, a. 4; *Commentary on the Sentences* Lib. III, dist. 33, qu. 3, a 1, qu. 2; for *synesis, Summa theologica* Ia, IIae, qu. 57, a.6. The instrumentalist consequences of this shift may be seen in the fact that "judgment" is by contraries, and is explicated by the analogy of the carpenter's rule, which is the test (κριτής) of the straight and the crooked (cf. *De anima* i. 5. 411ª2–7).

116. *Nic. Eth.* i. 3. 1094b27–1095ª2; ii. 9. 1109b20–23; iv. 5. 1126b2–4; *De part. anim.* i. 1. 639ª1–639b14. It should be noted that the general "criticism" is of method and has no bearing on substantive truth or falsity. Cf. *Posterior Analytics* ii. 19. 99b35; and for the psychological bases of judgment in sensation cf. *De anima* ii. 11. 424ª5–6; iii. 9. 432ª15–16, ˋ12. 434b3–4.

117. The good man judges well of good and noble things; cf. *Nic. Eth.* i. 9. 1109ª22–24; iii. 4. 1113ª29–31. It is difficult to judge pleasure impartially (cf. *ibid.* ii. 9. 1109b7–9). Judgment is the result of deliberation and is antecedent to choice (cf. *ibid.* iii. 3. 1113ª2–14). Responsibility depends on the source of the power to judge (cf. *ibid.* 5. 1114b5–8).

of the critical faculty on sensible, objects,[118] and in practical matters judgment of fact takes precedence over the opinions of the wise.[119] When one proceeds from the sphere of ethics to that of politics, the function of criticism or judgment increases, for the transition is by way of the virtue of justice, and legal justice is defined as the judgment of the just and the unjust.[120] Something of the Platonic distinction between ruling and judging appears in the political discussion of judgment, for those who govern must command and judge, while those who are governed must judge and distribute offices.[121] The citizen is therefore defined by his participation in the deliberative and judicial processes of the state.[122] Judgment applies not only to the decision of the law court,[123] and to the action of magistrates and assembly,[124] but also to the general determination of public interest and justice,[125] and is finally involved also in deliberation.[126] These considerations of the function of judgment or criticism in politics determine its central place in rhetoric, since that art exists to affect judgments.[127]

To be a good judge in moral and political questions, then, one must have had experience in the sense of having performed actions by which habits have been formed, while one may be a good judge in most of the arts by means of knowledge and a kind of science of how the thing is made. The teaching of the science of politics presents peculiar problems, because it is a *science* or *art* of *actions*, and the application of knowledge to actions is not direct. Aristotle elucidates the difficulty by the analogy of the arts. Unlike the other sciences and arts, politics is not taught by those who practice it, for politicians seem to rely more on experience than on abstract reason, while the Sophists profess to teach it but are ignorant of the science and its subject, since they confuse it with rhetoric and imagine that constitutions can be framed by making collections of existing laws reputed to be good. The kind of teaching and learning that is possible in

118. *Ibid.* x. 4. 1174ᵇ31–1175ᵃ3.

119. *Ibid.* 8. 1179ᵃ9–20.

120. *Ibid.* v. 6. 1134ᵃ30–32; cf. also *ibid.* 9. 1136ᵇ32 ff.

121. *Pol.* vii. 4. 1326ᵇ12–20.

122. *Ibid.* iii. 1. 1275ᵃ22–23; 1275ᵇ11–21; 6. 1281ᵇ31.

123. *Ibid.* v. 6. 1306ᵃ36–38.

124. *Ibid.* iv. 15. 1298ᵃ28–33, 1299ᵃ25–28; ii. 8. 1273ᵇ9–13.

125. *Ibid.* iii. 9. 1280ᵃ14–16; vii. 9. 1328ᵇ13–24.

126. *Ibid.* iii. 10. 1286ᵃ21–35; this is particularly true in questions of equity (*ibid.* 11. 1287ᵇ14–18).

127. *Rhetoric* ii. 1. 1377ᵇ21–29, 1378ᵃ20–23, 18. 1391ᵇ8–20. The kinds of listeners determine the purposes of speeches and therefore the classification of kinds of oratory: the familiar distinction of contemplative from critical reappears among the kinds of hearers (cf. *ibid.* i. 3. 1358ᵇ2–4). Similarly, the commonplace concerning the prudent man is stated in terms of the credit to be given to his powers of judgment (cf. *ibid.* 7. 1164ᵇ11–14).

subjects pertinent to political judgment and criticism is illustrated by music, which differs from the other arts in the knowledge and experience required for its understanding. Even selection among constitutions involves "intelligence" and the ability to "judge" correctly; and, as in music, those experienced in this art are alone able to judge rightly the works produced in it and understand how and by what means they are perfected and what harmonizes with what, while those inexperienced in the art must be content if they do not fail to discern, as they do in painting, that the work is well or badly made. The works of the art of politics are laws, and, though collections of laws may be useful to those who are able to "contemplate" and "judge" them, those who approach them without such trained habits cannot "judge" them correctly, except by chance, and it is only possible that their "intelligence" may be improved by the study of the laws.[128] Music differs from the other arts in that it alone imitates the passions and the virtues, for the objects of other senses than hearing can be signs but not imitations of virtues.[129] The one way to become a competent judge of music, since it is directly concerned with virtues and passions, is to become a performer, notwithstanding the contrary conviction of the Lacedaemonians that one could acquire the ability to judge or criticize music by only listening.[130] The other arts, particularly painting and poetry, are imitations, too, but of agents and actions, not of virtues and passions.[131] The object of art may therefore be treated in those arts as an entity in itself, an artificial object related both to the actions it represents and to the emotions it causes, but not itself a state of mind; in the strict sense, therefore, knowledge rather than criticism is pertinent to those arts, and the "poetic sciences" follow the analogy of the theoretic sciences, which are concerned with entities and actualities, more closely than they do that of the practical sciences, which are concerned with habits and institutions.

The investigation of the nature of tragedy in the *Poetics* proceeds through three stages. Aristotle first differentiates poetry from the other arts by three characteristics possessed by any imitation—its object, its means, and its manner—and uses these distinctions to account for the origin of poetry and its differentiation into kinds. The origin of poetry is traced to two natural causes: imitation is natural to man and it is also natural for man to delight in imitation.

128. *Nic. Eth.* x. 9. 1180^{b}28–1181^{b}12.

129. *Pol.* viii. 5. 1340^{a}12–1340^{b}19. Cf. Dewey's treatment of the emotional character of hearing as distinguished from sight (*Art as Experience*, pp. 237–38); Reynolds, on the other hand, maintains that music and architecture are not imitative arts because they apply directly to the imagination (*Discourses Delivered to the Students of the Royal Academy*, ed. with Introduction and notes by Roger Fry [New York, n.d.], "The Thirteenth Discourse," p. 365)

130. *Pol.* 1339^{a}42–1339^{b}4; 6. 1340^{b}20–39.

131. *Poet.* 2. 1448^{a}1 ff.; 6. 1449^{b}24–28; and esp. 1450^{a}15–38 and *passim*.

Both causes are discussed in terms of the process of learning, for man learns first by imitation and the pleasure he takes in art is due to the fact that he learns from it. "Learning," however, is one manifestation of "intelligence," distinct from "criticism" because it treats of particulars which fall under science rather than the particulars proper to prudence.[132] This investigation of the origin and history of poetry, therefore, supplies the distinguishing features of tragedy and comedy—among which one significant conclusion is that the person who "knows" (not "judges" or "criticizes") about tragedies, good and bad, knows also about epics, since their parts are the same[133]—and it lays the foundation for the treatment of tragedy as such. The isolation of tragedy is accomplished by comparing the various arts as imitations in their relations to the artist's use of means, manner, and object of imitation. Once isolated, tragedy may be considered as itself a kind of whole or object. The distinctions which had previously been made in terms of external agents and exemplars may be translated into traits discoverable in the poem, and the poem may be analyzed in terms of its unity and structure as part and whole (in which the plot, defined as the arrangement of incidents and as the imitation of action, is the principle or soul of tragedy) and in terms of the adaptation of means to ends (in which the plot is the most important part and the end of tragedy).[134] As a poetic science the results of such inquiry will serve equally for instruction of poets and amateurs, and they are stated, therefore, indifferently as what poets should do or what they have done. This second stage of analysis is knowledge or science as it is possible in and appropriate to the arts. It is supplemented, finally, by a consideration of tragedy in comparison with the closely related art of epic poetry, first, by analysis of both as parts and wholes, second, by analysis of them with respect to the means used to achieve their comparable ends and the success or failure of those means. Such comparative considerations yield "evaluation" or "censure" (ἐπιτίμημα), for in addition to the task which the poet faces in the construction of his play he faces "problems" which take the form of objections to "errors" (ἁμαρτία) he has committed. Since they are concerned with "errors," these problems are solved by inference from postulates or assumptions which the poet lays down concerning his art, such as would justify him in using as means to his end (which becomes at this third stage the proper pleasure caused by his work) devices that may be subject to some defect relative to a science or to morals but irrelevant to the considerations of his art. One of these assumptions is that the standard of rightness in poetry differs from that of politics and other arts, for two kinds of error are possible in poetry: failures

132. *Ibid*. 4. 1448^b4–19; cf. above, p. 512.

133. *Poet*. 5. 1449^b17–20.   134. *Ibid*. 6. 1450^a15–36.

of art when the poet intended to describe a thing correctly, and technical errors, proper to some other art or science, which might be justified for the purposes of the poetic art.[135] "Evaluation" or "censure" differs, therefore, from "judgment" or "criticism" as art and science differ from politics and morals: the former is the solution of a problem by demonstration that the end envisaged in the art is achieved by the means employed despite their possible deviation from other standards; the latter is the discrimination, by means of intelligence and in accordance with the command of prudence, of the contingent circumstances pertinent to actions determined by moral habits and political institutions.

The literal tradition treats of the objects of art or their production or appreciation as something apart from other objects, actions, or sciences. Three ways in which art may be isolated are suggested by Aristotle's cautious procedure and inquiry; and three kinds of treatment may be differentiated, each literal both in the sense that it is concerned only with art, or only with art of a given species or kind, and in the sense that it is sharply differentiated from other attempts to make criticism literal. It may be concerned with the work of art itself and attempt to make "scientific" generalizations or rules; it may be concerned with the work of art as illuminated by consideration of the poet's thought and attempt to make "critical," though poetic not moral, discriminations; it may be concerned with the work of art as effective of an end and attempt to make technical or artistic "evaluations." Poetic "science" differs from theoretic and practical sciences, for it is concerned neither with knowledge as such nor with action but with artificial objects and products; and if such objects are to be isolated for consideration in themselves, there must be some preliminary consideration of the conditions of their production and some supplementary consideration of the effects of their contemplation. "Criticism" is the consideration of the work of art primarily in its relation to the artist, and the problem of "making" may therefore be treated either in terms significative of thoughts and emotions (which had been reserved as the material of the practical sciences) in the discrimination and judgment of states of mind and their expression, or in terms significative of facts and knowledge (which had been used as the material of the theoretic sciences) for the resolution of problems involved in the circumstances of the poet or in the interpretation of his statements. "Evaluation" is the consideration of the work of art primarily in its relation to the audience, and the change of orientation from poet to audience involves a shift in the uses to which the basic terms are put, for the terms of thought and emotion, of imagination and fancy, are now used for the resolution of problems involved in the effectiveness of devices and the selection of con-

135. *Ibid.* 25. 1460^{b}6–21; cf. above, n. 113. On the implications of "censure" and its kinds cf. I. Bywater, *Aristotle on the Art of Poetry* (2d ed.; Oxford, 1909), pp. 328 ff.

tent, while the terms of knowledge and fact are used for precepts to guide the combination of thought and expression and the adaptation of both to circumstances. Criticism and evaluation or censure may then be distinguished from poetic science as variant attempts to set forth the nature and achievements of the arts literally in terms of the objects produced by artists and appreciated by audiences, and all three may be distinguished from the treatment of art in the total context of nature, thought, and experience in which knowledge, criticism, and evaluation are achieved at once and by single analogies or reductions.

The devices of "criticism," like those of "poetic science," bear on the work of art itself, but they are limited to questions similar to those initial considerations of Aristotle's *Poetics* in which the work of art is treated in relation to the artist and the conditions of its production. Criticism may, therefore, consist either in appealing to the known artist or judge or critic of works to be judged or in reconstructing the sense of those works and judging their value by learned commentary. Longinus, in the first manner, undertakes to seek a knowledge (ἐπιστήμη) and critical appreciation (ἐπίκρισις) of the sublime, realizing that judgment (κρίσις) in literature is the result of ripe experience and hoping to express the critical appreciation he seeks in rules and precepts.[136] The basic terms of his discussion are "nature" and "art," but the nature he is concerned with is the natural genius of the artist which is perfected or curbed by art,[137] and his rules are stated for the most part in terms of the virtues or faults of artists, which may be discerned by the artist as critic, by the expert, or by all mankind. Natural genius is fundamental, and sublimity is the true ring of the noble mind,[138] but the achievements of great authors may be used as touchstones and for emulation.

Accordingly it would be well for us, too, when we labor at anything which requires sublimity of style and loftiness of thought, to formulate in our minds how Homer would perhaps have said the same thing, how Plato or Demosthenes or, in history, Thucydides would have expressed it with sublimity. For these illustrious personages, presenting themselves to us for emulation and being as it were preeminent, will elevate our souls in some manner to the standards which our souls conceive. It will however be much more efficacious if we present this also to our mind: how Homer, if he had been present, or Demosthenes would have listened to such or such thing which I say, or how they would have been affected by it. This is truly a great contest, to submit our own statements to such a tribunal and audience, and to make believe that we are submitting the censure [εὔθυνα] of our writings to such great heroes as judges [κριτής] and witnesses. It would be even more stimulating to add: How will all posterity after me hear these writings of mine?[139]

136. *On the Sublime* vi.

137. *Ibid.* ii. 1–3.

138. *Ibid.* ix. 1–2.   139. *Ibid.* xiv. 1–3.

Treatment of literature in terms of the "judgment" of great writers yields rules which constitute a kind of "science" as well as standards for "evaluation," for the prudential discriminations of judgment become the type of knowledge and the basis for the technical and experiential censures of evaluation. The truly sublime is so constituted in nature that it elevates our souls; moreover, any man of prudence and experience (ἔμφρων καὶ ἔμπειρος) will recognize it; and finally all doubt will be removed concerning both the beautiful and the sublime if all mankind agrees despite differences of circumstances in the judgment (κρίσις).[140] Criticism in this first sense bears on the high moments of any branch of literature—poetry, rhetoric, history, or philosophy—and the genius is envisaged as a man of insight and feeling; criticism in the second sense bears on the meanings of all kinds of writings in a literal sense, as well as on the recondite meanings that might be found in poetry and fables, and in both the author is envisaged only in terms of the knowledge or learning to which criticism is an aid. Bacon makes use both of criticism and of "interpretation," the former applicable to all books, the latter limited to a kind of poetry and to myths.

There remain two appendices touching the tradition of knowledge, the one Critical, the other Pedantical. For all knowledge is either delivered by teachers, or attained by men's proper endeavours: and therefore as the principal part of tradition of knowledge concerneth chiefly writing of books, so the relative part thereof concerneth reading of books. Whereunto appertain incidently these considerations. The first is concerning the true correction and edition of authors; wherein nevertheless rash diligence hath done great prejudice. For these critics have often presumed that that which they understand not is false set down: as the Priest that where he found it written of St. Paul, *Demissus*

---

140. *Ibid.* vii. 2–4. The presuppositions which underlie this transition from the judgment of the genius to that of posterity are well expressed by Ch. Labitte, *Études littéraires* (Paris, 1846), I, 181: "Pour moi, ce me semble, il n'est qu'une manière un peu précise de songer à la posterité quand on est homme de lettres, c'est de se reporter en idée aux anciens illustres, à ceux qu'on préfère, qu'on admire avec prédilection, et de se demander: 'Que diraient-ils de moi? à quel degré daigneraient-ils m'admettre? s'ils me connaissaient m'ouvriraient-ils leur cercle? me reconnaîtraient-ils comme un de leurs, comme le dernier des leurs, le plus humble?' Voilà ma vue rétrospective de postérité, et celle-là en vaut bien une autre." The same rhetorical criterion of insight and agreement may be applied to other subjects, as when the mark of philosophy is sought in the "common experience" of men as opposed to the "special experience" of the sciences. Gibbon's record of his reading of Longinus illustrates the operation of this mode of criticism. On September 14, 1762, he writes (*Gibbon's Journal to January 28th, 1763*, ed. D. M. Low [New York, 1929], p. 142): "As yet I read my author more as a man of Genius, than as a man of taste: I am pleased and astonished rather than instructed." On October 3 he writes (*ibid.*, pp. 155–56): "The 9th chapter, which treats of the first of these, (the elevation of the ideas,) is one of the finest monuments of Antiquity. Till now, I was acquainted only with two ways of criticizing a beautiful passage; The one, to shew, by an exact anatomy of it, the distinct beauties of it, and from whence they sprung; the other, an idle exclamation, or a general encomium, which leaves nothing behind it. Longinus has shewn me that there is a third. He tells me his own feelings upon reading it; and tells them with such energy, that he communicates them. I almost doubt which is most sublime, Homer's Battle of the Gods, or *Longinus's* apostrophe to *Terentianus* upon it."

est per sportam, [he was let down in a basket,] mended his book, and made it *Demissus est per portam*, [he was let out by the gate]; because *sporta* was an hard word, and out of his reading; and surely their errors, though they be not so palpable and ridiculous, are yet of the same kind. And therefore as it hath been wisely noted, the most corrected copies are commonly the least correct.

The second is concerning the exposition and explication of authors, which resteth in annotations and commentaries; wherein it is over usual to blanch the obscure places, and discourse upon the plain.

The third is concerning the times, which in many cases give great light to true interpretations.

The fourth is concerning some brief censure and judgment of the authors; that men thereby may make some election unto themselves what books to read.

The fifth is concerning the syntax and disposition of studies; that men may know in what order or pursuit to read.[141]

In the more restricted region of poetry, however, the one relevant deficiency which Bacon notes is in the philosophic interpretation of ancient parables which he illustrates by developing the legends of Pan, Perseus, and Dionysus into significances applicable, respectively, in natural, political, and moral speculation.[142] Criticism may be achieved, in general, by appeal to what is universal or best in men's minds, or to the reconstruction of what one man said, or to the interpretation of the allegory concealed in stories and histories; the censure that accompanies these criticisms is by standards determined by comparison with great geniuses, or with other books in the field, or with the principles of philosophers. Broadly conceived, criticism so practiced is concerned either with sublime and beautiful feelings and the means by which they are expressed

141. *Of the Proficience and Advancement of Learning*, Book II (*Works*, III, 413–14). Cf. *De augmentis scientiarum*, Book VI, chap. iv (*Works*, IV, 493–94), where Bacon emphasizes the place of judgment in the critical processes: "There belongs thirdly to the critical part (and from this indeed it derives its name) the insertion of some brief judgment concerning the authors edited, and comparison of them with other writers on the same subjects; that students may by such censure be both advised what books to read and better prepared when they come to read them. This last office is indeed, so to speak, the critic's chair; which has certainly in our age been ennobled by some great men,—men in my judgment above the stature of critics." Machiavelli made excellent use of both fable and history (cf. *ibid.*, Book VIII [*Works*, V, 56]; *Of the Proficience and Advancement of Learning*, Book II [*Works*, III, 345, 453]), yet the Stoic use of the allegorical interpretation of poets seemed to Bacon vain: "Nevertheless in many the like encounters, I do rather think that the fable was first, and the exposition devised, than that the moral was first, and thereupon the fable framed. For I find it was an ancient vanity in Chrysippus, that troubled himself with great contention to fasten the assertions of the Stoics upon the fictions of the poets. But yet that all the fables and fictions of the poets were but pleasure and not figure, I interpose no opinion. Surely of those poets which are now extant, even Homer himself, (notwithstanding he was made a kind of Scripture by the later schools of the Grecians,) yet I should without any difficulty pronounce that his fables had no such inwardness in his own meaning; but what they might have upon a more original tradition, is not easy to affirm; for he was not the inventor of many of them" (*ibid.*, III, 345).

142. *Ibid.*, pp. 318–35; cf. *On Principles and Origins According to the Fables of Cupid and Coelum* (*Works*, V, 461–500).

or with the learned and critical interpretation of statements and the meanings they express.

The consideration of the work of art itself may be in terms of its effects rather than in terms of its organization or its author, and then the processes of "evaluation" will take precedence over those of "criticism" or "science." If appeal is made directly to audiences, rather than to posterity or any other universal audience which will approve only of the greatest artists, audiences are diversified and numerous; and if meanings are sought directly in words, rather than in the comparison of works on the same subject, the effects to be achieved by words are relatively few. The basic terms of evaluation are words and things, style and content, and the subject of censure may be either the suitability of the manner of statement to achieve effects on various audiences, or faults and improprieties from bad combinations of diction, composition, and subject in various styles. As the concern with the character of the poet and with his treatment of subject matter suggested analogies to the first part of Aristotle's analysis, so the concern with effects on an audience and with the relative effectiveness of various poetic genres may be viewed as a translation of the topics treated in the third part of Aristotle's analysis to a place of central importance. Horace's constant worry over the tastes of actual audiences yields emphases opposite to those which Longinus derives from his audience of heroes: popular judgment is fickle;[143] the public is sometimes right, sometimes wrong, but its particular error is to esteem the ancient poets and to censure other works, not because they are coarse or inelegant in style, but because they are modern;[144] the absence of a discerning critic of unmusical verses has an unfortunate effect on Roman poetry;[145] the recommendation to the poet, therefore, is to choose subjects suited to his own powers, and if Horace imitated Archilochus it was in spirit and meter, not in words or in subjects, so that even the imitation was a novel departure by which he was the first of the Romans to use those numbers:[146] the preferred critic is the good and prudent man who censures lifeless lines.[147] Similarly, Horace's treatment of kinds of poetry yields the familiar

143. *Epistles* i. 19. 37; cf. also i. 1. 71–76, where he speaks of the public as a many-headed monster imposing its "judgments"; and *Satires* i. 10. 72–77, where he advises the poet not to try to please the crowd but to be content with a few readers. The differentiation of audiences and their preferences or faculties is never far removed from the moral considerations from which this form of criticism takes its origin; cf. Reynolds, *op. cit.*, p. 354: "Such men will always prefer imitation to that excellence which is addressed to another faculty that they do not possess; but these are not persons to whom a painter is to look, any more than a judge of morals and manners ought to refer controverted points upon those subjects to the opinions of people taken from the banks of the Ohio, or from New Holland."

144. *Ep.* ii. 1. 63–92.

145. *Ars poetica* 263–64; the term used is *iudex;* cf. *Sat.* i. 10. 38, where Horace thinks of his poems as competing before Tarpa as judge: *certantia iudice Tarpa.*

146. *Sat.* 38–40; *Ep.* i. 19. 21–34.   147. Cf. above, n. 47.

genres rather than the parts of learning which emerge from Bacon's treatment. The effect of literature on audiences, however, may also be sought in the differentiation of styles, for in the rhetorical tradition in which Aristotle undertook to classify kinds of rhetoric in terms of audiences Theophrastus studied the "virtues," not of authors or of audiences, but of styles, and Cicero, Quintilian, Dionysius, and Demetrius classified first three, then four, styles in terms of their respective qualities and faults. Unlike Bacon, who treated words as the form, the content of statements being the matter, Cicero thought of words and speech as the material from which verse and the styles of prose are formed, and the styles are fitted to our thought.[148] Demetrius' classification of the elevated, the elegant, the plain, and the forcible styles depends at once on organizing parts into wholes and at the same time on fitting words and compositions appropriately to thoughts, so that his analysis of style differs from Horace's as the respective ends which they both derive from audiences differ, while in the place of the kinds of poetic composition, as classified by Horace or by Bacon, Demetrius arrives at kinds of style because the parts and wholes defined by thought in his analysis are verbal: members, phrases, periods. Finally, unlike Longinus' analysis, which is fixed on the expressions of the loftiest genius, Demetrius' inquiry is concerned with ways of fitting words to a variety of thoughts and with the faults corresponding to each of the possible styles. Evaluation may be achieved, in general, by comparing the effects of what is written on actual or chosen audiences or by measuring it against the canons for statements of the "kind" to which it belongs; the judges are either men conceived by various standards to be good and prudent or men judged to be expert in rhetoric or some other appropriate science of expression. Broadly conceived, evaluation so practiced is concerned either with qualities of genres of literature and art or with the virtues of style and expression.

III

The words used in criticism are relative to their subject matter, but the subject matter changes with changes of philosophic principle. The vocabulary of criticism is therefore applied now to all things—natural or artificial—and again only to artificial things or even to the things made in one art; and so restricted it applies now to entities, now to states of mind, and again to activities or expressions. Moreover, the consequent ambiguity in critical terms is not readily removed by stating critical or philosophic principles—whether for purposes of elucidating relative meanings or laying down the law of the true meaning—since the critic sometimes employs philosophic principles for the interpretation of art, sometimes uses criticism to dictate the principles of both philosophy and

148. *De oratore* iii. 45. 177.

art, and sometimes operates as artist, justifying at most his suspicion of philosophic or critical principles; or, again, if he thinks of his function as in some sense scientific, he conceives his knowledge on the model sometimes of the theoretic sciences, sometimes of the moral or practical sciences, sometimes of the aesthetic or poetic sciences. Changes of subject matter and changes of principles or manner of use of principles are rarely indicated by the introduction of new terms, and, even when they are, coined words or words borrowed from other disciplines merely illustrate anew the fashion in which the meanings of words shift within a discipline or by passage from one discipline to another. The history of critical discussions could be written in terms of a small number of words, which with their cognates and synonyms have moved back and forth from obscurity to prominence in the aesthetic vocabulary, or from neighboring vocabularies to criticism, or from one significance to another in different modes of criticism. Yet such relativity does not mean that standards are impossible or insignificant in criticism. It means rather that significances must be sought in the sense and application which statements of critical doctrines have in their context and relative to their purpose. It means, secondly, that the evaluation of critical statements should consist in a determination of their adequacy to the end for which they were formulated and of the relevance of that end to the explication of art and objects of art. The differentiation of meanings according to the variety of systems and purposes is itself neither criticism nor philosophy but a device preliminary to both and a substitute for the easy acceptance or refutation of statements according to preferred meanings which the reader justifies because (whether or not they leave the writer who is being interpreted much sense or consistency) they are determined by the *real* nature of art, or the *actual* limits of criticism, or the *true* precepts of philosophy.

The shifts of meaning do not, of course, occur as gross phenomena discernible in an idle glance, describable by simple tags, or remediable by semantic precepts and prohibitions. A purely "analogical" or a wholly "literal" set of terms is as mythical as "climates of opinion" or "dialectics of history" or any of the sets of terms that have been used to give meaning to such devices of explanation and discrimination—like realism, nominalism, conceptualism, or dogmatism, skepticism, criticism, or idealism, materialism, naturalism, and so through the dreary list of tags by which significant explanations are reduced to props for one more explanation that will in turn be honored and dismissed with a technical name. In the mixed tradition of discussion, however, the two usages are distinguishable by two movements in the meanings of terms: the analogical, by a dialectical doubling in which a word takes on two differentiated meanings, one good and one bad, or by a dialectical reduction in which a word retains only the minimal and slightest of its dialectical meanings; the literal, by a shift of the terms from subject matter to subject matter with accompanying changes of meaning.

These two kinds of change are rendered possible, and in turn are obscured, by the fact—on which the peculiarities of refutation and inference depend— that any statement or theory of criticism may be read and interpreted by any method of criticism and according to the principles of any philosophy. In the long history of variant uses to which Aristotle's *Poetics* has been put, for example, it would not be difficult to illustrate the fashion in which statements have been interpreted and reinterpreted to assume almost any philosophic form and significance, and have in turn been criticized for failing to take into account some implication of every significance that has been attached to them. Thus, the term "imitation" undergoes a typical series of literal shifts of meaning from Aristotle's application of it to the work of art as an imitation of nature, to the Hellenistic and Renaissance application of it to the artist imitating artists,[149] to the modern application of it to the amateur imitating the work of art or the artist.[150] Yet none of these need be literal, since man's imitation of man may be taken as essentially the same as his imitation of objects or as the objects' imitation of models which are of a higher degree of reality than man or human arts: the term "imitation" undergoes a typical series of analogical doublings and reductions, which may in turn be given literal definitions, from Plato's use of it to

149. Cf. above, pp. 168–69. The doctrine that the arts, or at least some of them, are essentially imitative of external things is, of course, not limited to antiquity but has had advocates in all the later ages, including the modern; cf. T. B. Macaulay, "Moore's Life of Lord Byron" (*Miscellaneous Works of Lord Macaulay*, ed. Lady Trevelyan [New York, n.d.] I, 476): "Poetry is, as was said more than two thousand years ago, imitation. It is an art analogous in many respects to the art of painting, sculpture, and acting. . . . Thus the objects of the imitation of poetry are the whole external and the whole internal universe, the face of nature, the vicissitudes of fortune, man as he is in himself, man as he appears in society, all things which really exist, all things of which we can form an image in our minds by combining together parts of things which really exist. The domain of this imperial art is commensurate with the imaginative faculty." Cf. also I. Babbitt, *The New Laokoon* (New York, 1910), chap. i, "The Theory of Imitation," pp. 3–19.

150. Cf. Dewey, *Art as Experience*, p. 325: "We lay hold of the full import of a work of art only as we go through in our own vital processes the processes the artist went through in producing the work." In the doctrine of *Einfühlung* or empathy the relation is between spectator and object, but it is contemplative rather than practical, and it is individualized to each spectator; cf. V. Lee, *The Beautiful: An Introduction to Psychological Aesthetics* (Cambridge, 1913), chap. ii, "Contemplative Satisfaction," and pp. 74–75: "I am speaking once more of that phenomenon called *Inner Mimicry* which certain observers, themselves highly subject to it, have indeed considered as Empathy's explanation, rather than its result. In the light of all I have said about the latter, it becomes intelligible that when empathic imagination (itself varying from individual to individual) happens to be united to a high degree of (also individually very varying) muscular responsiveness, there may be set up reactions, actual or incipient, *e.g.* alterations of bodily attitude or muscular tension which (unless indeed they withdraw attention from the contemplated object to our own body) will necessarily add to the sum of activity emphatically attributed to the contemplated object."

apply to nature, science, and art (in which the imitation of art is condemned unless it is with knowledge of the true), to the application of it to art in two senses, one good and one bad,[151] to the use of it in a sense in which it is opposed to genius and the antithesis of art.[152]

151. Coleridge, *Biographia literaria*, chap. xviii (*Works*, III, 421): "This and the preceding arguments may be strengthened by the reflection, that the composition of a poem is among the imitative arts; and that imitation, as opposed to copying, consists either in the interfusion of the same throughout the radically different, or of the different throughout a base radically the same." Both terms may be given literal definitions, as in Bryant, *Lectures on Poetry*, Lecture IV, "On Originality and Imitation" (*Prose Writings*, I, 35): "I propose in this lecture to say a few words on the true use and value of imitation in poetry. I mean not what is technically called the imitation of nature, but the studying and copying of models of poetic composition. There is hardly any praise of which writers in the present age, particularly writers in verse, are more ambitious than that of originality. This ambition is a laudable one, for a captivating originality is everything in art. Whether it consists in presenting familiar things in a new and striking yet natural light, or in revealing secrets of emotion and thought which have lain undetected from the birth of literature, it is one of the most abundant and sure sources of poetic delight." Or, again, the two senses of imitation—good and bad—and the two kinds of imitation—of nature and of artists—may be combined dialectically in such fashion that each meaning is set off by the others, as in Reynolds, *Discourses*, where the initial distinction between genius or natural ability and the study of authentic models leads to insistence on the importance of teaching young students to draw correctly what they see ("The First Discourse," pp. 7–13) and is then developed into a distinction between mere copying or exact imitation and selective imitation of the masters ("The Second Discourse," pp. 24–30), and, finally, mere imitation of masters and of nature is contrasted to the contribution of imagination, poetical enthusiasm, the grandeur of ideas and an ideal beauty, superior to what is to be found in individual nature but discernible by diligent study of the works of our great predecessors and the works of nature; cf. "The Third Discourse," pp. 49–53: "The first endeavours of a young Painter, as I have remarked in a former discourse, must be employed in the attainment of mechanical dexterity, and confined to the mere imitation of the object before him. Those who have advanced beyond the rudiments, may, perhaps, find advantage in reflecting on the advice which I have likewise given them, when I recommended the diligent study of the works of our great predecessors; but I at the same time endeavour to guard them against an implicit submission to the authority of any one master, however excellent; or by a strict imitation of his manner, precluding themselves from the abundance and variety of Nature. I will now add, that Nature herself is not to be too closely copied. There are excellences in the art of Painting beyond what is commonly called the imitation of Nature; and these excellences I wish to point out. The Students who, having passed through the initiatory exercises, are more advanced in the Art, and who, sure of their hand, have leisure to exert their understanding, must now be told, that a mere copier of Nature can never produce anything great; can never raise and enlarge the conceptions, or warm the heart of the spectator. . . . Could we teach taste or genius by rules, they would be no longer taste and genius. But though there neither are, nor can be, any precise invariable rules for the exercise or the acquisition of these great qualities, yet we may truly say, that they always operate in proportion to our attention in observing the works of Nature, to our skill in selecting, and to our care in digesting, methodising, and comparing our observations. There are many beauties in our Art that seem, at first, to lie without the reach of precept, and yet may easily be reduced to practical principles." Invention is the power of representing a mental picture on canvas, and the great end of the art, in turn, is to strike the imagination ("The Fourth Discourse," pp. 73, 74). But painting is intrinsically imitative, and therefore imitation "in its largest sense" must be contrasted to imitation in the sense of following other masters; even genius is the child of imitation, and we learn to invent by being conversant with the inventions of others, while even nature, which is the source of all excellences in art, may be known through the selections made by great minds of what is excellent in nature ("The Sixth Dis-

While the word "imitation" undergoes these changes, related terms go through like or proportional alterations. When art is an imitation of nature, and tragedy an imitation of action, the analysis may be, as Aristotle's was, in terms of parts of tragedies of which the plot, itself a combination (σύστασις) or a composition (σύνθεσις), is the most important. Plot is important in an analysis of objects of art because it is a combination of things or incidents (σύστασις πραγμάτων),[153] and it may be viewed for analytic purposes as synthesis or composition (σύνθεσις) of things, while only diction is analyzed as a composition of words.[154] Moreover, since beauty requires size as well as order and arrangement, the beautiful object of art is comparable as a structure (σύστημα) to beautiful organisms or animals.[155] Again, literature may be viewed, as it was by Longinus, in terms of the constituents (σύστασις) which yield sublimity; and of the five constituents chosen, two are natural, being

---

course," pp. 142–43, 145, 148, 152). If a more liberal style of imitation is distinguished from mere servile imitation of one master (*ibid.*, pp. 156–68), imitation is the one means by which an artist may perfect his art; cf. *ibid.*, p. 171: "Thus I have ventured to give my opinion of what appears to me the true and only method by which an artist makes himself master of his profession; which I hold ought to be one continued course of imitation, that is not to cease but with his life." The fact that art is an imitation of nature does not mean, however, that he who imitates her with the greatest fidelity is the best artist, for nature is not constituted of particularities ("The Seventh Discourse," pp. 193–94). The Platonic sources of this dialectic are apparent in the dependence of art as imitation on an eternal beauty; cf. "The Tenth Discourse," p. 270: "Imitation is the means, and not the end of art; it is employed by the sculptor as the language by which his ideas are presented to the mind of the spectator. Poetry and elocution of every sort make use of signs, but those signs are arbitrary and conventional. The sculptor employs the representation of the thing itself; but still as a means to a higher end— as a gradual ascent always advancing towards faultless form and perfect beauty." Therefore the art of seeing nature or, in other words, the art of using models is the point to which all art studies are directed ("The Twelfth Discourse," p. 344). Yet, consistently with this doctrine, Reynolds could object to the treatment of painting as only an imitative art, attributing the theory to Plato, and could differentiate the respects in which painting imitates nature from the respects in which it, and all the other arts, depart from nature for the purpose of inspiring the imagination ("The Thirteenth Discourse," pp. 353–66).

152. Kant, *Critique of Judgement*, Part I, Div. I, §§ 46–47, pp. 188-90: "*Genius* is the innate mental disposition (*ingenium*) *through which* Nature gives the rule to Art. . . . Every one is agreed that genius is entirely opposed to the *spirit of imitation*." Yet, even for Kant, imitation has its purposes and uses in separating genius from teaching, and to make that distinction Kant repeats Aristotle's separation of judgment and knowledge, but assigns judgment, not to moral questions, as Aristotle did, but to the determination of the beautiful; cf. *ibid.*, pp. 191–92: "If now it is a natural gift which must prescribe its rule to art (as beautiful art), of what kind is this rule? It cannot be reduced to a formula and serve as a precept, for then the judgment upon the beautiful would be determinable according to concepts; but the rule must be abstracted from the fact, *i.e.* from the product, on which others may try their own talent by using it as a model, not to be *copied* but to be *imitated.*"

153. *Poet.* 6. 1450ª15, 32, 1450ᵇ22; 14. 1453ᵇ2, 1454ª14; 15. 1454ª34.

154. *Ibid.* 6. 1450ª5; cf. also 1449ᵇ35; 12. 1452ᵇ31, 1453ª3, 19, 23. A riddle is a σύνθεσις τῶν ὀνομάτων (22. 1458ª28).

155. *Ibid.* 7. 1450ᵇ36–1451ª6. For the similar conditions of beauty in nature cf. *De part. anim.* i. 5. 645ª17–26 and 645ᵇ14–20, and *Metaph.* xiii. 3. 1078ª31 ff.

concerned with thought and emotion, while three are the contribution of art, being concerned with words, and of these verbal constituents the last, composition (σύνθεσις), when it achieves dignity and elevation, embraces all the rest.[156] Composition becomes the mere arrangement of words,[157] and it may be analogized, when the concern is with grandeur, to the structure (σύστημα) of the animal organism.[158] Finally, the problems of literature may be conceived, as Demetrius conceived them, entirely in terms of composition (σύνθεσις), which becomes a verbal organization to be contrasted to the intellectual meaning and combination (δύναμις καὶ σύστασις) imposed by argumentation.[159] In addition to moving literally in this fashion from subject to subject, the concept of "composition" undergoes the dialectical doubling in which verbal composition is contrasted to a higher or freer or more natural composition of feelings or ideas, as well as a dialectical reduction in which it becomes an improper term for aesthetic discussion. According to Goethe, it is a "thoroughly contemptible word."

How can one say, Mozart has *composed* [*componirt*] Don Juan! Composition! As if it were a piece of cake or biscuit, which had been stirred together out of eggs, flour, and sugar! It is a spiritual creation, in which the details, as well as the whole, are pervaded by *one* spirit, and by the breath of *one* life; so that the producer did not make experiments, and patch together, and follow his own caprice, but was altogether in the power of the daemonic spirit of his genius, and acted according to his orders.[160]

The terms for imitation were applied to things before imitation became psychological or verbal, and the terms for composition have persisted in their verbal associations and connotations after they have ceased to be applied to thoughts in their relations to one another and to words and to things in their artificial combinations and organic structures. Between these two sets of terms, controlling them and controlled by them, an even larger set of psychological terms undergoes similar alterations.

Thought (διάνοια) may be conceived, as it was by Aristotle, as one of the proper parts of tragedy distinct from character and plot, but relative to the object of imitation, while diction is treated as the means of imitation.[161] Or

156. *On the Sublime* viii. 1.

157. *Ibid.* xxxix.

158. *Ibid.* xl.; cf. also xi.

159. *On Style* i. 30–31. For "synthesis" or composition in Demetrius, cf. *ibid.* 4, 8, 9, 11; ii. 38, 40, 43, 45, 48, 49, 58, 68, 74, 92, 117, 121; iii. 179, 180, 186, 189; iv. 204, 221, 237, 239; v. 241, 246, 248, 299, 301, 303.

160. *Conversations with Eckermann and Soret*, trans. J. Oxenford (London, 1913), Sunday, June 20, 1831, p. 556.

161. *Poet.* 6. 1450ᵃ7–15, 1450ᵇ4–8.

thought and emotions may be contrasted as nature to words and expression as art, both thought and words being sources of the sublime, as Longinus held, since the ring of the sublime is due to thought (διάνοια) no less than to melody,[162] and the thought (νόησις) and diction of a statement may be mutually explanatory, beautiful words being the very light of thought.[163] Or thought (διάνοια) may be set forth in words, which, according to Demetrius, express in periods either whole thoughts or parts of whole thoughts.[164] In the analogical tradition thought may appear, not among the parts but among the criteria of art, as when Plato requires that the poet compose with knowledge of the truth, thereby satisfying both moral and theoretic criticism, since virtue is knowledge;[165] or thought may function neither as part nor criterion, practical or theoretic, and the region of art may be found in the interplay of understanding and imagination, as when Kant distinguishes judgment from both pure and practical reason;[166] or thought may be invoked in its practical guise, controlling or guiding the passions and emotions, as when modern critics, like Newman, Tolstoy, or D. H. Lawrence, argue that art is essentially moral.[167] When psychological functions are distinguished in aesthetic theory, reason is recon-

162. *On the Sublime* xxxix. 4.

163. *Ibid.* xxx. 1.

164. *On Style* i. 2–3; cf. 30–31; ii. 38, 115; iii. 187; iv. 236, 239. It is worthy of note that in actual discussion thought seems to be equated to subject matter (πρᾶγμα); cf. *ibid.* ii. 75–76, where poetry and painting are compared; iii. 132–36, 156–62; iv. 190; iv. 239; v. 240, 302, 304.

165. Cf. Sidney, who borrows from the Aristotelian terminology to argue that poetry is the architectonic science (*op. cit.*, pp. 11–12).

166. In Kant's division of philosophy into theoretical and practical, the phenomena of art fall in neither since the feeling of pleasure and pain is intermediate between the faculty of knowledge and the faculty of desire (*Critique of Judgement*, § i, pp. 7–8; § iii, pp. 14–17). Croce, dividing philosophy into theoretic and practical in terms of activities rather than faculties, finds art one of the two divisions of the *theoretic* and aesthetics a science of expression and general linguistics (*Estetica come scienza dell'espressione e linguistica generale* [6th ed.; Bari, 1928], chap. viii, pp. 68–69). Maritain, distinguishing in terms of virtues, finds art one of the two domains of the *practical* order (*Art et scolastique* [Paris, 1927], chap. iii, p. 8).

167. Newman, *op. cit.*, p. 21: "We do not hesitate to say, that poetry is ultimately founded on correct moral perception; that where there is no sound principle in exercise there will be no poetry; and that on the whole (originality being granted) in proportion to the standard of a writer's moral character will his compositions vary in poetical excellence." Tolstoy, *What Is Art?* p. 307: "So that were the question put: Would it be preferable for our Christian world to be deprived of *all* that is now esteemed to be art, and together with the false to lose *all* that is good in it? I think that every reasonable and moral man would again decide the question as Plato decided it for his *Republic*, and as all the early Church-Christian and Mohammedan teachers of mankind decided it, that is, would say, Rather let there be no art at all than continue the depraving art, or simulation of art, which now exists." D. H. Lawrence, *Studies in Classic American Literature* (New York, 1923), p. 254: "The essential function of art is moral. Not aesthetic, not decorative, not pastime and recreation. But moral. The essential function of art is moral."

ciled with or opposed to the passions[168] and imagination.[169] In the relations of reason, imagination, and the passions, again, the literal tradition sets up distinctions which are in turn the subject of fruitful comparison by use of the analogical method. In the literal tradition pleasure may be selected among the passions as the distinctive mark of beauty[170] or the end of poetry;[171] or a particular pleasure of pity and fear may be the mark of tragedy.[172] Or, in turn, the passions may be broadened analogically to embrace poetry, which may be defined as the spontaneous overflow of powerful feelings,[173] or the expression of any feelings[174] or of certain moral feelings;[175] or art may be

168. Hazlitt, *op. cit.*, p. 3: "Plato banished the poets from his Commonwealth, lest their descriptions of the natural man should spoil his mathematical man, who was to be without passions and affections, who was neither to laugh nor weep, to feel sorrow nor anger, to be cast down nor elated by any thing. This was a chimera, however, which never existed but in the brain of the inventor; and Homer's poetical world has outlived Plato's philosophical Republic." Cf. Plato *Rep.* x. 605A–607A.

169. Addison, *Spectator*, No. 421: "The Pleasures of the Imagination are not wholly confined to such particular Authors as are conversant in material Objects, but are often to be met with among the Polite Masters of Morality, Criticism, and other Speculations abstracted from Matter, who, tho' they do not directly treat of the visible Parts of Nature, often draw from them their Similitudes, Metaphors, and Allegories. By these Allusions a Truth in the Understanding is as it were reflected by the Imagination; we are able to see something like Colour and Shape in a Notion, and to discover a Scheme of Thoughts traced out upon Matter. And here the Mind receives a great deal of Satisfaction, and has two of its Faculties gratified at the same time, while the Fancy is busie in copying after the Understanding, and transcribing Ideas out of the Intellectual World into the Material." Cf. also Hobbes, *op. cit.*, 1. 8 (*Works*, III, 58): "In a good poem, whether it be *epic*, or *dramatic*; as also in *sonnets*, *epigrams*, and other pieces, both judgment and fancy are required: but the fancy must be more eminent; but ought not to displease by indiscretion." In Hobbes's table of the sciences, poetry figures as one of the sciences which treat of consequences from the qualities of men in special, since its subject is consequences from speech manifested in magnifying, villifying, etc. (*ibid.*, p. 73).

170. Hume, *A Treatise of Human Nature*, ed. L. A. Selby-Bigge (Oxford, 1896), Book II, Part I, sec. 8, p. 299: "Pleasure and pain, therefore, are not only necessary attendants of beauty and deformity, but constitute their very essence."

171. Dryden, "Defence of an *Essay of Dramatic Poesy*" (*Essays of John Dryden*, ed. W. P. Ker [Oxford, 1926], I, 113): "I am satisfied if it [verse] cause delight; for delight is the chief, if not the only, end of poesy: instruction can be admitted but in the second place, for poesy only instructs as it delights."

172. *Poet.* 14. 1453ᵇ8–14.

173. Wordsworth, *op. cit.*, pp. 82, 96.

174. Hazlitt, *op. cit.*, p. 2: "Fear is poetry, hope is poetry, love is poetry, hatred is poetry; contempt, jealousy, remorse, admiration, wonder, pity, despair, or madness, are all poetry." Or the circle may be rounded, and the passions may return to truth, beauty, and power by way of imagination and fancy; cf. Hunt, *op. cit.*, p. 377: "Poetry, strictly and artistically so called,—that is to say, considered not merely as poetic feeling, which is more or less shared by all the world, but as the operation of that feeling, such as we see it in the poet's book,—is the utterance of a passion for truth, beauty, and power, embodying and illustrating its conceptions by imagination and fancy, and modulating its language on the principle of variety in uniformity. Its means are whatever the universe contains; and its ends, pleasure and exultation."

175. Newman, *op. cit.*, p. 23: "According to the above theory, Revealed Religion should be especially poetical—and it is so in fact. . . . It may be added, that the virtues peculiarly Christian are especially poetical—meekness, gentleness, compassion, contentment, modesty,

concerned with emotions only if they are joined to materials,[176] or with pleasure only if joined to utility,[177] or, finally, the beautiful may be separated wholly from interest or pleasure.[178] Imagination, in turn, apart from its relation to or distinction from understanding and the passions may require causal differentiation into genius as a source and taste as a standard of beauty, or dialectical doubling into imagination and fancy.

Such shifts in the meanings of individual terms, of course, select different subject matters for the proper domain of criticism and are selected by principles which determine the interrelations and compendency of terms. But, in addition to their factual consequences and philosophic implications, terms and their meanings may be examined in their interplay in each of the modes of criticism in which they approximate systematic use in individual writers and particular traditions, and in the influence of modes of criticism on one another in the evolution and development of terms and meanings. If terms like "imitation," "imagination," and "communication" change their meanings as they move from context to context, it should be possible not only to trace the pattern of individual changes in such terms but also to sketch the analytic schemes which determine the various meanings and the stages of change.

The intermixture of analogical and literal elements in the discussion of art suggests a classification according to six modes as a means of ordering the many forms of aesthetic analysis that have been practiced and that still continue to contest the interpretation, criticism, and evaluation of art. The six modes are differentiated by the variables and constants that are appropriate to their sets of terms and by the means which are used to delimit or define them.

"Dialectical" criticism may be viewed as a single mode among these six, comprising a vast, sometimes amorphous, series of forms, which merge or move from one emphasis to another to take up in altering but appropriate terms the continuing opposition of dialectical criticism to each of the five remaining forms of "literal" criticism. It is a single mode, despite its diversity, since the full universality of subject matter and scope which it achieved in the

---

not to mention the devotional virtues; whereas the ruder and more ordinary feelings are the instruments of rhetoric more justly than of poetry—anger, indignation, emulation, martial spirit, and love of independence."

176. Dewey, *Art as Experience*, p. 69: "Yes, emotion must operate. But it works to effect continuity of movement, singleness of effect amid variety. It is selective of material and directive of its order and arrangement. But it is not *what* is expressed."

177. Plato *Rep.* x. 607D.

178. Kant, *Critique of Judgement*, Part I, Div. I, § 4, pp. 50–51: "In order to find anything good, I must always know what sort of thing the object ought to be, *i.e.* I must have a concept of it. But there is no need of this, to find a thing beautiful. . . . The satisfaction in the beautiful must depend on the reflection upon an object, leading to any conception (however indefinite); and it is thus distinguished from the pleasant which rests entirely upon sensation."

hands of Plato is possible in any of the forms which it has assumed since his time. Since it is a dialectical mode, however, that achievement must await, in each form, a great dialectician or poet, while in the hands of lesser critics the mode deteriorates to timid and common-sense apologies for what seems extravagant or sophistical in the moral judgment of art or to literal repetitions of those judgments in limited—and sometimes trivial, sometimes oppressive—applications. In any of its forms, the terms of dialectical criticism reflect the two moments or aspects of the method: the differentiation of terms in application to subjects and their reduction in the solution of problems. In the form which Plato employed, it is a dialectic of things; and his analysis of art and making in terms of imitation, therefore, requires the differentiation of object of imitation (which itself has a quality or value), the imitation (whose value depends on its correctness and the value of its object), and the execution of the imitation (which adds considerations of skill and medium to the previous two criteria). The reduction of these differentiations is achieved by Plato's distinction between being and becoming, knowledge and opinion, for the criterion of excellence is in each case—within art itself as in science, action, and being—found in the eternal pattern of ideas. When the dialectic shifts in the use of other writers to a dialectic of knowledge, it retains its scope in the dimension left free for the judgment of beauty or the practice of art within a rigid and literal distinction between theoretic and practical. This may be accomplished in either of two ways, depending on whether knowledge is conceived in terms of the human faculties or in terms of the branches of learning. Kant, in the first manner, differentiated the objects and laws of nature from those of freedom—thereby separating natural philosophy from moral philosophy, the metaphysics of nature from the metaphysics of ethics—and in the region between the theoretical and practical uses of reason he found the place of judgment and imagination in the free interplay of the human faculties, unlimited in the sense that they embrace art and nature, beauty, sublimity, and purpose. As a consequence, there is a doubling of both subject matters and problems, for the beautiful is distinguished from the sublime (which is certainly included in the concept of beauty developed in the *Symposium*), and the problems of appreciation are separated from those of production in the distinction of taste from genius (whereas the problems of the poet, the interpreter, and the amateur are inextricably involved in one another as treated in the *Ion*). Art is no longer imitation in this reduction to judgment; but the rules of the arts have become basic and unchanging, and the operation of taste might be made to yield the rules governing the individual objects proper to each of the arts, while the operation of genius might adumbrate the guiding rules of nature. Comte, in the second manner, divides all human activities into theoretic and practical, the latter being the application of the former by means of intermediary arts.[179] The result is again the doubling of subject matter and problems, for abstract laws are distinguished from concrete actions, and the objective method which leads to that distinction must be supplemented by a subjective method by which the supremacy of morals and sociology is established.[180] The logic of poetry is to be found midway between the logic of thought and the logic of feeling.[181] When the judgment of beauty is assigned to the free activity of imagination and taste, located midway between the pure and the practical reason, there is some danger that the rules regulating the beautiful in art will receive only such vague formulation as is customary in the delineation of taste or the designation of genius; when the operation of art is assigned to a logic of imagination, operating midway between a logic of thought and a logic of feelings, there is some danger that it will appear primarily in the guise, not of fine art, but of incidents pertinent to morals and sociology or explicable in psychology. The dialectic may undergo a third shift, however, to a dialectic of processes and relations, in which Plato's three basic differentiations appear in the altered form they assume in the realm of becoming: communication or expression takes the place of imitation (with sincerity in the artist taking the place of correctness in the

179. *Cours de philosophie positive*, ed. E. Littré (3d ed.; Paris, 1869), I, 50: "Tous les travaux humains sont, ou de spéculation, ou d'action. Ainsi, la division la plus générale de nos connaissances réelles consiste à les distinguer en théoriques et pratiques." *Ibid.*, p. 55: "On concevra d'autant mieux la difficulté de construire ces doctrines intermédiaires que je viens d'indiquer, si l'on considère que chaque art dépend non-seulement d'une certain science correspondante, mais à la fois de plusieurs, tellement que les arts les plus importants empruntent des secours directs à presque toutes les diverses sciences principales. C'est ainsi que la véritable théorie de l'agriculture, pour me borner au cas le plus essentiel, exige une intime combinaison de connaissances physiologiques, chimiques, physiques et même astronomiques et mathématiques: il en est de même des beaux-arts. On aperçoit aisément, d'après cette considération, pourquoi ces théories n'ont pu encore être formée, puisqu'elles supposent le développement préalable de toutes les différentes sciences fondamentales. Il en résulte également un nouveau motif de ne pas comprendre un tel ordre d'idées dans un cours de philosophie positive, puisque, loin de pouvoir contribuer à la formation systématique de cette philosophie, les théories générales propres aux différents arts principaux doivent, au contraire, comme nous le voyons, être vraisemblablement plus tard une des conséquences les plus utiles de sa construction."

180. *Système de politique positive* (Paris, 1851), I, 433–35 and 447–49; IV, 171–84, esp. 171: "Les lois abstraites constituent donc le domaine commun de la science et de l'art, qui les destinent respectivement à discipliner notre intelligence et régler notre activité."

181. *Ibid.*, I, 451–52; "Quelle que doive être l'aptitude naturelle du nouveau régime envers la logique rationelle, principalement destinée aux philosophes, il est donc encore plus indispensable pour construire et développer la logique morale, essentiellement propre aux femmes et aux prolétaires. Entre ces deux voies extrêmes, la logique des vrais poëtes, qui procède surtout par images, vient placer un lien général qui complète la constitution, à la fois spontanée et systématique, de la méthode humaine. Jusqu'ici l'image ne fut guère employée que pour perfectionner la manifestation, soit du sentiment, soit de la pensée. Désormais elle secondera surtout leur élaboration respective, d'après leur réaction mutuelle, dont elle constitue l'agent naturel. Tantôt l'image, rappelée sous le signe, fortifiera la pensée par le réveil du sentiment; tantôt, au contraire, l'effusion suscitera l'image pour éclaircir la notion."

imitation as a criterion), the emotions subsume the relevant problems of execution (for emotion is selective of material or of the ordering of material), and content is determined, not by the nature of the objects imitated, but by the interests of audiences or the interest of artists (for it is justified by its importance to the one or its pertinence to the intention of the other) or its appropriateness to the medium of expression.[182] Three problems emerge, where Plato treats the one problem of imitation and Kant the two problems of the production and the appreciation of beauty, for the reduction now operates on the artist (who is conditioned by experience or by his times and circumstances), and the art object (which cannot be considered in isolation), and the audience (which should reproduce in itself the operations of the artist and the structure of the art object) either by means of such inclusive and universal concepts as "experience" or the "brotherhood of man," which reconcile oppositions, or by means of the universalism of symbols which communicate emotions by expressing them and relate objects by signifying them. The resolution remains that appropriate to a dialectic of process and becoming; and, although some philosophers who take their subject matter from events and relations have, like Whitehead, returned to a Platonic dialectic of eternal objects, no modern semanticist has yet recognized his heritage by enunciating the logos-doctrine that haunts his study.

The terminologies of the five literal modes of criticism bear a double relation to the terminologies of the various forms of the dialectical mode: the terms employed in any form of the dialectical mode are usually also subjected to a literal treatment, intended to define them in the respects to which they were vague and to relate them to clearly distinguished matters, and those literal distinctions are usually analogized, at the next stage of discussion, in a dialectical treatment designed either to broaden them in more sensitive application or more reasonable definition or to show that they correspond to nothing real or essential in art. Since these attempts at literal definition are concerned to establish sharp boundaries, there results from them, not a single variegated mode of criticism, but a series of literal modes more or less sharply and successfully separated from one another and from the dialectical mode.

The mode of criticism which balances Plato's form of dialectical criticism, Aristotle's "scientific" criticism, may therefore be taken as the second mode, instituted in terms closely related to those of Plato's dialectic. In spite of the similarity of terms, however, the "scientific" method of the *Poetics* is distinct from the dialectical criticism of Plato; and much as dialectic, which is the method of science and philosophy for Plato, became a second-best

---

182. For Tolstoy's use of these distinctions cf. above, pp. 480 and 486; for Dewey's use cf. *Art as Experience*, pp. 69, 18, and *passim*.

method, based on opinions rather than on knowledge of things, for Aristotle, so, too, the treatment of imitation—in terms of object of imitation, the imitation itself, and its execution, which was easily translated in the dialectical tradition to audience, art object, and artist—formed the structure of Aristotle's rhetoric rather than of his poetics. He made use of a scientific method, rather than dialectic or rhetoric, to place his analysis of tragedy, considered as an object, in the context of his philosophic inquiries, for the first five chapters of the *Poetics* treat of phases of the operation of the artist in terms of object, means, and manner of imitation prior to analyzing tragedy in terms of construction and parts, while the last four chapters compare tragedy to a related art form and formulate replies to censures which ignore the ends governing the construction of tragedy. The scientific analysis which is framed between these preliminary and supplementary treatments of tragedy in terms of its efficient causes and its end brings the formulation of the circumstances and purposes of tragedy to bear on the analysis of tragedy as a whole consisting of six parts—plot, character, and thought arising from the object, diction and melody arising from the means, and spectacle from the manner of imitation—by finding a prime importance in plot and by treating plot at once as a combination of incidents, or, more literally, of things, and as the organizing principle of the tragedy. A criterion of unity and structure is thereby rendered available, and on it the possibility of a poetic science depends, for otherwise the analysis of an object of art must reduce the diversity of concepts that might be included under Aristotle's six terms to two broad analytic elements—form and matter—and must go for its criteria directly to the intention of the artist, or the reaction of the audience, or the technical achievement of the structure.

Such a criterion of unity disappears when the terminology of criticism is taken, not from things (the tragedy as an artificial thing and the incidents or "things" that compose its action) but from thoughts and aspirations, conceived either as universal, shared by all mankind but given particular expression by the poet, or as peculiar to the poet, and in need of explanation by his life and circumstances to make them intelligible to other men. Following the former principle, Poe could argue plausibly that "the phrase, 'a long poem,' is simply a flat contradiction in terms," for the poetic principle is the human aspiration for supernal beauty and the elevating excitement it occasions cannot be of long duration;[183] following the latter principle, T. S. Eliot could be moved to maintain that it is impossible to understand Shakespeare from any one of his plays, since the relation between the plays taken in order must be studied for years before any slight interpretation may be ventured,[184] and that Shakespeare indeed sup-

183. Poe, *op. cit.*, pp. 3 ff.
184. Eliot, "Dante," *Selected Essays, 1917–1932* (New York, 1932), p. 207.

plies in this personal and individual way a unity, not merely to his work, but to his times.[185] The two modes of criticism which employ these two principles approximate the equivalent forms of "dialectical" criticism more closely than other modes of literal criticism do, for the mind assumes a synoptic universality embracing things known and actions contemplated whether they are included analogically within its nature or separated literally from its proper activity.

The third mode of criticism, "poetic" criticism, proceeds from the poet, or more broadly the author, conceived as universal in the sense of being possessed of lofty thoughts and inspired by vehement emotions intelligible or moving to all mankind, to the particular language of the author's expression. The "objects of imitation" have been translated into the ideas and feelings which are the matter or content of the author's statement, and his "composition" is examined in a part-whole analysis into "periods" and "figures." This mode of criticism is properly called "poetic" both in the sense that it proceeds from the conceptions and expressions of great authors and uses them as touchstones for other statements, and in the sense that the critic's own expression must arouse reactions like those caused by the poet if the criticism is to be effective as a guide. It differs (as practiced, for example, by Longinus) from the equivalent form of dialectical criticism (as developed, for example, by Kant) in that it is concerned not with the conditions of the judgment of beauty and sublimity in general, but exclusively with their sources in literature.

The fourth mode of criticism, "scholarly" criticism, reverses this procedure and attempts to reconstruct the peculiar character and significance of an author from the corpus and development of his work. It was in this mode that the *ars critica* developed to such massive importance in the seventeenth and eighteenth centuries,[186] laying the foundations of the higher biblical criticism, furnishing the example of classical, and later modern, philology, and in the process revolutionizing historical method. It is based on the truth, converse to the basic truth of "poetic" criticism that poets are universal—and quite as obvious as it—that poets are particular, that their words, their references, and their intentions must be understood, if their statements and inventions are to be appreciated; that their various works have relations to one another and to the works of other authors, as well as individual marks of unity and particular high points of

185. Eliot, "Shakespeare and the Stoicism of Seneca," *ibid.*, p. 119: "It has been said that Shakespeare lacks unity; it might, I think, be said equally well that it is Shakespeare chiefly that *is* the unity, that unifies so far as they could be unified all the tendencies of a time that certainly lacked unity."

186. For an excellent review of "critical" literature as it bears on theological and historical problems in the seventeenth century see S. von Dunin Borkowski, *Spinoza*, IV: *Aus den Tagen Spinozas* (Münster i.W., 1936), 136–308 and 523–50.

excitement; that even when most original they seldom originate, but what is novel in their accomplishment may be understood by knowing what they, in turn, experienced and esteemed; and that the patterns of their lives and works are more easily perceived when the elements of which their works are composed are known independently. It differs (as practiced, say, by F. A. Wolf or Dover Wilson) from the equivalent form of dialectical criticism (as practiced, say, by Fechner) in that it is concerned, not with the formulation of scientific aesthetic principles, derived from the natural or biological sciences, to be applied in criticism to specific objects, natural or artificial, but with the use of the devices of the historical sciences to explain the significances of objects of art. The principles of scholarly criticism are the same as those of poetic criticism—expression and thought or emotion; form and content—but, whereas the poetic critic goes to other great authors to test the universal achievement of a given expression, the scholarly critic goes to other sources of information and other statements to elucidate the particular meaning of a given statement. Whereas the poetic critic proceeds from the elevation of soul caused by a statement to the examination of the manner of expression, the scholarly critic proceeds from the recovery of the author's meaning to the discovery of its effectiveness and value. As one consequence of this difference the poetic critic is concerned only with mall bits which constitute the high achievement of the author, whereas the scholarly critic tends to treat the whole body and context of his work. The poetic critic will proceed from the consideration of principles like the "good sense," "fancy," and "imagination" analyzed by Coleridge to abstract by practical criticism the marks characteristic of original poetic genius.

In the application of these principles to purposes of practical criticism, as employed in the appraisement of works more or less imperfect, I have endeavored to discover what the qualities in a poem are, which may be deemed promises and specific symptoms of poetic power, as distinguished from general talent determined to poetic composition by accidental motives, by an act of the will, rather than by the inspiration of a genial and productive nature.[187]

The scholarly critic will examine all the data bearing on the establishment of the text and its interpretation before venturing an evaluation of the quality of any part of it or the sense or imagination of its author.

Such considerations of genius and the author's circumstances disappear, in turn, when the terminology of criticism is taken, not from thoughts and feel-

---

187. *Biographia literaria*, chap. xv (*Works*, III, 375). The characteristics of genius are found in language and thought: (1) in the sweetness of the versification and its adaptation to the subject, (2) in the choice of subjects remote from the private interests and circumstances of the writer, (3) in images modified by a predominant passion or by associated thoughts or images awakened by that passion, (4) in depth and energy of thought. It is in virtue of the last characteristic that Coleridge argues that "no man was ever yet a great poet, without being at the same time a profound philosopher" (p. 381).

ings, whether in their universality or particularity, but from consideration of the effects of their expression. Such a causal analysis may be conducted either by studying the relation of the work to the audience to determine the *effects* that are produced or ought to be produced, or by studying the relation of the content to the style to determine the *means* that are effective or ought to be effective.

The fifth mode of criticism, "technical" criticism, which is developed in "arts" of poetry, constructs its precepts about what pleases or instructs audiences in terms relevant to thought and expression in a manner similar to poetic criticism. Yet the terminology which these two modes largely share is put to different applications and assumes different significances. The concern of poetic criticism is with the sublime and elevated moments achieved by literature; the concern of technical criticism, as practiced by Horace, Vida, or Boileau, is with any device which achieves a pleasant or a profitable effect. Therefore, the criterion for thought and expression is not the loftiness of thought, of expression, or of both together, but the decorum which relates them to each other and to the audience; its application is not limited to isolated moments, since it may apply significantly to the structure and unity of a work; and its incidence falls less upon content than upon devices and style.

The sixth mode of criticism, "formal" criticism, reverses the procedure of technical criticism, beginning with the work and the effort to express rather than with the audience and the effect of the expression. Its terminology, like that of technical criticism, bears a close relation to the terms used in poetic criticism, but the analysis is not limited to elevated thought but runs through a variety of contents and yields, not a single analysis, but a classification of styles (as in the case of Demetrius) or of uses of language (as in the case of I. A. Richards and some of his various rival semanticists). The concern of formal criticism is with the analysis of compositions or communications into their constitutive parts to evaluate the effectiveness or appropriateness of devices to purposes: figures of speech relative to subject matters and effects in the older analysis, strategies and devices of evocation relative to objectives and attitudes in the newer; it proceeds by a part-whole analysis from words or phrases to the composition as a whole; and the controlling consideration is the characteristic or thought which determines the devices suited to it. Consequently, the consideration of audiences and circumstances in technical criticism yields canons and censures for composition, whereas the consideration of the devices of language in formal criticism, since it takes language (according to the phrase of Demetrius) as a lump of wax from which anything may be molded, yields differentiations in effects to be achieved.

The principles employed by these various modes of criticism and the subject matters to which they are relevant are in the case of most of them so distinct from those of the others that statements constructed of the same words often turn out on examination of their meanings to be unrelated when apparently contradictory or equivalent when apparently opposed. It is important to recognize these variations of meanings, however, not because terms are necessarily inexact and criteria vague in criticism, but rather because the varieties of meanings are determined by the purposes and methods of the modes. Even the most impressionistic and subjective critic writes with the conviction that the expression at least of a personal or skeptical opinion is intelligible and to that minimum extent effective as communication; and in varying manners and degrees the critic works on the assumption that the appreciation, judgment, and evaluation of art follow laws which may be stated in terms of the matter or the form of objects of art, or the imagination, feelings, or reason of man, or his experience, his conditions actual or projected, or his manner of expression. It is therefore true (if the statement be interpreted in the dialectical mode of criticism) that the philosopher, the critic, the artist, and the amateur express the same thing, when each is sensitive and successful, the philosopher by choosing, through his principles, pertinent and analyzable characteristics, the critic by treating such characteristics in the objects he judges, the artist by embodying them in his appropriate medium, and the amateur by reacting to them in his experience of the object of art. What the critic directs attention to is the result of the labor of the artist and an ingredient in the experience of the intelligent amateur, even though neither would have made the explicit statement of the critic, and it should find a place and explanation in the system even of philosophies antagonistic to the critical presuppositions on which it depends. There are three dimensions of variability in the discussion of art. The artist at work with the natural materials which constitute his media and with the ideas and emotions which he seeks to express has a latitude of choice in the construction of his work and the effecting of his purposes, for the media may be used in a variety of ways and the responses may be secured by new and old devices: among the influences which might bear on the solution of his problem are the devices of other artists, the statements of critics, and the assumptions of philosophers. The critic contemplating the finished work of art finds in it as great a latitude for his interpretations as the artist found in the artistic materials for his manipulations: the example of other artists, the refutation or application of what other critics or scientists have said, and the substantiation of a philosophy may be among the influences which determine his choice. A changed conception of the imagination, or the rise of the proletariat, or the unbelief of the upper classes may lead to the institution of new critical systems and applications even in a single mode of criticism; and yet the three modern forms of dialectical criticism which have resulted from such changes apply to empirical data which overlap little or not at all: the Humanist critics to cultural, the Marxist to economic, and the Tolstoyan to moral and religious data. The philosopher, finally, takes the phenomena of art, the judgments of criticism, and the formulations of other philosophies among his subject matters, resolving their oppositions and contradictions within the scope of his own principles, and his resolutions become in turn one of the matters which the next philosopher may be concerned to explain. Even though principles do not achieve finality and universal adherence in philosophy, they do serve to state the purposes of the artist and the criteria of the critic. The shifts of artistic styles, critical evaluations, and philosophic principles illustrate the importance of standards and principles, and the alternations of advocacy of a set of principles and attack upon them do not constitute evidence for those who think to avoid the discussion of principles as stultifying in art, futile in criticism, and fantastic in philosophy. For even the technical questions of art and criticism—questions of materials and production, taste and judgment, intention and interests—have philosophic bases which serve to clarify the solutions to those problems and their relations to other proposed solutions.

The purposes and relative effectiveness of the various forms of dialectical criticism may be stated and judged in the terms used in the development of those forms of criticism, for the dialectical process employed in the discussion of art also determines the transition from one form of the dialectic to another and the issues which emerge in the oppositions of forms. The terms of that continued dialectic—largely the same and different primarily by the addition of technical terms to attach new significances to the continuing terms—are determined in their use and the differentiation of their significances by the things to which they are applied in the reductive scheme of each form of the dialectic. When the reduction is to things, as in the criticism of Plato, the characteristics of art are found in objects: the object of imitation, the object of art itself, and its objective characteristics or style. When the reduction is to faculties of the mind or to thoughts, as in Kant's analytic and dialectic, the characteristics of art are found in the taste by which it is judged and the genius by which it is produced: the objects of art and their relations to nature may be envisaged from rules derived from taste and genius. When the reduction is to processes and events, as it is in Tolstoy's or Dewey's operational inquiries, the characteristics of art are found in the act of expression: the emotions of the artist, the sophistication of the audience's reaction, and even the object of art may be differentiated as moments in the "union of moral community" or the identity of process and product. There is no reason why the complete dialectical development should not be possible in any of these reductive schemes. The peculiar virtue of dialectical criticism, however, is not in the isolation of art from other phenomena or of the aesthetic aspects in art as peculiar phenomena, but rather in the return of both to a broader context in which each object is considered in terms of the good, the true, and the beautiful, or as subject to the operation of pure reason, practical reason, or judgment, or as incident to the living processes of experience.

There are, however, three dangers which the analysis of art encounters in the dialectical mode of criticism which arise from the successive domination of one of the dialectical triad: the good, the beautiful, and the true. The moral implications of Plato's criticism have attracted more attention in the later discussions of art than the role which beauty plays in his conception of the nature of things or in the motivations of human actions; and, although under his influence art takes on a metaphysical significance in the philosophy of Plotinus, the meanings of Platonism have been exploited chiefly by moral critics from the Christian Church Fathers to Tolstoy. Kant, on the other hand, supplied analytical and dialectical devices to isolate beauty and the sublime from the subject matters of science and morality, but he did not himself state the rules which determine the objects of art as fully as he explored those involved in the activities of the pure and practical reason; and his heritage has been exploited less by critics who treat the phenomena of art than by idealists who, like Schelling, make aesthetics the center of philosophy and who do not consider art as a particular phenomenon but, on the contrary, construe the universe itself in the form of art and philosophy as the science of the universe in the potency of art. Dewey, in turn, has found in concepts like "inquiry," "instruments," and "experience," the dialectical device by which to reduce and confute all the distinctions made by idealists and by other philosophers: beauty and utility, art and science, practice and theory, morals and science, mechanical arts and fine arts, experience and nature, inquiry and knowledge—these and all like separations introduce distinctions which are unreal and problems which are false according to the principles of his philosophy; but the therapeutic effect of Dewey's dialectic depends rather on the abundance of mistaken distinctions which he can reduce to experience, thereby giving the concept a kind of refutative richness, than on specific or positive characteristics isolated in art or on methods evolved for the elucidation of art. As in the analyses of Plato and Augustine, the treatment of art recommended by Dewey is in the context of a synoptic analysis, and the direction of his thought is most nearly analogous to the hope repeatedly expressed by writers on aesthetics that at last, if their respective suggestions are followed, the inquiry will become scientific and the object of art or the appreciation of art will become an instance of physiological, psychological, sociological, ethnological, economic, or psychopathic phenomena, to be explained, used, and, when the circumstances warrant and the techniques are adequate, even cured as such.

The five modes of literal criticism, on the other hand, treat art as art, in some sense, by techniques and according to criteria distinct from those of other disciplines and sciences. The sharpness of this difference, however, does not preclude the possibility that dialectical criticism, sensitively and intelligently employed, may lead to the same conclusions in application to a particular set of problems as those justified by the use of a mode of literal criticism, for the intermingled universal principles of dialectic may, of course, be brought to bear on particular instances, and the specific principles of a literally aesthetic analysis may be supplemented by the application to the same object or event of principles proper to politics, ethics, psychology, or physics. The hope of universality in philosophy, indeed, depends on the possibility of such equivalences among the results of intellectual labor painstakingly and accurately carried forward in different perspectives, and the dangers of error indicated by disagreements arise from the misapplications, the miscarriages, and the mistaken interpretations of any given method rather than from the oppositions of methods. The dangers in the dialectical method are to be found in the loss of balance consequent on a dogmatic freezing of the dialectic in defense of an unexamined faith, for as a result the consideration of art or of any other subject may be submerged in other concerns or become itself the ruling principle of other considerations. The dangers in literal criticism arise from pedantic concentration on a trait proper to a form of literal criticism and the treatment of it subtly and in detail in isolation from the causes from which it originated, the effects which it might explain, and the phenomena with which it is related. The five modes of literal criticism which have been enumerated are related to one another in their common concern with the object or phenomenon of art as such. They differ from one another in the qualities selected as essential to art and the methods proper to the analysis of art. They may therefore be in opposition to one another; they may supplement one another; and any one of them may be the subject of such exclusive devotion—as program of research or manifesto of art—as to make it the peculiar interest of a school rather than a technique for inquiry or elucidation. Any one of them, finally, may suggest the terminology and the distinctions for a recrudescence of dialectical criticism devoted to the attempt either to give generality and therefore vitality to the distinctions used in a restricted fashion in literal criticism or to reduce and therefore rectify its separations.

The respective purposes and subject matters of the five modes of literal criticism may be isolated by consideration of the use they make of the causal analysis—the causes which contribute to the construction of the work and the effects which may be traced back to the work—and of the analysis of form and content or whole and part. In "scientific" criticism, as practiced by Aristotle, the causes and effects—the peculiarities of poets, their media, and their subjects, the proper pleasures of art forms, their peculiar structures, and probable criticisms—are translated into terms which may be identified in the work of art itself, and therefore the probability and necessity by which incidents are knit together in the unity of the plot may be distinguished from the natural probability which is imitated in the manner appropriate to the medium; character and thought in tragedy may be subordinated to the needs and end of plot; and diction may be treated as the matter whose potentialities are exploited in the construction of forms. In "poetic" criticism, as practiced by Longinus, natural causes are not translated into artistic causes, but nature and art alike contribute to the production of the sublime, for the causal analysis is analogical, the prime element in all natural production and therefore in literary effectiveness is the exemplar, and the function of scientific method is to control the effects of natural genius, not to explain the product of art.[188] The sublime, therefore, is contrasted as an overwhelming excellence and distinction of language to the arrangement and economy of things,[189] and the ideas and content become the "matter" organized in the organic whole of the composition of a great genius.[190] Thought, metamorphosed from the function it has for Aristotle as expressive of character and subservient to plot, has become the thought of the author and matter for his composition, and the effect of the sublime is not dependent primarily on the form and arrangements of facts or things. In "technical" criticism, as practiced by Horace, the diversification of effects considered is derived from the character of audiences, and therefore his analysis, like that of Longinus, depends on the nature of the poet and proceeds by considering content and expression, but the exemplar is found in the life and custom to be portrayed rather than in the performance of genius, and words no longer achieve effects independent of the persuasiveness of matter but follow the matter that is given. Horace's analysis, like that of Aristotle, embraces larger units than the analysis of Longinus and supplies even a criterion of unity; but, where Aristotle thought the complex plot preferable, Horace's methods incline him to simplicity. All three modes of criticism treat of causes to account for literary forms: the scientific mode treats the formal cause of objects of art by

188. *On the Sublime* ii. 1–3.

189. *Ibid.* i. 3–4. Where the plot had been a combination of "things" for Aristotle, the composition becomes for Longinus the means of adumbrating slowly the arrangement and economy of things (τάξις καὶ οἰκονομία τῶν πραγμάτων). Cf. the treatment of arrangements of thought and words in the consideration of the figure Inversion (*ibid.* xxii. 1–2).

190. *Ibid.* x. 1; xiii. 4.

analyzing their structure; the poetic mode finds form in that union of thought and expression which is consequent on the causality of the poet; the technical mode finds form in the verbal structure which secures effects in audiences. The virtues of the scientific mode are to be found in the analytic technique it supplies; the virtues of the poetic mode are in its manuductive guidance for judgment among monuments of art; the virtues of the technical mode are in the devices for censure and evaluation which may be derived from technical or strategic rules of the artist's craft.

The perversions of the three modes are likewise characteristic: the scientific mode may be reduced to a routine and dialectical application of "classical" rules for the unity of action, time, and place, the genealogical nobility of characters, and the rigid elevation of thought; the poetic mode may be translated from a method of judgment to a random dialectical biography of the adventures of a soul and the dialectical justification by selective example of any preference; the technical mode may degenerate from the canonic reaction of a selected audience as a standard—the Roman audience of Horace, the prince's court during the Renaissance, the urban population of Reynolds, the plain men of Tolstoy, the proletariat of the Marxists, or even a vaguely envisaged posterity which will rectify the errors of contemporary evaluation—to a dialectical relativity in which standards may be treated either in a history of the themes, forms, and media that were successively esteemed or in a canon of methods to achieve any results thought to be effective on the audiences of the moment.

The excesses or perversions of these three literal modes are avoided or rectified by other devices of literal criticism and by other subject matters to which those devices are applied. The "scientific" analysis usually occurs in the context of other methods appropriate to other aspects of art phenomena, and therefore the consideration of the form, structure, and material of works of art may be balanced by the consideration, in other sciences, of its psychological origins, social effects, and historical developments, which return the art object to its context in nature and society. "Scholarly" criticism, in like fashion, returns the genius and his expression from a universal and sublime isolation to the conditions of his life, times, and interests, which determined the idiom and manner of his expression as well as the temporal and local peculiarities of his objects. "Formal" criticism marshals the verbal or other technical devices by which a medium may be made to achieve any of the effects of which it is capable and from which the artist may choose, or the amateur recognize, devices and means. All three modes of criticism treat of content and form to account for the peculiarities of literary and artistic objects: in literature the scientific mode treats words as matter and other scientific methods are designed to seek the other manners in which the forms—the actions and incidents, the necessities and probabilities—appropriately expressed in literature may exist; the scholarly mode seeks in the circumstances of the artist the matter to which he gave form; the formal mode analyzes the verbal forms in which the vast variety of matters may be presented effectively. The virtues of the scientific mode are in the distinctions it makes possible between natural and artistic forms by means of their respective matters, and in the analysis that is therefore possible of particular artistic forms; the virtues of the scholarly mode are in the concrete significance it may give to the forms of an artist by considering the matters assembled in his experience and life and in the poetic appreciation and critical understanding that are thereby rendered possible of particular works; the virtues of the formal mode are in the differentiation of means of presenting the varieties of matter appropriate to communication, and in the practical evaluation and comparison of particular devices that is therefore possible. The scientific mode is perverted when artistic form or cause is confused dialectically with natural thing or cause, and art is treated as the exclusive or peculiar subject of some other science than the poetic; the scholarly mode is perverted when the investigation of the circumstances of the artist is pushed into details irrelevant to the traits of the art objects he produced, and still further perverted when those irrelevant traits are dialectically converted into the only explanation of his art; the formal mode is perverted when the machinery and terminology of distinction are carried to such refinements in the dialectical ordering and discrimination of tropes and figures that differences of effects and of matter are obscured or lost.

Needless to say, a given critic may successively employ more than one of these modes of criticism and may even combine two or more of them, crudely or effectively, in a single theory or application of criticism. Purity in adherence to a single mode is not necessarily a virtue in criticism since the differentiation of modes is in terms of the purposes envisaged in the criticism, and the identification of the mode employed by a critic is only a step toward the evaluation of his achievement in so far as such identification may indicate the appropriate criterion and thereby contribute to both the understanding and the judgment of his statements.

The pertinence of an examination of philosophic and critical principles in relation to art and criticism may, therefore, be illustrated by applying the distinctions treated in this essay to the essay itself. It is an essay in the dialectical mode of criticism, using as its reductive device concepts derived from semantics. It does not, however, use those semantic concepts in the form of dialectic in which the controlling principles are processes or symbols (as I. A. Richards, for example, reduces all meanings to symbolic or emotive uses of language) but rather takes advantage of the possibility of achieving full dialectical scope in any form of the dialectical mode of criticism to return to a dialectic of things on the model of Plato's usage. The manner of adherence to that mode may be seen in the subjects of the three parts into which the essay is divided: they are concerned in turn with the objects of criticism, criticism itself, and the terms of criticism, which are an adaptation of what Plato said about the criticism of art to the criticism of criticism, whereas the semantic mode of dialectic would translate these three (as was pointed out above when the three forms of dialectical criticism were considered) into some such considerations as the intention of the critic, the form of his criticism, and its pertinence to or effects on the audience. The effect envisaged in the three-fold division of subjects employed in the essay is to prevent the reduction of the treatment of criticism to some partially literal dialectic frozen to some one conception of the nature of art, or of the domain of criticism, or of the principles of philosophy. The essay is not, however, concerned directly with the criticism of art but with the criticism of criticism. It might be made the propadeutic to an essay in the criticism of art which would then, under the guidance of the criteria and subject matters distinguished in the six modes of criticism, pursue one mode in an appropriate manner and to a relevant conclusion with some grounds for the expectation that its meaning and purpose might be more clearly perceived. But, although it adumbrates no solution of the problems of art or beauty, it may pretend to adequacy in treating what has been said about art and beauty, for being a dialectic of what medieval philosophers used to call second, as distinct from first, intentions, it accounts for the literal modes, as well as for the dialectical mode in which it is couched, without distortion or prejudice, since in the positive operation of the dialectic the virtues of each mode may be isolated and the refutative elenchus may disclose indifferently the failures and perversions of each mode.

AN OUTLINE OF POETIC THEORY[1]

ELDER OLSON

I

WHEN, in any field of learning, discussions of the subject are based upon different principles, employ different methods, and reach different conclusions, such differences tend to be interpreted, by expert and layman alike, as real disagreement. The differences are not of themselves dangerous to the subject; the tendency to interpret them as contradictions is. The dogmatist, however sound in his own method, usually regards them as signs of the chaos that must await any who depart from his position. The syncretist regards them as signs that all positions are at least partly false, and collects "truths," which frequently lose, in his synthesis, not only their supporting arguments but their original significance as well. The skeptic, finally, interprets such differences as implying the impossibility of philosophical knowledge in the field. All these views are potentially harmful to learning in so far as, in suppressing discussion, they suppress some (and in the case of skepticism, all) of the problems and because, consequently, they retard or even arrest progress within the subject. Skepticism, indeed, is most dangerous of all, for it does not arrest progress merely in certain respects but arrests it wholly; and, once given head, it does not pause until it has also canceled whatever has been achieved in the past.

Criticism in our time is a sort of Tower of Babel. Moreover, it is not merely a linguistic but also a methodological Babel; yet, in the very pursuit of this analogy, it is well to remember that at Babel men did not begin to talk nonsense; they merely began to talk what *seemed* like nonsense to their fellows. A statement is not false merely because it is unintelligible; though it will have to be made intelligible before we can say whether it is true. The extreme diversity of contemporary criticism is no more alarming than—and, indeed, it is connected with—the similar diversity of contemporary philosophy; and the chief import of both is of the need for some critique which shall examine radically how such diversity arises, by considering what aspects of a given subject are amenable to treatment, what problems they pose, and how these may be

---

1. Reprinted from *Critiques and Essays in Criticism, 1920–1948*, ed. Robert Wooster Stallman (New York: Ronald Press Co., 1949). This essay represents, in a very condensed form, an argument developed much more fully in a forthcoming book to be entitled "General Criticism and the Shorter Forms of Poetry."

diversely formulated. For the diverse may be contradictory or not; theories of criticism which are not contradictory or incompatible may be translated into one another or brought to supplement one another, and a just decision may be given between those which are really contradictory, provided that we can isolate the differences of formulation from the differences of truths and falsities. True interpretation is impossible when one system is examined in terms of another, as is true refutation when the refutative arguments are systematically different from those against which they are directed. To propose such a critique is, in effect, to state the possibility of a fourth philosophic attitude: that of pluralism. Dogmatism holds the truth of a single position and the falsity, in some degree at least, of all others; syncretism holds the partial falsity of all; skepticism the total falsity of all. All these take into their consideration doctrines alone; pluralism, taking both doctrine and method into account, holds the possibility of a plurality of formulations of truth and of philosophic procedures—in short, of a purality of valid philosophies.

Such pluralism is possible both in philosophy and in criticism because criticism is a department of philosophy. A given comprehensive philosophy invariably develops a certain view of art; the critical theories of Plato, Aristotle, Hume, and Kant, for instance, are not any random views but are generated and determined by their respective philosophies. And while a given criticism or theory of art may not originate in a comprehensive philosophy and may resist reference to one already existent, it is not therefore really independent of a more comprehensive system, for the discussion of art must entail assumptions which involve more than art; it is merely part of a whole as yet undeveloped. In short, since criticism or the theory of art is part of philosophy, it has the same bases as philosophy and is determinate or variable according to the same principles.

It is impossible within the scope of this essay to discuss all the factors in the foundations of philosophies and criticisms; but perhaps a rough and partial statement may serve for illustration. I propose that the number of possible critical positions is relative to the number of possible philosophic positions and that the latter is determined by two principal considerations: (1) the number of aspects of a subject which can be brought into discussion, as constituting its *subject matter*; (2) the kinds of basic dialectic which may be exerted upon that subject matter. I draw this distinction between the subject and the subject matter: the subject is what is talked about; the subject matter is that subject in so far as it is represented or implied in the discussion. Philosophers do not discuss *subjects themselves*; they can discuss only so much as the terms or materials of the discussion permit; and that is the subject matter. We cannot discuss what we cannot, first of all, mention, or what we cannot bring to mind. In other words, any discussion of a "subject" is relative to its formulation. But, further, any discursive reasoning must employ some method of reasoning or inference; and, since there are various possible systems of inference, we may say that a given discussion is a function of its subject matter and of the dialectic, i.e., system of inference, exerted upon that subject matter.

Whatever art in itself may be, as a *subject*, it is clear that criticism has employed certain aspects of it as subject matters. Thus one aspect of an art is its product; another, the instrumentality, active or passive, which produced the product; another, the product as relative to or determined by that instrumentality, and hence as a sign of the nature of that instrumentality, whether this last be viewed as actual or potential. Another is the relation of an art to a certain subject or means, as a consequence, and hence as a sign, of these; still another aspect is its production of a certain effect, either of activity or of passivity, upon those who are its spectators or auditors; and, lastly, there is the art viewed as instrumental to that effect. We may sum up all this by saying that criticism has viewed art variously as a product; as an activity or passivity of the artist; as certain faculties or as a certain character of the artist; as a certain activity or passivity of the audience; as certain faculties or as a certain character of the audience; as an instrument; or as a sign, either of certain characteristics of the artist or his audience or of something else involved in art, e.g., its means, subject, etc.

The significances which the term "poem" assumes in critical discussions may illustrate this. In its most obvious meaning it refers to the product of the poetic art; but critics have often used it to refer to what they considered more important aspects of poetic art or have differentiated it by reference to such aspects. Thus those who think that it is characterized by its instrumentality mean by "instrumentality" either the poet or the poetic powers; those who define poetry in terms of the poet see the poet as active craftsman or as the passive instrument of his inspiration or as a mixture of the two; while those who define poetry in terms of poetic powers see the poet as possessed of faculties or qualities either of a certain kind or of a certain degree. With these differences, both consequently view the poem as a kind of behavior of the poet; and, for both, the literal poem—the product—becomes a sign of that behavior, which is, in turn, a sign of the poetic character or faculties. Others find that the poem properly exists in the audience; the audience is the true poet, for, without it, the poem could never come to life; and the audience, like the poet, can be viewed as actualizing certain active or passive potentialities or merely as possessing such potentialities—hence the theories of "audience-participation" (the active view) or "art as experience" (the passive view), etc. Finally, "poem" may mean the end to which the product is instrumental, e.g., the psychological cure or ethical or political attitude or behavior.

These seem like "conflicting views"; hence they have been treated so in the history of criticism. If "conflicting" merely means "different," there is no quarrel, for these views are different enough. But if it means "contradictory" or "inconsistent," nothing could be more absurd. For, in the first place, all these doctrines have different references, and it is impossible to have contradiction except in the same reference; and, secondly, where contradiction exists, one view must be false if the other is true, whereas all these views are perfectly true in their proper senses, for all are founded upon perfectly obvious aspects of art, poetic or otherwise. Nor, if they are not contradictory, are they inconsistent, in the sense that they proceed from, or result in, contradiction; for, asserting the existence of certain aspects of art as they do, they are all true in some sense, and it is impossible for true propositions to be inconsistent. Indeed, nothing prevents certain philosophers, like Plato and Aristotle, from investigating all these aspects of art.

Whatever aspect of art a critic may fix upon, he usually seeks to explain its nature by reference to certain causes or reasons; thus those who are concerned with the product of art, for instance, have thought to explain the nature of the product by reference to its matter or medium, to the subject represented or depicted, to the depictive method of the artist or some other productive cause, or to the end or effect of the product; and some have employed merely one of these causes or reasons, while others have used several or all. Aristotle, for instance, employs differentiations of object, means, manner, and effect to define tragedy, whereas a critic like Richard Hurd finds the nature of poetry adequately defined by its subject matter.

I have remarked that the kind of dialectic exerted upon the subject matter is the other determinant of a given mode of criticism. The variety of dialectics is an exceedingly complex question, but we may occupy ourselves here only with a single characteristic of dialectics—their concern with likeness or difference, or both. The integral or likeness-dialectic reaches solutions by combination of like with like; the differential or difference-dialectic, by the separation of dissimilars. Thus a criticism integral in its dialectic resolves its questions by referring poetry, for example, to some analogue of poetry, finding characteristics of poetry which are shared by the analogue; whereas a criticism differential in its dialectic resolves its questions by separating poetry from its analogues, finding characteristics which are peculiar to poetry.

Thus—to confine our illustrations to the various criticisms which deal with the product of art—we find criticisms differing as they center on either the subject matter of art or its medium or its productive cause or its end or several of these, and as they proceed integrally or differentially. Subject-matter criticism of the integral kind resolves the subject matter of the arts into something not peculiar to the arts, on the basis of likeness; and the principles of art, when so found, are always the principles of things other than art as well. Thus Plotinus finds the beautiful in art to consist in the imitation of the beautiful; but inquiry into that characteristic, for him, shows it to be common also to natural objects and to actions, and so upward to the Beauty which is almost indifferentiable from the Good; and the ultimate solution of artistic as well as of all other problems lies, for him, in the contemplation of God. Differential criticism of this order, on the other hand, separates the kinds of subject matter and argues on the basis of such separation, either to distinguish the arts from other faculties or activities or to distinguish them *inter se*.

In pure subject-matter criticisms, once the subject matter has been found, it determines all other questions, e.g., of artistic capacity or character or of the techniques, forms, processes, criteria, and ends of art. For example, if the subject matter in the raw, so to speak, is all-sufficient, the characteristics of the artist tend to appear as sharpness of observation and readiness of comprehension; if the subject matter requires order and selection, correlative capacities for order and selection are constituents of the artistic character; and so on. A similar determination operates throughout all other problems: criteria, for instance, are produced from some correspondence or opposition, absolute or qualified, between the subject and the medium, or the artist, or the effect. Thus many of the theories of artistic realism have as their criterion the absolute correspondence of the effects of art with those of reality itself; art is thus copyistic, and the work is a "slice of life," all formal criteria (such as order) being supplanted by attributes of the reality. Where the subject matter of art is opposed to the reality, however—whether it requires an order and selection not found in reality or differs from reality even more radically—such correspondence is qualified, or even negated, as in modern nonrepresentationalist theories.

Comparably, criticisms centering on the medium can be integral or differential, and solve their problems through reference to the medium. The integral criticism of this order is exemplified in the innumerable attempts to find general criteria for all literature, whether poetic, historical, philosophic, or personal, on the ground that all literature employs words; and the differential criticism is exemplified in the theories of men like I. A. Richards and Cleanth Brooks, who seek to differentiate poetry from prose by differentiation of the kind of diction employed in each, in order to discriminate appropriate criteria for each.[2] The character of the artist varies as the character of the medium is stated; where the medium is viewed as indifferent to form, the capacities of the artist are at the maximum, and, conversely, where the medium is viewed as tending toward form, the artist frequently appears as a kind of midwife to nature,

2. See above, pp. 46 ff., 92 ff.

assisting the bronze or the marble to a form which it implicitly contains. Criteria, again, can be found, by consideration of the degree to which a given work actualizes or fulfils the potentialities of the medium.

When the productive cause is central, the integral criticism establishes analogies between the artist or the artistic process and some more general cause, e.g., nature or natural process, or God and the divine creative process (Coleridge). Extreme criticisms of this order reduce the art-product almost to a by-product of the artistic character; Fracastoro and Carlyle, for example, refuse to limit the name of poet to those who actually write poems, since poetry is merely incidental to the possession of poetical character. Differential criticism of this kind, again, confines the conception of the artist to the unique maker of a certain product. When discussion centers on the natural elements of the artist, the artistic character lies outside the possibility of any deliberate achievement, as in Hazlitt; conversely, when the artistic character is defined in terms of acquired traits or disciplines (as in Reynolds), discussion of genius and inspiration is at a minimum, and the artistic character itself appears as amenable to art and, indeed, often as the *chef d'œuvre* of the artist.

When criticism turns on the ends of art, integral and differential dialectics are again possible; the ends of art can be analogized to other purposes of men or to some natural or divine teleology or, conversely, can be differentiated from all else. And, here, as above, the nature of the problems and of their solutions is determined by the choice of the ground-term.

All such criticisms may be called "partial," for each attempts to resolve all problems by consideration only of a part. All fix upon a single *cause*, in Aristotle's sense of the word, and account for everything in terms of it, as if one were to account for a chair merely in terms of its wood or merely in terms of its maker. None permits a full account, for the respects in which art is compared with, or contrasted to, other things are always only a part of its actual characteristics. This partiality remains, even if several of these causal factors are combined, unless, indeed, all are involved.

As opposed to such partial criticisms, there are comprehensive criticisms such as those of Plato and Aristotle, the former being primarily integral, the latter primarily differential, although each includes both likeness and difference. These systems permit not only the discussion of all aspects of art but a full causal account; for, whereas Aristotle makes the maximum differentiation of causes, Platonic dialectic employs only a single cause, but one subsuming all. The difference—not in truth or in cogency of argument but in *adequacy*—between comprehensive and partial systems can be readily seen by comparing, say, Aristotle with the "Aristotelian" Scaliger: Aristotle can discuss any aspect of poetry, but Scaliger, basing all merely upon the medium and viewing that only in its most general light—the universal power of language being to express fact or opinion—thereby confines himself to the treatment of poetry only as the instrument of instruction.[3]

Recognition of the methodological differences between systems of criticism, and of their consequent respective powers and limitations, quickly establishes the fact that twenty-five centuries of inquiry have not been spent in vain. On the contrary, the partial systems of criticism correct and supplement one another, the comprehensive intertranslate, to form a vast body of poetic knowledge; and contemporary theorists, instead of constantly seeking new bases for criticism, would do better to examine the bases of such criticisms as we have and so avail themselves of that knowledge. Many a modern theory of criticism would have died a-borning, had its author done a little more reading as he thought, or thinking as he read. Critical knowledge, like all knowledge, must be constantly extended; but no one is very likely to extend it who is not fully aware of what has already been accomplished or of what consequences follow from such accomplishments.

If a plurality of valid and true kinds of criticism is possible, choice must still be exercised, for it is impossible to employ all methods simultaneously, and the selection of method is by no means a matter of indifference. Choice is determined by the questions one wishes to ask and the form of answer one requires and by the relative adequacy of given systems. The discovery of properties peculiar to a given kind of poetry demands a differential method, as that of properties which poetry holds in common with other things requires an integral method. If one wishes to know the nature of a given kind of poetry, as a certain *synolon* or composite, a whole and its parts specified with the maximum differentiation possible without the destruction of the universals upon which science depends, an Aristotelian criticism is requisite; if one proposes to view poetry in terms of principles of maximum community, a Platonic criticism is demanded. Every philosophy is addressed only to certain questions and can answer them only in certain forms.

II

In the method of Aristotle, which underlies the following sketch, poetics is a science concerned with the differentiation and analysis of poetic forms or species in terms of all the causes which converge to produce their respective emotional effects. Scientific knowledge falls into three classes: theoretical, practical, and productive. The end of the first class, comprising metaphysics, mathematics, and the natural sciences, is knowledge; that of the second, com-

3. Cf. Bernard Weinberg, "Scaliger versus Aristotle on Poetics," *Modern Philology* XXXIX (1942), 337-60.

prising ethics and politics, is action; that of the third, comprising the fine and the useful arts, is some product over and above the actions which produce. Only the theoretical sciences are exact; the productive sciences, or arts, are less exact than the practical, since they involve a greater number of principles, and principles derived from many other sciences.

The poetics of a given species takes as its starting point the definition of the product, i.e., a statement of the nature of the whole composite produced by an art, and thence proceeds by hypothetical reasoning to treat of the questions specific to that whole and its parts. Such analysis does not exhaust all aspects of the art; but any which it excludes are referred to other sciences. Thus the consideration of art as a skill falls under ethics; that of art as a political and social instrument, under politics; and that of art as a mode of being, under metaphysics, in accordance with the general Aristotelian practice of assigning questions to their appropriate sciences. A given special poetics, therefore, does not treat centrally of the faculties requisite for production, or of the effects to be produced by art, but of the special product, viewed as a differentiable synthesis of differentiable parts, and, as such, having the capacity or power (*dynamis*) of producing certain peculiar effects.

Before we can consider the various special arts of poetry, however, we must discuss the significance of certain concepts of a more general nature. Unity, beauty, and imitation, for instance, relate to things other than poetry but are not therefore less important to poetic discussion. The term "imitation" is used coextensively with "artificial"; it differentiates art from nature. Natural things have an internal principle of motion and rest, whereas artificial things—a chair or a table—have, qua products of art, no such principle; they change through propensities not of their form but of their matter. Natural and artificial things alike are composites of form and matter; but art imposes a form upon a matter which is not naturally disposed to assume, of itself, such a form. The acorn of itself grows into the oak; the stone does not of itself become a statue or tend to become a statue rather than a column. Art may be said to imitate nature either in the sense that the form of the product derives from natural form (e.g., the human form in the painting resembles the natural human form) or in the sense that the artistic process resembles the natural (e.g., artificial fever in the art of medicine does what fever does naturally). The useful and the fine arts are both imitative; but the latter have as their end the imitation itself, as a form possessed of beauty. Since every imitation has some form imposed somehow upon some matter for some end, specification of all these factors results in a definition of a given species of art; e.g., by specifying *what* is imitated in tragedy (object of imitation), *in what* (means of imitation), *how* (manner of imitation), and to what effect we construct the definition of tragedy. Such definitions are the principles from which reasoning proceeds in the arts; if a certain product or whole is to be produced, it will have a certain number of parts of a certain nature ordered in a certain way, etc.[4]

A poem has unity in the sense in which anything which has continuity is unified; but, more than that, it is one in that it has a single form and is an ordered and complete whole. A piece of wire is one because it is continuous, and if you break the continuity you have two pieces; but some things are totals rather than wholes—a cord of wood, for instance, because the parts need merely be present, and not in any particular arrangement—and others are wholes proper, because they are not only complete and have all their parts but also have them in the proper arrangement, i.e., the least important ordered to its superior part, and so on until the principal part is reached. Parts of a shoe stitched together anyhow are one in the sense of continuity, but not one in the sense of assemblage into a certain single form, the shoe; a poem is similarly an ordered and complete whole.

Moreover, it is not only a whole, but one of a certain nature; it is an imitation in a certain means; hence, since a given means can imitate only certain objects (color and line cannot imitate the course of thought, or musical tones a face), poetry must imitate action, character, or thought; for a given means can be used to imitate only something having the same characteristics as it or something of whose characteristics its own characteristics are signs, and speech (the medium of poetry) is either action or the sign of action, character, and passion. (For example, painting can represent color directly, but the third dimension only by signs, such as perspective diminution, faintness, etc., of objects.) Media are not such things as certain pigments or stones but such as line, color, mass, musical tones, rhythms, and words. The object imitated, therefore, must be some form which these can take or which they can imply by signs. Hence inference plays a large role in all the arts.

Inference and perception serve to institute opinions and mental images concerning the object, and opinions and mental images produce emotion. We see or infer the object to be such and such, and, according to our opinion of what it is, we react emotionally in a certain specific way. If we have the opinion, we react, whether the thing, in fact, is so or not; and if we do not have it, we do not react, whether the thing is so or not. The opinion that a disaster is imminent produces fear; and the opinion that the victim suffers undeservedly produces pity; and so on.

Emotions are mental pains (e.g., pity), pleasures (e.g., joy), or impulses

---

4. It should be borne in mind that the present discussion applies strictly only to what I have elsewhere called "mimetic," as distinguished from "didactic," poetry. See above, pp. 65 ff., and below, pp. 588 ff.

(e.g, anger) instigated by opinion. The basis of our emotions toward art may be explained as follows: We feel some emotion, some form of pleasure or pain, because our desires are frustrated or satisfied; we feel the desires because we are friendly or hostile to, or favor or do not favor, the characters set before us and because we approve or disapprove the events; and we are friendly or hostile to the characters because of their ethical traits; in brief, we side with the good against the bad or, in the absence of significant differentiations of moral character, upon grounds still moral, as with the oppressed against the oppressor, with the weak against the strong, etc., our judgment now being primarily of the action rather than of the agents.

Since the object of imitation as we conceive it determines the emotions which we feel and since moral differentiation lies at the basis of our conception of the object, the possible objects of imitation in poetry, drama, and fiction may be schematized in terms of extremes, as follows: The serious, i.e., what we take seriously, comprises characters conspicuously better or worse than we are or at any rate such as are like ourselves and such as we can strongly sympathize with, in states of marked pleasure or pain or in fortunes markedly good or bad. The comic, i.e., the ridiculous, comprises characters as involved in embarrassment or discomfiture to whom we are neither friendly nor hostile, of an inferiority not painful to us. We love or hate or sympathize profoundly with the serious characters; we favor or do not favor or condescend to the comic. Serious and comic both divide into two parallel classes: the former into the tragic kind, in which the character is better than we, and the punitive, in which the character is worse; the latter into what may be called "lout-comic," in which the character, though good natured or good, is mad, eccentric, imprudent, or stupid, and the "rogue-comic," in which the character is clever but morally deficient. These kinds are illustrated in drama by *Hamlet, The Duchess of Malfi, She Stoops To Conquer,* and *The Alchemist;* the protagonists in these are, respectively, a man better than we, wicked men (the brothers of the Duchess), a good man with a ridiculous foible, and rogues. Between these extremes of the serious and the comic lie what I have called the "sympathetic" or the antipathetic; i.e., forms in which the morality of the characters does not function in the production of emotional effect so much as does our judgment of the events as, for example, just or unjust; the man is indifferent, but the suffering is greater than even a criminal should undergo, etc. The emotions produced by the contrary objects are themselves contrary; for instance, the pity and fear of tragedy are opposed by the moral vindictiveness and the confidence of retribution in the punitive kinds. Again, the emotions are contrary as the events are contrary; that is, the spectacle of a good man going from good fortune to misfortune or from a pleasant to a painful state effects emotions contrary to those evoked by the spectacle of a good man going from misfortune to fortune or from pain to pleasure. Again, comic "catastrophe" is mere embarrassment or discomfiture, and effects emotions contrary to those produced by catastrophe in the serious forms.

In short, the emotions we feel in poetry are, generally speaking, states of pleasure and pain induced by mental images of the actions, fortunes, and conditions of characters to whom we are well or ill disposed, in a greater or lesser degree, because of our opinions of their moral character or, such failing, because of our natural sympathy or antipathy; or, in other words, our emotions are determined by the object of imitation and vary with it.[5] Emotion in art results, thus, not because we believe the thing "real" but because we vividly contemplate it, i.e., are induced by the work of art to make mental images of it. Compare such expressions as "He was horrified at the mere thought of it," "The very notion filled him with ecstasy," etc.

Pleasure, in general, is a settling of the soul into its natural condition; pleasure in poetry results primarily from the imitation of the object and secondarily from such embellishments as rhythm, ornamental language, and generally any such development of the parts as is naturally pleasing. Where the object of imitation is itself pleasant and vividly depicted, pleasure is direct; when the object is unpleasant, pleasure results from the catharsis or purgation of the painful emotions aroused in us, as in tragedy. Pleasure is commensurate, in other words, with the beauty of the poetic form; and distinctive forms, as they have peculiar beauties, evoke peculiar pleasures.[6]

By "beauty" I mean the excellence of perceptible form in a composite continuum which is a whole; and by "excellence of perceptible form" I mean the possession of perceptible magnitude in accordance with a mean determined by the whole as a whole of such-and-such quality, composed of such-and-such parts. Assuming that parts of the number and quality required for the whole have been provided and ordered hierarchically to the principal part, the whole will be beautiful if that prime part is beautiful; and that part, as a continuity, must have magnitude and be composed of parts (e.g., plot, the prime part of tragedy, has magnitude and has parts); since it has magnitude, it admits of the more and the less, and hence of excess and deficiency, and consequently of a definite and proper mean between them, which constitutes its beauty. Specifically, in terms of the form itself, this mean is a proportion between whole and part and, consequently, is relative to the different wholes and parts; in reference to perception, it is a mean between such minuteness of the parts and such

5. But cf. above, p. 71.

6. For a further discussion of the relation between pleasure and poetry see below, pp. 588–89.

extension of the whole as would interfere with the perception of the parts, as of their proper qualities, and as in interrelation with each other and the whole. Thus in tragedy the mean of plot-magnitude lies between the length required for the necessary or probable connection of the incidents and the limit imposed by the tragic change of fortunes. The constituents of beauty are, therefore, definiteness, order, and symmetry; the last being such commensurability of the parts as renders a thing self-determined, a measure to itself, as it were; for example, plot is symmetrical when complication and denouement are commensurate. As a thing departs from its proper magnitude, it either is spoiled (i.e., retains its nature but loses its beauty) or is destroyed (i.e., loses even its nature). Compare a drawing of a beautiful head: alter its definitive magnitude to a degree, and the beauty is lost; alter it further, and it is no longer recognizable as a head.

III

These questions are not peculiarly poetic ones but rather matters belonging to metaphysics, psychology, and ethics. The problems we now approach, however, are poetic and may be divided into two kinds—general questions, common to all the poetic arts, and special questions, peculiar to a given poetic art. Biology offers a parallel; for some attributes are common to all forms of life, others are peculiar. Similarly with poetics; some questions come about merely because the imitation is of action, like Aristotle's discussion of plot prior to chapter 13, others because of something specific, like his discussion of the tragic plot, imitating a certain kind of action. I shall here deal with both kinds, though illustratively only, and take up first the question of the definition of forms.

In their scientific order, all the arts, as I have said, begin with definitions of their specific products as wholes, which they utilize as the principle or starting point of their reasoning. These definitions, far from being arbitrary resolutions, must be collected from a conspectus of the historical growth of the species to which they relate; a kind of art, to be known and defined, must first actually exist. Not every aspect of the growth of artistic species, however, is relevant to their artistic character; hence their historical development must be examined in terms of their character as imitations. No single line of differentiation suffices for the separation of species. Most broadly, the arts are distinguished in terms of their media, for, since nothing can be made actual which is not potentially in the medium, the potentialities of the medium, as matter, determine all else; yet the means, even when fully differentiated, singly and in combination, is insufficient for specific distinction, for arts which have the same means may imitate opposite objects, as do comedy and tragedy. In turn, objects may be differentiated, but even such further differentiation is not definitive, for imitations may still differ in manner, although the possibilities of manner are now broadly determined. With the distinction of modes or manners of imitation, the account of the parts of imitation qua imitation is complete, and the historical survey of the rise of the arts—the synthesis of these differentiated parts into distinct wholes—is now possible. Such history begins as the causes emerge. The poetic arts, like the other fine arts, originate in instinct, some matter being given a form not natural to it, by an external efficiency, for the sake of the pleasure produced. Yet, though imitation is natural to man, instinct is insufficient to account for the further development of art; for art ramifies rather than remains constant, as the universal cause of instinct would suggest; and its ramifications are determined by the character of the artist: the noble minded imitate the noble, the low-minded the low. Even so, the tale is not complete: for art develops further until a form is achieved and valued for its own sake. Art passes, thus, through three stages—the instinctive, the ethical or practical, and the artistic—the first two of which are determined by the nature and character of the artist, and the last by the form. The achievement of form is signalized by a revolution in the ordering and constitution of the parts: once the specifically pleasurable effect has luckily been produced, the part which is primarily effective becomes principal, develops its proper extension and qualities, and all other parts readjust to it, in their proper artistic order. A distinctive synthesis—a species of art—has now formed, and its poetics may begin, for the formulation of the distinctive means, object, manner, and effect of the synthesis gives all four of the causes which are collectively, but not singly, peculiar to it, and a definition results.

Aristotle has frequently been defended on the ground that all poetic species reduce to those which he has enumerated, and more frequently attacked on the ground that they do not. Both defense and attack are mistaken, the former because it makes poetics predictive, the latter because it assumes that, since Aristotle did not define certain species, his theory could not afford a basis for their definition. In fact, as the above account has shown, the poetics of a given species must always develop after the species has come into actual being, the definition being formed by induction; but, on the other hand, the poetic arts in their development do not leave their bases; they do not cease to have means, objects, and manners, or even the differentiations of these mentioned by Aristotle; they merely differentiate these further and produce new syntheses. The distinction between narrative and dramatic manner, for instance, has not been rendered obsolete, although it affords no significant distinction, in itself, between Homer and Henry James; yet, to distinguish them, we must begin with the different possibilities of telling, as opposed to impersonating, and discriminate the various complexities of narrative device.

Once object, means, manner, and effect have been specified to the emerging species, the definition of the artistic whole which so results permits an analysis into parts; and when the principal part has been identified and the order of importance of the remaining parts established, the proper construction of the principal part must be ascertained. That part is itself a whole composed of parts, and these parts—its beginning, middle, and end—must be determined, and the character of their conjunction—necessity and probability—must be shown. But the whole is not only a whole, but a whole of some magnitude; and, since it is, moreover, to be a beautiful whole, it must be a whole of some definite magnitude. As I have remarked, this definite magnitude lies in a mean between excess of the part and excess of the whole, the former producing such vast extension that the whole cannot be comprehended, the latter such minuteness that the parts cannot be apprehended. This formula, however, is general and must be specified to the species of art involved. Relatively to perception, it must always be determined in the temporal arts by the limits of memory, since in these arts the parts are not coexistent but successive and, consequently, must be remembered if the whole is to be comprehended; but even this is relative to the species, differences of the parts and wholes of which impose different burdens upon the memory. (A given lyric might be too long to be remembered, while a given tragedy might not.) The wholeness, completeness, and unity of the principal part once established, the part can be divided into its species; hence, for example, Aristotle divides plots into simple and complex, which are different wholes, since the complex plot consists of differentiable parts (peripety and discovery) according to the efficient cause of the change of fortunes with which tragedy is concerned.

"Aristotelian" criticism has frequently centered merely upon this much, to produce mere *Formalismus;* but Aristotle himself goes farther. The principal part is only materially a whole, complete, one, etc.: formally, it has an effect or power of a certain specific order; tragic action, for instance, is not merely action, nor even serious action, but action differentiated by a certain act—the tragic deed committed in a certain way by the tragic hero—and Aristotle, investigating the possibilities of character and action, determines which of these result in the tragic effect, for that effect—the "working or power" of tragedy —is the form. Comparably, the poetics of any species must be addressed to the differentiation of its principal part, since it is this that primarily determines the emotional effect.

Once the principal part has been treated, the subordinate parts can be dealt with in the order of their importance and according to their causes, the final cause of each being to serve its superior part, the formal cause being the beauty of the part itself. The whole analysis, thus, not merely indicates the possibilities of poetic construction but discriminates among them as better or worse, to exhibit the construction of a synthesis beautiful as a whole, composed of parts of the maximum beauty consistent with that whole, and productive of its proper emotional effects to a maximum degree.

The method—one of multiple differentiation and systematic resolution of maximal composites into their least parts—may obviously be extended to poetic species which have emerged since Aristotle. Aristotle distinguishes broadly and between extremes; later theorists in his method must follow the basic lines and go farther. For example, his poetics, as we have it, deals only with such poetry as has plot, i.e., such as imitates a *system* of actions. These are maximal forms; there are, that is, no "larger" poetic forms or any which have more parts than these; smaller forms, such as the species of lyric, can be treated by carrying such systems back to their elements.

Four kinds of action or behavior can thus be distinguished, without regard to seriousness or comicality, etc.: (1) a single character acting in a single closed situation. By "closed situation" I mean here one in which the character's activity, however it may have been initiated or however it may be terminated, is *uncomplicated* by any other agency. Most of what we call lyric poetry belongs here: any poem in which the character commits some verbal act (threatening, persuading, beseeching) upon someone existing only as the object of his action (Marvell's "To His Coy Mistress"), or deliberates or muses (Keats's "Ode to a Nightingale"), or is moved by passion (Landor's "Mother, I Cannot Mind My Wheel"). (2) Two or more characters in a single closed situation. "Closed situation" here means "uncomplicated by any other agency than the characters originally present and remaining so throughout." This parallels the notion of "scene" in French classical drama; here belong all the *real* colloquies of persons acting upon and reacting to one another (e.g., Browning's "The Bishop Orders His Tomb"), although not the metaphorical colloquies, such as dialogues between Body and Soul, etc. (3) A collection of such "scenes" as I have just mentioned about some central incident, to constitute an "episode" (Arnold's *Sohrab and Rustum*). (4) A system of such episodes, constituting the grand plot of tragedy, comedy, and epic which is treated by Aristotle.

These are whole and complete "actions"; hence the first differs from a speech in a play, the second from a dramatic scene, the third from a fragment of a tragedy; nevertheless, it is clear that, *in a sense*, the combination of speeches produces a scene, that of scenes an episode, that of episodes a plot. These classifications must not be confused with species; they are not poetic species but lines of differentation of the object of imitation which must be taken into account in defining species. Similar analysis of means and manner would extend Aristotle's system to include all poetic forms.

So much for Aristotle's general method and his apparatus for the definition of forms; I shall presently return to such questions again, in order to sketch a special poetics, but for the moment I wish to deal with three more problems of general poetics: those of unexpectedness, suspense, and representation, although we can do little more here than touch on general points.

All emotions are greater if produced from their contraries—for example, fear in one who has been confident—and the unexpected effects just this. Like suspense, it is common to all temporal arts, the parts as well as the wholes, for whatever involves temporal succession may involve anticipation, and wherever we have anticipation we may have the unexpected. Expectation is the active entertainment of the opinion that something is necessary or probable at a given time, place, in certain relations, etc. The audience must infer, and infer incorrectly; they have the premises, so to speak, for otherwise what happens would be improbable; but they cannot connect them to infer correctly, for otherwise what happens would be expected. Since they do not infer the probable, and do infer the improbable, two things must be noted: the causes of wrong inference and the causes of failure to infer rightly. Since the premises must be considered together for inference and since the audience will reason only from premises which they actively entertain and take to be true, failure to infer will be due to (1) forming no opinion or forming a contradictory one, so that one or both of the premises will not be used; (2) failure to collect the premises, although both are entertained; (3) failure to infer correctly, although both are entertained and collected. All these can be developed to show what the poet may possibly do: for instance, opinion can be prevented by the use of remote signs (i.e., such as involve many inferences), or many and apparently contradictory signs, ambiguity of words or acts; acceptance as true can be prevented by the use of unusual consequents, by contrariety to general belief, by dependence upon the words of an apparently untrustworthy character, or by contradiction of an apparently trustworthy one; and so on.

All these things lead to nonexpectation; but the truly unexpected comes about when the thing is not only not expected but contrary to expectation. This will happen if the poet provides premises which seem to prove the contrary. It is best when failure to infer the right thing and the faulty inference are brought about by the same premises. This is effected by the use of qualification. For example, if A happens, B usually follows, except in circumstance C, but if that circumstance happens, the opposite of B results; now if C is bound to happen, but people do not know that, they will expect B after A, whereas the opposite results. Surprise will vary in degree with expectation of the contrary; consequently, the audience will be most surprised when they are most convinced that B will happen. The less important, apparently, the reversing circumstance, the more surprise. Again, since the all-but-completed process makes its end most probable, expectation will be highest here; hence reversal just before the end will be most surprising. This underlies many "hair's-breadth escapes." Most surprising of all is the double unexpected, which occurs when from A comes the unexpected result B, which leads to the previously expected result C, which is now unexpected as the result of B. This is exemplified in Sophocles' *Oedipus*, where the inquiry into blood-guilt leads to the question of parentage, which seems at some remove; but the question of parentage resolves unexpectedly the question of blood-guilt.

Suspense is anxiety caused by extended anticipation—hence (1) by the uncertainty of what we wish to know and (2) by delay of what we wish to have happen, although we know it already. (Gossips are in the first state before they have been told the scandal, in the second until they impart it.) The first results whenever we want to know either the event or the circumstances of the event, whether in past, present, or future time; hence the poet must avoid the necessary, the impossible, or the completely probable, or that which is unimportant either way, for we are never in suspense about these; instead, he must choose the equally probable or else that which is probable with a chance of its not happening, and something which is of a markedly pleasant, painful, good, evil, or marvelous nature. Suspense of the second order is produced by unexpected frustration, by having the thing seem just about to happen, and then probably averting it. The anticipated thing must have importance exceeding the suspense; otherwise irritation and indifference result.

Representation—what parts of the action are told or shown, and how, and what is left to inference—is a question of manner of imitation. Obviously, poets sometimes exhibit more than the action (e.g., tragic poets exhibit events which are not part of the plot), sometimes less, leaving the rest to inference; sometimes follow the plot-order, sometimes convert it (e.g., using flashbacks); exhibit some things on a large and others on a small scale; and there are many other possibilities as well. It is impossible here to do more than suggest; in general, representation is determined by necessity and probability, emotional effect, and ornament, i.e., these are the main reasons for representing something. The poet must represent things which by their omission or their being left to inference would make the action improbable; hence, if an event is generally improbable but probable in a given circumstance, it must be represented in that circumstance (e.g., Antony's speech in *Julius Caesar*). Again, he must omit whatever would contradict the specific emotional effect (hence disgusting scenes, such as the cooking of Thyestes' children, are omitted, since disgust counteracts pity) or include what would augment the effect (hence scenes of lamentation and suffering in tragedy, since these make us poignantly aware of the anguish of the hero). Masques, pageants, progresses, etc., are ornaments. Representation, whether narrative or dramatic, always makes things more vivid, and the latter is more vivid than the former; and it affords the audience knowledge, whether directly or through inference by signs. In any poetic work the audience must at certain times know some things and not know others; generally the denouement discloses all, except in works which have wonder as their prime effect. Unless the audience knows somewhat, emotion is impossible, for emotion depends upon opinion; and unless it is ignorant of certain things, unexpectedness and some kinds of suspense are impossible. Hence in any work something is withheld until the end: either how the action began or continued or how it ends; the audience is ignorant of one or several of the following circumstances: agent, instrument, act, object, manner, purpose, result, time, place, concomitants. What must be concealed is the primary question; the next is the order in which things must be disclosed; and theory can make available to the poet a calculus of the frame of mind of the audience, of the nature of emotions, etc., to determine the order of representation which will produce the maximum emotional effect.

All these questions can be developed to afford a vast body of working suggestions for the poet and of criteria for the critic; I shall be happy if I have suggested, even faintly, the character of the problems and the method of their treatment.

IV

We have seen that in any special poetics—whether that of tragedy or epic or some kind of lyric or novel—reasoning proceeds from the distinctive whole which is the product of the art to determine what parts must be assembled if such a whole, beautiful of its kind, is to result, and that such terms as "whole," "part," "beauty," etc., must be specified to the given art, because, for example, the beauty of a tragedy is not the same as the beauty of a lyric, any more than the distinctive beauty of a horse is the same as that of a man. Indeed, lyrics and tragedies even have some different parts; for instance, a lyric does not have plot, but plot is, in fact, the principal part of tragedy.

We may illustrate the nature of a special poetics a little further by outlining briefly that of the species to which Yeats's "Sailing to Byzantium" belongs.[7] It is a species which imitates a serious action of the first order mentioned above, i.e., one involving a single character in a closed situation, and the

7. For a detailed "grammatical" analysis see the (University of Kansas City) *University Review*, VIII (1942), 211–15.

character is not simply in passion, nor is he acting upon another character, but has performed an act actualizing and instancing his moral character, that is, has made a moral choice. It is dramatic in manner—the character speaks in his own person; and the medium is words embellished by rhythm and rhyme. Its effect is something that, in the absence of a comprehensive analysis of the emotions, we can only call a kind of noble joy or exaltation.

There are four parts of this poetic composite: choice, character, thought, and diction. For choice is the activity, and thought and character are the causes of the activity, and diction is the means. The choice, or deliberative activity of choosing, is the principal part, for reasons analogous to those which make plot the principal part of tragedy. Next in importance comes character; next thought; and last, diction.[8]

8. Nowadays when the nature of poetry has become so uncertain that everyone is trying to define it, definitions usually begin: "Poetry is words which, or language which, or discourse which," and so forth. As a matter of fact, it is nothing of the kind. Just as we should not define a chair as wood which has such and such characteristics—for a chair is not a kind of wood but a kind of furniture—so we ought not to define poetry as a kind of language. The chair is not wood but wooden; poetry is not words but verbal. In one sense, of course, the words are of the utmost importance; if they are not the right words or if we do not grasp them, we do not grasp the poem. In another sense, they are the least important element in the poem, for they do not determine the character of anything else in the poem; on the contrary, they are determined by everything else. They are the only things we see or hear; yet they are governed by imperceptible things which are inferred from them. And when we are moved by poetry, we are not moved by the words, except in so far as sound and rhythm move us; we are moved by the things that the words stand for.

A gifted British poet, G. S. Fraser, has objected to these remarks on diction ("Some Notes on Poetic Diction," *Penguin New Writing*, No. 37 [1949], pp. 116 ff.): "I think, on the contrary, that criticism should pay a very close attention to diction. I agree with Mr. Allen Tate: 'For, in the long run, whatever the poet's philosophy may be, however wide may be the extension of his meaning . . . by his language shall you know him.' And I do not find that Mr. Olson's sturdy-looking piece of reasoning stands up very well to my regretful probing. In what sense is it true that we are simply 'moved by the things that the words stand for,' and not by the words themselves? Certainly not in any sense in which other words would do as well: in which the fullest paraphrase, or the most intelligent exposition, would be a substitute for the original poem. And certainly not in any sense in which the situation that the poem refers to, if we were capable of imagining that *without* words—if, for instance, we could draw a picture of it—would be a substitute for the original poem, either. Not, that is, in any sense, in which 'the things the words stand for' means merely the kind of physical object, abstract concept, or emotional state at which the words point. The pointing is the least of it."

I willingly concede what I have never debated: that diction is very important to poetry; that, as Tate suggests, distinction of language is an important index of poetic power (although I cannot agree that it is the sole index or even the prime index); that criticism ought to pay the utmost attention to diction; that, as T. S. Eliot has said, the poet is likely to be extraordinarily interested in, and skilful with, language; that we are not "moved by the things that the words stand for" in any sense that would allow us to dispense with the particular words by which the "things" are constituted for us; and all similar propositions. The point is not whether diction is important, but whether it is more or less important than certain other elements *in* the poem. In one respect, I repeat, it is the most important; the reader, if he does not grasp the words, cannot grasp anything further, and the poet, if he cannot find the appropriate words and arrange them properly, has not written a poem. In another respect, however, the words are the least important, in that they are governed and determined by

The "activity" of the character is thought or deliberation producing choice determined by rational principles; it is thus, as I once remarked, a kind of argument or arguing. But there is a difference between logical proof and such poetic argument as we have here; in logical proof the conclusion is determined by the premises; here it is, of course, mediated by the character of the man arguing, just as argument in a novel or a play is not supposed to be consistent with the premises but with the character. The limits of the activity are the limits of the deliberation; the parts of the activity are the phases of that deliberation, and they are conjoined by necessity and probability.

This species of poem, then, if it is to be beautiful, must have a certain definite magnitude as determined by the specific whole and its parts; and the proper magnitude will be the fullest extension possible, not exceeding the limits mentioned above, and accomplished by phases connected necessarily or probably. This is, it will be noted, different from the magnitude proper to comedy or tragedy, and even different from the magnitude proper to a speech exhibiting choice in any of these; for example, tragedy does not aim at making its constituent speeches or actions as full and perfectly rounded as possible absolutely, but only qualifiedly, in so far as that is compatible with the plot. Hence in properly made drama there are few if any "complete" speeches, let alone speeches developed to what would be their best proportions independently of the whole; this is true even in declamatory drama, where the speeches are of more importance than in the better kinds.

The activity, however, is not merely to be complete and whole, with its parts probably interrelated; it must effect certain serious emotions in us by exhibiting the happiness or misery of certain characters whom we take seriously. Hence the character must be better than we, but not so completely noble as to be beyond all suffering; for such people are godlike and can awaken only our admiration, for they are in a sense removed from such misfortunes as can excite dolorous emotions. Moreover, the choice imitated cannot be any choice, even of a moral order, but one which makes all the difference between happiness and misery; and, since it is choice, it must be accomplished with full knowledge and in accordance with rational principle, or as the man of rational prudence

---

every other element in the poem. There is agreement on all hands that words "function" in poetry; there should be no difficulty therefore, no matter how we conceive of the structure of poetry, in seeing that words must be subordinate to their functions, for they are selected and arranged with a view to these. Mr. Fraser himself has no difficulty with this fact, although he is disturbed by my statement of the fact; for he goes on to discuss (pp. 123 ff.) "a wide-scale current use of poetic diction in a really vicious sense to disguise a failure of choice, a confusion of character, or a lack of clear thought"; and he also remarks (p. 126) that "one cannot ask people to express themselves as confusingly as possible, in the hope that their confusions will prove to have a clear underlying structure; for, as Mr. Schwartz truly says, 'if this were the only kind of poetry . . . most poetry would not be worth reading.' " On this whole question see above, pp. 71 ff.

would determine it. Again, it must be choice not contingent upon the actions or natures of others, but as determined by the agent. And there must be no mistake (*hamartia*) here, as in tragedy; for, since this is a single incident, *hamartia* is not requisite to make future consequences probable.

We could proceed indefinitely here, as on all of these points; my intention, I repeat, is the merest illustration.

V

Thus far we have proceeded on the supposition that the imitative poetic arts have as their ends certain pleasures, produced through their play upon our emotions. Certainly, these are ends of art and such as any consideration of art must embrace; but to suppose that art has no further effect and that it may have no further ends relative to these is vastly to underestimate the powers of art. It exercises, for example, a compelling influence upon human action—individual, social, or political—for among the causes of the misdirection of human action are the failure to conceive vividly and the failure to conceive apart from self-interest; and these are failures which art above all other things is potent to avert, since it vivifies, and since in art we must view man on his merits and not in relation to our private interests. It is not that art teaches by precept, as older generations thought, nor that it moves to action; but clearly it inculcates moral attitudes; it determines our feelings toward characters of a certain kind for no other reason than that they are such characters. The ethical function of art, therefore, is never in opposition to the purely artistic end; on the contrary, it is best achieved when the artistic end has been best accomplished, for it is only a further consequence of the powers of art. The same thing is true of any political or social ends of art, provided that the state be a good state or the society a moral society. To reflect on these things is to realize the importance and value of art, which, excellent in itself, becomes ever more excellent as we view it in ever more general relations.

Yet these relations can scarcely be recognized unless we first recognize the distinctive powers of each form of poetic art; these relations are possible, indeed, because art has, first of all, certain powers. And it is to these powers, in all their variety and force, that the poetic method of Aristotle is directed. Indeed, the most distinctive characteristic of Aristotle as critic seems to be that he founds his poetic science upon the emotional effects peculiar to the various species of art and reasons thence to the works which must be constructed to achieve them.

A DIALOGUE ON SYMBOLISM

ELDER OLSON

I HAVE just been wondering about something. You must have observed often enough that the bulk of criticism in any one age tends to center about certain favorite terms and concepts. Sometimes the favorites are taken from a quality, such as sublimity or correctness or liveliness; sometimes from a technical device which happens to be in fashion, such as irony or paradox; sometimes from some faculty supposedly essential to appreciation—taste, for instance—or to creation—for example, imagination. And you must have observed that, however they are derived, they exercise a considerable influence.

Indeed they do; they determine the ways in which critics of the period define poetry or any of the various kinds of literature; they enter into the formulation of principles and criteria, and in general establish precision in the whole discussion of literary matters.

And I suppose they must be terms and concepts of the most precise order, since, as you say, they give precision to everything else?

Well—

And, since they possess almost unquestioned sovereignty, the grounds of that sovereignty must be as clear and firm as possible?

These are just the points that always puzzle me. Theoretically, what you are suggesting ought to be true; but I, at least, have always had a great deal of trouble in finding out what these important terms meant, or why they should have been so important; and I have never found any very satisfactory answers. For example, I think it is much easier to say what Dryden meant by "tragedy" than to say what he meant by "justness" or "liveliness." I suppose some such circumstance must have led Professor Elton to make a glossary of critical terms in our own age.

Doubtless our criticism is safe, then—thanks to Elton. It is comforting to think that one age, at least, has founded on rock.

You needn't be so sarcastic. Elton merely had a little card-file, with words like "ambiguity" and "symbol" written on the cards; and under each such title he set down a few remarks by Richards, Empson, Ransom, or some other distinguished critic. It was merely lexicography—perhaps not very good lexicography, either. It reminds me of Kant's notion of a lecture as a process by which ideas pass from the notebook of the professor to the notebook of the student, without passing through the head of either.

You think the glossary useless, then, because it involved no intellectual process?

Well—not utterly useless. But our age, like other ages, has its favorite central concepts, which I think are far from clear; and I can't see that Elton throws much light on them. We talk constantly these days about meaning, implication, suggestion, sign, image, symbol, metaphor, allegory, myth, and so forth; I am not sure that we know what we mean by these words; and when I look into Elton, I hear only the Tower of Babel. And, of course, given his sort of task, he can hardly be expected to deal with the cardinal questions.

The *cardinal* questions?

I was thinking of the term as Dante used it in its etymological sense. The questions on which these others turn, as a door on its hinge.

And these would be—?

The questions of the concepts back of the words. I doubt if you can have a good dictionary even of usages, if the concepts aren't clear. Put it this way: the cardinal question is not what this or that critic *means* by the term "symbol," but what a symbol *is*. Yes; I really think that, since poets are being so much praised or blamed for their use of symbols and are working so hard to invent and use them—since criticism has become so much a matter of symbolic exegesis—and since a lot of new theories of art declare art itself to be symbolic structure, we ought to know what a symbol is.

What a task you propose! You want to know, not the meaning of the word, but the nature of the thing meant by the word.

Precisely.

And how are you going to try to discover this?

Oh, I have no idea of attempting it by myself. But since we've opened the question, why not discuss it?

I hope you will not expect me to play Socrates.

No; why should we need Socrates? I have great faith in ordinary conversation. Perhaps you could just jog my mind with a few questions, and a few right answers might possibly fall out.

This seems to be a kind of piggy-bank theory of knowledge.

What if it is?

Very young children simply shake the bank any way at all, and get only a few coins after a great deal of effort. Older and more experienced ones learn to introduce a knife into the slot to guide the coins, and they very soon empty the bank.

Well?

I think we might do well to use a knife. Surely you know that in any inquiry the question must have a great influence upon the answer. If we were defining justice, and I asked you whether justice was a virtue or a vice, you would learn at least that justice is a virtue; whereas if I asked you whether it was pink or not-pink, you would learn that it is not-pink, which seems to me not nearly so useful. Socrates knew the sort of questions to ask; I don't. So, unless you are willing to play Socrates yourself—

I see; it appears we must have Socrates after all. Very well; invite him at once.

He is now, you must remember, only the shade of Socrates; he has suffered not only the oblivion of birth but the forgetfulness which follows death. I feel that he may come; the clock is striking midnight, a good hour for ghosts; and I will pour him a glass of this excellent muscatel, since a shade is supposed to drink the fragrance as we drink the wine.

A neat trick to get yourself an extra.

I, the shade of Socrates, have overheard you.

What, here so quickly?

I am present at all conversations where there is serious inquiry.

We were talking of modern critics.

I know nothing of them. But your predicament reminds me of a myth. May I tell it?—for it has never been recorded, and I think you are hardly likely to be acquainted with it.

By all means.

Well, then, I will tell you about the city of shadows. According to ancient legend, there was once a race of heroes, so remarkable for virtue and wisdom that they were godlike; and so the gods decided to admit them, mortal as they were, into heaven. Yet, because the heroes were mortal, they had shadows; and since heaven is a place of purest light, they were required to leave their shadows behind them on earth, so as not to sully that brightness. Thus the heroes passed into brilliance and joy; but their shadows languished behind them in darkness and misery, houseless and bodiless and, worse than either of these, inextricably entangled with one another—for, you must know, a shadow fears and detests absolute darkness even more than he does absolute light; in the latter he merely ceases to exist, while in the former he lies bound and wound and entangled with darkness and with other shadows and loses all identity and distinction. Thus it was with these shadows, until a god, I have forgotten which one, heard their lamentations and took pity on them. He built them a shadowy city of their own and, within it, a temple, wherein he set an altar; and upon this altar he placed a small piece of Reality, girdled with the fairest light, so that a shadow might have some knowledge of substance. In order to mark the way to this temple, he set faintly luminous signs in all the streets; and he gave them also such light as would confer identity upon them and permit them to see.

Very considerate.

So it was. However, the shadows were so taken with the signs that they neglected the Reality; they disputed endlessly as to which sign gave a clearer light or marked a better road; so that the god grew angry at last and turned the whole city into a maze and caused a great wind to cast down all the signs. Now the shadows were in utter confusion, quarreling as to which sign belonged where, until, at last, one who had been the shadow of the best of the heroes realized the vanity of such contentions and determined to seek out the Reality itself; for he thought that, once he had found it, he would possess the true treasure and, besides that, he would be able to restore order among the signs, for he would know which way they would have to point. His name, if I remember, was Lur; and I am told he obtained success. Now, it seems to me that this applies to your case.

That would seem to make us shadows.

So you are; and I, too, am a shade; and therefore we require, not true Philosophy, but its shadow—shall we say, skiatology? And yet this should be sufficiently nourishing to us; you have often seen that when a man eats, his shadow eats the shadow of his food, and leaves off eating when he does, so that presumably it, too, is full-fed? Let us, then, proceed to our shadow-banquet. You see I am holding something in my hand.

Yes, Socrates.

What is it?

I should say, a disk.

Look more closely at it.

It is made of metal.

Then you would say "metal disk" is an adequate name for it?

Yes.

And those disks you wear on your clothing—they are metal disks also?

No, Socrates, they are made of bone.

And then "bone disk" would be a good name for them?

No; they are called buttons, because of their use.

Then if this disk of mine has a use, it should be named according to its use, and not be simply called a disk.

Presumably.

And if I told you its use was to mark a place on a map, you would, say, call it a marker?

Yes.

And if I said it was to be used as money, you would call it a coin?

Yes.

If you will examine it now, closely, you will see that it is, in fact, a coin, although badly worn with age and use, I fear; and you will see that it is broken into two parts, which fit very closely together.

So it is.

We Greeks had a custom of breaking a coin thus when we made a contract; we called the broken halves *symbola*.

I have heard of that custom.

The broken coin, then, betokens a contract; and when we say that something is a "symbol," I suppose we mean that it betokens something.

Undoubtedly.

And if it were used in token of divorce or death or whatever, it would still be used as a symbol, and be called a "symbol"; but if used in token of nothing, it is simply a broken coin?

Quite so.

And what is meant by betokening something?

I should say it meant representing something.

Your photograph represents you?

Yes.

Does it symbolize you?

No; not necessarily.

You mean that not everything that represents is a symbol? For instance, if I were selling sand and showed you some grains, telling you that the rest would be of that order, these would represent, but not be symbols?

I should call them a sample.

What if you did not know what a book was, and I showed you this one as representative? Is that a symbol or a sample?

I should call it an example.

And that plaster bust on your bookshelf, which I observe that someone has labeled "Socrates"?

That is a copy, Socrates, of a very famous bust of you.

It is a copy, then, of some original bust, but not a sample or example of it?

Yes.

And the original—is that a copy or sample or example or symbol of me?

I should say rather that it was an imitation, in Aristotle's sense of the term.

I think I have heard of him and of his sense of the word "imitation." You mean by it, I presume, that the sculptor was not merely concerned with making a likeness of me but wanted also to make a good piece of sculpture, so that the bust, although it does not portray a handsome man, God knows, or portray an ugly man as handsome, is nevertheless a handsome work of art; whereas a copy gives only a replica and is handsome, middling fair, or ugly quite according to the original thing copied. I suppose that is what Aristotle also must have meant.

Yes, I should think so.

And I suppose you mean that "sample" should be used only when the things are homogeneous, like water or wine or honey or sand or cloth which is all of the same pattern and texture, so that a little represents the remainder, or the part, the whole; whereas an example is always one class of things or some individual as representative of a class into which it falls; and a copy, again, is a likeness of some individual thing.

Exactly.

But if representations differ thus, are they alike in any way?

They are alike in that they are all based upon some likeness.

So that a symbol, if it represents, must always bear some likeness to that which is symbolized.

Yes.

How marvelous, then, is the substance of air!

I do not follow you.

Spoken words are symbols, are they not?

Of course.

Then air in its motion must be able to make likenesses of everything which can be conceived.

You puzzle me.

And your photograph, after all, must be a symbol of you, and the best symbol, since it bears a very great likeness.

No; it is not a symbol at all, unless someone makes it so.

Then likeness and unlikeness are not necessarily connected with symbols?

Apparently not.

So a symbol may stand for anything, however unlike it?

So it would seem.

I suppose many poets must have used the sun as the symbol of darkness, or ice as the symbol of heat, and that you can quote some of these?

No, Socrates, I cannot; and I must admit that I cannot even conceive of the possibility.

We will accept that for the moment, although I am uncertain whether we are discussing the impossibility of the thing or the limitations of your powers of conception. Let us take another tack: your photograph, though it represents you as a likeness, does not, you say, represent you, therefore, as a symbol; how might it represent you as a symbol?

I suppose by being taken for me.

I thought you implied earlier that knowledge, and not ignorance or madness, was necessary before something could be a symbol; for you said, I believe, that "bone disk" was not a good name for a button and that "button" was so called on account of knowledge of its use.

So I did.

Then if I took your photograph for you, would that not be ignorance?

Not if you did it deliberately, with the knowledge that it was not I.

But if I did such a thing deliberately, would not that be madness?

Not if you did not really take it for me.

So a symbol is something which is taken for something and yet not taken for it?

I am sorry, Socrates; perhaps I should have said "pretendedly taken for something."

So the user of symbols is a practitioner of one of the arts of pretense?

I think I see where that will land us, and I refuse to go that way. May I retract my statement that a symbol is something taken for something and start afresh?

By all means.

I will say, then, with Thomas Aquinas that a symbol is that thing which, to an intellective power, stands for something other than itself.

I do not understand.

It is used in place of something—a kind of substitution.

You mean that if you took down these curtains and put certain others in their place, the second would be symbols of the first?

No, not at all. A symbol is a convenient substitute for something impossible or difficult to use in itself, or to achieve, or something of the sort.

And, since it is used for it, has the same use?

Yes.

You have evidently found it impossible to obtain a doorstop; I presume that the book which holds the door open symbolizes the doorstop.

No, I should say it was used as a doorstop.

Yet the word "doorstop" symbolizes a doorstop?

Yes.

But surely the word itself could not be used as a doorstop.

Yes, but—a symbol is quite certainly used as some sort of substitute; words, for instance, are substitutes for thought.

I suppose that is why those who find thought impossible or inconvenient talk so much. But let us go back a little in the argument. When we were talking of likeness and unlikeness, a certain thought occurred to me, and I should like to present it to you. I imagine I could use the book on your table as a symbol of knowledge.

Of course.

The book, however, remains exactly what it is?

Yes.

And so does knowledge remain what it is?

Yes.

Then both the symbol and the symbolized are such without any alteration of their natures?

Yes.

Then their natures could scarcely be the cause of one symbolizing the other —for, if their natures were the cause, it would be of the nature of the one to be a symbol and of the other to be the symbolized?

Yes.

Hence, if their natures are indifferent to this question, likeness and difference would also be indifferent; for the nature of a thing determines its similarity to, or difference from, another?

I have already told you, Socrates, that nothing is a symbol of itself.

Good; and you have also told me that anything can be a symbol of anything. Perhaps you will explain yourself.

I mean that the book is potentially a symbol; actually, it is not, unless something else makes it so.

To be something potentially and then to become it actually is to change?

Of course.

Will you explain how the book has changed? We have not touched it, and I see no difference between what it was and what it is. Yet, without changing, it seems now to be what it was not.

It has not changed in itself; it has changed in its relation to something else, wisdom.

My dear fellow! The relations between things must always be based upon characteristics of the things related?

Yes.

And while the characteristics remain the same, the relationship is the same, and when the characteristics differ, the relationship will differ also?

Yes.

Hence, surely, if the relationship has changed, the things have changed.

I am afraid you have the better of me; I am puzzled.

I wonder if we are in any difficulty after all. I suppose I could use your paper knife, there, to cut book leaves.

Certainly.

In doing so, I should have to handle the knife itself and affect and change it some way or other. Using it often enough, I should even wear it out.

Certainly.

But I used the book as a symbol, without handling it. And it does not show much wear as a result.

Of course not; that was a purely mental employment of the book.

I don't follow you.

You did not really use the book.

But if I did not really use the book, and a symbol must be used to be a symbol, then the book could not possibly be a symbol?

I can't see how it could be a symbol.

And yet we made a symbol, without the physical use of anything?

Yes.

Clearly, then, a symbol exists independently of any physical use?

Yes.

And this would hold good in all instances, would it not, regardless of what physical object was supposed to be involved?

Yes, Socrates.

Then I imagine that your Thomas Aquinas, as well as your contemporaries who talk of a symbol as a thing standing for some other thing, could scarcely have meant that or known what they were saying if they did mean it. For we have just seen that no thing can stand for any other thing.

So it seems.

Well, then, if I did not really use the book, what did I use as a symbol?

I know you will catch me out, but may I tentatively say the idea or notion of the book?

Tentatively. And you may also tell me tentatively how one uses an idea or notion.

We have already suggested, Socrates, that a relation is involved; I shall say, therefore, a relationship of ideas or notions. Quite certainly there is some sort of mental conjunction; the idea book is connected with the idea of knowledge.

How do you mean, "connected"?

Identified.

My dear man; you told me that in order to recognize a symbol it was necessary to distinguish it from the symbolized, or something to that effect; how is this possible if the symbol and the symbolized are identified?

I will withdraw; I should have said there is a kind of attribution or affirmation.

As when I say "The boy is brave" and conjoin the ideas of the boy and bravery?

Yes, something like that.

Then the concept of the boy symbolizes the concept of bravery?

No, hang it! I shouldn't say that either. It must be some sort of fusing, some sort of unifying of the ideas, so that they become one and the same.

My friend, this is a strange task you impose on me and any other symbolmaker. I can grasp the idea of blackness and the idea of sphere, and thus compound the concept of a black sphere; but I do not tell myself that I have made the idea of blackness identical with the idea of sphericity or that I have made one idea out of two. If I really went on in that style, I should end up after all my thinking with only one idea. Rather it seems that I get, in my own way, three, and I prefer that. In any case, this has nothing to do with symbolism, for these ideas do not symbolize each other.

Very well; I will hazard again. A concept is a symbol when it has been so frequently associated with another in experience that it brings the latter at once to mind.

By heaven! You speak as if you never took off your shoes before going to bed or before taking a bath; or as if you did so only infrequently.

I don't follow you.

You do remove your shoes on such occasions, I hope, and I hope also that these occasions are not too infrequent?

Of course.

But does the removing of shoes symbolize bathing or going to bed?

Not necessarily.

On the other hand, we could make their removal symbolize these things even without the habitual association you speak of?

Yes.

Then, clearly, inquiry into association will not help us much here.

I am afraid you are right. I suppose you will go on now to prove that it is impossible there should be symbols in the mind, just as you proved there were none outside the mind; so that we shall have no such thing as a symbol after all.

I have a similar dread myself; I should be very much disheartened, were it not that our conversation has suddenly reminded me of something.

What?

We sound like men who are looking at bricks and other building materials; men who have a vague idea of what a house is but are utterly ignorant of any such thing as an architect or an art of architecture, and who are consequently much puzzled as to how the materials could ever be assembled into a house.

I do not see how that helps any.

What would you advise such men to do? Would you not suggest that they learn about the architect and his powers?

I suppose so.

It seems to me that the architect, in this case, would be the soul.

Oh, Lord, Socrates! This is the twentieth century; the soul is now out of fashion.

I observe that it is indeed, in more ways than one. Why should that deter us?

Many now would refuse to admit its existence.

I suppose our most formidable opponents would claim it to be impossible?

Yes, certainly.

Well, then, let us cheerfully confront our strongest enemies at once and deal with them, and perhaps the others will not trouble us. I suppose that by calling the soul "impossible" they mean that there must be some cause why it could not be?

Yes.

This cause would have to be eternal—for if it ceased to exist for one moment, it would be false to say the soul is impossible?

Yes.

I should be most interested in their evidence for the eternal existence of this cause. However, let that be; let me ask you instead: for something to be actual, its potentiality must be existent first?

Of course.

For any act or operation to be performed, there must be something capable of performing that act or operation?

Yes.

That something itself must, however, exist actually and not merely potentially? For instance, if a man becomes a father, the power of reproduction must have been in him; but that power must have been an actuality and not existed merely in potential form—as in the man, say, when he was himself still a fetus.

Quite so.

And this, far from being impossible, is necessary.

Yes.

And by "necessary" we mean "impossible that it should not exist"?

Yes.

But, obviously, we are actually capable of mental acts, and the power to do these must therefore exist and have actual existence, and that necessarily?

Yes.

This, then, whatever it is, I will call the "soul"; I shall treat it discreetly and modestly, attributing to this mystery only such powers as it itself evinces in action. Are our enemies still on the field?

I believe they have withdrawn.

Good! Now, we obviously can compare ideas?

Certainly.

We can separate and conjoin them, distinguish and liken them?

To be sure.

Affirm, deny? Order the less general under the more general?

Yes.

Distinguish the true, the false, the probable, improbable, possible, necessary, impossible? And otherwise evaluate?

Yes.

Believe, disbelieve; and suppose that which we do not believe?

Yes.

Then the soul must have these powers?

Necessarily.

And be able to form pictures of some particular thing, and to turn these into ideas which are more general; and again to convert these ideas back into pictures? For instance, to form a picture of a certain tree, and out of it to get the idea of a tree; and again, having the idea of a tree, to envision a tree?

Yes.

And, surely, with all this activity, the soul must be busy?

Very.

I think I see in my mind's eye this busy soul of ours, seated amid her many treasures, counting and evaluating and ordering them. Such as she can deal with quickly and easily, she handles directly; but treasures are brought in to her constantly, in enormous measure; and in her haste and business she must often assign to one thing the value of another.

Doubtless.

Certainly, too, with all this business, she is sometimes fatigued and confused, and reckons the false as true, and the true as false, and is then in error.

Yes.

But sometimes she supposes something to have the value of another quite deliberately, although she knows it does not; for she is in haste to get on with her reckoning and hopes to set all her accounts in order one day.

Indeed.

There is no doubt that whatever evaluation she sets upon such things will have to stand in her accounts until she is ready to give a better reckoning.

No doubt at all.

Doubtless, too, these ideas may be said to have values in themselves; but, until the true reckoning, these values are superseded by the assigned values. Shall we give a name to these?

Why not?

What shall we call them?

Socrates, I know that, if I do not call them "symbols" immediately, you will presently force me to; so I yield at once. Let us call them "symbols."

I think we should rather call them the "symbolized."

Very well: the symbolized.

The concept or idea which is a symbol will have its own value, but the soul will deal with it as having the value assigned to it. This value is not of truth or falsity, or goodness or badness, but of meaning. The concept of physical sight, for instance, may have the value of intellectual vision; it will then mean intellectual vision. Otherwise it remains simply the concept of physical sight.

I see.

But will the world not think we are mad? Are not words, whether spoken or written, considered symbols by everybody—whereas we have shown that only a mental idea or concept can be a symbol?

I suppose the world will be furious.

Let us, then, to lessen its rage, call words "secondary symbols." For they are only a sort of signal to entertain a concept; and, without such a relation of concepts as we have described, they could never be symbols in any sense.

Please explain.

A spoken word is merely a sound, is it not, and capable on utterance only of raising the impression or idea of itself as sound in the mind of the hearer. That is, unless the idea of that sound is given the value of a certain other concept by the soul.

I see.

It would appear, then, that symbolism has to do not with things but with a mode of conception; a supposition, contrary to known fact, that one concept has the value of some other concept; does it not seem so?

Yes, it does.

I should now like to distinguish symbols from other things which are often confused with them.

Proceed.

They are different, for instance, from signs. Fever, for example, is a sign of illness, because it is an effect of which illness may be a cause; since it is a sign, we may infer from its presence that illness exists. But fever is not a symbol of illness. For if the concept of fever is given the value of the concept of illness, the inference from fever to illness would be absurd, seeing that, in granting the fever to be illness, we have already assumed the point to be inferred.

The question would be begged, undoubtedly.

A sign, therefore, must be said to have implication rather than meaning; we must reserve meaning for symbols.

True.

Meaning depends always upon knowledge of the symbols, singly and in conjunction, and never upon implication or inference, unless certain of the symbols are unclear or lacking, as in unfinished sentences or as in innuendoes, which are a kind of incompletely stated argument; or unless some apparent impossibility of meaning arises, as in irony.

I do not quite follow that.

Why, you would surely know, let us say, such individual words as "Socrates," "Plato," "is," "well," "ill," "and," "but," "not," and so on?

I think I can be credited with that much.

Some of these are significs, having meaning in themselves, and others have no meaning in themselves but show how the significs are to be related to one another—would you not agree?

Yes.

And if I said "Socrates" or any other of these words, there would be no necessity of inference, unless you did not know what the word meant?

Yes.

Then if I said "Socrates is ill," there would be no question of inference; the meaning of the parts would immediately give the meaning of the whole, since all parts of the meaning are expressed?

Yes.

But, should I say "Socrates is ill, but Plato . . . ," something is missing? And you would have to infer the missing part, would you not?

I see.

And similarly, in innuendo, one expresses the part which implies what one really means but does not express what one really means; and in irony, one says the opposite of what one means, counting on the fact that the hearer will recognize the impossibility of what is being said and infer the contrary, which one really intends.—Heaven forgive us!

What is the matter?

Here we have been sitting and chatting like two old women about things that are not symbols, as if our business were finished and we could be at leisure, when we have hardly begun.

What do you mean?

It seems to me that we have discussed symbols only in their poorest and barest variety, when they barely deserve that name, and we have said nothing of the truer and better variety.

You leave me in the dark.

Suppose you saw me pounding a nail with a stone—I should in a sense be hammering, should I not?

Yes.

And yet a stone is hardly a hammer and would deserve its name only from its use in this instance, and barely at that.

Yes.

I should be ridiculous if I said that I owned a hammer or knew how to use one, if that were all I had and knew how to use.

True.

I should be—should I not?—like a man riding a pig and vaunting it for a charger?

Very much.

By heaven! Now that I have ridden my pig and seen it for such, I will never rest until I have mounted a noble charger. Will you help me into the saddle?

Gladly; but how?

We were right, were we not, in insisting that nothing can be called a symbol in the true sense unless it can be used as a symbol; just as nothing can be called a hammer if it is utterly incapable of being used as a hammer—however much it might resemble a hammer?

I think so.

So that a painting of a man is not really a man, and the painted eye not really an eye, no matter how good the likeness to man or eye. These are mere appearances or falsities because they will not fulfil the functions of the things they mimic?

I agree.

We have, then, it appears, four classes of things. Shall I tell you what they are? The first is the class of things that have neither the use nor the appearance of certain others and hence are never confused with them. The second is the class of resemblances and appearances, which, however, are utterly useless with respect to the function of the things they resemble. Here, in our case, belong all sophistry and word-jugglings and meaningless distinctions and such speeches as the speaker himself does not understand. Thirdly, the class of things which may be used for a given purpose, but only crudely; for their nature does not suit that purpose; they are used only out of necessity or convenience, for lack of a better; they are hammers and knives and what-not only because something else wills them to be. It was amid these that we sat down so contentedly, thinking they were symbols, like barbarians happy with their stone trash and never dreaming of the marvelous tools of civilization.

Enough metaphors. Go on.

Well, then, there is a fourth class—that of the things which have both a use and a nature suited to the use. The real hammer, I suppose, has a form and material exactly suited to its special use, and to the circumstances of its use? And so our true symbol must also have a form and matter especially suited to its function?

Yes.

Since symbols are ideas, I suppose their materials must be the ideas which are parts of them.

I don't follow.

You have the idea of a circle?

Yes.

Surely the parts of this idea are center-point and curved line and radius and so on?

I don't see that; surely I can envision a circle without them.

You could prove, I suppose, that this circle you envision is really a circle? Or do you mean that you use the term loosely?

I see what you mean, and I withdraw. You mean that the idea of a circle cannot be formed without reference to some such parts as you mention; I, of course, was speaking only of an image or fantasm.

I suppose the form of an idea will be the synthesis of the parts of this idea; as the idea of a circle is the synthesis of the parts of the idea circle. Your fantasm, too, had a form; the curved line which made it had to be conceived as complete in all its parts, or you would not have envisioned a full circle.

Yes.

Similarly, the idea of a black sphere would be impossible without concepts of blackness and sphericity? For these are its immediate parts?

Yes.

And this indifferently whether the black sphere is the symbol or the symbolized?

I cannot see how there could be any difference.

Well, now; suppose I were trying to symbolize the concept of a sphere; would the concept of a circle or of a triangle be a better symbol?

I should say, the circle.

The sphere could exist without the triangle, but not without the circle? For the sphere is a circle fully revolved on a diameter, and any plane passing through it must always produce a circle; but a triangle could never generate a sphere, or form any part of it as sphere; and spheres could be if triangles had never existed.

I see.

The circle is, then, a cause of the existence of the sphere, whereas the triangle is not?

Yes.

And the keystone, because it is the cause of the existence of the arch, would be a better symbol of it than any other stone.

Doubtless.

The materials of the concept of the symbol, then, must always be drawn from some part of the concept of the symbolized, without which that latter could not be? That is, from a cause?

That seems reasonable enough.

The symbol gives a kind of understanding of the symbolized; this is scarcely possible without conveying a cause?

I think that makes it clearer.

There must be five ways, then, in which the symbolized is connected with the symbol, must there not? Resemblances of form or shape or nature would, I think, be one of these; such was the case with our circle and sphere.

Yes.

Again, the parts would stand for the whole, or the materials for the synthesis. For instance, the keystone or the arch might stand for the house, I think, or the victim for the murder.

No doubt.

And any instrumental causes as well; thus sword and shield might symbolize the art of war; and any agency might symbolize whatever was done by it. This is why workman's tools are so often chosen as symbols of their craft or trade.

Certainly.

And, surely, of things that have a use, purpose, function, or result, each may be symbolized by its proper work or use? The shipbuilder will, I think, be willing to have his art represented by a ship, and the engineer to have his represented by bridge or bastion.

True.

Lastly, we shall have a whole class of accidental concomitants of the aforementioned classes, arising out of confusion with the true causes just mentioned or out of historical happenings or customs or legends or analogies, and so forth. For example, members of a given religious cult will be most likely to take as symbols things connected with the most crucial articles of their faith, or a nation will accept something connected with some important event or period in its history.

Yes.

That which is distinctive and more immediately connected with the symbolized will always be the better symbol, will it not? I think, for example, that bricks are a better symbol of the building art than, say, clay; for clay is also used by the potter and the sculptor and the brickmaker; and something more immediately connected with the building art will be better still.

Certainly.

This is because whatever is immediate will always bring the symbolized more powerfully and vividly to mind than would the remote.

Beyond question.

Yet, it seems to me, we are no closer to our symbol, our true symbol, than an account of general attributes would be to a definition or than a description would be to an image.

Please explain.

I presume that an account of general attributes and a definition are alike in that they present to the mind some concept or idea, which is never of any particular thing but always of some universal?

Quite so.

And in this they differ from description and image, which are of the particular and present to the mind not a concept or idea but a fantasm or picture?

Yes.

The fantasm is to the idea as the particular to the universal, is it not?

Yes.

And an account of general attributes and a definition have nothing to do with the accidents connected with the particular thing, but with its essence; whereas for description and image it is the accidents which are more important than the essence, for they convey more of the particular? You would insist, for instance, if I described a particular man, that I should not simply call him man or unfeathered biped or rational animal, but that I should include his height, shape, size, facial appearance, colors, and other particulars, all of which are, however, no part of the concept "man" but are accidental to the individual?

I would.

A concept is surely distinct from a fantasm? Although the mind cannot think without fantasms which attend thought, so that you cannot think circle without envisioning a circle, there is still a difference between the idea, which is not a picture, and the fantasm, which is?

True.

I am glad you have not gone astray on that point, which confused so great a philosopher even as David Hume. Our general account and our definition must differ, then, from description and image.

Yes.

But surely an account of attributes is not the same as a definition? The account contains attributes which are true and sometimes essential, without resulting in a clear idea of the nature of the thing; until the proper attributes are selected from among these and gathered in proper arrangement into the unity of a definition, no clear idea of the nature of the thing results; but it results immediately from the definition. I speak, of course, only of true accounts and definitions.

Yes.

So the account provides, as it were, materials only for the definition.

Yes.

The same is true, I think, of the relation between description and image. For the description gives a mass of characteristics of the thing, characteristics which the thing might possess under any and all circumstances; from these the mind might frame a number of pictures, but only because it happened to frame them, just as the mind, if it chose, might assemble the characteristics of an account into a number of definitions or notions of the nature of something.

True.

Whereas a definition impels the mind to a single notion which is the notion of the nature of the thing, and an image impels the mind to a single fantasm.

Yes.

Similarly, I suppose, we must distinguish the materials of the symbol from the true symbol—which surely possesses the power to set before the mind the concept intended, and no other?

Surely.

What, then, shall we say about the form of our symbols? For our argument has gone to show that we must not talk merely about their matter if we are to have true symbols.

I am afraid I cannot help you, Socrates.

I presume that, possessing the concept of the symbol, however compounded of certain materials, we should have only that concept and no more? For instance, while a circle could symbolize a sphere, having the concept of a circle is to have that concept and not that of a sphere?

Right.

Unless, to be sure, that concept contains some indication that it is more than that concept.

How could it do that?

I have observed that even your cartoonists, when they represent a sphere by a circle, always add to the circle something to indicate that it is more than a circle; they give it shading or a high light or something of the sort, which a mere circle would not have.

You are right.

And, by this indication of something which is incompatible with circle, they show that something more than circle is intended?

Yes.

Without such indication, I presume, the mind would be content to take circle as circle; but meeting a contradiction, it is restless and will not be satisfied until it has resolved that contradiction?

Even so.

The contradiction between circular form and spherical high light will, however, be resolved when the mind discovers that a sphere is intended?

True.

Then we must advise our symbolists to be sure to have some such indication in their symbols, to give them power to force the mind toward that which is intended, or their symbols will not be recognized as symbols.

Certainly we must.

But the indication will have to be a true index of the thing symbolized; otherwise our circle will be taken erroneously for a wheel or something other than the sphere intended.

Yes.

But, given the proper selection of the proper materials and such an index, the mind will pass instantly to the symbolized, being impelled by the symbol.

Beyond doubt.

Since we do not only think but also often feel toward that which we think and since the thing symbolized will have a certain nature which may be good or bad, and hence lovable or hateful, presumably our index and all other parts of our symbol will have to be so framed that the appropriate emotions will be evoked. For example, if a man conceives Death as benign and merciful, it would be absurd to symbolize it by some concept which was hideous and evil, like that of a rotting skeleton.

Certainly.

Anyone who wishes to invent true and powerful symbols will have, therefore, to study that concept which he wishes to symbolize and determine its most striking and important attributes, that is, those which determine the conception and our emotions toward it; next, he will have to find or invent something which incorporates these attributes; and with these he will have to combine the index. Suppose, for example, that a symbol-maker conceived of a certain way of life, which concept he wished to symbolize; and suppose, on casting about in his mind, he thought it best typified by the kind of life led in a certain city—say, Byzantium. Now, it seems to me that if his thought runs on "life such as at Byzantium," he has only an example; if on "life like that at Byzantium," only an analogue, so that, on putting it into words, a metaphor will result; but if he so frames his conception of Byzantium that it is not a mere mirror, as examples and analogues are, but, as it were, a window, a trans-

parency through which we see the thing he truly intends; then and then alone
has he made a symbol.

You seem to think that symbols are not, after all, metaphors.

And should I? Whatever name we give to our symbol will now apply
immediately to the symbolized, and thus differ from metaphor; for a metaphor
is only the name of a certain thing transferred to its similar in respect to a certain similarity, although their concepts remain distinct; whereas the name of the
true symbol will stand not metaphorically but directly for the symbolized; because the concept of the symbol has been identified with that of the symbolized.

I think you are right.

And shall we let this stand, then, for our account of symbols?

I think we may well do that.

Yet it seems to me that we have said nothing of symbolic poetry.

How is that? Isn't it simply poetry which utilizes such symbols as you have
described?

My friend, in the first sense in which we talked of symbols, any user of
language is a symbolist; the poet, since he uses language, can hardly avoid
symbols of that sort.

That is true; but what of those who use the last kind of symbols you mentioned?

Could not such symbols be used in any form of composition?

I suppose they might.

Then it seems to me that we have said nothing about symbolic poetry because we have never discussed poetry; and therefore we must push farther, if
you are willing.

I am willing.

We should be talking again of materials only, and of only part of these, if we
discussed symbols; we must consider what the poet distinctively does as a
poet, if there is one kind of poet only, or what the several kinds do if there are
several, since one account for very different kinds might be so general that, in
fitting all, it fitted none.

I agree.

The poet, it seems to me, builds wholes; in this he is unlike the binder of
faggots or the money-tellers, who care only about totals.

I wish you would explain that.

If you bought a shoe from me, you would be very much surprised, I think,
if I handed you merely a number of pieces, even if they were all correctly
shaped and if all the necessary parts were there; you would demand to have
them assembled, and not stitched together anyhow, but assembled correctly;

for a shoe is a whole and not a total; whereas a sum of money or a bundle of faggots is merely a total and requires no particular arrangement.

I see.

A poet, then, constructs wholes. For he does not throw the parts together anyhow, but assembles them, and that properly according to his art, and is much annoyed if anyone spoils the order, say, by transposing lines or stanzas.

Yes.

And that which has a certain characteristic, as a whole, is surely more possessed of that characteristic than that which possesses it only in part? For instance, that which is beautiful as a whole is more beautiful than that which is beautiful only in part, and that which as a whole is good is better than that which is good only in a part?

Surely.

Then the poet whose poem is symbolic as a whole will be more truly a symbolic poet than one whose work is symbolic only in part?

Yes.

Then it seems to me that we must examine these wholes, and that according to their differences. For if we say that all art is symbolic, we say nothing of the poet save that he is an artist; if we say that all poetry is symbolic, we say merely that he is a poet.

Certainly.

Well, then, consider: does it not seem to you that there are two very broadly different kinds of poets, according to the different wholes which they make?

I am sure it will seem so if you discuss them.

On the one hand, there are those who set some kind of human activity before us, whether with many episodes and characters, as your novelists do, or with only a single character at a moment of passion or decision, as lyric poets so often do. In setting such activity before us, they are concerned primarily with the beauty of the poem, which, being beautiful, must give us pleasure.

I fancy, Socrates, that you will not find many critics at present who think pleasure important enough to be the end of poetry.

Then I should ask them with what swine they have lain, to have so low a conception of pleasure?

I merely present their objection; I do not share their opinion.

I wonder if they would think the lot of the just man less pleasurable or more painful than the lot of the unjust; or if they think there is no difference between the pleasures of noble and ignoble men. For they talk as if they suffered from profound moral ignorance. But to resume: I was speaking of high art, not of a swine's swill; and I was saying that certain poets sought to effect beauty by their imitation. I did not say that they sought to give us pleasure; the beauty is not for the sake of the pleasure but, rather, *results* in pleasure: two very different things. Let us call them "imitators" or "mimetic poets."

Very well.

On the other hand, there are those who seek to persuade us of some doctrine, that is, either merely to instruct us or to get us to feel a certain emotional disposition toward it. Now that I think of it, I suppose there is a third group in between these; the group of the entertainers, who are concerned merely with giving pleasure and offer only so much beauty or instruction as will be conducive to pleasure. Here belong your comedians, who will do anything to raise a laugh, and the sentimentalists, who will do anything to start a pleasant tear, and your popular moralists, who deal in what everyone knows because those who utter what we have always approved flatter us and give us pleasure. I can scarcely, however, consider them real poets; so perhaps, after all, we have two classes of poets—the mimetic and the didactic.

Very well; but I doubt also whether critics will accept this distinction, for they are likely to claim that all poetry is didactic, or something of the sort.

They would admit, I hope, some difference between Homer and Dante?

I doubt whether they would admit anything.

Then we must show them. If you were seeking to imitate an action, the action itself would give unity to the imitation?

I think so.

But if you were to inculcate some doctrine by way of representing some action—as in moral allegory, for example—completeness would depend not upon the action but upon the doctrine? Your poem would be complete only when the doctrine was completely expressed and when you had done everything you could to advance it?

Yes.

And the parts of the mimetic action would depend upon the action itself and whatever was necessary or probable within that, but the parts of the doctrinal action would be selected with a view to the doctrine and its statement?

True.

Homer and Dante you would regard, I presume, as both successful poets.

Very.

Is there any doctrine which as a whole binds the poem of Dante together?

I think there is.

Will you state it?

There are several levels of significance, and doctrines corresponding to each of these, all binding the work together as a whole; the allegorical subject, which is "man as by good or ill deserts, occasioned through free choice, he becomes liable to rewarding or punishing justice," is intended to enforce certain moral doctrines, practically, with the end of "removing those living in this life from the state of misery and leading them to a state of felicity."

And you would say that the parts and the whole are regulated by the moral doctrine and selected and shown in reference to it?

I would, since Dante himself says so.

Would you tell me what doctrine similarly underlies Homer?

That, I think, would be very difficult to say, whether you talked of the *Iliad* or the *Odyssey*.

And what would you say if I tried to persuade you of something and never made clear what it was of which I sought to persuade you?

I should say that you had not been very successful.

But Homer is successful, I think you said.

He is successful in a quite different way.

Then there must be those two different kinds of poets and poetry?

It would appear so.

It would be dreadful to confuse these two poets, would it not? For if we regard both as didactic, Dante appears excellent and Homer very poor, inasmuch as we cannot even tell what he is urging upon us; or if we regard both as mimetic, the reverse would be the case; for surely Dante is not much of a plot-maker; his incidents do not follow on each other as incidents, but as incidents representing a doctrine.

True.

To read them without regard to this distinction would be also, I think, to plunge ourselves into totally incorrect interpretation; we should puzzle ourselves indefinitely trying to find the doctrine behind Homer or trying to justify the practice of Dante without regard to the doctrine.

I agree in part; but I do not understand how, unless we are forced to the doctrine, that is, persuaded of it, we can get much out of Dante as you describe him; whereas I myself remain unpersuaded of it, and yet—quite illicitly, it would appear by your argument—get pleasure out of him, just as out of Homer.

My friend, I observe that you have Cicero and Demosthenes and many other orators on your shelves. I hope you read them with pleasure.

I do. Invariably.

They inevitably persuade you?

No. I see what you mean; I am pleased by the art of the orator, even though I am not persuaded.

Precisely; and, besides, we have not said that the one kind does not please and the other does not instruct, or anything so foolish; we have said that the one is concerned with beauty of form and the other with inculcation of doctrine.

I think I see it better.

To return to our distinction: we should find a similar distinction, I think, between the comic poet and the satirist, even if the latter is what we call "comic" and even if he deals with the general rather than, as do the writers of invectives and lampoons, with the particular. For the comic poet merely presents the ridiculous, whereas the comic satirist seeks to convince us that something *is* ridiculous.

Yes.

Then the mimetic and the didactic poets build different wholes?

Yes.

And these different wholes may involve different parts?

Yes.

The mimetic poem will have to include as its parts the action, I presume, and that along with character and thought; for it will imitate not merely a string of unqualified events, at which we might laugh or weep as we chose, but morally determinate actions, which would govern our feelings. For I suppose even death and murder might be considered serious or amusing, depending on the light in which they are regarded.

Yes; people are nowadays very much amused by things like *Kind Hearts and Coronets* and *Arsenic and Old Lace*, both of which involve a string of murders; and they are also greatly amused by the cartoons of Charles Adams, dealing with subjects which, in their usual conception, would be horrible and morbid.

The mimetic poet will also present what he is imitating in a certain manner— for instance, either dramatically or narratively; and he may either present the action in its proper order or convert it, and there are many other things relating to manner of representation, I should imagine. All this will be a second part. Lastly, there is the part of the medium, or words.

Yes.

And symbols are possible in all these parts, I think; for example, the characters and their actions and, in short, the plot as a whole may be symbolic.

As in Kafka's *The Castle* or Joyce's *Ulysses*.

Or there may be symbolism of narrative or dramatic manner.

Yes; a play called *Our Town* would exemplify that, for, while the plot is not symbolic, the dramatic representation is.

Or, finally, there is symbolism of diction; for a poet might symbolize brute nature by a tiger or a hawk, and call it by their names; and this would be like metaphor, and yet different from it, as we have argued.

Yes.

But poems are wholes, and a whole must always have some principal part?

Yes.

And surely it is the principal part which gives its nature to the whole, and not some subordinate part? And here the principal part would be the action, since it is the thing imitated? For without it I fear we should have no imitation at all.

Surely.

Our true symbolic poet of the mimetic kind must then make his action symbolic, if he wishes to impart the symbolic character to the whole.

Yes; and with a few exceptions like William Blake, poets have done this only recently. But Rimbaud and Joyce and Yeats and Kafka are certainly of that order, and so is Eliot.

And what of our didactic poet? The parts of the whole which he makes seem to me to be very different.

How?

He must make or intimate clearly some statement, which is his doctrine or thesis in the emotional or intellectual light in which he wishes us to accept it; and he must offer some sort of proof, whether logical or the kind of thing that in a certain frame of mind we should accept as logical, even if he merely presents himself as a good man and indicates that all good men must think or feel as he does in the matter. And there are many ways of proof; for example, he may offer us a story which implies his thesis, either by induction, as in the exemplum, or by deduction, as in the allegory, or by analogy, as in the parable and the fable. All this, thesis and proof alike, belongs to what we may call the "argument."

Why not?

On the other hand, he must use words. So there is a second part, clearly subordinate, I think, to the first part; for the words would be selected with a view to the argument and not, I should hope, the arguments selected with a view to the words—I cannot imagine the latter procedure as convincing anyone.

Nor can I.

The argument, therefore, is clearly the principal part; and our didactic poet will be a symbolist if that is made symbolically.

I suppose Ezra Pound's *Cantos* is of that sort, and perhaps certain things of Robinson Jeffers.

Now, I think, we have fashioned our mimetic and our didactic poets, noble fellows both, and we are able to say when either will or will not be a symbolist. Are you satisfied with our account?

I think I have still a few difficulties, Socrates; not so much with what you have said as with what arises beyond all this. I am still uncertain about whether allegorists and myth-makers are symbolists; and I am not clear, therefore, whether Dante and Spenser are symbolists or not.

By "allegorist" you mean, I presume, someone who uses personification and makes such abstract things as the virtues and vices into people?

Yes.

And does the rendition and elaboration of his poem depend upon the virtue or vice, primarily, or upon the convention that he is representing them as persons and must therefore assign them appropriate costumes, appearances, and so on?

Upon the latter, I should say.

Whereas the rendition of the symbol is rather determined by the thing symbolized, is it not?

I see; they are in a manner the reverse of each other.

Moreover, symbolism is possible apart from analogy—is it not?—whereas allegory never would be.

I agree.

And allegory is finite, since, once one has carried the traits from the personification to the quality personified, the process is complete; whereas, once one has reached the concept symbolized, one is left with the contemplation of it; and besides, it in turn may be made the symbol of something further?

Yes, I see; there is something transparent, as you said, about symbols and something opaque about allegory. But what of the myth-makers?

My friend, we saw that the poet, whether mimetic or didactic, required knowledge of some sort, both of his craft and of that which he represented?

Yes.

Apart from knowledge, he could never achieve plausibility of action or character or argument?

He could not.

So long as he presents this knowledge in terms of its manifestations in particular causes, we may call him "poet" and nothing more; a very honorable thing. But what if he seeks to convey this knowledge itself, wholly divorced from all particulars and accidents? He must needs do this by some myth or fable, and we may call him a "myth-maker" whether he uses symbol or parable or allegory; and that is to call him both "poet" and "philosopher." Surely, your Yeats did this in his work *A Vision;* and Eliot, also, in his myth of Wheel and still point.

I see.

And now I must be going, since it is nearly dawn and since the wine in the goblet has yielded nearly all its fragrance; but your question has reminded me that I left the myth of the shadow-city unfinished. May I finish, since only a word or two remains?

By all means.

Well, then: Lur, our shadow, found the place of the temple by his journey; but he discovered also that the god in his anger had locked the gates so that no one could enter. Yet a mirror had been hung in the vast hall, so that, although he could not see the Reality, yet he could see its reflection. And he saw that there were many other approaches to the temple by ways not his and that these too offered a view, although a different view from his, and like it only in that they too were of reflections only. And, being a shadow, he was content; for the shadow must be content with the shadow of knowledge and rise as if full-fed from the shadow of food. Are you not also content?

I am content.

EPISODE, SCENE, SPEECH, AND WORD: THE MADNESS OF LEAR

NORMAN MACLEAN

I

IT WOULD, of course, be an exaggeration to say that the history of the story of King Lear is a history of art. Far back of Geoffrey of Monmouth's *Historia regum Britanniae*, in which Lear's story makes its first appearance in literature, is a folk tale of a daughter who angers her father by telling him that she loves him as much as salt,[1] but this story already has shape, although the shape of art in embryo. It is a narrative riddle, depending upon the double meaning of a word, and when the real meaning is recognized by the father, through some device such as serving him a feast without salt, both the anger of the father and the story dissolve. That the story appears in many variants indicates the universality of its appeal, but the emotions it aroused must have been limited largely to common curiosity in verbal puzzles and the pleasure, not confined to children, of discovering that children are more subtle than their parents. A narrative riddle, then, such as might be added to the collections of the Grimm brothers is the prototype of the story that Shakespeare transformed into a tragedy. That the history of the Lear story concludes in a consummation of art is testified to by another kind of history—the history of men's literary affections: tragedy, on the whole, has proved to be the most moving of literary forms, and to most critics *King Lear*, although not the most flawless, is the most tragic of Shakespeare's tragedies.

The problem of artistic consummation, being the problem of magnitude in the highest degree, is imperiled by its own scope, but fortunately there is a part of *King Lear* that by assent is its most tragic region, the region where suffering takes on such dimension that even Shakespeare could find no better word than "madness" to contain it. Furthermore, since the madness of Lear is almost entirely Shakespeare's invention[2] and is crucial in the transformation of the many

1. Wilfrid Perrett, *The Story of King Lear from Geoffrey of Monmouth to Shakespeare* (Berlin, 1904), pp. 9 ff.

2. "Lear's madness has no place in the old story; it is Shakespeare's own invention" (George Lyman Kittredge, *The Complete Works of Shakespeare* [Boston, 1936], p. 1196). According to Perrett, certain versions of the story contain suggestions of madness (*op. cit.*, pp. 225–26), but these suggestions, as Perrett says, are remote and are limited to phrases (such as "crazed thoughts") and, moreover, they are probably stereotypes not intended to suggest actual madness, just as we speak only in figurative cliché when we say, "He was mad with rage."

stories of King Lear into the only *Tragedie of King Lear*, it brings us face to. face with both the tragic art and the tragic artist. Now, to speak of a consummate poetic accomplishment is to imply that the kind of criticism which views all a writer's problems as unique has overlooked a part of the whole of truth. For, to speak of an artistic attainment as possessing magnitude in the highest degree is to imply the existence of attainments somewhat analogous and in this and that common respect somewhat inferior; it implies either this or the existence of a critic who has some a priori conception of a poem more wonderful than any yet written, in which case the critic should change to a more wonderful profession and contribute its culminating splendor. For us at least, it is certainly easier and wiser to say that every writer in each particular act of composing faces problems that have various levels of universality, and, if this were not so, we could not recognize any uniqueness in his achievement; the chances are we could not even recognize what he had written. In only certain senses, then, does Shakespeare forever elude us and refuse to "abide our question," for, if there are general problems confronting every writer, we should be able to ask questions that Shakespeare of all men made no attempt to elude.

At a high level of universality, to write anything well, whether it be intellectual or imaginative, is to assume at least two obligations: to be *intelligible* and to be *interesting*. Intelligibility, too, has its levels of obligation, on the lowest of individual statements, and even on this level the obligation is never easy to fulfil and perhaps even to genius could be a nightmare if what the genius sought to represent was "madness." Only to a limited degree, however, can individual statements be intelligible—and in many instances and for a variety of reasons the individual statements are meant to be obscure, as in "mad" speeches. Since full intelligibility depends upon the relations of individual statement to individual statement, the concept of intelligibility, fully expanded, includes *order* and *completeness;* for a fully intelligible exposition or poem having relations has parts, and all the parts ought to be there and add up to a whole. The second major obligation, that of being "interesting," includes *unexpectedness* and *suspense*, for expository as well as imaginative writing should not be merely what the reader expected it would be—or why should it be written or read?—and the unexpected should not be immediately and totally announced (in other words, expository and imaginative writing should have suspense), for, if the whole is immediately known, why should the writer or reader proceed farther?

But the accomplished writer gives his selected material more than shape—he gives it proper *size*. For a piece of writing to have its proper size is an excellent thing, or otherwise it would be lacking in intelligibility or interest or both. Thus, if Lear's anger had been transformed into madness in a single scene, all the odds are that such a transformation would seem beyond belief, and it is just as certain that the play would have died in the memory of men for want of suspense. On the other hand, the madness of Lear could have been drawn at such length that the spectator, like Kent, could not continue to view the suffering or, worse still, until the spectator began to suspect an author was manipulating suffering for suspense—and in either case the spectator would feel that he had seen too much. Moreover, the size of any literary particle·is not a matter of quantity only. Every art has ways of making a thing seem bigger or smaller than the space it occupies, as Cordelia is more wonderful by far than the number of lines she utters and is even tragically present when she is tragically absent, and as Lear becomes more gigantic when he can utter only a few lines or broken lines or none at all.

We have come close to the special realm of imaginative or poetic writing, with its special obligations, two of which we shall refer to as *vividness* and *probability*. As poetic writing is the representing or "making" of human experience, so the poet is the writer who possesses the powers and devices that transfer "life" from flesh to words. These possessions of a poet are not merely a knowledge of "life"; Machiavelli knew much about successful and unsuccessful rulers and wrote *The Prince*, and analysts know much about madness and come no closer to *King Lear* than case reports. Shakespeare "made" many rulers, successful and otherwise, and one he "made" mad. In so far, then, as a poem possesses "life," it has *vividness*. A poem, however, makes not "life" only but a "world." Hence any of its parts, when related to the others, must seem *probable*. Not any living being may enter *Lear*, and the few who may are severely limited in freedom of thought, speech, and action. What may happen in a poem must be compatible with the general conditions of "existence" as postulated by the poem; and what actually does happen and the order in which it happens must appear as adequately caused by the constitution of the individual characters and by the circumstances in which they are placed. The same legendary figure may enter two worlds and in the early Elizabethan play may spell his name "Leir" and survive his misfortunes, but, having ventured upon the thick rotundity of Shakespeare's world, he cannot be saved, and certainly not by the alteration of any neoclassical poet.

In certain ultimate senses the world that is each poem is bound together so that it binds the hearts of those who look upon it, of whom the poet is one. To look upon a poem, then, as distinct from looking upon much of the succession of life, is to be moved, and moved by emotions that, on the whole, attract us to it and are psychologically compatible. All of us, therefore, seem to be asking for less than we expect when we ask that poems have *emotional unity;* but this is so commonly the language of the request that we shall assume it means what we expect it does—that the emotions aroused by any good poem should be psychologically compatible and also of a kind out of which attachments are formed. We may ask for many other things from poems—biographical information, or political or theological wisdom—but, in making any of these further requests, we should recognize that we are asking for what only certain good poems give, and then generally not so well as something else. What is here taken as ultimate in poetry is what is true of all good poems : they give a high order of distinctive pleasures, and it may be said summarily of high and distinctive pleasures that no man seems in danger of exceeding his allotment.

In a way a poet is untroubled about all this—about writing or writing poetry, for these are abstractions that cannot be engaged in, and he is trying to find the first or next word, and after "thick rotundity" he listens to "of" and is troubled, and then hears "o' " and so moves on to other troubles, leaving behind him "the thick rotundity o' th' world." In a way, then, even in a long life a poet never writes poetry—just a few poems; and in this sense a poet's problems do not begin until he closes in upon a piece of paper with something less abstract in mind than writing or writing poetry. He may wish, as many lyric poets have wished, to write a drama or a novel, but the story is so distinct from the lyric that few poets, despite a tendency of poets to be expansive in their ambitions, have been eminent in both poetic arts. Shelley and Keats had a maximum of aspiration but hardly a minimum of gift for plot and character, and even Browning, with his surpassing delineation of men and women in dramatic monologue, could not make anything happen in a drama. Coming closer to the paper on which *King Lear* was written, we also know that to have the characters tell their own story on a stage raises problems very distinct from those required for putting the story between the covers of a novel. It may seem that the distinction between manners of presenting a story is largely classificatory; yet stories are so locked artistically to those selected to tell them that great novels seldom remain great when they are strutted upon the stage, and vice versa. Particular manners of presentation are particular artistic problems, and particular artistic gifts are needed to solve these problems, and, if not, who are those who are both great novelists and great dramatists? And, more particular still, who among dramatists wrote both great comedies and great tragedies, although tragedy is only drama that moves certain emotions in us? Yet these two dramatic arts are so distinctive that Shakespeare is the single answer to the question of what dramatist eminently possessed both the tragic power and the power of moving to laughter. Even more specialized, personal, and unique are the problems to be focused on in this study—what confronted Shakespeare and Lear, who stood outside when a storm arose and a daughter ordered a door shut. Mind you, before this particular moment Lear had been a successful king and Shakespeare had written great tragedies, but neither had ventured far into madness.

This was a lonely moment in art; yet the moment that is the poet's moment is not his alone, and his problems that seem highly unique would not even occur if he were not concerned, however secretly and for whatever reasons, in loading each particular vein with what can generally be recognized as ore. It is true that he would have no poetic problems at all if each particular moment of art did not have to enter the general world of art, for unattended self-expression is another occupation, altogether lonely.

We propose to follow Lear and Shakespeare across the heath to the fields of Dover on what for both was a unique experience, and then to be even more particular, considering the individual scenes leading to this meeting of Lear and Gloucester when in opposite senses neither could see. And, for smaller particulars, we shall consider an incident from one of these scenes, a speech from this incident, and, finally, a single word. In this declension of particulars, our problems will be some of those that were Shakespeare's because he was attending Lear and at the same time was on his way toward a consummation in the art of tragic writing.

II

At the end of Act II night has come, an external storm threatens, and an external door is shut; in Act IV, scene 6, Lear, "fantastically dressed with weeds," meets Gloucester and Edgar upon the tranquil fields of Dover, the tempest now a tempest of the mind and at its worst. To view this large expanse of suffering as a single dramatic unit is also to see that, in the form of organic life called a poem, "parts" are "parts" and in certain senses "wholes." By the end of Act II the major external causes of Lear's madness have occurred; by Act IV, scene 6, they have brought Lear to "the sulphurous pit" and unrestrained madness, from which, even in the next scene, he is somewhat "restored." For a variety of reasons we shall state the unity of this dramatic episode in terms of a change that it brings about in Lear's thoughts and beliefs concerning man, the universe, and the gods, a change in thought that is both a cause and a projection of his madness.

Prior to this episode (and presumably always before it), Lear believed in a universe controlled by divine authority, harmoniously ordered and subordinated in its parts, a harmony reflected in the affairs of men by the presence of political and legal institutions, and social and family bonds. Men were the most divinely empowered of divine creations, and the special power of kings was a sign of their special divinity. At the end of this episode (Act IV, scene 6), the world that Lear tells Gloucester he should be able to see even without eyes is one in which man is leveled to a beast and then raised to the most fearful of his kind: the source of man's power, as with the beast's, is sex and self, but above the girdle which the gods inherit is the special gift of reason; only it is a kind of sadistic ingenuity by which man sanctifies his own sins—the universally inevitable sins of sex and self—by declaring them anathema for others ("Thou rascal beadle, hold thy bloody hand! / Why dost thou lash that whore? Strip thine own back"). Therefore, as king, Lear dismisses the phantom of the adulterer arraigned before him, because, all offending, "none does offend, none—I say none!"

The moment we imagine Shakespeare's pen in our hand and Act III unwritten, we begin to sense the immensity of the problem that arises merely from the first general requirement of all good writing, intelligibility. For the problem is to make clear that the mind of Lear progressively loses its clarity and comes at last to a moment everyone will recognize as "the worst" and be willing to take as "madness." Analogically, what is needed are recognizable circles of the inferno descending to the pit and ways of knowing when the pit has been reached. To present a character becoming more and more disintegrated emotionally, therefore, is fundamental but not enough, since emotions under pressure lack outline and precision, with the result that the best of lyric poets know their task is to find "objective correlatives" for what otherwise would remain in prison or confusion. In the next section, dealing with the scenes leading to Lear's madness, we shall see how Shakespeare uses actions, which are more discernible than emotions, to mark the descent into the pit; here we are concerned with the fact that Shakespeare added "thought" to action and emotion, and "thought" in many ways is more precise than either of the other two. In solving this problem of intelligibility, then, Shakespeare was "abundant," utilizing the maximum of means, and one way we have of knowing at what circle Lear is stationed for the moment is to learn what Lear for the moment believes is the nature of men, beasts, and gods.

When intelligibility was first discussed, it was expanded to include the concepts of "order" and "completeness." Order, being a matter involving all the parts, is a matter for later consideration, but we may already observe that the change in Lear's thought during this large episode is a complete change. Lear does not have merely different thoughts about the nature of the universe and of those who crawl upon it; the beliefs he has about the universe at the end of Act II are philosophically opposite to those he expresses upon the fields of Dover, and a complete change is one that goes as far as it can. Thus, because the change in Lear's thought is so bitterly complete, we recognize the pit when Lear has reached it. Shakespeare also took care that we should know where Lear started. Lear's last speech in Act II is the first one he gives in which thought of a general nature is directly expressed; it is appropriate to his character and the accumulated situation that at this moment he should say man is not man without some gorgeous possessions not needed to keep his body warm, and the speech is also a location point before the heath by means of which we can more easily see what a falling-off there was.

Ultimately, however, it is only of secondary importance that Lear's thoughts clarify our understanding; they lack the power of poetry if they are not moving. Let us begin less intensely, and therefore with the second requirement of all good writing, to be interesting, for, if we are not interested, we surely will not go farther and be moved. Until his last speech in Act II, Lear's thoughts have all been particular and have been concentrated upon the individual natures of his daughters and their husbands. This is appropriate to the circumstances and Lear's character, which is driven rather than given to philosophical speculation; yet, partly as a result, Lear is a character, even by the end of Act II, with whom we have only slight bonds of identification; he is an old man over eighty years, who, so late as this, is in the process of discovering that two of his daughters are nonhuman and that the one who could say "nothing" was alone worthy of all his love. In contrast to *Hamlet* and *Othello*, *King Lear* is a tragedy in the course of which the protagonist becomes worthy of being a tragic hero, and one dimension that Lear takes on is the power of thought. Moreover, his thoughts upon the heath and upon the fields of Dover are of universal significance and therefore "interest" us, for the question of whether the universe is something like what Lear hoped it was or very close to what he feared it was, is still, tragically, the current question.

Earlier we said that material of general, human interest could be handled by an artist in such a way as to take on an added interest—the interest of the unexpected or surprising. It is surprising in life or in literature for a serious man to reverse his philosophical beliefs about the common human problems, but Lear's change in thought is dramatically as well as philosophically unexpected, for the beliefs that have become the protagonist's by Act IV, scene 6, are his antagonists'—Goneril's, Regan's, and Edmund's—who also hold that sex and self are the sole laws of life. Lear has indeed "veered around to the opposite"; it is as if the tortured came to have the same opinion of the rack as the inquisitors.

There is, finally, the contribution that this change makes to the special emotional effects produced by tragedy. Now the tragic writer is also upon the rack, pulled always two different ways, for the deep emotions he stirs he also alleviates. A certain alleviation of fear and pity is necessary to make the emotional effect of tragedy one that we are consumed rather than repelled by; and proper tragic alleviation excludes any supposed consolation that might come from the avoidance of disastrous consequences after we have been asked to suffer emotions such as are aroused by clear premonition of disaster.

By the time that we and Edgar are confronted with the "side-piercing sight" upon the field of Dover, the grounds are many for fearing that Lear and all that is admirable are condemned by some hopelessly formidable perversity of power ultimately beyond challenge. Othello's fate was his own—at least many of us could have escaped it; but Lear's tragedy comes to a point where it threatens what we should wish to be with inevitable inclusion. As a very minimum, we know suffering such as the sufferer can account for only by believing the worst that can be thought of everything, including himself. The minimum, therefore, has some kind of maximum of fear and pity—we are almost certain that such suffering will leave him without the power to better his fortune and without the mental resources needed to gain a clear picture of what is the truth, if this is not it. And, indeed, in the end Lear is deprived of Othello's modicum of consolation—that of seeing the situation as it was—for he is not even permitted to believe that he and Cordelia can be God's spies (pitiful, imprisoned spectators of a conspiratorial universe), since in the same scene the role of a nonparticipant in the universe proves to be nonexistent, Cordelia is murdered, and the mind and body of Lear are asked to suffer no further vexation.

We perhaps do not think sufficiently of the other task of the poet who makes intense emotions—the task of constantly taking away something from them lest they become intolerable or change to some other emotions not intended or desirable, just as the unrestrained grief of Laertes at the grave of Ophelia produced contempt and indignation and not compassion in the heart of Hamlet. Our fear and pity for Lear are both magnified and mitigated. These terrifying thoughts are held by him when he is mad, and their validity is further denied by all those in the play who are intelligent, loving, and somewhat disengaged—their complete validity is called into question by even the existence of people such as Kent, Edgar, and Albany. In addition, the action is arranged from beginning to end (that is, from the beginning of Act III to Act IV, scene 6) in such ways that fear does not become horror, or pity some kind of excruciating anguish. In the first scene in Act III, before we see Lear on the heath, we are given subdued assurance that friends are organizing to rescue him and the kingdom. This scene can be criticized for its execution, because it is a scene merely of talk between Kent and a Gentleman, whose talk is obviously directed to us as much as to themselves, but the intention to save us from horror is right. Moreover, throughout the scenes leading to Lear's madness there are continuing preparations to remove him to Cordelia, and, oppositely, the intervening actions of the antagonists do not make their complete success probable, for Cornwall is killed, Albany becomes disillusioned, and jealousy turns Goneril and Regan upon themselves. And, finally, although scene 6 is constructed to magnify our fear and pity by confronting us with both Gloucester and Lear and their combined anguish, it is also designed to alleviate our suffering and serves as a superlative example of the paradoxical task of the tragic artist. The thoughts to be expressed by Lear upon the fields were Gloucester's as he approached the cliffs of Dover ("As flies to wanton boys are we to th' gods. / They kill us for their sport"), but Gloucester has been purged of these thoughts just prior to Lear's expression of them, and, since Lear and Gloucester have been made parallel in so many ways, one might assume that Shakespeare had constructed this scene to assure the beholder that the beliefs he is about to hear from Lear are not the final beliefs of either. We must recognize, however, that a certain number of critics read *King Lear* in such a way that Gloucester's lines are taken as a condensation of Gloucester's and Lear's and Shakespeare's ultimate "philosophy," although this seems to me to be an interpretation of another book, possibly one written by Hardy. Surely, though, by the end of the scene, if our feelings and the creator do not deceive us, the world is such as to make a man a man of salt—but for purposes more magnificent than the laying of autumn's dust.

III

So far our view of *King Lear* has been both panoramic and confined. In looking upon the large expanse of lines from the end of Act II to Act IV, scene 6, we have confined ourselves to the reversal in Lear's thoughts and feelings that occurs therein and makes it a single, though large, tragic episode. Lear and Shakespeare had conceptions of the tragic that mark them as men who saw "feelingly," but, as a dramatist, Shakespeare had his own set of dismaying problems—the dramatic problems of objectifying tragic thoughts and feelings into commensurate actions and then of dividing and arranging these actions into parts which would be themselves little tragedies and yet stations on the way to some more ultimate suffering. In making these problems ours, we become more particular and yet, in certain ways, closer to the general qualities of great writing which, in order to have a name, must also have a local habitation.

Many a tragic drama has itself met a tragic ending for lack of drama, and the odds increase that this will be the case when the tragedy in some central way involves internal changes, changes in thoughts and states of mind. Byron, too, wished to depict a soul in torment, and he produced *Manfred*, but, despite the subtitle, "A Dramatic Poem," it is largely a series of soliloquies addressed to the Alps in inclement weather. Drama is movement, and, in the four scenes depicting the increasing tempest in Lear's mind, the stage is also in flux—the actors on it move naturally and interestingly, and other characters enter mysteriously and leave on secret missions. Moreover, these actions are designed not merely to keep the stage from becoming static while everything else is dynamic; they are in a higher sense dramatic actions, actions involving an *agon*, "objective correlatives" to the conflict in Lear's mind. Lear challenges the storm; he arraigns his daughters before a justice so perverted that it is represented by the Fool and Edgar disguised as a madman; he imagines impotently that he is raising an avenging army and is distracted by a mouse; and he assumes he is judging a culprit guilty of adultery and finds no sin because he finds the sin universal. Such are the inventions of a dramatic poet, and by them he makes the passage of Lear's tortured soul intelligible, probable, and tragically moving. Scholars are still in search of the exact meaning of certain speeches in each of Shakespeare's great tragedies—and we should like to assume that those who saw these plays for the first time did not have perfect understanding of all of the lines—but so great was Shakespeare's power to conceive of action from which thought and feeling can be readily inferred that all of us know Lear, Hamlet, and Macbeth more intimately than we know many men whose remarks we understand perfectly.

Yet a master of tragic drama would also sense that, in scenes depicting a great change in thought and state of mind, action should be kept to a certain minimum, lest too much outer clangor obscure the inner vibrations and tragedy pass over into melodrama. He would sense, too, that language suggesting madness, if sufficiently understood, would put tremendous demands upon our powers of concentration. Three scenes lead to the madness of Lear and are alternated with three leading to the blinding of Gloucester. Unlike the "internal" Lear scenes, the other three are action cut to the bone; and unlike the clogged language of Lear, the Fool, and Poor Tom, the speech of the conspiracy is lean, bare, and cruel. Removing us momentarily from Lear, these scenes relieve both our understandings and our feelings, but tragic "relief" quickly becomes tragic illusion, when the master-touch is upon it. We turn our eyes away from an old man seeking in suffering to discover the final cause of suffering, only to have it dawn on us that we have turned to a horrible replica of the action that was the immediate cause of this suffering, another old man tortured by his offspring and by Lear's as well. Suffering, then, as it works out its lonely and final course upon the heath, is combined with action such as initiated it. Moreover, in another way the two tragedies are one—Gloucester's attempts to rescue Lear from his suffering are the immediate cause of bringing on his own. Thus the interplay of these two tragedies gives to both more than either singly possesses of intelligibility, suspense, probability, and tragic concern.

But, although Gloucester's tragedy is also Lear's, our concentration is upon those scenes in which Lear goes mad and which collectively make intelligible the scene upon the fields of Dover, where his madness is complete. It is not enough, therefore, that action in these scenes is kept at a certain minimum and within this guarded minimum is maximal, or that the action also is dramatic, involving conflict. It has also to be action everywhere suggesting "madness," and, secondly, it has to be arranged in such a way as to lead Lear to "madness." Let us consider first the materials and then the order out of which such disorder is made.

Certainly, Shakespeare's choice was right in introducing no totally new material in these scenes that center in the depth of Lear's mind; they are made out of materials already in the play—Lear's Fool, Edgar who previously had decided to disguise himself as a madman, and the storm. Distraction that is great and is not the general confusion of a battle but centered and ultimately internal is rightly made out of a certain minimum of material that can be assimilated and out of material already somewhat assimilated. Moreover, such a reduction of material not only helps our understanding at a moment in literature when it stands most in need of help; actually, art attains the maximum of unexpectedness out of restricted sources (as a good mystery story limits the number of possible murderers) and out of material already introduced and about which we have expectations (as the best mystery stories are not solved by material that has been kept from us by the detective and the writer until the end). While on the heath, Lear might have been attacked by a gang of robbers and, in culminating suffering, have thought this some symbolic act, signifying that all men are beasts of prey; surely, it is much more surprising that it is the legitimate son of Gloucester, counterpart of Cordelia, who makes him think this.

Out of a proper economy of material, then, a maximum of madness is made, and everyone who has read *King Lear* has sensed that the heath scenes are composed of complex variations upon the theme of madness—a noble man going mad, accompanied by a character professionally not "normal," meeting a character whose life depends upon his appearing mad, amid a storm such as makes everyone believe that the universe and even the gods are not stable. We add that Kent, too, is present in these scenes and that a point constantly calm is useful in the art of making madness.

The musical analogy of a theme with variations must be used only up to a certain point and then dropped lest it stop us, as it has stopped some others, from going farther and seeing that these scenes are a part of a great poem and that in this part a noble man goes mad, which is something more than orchestration, although orchestration has its purposes. Ultimately, we are confronted with a poetical event; and the storm, the Fool, and Poor Tom are not only variations on madness but happenings on the way which collectively constitute the event. That is, the setting and two characters, all previously somewhat external to Lear, successively become objects of his thought, and then become himself transubstantiated. The storm becomes the tempest in his mind; the Fool becomes all wretches who can feel, of whom Lear is one, although before he had not recognized any such wide identity; and then a worse wretch appears, seemingly mad, protected against the universe by a blanket, scarred by his own wounds, and concentrating upon his own vermin. He is "the thing itself," a "forked animal," with whom Lear identifies his own substance by tearing off his clothes, which are now misleading. We know Lear, then, by Lear's other substances, which are dramatically visible.

There is another substance present with Lear, for the madness that comes upon him is more terrible than the madness that translates everything into the ego; in the mind of Lear, when his madness is complete, all substances—the universe, man, and Lear himself—have been translated into the substance of his daughters, and perhaps something like this is what is technically meant by a "fixation." Although actually never appearing, Lear's daughters are the central characters in the inverted and internal pilgrim's progress that occurs upon the heath, and ultimately we know the stage of Lear's progress by his daughters' presence. In the first appearance of Lear upon the heath (Act III, scene 2) the daughters are already identified with the storm and the underlying powers of the universe, and Lear dares to defy them and to confront the universe, even though he now sees what he began to see at the end of Act II, that the ultimate powers may be not moral but in alliance with his daughters. Either possibility, however, he can face with defiance: in his first great speech to the storm, he calls upon it, as he had called upon the universe before, to act as a moral agent to exterminate even the molds of ingratitude; his second speech is one of moral outrage ("O! O! 'tis foul!") against universal forces that may have joined "two pernicious daughters" in a conspiracy against his head. In the beginning of his next scene (scene 4), he has still the power of defiance, but it is only the storm as a storm that he can confront; he knows that he no longer dares to think of his daughters, for "that way madness lies." Almost at that moment Poor Tom emerges from the hovel, and with him in Lear's mind another substance ("Hast thou given all to thy two daughters, and art thou come to this?"). The shattering of the resolution not to think on this substance leads Lear down the predicted way, and first to a complete identification with a mad beggar; then his mind, rapidly disintegrating, leaves equality behind and, in deferential hallucination, transforms the mad beggar into a philosopher of whom he asks the ancient philosophical question, "What is the cause of thunder?" At the end of this scene, then, Lear's thoughts return to the storm, but it is no longer a storm that he might possibly endure. By many signs Lear's final scene in Act III is the final scene on Lear's way to madness. Poor Tom places Lear's mind in the underworld with his opening speech: "Frateretto calls me, and tells me Nero is an angler in the lake of darkness. Pray, innocent, and beware the foul fiend." With this speech, Lear's thoughts literally enter the pit, and here he finds the forbidden women. What he knew at the opening of the earlier scene that he must avoid now becomes his total occupation, and the mind now revels in what the mind once knew it could not endure. Elaborately and in elation Lear arraigns his daughters upon the shores of the lake of darkness,[3] and, just before drawing the curtain, he asks the final philosophical question, "Is there any cause in nature that makes these hard hearts?"

It is later, properly much later, when we see Lear again, since by then he has found in madness an answer to the questions that led him there. Then, looming upon his mind, is a universe the basic substance of which is female:

> Down from the waist they are Centaurs,
> Though women all above.
> But to the girdle do the gods inherit,
> Beneath is all the fiend's [Act IV, scene 6, ll. 126–29].[4]

In the opening of this section we promised to say something about these scenes as being tragic wholes as well as parts of a fearful and pitiful event, and already a good deal has been said indirectly about their separate natures. But their natures are not only separate; they are tragic, each one arousing and then to a degree purging the emotions of fear and pity. In the first of these scenes, our immediate fear and pity for Lear as we see him trying to outface the elements are intensified by his second address to the storm in which he realizes that the universe may be allied with his daughters "'gainst a head / So old and white as this!" But, shortly, Kent enters, and that makes things somewhat better; then Lear has an insight into the nature of his own sins, and although his sins are pitifully small by comparison, still self-awareness of sin is a good no matter the degree or the consequences—and it is a good to Lear, purging his feelings so that at the end of this little tragedy he turns to the Fool in new tenderness and in a new role, for the first time considering someone else's feelings before his own ("How dost, my boy? Art cold? / I am cold myself"). And such, in a general way, is the emotional movement of the other two scenes in which Lear appears in Act III—they begin with Lear alarmingly agitated; the agitation mounts (with the appearance of Poor Tom or with the prospect of arraigning his daughters in hell); but in the enactment of the enormous mo-

---

3. In the Folio Lear's arraignment of his daughters is omitted (ll. 18–59 in Kittredge). The Folio also omits Edgar's soliloquy concluding the scene. The Folio is far more accurate in editoral detail than the Quarto but is considerably shorter, most scholars surmising that it represents a version of the play that had been cut for acting purposes. As dramatic magnifications of states of mind and feelings already embodied in the play, both Lear's arraignment of his daughters and Edgar's soliloquy are made of material that is often cut if a cutting has to be made for stage purposes. Certainly, it is not difficult to understand the omission of the soliloquy, but the deletion of the trial upon the edge of hell removes from the scene a tremendous amount of its drama and tragedy.

4. All quotations from Shakespeare, unless otherwise specified, are from Kittredge's *The Complete Works of Shakespeare*.

ment he (and we) get some kind of emotional release for which undoubtedly there is some clinical term, not, however, known to me or to the Elizabethans or to most people who have felt that at the end of each of these scenes both they and Lear have been given mercifully an instant not untouched with serenity on the progress to chaos. "Draw the curtains. So, so, so."

There are many tragedies of considerable magnitude the effects of which, however, are almost solely macrocosmic. The greatest of tragic writers built his macrocosms out of tragedy upon tragedy upon tragedy.

IV

The third time that we shall consider Lear upon the heath will be the last, for the full art of tragedy has three dimensions, like anything with depth. The tragedy with depth is compounded out of a profound conception of what is tragic and out of action tragically bent, with characters commensurate to the concept and the act—and, finally, it is composed out of writing. The maximal statement of an art always makes it easier to see how many lesser artists there are and why; and thus the author of *The American Tragedy* could not write— a failing not uncommon among authors—and the author of *Manfred*, although a very great writer in many ways, was so concentrated upon his personal difficulties that he could form no clear and large conception of the tragic, and his tragic action is almost no action at all.

In addition to the remaining problem of writing, one of the general criteria introduced early in this essay has not yet been dealt with directly—vividness, or the powers and devices that make a literary moment "come to life." For a consideration of both, we need units smaller even than scenes, and so we turn to what may be regarded as a small "incident" in one of the scenes and, finally, to a speech from this incident and a single word from the speech. It is easy to understand why the moments of a drama usually singled out for discussion are those that are obviously important and splendid with a kind of splendor that gives them an existence separate from their dramatic context, like passages of Longinian sublimity; but this study is so committed to the tragic drama that it will forego the sublime—although few dramas offer more examples of it— and concentrate, instead, upon an incident and a speech, the importance and splendor of which appear largely as one sees a tragic drama unfold about them.

On a technical level, this incident is a unit because it is a piece of dramatic business—in these lines, Shakespeare is engaged in the business of introducing a character:

KENT: Good my lord, enter here.
LEAR: Prithee go in thyself; seek thine own ease.
            This tempest will not give me leave to ponder
            On things would hurt me more. But I'll go in.

[To the Fool]

In, boy; go first.—You houseless poverty—
Nay, get thee in. I'll pray, and then I'll sleep.

Exit [Fool]

Poor naked wretches, wheresoe'er you are,
That bide the pelting of this pitiless storm,
How shall your houseless heads and unfed sides,
Your loop'd and window'd raggedness, defend you
From seasons such as these? O, I have ta'en
Too little care of this! Take physic, pomp;
Expose thyself to feel what wretches feel,
That thou mayst shake the superflux to them
And show the heavens more just.

EDG.: *[within]* Fathom and half, fathom and half! Poor Tom!

Enter Fool [from the hovel]

FOOL: Come not in here, nuncle, here's a spirit. Help me, help me!
KENT: Give me thy hand. Who's there?
FOOL: A spirit, a spirit! He says his name's poor Tom.
KENT: What art thou that dost grumble there i' th' straw? Come forth.

Enter Edgar [disguised as a madman]

EDG.: Away! the foul fiend follows me! Through the sharp hawthorn blows the cold wind. Humh! go to thy cold bed, and warm thee.
LEAR: Hast thou given all to thy two daughters, and art thou come to this?
EDG.: Who gives anything to poor Tom? whom the foul fiend hath led through fire and through flame, through ford and whirlpool, o'er bog and quagmire; that hath laid knives under his pillow and halters in his pew, set ratsbane by his porridge, made him proud of heart, to ride on a bay trotting horse over four-inch'd bridges, to course his own shadow for a traitor. Bless thy five wits! Tom's acold. O, do de, do de, do de. Bless thee from whirlwinds, star-blasting, and taking! Do poor Tom some charity, whom the foul fiend vexes. There could I have him now—and there—and there again— and there!

[Storm still (Act III, scene 4, ll. 22–64)].

Now, the business of introducing a character can be transacted quickly in brackets—*[Enter Edgar, disguised as a madman]*—and when the character is some straggler in the play or not so much a character as some expository information, like a messenger, then the introduction properly can be cursory. But in the drama of Lear's madness, Poor Tom becomes "the thing itself," and the mere size of his introduction is a preparation for his importance. And artistic size, as we said earlier, has qualitative as well as quantitative aspects.

From the time Poor Tom first speaks until the end of this passage, his name is given five times, and it is given the first time he speaks. Yet a complete introduction does more than fasten on a name, especially if the person is distinctive and we should be warned about him. Three times before Poor Tom appears, he is said to be a "spirit," and after he appears he says three times that "the foul fiend" is pursuing him, so that, leaving out for the moment his confirmatory actions and speeches, we surely ought to be forewarned by his introduction that he is "mad." It is not always needful to be so elaborate and repetitive, even when introducing a character of importance, but when, in addition, the moment of introduction is tense emotionally and the character is abnormal, we are grateful, even in life, to have the name repeated. Or, if confirmation is sought from literature, we may turn to the opening of the first scene of *Hamlet* and note how many times in the excitement the names of Bernardo, Marcellus, and Horatio are called back and forth and how often the ghost is referred to before he appears. This introduction, then, has one of the qualities of all good writing, intelligibility, and in circumstances not favorable to understanding.

Moreover, this is an introduction achieving a maximum of unexpectedness and suspense, effects desirable in themselves as well as qualitative signs that the character being introduced is dramatically important. The king is about to escape from the storm into the hovel, but, before doing so, he turns to the heavens with a prayer in behalf of all "poor naked wretches." Not from above but from within the hovel a supernatural voice cries out, "Fathom and half!" If a lesser pen had turned Poor Tom loose upon the stage at this moment with no further identification, we would have been dismayed, and, furthermore, the suspense latent in the unexpected would not have been realized. When he does come forth, we have identified and awaited him, but unexpectedly and in consternation Lear identifies him—identifies him as himself. Then, surely, it is unexpected that the *alter* Lear goes into the singsong of a mad beggar whining for a handout.

As merely unexpected, the entry of Poor Tom is a diversion and serves a purpose, that of momentarily affording us much needed relief. The art of tragic relief is itself worth a study, although all its highest manifestations are governed by two conjoined principles—the moment of relief should be psychologically needed, but the moment of relief should be a momentary illusion which, as it is dispelled, only deepens the tragedy. Mere unexpectedness thus becomes consummate unexpectedness, with what seems to be a turning from tragedy an entry into darker recesses; and the entry of Poor Tom, viewed first as a piece of technical business, is the appearance of greater tragedy. Lear's prayer, among its many dramatic reasons for being, is preparation for the appearance of something worse. The audience, after it becomes confident in its author, quietly assumes that, when something big is said and something big immediately follows, there is a connection between the two, although not too obvious—as Shakespeare himself said earlier in *King Lear*, the entry should not be so pat as "the catastrophe of the old comedy" (Act I, scene 2, ll. 145–47). The prayer comes out of suffering which has identified Lear with the Fool and with a whole class whose feelings before were unknown to Lear, "poor naked wretches, wheresoe'er you are." And "wheresoe'er" might unexectedly be within the hovel at hand, which was to be a refuge from suffering, and the wretch who emerges, poorer and more naked than the Fool, might be fraught with greater suffering. "Fathom and half, fathom and half!" he has called from within, and this is certainly a mysterious cry and, in the circumstances, not a rational utterance, but it is also a sounding of depth. Of the two tragic emotions, it is fear that is aroused by this cry, and it is fear that sends the Fool running out of the hovel, and it is at least in alarm, a diminutive of fear, that Kent commands the "spirit" to come forth. Then Lear's tragic complement appears, and almost in the next moment the pity aroused by the sight of unprotected madness is transposed to the object about which all pity should be centered in a tragedy—the tragic protagonist, who in startled compassion asks the new thing if the two of them are not identical in substance. Poor Tom's answer to the tragic question on the surface and at first seems no answer at all, but what nevertheless might be expected of a mad beggar, a routine whine for alms, a routine that one of the most ancient professions has invariably divided into two parts—first a self-commiserating account of the beggar's own suffering and then a prayer that the possible giver be spared any such suffering, the prayer being, as it were, anticipatory repayment which, by implication, can be taken back and changed to a curse. Surely, the art of panhandling here comes to life, and literary moments that come to life have been called "vivid." But it is Shakespeare's art, referred to by so many as "abundant," to make two moments come to life in one, and, from a mad beggar's routine emerges an answer to Lear's question and hence a moment filled with tragedy and latent with tragedy to come. As Poor Tom's account of himself proceeds, it becomes apparent, although not to Edgar, that he is describing Lear and his own father. At first the multiple identification is scarcely noticeable, since it depends only upon similarity in immediate and outer circumstances—others besides Poor Tom are led through fire and flood. Then the similarity becomes both more inclusive and deeper as tragic flaws and tragic courses of action become parallel—Lear and Gloucester, in pride of heart, are also trotting over four-inched bridges and coursing their own shadows for traitors. And, since the prayer for the possible almsgivers that immediately follows ("Bless thy five wits! . . . Bless thee from whirlwinds, star-blasting, and taking!") approaches the tragic ultimate in vain request, perhaps enough has been said about the introduction of "such a fellow" as was to make both his father and Lear think "a man a worm."

V

Given the confines of this paper, the speech to be considered must be short, for the focus finally is upon the smallest unit of drama, a speech, and the smallest unit of speech, a single word. Moreover, given our other commitments, the speech should also be in essence dramatic and tragic. Let us take, then, the speech in which Lear first recognizes his identity with unprotected nakedness scarred with self-inflicted wounds:

Hast thou given all to thy two daughters, and art thou come to this?[5]

This is not one of those speeches, somewhat detachable as sententious utterances or lyric poems from which are collected *The Beauties of Shakespeare;* yet upon the heath it is one of the great moments. It is tragic drama contracted to its essences—fear and pity. The question is asked in consternation and commiseration; and it arouses in us, who are more aware of implications than Lear, fear and pity in some ways more enormous than his.

These two qualities of the speech—its shortness and its enormousness—at the outset may be considered as somewhat separate and paradoxical qualities. The speech is short not only in over-all measurement but in the individual words composing it, for all of them, with the exception of "given" and "daughters," are monosyllables, and all of them are short qualitatively, being ordinary, colorless words. Of conceivable adjectives that could be attached to the daughters who had brought Lear to this place, none could be more simple, neutral, or needless seemingly than the number "two." What, if anything, can be said of such a complete contraction of language? Well, as a simple beginning, it is easy to understand, and the moment demands understanding. Then, too, just as language, it is unexpected. In forty-odd lines called an "incident," there are the "superflux" of prayer, the eerie cry of Poor Tom, the scurrying prose of the Fool and Kent, the singsong and shivering rhythms of Poor Tom that rise into an actual line of song—and then this, to be answered by a long beggar's whine, colorful but seemingly confused, since the speaker, as announced, is from Bedlam. This is a great deal of dramatic dialogue for forty lines, and perhaps might be contrasted to certain modern schools of writers who have found the essence of drama and reality to be iteration and reiteration of monosyllables. But Shakespeare's contractions are not exhaustions of his language, which was almost limitless in its resources. Ultimately, the kind of verbal contraction here being considered is right because the immediate moment of tragic impact is a contraction—abdominal, in the throat, in the mind

5. The Folio reads: "Did's't thou give all to thy Daughters? And art thou come to this?" We shall analyze the speech as it is given in our text and as it appeared in the first Quarto. Although in several particulars the Folio has contracted the first half of the question, an analysis of either version of the speech would be substantially the same.

impaled upon a point. The vast tragic speeches of Shakespeare are anticipations of impending tragedy or assimilations of the event after its impact, like scar tissue after the wound. Thus every appearance of the ghost in the first act of *Hamlet*, being awaited, is immediately preceded by a long, imaginatively unbounded speech; but, when the ghost reveals his tragedy, his son, who makes many long speeches, can only exclaim, "O my prophetic soul! / My uncle?" Othello enters Desdemona's chamber with a culmination of tragic resolutions, and his opening speech ("It is the cause," etc.) has the magnitude of his fears and his resolutions; but he has no speech, not always even complete sentences, with which to answer the prayers of Desdemona; and her last prayer, that she be allowed to pray, he answers with the ultimate words, "It is too late." In Shakespeare, as in life, the instances are many that the enormous moment, precisely at its moment, contracts body, mind, and utterance.

From life, however, come only the suggestions for art's patterns, not art's final accomplishments. Specifically, life makes it right that Lear's speech at this moment is not a "speech"; yet art demands that no moment of such import call forth, as it often does in life, some truly little, inadequate response. It is the task of the artist to give the enormous its proper dimensions, even if, as in this instance, the illusion has to be preserved that only some little thing was said. Our task, therefore, is to look again at these few, short, ordinary words to see how they add up to what our feelings tell us is something very big. Here, as elsewhere, there can be but the suggestion of a complete analysis; and, in respect to words, the accomplished writer lifts this one and this one and this one and listens to both sound and significance.

Rhythmically and metrically, Lear has asked a tremendous question. Its return to iambic rhythm after seven lines of mad cries and scurrying conversation should in itself encourage the actor to add some dimension to its delivery, and metrically it is seven feet, for, although there is a pause after the fourth foot ("two daughers"), it is all inclosed within a question, and the second part ("and art thou come to this?") mounts above the first. A seven-foot mounting question is a big question. Moreover, the fact that the words, with two exceptions, are monosyllables gives them collectively a pounding effect, especially when they are blocked by so many dentals, only three of the fourteen words being without *d*, *t*, or *th*, and these ("given all" and "come") stand out as it were by their phonetic displacement, two of them being the verbs and "all" being probably more important than either. The fourth foot ("two daughters") has also properly been lengthened, "daughters" being terminal to the first half of the question and being, in addition, the largest word uttered. Rhythm, too, makes this foot speak out, for only a schoolboy would scan it as a foot with a feminine ending ("twŏ dáugh tĕrs"); although no one seemingly can be sure how "daughters" was pronounced at this time, anyone ought to be sure that in this place the second syllable of "daughters" gets as much emphasis as the first and the whole foot is as long roughly as this scansion ("tw̄o daúgh térs").

Grammatical mode of utterance brings us closer to significance. Some dimension, some significance, goes out of the speech if it is not a question but a declaration: "Thou gavest all to thy two daughters, and now art come to this." Gone is some of the immediacy of the moment, too big at its occurrence to be believed and recorded as fact. To a degree, then, fear and pity are made out of grammar, and, if we say that each point so far discussed is a little matter and singly is no great accomplishment, then all we have said is that much of art is composed of little brush strokes and that this is especially true when what is being composed is "the seemingly simple."

Yet there is one big word within this speech—the one right word, the one word that is not a touching-up of another word which could itself have remained without the notice of aftertimes. The right word is also in the right place; it is the last word, "this." Perhaps we are accustomed to thinking of the *mot juste* as a word giving a definite, irreplaceable image, and certainly *the* right word should be irreplaceable and in some sense definite; only there are moments so tremendous that their exact size is without any definite boundary. There are moments, moreover, which have a size that is unmentionable, moments which cannot, at least at the instant, be fully faced or exactly spoken of by those who must endure them. Poetry may make a perfection out of what would be an error in exposition, and moments such as these may set at naught the rule of composition teachers that "such," "it," and "this" should not be used without a definite, grammatical antecedent. Likewise, what has been said about "this" has a relevance to "all" in the first part of the question that is for this moment the exact question:

> Hast thou given *all* to thy two daughters,
> And art thou come to *this?*

There is always a test that should be made of such matters—can we, after searching, find something at least as good? The test does not always lead to humiliation, and always it should lead to some improvement of ourselves, but the most rigorous test of Shakespeare is Shakespeare himself. Marcellus' first question to Bernardo, both of whom have twice seen the ghost, is the forced mention of the enormous and unmentionable: "What, has this *thing* appear'd again to-night?" The ghost of Hamlet's father, as it is awaited, is "this thing," "this dreaded sight," "this apparition," sometimes "it," more often "'t," but never the ghost of Hamlet's father. In the first soliloquy Hamlet's thoughts move past the canons of the Everlasting, past the general un-profitable uses of the world, until they come to the loathsome point focal to his whole universe: *"That it should come to this! /* But two months dead! Nay, not so much, not two." So a second time in Shakespeare we have "come to this." And at the end Hamlet comes to his own tragic moment which he believes can-not be avoided: "If it be now, 'tis not to come; if it be not to come, it will be now; if it be not now, yet it will come: the readiness is all." In themselves, "it," "to come," "be," "will," and "all" are some of the smallest, least precise and colorful words in our language; but words are so important that from the least of them can be made the uttermost in meaning and emotion—the suffering of man triumphed over by some slight touch of serenity. "Let be."

THE CONCEPT OF PLOT AND THE PLOT
OF *TOM JONES*[1]

R. S. CRANE

O F ALL the plots constructed by English novelists that of *Tom Jones* has probably elicited the most unqualified praise. There is "no fable whatever," wrote Fielding's first biographer, that "affords, in its solution, such artful states of suspence, such beautiful turns of surprise, such unexpected incidents, and such sudden discoveries, sometimes apparently embarrassing, but always promising the catastrophe, and eventually promoting the completion of the whole."[2] Not since the days of Homer, it seemed to James Beattie, had the world seen "a more artful epick fable." "The characters and adventures are wonderfully diversified: yet the circumstances are all so natural, and rise so easily from one another, and co-operate with so much regularity in bringing on, even while they seem to retard, the catastrophe, that the curiosity of the reader . . . grows more and more impatient as the story advances, till at last it becomes downright anxiety. And when we get to the end . . . we are amazed to find, that of so many incidents there should be so few superfluous; that in such variety of fiction there should be so great probability; and that so complex a tale should be perspicuously conducted, and with perfect unity of design."[3] These are typical of the eulogies that preceded and were summed up in Coleridge's famous verdict in 1834: "What a master of composition Fielding was! Upon my word, I think the Oedipus Tyrannus, The Alchemist, and Tom Jones, the three most perfect plots ever planned."[4] More recent writers have tended to speak less hyperbolically and, like Scott, to insist that "even the high praise due to the construction and arrangement of the story is inferior to that claimed by the truth, force, and spirit of the characters,"[5] but it is hard to think of any important modern discussion of the novel that does not contain at least a few sentences on Fielding's "ever-to-be-praised skill as an architect of plot."[6]

1. Reprinted, with alterations and additions, from the *Journal of General Education*, January, 1950.

2. Arthur Murphy (1762), quoted in Frederic T. Blanchard, *Fielding the Novelist: A Study in Historical Criticism* (New Haven, 1927), p. 161.

3. *Dissertations Moral and Critical* (1783), quoted in Blanchard, pp. 222–23.

4. *Ibid.*, pp. 320–21.   5. *Ibid.*, p. 327.

6. The phrase is Oliver Elton's in *A Survey of English Literature, 1730–1780* (New York, 1928), I, 195. See also Wilbur L. Cross, *The History of Henry Fielding* (New Haven, 1918),

I

The question I wish to raise concerns not the justice of any of these estimates but rather the nature and critical adequacy of the conception of plot in general and of the plot of *Tom Jones* in particular that underlies most if not all of them. Now it is a striking fact that in all the more extended discussions of Fielding's masterpiece since 1749 the consideration of the plot has constituted merely one topic among several others, and a topic, moreover, so detached from the rest that once it is disposed of the consideration of the remaining elements of character, thought, diction, and narrative technique invariably proceeds without further reference to it. The characters are indeed agents of the story, but their values are assessed apart from this, in terms sometimes of their degrees of conformity to standards of characterization in literature generally, sometimes of the conceptions of morality they embody, sometimes of their relation to Fielding's experiences or prejudices, sometimes of their reflection, taken collectively, of the England of their time. The other elements are isolated similarly, both from the plot and from one another: what is found important in the thought, whether of the characters or of the narrator, is normally not its function as an artistic device but its doctrinal content as a sign of the "philosophy" of Fielding; the style and the ironical tone of the narrative are frequently praised, but solely as means to the general literary satisfaction of the reader; and, what is perhaps more significant, the wonderful comic force of the novel, which all have delighted to commend, is assumed to be independent of the plot and a matter exclusively of particular incidents, of the characters of some, but not all, of the persons, and of occasional passages of burlesque or witty writing.[7]

II, 160–61; Aurélien Digeon, *Les Romans de Fielding* (Paris, 1923), pp. 210–16; Elizabeth Jenkins, *Henry Fielding* (London, 1947), pp. 57–58; and George Sherburn, in *A Literary History of England*, ed. Albert C. Baugh (New York and London, 1948), pp. 957–58; cf. his interesting Introduction to the "Modern Library College Editions" reprint of *Tom Jones* (New York, 1950), pp. ix–x.

7. The explanation of this procedure lies, partly at least, in a still unwritten chapter in the history of criticism. When works of prose fiction became objects of increasingly frequent critical attention in the eighteenth century, it was natural that the new form should be discussed in terms of its obvious analogies, both positive and negative, to drama and epic and that critics of novels should avail themselves, consequently, of the familiar categories of "fable," "characters," "sentiments," and "language" which had been long established, in the neoclassical tradition, as standard devices for the analysis of tragedies, comedies, and heroic poems. In remote origin these distinctions derived from the four qualitative "parts" which Aristotle had shown to be common to tragedy and epic (cf. *Poetics* 5. 1449^{b}15 ff.; 24. 1459^{b}8–11). In the course of their transmission to the eighteenth century, however—as a result partly of the influence of Horace and partly of a complex of more general causes operative from the beginnings of Aristotelian commentary in the Renaissance (see above, pp. 319–48) —the analytical significance of the scheme had undergone a radical change. For Aristotle, concerned with the construction of poetic wholes that afford "peculiar pleasures" through their imitations of different species of human actions, the four terms had designated the essential elements upon the proper handling and combination of which, relatively to the in-

All this points to a strictly limited definition of plot as something that can be abstracted, for critical purposes, from the moral qualities of the characters and the operations of their thought. This something is merely the material continuity of the story considered in relation to the general pleasure we take in any fiction when our curiosity about the impending events is aroused, sustained, and then satisfied to a degree or in a manner we could not anticipate. A plot in this sense—the sense in which modern novelists pride themselves on having got rid of plot—can be pronounced good in terms simply of the variety of incidents it contains, the amount of suspense and surprise it evokes, and the ingenuity with which all the happenings in the beginning and middle are made to contribute to the resolution at the end. Given the definition, indeed, no other

---

tended over-all effect, the quality of a tragedy or epic necessarily depends. They are distinct parts in the sense of being variable factors in the complex problem of composing works which, when completed, will produce their effects, synthetically, as organic wholes. Hence it is that in the *Poetics* they are treated, not discretely as co-ordinate topics, but hierarchically in a causal sequence of form-matter or end-means relationships in which plot is the most inclusive or architectonic of the four, subsuming all the others as its poetic matter; in which character, while subordinated materially to plot and effect, is similarly a formal or organizing principle with respect to thought and diction; in which thought, while functioning as matter relatively to character, incident, and effect, is the form which immediately controls the choice and arrangement of language in so far as this is employed as a means to imitative rather than ornamental ends; and in which diction, though necessarily having a form of its own by virtue of its rhythmical, syntactical, and "stylistic" figuration, is the underlying matter which, as significant speech, at once makes possible all the other "parts" and is in turn, mediately or immediately, controlled by them. The nature of the four elements is such, in short, that, although a critic in his analysis of a given tragedy or epic may take any one of them as his primary object of attention, he can make no adequate judgment of the poet's success or failure with respect to it without bringing into his discussion all the others to which it is related, directly or indirectly, either as matter or as form.

Of this causal scheme only the general outlines survived in the doctrines of subsequent critics in the "Aristotelian" line. The distinction of the four parts was retained and, along with it, the substance of the rules which Aristotle had formulated for their handling; what disappeared was precisely the rationale which in the *Poetics* had justified not only the rules but the discrimination, definition, and ordering of the parts themselves. In its place various new principles and schemes of analysis were substituted by different theorists and critics, the general tendency of which was to make of poetics a practical rather than a productive art and hence to reduce tragedy and epic to modes of ethical or rhetorical discourse designed to serve, each in its specialized way, the common purposes of all such discourse, namely, the delight and instruction of mankind. The consequence was that, although critics continued to distinguish aspects of tragedies and epics that corresponded roughly with the Aristotelian "parts" and although these served to determine the framework of the discussion at least in the most systematic treatises and essays, the discussion itself no longer turned on the nature and functional interrelations of the four parts as elements in an artistic synthesis of a particular kind but on the general qualities which the poet ought to aim at in each, in order to enhance its independent power of pleasing, moving, and edifying spectators or readers. And when this apparatus was carried over from the statement of tragic or epic theory to the practical criticism of tragedies or epics (as in Addison's papers on *Paradise Lost* or Pope's Preface to the *Iliad*), the disjunction of the four elements tended to become still more marked. They were no longer functional parts in an organic whole but so many relatively discrete *loci* of critical praise and blame; and critics could write *seriatim* of the beauties or defects in the fable, characters, sentiments, and language of a given tragedy or heroic poem without assuming any synthesizing principles more specific than the decorum of the genre or the

criteria are possible, and no others have been used by any of the critics of *Tom Jones* since the eighteenth century who have declared its plot to be one of the most perfect ever planned. They have uniformly judged it as interesting story merely—and this whether, as by most of the earlier writers, "the felicitous contrivance and happy extrication of the story" is taken to be the chief "beauty" of the novel or whether, as generally nowadays, preference is given to its qualities of character and thought. It is clearly of plot in no completer sense than this that Oliver Elton is thinking when he remarks that, although some "have cared little for this particular excellence, and think only of Partridge, timorous, credulous, garrulous, faithful, and an injured man; of Squire Western, and of the night at Upton, and of wit and humour everywhere," still "the common reader, for whom Fielding wrote, cares a great deal, and cares rightly, for plot; and so did Sophocles."[8]

When plot is conceived thus narrowly, in abstraction from the peculiar characters and mental processes of the agents, it must necessarily have, for the critic, only a relatively external relation to the other aspects of the work. That is why, in most discussions of *Tom Jones*, the critical treatment of the plot (as

---

necessity (e.g.) that the sentiments expressed should be consonant with the characters of the persons who uttered them (many illustrations of the procedure may be found in H. T. Swedenberg, Jr., *The Theory of the Epic in England, 1650–1800* [Berkeley and Los Angeles, 1944]; cf. the Index under "Fable or action," "Characters," "Sentiments in the epic," and "Language of the epic").

It was at this stage in the history of the Aristotelian "parts" that they entered into the criticism, both general and applied, of modern prose fiction. See, for example, besides many notices of novels in the *Monthly Review* and the *Critical Review*, the anonymous *Critical Remarks on Sir Charles Grandison, Clarissa, and Pamela* (1754); Arthur Murphy's "Essay on the Life and Genius of Henry Fielding," in *The Works of Henry Fielding* (1762); James Beattie's "On Fable and Romance," in his *Dissertations* (1783); and John More's "View of the Commencement and Progress of Romance," in *The Works of Tobias Smollett* (1797). In spite of the general indifference of criticism since about 1750 to questions specific to the various poetic kinds (see above, pp. 14, 459), the tradition of method thus established has persisted, especially in academic circles, to the present day; its influence still lingers in the topical divisions of treatises or textbooks dealing with the technique of fiction; and it still provides the commonplaces of a good many "studies" of novelists and novels (e.g., the pages on *Tom Jones*, already referred to, in Elton's *Survey*). The undoubted deficiencies of the scheme (in its neoclassical degradation) as an instrument of critical analysis and judgment have not passed unnoticed in recent years, particularly among critics of the *Scrutiny* group, who point out, justly enough, that "plot" and "character" are treated in a fashion that abstracts them unduly from the continuum of the novelist's language through which alone they affect us. These critics, however, are usually content to offer, as a positive substitute for the traditional scheme, only a still more extreme reduction of Aristotle's principles, in which everything in the discussion of a novel is made to turn on the relations between diction, in the sense of the author's "verbal arrangements," and thought, in the sense of the "experience" which he communicates by imposing "the pattern of his own sensibility" on the reader through the medium of language. See, for example, Martin Turnell, "The Language of Fiction," *Times Literary Supplement*, August 19, 1949, pp. 529–31; reprinted in his *Novel in France* (New York, 1951).

8. *Op. cit.*, I, 195.

distinguished from mere summary of the happenings) is restricted to the kind of enthusiastic general appreciation of which I have given some examples, supplemented by more particular remarks on various episodes, notably those of the Man of the Hill and of Mrs. Fitzpatrick, which appear to do little to advance the action. The plot, in these discussions, is simply one of several sources of interest and pleasure afforded by a novel peculiarly rich in pleasurable and interesting things, and the problem of its relation to the other ingredients is evaded altogether. Occasionally, it is true, the question has been faced; but even in those critics, like W. L. Cross and Oliver Elton, who have made it most explicit, the formulas suggested never give to the plot of *Tom Jones* the status of more than an external and enveloping form in relation to which the rest of the novel is content. It is not, as they see it, an end but a means, and they describe it variously, having no language but metaphor for the purpose, as a "framework" in which character (which is Fielding's "real 'bill of fare' ") is "set"; as a device, essentially "artificial," for bringing on the stage "real men and women"; as a "mere mechanism," which, except now and then in the last two books, "does not obtrude," for keeping readers alert through six volumes.[9]

I do not believe, however, that it is necessary to remain content with this very limited and abstract definition of plot or with the miscellaneous and fragmentized criticism of works like *Tom Jones* that has always followed from it. I shall assume that any novel or drama not constructed on didactic principles[10] is a composite of three elements, which unite to determine its quality and effect —the things that are imitated (or "rendered") in it, the linguistic medium in which they are imitated, and the manner or technique of imitation; and I shall assume further that the things imitated necessarily involve human beings interacting with one another in ways determined by, and in turn affecting, their moral characters and their states of mind (i.e., their reasonings, emotions, and attitudes). If this is granted, we may say that the plot of any novel or drama is the particular temporal synthesis effected by the writer of the elements of action, character, and thought that constitute the matter of his invention. It is impossible, therefore, to state adequately what any plot is unless we include in our formula all three of the elements or causes of which the plot is the synthesis; and it follows also that plots will differ in structure according as one or another of the three causal ingredients is employed as the synthesizing principle. There are, thus, plots of action, plots of character, and plots of thought. In the first, the synthesizing principle is a completed change, gradual or sudden, in the situation of the protagonist, determined and effected by character and thought (as in *Oedipus* and *The Brothers Karamazov*); in the second, the

9. Cross, *op. cit.*, II, 159–61; Elton, *op. cit.*, I, 195–96.
10. See above, pp. 65–68, 588–92.

principle is a completed process of change in the moral character of the protagonist, precipitated or molded by action, and made manifest both in it and in thought and feeling (as in James's *The Portrait of a Lady*); in the third, the principle is a completed process of change in the thought of the protagonist and consequently in his feelings, conditioned and directed by character and action (as in Pater's *Marius the Epicurean*). All these types of construction, and not merely the first, are plots in the meaning of our definition; and it is mainly, perhaps, because most of the familiar classic plots, including that of *Tom Jones*, have been of the first kind that so many critics have tended to reduce plot to action alone.[11]

If this is granted, we may go farther. For a plot, in the enlarged sense here given to the term, is not merely a particular synthesis of particular materials of character, thought, and action, but such a synthesis endowed necessarily, because it imitates in words a sequence of human activities, with a power to affect our opinions and emotions in a certain way. We are bound, as we read or listen, to form expectations about what is coming and to feel more or less determinate desires relatively to our expectations. At the very least, if we are interested at all, we desire to know what is going to happen or how the problems faced by the characters are going to be solved. This is a necessary condition of our pleasure in all plots, and there are many good ones—in the classics of pure detective fiction, for example, or in some modern psychiatric novels—the power of which depends almost exclusively on the pleasure we take in inferring progressively, from complex or ambiguous signs, the true state of affairs. For some readers and even some critics this would seem to be the chief source of delight in many plots that have obviously been constructed on more specific principles: not only *Tom Jones*, as we have seen, but *Oedipus* has been praised as a mystery story, and it is likely that much of Henry James's popularity is due to his remarkable capacity for provoking a superior kind of inferential activity. What distinguishes all the more developed forms of imitative literature, however, is that, though they presuppose this instinctive pleasure in learning, they go beyond it and give us plots of which the effects derive in a much more immediate way from the particular ethical qualities manifested in their agents' actions and thoughts vis-à-vis the human situations in which they are engaged. When this is the case, we cannot help becoming, in a greater or less degree, emotionally involved; for some of the characters we wish good, for others ill, and, depending on our inferences as to the events, we feel hope or fear, pity or satisfaction, or some modification of these or simi-

11. This accounts in large part, I think, for the depreciation of "plot" in E. M. Forster's *Aspects of the Novel*, and for his notion of a rivalry between "plot" and "character," in which one or the other may "triumph." For a view much closer to that argued in this essay see Elizabeth Bowen, "Notes on Writing a Novel," *Orion*, II (1945), 18 ff.

lar emotions. The peculiar power of any plot of this kind, as it unfolds, is a result of our state of knowledge at any point in complex interaction with our desires for the characters as morally differentiated beings; and we may be said to have grasped the plot in the full artistic sense only when we have analyzed this interplay of desires and expectations sequentially in relation to the incidents by which it is produced.

It is, of course, an essential condition of such an effect that the writer should so have combined his elements of action, character, and thought as to have achieved a complete and ordered whole, with all the parts needed to carry the protagonist, by probable or necessary stages, from the beginning to the end of his change: we should not have, otherwise, any connected series of expectations wherewith to guide our desires. In itself, however, this structure is only the matter or content of the plot and not its form; the form of the plot—in the sense of that which makes its matter into a definite artistic thing—is rather its distinctive "working or power," as the form of the plot in tragedy, for example, is the capacity of its unified sequence of actions to effect through pity and fear a cartharsis of such emotions.

But if this is granted, then certain consequences follow for the criticism of dramas and novels. It is evident, in the first place, that no plot of this order can be judged excellent *merely* in terms of the unity of its action, the number and variety of its incidents, or the extent to which it produces suspense and surprise. These are but properties of its matter, and their achievement, even to a high degree, in any particular plot does not inevitably mean that the emotional effect of the whole will not still be diffused or weak. They are, therefore, necessary, but not sufficient, conditions of a good plot, the positive excellence of which depends upon the power of its peculiar synthesis of character, action, and thought, as inferable from the sequence of words, to move our feelings powerfully and pleasurably in a certain definite way.

But this power, which constitutes the form of the plot, is obviously, from an artistic point of view, the most important virtue any drama or novel can have; it is that, indeed, which most sharply distinguishes works of imitation from all other kinds of literary productions. It follows, consequently, that the plot, considered formally, of any imitative work is, in relation to the work as a whole, not simply a means—a "framework" or "mere mechanism"—but rather the final end which everything in the work, if that is to be felt as a whole, must be made, directly or indirectly, to serve. For the critic, therefore, the form of the plot is a first principle, which he must grasp as clearly as possible for any work he proposes to examine before he can deal adequately with the questions raised by its parts. This does not mean that we cannot derive other relevant principles of judgment from the general causes of pleasure operative in all artistic imitations, irrespective of the particular effect, serious or comic, that is aimed at in a given work. One of these is the imitative principle itself, the principle that we are in general more convinced and moved when things are "rendered" for us through probable signs than when they are given merely in "statement," without illusion, after the fashion of a scenario.[12] Critical judgments, valid enough if they are not taken absolutely, may also be drawn from considerations of the general powers of language as a literary medium, of the known potentialities or requirements of a given manner of representation (e.g., dramatic or narrative), and of the various conditions of suspense and surprise. We are not likely to feel strongly the emotional effect of a work in which the worse rather than the better alternatives among these different expedients are consistently chosen or chosen in crucial scenes. The same thing, too, can be said of works in which the thought, however clearly serving an artistic use, is generally uninteresting or stale, or in which the characters of the agents, though right enough in conception for the intended effect, are less than adequately "done" or fail to impress themselves upon our memory and imagination, or in which we perceive that the most has not been made of the possibilities implicit in the incidents. And there is also a kind of judgment, distinct from any of these, the object of which is not so much the traits of a work that follow from its general character as an imitative drama or novel as the qualities of intelligence and moral sensibility in its author which are reflected in his conception and handling of its subject and which warrant us in ascribing "greatness," "seriousness," or "maturity" to some products of art and in denying these values to others no matter how excellent, in a formal sense, the latter may be.

Such criticism of parts in the light of general principles is indispensable, but it is no substitute for—and its conclusions, affirmative as well as negative, have constantly to be checked by—the more specific kind of criticism of a work that takes the form of the plot as its starting point and then inquires how far and in what way its peculiar power is maximized by the writer's invention and development of episodes, his step-by-step rendering of the characters of his people, his use and elaboration of thought, his handling of diction and imagery, and his decisions as to the order, method, scale, and point of view of his representation.

All this is implied, I think, in the general hypothesis about plot which I have been outlining here and which I now propose to illustrate further in a reexamination of the "ever-to-be-praised" plot of *Tom Jones*.

12. The meaning and force of this will be clear to anyone who has compared in detail the text of *The Ambassadors* with James's preliminary synopsis of the novel (*The Notebooks of Henry James* [New York, 1947], pp. 372–415). See also the excellent remarks of Allen Tate, apropos of *Madame Bovary*, in his "Techniques of Fiction" (*Forms of Modern Fiction*, ed. William Van O'Connor [Minneapolis, 1948], esp. pp. 37–45).

II

It is necessary to look first at its matter and to begin by asking what is the unifying idea by which this is held together. Elementary as the question is, I have not read any answers to it that do not, in one way or another, mistake one of the parts of Fielding's novel for the whole. Doubtless the most common formula is that which locates the essence of the story in the sustained concealment and final disclosure of Tom's parentage. "It is pleasant," writes Oliver Elton, "to consider *Tom Jones* as a puzzle and to see how well the plan works out." For others the most important unifying factor is the love affair of Tom and Sophia; for still others, the conflict between Tom and Blifil; for others again, the quasi-picaresque sequence of Tom's adventures with women and on the road. The novel, it is true, would be quite different in its total effect if any of these four lines of action had been left out, but no one of them so subsumes all the rest as to justify us in considering it, even on the level of material action, as the principle of the whole. A distinctive whole there is, however, and I venture to say that it consists, not in any mere combination of these parts, but rather in the dynamic system of actions, extending throughout the novel, by which the divergent intentions and beliefs of a large number of persons of different characters and states of knowledge belonging to or somehow related to the neighboring families of the Allworthys and the Westerns are made to cooperate, with the assistance of Fortune, first to bring Tom into an incomplete and precarious union, founded on an affinity of nature in spite of a disparity of status, with Allworthy and Sophia; then to separate him as completely as possible from them through actions that impel both of them, one after the other, to reverse their opinions of his character; and then, just as he seems about to fulfil the old prophecy that "he was certainly born to be hanged," to restore them unexpectedly to him in a more entire and stable union of both affection and fortune than he has known before.

The unity of *Tom Jones* is contained in this formula, but only potentially; and before we can properly discuss the plot as an artistic principle we must examine, in some detail, the intricate scheme of probabilities, involving moral choices, mistaken judgments, and accidents of Fortune, which binds its many parts together from the time we first see Tom in Allworthy's bed until we leave him, calmly enjoying his double good luck, at the end of Book XVIII.

There are three major stages in the action, the first of which, constituting in relation to the other two stages a "beginning," is complete by chapter vii of Book V. The starting point of everything is Bridget's scheme to provide security for both herself and her illegitimate son by palming off Tom on Allworthy as a foundling, with the intention, however, of ultimately informing her brother of the truth. The first part of the plan works beautifully: the affection which "the good man" at once conceives for the child assures Tom of a proper home and upbringing, and suspicion is diverted from his mother by Allworthy's discovery of parents for him, first in Jenny Jones (who, as Bridget's agent, is in the secret) and then in Partridge (who is not), and by the consequent departure of both of these from the neighborhood. In the end, too, Bridget's second purpose is fulfilled; but meanwhile she has put both parts of her scheme for Tom in jeopardy by her marriage (facilitated, again, by Allworthy's "penetration") with Captain Blifil. As a result, no early disclosure of Tom's true parentage is possible, and in addition the boy acquires a potential rival, in the younger Blifil, for both the affection and the fortune of Allworthy. On the other hand, although the intrigue against him begins immediately after the marriage, its only result at this stage, thanks to the goodness of Allworthy and the obvious innocence of Tom, is to make him thought of henceforth as the son of Partridge. This damages him in the eyes of the "world," but his status as protégé and heir, along with young Blifil, of the benevolent Allworthy is still secure and will remain secure so long as his protector has no reason to think him unworthy of his favor.

A second phase of the "beginning" opens in Book III, with the emergence of moral character in the two half-brothers. There are now, so far as Tom is concerned, two main problems. The first has to do with his relation to Allworthy, for whom by this time he has come to feel as strong an affection as Allworthy has felt, and continues to feel, for him. There can be no change on his part no matter what Allworthy does, since his feelings are based not on any opinion of interest but on the instinctive love of one good nature for another; and there can equally be no change on Allworthy's part that will lead to a separation between them unless something happens to convince him that Tom's nature is after all bad. That under certain circumstances Allworthy should be capable of such a verdict on Tom is made probable, generally, by the excessive confidence in his ability to judge of character which has led him long before to condemn Partridge, and, particularly, by his implicit and, in the face of Bridget's favoritism for Tom, even aggressive belief in the good intentions of young Blifil, as well as in the integrity of the learned men he has chosen, in his wisdom, as tutors for the two boys.

Occasions for passing judgment on Tom present themselves increasingly from his fourteenth year; and Blifil, seconded by Thwackum and Square, misses no chance of using them to blacken his character in his guardian's eyes. The occasions are given by Tom's well-intentioned but quixotic and imprudently managed actions toward Black George and his family, before and after his seduction by Molly. In the first series of these, no harm, in spite of Blifil, is done; on the contrary, as we are told, Tom by his generosity has "rather improved than injured the affection which Mr. Allworthy was inclined to entertain for him." And it is the same at first with the actions that culminate in Tom's mistaken confession that he is the father of Molly's child; angry as Allworthy is at Tom's incontinence, he is "no less pleased with the honour and honesty of his self-accusation" and he begins "to form in his mind the same opinion of this young fellow, which, we hope, our reader may have conceived"; it is only later, after having pardoned him, that he is induced by the sophistry of Square to entertain his "first bad impression concerning Jones." But even this is not fatal to Tom: he is assured again after his injury, though with a warning for the future, that what has happened is "all forgiven and forgotten"; he remains a beneficiary, in proportion to his supposed status, in Allworthy's will; and he is thought of by Allworthy, as we learn from the latter's speech in Book V, chapter vii, as one who has "much goodness, generosity, and honour" in his temper and needs only "prudence and religion" to make him actually happy. Fortune is still, however hesitatingly, on the side of Tom.

The other problem concerns the attachment that has been developing meanwhile between Tom and Sophia. The basis of the attachment is again one of likeness of nature, and the function of the incidents in Books IV and V in which the two are thrown together (Tom's intervention on behalf of Black George, his rescue of Sophia and his convalescence at her house, the affair of the muff, etc.) is simply to make credible its rapid progress, in spite of Tom's initial indifference and his entanglement with Molly, to the stage of mutual recognition reached in Book V, chapter vi. From this point on, we need not expect any change in Tom's feelings toward Sophia, no matter what he may do in his character as gallant; and there is an equally strong probability, in terms of her character, that Sophia will never cease to love Tom. She is, for one thing, a better judge of persons than Allworthy and is in no danger of being deceived, as he is, by the formal appearances of virtue in Blifil and of vice in Tom. "To say the truth, Sophia, when very young, discerned that Tom, though an idle, thoughtless, rattling rascal, was nobody's enemy but his own; and that Master Blifil, though a prudent, discreet, sober young gentleman, was at the same time strongly attached to the interest only of one single person . . ." (IV, v). She has, moreover, been even more completely aware than Allworthy of Tom's affair with Molly, and yet, for all her hurt pride, she has not altered her opinion of his worth; Tom will have to behave, or appear to behave, much worse than this before she will decide to cast him off. In the meantime, however, their union is apparently condemned by circumstances to be one of affection only. Her father, though very fond of Tom, will not approve a marriage which offers so little prospect of fortune for his beloved daughter; she will not act counter to her father's wishes, even though she will not agree to marry against her own feelings; and as for Tom, though his life is now "a constant struggle between honour and inclination," he can do nothing that will injure Sophia, show ingratitude to Western, or violate his more than filial piety toward Allworthy. The only possible resolution of their problem, it is plain, must be some event that will alter fundamentally Tom's position as a foundling.

Such an event is indeed impending at precisely this point in the action. For Bridget, dying, has just confided her secret to her attorney Dowling and has commanded him to carry the all-important message to Allworthy in fulfilment of the second part of her original design.

Blifil, however, aided by Fortune (which now turns temporarily against Tom), here intervenes, with two important results: immediately, that a chain of happenings is set in motion, constituting the "middle" of the plot, which leads to the complete separation of Tom from both Allworthy and Sophia; and remotely, that, when Bridget's message is at last delivered in Book XVIII, the position to which Tom is then restored is made, by reason of the delay, one of even greater security and happiness than would have been possible had his relationship to Allworthy become known at the time Bridget intended to reveal it.

The action from the moment when Bridget gives Dowling her message to the moment, many weeks later, when Allworthy receives it falls into three main parts. The first begins with Allworthy's illness and ends with Tom's expulsion and Sophia's flight. The events in this stage form a single complex sequence, in which Fortune conspires with the malice and ambition of Blifil, the pride and family tyranny of the Westerns, and the easily imposed-on sense of justice of Allworthy, first to thwart the purpose of Bridget and then to turn the indiscreet manifestations of Tom's love for Allworthy and joy at his recovery and of Sophia's love for Tom into occasions for the condemnation and banishment of Tom as "an abandoned reprobate" and for the persecution of Sophia as a recalcitrant daughter. The separating action of the novel thus comes to its first major climax, with Tom now resolved, for the sake of Sophia, to renounce her and leave the country, and with Sophia, unable to endure the prospect of a marriage with Blifil, determined to seek refuge in London with her cousin Lady Bellaston, not without hopes of again seeing Tom. Blifil, now dearer than ever to Allworthy because of Tom's "ill-treatment of that good young man," has apparently triumphed, though not completely, since Sophia is still out of his grasp. In reality, he has already made his fatal mistake, the mistake that will inevitably ruin him and restore Tom if and when Allworthy discovers it; and in addition, by driving Tom out, he has made it more rather than less probable that the truth he has concealed will eventually come to light, since, besides himself, it is also known, in part or in whole, to three other persons—Partridge, Jenny Jones, and Dowling—any or all of whom it is more likely now than before that Tom will meet.

This is, in fact, what happens during the next stage of the action, all the incidents of which converge on bringing Tom into contact, first with Partridge, then with Dowling, and finally with Jenny (now Mrs. Waters). The first meeting leads to a kind of negative resolution: Tom now knows that he is not Partridge's son. From the meetings with the others, who alone, save Blifil, know the whole truth, no resolution immediately follows, being prevented in both cases by the same causes that have determined Tom's fate hitherto: in the case of Jenny by Fortune, which sees to it that there is no encounter between her and Partridge at Upton; in the case of Dowling, who is ready to sell his knowledge for a price, by Tom's quixotic disinterestedness. The crucial discovery is thus postponed, but when we consider that Tom is now known to Dowling and to Jenny (though to the latter not as Bridget's son) and that both of these now become attached to persons in the Allworthy-Western circle—Jenny to Sophia's cousin-in-law Fitzpatrick and Dowling to Blifil—it is clear that the probability of its eventually taking place, and possibly in more auspicious circumstances, is increased rather than diminished by what has occurred.

In the meantime, with the happenings at Upton, the complication has entered its last and longest and, for Tom, most distressing phase, the climax of which, at the end of Book XVI, is his receipt in prison of Sophia's letter of condemnation and dismissal. The principal villain is again Fortune, which as we have been told (V, x), "seldom doth things by halves," and which, having already robbed Tom of the good will of Allworthy, now seems bent on completing his unhappiness by using his too complaisant good nature and his capacity for indiscretion to deprive him of Sophia and perhaps even of his life. It all begins with the chapter of accidents at the inn, where, because of his gallantry to Jenny, Tom first has an angry encounter with Fitzpatrick (who is seeking his runaway wife) and then misses Sophia, who departs at once on learning of his infidelity and makes her way, in the company of Mrs. Fitzpatrick, to London and Lady Bellaston. Some harm has now been done, but not much, as Tom learns when, having pursued her to London, he finally meets her again at Lady Bellaston's and is told, in a tender scene, that what has really disturbed her has not been so much his misconduct with Jenny, which she can forgive, as Partridge's free use of her name in public.

This happy resolution, however, comes too late; for already, although with the best intentions—namely, of finding his way to Sophia—Tom has been seduced into the affair with Lady Bellaston which is his closest approach, in the novel, to a base act. The affair does indeed lead him to Sophia, but only by chance, and then under circumstances which, while they do not betray him to Sophia, turn the wrath of his new mistress against her and lead to a fresh series of efforts to separate her from Tom. The first of these, the attempted rape by Lord Fellamar, is thwarted when Western, having learned of his daughter's whereabouts, rescues her in the nick of time and carries her away to his lodgings to face another course of family persecution and threats of imminent marriage to Blifil. It is on hearing of this that Tom, his thoughts now centered wholly on Sophia in spite of his despair of ever winning her, decides to break with Lady Bellaston, and adopts the expedient for doing so without dishonor which nearly leads to his ruin. For the effect of his proposal of marriage is to draw the Lady's vengeful feelings upon himself and Sophia at once, with the result that she arranges for his kidnapping by a press gang at the same time that she makes sure Sophia will never marry him by sending her the letter of proposal as proof of his villainy. With Sophia her scheme succeeds, so incapable of any other interpretation does the evidence seem. She is foiled, however, in her design against Tom, and once more by a delayed effect of the events at Upton. But the meeting which Fortune brings about with the still angry Fitzpatrick, though it saves Tom from being pressed into the navy, spares him only for what promises to be a worse fate.

The separating action has now come to its second major climax—much the more serious of the two for Tom, since he has not only lost Sophia as well as Allworthy but lost her, he thinks, as a direct result of his own vice and folly. He can still, if Fitzpatrick dies, be separated from his life, but otherwise all the possibilities of harm to him contained in his original situation have been exhausted. Not, however, all the possibilities of good; for the very same incidents proceeding from the affair at Upton which have so far been turned by Fortune against Tom have also had consequences which Fortune, bent upon doing nothing by halves, may yet exploit in his favor.

The most important of these in the long run is the moral change produced by his recent experiences in Tom himself, as manifested by his break with Lady Bellaston and by his rejection of the honorable advances of Mrs. Hunt and the dishonorable advances of Mrs. Fitzpatrick. It is not so much what he is, however, as what he is thought to be by Allworthy and Sophia that immediately counts; and he has had the good luck, by virtue of coming to London, of acquiring in Mrs. Miller a character witness who knows the best as well as the worst of him and who will at least be listened to by her old friend and benefactor Allworthy and perhaps by Sophia. There is, moreover, as a result of what has happened, rather less danger than before that Sophia, who, in spite of her reason, still loves Tom, will be forced to marry Blifil; for, though she is again in the power of her family, the machinations of Lady Bellaston have led to a conflict between the two Westerns over the rival merits of Blifil and Lord Fellamar. Time has thus been gained for Tom; and meanwhile Allworthy and Blifil have come up to town in response to Western's summons and have taken lodgings with Mrs. Miller. Dowling has come too, and so also has Jenny, now living with Fitzpatrick in lieu of the wife he has been seeking since Upton and whose whereabouts he has just learned. All those, in short, who know Bridget's secret—and Blifil's villainy in suppressing it at the time of her death—are now assembled, for the first time, in close proximity to Allworthy. And then Blifil, made overconfident by his success and believing Fitzpatrick about to die of his wound, decides to use the opportunity afforded by the presence of Lord Fellamar's press gang at the duel to strike one last blow at Tom.

But this time all the acts of Fortune work to the advantage of our hero, and the resolution moves rapidly to its end, first by the reunion of Tom with All-worthy and then by his reunion with Sophia. The first requires a reversal of Allworthy's judgment of Tom's character and actions at the time of his banish-ment. This is prepared by Mrs. Miller's insistence upon his present goodness and the services he has rendered her family, but the decisive event is the letter from the dying and repentant Square, which sets in a new light Tom's acts during Allworthy's illness, although without clearly implicating Blifil. The result is to restore Tom to his foster-father's affections more or less on the footing which he had at the beginning of Book V, but with the added circum-stance that he has since suffered unjust persecution. The new Tom is not yet fully known, or the entire extent and cause of the injuries that have been done him. Mrs. Miller indeed suspects, but the blindness of Allworthy prevents a discovery; and it requires a second intervention of Fortune, aided by the rash-ness of Blifil, to bring the revelation about. For not only does Blifil think Fitzpatrick's wound more serious than it is, but in his zeal to gather all possible evidence damaging to Tom he has made it inevitable that Jenny will come to know who Tom is, that she will at once go to Allworthy with her story, that Dowling will then be questioned, and that he, seeing where his profit now lies, will tell the truth about the suppression of Bridget's dying message. Thus here again Fortune has done nothing by halves, with the result that the exclusive place which Blifil has all along sought for himself in Allworthy's fortune and favor is now, with his unmasking and subsequent banishment, properly ac-corded to Tom. In relation to the original conditions of the action, moreover, the reversal is equally complete: Bridget's intended disclosure of her secret has at last been made, and with it both of her mistakes—of concealing Tom's parentage and then of marrying the elder Blifil—are finally canceled out.

The reunion with Sophia is likewise prepared by Mrs. Miller, who is able to convince her that Tom's letter proposing marriage to Lady Bellaston was at worst an indiscretion. But though Allworthy also intervenes on his nephew's behalf and though Western is now as violent an advocate for Tom as he has earlier been for Blifil, the resolution comes only when Sophia, faced with the repentant young man, finds once more (as after his previous affairs with Molly and Jenny) that her love for him is stronger than her injured pride and that it is now a pleasure to be able to obey her father's commands.

It is in nothing short of this total system of actions, moving by probable or necessary connections from beginning, through middle, to end, that the unity of the plot of *Tom Jones* is to be found. It is the unity, clearly, of a complex plot, built on two continuous but contrary lines of probability, both stemming from the double scheme of Bridget respecting Tom and from her marriage with Captain Blifil, and both reinforced, from Book III onward, by the combination in Tom's character of goodness and indiscretion: the one producing immediately, throughout the complication, ever more bad fortune and distress for Tom, the other at the same time preparing for him the good luck he finally comes to enjoy after the discovery and reversal in Book XVIII. It is no wonder that this "plot," in which so many incidents, involving so many surprising turns, are all subsumed so brilliantly under one principle of action, should have been praised by all those critics from the eighteenth century to the present who have had a taste for intricate and ingenious constructions of this kind.

If the plot of *Tom Jones* is still to be praised, however, it ought to be for reasons more relevant than these to the special artistic quality of the novel we continue to read. For what has just been outlined as the "plot" is obviously something from which, if we had never read the work itself, we could hardly predict with any assurance how Fielding's masterpiece, as composed for readers in a particularized sequence of words, paragraphs, chapters, and books, would be likely to affect our opinions and feelings. It is therefore not the plot proper of this novel but, at most, its necessary substrate of unified and probable action; and, if we are to say what the plot proper is and be able to use our account for critical purposes, we must go beyond the material system of happenings—however intrinsically admirable this may be in its ordered magnitude—and look for the formal principle which makes of this system a definitely effective whole and which actually operates, in so far as we concentrate closely on the text, to direct our emotionalized expectations for Tom and the others and our subsequent responses when the hoped-for or feared events occur.[13]

13. The distinction can also be stated in terms of the decisions Fielding had to make in writing the novel. It would obviously not have been the novel it is, had he not conceived, at some stage of the process of construction, the particular system of actions I have sketched above; but, on the other hand, the conception merely of this intricate scheme of incidents would have been insufficient to allow him to proceed securely in the writing without a further decision, or complex of decisions, as to the precise nature of the over-all effect, among

III

In stating this principle for any plot, we must consider three things : (1) the general estimate we are induced to form, by signs in the work, of the moral character and deserts of the hero, as a result of which we tend, more or less ardently, to wish for him either good or bad fortune in the end; (2) the judgments we are led similarly to make about the nature of the events that actually befall the hero or seem likely to befall him, as having either painful or pleasurable consequences for him, and this in greater or less degree and permanently or temporarily; and (3) the opinions we are made to entertain concerning the degree and kind of his reponsibility for what happens to him, as being either little or great and, if the latter, the result either of his acting in full knowledge of what he is doing or of some sort of mistake. The form of a given plot is a function of the particular correlation among these three variables which the completed work is calculated to establish, consistently and progressively, in our minds; and in these terms we may say that the plot of *Tom Jones* has a pervasively comic form. The precise sense, however, in which the form is comic is a rather special one, which needs to be carefully defined.

To begin with, it is obviously a plot in which the complication generates much pain and inner suffering for the hero, as a result of misfortunes which would seem genuinely serious to any good person. He is schemed against by a villain who will not stop even at judicial murder to secure his ends, and, what is worse in his eyes, he loses the good will of the two people whom he most loves, and loses it as a consequence not simply of the machinations of his enemies but of his own mistaken acts. From near the beginning until close to the end, moreover, he is made to undergo an almost continuous series of distressing indignities : to be insulted on the score of his birth, to be forbidden the sight of Sophia, to see her being pushed into a hated marriage with Blifil and persecuted when she refuses, to be banished abruptly from home, to be reduced to poverty and forced to take money from Lady Bellaston, to be laid in wait for by a press gang, to be compelled to run a man through in self-defense, and finally, in prison, to be faced with the prospect of a disgraceful death.

The hero, furthermore, to whom all this happens is a naturally good man—

---

several more or less distinct possibilities, he wished his story to have on its readers. The plot proper of *Tom Jones* is thus not its system of actions alone but this system so qualified, with respect to its "working or power," as to determine specifically rather than generally the successive artistic problems which Fielding faced in putting it into words. It is only in this sense that we can speak intelligently or usefully of "plot" as a constructive first principle in *Tom Jones* or in any other imitative novel or drama.

I should add that several of my friends, while willing to accept the foregoing analysis, would prefer that I should use some other word than "plot" to designate the formal principle I have been attempting to define. I am inclined to agree with them, and only wish that they or I could think of a better term.

not notably virtuous, but, for all his faults, at least the equal of ourselves and of any other character in the novel in disinterestedness, generosity, and tender benevolent feeling. These traits are impressed upon us in the third book and are never obscured even in the worst of Tom's troubles in London; they are, in fact, revivified for us, just at the point when we might be most tempted to forget them, by the episodes of Anderson and of Mrs. Miller's daughter. We favor Tom, therefore, even if we do not admire him, and we wish for him the good fortune with Allworthy and Sophia which he properly wishes for himself and which, in terms of his basic moral character, he deserves to get. We follow him through his troubles and distresses, consequently, with a desire that he will eventually be delivered from them and reunited to his friend and mistress, and this all the more when, at the climax of his difficulties, we see him acting, for the first time, in a way we can entirely approve; in the end, when our wishes for him are unexpectedly realized, and to a fuller degree than we had anticipated, we feel some of the satisfaction which Fielding says (XVIII, xiii) was then felt by the principal characters themselves. "All were happy, but those the most who had been most unhappy before. Their former sufferings and fears gave such a relish to their felicity as even love and fortune, in their fullest flow, could not have given without the advantage of such a comparison."

Having conceived a plot in which so sympathetic a character is subjected in the complication to experiences so painful, it would have been relatively easy for Fielding to write a novel similar in form to his *Amelia*, that is to say, a tragicomedy of common life designed to arouse and then to dissipate, by a sudden happy resolution, emotions of fear and pity for his hero and of indignation toward his enemies. There is, indeed, an even greater material basis for such an effect in *Tom Jones* than in the later novel: the evils that threaten Tom and the indignities he undergoes are, in the abstract, more serious than anything Booth has to fear, and the same thing is true of the persecutions endured by Sophia as compared with those which Amelia is made to suffer. And yet nothing is more evident than that, whereas the emotions awakened in us by the distresses of Booth and Amelia are the graver emotions of anxiety and compassion that yield what Fielding calls "the pleasure of tenderness,"[14] our feelings for Tom and Sophia, as we anticipate or view in actuality the greater evils that befall them prior to the final discovery, partake only in the mildest degree of this painful quality. We do not actively fear for or pity either of them, and our indignation at the actions of their enemies—even the actions of Blifil—never develops into a sustained punitive response.

Nor is the reason for this hard to find. It is generally the case that whatever tends to minimize our fear in a plot that involves threats of undeserved misfor-

14. *Amelia*, Book III, chap. i.

tune for the sympathetic characters tends also to minimize our pity when the misfortune occurs and likewise our indignation against the doers of the evil; and fear for Tom and Sophia as they move toward the successive climaxes of their troubles is prevented from becoming a predominant emotion in the complication of *Tom Jones* chiefly by two things.[15]

The first is our perception, which in each case grows stronger as the novel proceeds, that the persons whose actions threaten serious consequences for the hero and heroine are all persons for whom, though in varying degrees, we are bound to feel a certain contempt. The most formidable of them all is of course Blifil. As a villain, however, he is no Iago but merely a clever opportunist who is likely to overreach himself (as the failure of his first schemes shows) and whose power of harm depends entirely on the blindness of Allworthy; he deceives Tom only temporarily and Sophia and Mrs. Miller not at all; and after we have seen the display of his personal ineptitude in the proposal scene with Sophia, we are prepared to wait, without too much active suspense, for his final showing-up. Blifil is too coldly selfish, perhaps, to strike us as positively ridiculous, but in the characters of the other agents of misfortune the comic strain is clear. It is most obvious, needless to say, in Squire Western and his sister: who can really fear that the persecutions directed against the determined and resourceful Sophia by such a blundering pair of tyrants can ever issue in serious harm? For Allworthy, too, in spite of his excellent principles, it is hard for us to maintain entire respect; we should certainly take more seriously his condemnation of Tom in Book VI had we not become accustomed, as a result of earlier incidents in the novel, to smile at a man who could believe in the goodness of the two Blifils and whose pride in his own judgment could make him dispose so precipitously of Jenny and Partridge. There are evident comic traits also in all the persons who cause trouble for Tom and Sophia in the later part of the action: in Dowling, the man always in a hurry; in Lady Bellaston, the great dame who pursues a plebeian with frenzied letters and nocturnal visits to his lodgings; in Lord Fellamar, the half-hearted rake; in Fitzpatrick, the unfaithful but jealous husband who will not believe the evidence of his own eyes. In respect of her relations with Tom, though not otherwise, Sophia, too, must be added to the list, as a virtuous girl with a proper amount of spirit (not to say vanity) whose good resolutions against Tom never survive for long in the presence of her lover. These are all manifestations of the ineffectual or ridiculous in a plot in which the impending events are materially painful, and

15. I confine myself here to devices in some sense implicit in the plot itself as distinguished from devices, serving the same purpose, which involve Fielding's manner of representation; on the latter, see Section IV, below. A full solution of the problem would also have to take into account, as one of my friends reminds me, such things as the choice of names for the characters and the general nonserious expectations suggested by the title of the work.

they contribute, on the principle that we fear less or not at all when the agents of harm to a hero are more or less laughable persons, to induce in us a general feeling of confidence that matters are not really as serious as they appear.

A second ground of security lies in the nature of the probabilities for future action that are made evident progressively as the novel unfolds. From the beginning until the final capitulation of Sophia, the successive incidents constantly bring forth new and unexpected complications, each seemingly fraught with more suffering for Tom than the last; but as we read we instinctively infer from past occurrences to what will probably happen next or in the end, and what steadily cumulates in this way, in spite of the gradual worsening of Tom's situation, is an opinion that, since nothing irreparable has so far happened to him, nothing ever will. In one sense—that which relates to its material events— the action becomes more and more serious as it moves to its climax, in another sense—that which relates to our expectations—less and less serious; and I think that any close reader who keeps in mind the earlier parts of the novel as he attends to the later is inevitably made aware of this, with the result that, though his interest mounts, his fear increasingly declines. We come thus to the first climax in Book VI recalling such things as Jenny's assurance to All- worthy that she will someday make known the whole truth, the sudden re- versal of the elder Blifil's sinister plans, the collapse, after initial success, of young Blifil's first scheme against Tom, and Tom's return to favor with All- worthy after the incident of Molly's arrest; and all these memories inevitably operate to check the rise of any long-range apprehensions. And it is the same, too, with the second and apparently much more serious climax at the end of Book XVI, when Tom, dismissed by Sophia, lies in prison awaiting the death of Fitzpatrick, who has been given up by his surgeon: we cannot but remember how, in the affairs of Molly and then of Mrs. Waters, Sophia has more than once demonstrated her inability to inflict any great or prolonged punishment on Tom for his sins with other women and how, on the occasion of Allworthy's illness in Book V, the outcome had completely disappointed the gloomy pre- dictions of the doctor.

The attenuation, in these ways, of fear, pity, and indignation is a necessary condition of the peculiar comic pleasure which is the form of the plot in *Tom Jones*, but it is only a negative and hence not a sufficient condition. A comic effect of any kind would be impossible if we took Tom's increasingly bad prospects with the same seriousness as he himself takes them, but what in a positive sense makes Fielding's plot comic is the combination of this feeling of security with our perception of the decisive role which Tom's own blunders are made to play, consistently, in the genesis of all the major difficulties into which he is successively brought—always, of course, with the eager assistance of Fortune and of the malice or misunderstanding of others. The importance of this becomes clear when we consider how much trouble he would have spared himself had he not mistaken his seduction by Molly for a seduction of her by him; had he not got drunk when he learned of Allworthy's recovery or fought with Blifil and Thwackum; had he not suggested to Western that he be allowed to plead Blifil's case with Sophia; had he not allowed himself to be seduced by Jenny at Upton; had he not thought that his very love for Sophia, to say nothing of his gallantry, required him "to keep well" with the lady at the masquerade; and, lastly, had he not accepted so uncritically Nightingale's scheme for compelling her to break off the affair.

The truth is that each successive stage of the plot up to the beginning of the denouement in Book XVII is precipitated by a fresh act of imprudence or indiscretion on the part of Tom, for which he is sooner or later made to suffer not only in his fortune but his feelings, until in the resolution of each sequence, he discovers that the consequences of his folly are after all not so serious as he has feared. This characteristic pattern emerges, even before the start of the complication proper, in the episode of Tom's relations with Molly and Sophia in Book IV and the first part of Book V; it dominates the prolonged suspense of his relations with Allworthy from the time of the latter's illness to the final discovery; and it determines the course of his troubles with Sophia from Upton to the meeting in London and from the ill-conceived proposal scheme to her sudden surrender at the end.

The comic pleasure all this gives us is certainly not of the same kind as that produced by such classic comic plots as (say) Ben Jonson's *The Silent Woman* or, to take a more extreme instance of the type, his *Volpone*, in which a morally despicable person is made, by reason of his own folly or lapse from cleverness, to suffer a humiliating and, to him, though not to others, painful reversal of fortune. The comedy of Blifil is indeed of this simple punitive kind,[16] but our suspense concerning Blifil is only in a secondary way determinative of the effect of Fielding's novel, and the comedy of Tom and hence of the plot as a whole is of a different sort. It is not simple comedy but mixed, the peculiar power of which depends upon the fact that the mistaken acts of the hero which principally excite our amusement are the acts of a man for whom throughout the plot we entertain sympathetic feelings because of the general goodness of his character: we do not want, therefore, to see him suffer any permanent indignity or humiliation, and we never cease to wish good fortune for him. This favorable attitude, moreover, is not contradicted by anything in the acts themselves from which his trouble springs. We perceive that in successive situations, in-

---

16. I borrow this term from Elder Olson's "An Outline of Poetic Theory" (see above, p. 555).

volving threats to his fortune or peace of mind, he invariably does some imprudent or foolish thing, which cannot fail, the circumstances being what, in
our superior knowledge, we see them to be, to result for him in painful embarrassment and regret; but we realize that his blunders arise from no permanent weakness of character but are merely the natural errors of judgment,
easily corrigible in the future, of an inexperienced and too impulsively generous
and gallant young man. We look forward to the probable consequences of his
indiscretions, therefore, with a certain anticipatory reluctance and apprehension—a kind of faint alarm which is the comic analogue of fear; it is some such
feeling, I think, that we experience, if only momentarily, when Tom gets
drunk and goes into the wood with Molly and when, much later, he sends his
proposal letter to Lady Bellaston. We know that trouble, more trouble than the
young man either foresees or deserves, is in store for him as a result of what
he has done, and since, foolish as he is, we favor him against his enemies, the
expectation of his inevitable suffering cannot be purely and simply pleasant.

And yet the expectation is never really painful in any positive degree, and
it is kept from becoming so by our counter-expectation, established by the
devices I have mentioned, that, however acute may be Tom's consequent sufferings, his mistakes will not issue in any permanent frustration of our wishes
for his good. In this security that no genuine harm has been done, we can view
his present distresses—as when he anguishes over the wrong he thinks he has
done to Molly, or finds Sophia's muff in his bed at Upton, or receives her
letter—as the deserved consequences of erroneous actions for which any good
man would naturally feel embarrassment or shame. We do not therefore pity
him in these moments, for all his self-accusations and cries of despair, but
rather laugh at him as a man who has behaved ridiculously or beneath himself
and is now being properly punished. And our comic pleasure continues into the
subsequent resolving scenes—the discovery of Molly in bed with Square, the
meeting with Sophia in London, and the final anticlimax of her agreement to
marry him the next morning—when it appears that Tom has after all worried
himself overmuch; for we now see that he has been doubly ridiculous, at first
in not taking his situation seriously enough and then in taking it more seriously
than he should. But Tom is a good man, and we expect him to get better, and
so our amused reaction to his sufferings lacks entirely the punitive quality that
characterizes comedy of the Jonsonian type. If the anticipatory emotion is a
mild shudder of apprehension, the climactic emotion—the comic analogue of
pity—is a kind of friendly mirth at his expense ("poor Tom," we say to ourselves), which easily modulates, in the happy denouement, into unsentimental
rejoicing at his not entirely deserved good fortune.

This, however, is not quite all; for not only does Tom's final good fortune seem to us at least partly undeserved in terms of his own behavior, but we realize, when we look back from the end upon the long course of the action, that he has, in truth, needed all the luck that has been his. Again and again he has been on the verge of genuinely serious disaster; and, though we expect him to survive and hence do not fear for him in prospect, we perceive, at the resolution of each of his major predicaments, that there has been something of a hair's breadth quality in his escape. The cards have indeed been stacked against him; from the beginning to the ultimate discovery, he has been a young man whose lack of security and imprudence more than offset his natural goodness, living in a world in which the majority of people are ill-natured and selfish, and some of them actively malicious, and in which the few good persons are easily imposed upon by appearances. It is against this background of the potentially serious—more than ever prominent in the London scenes—that the story of Tom's repeated indiscretions is made to unfold, with the result that, though the pleasure remains consistently comic, its quality is never quite that of the merely amiable comedy, based likewise upon the blunders of sympathetic protagonists, of such works as *She Stoops To Conquer* or *The Rivals*. We are not disposed to feel, when we are done laughing at Tom, that all is right with the world or that we can count on Fortune always intervening, in the same gratifying way, on behalf of the good.

IV

This or something very close to this, I think, is the intended "working or power" of *Tom Jones*, and the primary question for the critic concerns the extent to which Fielding's handling of the constituent parts of the novel is calculated to sustain and maximize this special pleasure which is its form.

It must be said that he sometimes fails. There are no perfect works of art, and, though many of the faults that have been found in *Tom Jones* are faults only on the supposition that it should have been another kind of novel, still enough real shortcomings remain to keep one's enthusiasm for Fielding's achievement within reasonable bounds. There are not infrequent *longueurs*, notably in the Man of the Hill's story (whatever positive values this may have), in Mrs. Fitzpatrick's narrative to Sophia (useful as this is in itself), in the episode of Tom's encounter with the gypsies, and in the final complications of the Nightingale affair. With the best will in the world, too, it is impossible not to be shocked by Tom's acceptance of fifty pounds from Lady Bellaston on the night of his first meeting with her at the masquerade and his subsequent emergence as "one of the best-dressed men about town"; it is necessary, no doubt, that he should now fall lower than ever before, but surely not so low as to make it hard for us to infer his act from our previous knowledge of his character and of the rather modest limits hitherto of his financial need; for the moment at least, a different Tom is before our eyes. And there are also more general faults. The narrator, for one thing, though it is well that he should intrude, perhaps intrudes too much in a purely ornamental way; the introductory essays, thus, while we should not like to lose them from the canon of Fielding's writings, serve only occasionally the function of chorus, and the returns from them, even as embellishment, begin to diminish before the end. What chiefly strikes the modern reader, however, is the extent of Fielding's reliance, in the novel as a whole, on techniques of narrative now largely abandoned by novelists who have learned their art since the middle of the nineteenth century. It could be shown, I think, that as compared with most of his predecessors, the author of *Tom Jones* had moved a long way in the direction of the imitative and dramatic. Yet it cannot be denied that in many chapters where he might better have "rendered" he merely "states" and that even in the most successful of the scenes in which action and dialogue predominate he leaves far less to inference than we are disposed to like.[17]

Despite all this, however, there are not many novels of comparable length in which the various parts are conceived and developed with a shrewder eye to what is required for a maximum realization of the form.[18] A few examples of this will have to serve, and it is natural to start with the manner in which Fielding handles the incidents that follow directly from Tom's mistakes. The pattern of all of these is much the same. Tom first commits an indiscretion, which is then discovered, and the discovery results in his immediate or eventual embarrassment. Now it is clear that the comic pleasure will be enhanced in proportion as, in each incident, the discovery is made unexpectedly and by precisely those persons whose knowledge of what Tom has done will be most damaging to him, and by as many of these as possible so that the consequences for him are not simple but compounded. Fielding understood this well, and the effects of his understanding are repeatedly evident in *Tom Jones*, from Book IV to the end of the complication. Consider, for example, how he manages the discovery of Tom's original entanglement with Molly. It is necessary, of course, when Molly is arrested after the fight in the churchyard, that Tom should at once rush to Allworthy with his mistaken confession; but it is not necessary—only highly desirable—that he should intervene in the fight himself as Molly's champion, that Blifil and Square should be with him at the time, that the news of the arrest should reach him while he is dining with Western and Sophia, whose charm he is just beginning to perceive, and that, when he leaves in a

17. Perhaps the chief exception to this, in its relatively large use of "intimation," is the scene of Tom's conversation with Dowling in Book XII, chap. x.

18. I am indebted for several points in what follows to an unpublished essay by one of my students, Mr. Melvin Seiden.

hurry, the Squire should joke with his daughter about what he suspects. Or, again, there is the even more complicated and comically disastrous sequence that begins with Tom's drunkenness after Allworthy's recovery. This in itself is ridiculous, since we know the illness has never been serious; but observe how the succeeding embarrassments are made to pile up: Tom's hilarious joy leading to his fight with Blifil; this to his retirement to the grove, his romantic meditation on Sophia, and his surrender to Molly; this to the discovery of his new folly by Blifil and Thwackum; this to the second fight, much bloodier than the first; and this in turn, when the Westerns unexpectedly appear on the scene, to Sophia's fresh discovery of Tom's wildness and, what is much more serious, to the misconstruction of her fainting fit by her aunt, with results that lead presently to the proposal of a match with Blifil, the foolish intervention of Tom, the discovery by Western of the true state of affairs, his angry appeal to Allworthy, Blifil's distorted version of what has happened, Tom's expulsion from home, and Sophia's imprisonment. All this is probable enough, but there is something of the comically wonderful in the educing of so many appropriately extreme consequences from a cause in itself so apparently innocent and trivial. And the same art of making the most out of incidents for the sake of the comic suspense of the plot can be seen at work through the rest of the novel: in the great episode at Upton, for example, where all the happenings are contrived to produce, immediately or remotely, a maximum of pseudo-serious suffering for Tom, and also in the various later scenes in which the discovery to Sophia of Tom's intrigue with her cousin is first narrowly averted, with much embarrassment to him, and then finally made under circumstances that could hardly be worse for the young man. A less accomplished artist seeking to achieve the same general effect through his plot would certainly have missed many of these opportunities.

A less accomplished artist, again, would never have been able to invent or sustain characters so good for the form, as well as so interesting in themselves, as the two Westerns and Partridge. We need not dwell on the multiple uses to which these great humorists are put; it is more important, since the point has been less often discussed, or discussed in part to Fielding's disadvantage, to consider what merits can be found in his handling of the other characters, such as Tom himself, Allworthy, Sophia, and Blifil, who are intended to seem morally sympathetic or antipathetic to us and comically inferior only by virtue of their erroneous acts. With the exception of Sophia, who is made charming and lively enough to constitute in herself good fortune for Tom, they are not endowed with any notably particularized traits, and the question for criticism is whether, given the comic form of the novel as a whole, any more lifelike "doing" would not have entailed a departure from the mean which this imposed. I think the answer is clear for Blifil: he must be made to seem sufficiently formidable in the short run to arouse comic apprehension for Tom but not so formidable as to excite in us active or prolonged feelings of indignation; and any further individualizing of him than we get would almost certainly have upset this balance to the detriment of the whole. The answer is clear also, I think, for Tom. We must consistently favor him against his enemies and think it probable that he should suffer acute embarrassment and remorse when he discovers the consequences of his mistakes; but, on the other hand, any appreciably greater particularizing of his sympathetic traits than is attempted would inevitably have made it difficult for us not to feel his predicaments as seriously as he does himself, and that would have been an error; it is not the least happy of Fielding's inventions, for example, that he repeatedly depicts Tom, especially when he is talking to Sophia or thinking about her, in terms of the clichés of heroic romance. There remains Allworthy, and concerning him the chief doubt arises from a consideration of the important part he is given, along with Sophia, in the definition of Tom's final good fortune. For the purposes of the comic complication it is sufficient that we should see him acting in the character of a severely just magistrate who constantly administers injustice through too great trust in his knowledge of men; it is not for this, however, but for his "amiability" that Tom loves him and cherishes his company in the end; yet of Allworthy's actual possession of that quality we are given few clear signs.

A whole essay, finally, could be written on the masterly way in which Fielding exploited the various devices implicit in his third-person "historical" mode of narration in the service of his comic form. Broadly speaking, his problem was twofold: first, to establish and maintain in the reader a general frame of mind appropriate to the emotional quality of the story as a whole and, second, to make sure that the feelings aroused by his characters at particular moments or stages of the action were kept in proper alignment with the intended over-all effect.

That the first problem is adequately solved there can be little doubt; long before we come to the incidents in which Tom's happiness is put in jeopardy by his own blunders and the malice of Blifil, we have been prepared to expect much unmerited calamity and distress for him, and at the same time to view the prospect without alarm. Our security would doubtless have been less had not Fielding chosen to represent at length the events contained in Books I and II, with the vivid impressions they give of the fallibility of Allworthy on the one hand and of the impotence for permanent harm of the elder Blifil on the other: we cannot but look forward to a repetition of this pattern in the later parts of the novel. This is less important, however, as a determinant of our frame of mind than the guidance given us by the clearly evident attitude of

Fielding's narrator. He is, we perceive, a man we can trust, who knows the whole story and still is not deeply concerned; one who understands the difference between good men and bad and who can yet speak with amused indulgence of the first, knowing how prone they are to weakness of intellect, and with urbane scorn, rather than indignation, of the second, knowing that most of them, too, are fools. This combination of sympathetic moral feeling with ironical detachment is bound to influence our expectations from the first, and to the extent that it does so, we tend to anticipate the coming troubles with no more than comic fear.

It is when the troubles come, in Book V and later, that Fielding's second problem emerges; for, given the kinds of things that then happen to Tom and especially the seriousness with which, as a good man, he necessarily takes them, there is always a danger that our original comic detachment may give way, temporarily, to tragicomic feelings of fear, pity, and indignation. That this seldom happens is another sign of how successfully, in *Tom Jones*, the handling of the parts is kept consonant with the formal demands of the whole. It is a question primarily of maximizing the general comic expectations of the reader by minimizing the possible noncomic elements in his inferences about particular situations; and the devices which Fielding uses for the purpose are of several kinds. Sometimes the result is achieved by preventing our attention from concentrating long or closely on potential causes of distress for Tom; it is notable, for example, that we are given no representation of Blifil scheming Tom's ruin before his speech to Allworthy in Book VI, chapter xi, and that from this point until Book XVI Blifil and his intentions are not again brought to the fore. Sometimes the device consists in slurring over a painful scene by generalized narration and then quickly diverting us to an obviously comic sequence in another line of action: this is what Fielding does, to excellent effect, with the incident of Tom's condemnation and banishment; we should feel much more keenly for him if, in the first place, we were allowed to hear more of his talk with Allworthy and, in the second place, were not plunged so soon after into the ridiculous quarrels of the Westerns. Or, again, the expedient may take the simple form of a refusal by the narrator to describe feelings of Tom which, if they were represented directly and at length, might easily excite a non-comic response; as in the accounts of his "madness" at Upton after he finds Sophia's muff and of the torments he endures ("such that even Thwackum would almost have pitied him") when her message of dismissal comes to him in prison. And the same general minimizing function is also served by the two episodes in the middle part of the novel which have occasioned so much discussion among critics. Both the story told to Tom by the Man of the Hill and that recounted to Sophia by Mrs. Fitzpatrick, however much they owe to the convention of interpolated narratives which Fielding had inherited, along with other devices, from the earlier writers of "comic romance," are clearly designed as negative analogies to the moral state of the listeners, from which the reader is led to infer, on the eve of the most distressing part of the complication for the hero and heroine, that nothing that may happen to them will be, in comparison, very bad.

The controlling influence of the form can be seen in all these expedients, and it is no less apparent in Fielding's handling of the intrigue upon which the action of the novel ultimately depends—Bridget's affair with Summer, her scheme of temporary concealment and eventual disclosure of Tom's parentage, and the frustration of the second of these intentions, until the denouement, by Blifil. Without this series of events and the consequences they entail in the opinions and acts of the characters, the plot as we have it could not have existed; but there was nothing in the nature of the events themselves to prescribe the particular manner in which they must be brought before the reader. At least two alternative modes of procedure were open to Fielding besides the one he actually chose. He could, on the one hand, have let the reader into the secret, either from the beginning or at the point in Book V where Bridget's dying message is brought by Dowling: in the former case a brief statement by the narrator would have been sufficient (since he plainly knows the facts); in the latter case, a brief report, for which there are precedents elsewhere in the novel, of Blifil's thoughts. Or, on the other hand, he could have contrived to keep our curiosity regarding the mystery more continuously and actively awake, especially in the long stretches of the story between Book III and the final scenes in London: this need not again have required any invention of new incidents, but only manipulations of the narrative discourse, such as an explicit direction of the reader's mind to the circumstance that Dowling brought a letter from Bridget as well as the news of her death, a hint that Blifil now had some new and surprising information about Tom, and an occasional reminder thereafter that the full truth concerning Tom's birth was still to be learned and that it might, when known, have important bearings, for good or possibly for ill, upon his fortunes.

Given, however, the form which Fielding, according to our hypothesis, was attempting to impose on the materials of his plot, with its distinctive line of seriocomic expectations and desires, either of these two courses would clearly have been incorrect. The second would have injected into the middle sections of the narrative a competing principle of suspense, diverting our attention unduly from the question of what is likely to befall Tom as a result of his mistakes to the question of who he is; the novel would then have become in fact the mystery story which, on a partial and erroneous view, it has sometimes been taken to be. And the consequences of the other course would have been equally, perhaps more, disruptive. For the complication in that case would have become, in large part, the story of a completely foreseen and wished-for discovery repeatedly deferred, with the result, on the one hand, that our complacency about the eventual outcome would have been increased to such a degree as sensibly to lessen our comic fear and hence our comic mirth in the successive anticlimactic reversals and, on the other hand, that our preoccupation with the comic aspects of Tom's well-intentioned blunderings would have tended to give way excessively to a concern with the original injustice done him by Bridget and with the villainy of Blifil. A mean between emphasis on the existence of a mystery and full revelation of the secret to the reader was therefore indicated as the right technique, and it was his perception of this that guided Fielding's procedure both in Books I and II, where the question of Tom's parentage is formally inquired into by Allworthy and settled to his own satisfaction, and in Books V–XVII, where the question is reopened, in intent but not in result, first by the confession of Bridget and then by the advances of Dowling to Tom. Something close to the proper mean is achieved by concentrating the narrative in the opening books on the objective acts and declarations of Bridget, Jenny, and Partridge subsequent to the finding of Tom in Allworthy's bed and representing these by signs sufficiently ambiguous so that, although we discount the inferences drawn by Allworthy from the behavior of the two supposed parents, we are yet given no adequate premises from which to reason to any particular alternative explanation. We surmise that one will ultimately be forthcoming, but in the meantime we are easily persuaded by the narrator to suspend our curiosity, especially since we perceive that neither of Allworthy's discoveries will make any difference in his treatment of Tom. We are predisposed therefore to yield our attention to the events recounted in the middle books of the novel without active speculation concerning their remoter causes or growing impatience for further disclosures. Ambiguous disclosures do indeed continue to be made. There is the pervasive irony (in the world of this novel) of a young man assumed by nearly everyone in his circle, including himself, to be base-born who yet manifests all the signs, in appearance and sensibility, of being a gentleman and is regularly taken as one by strangers until they learn his story; and there are also the more specific clues to the real state of affairs afforded by Bridget's increasing preference for Tom as he grows up, the suddenly intensified animosity of Blifil toward the foundling after he learns the content of Bridget's message, Partridge's disavowal of the role in which he has been cast as Tom's father, and, most pointed of all, Dowling's sly reference to "your uncle" in the interview which he forces on Tom in Book XII. But though hints of the truth are thus given in the events themselves, it is only in retrospect, at the moment of the discovery scene in Book XVIII, that we grasp their cumulative import; so effectively, in the narrator's discourse up to the very eve of this scene, has the question of who Tom is been kept subordinate to the question, upon which the main comic effect depends, of what will immediately follow from his imprudent acts.

V

These are only a few of the things that can be said, in the light of our general hypothesis about plot, concerning the plot of *Tom Jones* and the relation to it of the other parts of the novel. I have given no consideration, thus, either to the functions served by the minor characters and by the many passages of extra-dramatic thought in defining the moral quality of the "world" in which the action takes place, or to the formal purposes governing Fielding's highly selective use of dialogue, or to the manner in which the diction and imagery of the narrative parts help to hold our responses to the right comic line even when the incidents themselves seem most serious.

An adequate study of the plot of *Tom Jones* considered as a first principle of artistic construction would require answers to these and possibly still other questions, all of them of a kind which the traditional ways of discussing works with "plots" have tended to leave out of account. My intention, however, has been not so much to attempt a revaluation of *Tom Jones* as to make clear the assumptions and illustrate some of the possibilities for practical criticism of a kind of whole-part analysis of narrative compositions such as has not too often, I think, been undertaken. Like all critical methods it has its limitations, and it must be judged, accordingly, in terms not only of the problems it is peculiarly fitted to deal with but of those which lie beyond its scope. Its distinctive character derives, in the first place, from the fact that it views a work of art as a dynamic whole which affects our emotions in a certain way through the functioning together of its elements in subordination to a determinate poetic form. It is better suited, therefore, to exhibit the degree of efficiency with which the parts of a work or section thereof contribute to the maximum achievement of its effect than to do full justice to the qualities over and above this which characterize, in all fine works, the development of the parts themselves: there are many strokes in the representation of Partridge, for instance, which no one would wish away, yet which are bound to seem gratuitous when considered merely in the light of his somewhat minor role in the evolution of the comic action.[19] The method, again, is specific, in the sense that it seeks to appraise

19. The kind of thing I have in mind is well illustrated by the late George Orwell's remarks on the "unnecessary detail" in Dickens (see his *Dickens, Dali & Others* [New York, 1946], pp. 59–65). Of the same order is the following sentence from the account of the fight with the captain in *Joseph Andrews*, Book III, chap. xi (italics mine): "The uplifted hanger

a writer's performance in a given work in relation to the nature and requirements of the particular task he has set himself, the assumed end being the perfection of the work as an artistic whole of the special kind he decided it should be. It is a method better adapted, consequently, to the appreciation of success or failure in individual works than it is to the making of comparative judgments based on criteria of literary "greatness" or "seriousness" that transcend differences of kind: we clearly need other terms and distinctions than those provided by a poetics of forms if we are to talk discriminatingly about the general qualities of intelligence and feeling reflected in *Tom Jones* or even be able to defend Fielding against the recent, and surely somewhat insensitive, judgment that his "attitudes and his concern with human nature, are simple, and not such as to produce an effect of anything but monotony (on a mind, that is, demanding more than external action) when exhibited at the length of an 'epic in prose.' "[20] Finally, the method is one which depends on the analytical isolation of works of art, as finished products, from the circumstances and processes of their origin. It is therefore better fitted to explain those effects in a work which would be specifically the same in any other work, of whatever date, that was constructed in accordance with the same combination of artistic principles, than those effects which must be attributed to the fact that the work was produced by a given artist, in a given period, at a given stage in the evolution of the species or tradition to which it belongs: we have obviously to go beyond formal criticism if we would assess Fielding's originality as a writer of "comic romance" or account for that peculiarly eighteenth-century flavor in *Tom Jones* which causes us to reflect that, unique and unrepresentative as Fielding's novel is when considered as a whole, it could yet have been written at no other time.

The criticism of forms needs thus to be supplemented by the criticism of qualities, in both of the senses just indicated, and also by historical inquiries of various sorts. This granted, however, two things can be said, the first of which is that, although the criticism of forms is only one among a number of valid and useful critical methods, it is still the sole method capable of dealing adequately—i.e., with a minimum of unanalyzed terms—and at the same time literally—i.e., in terms of causes and effects rather than analogies—with those characteristics and values in any literary work which derive from its construction as a self-contained whole endowed with a power of affecting us in a par-

---

dropped from his hand, and he fell prostrated on the floor with a lumpish noise, *and his half-pence rattled in his pocket*. . . ." It is difficult to conceive of any functional analysis, however refined its principles, that would afford premises for the discussion of such traits; and yet their presence or absence is obviously an important factor in our discrimination between distinguished and undistinguished writing.

20. F. R. Leavis, *The Great Tradition* (New York, [1949]), p. 4.

ticular way by virtue of the manner in which its internal parts are conceived and fitted together. It is a method, therefore, which ought to have a strong appeal to the many students of literature in our time who wish to consider their subject, in a now famous phrase, "as literature and not another thing," but who are temperamentally averse to analogical procedures and intellectually dissatisfied with those modern critical systems which, however literal, provide no analysis of any except one or two of the internal causes of literary effects. And the second point is perhaps equally clear: namely, that although the criticism of qualities and the investigation of historical origins and significances may achieve important results independently of the criticism of forms, as the past history of practical criticism and literary scholarship shows, both of these modes of judging literary productions would gain considerably in rigor and scope if they were founded on, and hence controlled by, a prior analysis of works from the point of view of their peculiar principles of construction and the special artistic problems which these presented to their writers. We should then, perhaps, have less qualitative criticism of the dogmatic sort which reproaches writers of poems, dramas, and novels perfect enough in their respective kinds for not exhibiting virtues of language or thought incompatible with the specific tasks these writers chose to undertake, and likewise fewer literary histories in which the achievements of authors are discussed exclusively in terms of materials and techniques without reference to the formal ends that helped to determine how these were used.

ACKNOWLEDGMENTS

For valuable suggestions and other assistance in the publication of this volume, the writers are indebted to Mr. Gwin J. Kolb, of the University of Chicago, and Miss Calla Guyles, of Madison, Wisconsin. They also wish to make grateful acknowledgment to the following persons and organizations for permission to reprint the fourteen essays contained in the volume which have already appeared elsewhere and for permission to quote from copyrighted materials:

Harcourt, Brace and Company for permission to quote from *Interpretation in Teaching* by I. A. Richards (copyright 1938), and from *The Well Wrought Urn* by Cleanth Brooks (copyright 1947).

Robert B. Heilman and the Louisiana State University Press for permission to quote from *This Great Stage* by Robert Bechtold Heilman (copyright 1948).

The Mediaeval Academy of America and the editors of *Speculum* for permission to reprint the essay "Rhetoric in the Middle Ages" by Richard McKeon.

New Directions (Norfolk, Conn.) for permission to quote from *Seven Types of Ambiguity* by William Empson (2d ed.; copyright 1947).

The Ronald Press Company for permission to reprint the essay "An Outline of Poetic Theory" by Elder Olson from *Critiques and Essays in Criticism, 1920–1948*, edited by Robert Wooster Stallman (copyright 1949).

Joseph T. Shipley for permission to reprint the essay "English Neoclassical Criticism: An Outline Sketch" by R. S. Crane from *The Dictionary of World Literature*, edited by Joseph T. Shipley (copyright 1943).

The University of Chicago Press for permission to reprint the essays contained in this volume which appeared originally in the following journals: *Classical Philology*, *Ethics*, *Journal of General Education*, and *Modern Philology*.